WITHDRAWN

The Presidential Medal of Freedom

The Presidential Medal of Freedom

WINNERS
AND
THEIR
ACHIEVEMENTS

———■———

BRUCE WETTERAU

CONGRESSIONAL QUARTERLY INC. WASHINGTON, D.C.

Typography, book, and cover design by Anne Masters Design, Inc., Washington, D.C.

Illustration credits begin on page 529, which is to be considered an extension of the copyright page.

LIBRARY OF CONGRESS CATALOGING-IN-PUBLICATION DATA

Wetterau, Bruce.
    The Presidential Medal of Freedom:
winners and their achievements / Bruce Wetterau.

    p. cm.
    Includes bibliographical references and index.
    ISBN 1-56802-128-3 (alk. paper)
    1. United States —Biography. 2. Presidential Medal of Freedom.
I. Title.
CT220.w48 1996
920.073—dc20
[B]   96-24499

Contents

Preface

The Presidential Medal of Freedom has been awarded for more than thirty years, and as the nation's highest civilian honor—the equivalent of the military Medal of Honor—it has provided recognition for a prodigious record of achievement. Leading statesmen, writers, artists, musicians, business executives, labor leaders, and humanitarians, to name but a few, are among those who have been honored for their contributions to American society or to the world at large. It is indeed a distinguished group of recipients who have received this award, which makes it all the more surprising that there has never been a book about it before.

The Presidential Medal of Freedom: Winners and Their Achievements fills this void with the first detailed history of the award, coverage of the selection process and award ceremonies, and an extensive section of biographical sketches of the more than three hundred distinguished award winners—including all of President Bill Clinton's awardees through mid-1996. The book also contains a complete index.

Part I, the award history, begins with an overview of the evolution of American medals from colonial times to the present, including both military and nonmilitary medals. The focus then shifts to the Presidential Medal of Freedom itself, documenting President John F. Kennedy's efforts to create the new award program and President Lyndon B. Johnson's presentation of the first awards after Kennedy's death. Here, documents from the JFK and LBJ presidential libraries, as well as from the U.S. Army Institute of Heraldry, helped illuminate this important phase of the award's history.

The uncertain fate of the medal during the Johnson administration also came to light through archival records, particularly in an oral history donated to the LBJ library by Civil Service Commission Chairman John Macy, who played an important role in keeping the award program alive during both the Johnson and early Nixon administrations. Without his efforts, the Presidential Medal of Freedom might not have been revived by President Johnson in the closing months of his presidency.

The Nixon Project—which currently controls President Nixon's papers for the National Archives—the Gerald Ford Presidential Library, and the Carter Presidential Library all proved helpful in sorting out questions relating to the medal history during these administrations. Both the Reagan and Bush libraries also were consulted, although much of the basic work on classifying papers remains to be done at these facilities.

No one but the presidents themselves can say why they chose the people they did for the Presidential Medal of Freedom, but the section on the selection process examines how proposed nominees reached the attention of the president as well as how many people were finally awarded medals. There is ample discussion of the general trends in the selection process that have become apparent over the years, including a look at both the array of occupations represented and the fields where the medal is most often awarded.

The last section of Part I covers the award ceremonies themselves. In addition to background information on the ceremonies—including where they have been held, and how many there have been—this section features an interesting and sometimes inspiring series of excerpts from speeches the presidents and occasionally the recipients gave during the award ceremonies.

Part II, which makes up the bulk of the book, presents biographical sketches of all the award winners to date. Illustrated with more than one hundred photographs, these biographies are arranged by presidential administration and ceremony date, which provides a chronological view of the award and highlights the choices of each president. While the sketches are necessarily brief and to the point, they begin with the full citation accompanying the award and cover details of the recipient's early life, climb to success, and accomplishments, as well as important facts about later life. A significant portion of this material cannot be found in any other readily available source. It should be noted that coverage is fuller for some recipients than others. This may reflect either the extent of the recipient's accomplishments or the lack of biographical information for some individuals.

In sum, the book presents a picture of the Presidential Medal of Freedom and its recipients that is as complete as possible. I hope that this first book on the medal will not only serve as a useful reference on the award, its history, and its recipients, but also help promote greater awareness of the medal program itself.

ACKNOWLEDGMENTS

As always with books of this size and scope, the author must depend to one degree or another on the help of others. Researching the biographical sketches proved a large and time-consuming process, and several researchers contributed to this effort, including Cindy Remington, Tyler Pender, Sally Bunch, Mike Brady, and Jesse Haden. I want also to thank Ann Marr, who drafted a batch of biographical entries to help keep the project on schedule.

Linda Hansen at the LBJ Presidential Library and William Joyner at the Nixon Project gave considerable advice and counsel, as did Tom Proffit at the U.S. Army Institute of Heraldry. Tim Saunders at the White House Executive Clerk's office kindly located material needed to complete the book. James A. Yancey, Jr., and others on the Carter Presidential Library staff and Warren Finch at the Bush Presidential Materials Project also deserve thanks.

Once again the University of Virginia library staff proved most helpful, particularly Barbara Selby, John Price, and others in the government documents sections. I would also like to thank Alex Cannon at the office of Representative Thomas J. Bliley, Jr., for digging out a report prepared by the Eisenhower administration, and Representative Ileana Ros-Lehtinen's office for help in finding material on Claude Pepper after I had run out of leads.

There were of course many others who contributed in one way or another to locating sources or missing information. Freelance photograph researcher Jamie Holland tracked down virtually all the illustrations for this wide-ranging group of medal recipients. As for completing the manuscript, I would like to thank acquisitions editor Shana Wagger for both her patience and contributions, and copy editor Elizabeth Helfgott and editorial assistant Megan Campion for their work in bringing the book through the final production stages.

Bruce Wetterau
Earlysville, Virginia

Part I

The Presidential Medal of Freedom

The Medal—Yesterday and Today

Established by President John F. Kennedy in 1963, the Presidential Medal of Freedom is the country's highest civilian award. The medal recognizes especially meritorious contributions to the country's security or national interests, to world peace, or to cultural or other notable public or private endeavors, and can be awarded only by the president of the United States. In the thirty-two years since the medal was created, just 331 people have received the honor, and being awarded the medal remains a rare privilege today.

Past medal winners, who represent virtually every field of endeavor, range from writers, artists, and scientists to business executives, labor leaders, government officials, and civil rights activists. And astronauts, movie stars, sports legends, and even a race-car driver (Richard Petty) have won it, too. Giants of this century—the architect Ludwig Mies van der Rohe, pioneering photographer Edward Steichen, industrialist Henry Ford II, DNA discoverer James D. Watson, and world-famous comedienne Lucille Ball—stand alongside other, sometimes lesser-known individuals who nevertheless distinguished themselves in a career of public service, work for a worthy cause, or some other notable pursuit.

While most people today would recognize the names of the nationally and internationally famous medal recipients, few know what the president's medal actually looks like. Be assured it is every bit as impressive looking as it is prestigious. A two-inch white enamel star with a gold border, the medal has a circular blue enamel center with thirteen gold stars, representing the original thirteen states. Gold eagles stretch their wings between the arms of the dominating white star, and their talons rest on red triangles infilling the small space where the arms intersect. There also is a higher degree of the medal, the Presidential Medal of Freedom "with distinction," which looks essentially the same. The star is larger, though, three inches across instead of two inches, and the award is worn along with a distinctive blue sash. All medals, whether first or second degree, are presented with a citation recording the awardee's outstanding achievements.

From the very outset in 1963, the idea of a president's award was well received, though not without a mild misgiving or two aired in the press about who might get the award. As a *Life* magazine editorial praising the newly created award noted, even the highly regarded British Honors List was subject to occasional abuses, notably some political back-scratching in deciding who was to be included. But the White House itself soon came upon the fundamental problem that invariably accompanies such a prestigious award program. Selecting

The Presidential Medal of Freedom

nominees for the Presidential Medal of Freedom, which can be awarded to people from virtually any walk of life, was proving genuinely difficult. As one White House staffer noted in the early days of the medal, potential nominees amounted to "an embarrassment of riches," and there were only a precious few medals to give out.

When Napoleon created the famed Legion of Honor in 1802, he said, "Show me a republic, ancient or modern, in which there have not been decorations. Some people call them baubles. Well, it is by means of baubles that one leads men." That, too, has been, and will continue to be, a part of the Presidential Medal of Freedom. The very first group of thirty-one medal recipients, selected from hundreds of possible candidates, bore the indelible stamp of the Kennedy administration, its aspirations, its likes and dislikes. Every president since then has done likewise.

Awards, like the outstanding achievements they recognize, are at bottom human endeavors, subject to all the frailties of the species. Hundreds of distinguished people may deserve recognition, but only a few among them may actually receive it. Of these there will always be people who get it because their achievements are somehow politic or symbolic, because they have the good luck, and good sense, to do the right thing at the right time, because they happen to be just down the corridor of power, or because they unabashedly lobby for it. But that should not cloud the essential fact that each medal winner, past and present, has a distinguished record of achievement and in one way or another has contributed significantly to the nation or the world at large.

Heroes, History, and the Presidential Medal of Freedom

Though a fairly recent innovation, the Presidential Medal of Freedom springs from a long history of recognizing meritorious service. The earliest American medals, given only sporadically during the first hundred years or so of the country's existence, and the array of other military and civil honors created since, ultimately provided the foundation for the Presidential Medal of Freedom award program.

WAR HEROES AND THE FIRST MEDALS

The very first medals awarded in the United States went to soldiers, for meritorious deeds in combat or for taking part in a particular war or campaign. But these military medals, common in other countries and cultures throughout history, were at first given in America only when the act sufficiently moved Congress to legislate an award for an individual. In fact, Congress did not establish a permanent military award program for outstanding bravery in battle until the Civil War, nearly ninety years after the United States declared independence from Great Britain.

The fledgling government of the United States knew well enough the importance of rewarding success on the battlefield, though. The country's first medal, the Congressional Gold Medal, was presented to none other than General George Washington in 1776 for driving the British from Boston at the outset of the Revolutionary War. Just a few years later in 1780 three militiamen each received specially struck "Andre" medals and a $200–per-year stipend from Congress for cap-

★ ★

Early Congressional Medals for Military Heroism

In the first decades after the Declaration of Independence, both the Continental Congress and the United States Congress voted from time to time to strike special medals rewarding heroic acts in wartime. (Source: U.S. Army Institute of Heraldry.)

1776 Continental Congress voted to award the country's first congressional gold medal to General George Washington for driving the British out of Boston. The measure also offered gratitude to those under his command.

1777 Major General Horatio Gates was voted a gold medal for forcing the surrender of Lieutenant General John Bourgoyne after the Battle of Saratoga (1777). Congress also commended the officers and men of Gates's command.

1779 General "Mad Anthony" Wayne was voted a gold medal for his daring raid on a supposedly impregnable British fort at Stony Point, New York. The capture of the fort provided a much-needed boost to the Continental Army's morale and moved Congress to also award silver medals to two of Wayne's subordinate officers.

1780 Continental Congress voted silver "Andre" medals to the three soldiers who caught the British spy Major John Andre—John Paulding, David Williams, and Isaac Van Wert. Congress cited their "virtuous and patriotic" conduct in turning down Andre's offers of large bribes for his release.

1781 Brigadier General Daniel Morgan, who inflicted a bloody defeat on the British at the Battle of Cowpens in South Carolina (1781), was voted a congressional gold medal.

1787 Naval hero John Paul Jones was voted a congressional gold medal for his outstanding service as a naval commander during the Revolution.

1800 Congress voted a gold medal for Captain Thomas Truxtun, commander of the frigate *Constellation,* for his defeat of the French warship *La Vengeance* (1800) during the hostilities with France.

1805 Congress awarded Commodore Edward Preble a gold medal for his successful attack on Tripoli, the Barbary pirates' stronghold.

1813 Captains Isaac Hull (of the *Constitution*), Stephen Decatur (of the *United States*), and Jacob Jones (of the *Wasp*) were all voted congressional gold medals for their victories in the War of 1812. Congress gave silver medals to the officers serving aboard those ships.

1814 Captains Oliver Hazard Perry and Jesse D. Elliott were voted congressional gold medals for their signal victory over the British navy on Lake Erie during the War of 1812. All officers aboard the two American ships received silver medals.

★ ★

turing the British spy Major John Andre. Andre's arrest foiled General Benedict Arnold's treasonous plan to hand over West Point to the British, and the three militiamen—John Paulding, David Williams, and Isaac Van Wert—steadfastly refused Andre's attempts to bribe his way to freedom. Taking note of that, Congress had their specially designed medals inscribed with the word "Fidelity" in large letters.

Two years later in 1782 General Washington took up the idea of a regular medal for heroism, establishing the Badge of Military Merit. Pierre-Charles L'Enfant, the famous Frenchman who joined the American cause during the Revolutionary War, designed the award as a heart-shaped swatch of purple cloth with silver edging and the word "Merit" embroidered on it. Though Washington intended the award to be permanent, he gave it to just three American soldiers. With the Revolutionary War all but over by this time, Washington's award lapsed into disuse. It was not completely forgotten, though, and almost a century and a half later the distinctive heart-shaped design inspired the Purple Heart medal, which today is awarded to soldiers wounded in battle.

Congress finally enacted legislation in 1862 establishing the country's first permanent award for heroism in combat. With the Civil War in full fury, both the army and the navy were empowered to present Medals of Honor to soldiers who distinguished themselves by their gallantry in action. The first army Medals of Honor, fashioned from bronze in the shape of a five-pointed star and awarded "in the name of Congress," were presented on March 25, 1863. The six Union soldiers who received the medals were the surviving members of Mitchell's Raiders, who had been sent behind Confederate lines to sabotage a key railroad between Chattanooga, Tennessee, and Marietta, Georgia. The mission had failed, but there could be no question of the soldiers' courage and resourcefulness under fire.

As the nation's only official medal for bravery in combat, the Medal of Honor gained status and considerable popularity among veterans in the years after the Civil War. In fact, it was altogether too popular. Numerous imitations became generally available, questions arose about who had and who had not actually received the award, and, in the late 1860s, reports surfaced about men who had "surreptitiously" obtained the medal to further schemes for "soliciting charity." Meanwhile, ex-soldiers in increasingly large numbers began applying for the Medal of Honor, citing deeds without any credible documentation, and years after the fact as well.

Concerned about the dignity of the medal, the army imposed a new set of regulations for awarding it by the turn of the century, and in 1904 Congress passed a law requiring official documentation of deeds before a soldier could be considered for the medal. That same year officials changed details of the medal's design, gave the five-pointed star a gold finish (instead of bronze), and patented the medal to prevent manufacture of new imitations. (Congress passed a law against imitating the medal in 1923, when the patent ran out.)

By far the most drastic step to restore the honor of the medal came in 1916, when Congress passed an act specifying that the medal could be awarded only for heroism in actual combat, and then only in cases of conspicuous gallantry involving the risk of life. The secretary of war was then charged with reviewing all 2,625 Medals of Honor awarded since 1863 and in 1917 ordered 910 names stricken from the Medal of Honor roll.

Easily the largest group of revoked medals, 864 in all, had been given to a Civil War regiment from Maine whose enlistment was due to expire in late June of 1863. At about that time General Robert E. Lee's Confederate army had launched an invasion of Pennsylvania, which led to the decisive battle at Gettysburg a week later. Worried by the military situation, a desperate President Abraham Lincoln offered Medals of Honor to members of the Maine regiment who extended their military service a short time longer to help defend Washington, D.C. Only about three hundred of the soldiers remained until after Gettysburg had been won by Union forces, but because of a clerical error, the entire regiment ended up with medals. Under the more stringent 1916 rules for awarding the Medal of Honor, however, not even the Maine soldiers who actually did stay to defend Washington qualified, so all 864 medals were revoked.

The forty-six other revoked medals included those awarded to William F. "Buffalo Bill" Cody and to Dr. Mary T. Walker, for her lifesaving work as an Army Medical Corps assistant surgeon during the battle of Gettysburg.

The tough new regulations for awarding the medal created a problem when it came to recognizing acts that were clearly courageous yet not sufficiently heroic to deserve a Medal of Honor. What evolved over the next three decades was a military award hierarchy called the "pyramid of honor," with new awards being created and ranked from lowest to highest according to the degree of merit reflected in the deed itself. The lowest award was the one most frequently given and so formed the pyramid's base. The Medal of Honor, the nation's highest military honor and the least-often awarded, formed the pyramid's peak.

Beginning with the Distinguished Service Medal and the army's Silver Star, which were established during World War I, Congress, the president, and the military services over the next decades fleshed out the military's pyramid of honor by creating other, now familiar medals. Congress, for example, created the Distinguished Flying Cross in 1926 for achievement in aerial flight and the navy's Silver Star in 1942 for gallantry in action. An executive order created the Bronze Star in 1944 for heroic or meritorious service. The War Department instituted the Army Purple Heart in 1932 and the Navy and Marine Corps Purple Hearts in 1943.

The government devised numerous other medals for more specific types of military service and for promoting national security, especially during World War II. Among these awards was the Medal of Freedom, which would later influence the creation of the Presidential Medal of Freedom.

HEROES OF ANOTHER TYPE

While the number of soldiers' medals mushroomed between the first and second world wars, the practice of awarding medals for meritorious service outside the military also was evolving. Like the first military medals in the United States, this also was not an American idea. Napoleon, for example, created the French Legion of Honor in 1802 as an order of merit for civilians, as well as for soldiers, and the Order of the British Empire, instituted in 1917, could be awarded for exceptional service in such fields as science, medicine, diplomacy, law, literature, art, music, and sports.

As with the first soldiers' medals, a few, specially struck nonmilitary medals were given out by the president and Congress during the early years of the republic. In 1790 President George Washington presented special diplomatic medals to the outgoing French ambassador, the Marquis de la Luzerne, and to his successor, the Count de Moustier, setting a precedent for recognizing foreign diplomats' service to the country's national interests. Beginning some decades later, Congress also issued a few individual awards for nonmilitary acts of heroism, but Congress did not set up the first regular civilian medal program until 1874. These awards, the Life Saving Medals, were for rescuing people from shipwrecks and other accidents at sea, acts that like combat involved considerable risk of life and limb.

Little more was done to recognize extraordinary civilian achievements until the post–World War II period, though nonmilitary activities received increasing recognition from the 1920s onward. The Distinguished Flying Cross (DFC), established by Congress in 1926,

★ ★

Early Nonmilitary Medals for Heroism

Some of the first special medals voted by Congress honoring nonmilitary acts are included below. (Source: U.S. Army Institute of Heraldry.)

1858 British Navy surgeon Frederick Henry Rose was voted a congressional gold medal for volunteering to serve aboard the USS *Susquehanna* as the medical officer when nearly all the ship's crewmen were sick and dying of yellow fever.

1864 Congress voted "Commodore" Cornelius Vanderbilt a medal for donating a $1 million steamer to the U.S. government.

1866 Ship Captains Creighton, Stouffer, and Low were voted medals for rescuing the crew of the wrecked steamer *San Francisco*.

1871 George F. Robinson was voted a gold medal for saving the life of Secretary of State William A. Seward.

1874 Congress authorized the first Life Saving Medals for rescuing those in distress at sea.

★ ★

became a tenuous step in that direction. It recognized "heroism or extraordinary achievement while participating in an aerial flight," and appropriately enough Charles A. Lindbergh received the first DFC following his daring nonstop, solo flight across the Atlantic in 1927.

An overnight national hero after his successful flight, Lindbergh had made the venture as a civilian. But he was a U.S. Army reservist at the time and so had at least some connection with the military. Navy Commander (later Admiral) Richard E. Byrd also received the DFC at about this time, for his pioneering flight to the North Pole in 1926, a notable but decidedly nonmilitary achievement. Aviator Amelia Earhart, a former Canadian military nurse but otherwise an undiluted civilian, also received the DFC, but after 1927 the award was restricted to military flyers.

The 1930s and 1940s saw the creation of four different special medals for polar exploration, awarded to civilians for their participation in the expeditions. Medals went to members of Admiral Richard Byrd's Antarctic expeditions of 1928–1930, 1933–1935, and 1939–1941. In 1944 Congress approved the fourth medal, for members of Admiral Robert E. Peary's 1909 expedition, during which Peary was believed to have been the first person to reach the North Pole.

World War II, meanwhile, brought new awards for contributions to the war effort. In addition to creating various medals for meritorious service in the quasi-civilian merchant marines, President Franklin D. Roosevelt also established the Medal for Merit in 1942. This medal went to civilians of friendly foreign countries for performing outstanding services. Similarly, in the last days of the war, President Harry S. Truman created the Medal of Freedom to honor those soldiers and civilians whose actions in foreign countries advanced the national security of the United States or its allies.

Truman's medal could be awarded by the president and the secretaries of state, war, and the military branches. The secretaries and officials they designated gave out thousands of the medals immediately after World War II, but President Truman himself gave out only nine, all in 1946. President Dwight D. Eisenhower also awarded the medal sparingly, giving out only thirteen in his two terms during the 1950s, and President John F. Kennedy gave out just one, which also was the last.

On the final day of his presidency in 1953, President Truman also created the National Security Medal, by executive order. Coming at a high point in Cold War tensions, the award was intended to recognize those who contributed significantly to the country's intelligence efforts. Office of Strategic Services (OSS) Director William J. Donovan was among the few recipients of this award (1957).

THE MEDAL CONCEPT

President Eisenhower, a career military officer before he took office, firmly established the idea of awarding medals to civilians for exceptional service. The Distinguished Civilian Service Medal, created during his administration by the Department of Defense (1956), represented a first step in this direction. It recognized important service to the military by civilians outside the government employ.

A year later, in 1957, President Eisenhower issued an executive order setting up another award, the Distinguished Federal Civilian Service Award. Established as the highest honor for meritorious service by federal government employees, this second award recognized those who had given exceptional service in the public interest, made significant improvements in government service, or otherwise had a distinguished career. President Eisenhower envisioned that the medal would be awarded on a regular basis, and he set up a blue-ribbon committee, the Distinguished Civilian Service Awards Board, to provide lists of prospective recipients. That had the effect of institutionalizing the program, and since then medals have been awarded annually.

But President Eisenhower also had in mind an even broader civilian honors program that clearly foreshadowed the Presidential Medal of Freedom. During his 1955 State of the Union address, he proposed "that awards of merit be established whereby we can honor our fellow citizens who make great contributions to the advancement of our civilization and of this country." The following year he appointed a Committee on Civilian National Honors, and in 1957 the committee issued a report recommending the creation of a Presidential Medal for Civilian Achievement. President Eisenhower submitted the report to Congress in 1957, and though legislation to set up the award program passed the Democratic-controlled House, the Senate, also dominated by a narrow majority of Democrats, failed to act on it.

By this time ample precedent existed for establishing new medals by executive order, although these awards were more limited in scope. One of the earliest, if not the earliest, was the Nicaraguan Campaign Medal. President Woodrow Wilson created that medal by presidential directive in 1913 to reward U.S. Marines who occupied Nicaragua to quell a revolt there. Over the next decades Congress continued to pass legislation on the higher-ranking military medals, but Presidents Franklin D. Roosevelt and Harry S. Truman increasingly relied on executive powers to create them as well (the Good Conduct Medal and Bronze Star among them). Perhaps President Eisenhower risked seeking congressional approval for his civilian honors medal because of the potential importance of the award and because of its broad scope. Whatever the reason, the country's first concerted effort to establish a cultural award program died on Capitol Hill in the late 1950s.

Afterward, President Eisenhower appeared to turn to the old Medal of Freedom as a substitute, granting a series of awards to important public officials and others. Among them was a deathbed presentation of the medal to Secretary of State John Foster Dulles in 1959. The cumulative effect was to increase the prestige of the Medal of Freedom by virtue of those who were receiving it. By the end of Eisenhower's administration the award was regarded as one of the top civilian honors the government could bestow.

The task of actually establishing a new national medal for civilian achievement fell to Eisenhower's successor, President John F. Kennedy, who had been a senator at the time Eisenhower's medal program was being voted on in Congress. The idea of a civilian award for cultural achievement fit in well with the larger themes of the Kennedy administration. Kennedy put particular emphasis on academia, the arts, and public service, while actively seeking to infuse the country with a new sense of idealism and the promise of the nation's future. Highly publicized award ceremonies for public service and cultural excellence would only serve to underscore the message.

Soon after taking office, President Kennedy asked Secretary of Labor Arthur J. Goldberg to investigate the possibility of establishing an award for distinguished civilian achievement, and Goldberg in turn assigned the task to Assistant Secretary of Labor Daniel Patrick Moynihan. Moynihan, later a Democratic senator from New York, worked with Civil Service Commission Chairman John Macy, who would figure prominently in the ongoing medal program; Fred Holborn, a White House special assistant; and General C.V. Clifton, the president's military aide. Secretary Goldberg's appointment to the Supreme Court in 1962 curtailed his effective participation in the budding program, but during 1961 and 1962 Moynihan and the others prepared various background papers establishing the outlines of an award program, subject to President Kennedy's approval.

THE PLANNING

The problem, as Moynihan and others in this working group saw it, was threefold. The federal government already had in place a number of fairly specialized awards, such as the Distinguished Federal Civilian Service Award, the National Medal for Science, and the National Security Medal, although there was no high-ranking government award for outstanding achievement in the arts, education, industry, labor, public service, and the like. Furthermore, there was no clear hierarchy of civilian awards, as in the military's pyramid of honor, and there was no system for making the awards on a regular basis.

At the outset, the idea was to create a new, general-purpose president's medal as the top civil honor awarded by the U.S. government, on a par with such foreign national awards as the Order of the British Empire and the French Legion of Honor. But the working group also saw some advantage in possibly revamping an existing medal. By early spring 1962 the White House was still investigating the criteria for awarding various American medals, including the Medal of Freedom. Eventually, attention focused on the Medal of Freedom as a basis for the new president's medal.

Moynihan and the working group had a number of concerns about using the Medal of Freedom. For one thing, during the 1940s especially, thousands of the medals had been given away to members

★ ★

Medals of Freedom Awarded by the President

PRESIDENT TRUMAN

1946 William H. Charman, *British civilian, Combined Chiefs of Staff*

1946 George L. Howe, *War Department employee*

1946 Gordon T. Jackson, *American Red Cross*

1946 Richard Mazzarini, *Office of Strategic Services*

1946 Father Pierre A. Poullet, *Canadian civilian*

1946 Dennis Puleston, *War Department employee*

1946 Chen Sun, *Chinese Supply Commission*

1946 Norman H. West, *British civilian, Combined Chiefs of Staff*

1946 William M. Wheeler, Jr., *U.S. counterintelligence*

PRESIDENT EISENHOWER

1954 Genevieve de Galard-Terraube, *French nurse at Dien Bien Phu*

1955 Robert B. Anderson, *secretary of the navy*

1956 John Von Neumann, *scientist*

1957 Charles E. Wilson, *secretary of defense*

1958 Lewis L. Strauss, chairman, *Atomic Energy Commission*

1959 John Foster Dulles, *secretary of state*

1959 Neil McElroy, *secretary of defense*

1959 Donald A. Quarles, *deputy secretary of defense*

1961 James H. Douglas, *deputy secretary of defense*

1961 Thomas S. Gates, *secretary of defense*

1961 Gordon Gray, *special assistant to the president*

1961 Christian A. Herter, *secretary of state*

1961 George B. Kistiakowsky, *special assistant to the president*

PRESIDENT KENNEDY

Paul-Henri Spaak, *secretary-general, North Atlantic Treaty Organization*

★ ★

of various underground groups and to other foreign nationals who had helped the Allies win World War II. The Medal of Freedom could be (and was) awarded by people other than the president, including the secretary of state, the secretaries of the military branches, and any subordinate officers they might designate. But the only complete record of recipients was for those few medals awarded by the president himself. By the early 1960s it could not even be determined if more than the original twenty-two-thousand medals had been given away by the government. Even more problematic was the restriction that the medal be given only for contributions to the national security *outside* the United States.

By late 1962 the working group's plan called for a reconstituted Medal of Freedom, possibly called the Presidential Medal of

Freedom. Like the Medal of Freedom, the president's medal was to have three classes, designated as Gold Palm, Silver Palm, and plain, a slight change from the Medal of Freedom class designations, Gold Palm, Silver Palm, and Bronze Palm. An alternative plan named the degrees "with highest distinction," "with distinction," and ordinary.

But the big change was that the new medal would be awarded for achievements in culture, world peace, and the national interest, not just for national security. That would make it a true national award for civil honors. The group also suggested that all civil awards given out by the government be ranked in order of precedence, with the new president's medal as the nation's top civil honor.

Furthermore, they proposed that the awards be given on a regular basis, to a reasonably large number of persons (about thirty-five or so a year), and for a fairly wide range of activities. The idea of a regular award program, with winners announced on some fixed date, like July Fourth, seemed especially important to the planners. They noted that while the federal government now awarded a number of civil honors (such as the Enrico Fermi Award and the National Security Medal), the honors had been given out infrequently and in such small numbers that the general public was largely unaware of them. A regular award program with a suitable number of recipients would certainly make a bigger splash in the press.

The working group also offered a key suggestion aimed at establishing a system for regularly awarding the president's medal. They recommended expanding the Distinguished Civilian Service Awards Board, which President Eisenhower had established in 1957 to help select the recipients of the Distinguished Federal Civilian Service Award. The board would be expanded to include four non-government members and would then take responsibility for compiling a preliminary list of possible president's medal recipients. Once each year (April was suggested) the board would sift through nominations from government departments and agencies, private citizens and organizations, and submit its recommendations to the president. The president could add or delete names as he saw fit and, after announcing the final selections on a fixed date, say, July Fourth, could hold the award ceremony at any convenient date. The president could of course also award the medal to deserving individuals at other times during the year.

One crucial problem remained: how to get the civil award program established. Moynihan and the working group were well aware of President Eisenhower's unsuccessful attempt at getting an award bill through Congress, and by 1962 the Kennedy administration was having its own problems with Congress. Clearly an executive order offered the surest, safest route, because that could be done without congressional approval. Perhaps to further bolster their position, the working group suggested "building on the body of precedent and tradition" by writing a new executive order to reconstitute the old Medal of Freedom into the Presidential Medal of

Freedom. All the features of the new medal program could be spelled out in the executive order.

CREATING THE MEDAL

Meanwhile, the White House already had some definite ideas on how the new medal should look, and in December 1961 staffers contacted the Army Institute of Heraldry, which oversees design and development of medals, official seals, and the like for the armed forces and other government agencies. Among President Kennedy's early instructions were that the proposed medal have two degrees, the higher one to include a sash like those of some foreign awards and the other to be suspended from a neck ribbon, as in the case of the Medal of Honor. The medal was to be awarded exclusively by the president and had to be of a suitably dignified and impressive design.

The Institute of Heraldry provided the White House with an initial design proposal in late March 1962. That first design, a pentagon-shaped medal with an engraved representation of the torch of liberty in the center, was apparently passed over. The White House did not get back in touch with the institute until late September 1962, though, and then asked for further information on existing American awards.

President Kennedy's military aide, General C. V. Clifton, met with representatives of the Institute of Heraldry on December 11, 1962, shortly after the Kennedy administration had successfully concluded the Cuban Missile Crisis. General Clifton explained the current White House thinking on the medal and requested suggestions for a name for the new medal, as well as for three degrees of the medal, which the president was then considering. He also asked that a set of five new design proposals be made ready by December 20 so that President Kennedy could study them over the Christmas holidays.

The five new designs included a square medal overlaid with a cross, a six-armed design with a central field of thirteen stars, and a six-pointed star with a field of small stars in its center. This last design bore a strong resemblance to the final design of the new medal. Meanwhile, in a telephone call to the institute a week earlier, General Clifton had broached the idea of using the title Medal of Freedom for the new medal. But that idea was discouraged because of possible confusion with the existing medal.

With Moynihan's basic plan for the award program in hand and the design of the medal under way, the White House made the final decision to reconstitute the Medal of Freedom as a new medal by way of an executive order. As established by the order, the new medal, to be called the Presidential Medal of Freedom, was to be awarded solely by the president for "especially meritorious contributions to (1) the security or national interests of the United States, (2) world peace, or (3) cultural or other significant public or private endeavors." The White House also decided to award the medal in just two degrees, not the three previously discussed, and the

★ ★

What Do We Call It?

While preparations for establishing a president's medal for civil honors were well under way by late 1962, no name for the award had as yet been definitely decided upon. The U.S. Army Institute of Heraldry, enlisted to help create the award, offered this list of possible names along with its proposed medal designs.

The Presidential Award of Honor   The Presidential Award for Achievement
The Presidential Emblem of the Oak   The Presidential Emblem of Distinction
The Presidential Laurel   The Presidential Liberty Award
The Presidential Constellation Award   The Presidential Society of Merit
The Presidential Society of Distinction The Presidential Commendation Award
The Presidential Accolade   The Presidential Laurel of Acclaim

★ ★

Distinguished Civilian Service Awards Board was enlarged to include five members from outside the executive branch.

The White House officially announced Executive Order 11085 on February 22, 1963, noting that "in a period when the national government must call upon an increasing portion of the talents and energies of its citizens, it is clearly appropriate to provide ways to recognize and reward the work of persons, within and without the Government, who contribute significantly to the quality of American life." The press release pointed out that until then no program of regular awards of civil honors had existed, and it set July Fourth as the date for announcing recipients each year.

All was now in motion toward an award ceremony, with early July 1963 as an initial target date. The Distinguished Civilian Service Awards Board, chaired by Undersecretary of State George Ball, held its first meetings in early March to begin the process of selecting nominations for the first group of medal winners. Work on the medal design also proceeded apace, with three designs submitted to the White House by late February 1963. Final decisions on the design were needed as soon as possible, since creating the necessary molds and completing the finished medals would take upwards of three-months' time.

That proved crucial. Both President Kennedy and First Lady Jacqueline Kennedy became deeply involved in designing the medal, or perhaps redesigning it would be a better description. Unfortunately, the president and the first lady had different ideas about the medal, and as disagreements developed the Army Institute of Heraldry found itself caught in the middle. What began as a little slippage in April turned into a scheduling nightmare by July, forcing postponements of the award ceremony, first from July to September and then from September to early December 1963.

The first lady was taking part in the design process from at least as early as April, having indicated her first choice of the designs on April 11. She asked for some modifications of it, as well as for the creation of an entirely different badge to be attached to the sash accompanying the medal's higher degree ("with distinction"). The Institute of Heraldry began developmental work based on her design, and at the end of the month President Kennedy selected his first choice of the more detailed designs, deciding among other things in favor of the first lady's badge for the sash.

President Kennedy viewed preliminary samples of the medal at the White House on July 3 but, apart from making a few comments, refused to give his final approval until after the first lady had seen the samples over the July Fourth holiday at Hyannis Port, Massachusetts. By then officials at the Institute of Heraldry desperately needed a decision to make the then-September deadline, and the constant vacillation on design questions had nearly driven them to distraction. They had no choice but to wait, however. In one instance the president had suggested a border around the medal's white enameled star, and the institute produced a sketch of the medal with a blue border. The first lady overruled the design change, though, and the blue border promptly disappeared.

The weekend of July Fourth came and went without the long-awaited final design approval from the White House. In fact, the first lady and the president did not come to an agreement over that weekend and instead showed the medal samples to David Webb, a New York City custom jeweler and family friend. Webb said that he could improve the design and, with the weeks slipping by, eventually produced some sketches for the Kennedys. President Kennedy agreed, or perhaps capitulated, but in any event forwarded the sketches to the Institute of Heraldry on July 22, saying that the new design was what he now wanted. All previous development work was to be scrapped.

The effect on the schedule, not to mention morale at the Army Institute of Heraldry, was devastating. While Webb had retained the basic design, he called for changes that effectively forced the institute to start from scratch on manufacturing the medal. Even the sash ribbon with stars, which President Kennedy had personally approved in May, was changed (no stars). The September 15 deadline, already in doubt by July 3, was now out the window and costs threatened to run to four times the original estimates.

Perhaps President Kennedy was not fully aware of the problems caused by the repeated design changes, but by July 31 the White House was sufficiently concerned to ask the institute, "If the White House was to give its final design decision…on Friday, 2 August, just when could the president have his award party?" The answer— thirteen weeks hence—produced only a partial decision from the president. On August 2 he approved the obverse (front) of the new medal design but withheld a final decision on the reverse side and ribbon until talking with the first lady at Hyannis Port that weekend. The first lady's final approval was received on August 5.

Happily for the White House, the Distinguished Civilian Service Awards Board had been having far less trouble developing the

★ ★

President Kennedy's Selections for the First Presidential Medal of Freedom Awards

Preparations for establishing a president's medal for civil honors were well under way by late 1962, and the Distinguished Civilian Service Awards Board developed a list of potential nominees for the first award ceremony. President Kennedy added his selections, then decided on these people to be be the first recipients of the award.

Marian Anderson, *contralto*

Ralph Bunche, *statesman*

Ellsworth Bunker, *statesman*

Pablo Casals, *cellist*

Genevieve Caulfield, *educator*

James B. Conant, *educator*

John F. Enders, *bacteriologist*

Felix Frankfurter, *jurist*

Karl Holton, *youth authority*

Robert J. Kiphuth, *athletic director*

Edwin H. Land, *inventor*

Herbert H. Lehman, *statesman*

Robert A. Lovett, *statesman*

J. Clifford MacDonald, *educator*

John J. McCloy, *banker and statesman*

George Meany, *labor leader*

Alexander Meiklejohn, *philosopher*

Ludwig Mies van der Rohe, *architect*

Jean Monnet, *European statesman*

Luis Muñoz-Marín, *governor of Puerto Rico*

Clarence B. Randall, *industrialist*

Rudolf Serkin, *pianist*

Edward Steichen, *photographer*

George W. Taylor, *educator*

Alan T. Waterman, *scientist*

Mark S. Watson, *journalist*

Annie D. Wauneka, *public-health worker*

E.B. White, *author*

Thornton Wilder, *author*

Edmund Wilson, *author and critic*

Andrew Wyeth, *artist*

★ ★

proposed list of distinguished nominees for the first award ceremony. To be sure, considerable effort went into its creation, and the president himself spent still more time adding and deleting names. After President Kennedy made his final selections, the White House sent out telegrams on July 1 congratulating each of the thirty-one recipients and notifying them of a planned September award ceremony (which was later postponed). Soon afterward the White House released the recipients' names to the press.

The list was both impressive and varied, containing some of the most renowned artists, musicians, educators, statesmen, scientists, and business and labor leaders of the day. While largely focusing on those who had achieved national prominence, the president also named a few lesser-known individuals, like the youth authority Karl Holton and public-health worker Annie D. Wauneka, whose devoted service to others merited special attention.

All that was lacking were the medals themselves, and once the final design decisions had been made, the Institute of Heraldry pushed development and manufacture ahead as quickly as possible. Thanks to the efforts of the institute designers, the thirty-one medals arrived at the White House on October 31, 1963, a day before the revised deadline, engraved and ready for presentation. By all accounts they were indeed beautiful and impressive medals, fitting emblems of the nation's highest civilian honor.

THE FIRST CEREMONY

With the medals now in hand, the White House at last announced the award ceremony for December 6. Civil Service Commission Chairman John Macy wrote the plan for the ceremony, which involved both an awards presentation and a luncheon afterward, and took care of sending out invitations, printing programs, and a multitude of other details as the days of November slipped by. On the twenty-first of the month, with the ceremony fast approaching, President Kennedy's special assistant, Frederick Holborn, passed along a routine request to have the Marine String Orchestra play at a reception for the medal winners. Neither Holborn nor anyone else at the White House could have known it was the last full day of President Kennedy's life. On November 22 President Kennedy was assassinated while riding in a presidential motorcade through Dallas, Texas.

The president's murder stunned the nation and thrust Vice President Lyndon B. Johnson into the presidency. Through the last bewildering days of November the nation seemed to drift, as Americans mourned Kennedy's tragic death and tried to understand how it could have possibly happened. But after Kennedy had been laid to rest, the time came to begin healing the nation, to get back a sense of direction. The award ceremony provided one of the first opportunities to begin that process, and both Jacqueline Kennedy and President Johnson insisted on holding it as scheduled on December 6.

The emotional burden on everyone at the White House was enormous in the aftermath of the assassination, but no one bore a greater burden than Mrs. Kennedy—or displayed anything approaching her dignity. Though the fact was not made public, President Johnson was moved to award her a Presidential Medal of Freedom, "with distinction," at the upcoming ceremony, along with one for the late president. Both medals were engraved and delivered to the White House, but Mrs. Kennedy declined her award.

In the last hours before the ceremony on December 6, President Johnson had serious misgivings about taking part in the event and almost backed out of it altogether. Civil Service Chairman Macy later recalled the incident in an oral history donated to the Johnson Presidential Library, saying he argued vigorously with President Johnson to go ahead with the ceremony. In tough terms, Macy said, he argued "that this was important—not just to honor President Kennedy— but I felt it was very important for the presidency as an institution." President Johnson put aside his doubts, and the White House ceremony began as scheduled at noon in the State Dining Room. It was a high-prestige event with members of the cabinet, Congress, and the Supreme Court, and other distinguished guests attending, yet there was no escaping the lingering sense of loss in the room. Mrs. Kennedy was understandably absent, but Attorney General

Robert F. Kennedy was on hand to represent his late brother and his brother's family.

Undersecretary of State George Ball, who had chaired the Distinguished Civilian Service Awards Board, gave the opening remarks.

Today, the President of the United States is expressing the appreciation of a great Nation for the extraordinary achievements of a remarkable group of men and women, achievements spanning a wide spectrum of human endeavor …. For the first time, the president is establishing what we can proudly call an American civil honors list ….

The ceremony today has a dual significance. We are joining President Johnson not only in honoring the recipients of the Presidential Medal of Freedom and the high endeavors that have won them this acclaim but also in paying tribute to the man responsible for this new decoration.

It was characteristic of President Kennedy that early in his administration he should turn his mind to the means by which we could give appropriate encouragement to deeds well done. He felt deeply that our nation should pay full homage to those who contribute to enriching the qualities of American life, strengthening the security of free men and building the foundations for peace …. President Johnson shares with his great predecessor a deep respect for distinguished achievement and a desire to give gratitude and recognition to those who nobly serve the cause of humanity. He has come here today to pay honor to a bright constellation of talent and achievement.

President Johnson spoke next, beginning his speech by recalling the tragic events leading up to the ceremony.

Over the past two weeks, our nation has known moments of the utmost sorrow, of anguish and shame. This day, however, is a moment of great pride.

In a shattering sequence of events that began fourteen days ago, we encountered in its full horror man's capacity for hatred and destruction. There is little we do not now know of evil, but it is time to turn once more to the pursuits of honor and excellence and of achievement that have always marked the true direction of the American people.

So we meet today to confer the nation's highest civil honor on thirty-one of the nation's most distinguished citizens, citizens of the free world … in joining with my fellow countrymen to express the nation's gratitude to each of you, I want particularly to thank you for reminding us that whatever evil moments may pass by, we are and we shall continue to be a people touched with greatness, called by high destiny to serve great purposes.

Undersecretary Ball next read the recipients' names, one by one, while President Johnson read the citations accompanying each of the medals.

"Miss Marian Anderson."

"Artist and citizen, she has ennobled her race and her country while her voice has enthralled the world."

"Miss Genevieve Caulfield."

"Teacher and humanitarian, she has been for four decades a one-woman Peace Corps in Southeast Asia, winning victories over darkness by helping the blind to become full members of society."

"Dr. John F. Enders."

"Physician and researcher, he has opened new pathways to medical discovery and has been an example and companion to two generations of doctors in the demanding quest for scientific truth."

And so it went through the list, twenty-four winners of the regular Presidential Medal of Freedom, followed by seven who won the medal "with distinction."

After brief remarks on behalf of the recipients by the former World Bank President John J. McCloy, President Johnson announced that he had decided to award posthumous Presidential Medals of Freedom to two others, Pope John XXIII, who had died earlier in 1963, and the late president Kennedy. Though few people noticed, Mrs. Kennedy appeared at that moment in a small anteroom opening onto the State Dining Room. Standing there alone, she listened to President Johnson's remarks honoring her late husband.

President Johnson began gravely. "John Kennedy is gone. Each of us will know that we are the lesser for his death. But each is somehow larger because he lived. A sadness has settled on the world which will never leave it while we who knew him are still here."

The America that produced him shall honor him as well. As a simple gesture, but one which I know he would not have counted small, it is my privilege at this moment to award the Presidential Medal of Freedom posthumously to John Fitzgerald Kennedy on behalf of the great republic for which he lived and died.

The citation reads: "John Fitzgerald Kennedy, 35th President of the United States, soldier, scholar, statesman, defender of freedom, pioneer for peace, author of hope—combining courage with reason, and combating hate with compassion, he led the land he loved toward new frontiers of opportunity for all men and peace for all time. Beloved in a life of selfless service, mourned by all in a death of senseless crime, the energy, faith and devotion which he brought to his extraordinarily successful though tragically brief endeavors will hereafter 'light our country and all who serve it—and the glow from that fire can truly light the world.'"

The final words of the citation were drawn from Kennedy's inaugural address in 1961. Robert Kennedy, who in 1968 also fell victim to an assassin's bullet, accepted the medal on behalf of his brother.

THE MEDAL BECOMES A TRADITION

Early in his administration, President Johnson seemed content to continue the award program. When the Distinguished Civilian

Service Awards Board forwarded its 1964 nominees list to the White House, Johnson spent considerable time sifting through the names. Then on July Fourth, according to the precedent set by Kennedy, the White House announced the names of twenty-nine recipients. Two months later, on September 14, President Johnson presented the awards at a ceremony in the White House East Room.

The president's award program appeared to be up and running smoothly. The word was getting out; the press had given the 1964 ceremony good coverage, and it seemed that the American civil honors award had indeed finally arrived. A year later in 1965 the awards board again delivered a nominees list, but this time the White House made no announcement of medal recipients on July Fourth. Months passed without a word on the medal. The awards board continued to sit, but the medal program virtually disappeared from the president's agenda and the public eye.

Part of the explanation lay in the times. President Johnson was stepping up America's commitment of men and materiél in the Vietnam War and was fast becoming the target of protests. Civil rights protests also were becoming more strident, and violent as well. While these events helped set the stage for President Johnson's decision to stop the awards in 1965, there also were more immediate, and personal, reasons for the lapse.

Civil Service Commission Chairman Macy later recalled in his oral history what he believed were the three main causes. "We'd had the abortive experience with the arts event that Eric Goldman put on where people being honored at the White House misbehaved. Also, one of the names on the [1965 nominees] list happened to be [the cartoonist] Herblock, and the day that the list reached the President, the cartoon with Valenti's words [a very satirical cartoon about Johnson] appeared in the *Washington Post*. And thirdly, several people with high ambition to receive the award were lobbying the White House very vigorously."

Whatever the reasons, President Johnson refused to award the medal from 1965 to nearly the end of 1967. Since the awards were given at the pleasure of the president, he had as much right to *not* give them as to give them. Macy tried to prod the president into reviving the award in an April 1966 memo, offering to reorganize and redesign the program "in order to give it the proper Johnson identification." Macy tried again in early 1967, only to be rebuffed by the president, who returned the note with "I don't want this" written on it.

Others made similarly unsuccessful attempts later that year, until finally in the last month of the year President Johnson opened the door just a crack. On December 23, 1967, while visiting Cam Ranh Bay, the massive U.S. military base in Vietnam, the president gave Presidential Medals of Freedom to Ellsworth Bunker (his second award), Robert W. Komer, and Eugene Murphy Locke for their contributions to the American effort in Vietnam. Two months later, on February 28, 1968, the president again awarded the medal, this time to a longtime member of his administration, Defense Secretary Robert S. McNamara.

The shift in presidential mood was not lost on Macy, who still firmly believed in the award program. Finally, during an October 30, 1968, meeting, President Johnson asked Macy to compile a list of outstanding American leaders who had contributed significantly to public programs during his administration. After compiling the list largely on his own, Macy sent a memo suggesting a ceremony in late December or early January, tactfully mentioning that the president should honor only those he personally believed deserved recognition. He also pointed out that the Distinguished Civilian Service Awards Board need not be involved in any of the selections.

As Macy said later in his oral history, though, nothing happened until the morning of January 20, 1969, the last day of President Johnson's term. That morning the president's appointments secretary called, saying the president had decided to award the medal at noon that day to eighteen people from the list. Macy gave the necessary background information for the official announcement, but a formal presentation ceremony that day was impossible. Then, at 11:45 A.M., the secretary called Macy back to say President Johnson planned to announce two other medal recipients along with the eighteen: McGeorge Bundy and John Macy. It was a surprise gesture by President Johnson that Macy never forgot.

Staffers of the incoming administration of Richard Nixon later took care of preparing the citations and sending out the medals.

Over the next decades the fate of the Presidential Medal of Freedom more or less depended on the personal preferences of the president in power. By 1969 all the civilian appointees to the Distinguished Civilian Service Awards Board had served out their terms, and no new appointments had been made.

Meanwhile, in the early months of the Nixon administration, Daniel Patrick Moynihan lobbied hard for restarting the formal award program, stressing the importance of a regular schedule to prevent its being neglected and to increase its prestige. He called for reestablishing the role of the awards board.

Nixon staffers also heard from Macy, who urged that the award program be continued, but with an informal selection procedure that allowed the president to make his own choices. Macy recommended abandoning the board concept because it formalized the process, took too much control away from the president, and was subject to outside pressure. He told staffers that the main reason President Johnson had abandoned the awards was because a group of people had been pushing the board to select a particular candidate.

President Nixon thereafter relied on his own staff to sift through outside suggestions and to compile lists of their own nominations, on the few occasions when such lists were needed. Gone was any attempt at the programmatic approach whereby awards went to leaders in a variety of fields during a single ceremony. For the most part President Nixon awarded the medals sparingly, in small ceremonies usually involving just one recipient, as in the president's first award, to Duke Ellington on April 29, 1969.

Meanwhile, on March 13, 1970, President Nixon issued an executive order formally ending the nominating function of the Distinguished Civilian Service Awards Board.

After the demise of the Nixon administration during the Watergate scandal, President Gerald R. Ford appointed a commission to consider further changes to the award program. A new executive order was drafted and approved within the White House but for some reason was never enacted. The chief aims of the order included establishing a blue-ribbon committee to suggest nominations, making the award criteria somewhat clearer, and removing the stipulation for a July Fourth announcement. As of mid-1996, it marked the last effort to significantly alter the president's medal program.

President Jimmy Carter, a populist at heart, showed little interest in awarding the medal after presenting two medals in 1977, to Dr. Jonas E. Salk, inventor of the first polio vaccine, and (posthumously) to Martin Luther King, Jr., the slain civil rights leader. He awarded just two additional medals during his first three years in office, rebuffing all proposals for further awards. In 1980, though, with the country entangled in the demoralizing hostage crisis, he relented and presented fourteen medals in a June ceremony. Some months later, during the last days of his administration in January 1981, he presented another fifteen medals at a White House ceremony.

President Ronald Reagan clearly enjoyed presenting the award, and in every year of his two terms as president, except 1982, he held a group-award ceremony at the White House. No effort was made to adhere to a rigid timetable as Kennedy's plan had envisioned, and the group ceremonies ran to only about ten to fifteen recipients, about half the number as at each of the first two group-award ceremonies, in 1963 and 1964. But President Reagan also regularly gave medals at small ceremonies involving only one or two recipients.

During the last two years of his administration, President Reagan reduced the number of awardees at the group ceremonies to a more manageable level of five to ten, while also awarding medals individually at other times of the year. This pattern—group awards usually involving no more than five to ten recipients roughly once a year and individual award presentations at other times—has held through the administrations of George Bush and Bill Clinton.

Selecting the Medal Winners

With so few medals to give, deciding who gets them inevitably becomes a difficult and largely undemocratic process. President Kennedy's original criteria—meritorious contributions to the national interest or security, world peace, or cultural or other notable private or public endeavors—are so vague and so all-encompassing as to include hundreds, if not thousands of distinguished Americans. And the award can be given to foreigners as well.

All of the medal winners are high achievers of one sort or another, but some broad trends in the selections have emerged over the years. More often than not, it seems, presidents tend to pick nationally recognized figures who are near or at the end of a long and distinguished career. The awardee not only gains recognition for a substantial record of accomplishment but also adds to the prestige of the award itself, which is something selection committees and the president must be concerned about. Posthumous awards have been given, but for obvious reasons honoring a living recipient is preferred. At times presidents have even made special arrangements to present an award to a recipient of advanced years who was seriously ill, as happened during the Carter administration.

Generally speaking, presidents have tried to select medal winners from a variety of backgrounds, including the arts, government, labor, business, public service, and humanitarian work. While a long record of achievement is most often recognized, specific, highly publicized accomplishments also have garnered awards. President Nixon, for example, gave president's medals to the astronauts of the history-making *Apollo 11* mission, on which Neil Armstrong became the first man to walk on the moon. There have been other awards for fairly specific accomplishments, such as President Bush's medals to Generals Colin Powell and H. Norman Schwarzkopf after the stunning allied victory in the Persian Gulf War. Usually, though, the specific event just serves to draw attention to an otherwise distinguished career.

At the very outset President Kennedy established another precedent, for awarding the medal to dedicated but little-known individuals engaged in public service, humanitarian, or other laudable work. In effect he used the prestige of the award to focus attention on idealistic but overlooked achievements, certainly a worthwhile idea and one that other presidents adopted in following decades. These awards also amounted to symbolic selections for the Kennedy administration, which stressed the need for greater public service in programs like the Peace Corps. In fact, the citation of one, Genevieve Caulfield, even called her a "one-woman Peace Corps." Political con-

★ ★

Foreign Recipients

Manlio Giovanni Brosio	Joseph M.A.H. Luns
Lord Peter Carrington	Jean Monnet
Pablo Casals	Javier Pérez de Cuéllar
Jacques-Yves Cousteau	General Carlos P. Romulo
T. S. Eliot	Anwar el-Sädät
Luis A. Ferré	Mother Teresa
Friedrich August von Hayek	Margaret Thatcher
Archbishop Iakovos	Lech Walesa
Pope John XXIII	

★ ★

siderations aside, though, she was as deserving a candidate for recognition as can be found—a blind American woman who found the courage to go overseas and set up desperately needed schools for the blind in Southeast Asia.

Another persistent theme in award-giving has been government service. Although Kennedy had included a few statesmen among the first medal recipients, President Johnson made a point of rewarding service in his administration with the president's medal, especially during his last year or so in office. Other presidents followed suit. President Nixon named Secretary of State William P. Rogers and Defense Secretary Melvin R. Laird, for example; President Ford named Vice President Nelson A. Rockefeller and Secretary of State Henry A. Kissinger; President Carter named his assistant for national security affairs, Zbigniew Brzezinski, and Deputy Secretary of State Warren Minor Christopher; and so on. About a third of the president's medals to date have gone to those who were or are in government, but the award is in no danger of becoming a medal for government service. Every president also has named leading American writers, musicians, movie stars, educators, business executives, and civil rights and labor leaders, and awardees from these other walks of life constitute the bulk of medal winners.

Presidential Medals of Freedom also have been given to foreigners, including dignitaries and representatives of the arts. President Kennedy, for example, included in his list the internationally renowned cellist Pablo Casals; President Johnson gave a posthumous president's medal to Pope John XXIII; and President Reagan gave a posthumous medal to slain Egyptian president Anwar el-Sädät. Medals to non-Americans, however, have been given out sparingly.

The Evolving Selection Process

Procedures for deciding who will receive the president's medal are less formalized today than they were at the outset, though the final decision still rests, as always, with the president. During the first years of the award program, the Distinguished Civilian Service Awards Board produced lists of proposed nominees that the president then used as a basis for picking the actual recipients. At that time, however, there was greater emphasis on large award ceremonies (to help capture public attention), and so more effort went into selecting recipients from a broad range of fields for each ceremony.

The awards board created by President Kennedy in 1963 was an expanded version of the board formed by President Eisenhower in 1957 in connection with the Distinguished Federal Civilian Service Award. In his executive order creating the Presidential Medal of Freedom, President Kennedy simply specified that new board members be added from outside the executive branch and charged the board with producing a list of possible awardees.

The enlarged board met and reviewed general guidelines for selecting nominees in early March 1963 and, soon after, the actual work of selecting candidates began. Each member compiled a list of prospective nominees (and their accomplishments), which was merged into a single list. In late April the board met again and voted name by name, eliminating those who did not get at least one vote. A general consensus emerged on the second round of voting, and the board forwarded to the president all names receiving at least three votes on this second ballot. President Kennedy then spent considerable time on the list, adding and deleting names until at last deciding on the first group of thirty-one recipients. The group included the first black (Marian Anderson, Ralph Bunche) and the first female (Anderson and Annie Wauneka) recipients.

Interestingly, the board also forwarded a separate recommendation nominating Pope John XXIII for a posthumous award, which President Kennedy decided against. Pope John, however, did get an award that year, one of two that President Johnson decided to award on his own at the December 6, 1963, ceremony, soon after Kennedy's assassination. The other was for Kennedy.

The board prepared a new list the following year for President Johnson, who, like Kennedy before him, put considerable effort into revising it. The result was a similarly large group of nominees—twenty-nine in all—covering a variety of disciplines and including such well-known individuals as Helen Keller, Edward R. Murrow, and John Steinbeck. Also in the group were the first recipients associated with popular culture, Broadway stars Alfred Lunt and Lynne Fontanne, and Walt Disney, though he might also have been considered for his notable achievements as an entrepreneur. Generally speaking President Kennedy's selections had emphasized a more academic view of culture, and it fell to President Johnson and others who followed to recognize leading figures from the world of entertainment and popular culture.

The board's list for 1965 was apparently its last, because that year Johnson turned against the award program altogether, for reasons already mentioned. He refused to name any medal winners at all

★ ★

The Distinguished Civilian Service Awards Board

The members appointed by President Kennedy are listed below. George Ball served as board chairman. John Macy was executive secretary.

EXECUTIVE BRANCH MEMBERS

George W. Ball, *undersecretary of state*
John Macy, *Civil Service Commission chairman*
Robert F. Kennedy, *attorney general*
W. Willard Wirtz, *secretary of labor*
Anthony J. Celebrezze, *secretary of health, education, and welfare*
Roswell L. Gilpatric, *deputy secretary of defense*

MEMBERS FROM OUTSIDE THE EXECUTIVE BRANCH

Henry Cabot Lodge, *former ambassador to the United Nations*
Dr. Lee A. DuBridge, *California Institute of Technology president*
Samuel I. Newhouse, *publisher*
Mary McGrory, *journalist*
Arthur J. Goldberg, *Supreme Court justice*

★ ★

until late 1967, and then only gave awards to three deserving members of his administration. After awarding a few other medals to other administration officials on his own initiative in 1968, President Johnson asked Civil Service Commission Chairman and awards board member Macy for a list of prospective nominees, which Macy prepared largely on his own. The president used the list as the basis for selecting his last twenty awards. At that point President Johnson selected the first comedian, show business legend Bob Hope, and the first Hollywood movie star, Gregory Peck.

When President Nixon took office, the board had effectively lapsed because the terms of members outside the executive branch had already expired and President Johnson had appointed no new members. After Macy himself urged the administration not to reconstitute the board, because, among other reasons, it forced the president to accept nominations that did not reflect his own preferences, President Nixon assigned a White House assistant the job of coordinating matters dealing with the medal. During his administration he selected medal winners based on staff suggestions, his own ideas, and some outside suggestions.

Nixon's first award was given in an individual presentation, to jazz musician Duke Ellington, early in his presidency, and he ultimately gave Presidential Medals of Freedom to twenty-seven people. The large award ceremony effectively disappeared while Nixon was president, though. All but one presentation involved three or fewer recipients, which of course also greatly simplified the selection process.

President Nixon introduced an interesting innovation, selecting several recipients from the same discipline and presenting their awards at a group ceremony. In this case, which was President Nixon's only large ceremony, he awarded medals to eight leading journalists in April 1970. President Clinton revived the idea more than two decades later when he presented medals to five noted reformers at a ceremony November 30, 1993.

President Ford considered restoring a selection board to the award-nominating process, but he dropped the idea and relied on his White House staff to provide suggestions from which he made the final selections, just as President Nixon had. President Ford, who served out only the remainder of Nixon's second term, selected twenty-one recipients in 1977 for what was to be the last of the big Presidential Medal of Freedom award ceremonies. The president made what appeared to be a conscious effort to select a broad range of recipients and succeeded admirably, including in the group songwriter Irving Berlin, agricultural scientist Norman Bourlag (originator of the Green Revolution), World War II hero Omar N. Bradley (the "GI's General"), historian Bruce Catton, novelist James Michener, and DNA discoverer James D. Watson.

Ford also named baseball great Joe DiMaggio, only the second athlete to receive the award. President Ford, who had himself been a professional football player, also selected the first athlete, track champion Jesse Owens, in 1976.

President Carter embarked on a determined policy of awarding fewer president's medals from the very outset of his administration. Like previous presidents, he assigned a White House staffer the task of coordinating matters dealing with the medal, including preparing lists of proposed recipients and responding to outside suggestions. In fact, in June 1977, staffer Greg Schneiders actively polled the senior White House staff, all department and agency heads, House Speaker "Tip" O'Neill, West Virginia Sen. Robert C. Byrd, and others in an effort to prepare a list of fifteen suggestions, from which the president might choose five.

Among the fifteen names sent to President Carter on this first list were such widely known and diverse figures as Supreme Court Justice William O. Douglas, Bob Dylan, and Ralph Nader, as well as three who later received the medal, Cesar E. Chavez (1994), Hubert H. Humphrey (1980), and Hyman Rickover (1980). The president's two final selections for the July 11, 1977, ceremony were there as well— Dr. Jonas E. Salk and Martin Luther King, Jr. President Carter later said he selected these two for having made contributions that significantly changed the lives of all Americans for the better.

For the next two years President Carter all but stopped selecting winners of the Presidential Medal of Freedom, awarding just one a year in 1978 and 1979 (Arthur J. Goldberg and Margaret Mead). The president rebuffed several staff proposals to hold award ceremonies during this time, including a 1978 memo by Schneiders calling for a

White House award dinner for perhaps five recipients. Schneiders pointed out that the awards would be a "positive, patriotic, non-controversial exposure for the president" and a way of recognizing important individuals and movements. Other staffers recommended medal presentations in conjunction with a Human Rights Day commemoration ceremony in late 1978 and at a proposed White House reception for the country's leading judges and bar officials in 1979. President Carter turned them all down.

Meanwhile, as had been the case since the award was established, the White House continued receiving outside suggestions for proposed medal recipients. Private individuals, government officials, and even past medal winners would, and still do, write to the White House to suggest people they feel are particularly deserving. In 1978 a member of Congress proposed American Civil Liberties Union leader Roger Nash Baldwin, for example, and in 1981 Baldwin was in the last group awarded medals by the Carter administration.

But in an unusual, and certainly ironic, coincidence involving outside suggestions, the White House received a letter from the Empress Farah of Iran supporting the nomination of Richard Buckminster Fuller, Jr., in the spring of 1978. The empress, whose husband had sought to rapidly modernize Iran, noted Fuller's work had greatly enriched the world and pointed the way toward "a more humane environment" in the future. In a diplomatic gesture, President Carter personally answered the empress's letter on May 9, 1978. But neither of them could have guessed then how quickly and powerfully events would overtake their respective countries. Coincidentally, just two days after President Carter sent his reply, Muslim fundamentalists began rioting in Tehran. Eight months after that, the rioting Muslim fundamentalists forced the Iranian emperor, the empress, and their family to flee the country. Later that year the United States and the Carter administration were drawn into the vortex when Muslim fundamentalists overran the U.S. embassy in Tehran and took fifty-two of the diplomatic staff hostage. The prolonged hostage crisis became a major embarrassment to the Carter administration and probably cost him the election in 1980. Buckminster Fuller had to wait for world events to run their course, but he eventually got a president's medal. President Reagan selected him for the award in 1983.

With the country embroiled in an international crisis in Iran, President Carter finally relented on the issue of presenting president's medals. In mid-1980 he selected fourteen recipients for a White House ceremony, the first big award event of his administration. His choices represented an eclectic assortment of winners, including John Wayne and Tennessee Williams, former president Johnson and ornithologist Roger Tory Peterson, ballet director Lucia Chase and Admiral Hyman Rickover, author Robert Penn Warren and Greek Orthodox Archbishop Iakovos. President Carter himself defined the common thread during his speech at the award ceremony.

Their widely differing styles and careers are united by just one thing—their passionate commitment to their own convictions and the compatibility of their convictions with the enhancement of the quality of American life. They have enriched our lives by broadening the scope of our vision and by deepening our understanding.

President Reagan genuinely enjoyed presenting the Presidential Medal of Freedom—he said so on several occasions—and selected a large number of medal winners during his two terms. In all, he gave the medal to eighty-six people, just short of the total number of recipients during the combined Kennedy-Johnson years.

As with all other presidents from Nixon onward, President Reagan named a White House assistant to coordinate the medal program and prepare lists of proposed recipients when needed. Senior staffers reviewed the selections, giving their input before passing it on to the president. President Reagan then would select from five to twelve names at most for group-award ceremonies. He also awarded a number of medals singly at ceremonies honoring just the one recipient.

President Reagan's selections were as varied as any previous president's, ranging from ballet choreographer George Balanchine to football coach Bear Bryant, from Mother Teresa to test pilot Chuck Yeager, and from pianist Vladimir Horowitz to Count Basie. As might be expected of a former Hollywood star, Reagan named some greats from the entertainment world—among them Pearl Bailey, James Cagney, Helen Hayes, Danny Kaye, Frank Sinatra, and Jimmy Stewart—perhaps more than any other president but still only a small fraction of his overall total. That long list also included some notable names from the religious world, including evangelist Billy Graham, Cardinal Terence Cooke, and theologian Norman Vincent Peale, as well as Mother Teresa.

A number of President Reagan's selections bore his conservative stamp, just as some in the Johnson and Carter years had given recognition to liberal activists. Perhaps Reagan's best known selection in this arena was the arch-conservative and unsuccessful presidential candidate in 1964, Barry Goldwater. But there were others, including the philosopher Sidney Hook; the founding editor of the conservative journal the *National Review*, James Burnham; and perhaps the most controversial of all, Whittaker Chambers, an editor at *Time* magazine whose testimony before Congress had sparked the Alger Hiss case in the late 1940s. Interestingly, these last three had all been involved with the Communist Party earlier in their lives but during the 1930s, though, had renounced those beliefs in favor of conservatism.

Business leaders formed another important thread in President Reagan's selections. He was not the first to name a business executive, as President Kennedy had included Clarence B. Randall, a steel industry leader, among his medal winners in 1963. But President Reagan over his two terms named several others, among them publishing magnate Walter Hubert Annenberg, drugstore chain president Justin Whitlock Dart, defense company president David Packard, and hotel magnate J. Willard Marriott.

President Bush selected thirty-seven medal winners during his one term in office. Like President Reagan, he gave the president's medal ample exposure through smaller, relatively frequent ceremonies that honored anywhere from one to ten recipients. Although President Bush named a fair number of government officials, eleven in all including former president Reagan, he also strove for the variety that characterized selections by previous administrations. To that end he picked such diverse personalities as renowned architect I.M. Pei, author and Holocaust survivor Elie Wiesel, and the hero of Poland's Solidarity movement, Lech Walesa.

President Bush awarded medals to a number of key players in the Mideast crisis of 1990 and 1991, including Generals Colin Powell and Norman Schwarzkopf, the heroes of Operation Desert Storm; and to Secretary of State James Baker; Secretary of Defense Dick Cheney; and National Security Adviser Brent Scowcroft, who oversaw various aspects of the successful effort to drive the Iraqis from Kuwait.

Two other threads in President Bush's selections are worth noting. He awarded medals to a number of notable women, including comedian Lucille Ball, politician Margaret Chase Smith, singer Ella Fitzgerald, First Lady Betty Ford, educator Hanna Gray, and actor Audrey Hepburn. He also selected several people who, like Lucille Ball, were known to literally millions of Americans—baseball great Ted Williams, television news anchor David Brinkley, former "Tonight Show" host Johnny Carson, and race-car driver Richard Petty.

During his first three years in office, President Clinton selected thirty medal winners and held both individual and group-award ceremonies. The president's first award went to Sen. James William Fulbright, the noted Arkansas Democrat, and others honored at individual ceremonies included tennis champion and AIDS activist Arthur Ashe, entertainer Martha Raye, and Desert Storm hero General Colin Powell. President Clinton awarded Powell his second Presidential Medal of Freedom on the occasion of Powell's retirement from the army. Powell was only the second person to receive the award twice, Ellsworth Bunker being the first.

For his first group-award ceremony, President Clinton selected five great reformers who changed America for the better: Marjory Stoneman Douglas, Joseph L. Rauh, Jr., Judge John Minor Wisdom, and Supreme Court Justices William Joseph Brennan and Thurgood Marshall. While Douglas's selection acknowledged environmental reform, the focus was on key civil rights and civil liberties reformers. Justice Marshall was a civil rights reformer who successfully fought segregation both as a lawyer before the Supreme Court and as a jurist from that bench. Rauh, a founder of Americans for Democratic Action, was a persistent champion of civil liberties. Judge Wisdom handed down the order integrating the University of Mississippi in 1962, and Justice Brennan wrote the Supreme Court's "one man, one vote" ruling that became the standard test for apportioning voting districts.

President Clinton's award selections for 1994 returned to the theme of presenting medals to winners with a broad range of backgrounds. Among the nine winners were cartoonist Herbert Block; Cesar E. Chavez, the leader of migrant farmworkers; former U.S. representative Barbara Jordan; then-AFL-CIO President Joseph Lane Kirkland; and former Peace Corps director Robert Sargent Shriver. They were, as the president noted, from "different eras, different races, different generations," yet they all sought in one way or another to "improve the lives of their fellow men and women, to improve the future for our children, to embody the best of what we mean by the term 'American citizen.'" President Clinton awarded another twelve medals in September 1995, honoring former surgeon general C. Everett Koop, Earth Day founder Gaylord Nelson, labor leader Walter Reuther, and others.

The Award Ceremonies

Since President Kennedy created the Presidential Medal of Freedom in 1963, over seventy ceremonies have been held to present the award. The award itself is of course a high honor, but receiving it from the president, and more often than not at the White House, adds immeasurably to the importance of the occasion. Then, too, there is the positive publicity the ceremony generates for all concerned, and for the medal itself.

Over the years a fairly standard format for single- and group-award ceremonies at the White House has developed. The one most popular location is in the White House East Room, although awards have been presented in the State Dining Room (for occasions involving many recipients and guests), the Roosevelt Room, the Oval Office, and the Rose Garden. Generally speaking the ceremony begins with a speech by the president, which honors the significance of the recipients' achievements either in detail or in larger terms. The Presidential Medals of Freedom are then presented to the recipients one by one, usually along with a reading of the accompanying citations. A White House luncheon for the recipients often follows the formal ceremony.

There have been many exceptions to this basic set-up, of course. After presiding over the first two large and formal presentation ceremonies at the White House, President Johnson in 1967 held the first award ceremony outside the executive mansion.

In fact it was also the first, and one of the few, held outside the country—at Cam Ranh Bay military base in what was then South Vietnam. President Nixon established the occasional practice of the president's traveling to award the medal for one reason or another. For example, he awarded president's medals to the three *Apollo 11* astronauts at a banquet honoring them in Los Angeles, to director John Ford at an American Film Institute dinner in Beverly Hills, and to movie producer Samuel Goldwyn, who was too ill to travel, at the Goldwyn home in Beverly Hills. Years later President Bush presented former member of Congress Claude D. Pepper's medal at Walter Reed Hospital, where Pepper was critically ill. Of the over seventy ceremonies held through 1995, though, just twenty-four have been held outside the White House.

Whenever possible presidents have given the award personally, but at times recipients have been unable to make the ceremony because of illness or other problems. The White House then has either mailed the award or had a government official near the recipient's home present the award on the president's behalf. In one unusual instance, President Johnson announced the names of twenty recipients on the last day of his administration. Two administration members, Walt Whitman Rostow and Cyrus Vance, got their medals that day, but the other eighteen awards were sent out later by the new Nixon White House staff.

President Carter's last award ceremony also involved unusual arrangements, because two of the recipients, Roger Nash Baldwin and Warren Minor Christopher, could not attend. Roger Nash Baldwin, then ninety-six, was unexpectedly confined to a hospital in New Jersey, but President Carter sent the award to the deputy U.S. ambassador to the United Nations, who presented it to Baldwin at exactly the time other awards were being given out at the White House. Meanwhile, Christopher was tied up in round-the-clock negotiations in Algiers, trying to win release of the American hostages in Iran. President Carter made special arrangements to have an open telephone line in the East Room, over which Christopher listened to the ceremony.

Over the years, presidents have differed considerably on how much emphasis they have placed on the Presidential Medal of Freedom. President Reagan held the most ceremonies (twenty-one), well ahead of President Nixon, who held the second most (sixteen). But because ceremonies in the early days of the award featured as many as thirty recipients, President Johnson has the distinction of having awarded medals to the most recipients, eighty-nine in all, though his first thirty-one were originally selected by President Kennedy. President Reagan came in a close second with eighty-six recipients during his two full terms.

President Carter, who served just one term, held the fewest award ceremonies (six), followed by Johnson (seven) and Ford (seven), who served only a partial term. President Clinton held award ceremonies seven times in his first three years in office.

WORDS OF THE PRESIDENTS AND THE MEDAL WINNERS

The award ceremonies have been a time for the president to not only honor the medal winners but also to speak about the significance of the winners' accomplishments. For the most part, presidents have focused directly on those achievements and what they have meant to the country. But from time to time, inspired by the importance of the occasion, presidents also have offered thoughts on such larger topics as freedom and the importance of the individual. At other times they have recorded glimpses of important events in the life of the nation.

At his second award ceremony in 1964, for example, President Johnson spoke about how important individuals are to America's success:

The history of America is a history of outstanding achievement by outstanding individuals—inventors and enterprisers, thinkers and doers, creators and constructors …. Only those who doubt the individual

*can be dubious of America's survival and success in this century of
contest .... It was this conviction that led President Kennedy to the
establishment of the Medal of Freedom as our highest civilian honor for
outstanding individuals—citizens who share an extra measure of individual excellence in the mainstream of our well-being and our
advancement. On the talents of such citizens rests the future of our
American civilization.*

In one of history's ironic twists, it was President Nixon who
decided to honor eight journalists in a single award ceremony in
1970. Just a few years later aggressive investigative reporting by
newspaper journalists would reveal the Watergate scandal and force
him out of office. At the time, though, President Nixon mused over
the role of newspapers in society:

*It was Jefferson, I think, who perhaps made the most cogent
comment about the relationship between the press and the
government .... Jefferson once said, as I recall, that if he had to make a
choice between government without newspapers and newspapers
without government, he would take the latter.*

Again it was President Nixon who, in presenting a Presidential
Medal of Freedom to Secretary of State William P. Rogers, told the
following story about Rogers and the nature of diplomacy. Referring
to a comment about Secretary Rogers by a French foreign minister,
the president recalled, "[The minister] said 'I am always happy when
he agrees with me, but I am never unhappy when he disagrees with
me. That is the mark of a very successful secretary of state.'"

President Carter presented his first Presidential Medals of
Freedom to Dr. Jonas E. Salk and (posthumously) to Martin Luther
King, Jr., in 1977. At the ceremony the president pointed out, "There
are many Americans who do great things, who make us proud of
them and their achievements, and who inspire us to do better ourselves. But there are some among those noble achievers who are
exemplary in every way, who reach a higher plateau of achievement."

Some years later at a 1981 award ceremony, President Ronald
Reagan focused on the individual's responsibility to society.

*Now, let me tell you how these six recipients have strengthened our
freedom by reading to you something the historian Edward Gibbon
wrote about ancient Athens, the first democracy and the fountainhead
of Western culture. He wrote that when the Athenians finally wanted
not to give to society but for society to give to them, when the freedom
they wished for was freedom from responsibility, then Athens ceased to
be free. The recipients today have given greatly to our society.*

President Clinton, while awarding General Colin Powell his
second Presidential Medal of Freedom in 1993, observed that Powell's

highly successful career was a victory "for the principle that in our nation, people can rise as far as their talent, their capacities, their dreams, and their discipline will carry them."

Clinton continued:

A long time ago, Thomas Jefferson wrote, 'The creator has not thought proper to mark those in the forehead who are of stuff to make good generals.' The creator has not thought proper to mark them by the color of their skin or the station of their birth or the place where they were born. Thank God for the United States that it is so.

And in a September 1995 award ceremony, President Clinton spoke of the importance of enduring values, even in times of great change.

In this time of change, where people's living patterns and working patterns are undergoing such dramatic transformation, it is necessary and fashionable to focus on new ideas and new visions of the future. We are here today to celebrate people who have always been for change and who have changed America for the better but who have done it based on the enduring values that make this country great: the belief that we have to give all of our citizens the chance to live up to the fullest of their God-given capacities; the conviction that we have to do everything we can to strengthen our families and our communities; the certainty that when the chips are down, we have to do what is good and right, even if it is unpopular in the short run; the understanding that we have the obligation to honor those who came before us by passing better lives and better opportunities on to those who come after.

Speeches given by presidents and medal winners have at times touched, in one way or another, on some great moments in our nation's recent history. While the record they present is by no means complete or even comprehensive, they serve as poignant reminders of past triumphs and tragedies, often providing a unique perspective on times gone by.

With protesters vigorously attacking his Vietnam policies at home in late 1967, for example, President Johnson traveled to Vietnam to award president's medals to three top diplomatic officials involved with the war effort. In his speech at Cam Ranh Bay military base, President Johnson expressed his continued determination to win and his optimism.

This is not the shortest route back to the White House from Australia—through Vietnam. But because it is almost Christmas and because my spirit would be here with you anyway, I had to come over here this morning .... I wish I could have brought you some tangible symbol of the great pride that the American people feel in you, back home .... All the debate that you read about can never obscure that pride. The slogans, the placards, and the signs cannot diminish the power of that love.

I wish I could have brought you, too, some sign that the struggle you are in will soon be over—some indication from the other side that he might be willing to let this suffering land finally heal its wounds.

I can bring you assurance of what you have fought to achieve: The enemy cannot win, now, in Vietnam. He can harass, he can terrorize, he can inflict casualties—while taking far greater losses himself—but he just cannot win. You—each of you—have already seen to that ....

Our leaders have had to meet an enemy that is hardened by experience of over 20 years of fighting—an enemy using his knowledge of the terrain to strike, to move, and to strike again. We have come from way behind.

All the challenges have been met. The enemy is not beaten but he knows that he has met his master in the field. He is holding desperately—he is trying to buy time—hoping that our nation's will does not match his will.

The landing of the *Apollo* astronauts on the moon was of course a happier time for America. President Nixon awarded Presidential Medals of Freedom to each of the *Apollo 11* astronauts soon after their return to earth in 1969. Each of the three astronauts spoke in turn, beginning with Michael Collins:

Mr. President, here stands one proud American, proud to be a member of the Apollo team, proud to be a citizen of the United States of America—which nearly a decade ago said that it would land two men on the moon and then did so, showing along the way, to the world, both the triumphs and the tragedies—and proud to be an inhabitant of this most magnificent planet.

As I looked at it from nearly a quarter of a million miles away, three weeks ago, the people of New York, of Chicago, and of Los Angeles were far from my mind, frankly.

But tonight, they are very close to my mind. I wish that each and every one of you could have been with us today to see their enthusiasm and the magnificent greeting which they gave us upon our return.

And, of course, now the Freedom Medal. I simply cannot express in words what that means to me.

Next came Edwin E. "Buzz" Aldrin, who spoke of the thousands of others who had helped make the Apollo landing possible and of explorations yet to come.

What Apollo has begun we hope will spread out in many directions, not just in space, but underneath the seas and in the cities, to tell unforgettably that we can do what we want to do.

Never before have travelers been so far removed from their homelands as we were. Yet, never before have travelers had so many human beings at their right hand.

There are footprints on the moon. Those footprints belong to each and every one of you, to all of mankind, and they are there because of

*the blood, the sweat, and the tears of millions of people. These footprints
are a symbol of the true human spirit.*

Lastly came Neil Alden Armstrong, who was first to set foot on
the moon after the lunar lander touched down at Tranquility base.

*I was struck this morning in New York by a proudly-waved, but
uncarefully scribbled sign. It said, 'Through you, we touched the moon.'
Through you, we touched the moon.*
It was our privilege today across the country to touch America.
*I suspect that perhaps the most warm genuine feeling that all of us
could receive came through the cheers and shouts and, most of all, the
smiles of our fellow Americans.*
*We hope and think that those people shared our belief that this is the
beginning of a new era when man understands the universe around
him, and the beginning of a new era when man understands himself.*

A year later the *Apollo 13* spacecraft was severely damaged by an
explosion on the way to the moon, and while the world watched and
waited anxiously, the three astronauts aboard succeeded in getting
safely back to earth. Like many people the world over, President
Nixon was deeply impressed by their courage. In announcing his
intention to award the astronauts and the mission ground controllers
president's medals, he told White House reporters:

*I feel that what these men have done has been a great inspiration to
all of us. I think also what the men on the ground have done is an inspiration to us. How men react in adversity determines their true
greatness, and these men have demonstrated that the American
character is sound and strong and capable of taking a very difficult situation and turning it into a really very successful venture …. This is a
superb achievement. It is one the whole nation is proud of.*

Later at the award ceremony, President Nixon said:

*I think it is important that out of this mission we recognize that it
was not a failure. I remember when I called Captain Lovell, he said he
was sorry that they were unable to complete their mission of landing on
the moon. I would reply this way: The three astronauts did not reach
the moon but they reached the hearts of millions of people in America
and in the world.*
*They reminded us in these days when we have this magnificent tech-
nocracy, that men do count, the individual does count. They reminded
us that in these days machines can go wrong and that when machines go
wrong, then the man or the woman, as the case may be, really counts.*

Some years afterward in 1976, President Ford awarded the
Presidential Medal of Freedom to a hero of a bygone era, track star

Jesse Owens. Recounting Owens's historic accomplishment, President Ford said:

In 1936 when Adolph Hitler was trying to turn the [Olympic] games into a spectacle that would glorify racist dogma of the Nazi state, there was a strong movement in the United States against our participation in the games. As it turned out, U.S. participation in those Olympics provided a sharp rebuke of Hitler's racist rubbish. Five black American athletes won eight gold medals in track and field. One American athlete in particular proved that excellence knows no racial or political limits. That man is Jesse Owens ....

In the 1936 Olympics Jesse Owens won four gold medals .... He personally achieved what no statesman, journalist, or general achieved at that time—he forced Adolph Hitler to leave the stadium rather than acknowledge the superb victories of a black American.

Fifteen years later, revisiting that same stadium, Jesse Owens received a standing ovation when he urged his audience, and I quote, 'to stand fast with us for freedom and democracy.' Giants like Jesse Owens show us why politics will never defeat the Olympic spirit. His character, his achievements have continued to inspire Americans as they did the whole world in 1936.

Desert Storm, the victorious allied offensive during the Persian Gulf War, was perhaps the single most important success of the Bush administration. Before presenting Presidential Medals of Freedom to the top military and civilian officials involved in the operation in 1991, President Bush described it this way:

We date our independence from the Declaration of July 4, 1776. But the truth is that in the eyes of the world, the full meaning of America's triumph remained in question well after our revolution was won. And it wasn't until the War of 1812 and the decisive defeat ... of the British forces ... at the Battle of New Orleans ... that America truly seized the world's attention and Americans truly believed that they had arrived as a nation. That victory helped shape our new Nation and move our country toward a destiny that few dreamed possible.

Like that early battle, Desert Storm marks another turning point in America's destiny. The young men and women we've welcomed home from the Gulf return to a Nation far different than the one they left. They come home to a country that is confident and proud, an America that is sure of itself and strong, an America other nations look to for leadership. That's been true in the past, but I think there is a newfound credibility around the world. And Desert Storm proved once more that America's strength of character begins in the heart of every individual.

Later that same year, President Bush welcomed home five American hostages, held for five years by Mideast terrorists, and awarded a president's medal to the one most responsible for their release, UN Secretary-General Javier Pérez de Cuéllar. Speaking of the hostages—Terry Anderson, Thomas Sutherland, Alan Steen, Jesse Turner, and Joseph Cicippio—President Bush said:

All over America people waited for the day your long ordeal would end. And all over America we share your joy, and we thank God that you are free ....

And all of you have survived an act of unspeakable uncivilized cruelty. Hostage-taking is hell on a human scale, not just for the innocents held captive, but for the families, for the families that they left behind. And no power on Earth can give back the years that you've lost. And yet no one can take from you the strength of the spirit that sustained you.

The world is now learning the horrors that you endured. But we're learning as well, and this is the good news, the story of your survival, the miracle that you fashioned from the hope your captors could not take away.

We know now you used the language of the deaf to communicate from cell to cell to speak to one another in silence, how you managed to learn from one another, laugh with one another, help each other sustain a stubborn indignity. And you demonstrated each day in captivity a defiant faith. You believed in your country and your families and your colleagues and yourselves. And you knew that one day you would go free.

Your triumph shines new light on a simple truth: The days and years apart burn away the trivial things we once thought had value to reveal what truly matters in life—family, faith, hope, and love. And seeing freedom through your eyes, even for a moment, frees us from the petty concerns that so often hold us hostage and distract us from life's larger joys, larger meaning.

On That Matter of Freedom

How freedom is defined often depends on one's particular perspective. But from time to time at presentation ceremonies for the Presidential Medal of Freedom, presidents and recipients alike have offered their thoughts on what it is, or what it should be.

The famed black jazz musician Duke Ellington received his president's medal on April 29, 1969, and after thanking President Nixon and assembled guests, he spoke a few words on his view of freedom.

We speak of freedom of expression and we speak of freedom generally as being something very sweet and fat and things like that.

In the end when we get down to the payoff, what we actually say is that we would like very much to mention the four major freedoms that my friend and writing-and-arranging composer, Billy Strayhorn, lived by and enjoyed.

That was freedom from hate, unconditionally; freedom from self-pity; freedom from fear of possibly doing something that may help someone else more than it would him; and freedom from the kind of pride that could make a man feel that he is better than his brother.

President Reagan, who spoke often on the subject of freedom, gave a similarly blunt definition of it at a 1986 award ceremony.

Freedom is important to all of us. As someone who spent many years making speeches, I have quoted many definitions of freedom—some very moving and eloquent. But I've always liked George Orwell's blunt and unadorned statement. He said, "Freedom is the right to say no." There's something kind of happily rebellious about that definition, and I thought of it this morning because I decided this year's recipients of the Medal of Freedom are distinguished by this. You're a group of happy rebels …. But it's probably true that there is little point to freedom unless it's accompanied by a big "Yes." And each of you has uttered a resounding Whitmanesque "Yes" to many things—excellence and risk and reach, to courage and the untried and the supposedly impossible.

As to America's responsibility for freedom in the world, President Reagan said this at an award ceremony just before leaving office in 1989:

America's freedom does not belong to just one nation. We're custodians of freedom for the world. In Philadelphia, two centuries ago, James Allen wrote in his diary that "If we fail, liberty no longer continues to inhabit this globe." Well we didn't fail. And still, we must not fail. For freedom is not the property of one generation; it's the obligation of this and every generation. It's our duty to protect it and expand it and pass it undiminished to those still unborn.

The 1989 ceremony in which Poland's national hero, Lech Walesa, received the Presidential Medal of Freedom served as a stark reminder of what life without freedom is like. President Bush recounted the dramatic story of Communist Poland's crackdown on the Solidarity movement:

Just before Christmas, 1981, a darkness descended across Poland for the third time this century. What had begun as a year of hope and freedom ended in violence and repression. In snow-filled crossroads and town squares across Poland, iron tanks rumbled to a stop. Lech Walesa made the sign of the cross on the foreheads of his sleeping children and was taken away into the night. Solidarity, a movement embracing the Polish Nation, was outlawed. Communications with the outside world were cut. And Poland awoke to snow and steel and silence, an entire nation imprisoned.
But you can't lock up a dream. One by one, candles lit the windows of Poland's farmhouses and tenements, silent beacons of liberty still burning in the hearts of a brave and ancient people ….
When spring came, a time of renewal and rebirth, Lech Walesa's fate

was still unknown. And as colleges and universities [in America] approached graduation, one by one, again and again, the same two names were heard, Lech Walesa and Solidarity. Of course, Lech Walesa could not come to accept those honorary degrees. And so, in crowded assembly halls and packed arenas across America...stage after stage held a single, unfilled place—an empty chair bearing only the Solidarity banner—awaiting the release of Lech Walesa.

...For eight years, these empty chairs and the American people have waited for you to come .... Lech Walesa, on behalf of the people of the United States, I am proud to say to you: Take your place in this house of freedom. Take your place in the empty chair ....

In just a few days, you will be the second private citizen from abroad—second in our history—to ever address a joint meeting of Congress, after the Marquis de Lafayette in 1824. And like him, you helped win an historic struggle. And like him, you represent not only a people but also an idea—an idea whose time has come. That idea is freedom. The time is now.

...The story of our times is the story of brave men and women who seized a moment, who took a stand. Lech Walesa showed how one individual could inspire others—in them a faith so powerful that it vindicated itself—[and] changed the course of a nation. History may make men, but Lech Walesa made history. And I believe history continues to be made every day by small daily acts of courage, by people who strive to make a difference. Such people, says Lech, "are everywhere, in every factory, steel mill, mine, and shipyard—everywhere."

Thank you, Poland, for showing us that the dream is alive. And thank you, Poland, for showing us that a dream wrought by flesh and blood cannot be stilled by walls of steel.

Part II

Medal Winners and their Achievements

Lyndon B. Johnson

Vice President Lyndon B. Johnson, a Democrat, became president on November 22, 1963, following the assassination of President Kennedy. He completed the remainder of Kennedy's term (1963–1965) and was elected to serve his own term (1965–1969).

MEDAL CEREMONIES

December 6, 1963 *The White House*

September 14, 1964 *The White House*

December 23, 1967 *Cam Ranh Bay, South Vietnam*

February 28, 1968 *The White House*

December 9, 1968 *The White House*

January 16, 1969 *Department of State*

January 20, 1969 *Department of State*

Marian Anderson

<small>ARTIST AND CITIZEN, SHE HAS ENNOBLED HER RACE AND HER COUNTRY WHILE HER VOICE HAS ENTHRALLED THE WORLD.</small>

★ ★ ★

President Lyndon B. Johnson awarded Anderson the Presidential Medal of Freedom with the above citation during a White House ceremony December 6, 1963. Anderson had been selected as a medal recipient earlier in 1963 by President John F. Kennedy, who was assassinated shortly before the award ceremony.

Often called the world's greatest contralto, Marian Anderson sang operatic arias and the works of such classical composers as Bach, Brahms, Handel, and Schubert, as well as spirituals and patriotic anthems. She is remembered today both for the stunning quality of her voice and as a pioneer in the movement for racial equality in America. In 1955, she became the first black singer to perform at New York's Metropolitan Opera.

Born in 1897 and raised in Philadelphia, she was the eldest of three daughters. Her interest in music flowered early; she joined the junior choir at age six and by age thirteen already possessed an impressive vocal range. Formal vocal training began during high school and continued for years after she graduated.

Anderson's first big success came in 1925 when she won a competition to perform as an operatic soloist with the Philadelphia Symphony Orchestra, then directed by Eugene Ormandy. Continuing her vocal training, Anderson gave a Carnegie Hall recital in 1929. But it was her European tour between 1933 and 1935 that firmly established her reputation as a leading contralto. She gave performances for the kings of Denmark and Sweden, and during the last engagement of that tour, conductor Arturo Toscanini told her, "A voice like yours is heard only once in a hundred years."

Anderson was destined to be more than a world-class singer, however. During the late 1930s, she toured both Europe and the United States, including many southern cities. But it was an engagement in Washington, D.C., that stirred a public outcry and became a famous skirmish in the movement for racial equality. In 1939 the Daughters of the American Revolution (DAR) refused to book Anderson at Constitution Hall, its headquarters, raising a storm of protest against racial discrimination. First Lady Eleanor Roosevelt joined other public figures protesting the incident and resigned from the DAR. Granted the use of the Lincoln Memorial, Anderson performed there on Easter Day 1939 before some seventy-five-thousand spectators.

She married Orpheus Fisher, an architect, in 1943 and toured for many years, sometimes giving as many as sixty concerts and recitals a year. Anderson again confronted racial barriers on January 7, 1955, this time as the first black singer to perform at the Metropolitan Opera in New York City. She sang the part of Ulrica in Verdi's *Un ballo in maschera.*

Anderson, who published *My Lord What a Morning! An Autobiography* in 1956, began her final singing tour in 1963 and retired upon its completion in 1965. The recipient of the Spingarn Medal from the National Association for the Advancement of Colored People, she also was awarded the Congressional Gold Medal in 1978. She died in 1993 at her nephew's home in Portland, Oregon.

Ralph Bunche

SCHOLAR AND DIPLOMAT, SERVANT OF THE EMERGING WORLD ORDER, HE HAS OPENED UP NEW VISTAS IN THE DEMANDING QUEST FOR INTERNATIONAL JUSTICE AND PEACE.

★ ★ ★

President Lyndon B. Johnson awarded Bunche the Presidential Medal of Freedom with the above citation during a White House ceremony December 6, 1963. The award was accompanied by the added accolade "with distinction." Bunche had been selected as a medal recipient earlier in 1963 by President John F. Kennedy, who was assassinated shortly before the award ceremony.

A high-ranking UN official, civil rights advocate, scholar, and educator, Ralph Bunche was among the most widely respected blacks during his lifetime. UN secretary-general U Thant once praised him as "an international institution in his own right, transcending both nationality and race in a way that is achieved by very few."

Bunche rose from modest beginnings to achieve this worldwide reputation. Born the son of a Detroit, Michigan, barber in 1904, he was raised in Los Angeles by his maternal grandmother after being orphaned in 1917. Despite the hardships, Bunche showed his academic brilliance and capacity for hard work early on. He finished high school first in his class and graduated summa cum laude from the University of California, Los Angeles, in 1927. After earning his master's degree in political science at Harvard in 1928, Bunche became an instructor at the predominantly black Howard University in Washington, D.C., where he founded and chaired the political science department. In 1930 he married Ruth Harris, an elementary school teacher.

Bunche continued striving to excel with characteristic energy during the 1930s and 1940s. He earned a doctorate in government and international relations at Harvard, the first black to do so, and began working to improve conditions for blacks in America through civil rights activism. He helped found the National Negro Congress in 1936 and published *A World View of Race* the same year. In 1949, Bunche joined the National Association for the Advancement of Colored People board of directors, a position he held for over two decades.

Though Bunche continued supporting civil rights causes in the United States, World War II thrust him into international affairs, first as head of the Office of Strategic Services (OSS) Africa section and then as a member of the State Department planning group for the postwar colonial world. At the State Department, he helped organize the United Nations in 1945 and had an important role in drafting sections of the UN charter on colonial territories.

Bunche joined the UN staff as the trusteeship division head in 1946. During the first Arab-Israeli war in 1948 he became the UN mediator and eventually negotiated individual armistice agreements between Israel and the major Arab combatants. Bunche's diplomatic skill and determination in resolving the conflict won him the Nobel Peace Prize in 1950, making him the first black recipient.

His career was far from over, however. Remaining a top-level UN adviser and trouble-shooter, Bunche eventually rose to under-secretary-general for special political affairs. Besides taking part in organizing the UN Development Program and the UN Atomic Energy Agency, he also helped arrange UN peacekeeping operations during the second Arab-Israeli war and during later conflicts in the Congo, Cyprus, Yemen, and Pakistan.

Bunche died in 1971, shortly after retiring from the UN. He was sixty-seven years old.

Ellsworth Bunker

CITIZEN AND DIPLOMAT, HE HAS BROUGHT INTEGRITY, PATIENCE AND A COMPASSIONATE UNDERSTANDING OF OTHER MEN AND NATIONS TO THE SERVICE OF THE REPUBLIC UNDER THREE PRESIDENTS.

★ ★ ★

President Lyndon B. Johnson awarded Bunker the Presidential Medal of Freedom with the above citation during a White House ceremony December 6, 1963. The medal was accompanied by the added accolade "with distinction." Bunker had been selected as a medal recipient earlier in 1963 by President John F. Kennedy, who was assassinated shortly before the award ceremony. [Bunker was awarded a second Presidential Medal of Freedom on December 23, 1967. See p.134.]

One of only two people who have received the Presidential Medal of Freedom twice, Ellsworth Bunker capped his twenty-four-year career as a sugar company executive with twenty-seven years in the diplomatic service. *(See also the entry for Colin Powell, p. 440).* He was born in Yonkers, New York, in 1894. His father owned the National Sugar Refining Company, and after Bunker graduated from Yale in 1916, he learned the business from the bottom up. Starting out as a dockworker in the company's shipping department, he worked his way up to director by 1927. He was National Sugar's president from 1940 to 1948 and served as the board chairman from 1948 to 1951.

Bunker's diplomatic career began after Secretary of State Dean Acheson, his classmate at Yale, recommended him for an appointment as ambassador to Argentina. Bunker's extensive business dealings in South America made him an ideal candidate, and in 1951 President Harry S. Truman appointed him. Bunker's next assignment, as Italy's ambassador, lasted from 1952 until President Dwight D. Eisenhower succeeded Truman in 1953. Recognizing Bunker as a skilled diplomat, President Eisenhower named him ambassador to India in 1956, a post Bunker held until 1961. During that time he also served as ambassador to Nepal (1956–1959).

Special assignments during the 1960s helped Bunker win his reputation as a diplomatic trouble-shooter and skilled negotiator with a knack for finding workable compromises. He resolved disputes between the Netherlands and Indonesia over possessions in New Guinea (1962), between the Saudis and Egyptians over interference in the Yemeni civil war (1963), and between the United States and Panama over bloody riots by Panamanians in the Canal Zone (1964).

From 1964 to 1966 Bunker served as chairman of the Council of the Organization of American States and during that time helped ease the crisis in the Dominican Republic resulting from a right-wing military coup. President Johnson appointed him ambassador to South Vietnam in 1967, an assignment that lasted through the most troubled years of the Vietnam conflict. (President Richard Nixon kept him on in Vietnam until the 1973 peace settlement ending U.S. involvement there.) Meanwhile, in 1964, Bunker married career diplomat Carol Clendening Laise, his first wife having died a few years earlier.

As ambassador at large, Bunker represented the United States during the 1973 Geneva peace conference between the Arabs and Israelis. That same year he took over the U.S. delegation in the Panama Canal Treaty talks. Bunker spent years negotiating the controversial treaty, which turned the Panama Canal over to Panama and was concluded in 1978. It was probably his most important accomplishment.

Bunker retired that same year at age eighty-four. He then served as founding chairman of the Georgetown University Institute for the Study of Diplomacy until his death in 1984. He was ninety.

Pablo Casals

STATESMAN OF MUSIC, HE HAS INCARNATED THE FREEDOM OF ART, WHILE THE CELLO UNDER HIS FINGERS HAS TOUCHED THE HEART OF THE WORLD.

★ ★ ★

President Lyndon B. Johnson awarded Casals the Presidential Medal of Freedom with the above citation during a White House ceremony December 6, 1963. Casals, the first foreign recipient of the medal, had been selected earlier in 1963 by President John F. Kennedy, who was assassinated shortly before the award ceremony.

Pablo Casals, the second of eleven children, was born in Catalonia, Spain, in 1876. He began studying music at age five, composing at seven and playing the cello at ten. With his mother's help, Casals continued studying music and in 1899 made his Paris debut as a cello virtuoso. He also began giving public performances of Bach's unaccompanied suites for cello, which by the richness of his interpretations introduced them to modern audiences.

Casals's musical career was firmly established from this time forward. He toured Europe regularly and traveled to the United States more than a dozen times over the next twenty years. He founded the Pau Casals Orchestra at Barcelona in 1920, which he conducted and supported financially to bring orchestral music to his native Catalonia.

Casals, who called orchestras "the greatest of all instruments," increasingly turned to conducting. He did guest performances with such prestigious orchestras as the Vienna Philharmonic, the London Symphony, and the New York Symphony and became famous for his interpretations of music by Bach, Beethoven, and others.

When Fascist dictator General Francisco Franco gained control of Spain in 1939, Casals went into self-imposed exile at Prades, France, along with other exiled Catalans. During World War II he gave no public performances, a self-imposed musical silence he continued afterward to protest Franco's Fascist regime in Spain. Finally, in 1950, he performed as a soloist and conductor at Prades for a Bach bicentenary festival. Casals organized the Prades Festival the next year, performing there annually for the next few years. In 1956 he began performing outside Prades again, moved to Puerto Rico, and established the annual Festival Casals there. Casals, who had divorced two previous wives, married his Puerto Rican cello student, Martita Angelica Montaner, in 1957.

Among the most renowned personalities in the music world by this time, he performed at the White House for President Kennedy in 1961. Two years later, in July 1963, President Kennedy recognized his outstanding accomplishments by selecting him as a recipient of the Presidential Medal of Freedom.

Casals developed modern techniques for playing the cello and helped establish a place for it as a solo instrument. Famed for his interpretations of the classical composers, he also wrote symphonies, sonatas, motets, string quartets, and songs, as well as solo pieces for the cello and violin. Casals died in 1973, about two months before his ninety-seventh birthday.

Genevieve Caulfield

TEACHER AND HUMANITARIAN, SHE HAS BEEN FOR FOUR DECADES A ONE-WOMAN PEACE CORPS IN SOUTHEAST ASIA, WINNING VICTORIES OVER DARKNESS BY HELPING THE BLIND TO BECOME FULL MEMBERS OF SOCIETY.

★ ★ ★

President Lyndon B. Johnson awarded Caulfield the Presidential Medal of Freedom with the above citation during a White House ceremony December 6, 1963. Caulfield had been selected as a medal recipient earlier in 1963 by President John F. Kennedy, who was assassinated shortly before the award ceremony.

The aunt of actress Joan Caulfield, Genevieve Caulfield was born blind in 1889. But she did not let her handicap restrict her life. In fact, she led a more adventurous life than many sighted people. After graduating from both the Overbrock School for the Blind and Columbia University, Caulfield went overseas to Japan, where she taught English.

Miraculously, she survived the 1923 earthquake that destroyed Tokyo and killed some 100,000 people soon after she arrived there. Caulfield continued teaching in Japan until 1938 when she moved to Thailand and there established a school for the blind (1939). Japanese authorities kept her under guard during World War II but allowed her to continue operating the school. After the war, her school for the blind prospered and in 1956 she set up a similar school in Vietnam.

Caulfield published her autobiography, *The Kingdom Within,* in 1960 and three years later received the Presidential Medal of Freedom from President Johnson for her work in Southeast Asia. She continued working there for the rest of her life and even traveled to South Vietnam during the war years. (She strongly supported U.S. involvement against the takeover of South Vietnam by the North Vietnamese.)

Caulfield died in 1972 while in Bangkok, Thailand. She was eighty-three.

James B. Conant

SCIENTIST AND EDUCATOR, HE HAS LED THE AMERICAN PEOPLE
IN THE FIGHT TO SAVE OUR MOST PRECIOUS RESOURCE—OUR
CHILDREN.

★ ★ ★

*President Lyndon B. Johnson awarded Conant the Presidential Medal
of Freedom with the above citation during a White House ceremony
December 6, 1963. Conant had been selected as a medal recipient
earlier in 1963 by President John F. Kennedy, who was assassinated
shortly before the award ceremony.*

Science became the key to James B. Conant's first successes, but it
proved to be just a steppingstone in his long and varied career. Born
in Dorchester, Massachusetts, in 1893, he showed an early interest in
chemistry. By 1916 he had earned both his bachelor's and doctor's
degrees in that field from Harvard University, and after a year in
poison gas research for the government during World War I, he
returned to Harvard in 1919 as a chemistry instructor. Conant
married Grace Thayer Richards in 1921.

Conant's research into the molecular structures of chlorophyll in
plants and hemoglobin in blood gained him a wide reputation in the
scientific community. By 1931 he had risen to chairman of the
chemistry department, but his tenure was brief. Just two years later
Harvard named him its president, even though he was only forty
years old. As president, Conant instituted new programs and continued his predecessor's policy of establishing strong professional
schools to enhance the core undergraduate program.

While remaining as Harvard president, he also played a key role in
organizing the U.S. scientific research effort during World War II.
The National Defense Research Committee chairman from 1941 to
1946, Conant helped organize the Manhattan Project to develop the
atomic bomb. Later he reportedly suggested Hiroshima as the target
for the first of two atomic bombs dropped to force Japan's surrender.

Conant's government work led him into a diplomatic career. In
1953 he became the U.S. high commissioner for West Germany,
resigning his post at Harvard to do so. President Dwight D.
Eisenhower next appointed him as U.S. ambassador to West
Germany in 1955, and Conant served until 1957.

Soon after returning to the United States, Conant's career took yet
another turn—this time into education reform. Armed with grants
from the Carnegie Corporation, he compiled a series of reports on
the U.S. education system that highlighted problems and suggested
reforms. The first, *The American High School Today,* appeared in 1959
with twenty-one recommendations for improving secondary schools.
Conant went on a nationwide tour promoting the reforms and the

following year issued his study of the junior high school system. Other studies followed during the 1960s, focusing public attention on such problems as unemployed, poorly educated youths in ghettos, teacher education, and state education bureaucracies.

Following a two-year stint as education adviser to the West Berlin government (1963–1965), Conant resumed his education reform work and in 1970 published his autobiography, *My Several Lives*. He died in 1978, at age eighty-four.

John F. Enders

PHYSICIAN AND RESEARCHER, HE HAS OPENED NEW PATHWAYS TO MEDICAL DISCOVERY AND HAS BEEN AN EXAMPLE AND COMPANION TO TWO GENERATIONS OF DOCTORS IN THE DEMANDING QUEST FOR SCIENTIFIC TRUTH.

★ ★ ★

President Lyndon B. Johnson awarded Enders the Presidential Medal of Freedom with the above citation during a White House ceremony December 6, 1963. Enders had been selected earlier in 1963 by President John F. Kennedy, who was assassinated shortly before the award ceremony.

During the 1940s and early 1950s a severe polio epidemic swept the United States. The dreaded viral disease left many children and young adults crippled for life, and medical researchers across the country sought ways to prevent the disease. But it was a small research team at Boston Children's Hospital, led by virologist John F. Enders, that made the key breakthroughs needed to produce a successful polio vaccine. For this and his subsequent work on viral diseases, Dr. Enders was awarded the Presidential Medal of Freedom.

Dr. Enders was born in 1897, the son of a West Hartford, Connecticut, banker. He graduated from Yale in 1920 after serving as a navy pilot during World War I, and completed his master's degree in English literature at Harvard in 1922. While continuing his graduate studies, he met Professor Hans Zinsser, head of Harvard's Department of Bacteriology and Immunology. Zinsser's enthusiasm for science proved infectious, and by 1927 Enders had switched fields and was working in Zinsser's research lab. Enders married his first wife, Sarah Frances Bennett, that same year. She died in 1943, and in 1951 he married Carolyn Keane.

Enders earned his doctorate in microbiology at Harvard in 1930 and began teaching at Harvard Medical School. Then in 1937 he reached a critical turning point, switching from bacterial research to the investigation of viruses. Ten years later, while still teaching at Harvard, Enders set up the Infectious Diseases Research Laboratory at Boston Children's Hospital.

Enders and his research team at Children's Hospital began their work at a crucial time. Little was known about viruses then, in part because the organisms had proved so hard to work with in the laboratory. Viruses needed living tissue to grow, and up until the 1940s researchers had only one highly complex and impractical method for culturing them. This made work on viruses that attack human cells especially difficult.

Focusing on the problem of human virus tissue culture, Enders and his researchers soon discovered a simple method for growing tissue in the laboratory. Next they succeeded in using their tissue culture to grow the chicken pox virus and in 1948 made what became a key discovery in the fight against polio. They found that the polio virus, once believed to grow only in human nerve tissue, could be cultured in various types of human tissue. Their work paved the way for an effective polio vaccine, and for their contribution Enders and two colleagues shared the 1954 Nobel Prize in physiology or medicine.

Continuing their work, Enders's team isolated the measles virus in 1954 and later identified a strain that safely produced immunity. Present-day measles vaccines come from this viral strain.

In 1962 Harvard named Enders a university professor, its highest faculty honor. After retiring from both Harvard and Children's Hospital in 1977, Dr. Enders died suddenly in 1985, at age eighty-eight.

Felix Frankfurter

JURIST, SCHOLAR, COUNSELOR, CONVERSATIONALIST, HE HAS BROUGHT TO ALL HIS ROLES A ZEST AND WISDOM WHICH HAVE MADE HIM TEACHER TO HIS TIME.

★ ★ ★

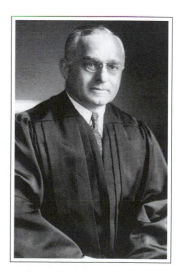

President Lyndon B. Johnson awarded Frankfurter the Presidential Medal of Freedom with the above citation during a White House ceremony December 6, 1963. The medal was accompanied by the added accolade "with distinction." Frankfurter had been selected as a medal recipient by President John F. Kennedy, who was assassinated shortly before the award ceremony.

As a Harvard Law School professor and Supreme Court justice, Felix Frankfurter ranked among the most highly regarded—and most controversial—legal figures of his time. The only naturalized U.S. citizen to become a justice, he was a proponent of such liberal causes as the American Civil Liberties Union, which he helped found, and the New Deal, which he helped shape as an adviser to President Franklin D. Roosevelt. As a justice, though, he angered liberals on and off the Court by opposing expanded protections for minorities and individual rights.

The son of a former rabbinical student, Frankfurter was born in Vienna, Austria, in 1882 and came to the United States in 1894 when his family moved to New York City. He was an outstanding student, graduating from an accelerated bachelor's program at the College of the City of New York in 1902 and finishing first in his class at Harvard Law School in 1906. Soon after, Frankfurter began working for Henry L. Stimson, the U.S. attorney of New York.

Stimson became a close friend and valuable contact, and when President William Howard Taft appointed him secretary of war in 1911, he got Frankfurter a job in the War Department. Frankfurter made important contacts in Washington, D.C., and began lifelong friendships with two important mentors, Justice Oliver Wendell Holmes and the future justice Louis D. Brandeis. In 1914 Frankfurter left Washington to become a professor at Harvard Law School.

Except for his wartime service between 1917 and 1920, Frankfurter spent the next twenty-five years teaching at Harvard. He established his reputation as a leading legal scholar during this time, and through Holmes, Brandeis, and others, he kept up his contact with the political scene. In 1920 he helped found the ACLU and became involved in various public debates of the day, among them the highly controversial Sacco-Vanzetti murder trial, which he criticized for lack of due process. Later, Frankfurter became an adviser to Franklin D. Roosevelt while the future president was still a governor. An enthusiastic supporter of Roosevelt's New Deal and its concept of government-sponsored social programs, Frankfurter continued as a trusted adviser after Roosevelt became president in 1933.

President Roosevelt named Frankfurter to the Supreme Court in 1939, where he succeeded Justice Benjamin Cardozo. He joined other Roosevelt appointees in supporting New Deal programs, but despite his strong liberal background, he firmly believed in judicial restraint. He was willing to let the government limit civil liberties of individuals and minorities unless those rights were essential to the broader framework of the Constitution. Among his most controversial opinions in this vein was *Minersville School District v. Gobitis* (1940). The Court upheld the suspension from school of Jehovah's Witnesses students who refused to salute the American flag.

Frankfurter retired from the high court in 1962, at age eighty, and died three years later. His wife, the former Marion A. Denman, survived him.

Karl Holton

Innovator in applying imaginative solutions to problems of juvenile delinquency, he has contributed generously to developing responsible citizenship among our youth.

* * *

President Lyndon B. Johnson awarded Holton the Presidential Medal of Freedom with the above citation during a White House ceremony December 6, 1963. Holton had been selected as a medal recipient earlier in 1963 by President John F. Kennedy, who was assassinated shortly before the award ceremony.

A top expert on juvenile delinquency, Karl Holton was born in 1898. He graduated from the University of Washington and went on to study sociology and psychology at the University of California and the University of Southern California.

Holton began working in the social services field in 1928 as a probation officer for the Los Angeles County Probation Department. Moving up the ranks he became chief of the department, and in 1943 he was appointed director of the California Youth Authority. He remained in that post until 1952, when he returned to Los Angeles to become head of the city's probation department. Holton retired in 1963.

During his long career, Holton focused on guidance work with youthful offenders and acted as a consultant for both the state and national correctional systems.

John Fitzgerald Kennedy

JOHN FITZGERALD KENNEDY, 35TH PRESIDENT OF THE UNITED STATES, SOLDIER, SCHOLAR, STATESMAN, DEFENDER OF FREEDOM, PIONEER FOR PEACE, AUTHOR OF HOPE—COMBINING COURAGE WITH REASON, AND COMBATING HATE WITH COMPASSION, HE LED THE LAND HE LOVED TOWARD NEW FRONTIERS OF OPPORTUNITY FOR ALL MEN AND PEACE FOR ALL TIME. BELOVED IN A LIFE OF SELFLESS SERVICE, MOURNED BY ALL IN A DEATH OF SENSELESS CRIME, THE ENERGY, FAITH AND DEVOTION WHICH HE BROUGHT TO HIS EXTRAORDINARILY SUCCESSFUL THOUGH TRAGICALLY BRIEF ENDEAVORS WILL HEREAFTER "LIGHT OUR COUNTRY AND ALL WHO SERVE IT—AND THE GLOW FROM THAT FIRE CAN TRULY LIGHT THE WORLD."

★ ★ ★

President Lyndon B. Johnson awarded Kennedy a posthumous Presidential Medal of Freedom with the above citation on December 6, 1963, during the first White House ceremony for presenting the new medal. The final quotation was from Kennedy's 1961 inaugural address. Attorney General Robert F. Kennedy received the award on his brother's behalf.

Among the best-remembered and most highly regarded presidents of this century, John F. Kennedy was born in Brookline, Massachusetts, in 1917. He was the second son in an affluent Irish Catholic family that grew to four sons and five daughters. His father, Joseph P. Kennedy, was a successful businessman who later actively supported Franklin D. Roosevelt and served in various appointive posts during the Roosevelt administration.

The young Kennedy was raised in a strict household where competition, intellectual development, and public service were held in high esteem. Frail and sickly as a child, he later became involved in sports and took a special interest in foreign affairs while at Harvard University. Graduating cum laude in 1940, Kennedy saw his senior essay, about Britain's failed policy of appeasing the Nazis during the late 1930s, become a bestseller, *Why England Slept* (1940).

The military rejected Kennedy because of his back problems, but he pulled strings to get into the navy during World War II. Eventually, the navy made him commander of the torpedo boat PT–109, and Kennedy saw action in the South Pacific—but not for long. In the summer of 1943 a Japanese destroyer rammed Kennedy's boat, throwing everyone aboard into waters covered with burning gasoline. While swimming to safety, Kennedy courageously towed a seriously injured crewman along with him. The writer John Hersey heard of the story and publicized Kennedy's heroism in a *New Yorker* article. Kennedy was sent back to the United States to recover from malaria and a new flare-up of back problems.

A year later, the war-related death of his older brother, Joseph Jr., proved an important turning point in Kennedy's life. Kennedy's father had expected that young Joseph would carry the family name into politics, but that role now fell to John Kennedy. Prodded by his father, he won a seat in the U.S. House as a representative from Massachusetts. He served three terms (1947–1953) before running successfully for a Senate seat in 1952. Just months after becoming a senator, Kennedy married Jacqueline Lee Bouvier.

During his Senate years, he voted for building the Saint Lawrence Seaway (1954), despite strong opposition at home in Massachusetts, and in the late 1950s helped push through measures for labor reform. In foreign policy he saw the Cold War as a power struggle and in the mid–1950s opposed U.S. intervention in Southeast Asia. Meanwhile, during recovery from back surgery, Kennedy wrote his famous book about American politicians who had stood up for principles despite the risks to their careers. *Profiles in Courage* (1956) won Kennedy the 1957 Pulitzer Prize for biography, and the following year he won reelection to the Senate.

Despite his youth and the fact that no Catholic had ever before been elected president, Kennedy ran in 1960 and won a narrow victory over Richard Nixon. Though Kennedy once called himself "an idealist without illusions," he sought to move the country in a new direction after eight years of Eisenhower conservatism. At home he appealed to the nation's patriotic spirit ("ask not what your country can do for you; ask what you can do for your country") and advanced his New Frontier program of proposed liberal reforms.

Meanwhile, he quickly became entangled in risky Cold War confrontations. Weeks after the complete failure of the CIA-backed Bay of Pigs invasion of Cuba in April 1961, the young Kennedy sat across the bargaining table from the wily old Soviet leader Nikita Khrushchev and proposed that the two superpowers refrain from enlarging their spheres of influence. Khrushchev flatly rejected the idea and threatened to force the United States out of West Berlin.

Kennedy activated reservists and started a near-panic by calling for a fallout shelter program to provide protection in the event of nuclear war. The East Germans put up the Berlin Wall two months later, and East-West tensions only continued to get worse.

The world held its collective breath the following year during the Cuban Missile Crisis. With the United States and the Soviet Union teetering on the brink of nuclear war, Kennedy scored a victory over Khrushchev by forcing him to withdraw Soviet missiles from Cuba. Relations with the Soviets improved after that, but the Cold War was far from over. Faced with a mounting Communist-backed rebellion in South Vietnam, President Kennedy sharply increased the number of

U.S. military advisers in South Vietnam (to more than 16,000) during 1962 and 1963 and approved some combat roles.

At home Kennedy's political clout was limited. He established the Peace Corps and proclaimed the goal of sending men to the moon by the end of the decade, but his New Frontier program—including aid to education, medical care for the aged, and civil rights legislation— was for the most part stalled by conservative opposition in Congress. Civil rights protests in the South were making headlines, though, forcing Kennedy to move faster than even he wanted.

At first President Kennedy resorted to his considerable executive powers to circumvent Congress—he ended segregation in interstate transportation, sent federal troops to back court-ordered desegregation at the University of Mississippi, and created the President's Committee on Equal Employment Opportunity, among other actions. But television coverage of the brutal police crackdown on Dr. Martin Luther King's marchers in Birmingham, Alabama, in the spring of 1963 forced President Kennedy to go further still, and he went on television to ask for sweeping new civil rights laws. He sent a major civil rights bill to Congress soon after. *(See also the entry for King, p. 253.)*

President Kennedy did not live to see the bill passed, however. While riding in a motorcade through Dallas, Texas, on November 22, 1963, he was killed by an assassin named Lee Harvey Oswald.

The debate over the Kennedy legacy continues even today. In the years immediately after his assassination, Kennedy was remembered as a martyr who might have accomplished great things had his life not been cut short. Certainly he aroused the ideals and expectations of many millions of Americans. His successor, President Lyndon B. Johnson, continued many of Kennedy's policies. *(See also the entry for Johnson, p. 266.)* Johnson not only won passage of much of the New Frontier program, but also enlarged upon it to create the Great Society program. So the spirit, if not the largesse, of the 1960s social reforms was Kennedy's.

President Johnson also vastly expanded U.S. involvement in Vietnam, building on Kennedy's earlier commitment (including U.S. complicity in the assassination of the corrupt dictator Diem). President Kennedy might well have steered clear of the trap Johnson fell into in Vietnam, but a key part of Kennedy's military policy—his strategy of "flexible response"—was to develop conventional forces for use in localized brushfire wars. In addition, though he might have wanted to pull out of Vietnam, the politics of the time were such that he would likely have faced serious political consequences at home and abroad. It would have been extremely difficult to abandon the long-standing American commitment to "containing" communism.

Robert J. Kiphuth

TEACHER AND COACH, HE HAS INSPIRED GENERATIONS OF
ATHLETES WITH HIGH IDEALS OF ACHIEVEMENT AND SPORTS-
MANSHIP.

★ ★ ★

*President Lyndon B. Johnson awarded Kiphuth the Presidential Medal
of Freedom with the above citation during a White House ceremony
December 6, 1963. Kiphuth had been selected as a medal recipient
earlier in 1963 by President John F. Kennedy, who was assassinated
shortly before the award ceremony.*

Called the greatest swimming coach in history, Yale's longtime
trainer Robert Kiphuth led teams to 528 dual-meet victories and 4
collegiate championships between 1918 and 1959. He also coached
four winning U.S. Olympic swimming teams during that time.
Amazingly, these accomplishments came from a man who did not
even like to swim.

Kiphuth was born in Tonawanda, New York, in 1890 and
graduated from high school in 1909. Short, heavily muscled, and pos-
sessing a booming baritone voice, he began working as the director
of physical education at the Tonawanda Young Men's Christian
Association (YMCA), while also using his summers to study physical
education at various colleges, including Harvard. But before Kiphuth
could complete his college studies, Yale hired him in 1917 as a
physical education instructor. Kiphuth married Louise DeLaney that
same year.

By 1918 he had begun what became a long and successful career as
Yale's swimming coach. He took the job reluctantly at first, because
he knew almost nothing about swimming. Kiphuth did not particularly like the water and by his own admission swam only a little; he
preferred the handball court to the swimming pool. But he
immersed himself in books about the sport and soon developed
what was then a highly unconventional, and amazingly successful,
conditioning program for swimmers.

Before Kiphuth's regime, swimming coaches frowned upon body-
building. But Kiphuth developed a demanding program of exercises
designed to produce "muscle and mileage." Swimmers went through
a month or two of calisthenics before being allowed to swim and
then had to swim mile upon mile during practice sessions. And
believing an underwater view better showed a swimmer's form,
coach Kiphuth would even don a diving helmet to study his team
members from the bottom of the practice pool.

The results were stunning. Between 1918 and 1924 Yale teams won 65
straight dual-team swim meets. Coach Kiphuth put together another
streak of 175 dual-meet wins from 1924 to 1937, as well as two others in

following years. During Kiphuth's entire career, his Yale teams lost only 12 dual meets. Under coach Kiphuth Yale swimmers also became four-time winners of the collegiate swimming "world series," the National Collegiate Athletic Association championship—in 1942, 1944, and 1953.

Kiphuth's successes were not confined to collegiate athletics, however. He also coached four winning U.S. Olympic swimming teams, those of 1928, 1932, 1948, and 1952. U.S. swimmers went on a history-making winning streak at the 1948 Olympics in London, winning all six swimming competitions and both diving championships. All told, Kiphuth's swimmers snatched up eleven of the eighteen possible medals that year.

Coach Kiphuth retired in 1959. He died eight years later, at age seventy-six.

Edwin H. Land

SCIENTIST AND INVENTOR, HE HAS BROUGHT HIS CREATIVE GIFTS TO BEAR IN INDUSTRY, GOVERNMENT AND EDUCATION, ENRICHING THE LIVES OF MILLIONS BY GIVING NEW DIMENSIONS TO PHOTOGRAPHY.

★ ★ ★

President Lyndon B. Johnson awarded Land the Presidential Medal of Freedom with the above citation during a White House ceremony December 6, 1963. Land had been selected as a medal recipient earlier in 1963 by President John F. Kennedy, who was assassinated shortly before the award ceremony.

The inventor of the revolutionary Polaroid Land camera, Edwin Land was born in Bridgeport, Connecticut, in 1909. As a child he showed an interest in photography and proved an exceptional student with a strong aptitude for physics. The youthful inventor also began researching polarized light in his home laboratory.

Entering Harvard University in 1926, Land continued his search for an inexpensive, practical means of polarizing light to reduce glare. At the time only fragile and expensive crystals could be used for that purpose, and he became convinced a synthetic sheet impregnated with aligned microscopic crystals could be developed. He succeeded by 1932 and formally presented his first major discovery in a scientific paper at Harvard that year. Soon after, Land completely abandoned his college studies and formed a company with Harvard physics instructor George Wheelwright III. By 1934 they were manufacturing the world's first synthetic sheet polarizer, which was used to eliminate glare in camera lenses, sun glasses, and various other optical equipment.

Land formed the Polaroid Corporation in 1937 with Wall Street backing, and the company flourished during the 1940s as a wartime supplier of polarizing filters for goggles, gun sights, range finders, bombsights, and other military gear. Meanwhile, far from the front lines, a seemingly inconsequential incident occurred that would eventually revolutionize still photography.

While on vacation in 1943, Land snapped a photograph of his three-year-old daughter. With childlike innocence she asked afterward why she could not see the picture immediately. The question she posed left Land wondering why not. All his past work with plastics, polarizers, microscopic crystals, and viscous liquids suddenly came to bear on the problem, and after only an hour's thought, he knew just how to make a camera with a one-step photographic process.

Land began work on the camera and its special film after the war, and by late 1947 he publicly demonstrated his revolutionary Polaroid Land camera for the first time. The camera, which produced sepia-toned prints in sixty seconds, was an immediate commercial success. Land steadily improved the camera, eventually reducing developing time to just a few seconds. His company introduced traditional black-and-white prints in 1950 and color prints in 1963.

Land continued as chief executive of the Polaroid Corporation until his retirement in 1980, developing cameras for the home market as well as for industrial, medical, military, and other applications. Land received more than 500 patents during his lifetime and also contributed to basic research in how humans perceive color. His experiments in this area showed that color perception is not entirely dependent on the proportion of blue, green, and red light striking the retina, as had been thought previously. Researchers under Land's direction discovered that the brain itself plays a major role in the color-image-forming process.

Land died in 1991, about two months before his eighty-second birthday. During his long career, he received many achievement awards and was inducted into the National Inventors Hall of Fame.

Herbert H. Lehman

CITIZEN AND STATESMAN, HE HAS USED WISDOM AND COMPASSION
AS THE TOOLS OF GOVERNMENT AND HE HAS MADE POLITICS THE
HIGHEST FORM OF PUBLIC SERVICE.

★ ★ ★

*President Lyndon B. Johnson awarded Lehman a posthumous
Presidential Medal of Freedom with the above citation during a White
House ceremony December 6, 1963. Lehman had been selected as a
medal recipient earlier in 1963 by President John F. Kennedy, who was
assassinated shortly before the award ceremony.*

A former New York governor, Herbert H. Lehman was born in New
York City in 1878 and grew up in an affluent German-Jewish community there. He graduated from Williams College in Massachusetts
in 1899 and then went to work for a cotton manufacturing firm.
Rising quickly to vice president and treasurer, he left the company in
1908 to join his brother's investment banking firm, Lehman Brothers.
Two years later, he married Edith Louise Altschul, whose family also
was involved in investment banking.

Lehman served as a Navy Department procurement officer in
World War I. Returning to investment banking during the 1920s, he
became involved in the Democratic Party and was a major backer of
Alfred E. Smith, the unsuccessful Democratic presidential candidate
in 1928. Lehman was elected New York State's lieutenant governor in
1928, serving under Gov. Franklin D. Roosevelt from 1929 to 1932.

When Roosevelt ran for president in 1932, Lehman was elected
governor. Reelected three more times, Lehman served until 1942. As
governor, Lehman generally supported Roosevelt's New Deal and
instituted his own "Little New Deal" in New York State. His reforms
were accompanied by conservative fiscal policies, though, resulting in
a state budget surplus by the late 1930s.

Early in World War II Lehman grew increasingly concerned about
the Nazis' treatment of European Jews, and in 1942 he became director
of the State Department's new Office of Foreign Relief and
Rehabilitation. In 1943 Lehman was named the first director of an international relief organization, what would become the UN Relief and
Rehabilitation Administration, and headed that effort for three years.

He lost his bid for a U.S. Senate seat in 1946 but persevered and
won a special election in 1949. Elected to a full term in 1950, Lehman
remained in the Senate until 1957 and generally supported President
Harry S. Truman's Fair Deal. He opposed the president's compulsory
health insurance plan, however. Lehman also was among the first
politicians to speak out against McCarthyism.

Remaining active in New York politics even after his retirement in
1957, Lehman died in 1963, the day before he was due to receive the

Presidential Medal of Freedom. He was eighty-five years old. His wife received the medal on his behalf at a special White House ceremony January 28, 1964.

Robert A. Lovett

SERVANT OF THE REPUBLIC, HE HAS SET HIGH STANDARDS FOR THE PRIVATE CITIZEN IN PUBLIC SERVICE BY HIS SELFLESS DEDICATION TO THE NATIONAL SECURITY UNDER FOUR PRESIDENTS.

★ ★ ★

President Lyndon B. Johnson awarded Lovett the Presidential Medal of Freedom with the above citation during a White House ceremony December 6, 1963. The award was presented with the added accolade "with distinction." Lovett had been selected as a medal recipient earlier in 1963 by President John F. Kennedy, who was assassinated shortly before the award ceremony.

A key figure in the phenomenal growth of U.S. Air Force during World War II, Robert A. Lovett was born in Huntsville, Texas, in 1895. He was the son of a prominent lawyer for the Union Pacific Railroad who became president of both the Union Pacific and Southern Pacific railroads after railroad magnate E. H. Harriman died in 1909. Raised in his father's world of business, high finance, and nineteenth-century enterprise, Lovett went off to Yale University just as World War I was beginning.

Lovett left college in his junior year to join the navy's fledgling air corps and during World War I flew many daring combat missions over Germany and occupied Belgium, winning the Navy Cross. After the war, in 1919, he married Adele Quartley Brown, an affluent neighbor from Long Island, New York, and that same year earned his bachelor's degree from Yale. Two years of graduate studies followed before Lovett began his career in finance as a lowly bank clerk. Soon after he moved to his father-in-law's investment banking firm, Brown Brothers, again landing on the bottom rung.

Lovett did not remain there long, though. Within five years he had become a partner in the firm and also had been elected a director of Union Pacific. Then, thanks to his connections with the Harriman family, he brought about the merger of Harriman banking interests with Brown Brothers, in 1931, creating Brown Brothers, Harriman and Company.

An influential figure in the financial community during the rest of the 1930s, Lovett focused on international investments, particularly in

Europe. Through those overseas business dealings he realized Hitler was building up German forces for a war and worried that the United States would be too weak militarily to meet the threat. Concentrating on the importance of air power, Lovett decided on his own to tour U.S. aircraft factories and then wrote a report on the need for a rapid buildup of the air force, which was then part of the army.

The army was so impressed that, in 1940, it made Lovett a special assistant. A few months later War Department Secretary Henry Stimson named him assistant secretary for air. In this post Lovett not only presided over the dizzying expansion of the U.S. air corps during World War II, but also maneuvered the army into giving it the semiautonomous status it maintained throughout the war (the Air Force was part of the army until 1947). Perhaps even more significant was his success in winning top priority for bomber production early in the war production effort, since strategic bombing became such an important part of the Allied victory in World War II. Having transformed the United States into the world's leading air power in just a few short years, Lovett was awarded the Distinguished Service Medal in 1945.

Lovett became undersecretary of state in 1947, serving as Secretary George Marshall's top trouble-shooter and an important figure in preparing the Marshall Plan aid program. During his term as undersecretary, he became involved in the U.S. refusal to give in to the Soviet's Berlin blockade and was in office when the massive Berlin airlift finally forced the Soviets to back down. Leaving the State Department with Marshall in 1949, Lovett became deputy secretary of defense a year later, at the outbreak of the Korean War. As deputy secretary, and then as secretary from 1951 to 1953, Lovett oversaw a new buildup of U.S. military forces in response to the Far Eastern crisis.

After 1953 he returned to his business interests, though he served on various presidential commissions concerned with military and other matters. Lovett retired from his Union Pacific directorship in 1978 but continued as a partner in Brown Brothers, Harriman for the rest of his life. He died in 1986, at age ninety.

J. Clifford MacDonald

Businessman and philanthropist, he has directed his concern to the quiet but noble work of enlarging the lives and opportunities of the physically and mentally handicapped.

★ ★ ★

President Lyndon B. Johnson awarded MacDonald a posthumous Presidential Medal of Freedom with the above citation during a White House ceremony December 6, 1963. Mrs. MacDonald received the award for her late husband. MacDonald had been selected as a medal recipient earlier in 1963 by President John F. Kennedy, who was assassinated shortly before the award ceremony.

J. Clifford MacDonald, whose mother was a writer, was born in Alexandria, Virginia, in 1902. After studying journalism at Columbia University, he worked first as a newspaper reporter and then published his own newspaper, *The Spectator,* in Saint Petersburg, Florida, during the 1920s. Moving to Tampa in 1926, he started the MacDonald Printing Company there and managed the plant until 1959, when a stroke forced him to retire.

MacDonald began working in behalf of handicapped children in 1942 after learning his only son was retarded. He founded the Hillsborough Association for Retarded Children in 1953 and, with help from other local groups, opened the MacDonald Training Center in Tampa. Three years later the center became part of a national research program on training retarded children.

MacDonald went on to organize the Florida State Council for Retarded Children, and from 1955 to 1957 he served as president of the National Association for Retarded Children. He also worked as chairman of the National Committee for Vocational Rehabilitation and Employment.

President John F. Kennedy announced MacDonald's selection for the Medal of Freedom in July 1963, but sadly neither man lived to see the presentation itself. The ailing Floridian died of a stroke just weeks after the announcement, at age sixty-one, and President Kennedy died after being struck by an assassin's bullet that November.

John J. McCloy

DIPLOMAT AND PUBLIC SERVANT, BANKER TO THE WORLD AND
GODFATHER TO GERMAN FREEDOM, HE HAS BROUGHT CHEERFUL
WISDOM AND STEADY EFFECTIVENESS TO THE TASKS OF WAR AND
PEACE.

★ ★ ★

*President Lyndon B. Johnson awarded McCloy the Presidential Medal
of Freedom with the above citation during a White House ceremony
December 6, 1963. The award was presented with the added accolade
"with distinction." McCloy had been selected as a medal recipient
earlier in 1963 by President John F. Kennedy, who was assassinated
shortly before the award ceremony.*

A prominent lawyer and adviser to eight presidents from Franklin D.
Roosevelt to Ronald Reagan, John J. McCloy served as president of the
World Bank in the late 1940s and as high commissioner of West
Germany in the early 1950s. He went on to become chairman of
several corporations, to serve on the Council on Foreign Relations,
and to play an important role in early efforts at disarmament.

An insurance auditor's son, McCloy was born in Philadelphia in
1895. His father died when he was six, and the young McCloy worked
his way through college at Amherst, graduating cum laude in 1916. At
Harvard Law School he studied under Felix Frankfurter, the future
Supreme Court justice, and after a stint in army during World War I
earned his law degree in 1921. *(See also the entry for Frankfurter, p. 55.)*

McCloy entered private practice in New York City, becoming a law
firm partner in 1929. A year later he married Ellen Zinsser and coincidentally began his work on the infamous "Black Tom" case, which
launched his career in government service. His diligent, nine-year
investigation (1930–1939) for his client finally proved that German
spies had caused an explosion at a New Jersey munitions plant
during World War I. McCloy's investigation so impressed Secretary
of War Henry Stimson that he brought McCloy to Washington in
1941 as an assistant secretary of war.

Stimson's trouble-shooter, McCloy was involved with many high-
level matters during World War II. He helped win congressional
approval of the lend-lease program to aid Britain and other Allies
against Nazi Germany, oversaw the internment of Japanese-Americans
during the war, helped formulate U.S. policy toward occupied areas,
and attended major wartime conferences among Allied leaders.

After the war McCloy served as president of the World Bank,
thereby playing a key role in rebuilding war-torn economies as well
as putting the bank itself on a sound operating basis. After two years
at the World Bank, he became high commissioner for occupied West
Germany in 1949. In this post he not only set up a civilian gov-

ernment in West Germany but also began the work of rebuilding the country's economy.

For the next four decades McCloy continued advising presidents and serving on government councils, while also heading the boards of various corporations and organizations. The chairman of the Council on Foreign Relations from 1953 to 1970 (and continuing as a member until 1989), he also chaired the Chase Manhattan Bank from 1953 to 1960 and the Ford Foundation from 1958 to 1965. He chaired the President's General Advisory Committee on Disarmament from 1961 to 1974, and served on the Warren Commission. Meanwhile he also represented dozens of corporate clients in need of his legal expertise and negotiating skills.

McCloy, who in his last years served as a foreign affairs adviser to the Reagan administration, died in 1989, at age ninety-three.

George Meany

CITIZEN AND NATIONAL LEADER, IN SERVING THE CAUSE OF LABOR, HE HAS GREATLY SERVED THE CAUSE OF HIS NATION AND OF FREEDOM IN THE WORLD.

★ ★ ★

President Lyndon B. Johnson awarded Meany the Presidential Medal of Freedom with the above citation during a White House ceremony December 6, 1963. Meany had been selected as a medal recipient earlier in 1963 by President John F. Kennedy, who was assassinated shortly before the award ceremony.

The iron-willed AFL-CIO president for nearly twenty-five years and one of the nation's most powerful labor leaders, George Meany was born in Harlem, New York, in 1894. He quit school at sixteen to follow his father into the plumbing trade, becoming a journeyman plumber and union member in 1915. Four years later he married Eugenia A. McMahon.

A frequent speaker at union meetings, Meany eventually moved up through the ranks of the union bureaucracy. Winning steadily more prestigious posts, he served as New York State president of the American Federation of Labor (AFL) from 1934 to 1939, secretary-treasurer of the AFL national organization from 1939 to 1952, and AFL president from 1952 to 1955.

What was perhaps Meany's greatest accomplishment came just a few years after he became AFL president. Unions had traditionally been organized according to crafts (as they were in the AFL), and until the 1930s unskilled workers in factories, assembly plants, and elsewhere had not even been organized. The rise of the Congress of Industrial Organizations (CIO), which recruited these unskilled workers in the 1930s, created a rift in the union movement that Meany set out to close after being elected AFL president. Three years of often delicate negotiations followed, but he succeeded in merging the AFL and CIO in 1955 and became the first AFL-CIO president.

Meanwhile, Meany also gained a reputation for battling union corruption. As early as 1953 the AFL president saw to the expulsion of the International Longshoremen's Association on grounds it harbored gangsters among its ranks, and in 1957, expelled Jimmy Hoffa's Teamsters union because of corruption. Both unions eventually rejoined the AFL-CIO.

As president of the 13.6-million-member AFL-CIO, Meany wielded considerable influence with business and government, as well as having his say in the overall direction of the labor movement. He was above all a "pork chop" unionist, seeking to promote the economic welfare of members through labor contracts and collective bargaining. In Congress Meany used AFL-CIO lobbyists to win increased minimum wages, protect union rights, promote healthcare legislation, and secure other benefits for workers. He remained a strident anticommunist when it came to U.S. foreign policy and opposed both détente and normalization of relations with China.

The AFL-CIO also gave Meany considerable clout within the Democratic Party, but he did not always get what he wanted. A hardline supporter of U.S. involvement in Vietnam, he refused to support George McGovern's presidential candidacy. Some years later Meany publicly criticized President Jimmy Carter for ignoring labor.

Meany's own conservative leadership was not immune to attack. Accused of foot-dragging on racial discrimination, he eventually approved an equal opportunity program that also was incorporated in the landmark Civil Rights Act of 1964. A few years later United Automobile Workers (UAW) chief Walter Reuther, a union activist who believed in the social vision and crusades of the 1960s, openly broke with Meany. Criticizing Meany's "rusty-bottomed conservatism," Reuther pulled the UAW out of the AFL-CIO in 1967.

Though Meany responded by listening more closely to blacks, farmworkers, and women, labor was already losing influence in the 1970s. Finally, with his health failing, the longtime labor leader retired from the AFL-CIO in 1979. He was succeeded by his close associate Lane Kirkland. *(See also the entry for Kirkland, p. 504.)* Meany died the following year, at age eighty-five.

Alexander Meiklejohn

EDUCATOR AND LIBERTARIAN, [A] TEACHER BY EXAMPLE AND
PHILOSOPHER IN PRACTICE, HIS FREE AND FERTILE MIND HAS
INFLUENCED THE COURSE OF AMERICAN HIGHER EDUCATION.

★ ★ ★

*President Lyndon B. Johnson awarded Meiklejohn the Presidential
Medal of Freedom with the above citation during a White House
ceremony December 6, 1963. Meiklejohn had been selected as a medal
recipient earlier in 1963 by President John F. Kennedy, who was assassinated shortly before the award ceremony.*

An unremitting champion of academic freedom and free speech,
Alexander Meiklejohn was born in Rochdale, England, in 1872. Eight
years later his father, a textile worker, moved the family to Pawtucket,
Rhode Island, and the young Meiklejohn went on to graduate from
Brown University in nearby Providence in 1893. After earning his
master's degree at Brown in 1895 he won his doctorate in philosophy at
Cornell University in 1897. Two years later he returned to Brown as a
philosophy instructor.

A talented teacher, Meiklejohn proved popular with students and
was named dean of students at Brown in 1901. A year later he
married Nannine A. LaVilla, and in 1905 Brown made him a full professor. Meiklejohn continued teaching philosophy and serving as
dean until 1912, when his successful record at Brown led to his
appointment as president of Amherst College.

Amherst had by some accounts reached a low point then, having a
curriculum consisting mainly of philosophy and the classics. As
president, Meiklejohn set about broadening the academic offering by
recruiting historians, political economists, and creative thinkers to
teach there. He once again proved popular with students. But
relations with most of the Amherst faculty soured, and in 1918 his
plan to create a uniform curriculum for the first two years of undergraduate study was rejected for lack of faculty support. The mutual
contempt between Meiklejohn and the faculty worsened over the
next years until he was forced to resign in 1923. That same year he
published *Freedom and the College.*

Three years later Meiklejohn was asked to create an experimental
liberal arts college at the University of Wisconsin. His new college
extended through the first two years of undergraduate work and
replaced classes and tests with conferences, lectures, and discussions.
The key to the experiment was shared living quarters in which
faculty and students intermingled to form an intellectual community. While the experimental school provoked an array of sensational accusations, including charges of communism and free love, it
ultimately failed after four years for lack of interested students.

Meanwhile, Meiklejohn married his second wife, Helen Everett, in 1926, his first wife having died the year before.

Moving to Berkeley, California, in 1932, he served as chairman of another short-lived experimental school, the San Francisco School for Social Studies. Afterward he made appearances as a speaker and visiting lecturer, and his writings included the books *Education Between Two Worlds* (1942) and *Political Freedom: the Constitutional Powers of the People* (1960). Following World War II he worked actively for the American Civil Liberties Union and became a staunch opponent of the House Un-American Activities Committee. In his later years especially, Meiklejohn sought to promote academic freedom, freedom of speech, and freedom of the press as absolute privileges that should not be restricted in any way.

Meiklejohn died in 1964, a year after receiving the Presidential Medal of Freedom. He was ninety-two years old.

Ludwig Mies van der Rohe

TEACHER, DESIGNER, MASTER BUILDER, HE HAS CONCEIVED SOARING STRUCTURES OF GLASS, STEEL AND CONCRETE WHICH AT ONCE EMBODY AND EVOKE THE DISTINCTIVE QUALITIES OF COURAGE.

★ ★ ★

President Lyndon B. Johnson awarded Mies van der Rohe the Presidential Medal of Freedom with the above citation during a White House ceremony December 6, 1963. Mies van der Rohe had been selected as a medal recipient earlier in 1963 by President John F. Kennedy, who was assassinated shortly before the award ceremony.

Among the preeminent architects of this century and a leading practitioner of the International Style of architecture, Ludwig Mies van der Rohe was born in Aachen, Germany, in 1886. He was the son of a master mason and became a contractor's apprentice at age fifteen. By 1905, at age nineteen, he was in Berlin working in various architects' offices, including that of Bruno Paul, who also was known as a furniture designer.

Mies landed his first commission in 1907 for the design of a traditional suburban house. That project led to a job offer by Germany's most progressive architect, Peter Behrens, who was impressed by the design. Mies then joined two other future leaders of the architectural world who also were getting their start at Behrens's office: Le Corbusier and Walter Gropius. Mies stayed with Behrens until 1912, when he was commissioned to design a house in the Netherlands. The following year he married Adele Auguste Bruhn, but the marriage was not destined to succeed (they lived apart after 1921).

After serving in the German military construction corps during World War I, Mies returned to his practice. But with the German economy in shambles, there were precious few projects. Though he joined several modernist architectural organizations and set up exhibitions during the 1920s, his most important work at this time was a series of designs for structures that were never actually built. Uncompromisingly modernistic, these designs embodied much of what went into his later work, including the stark simplicity ("less is more"), emphasis on structural elements, and meticulous attention to detail for which he became famous. Completed between 1919 and 1924, the designs included one of the first for a building made entirely of steel and glass.

As the vice president of the German group Werkbund, Mies planned what became a demonstration project near Stuttgart in 1927. Designed by sixteen of the leading modernist architects in Europe, including Mies and Le Corbusier, the complex of apartment buildings and houses became the first clear statement of the International Style of architecture. Two years later Mies completed the German Pavilion at the 1929 International Exposition at Barcelona and created the now-classic Barcelona chair for the pavilion. In 1930 Mies was named director of Germany's famous Bauhaus school.

Nazi interference forced Mies to close the school in 1933, and he emigrated to the United States five years later. On his arrival he became director of the architecture school at Chicago's Armour Institute of Technology (since renamed the Illinois Institute of Technology). Mies developed a rigorous new curriculum for training young architects and was given free reign to design the school's new campus, his first commission in the United States and a showcase for his work.

Under his direction for the next twenty years, the school achieved international fame. Meanwhile, Mies, who became a U.S. citizen in 1944, also kept up his private practice, completing about one project a year. His works of this period are largely of steel and glass, and his designs focused on the architectural aesthetics of structure and space. Among his buildings are the Lake Shore Drive Apartments in Chicago (1951), the Seagram Building in New York (1958), the Bacardi Building in Mexico City (1961), the Federal Center in Chicago (1964), the Washington, D.C., Public Library (1967), and the New National Gallery in Berlin (1968).

Mies, who lived alone in Chicago, died in 1969. He was eighty-three years old.

Jean Monnet

<small>CITIZEN OF FRANCE, STATESMAN OF THE WORLD, HE HAS MADE
PERSUASION AND REASON THE WEAPONS OF STATECRAFT,
MOVING EUROPE TOWARD UNITY AND THE ATLANTIC NATIONS
TOWARD A MORE EFFECTIVE PARTNERSHIP.</small>

★ ★ ★

*President Lyndon B. Johnson awarded Monnet the Presidential Medal
of Freedom with the above citation during a White House ceremony
December 6, 1963. The medal was presented with the added accolade
"with distinction." Monnet had been selected as a medal recipient
earlier in 1963 by President John F. Kennedy, who was assassinated
shortly before the award ceremony.*

The author of the Monnet Plan for rebuilding France's shattered
economy after World War II and the "spiritual father" of the
European Economic Community, Jean Monnet was born in Cognac,
France, in 1888. His father had started the J. G. Monnet & Co. brandy
firm and pressed Monnet into service as a brandy salesman immediately after his graduation from high school. Monnet enjoyed
success in the early 1900s selling the family wares in Canada, the
United States, Britain, and Egypt.

During World War I his international connections led to posts on
inter-Allied committees that provided arms, shipping, and food for
the war effort. From there the former brandy salesman moved into
the top echelons of international affairs as deputy secretary-general
of the League of Nations, a post he held from 1919 to 1923. Among
Monnet's duties at the league was the reconstruction of Austria.

After reorganizing the family business, he next went into
investment banking as a partner in a U.S. firm, Blair and Co. Monnet
became a key figure in refinancing Romania and Poland and recapi-
talizing the Diamond Match Company. He also helped set up the
China Development Corporation and arranged financing through
loans from various countries.

Early in World War II Monnet became chairman of the Franco-
British Economic Coordination Committee and after the fall of
France worked with Allied leaders to further the war effort. He is
credited with giving President Franklin D. Roosevelt the line, "We
must be the great arsenal of democracy."

The postwar years saw Monnet's greatest contributions, however.
Named director of France's National Economic Council by French
president Charles de Gaulle, Monnet formulated the plan to rebuild
and modernize the French economy after World War II. The government adopted the plan in 1947, but even then Monnet had still
larger projects in mind. He firmly believed that coal and steel production throughout Western Europe would be an important factor

in France's recovery and that a joint effort in these industries would benefit all the countries involved.

Monnet and French foreign minister Robert Shuman proposed creation of the European Coal and Steel Community (ECSC) in 1950, and the following year six nations, including France, West Germany, and Italy, became founding members. For Monnet, who served as the first ECSC president, from 1952 to 1955, the organization was but the first step toward what he believed would become a unified European economy and ultimately a united Europe.

Having left the ECSC to form an action committee to promote creation of the United States of Europe, Monnet nevertheless was deeply involved in negotiations that resulted in the founding of the European Economic Community (Common Market) in 1957. An unquestionable success, the Common Market flourished over the next decades and, especially after Britain was allowed to join, became a steppingstone for further unification of Europe. Monnet was named a Citizen of Europe in 1976 by the nine Common Market government leaders.

In his later years Monnet focused on promoting further unity, including steps toward a single European currency and his cherished dream of a United States of Europe. He published his *Memoirs* in 1978 and died the following year, at age ninety.

Luis Muñoz Marín

POET, POLITICIAN, PUBLIC SERVANT, PATRIOT, HE HAS LED HIS PEOPLE ON TO NEW HEIGHTS OF DIGNITY AND PURPOSE AND TRANSFORMED A STRICKEN LAND INTO A VITAL SOCIETY.

★ ★ ★

President Lyndon B. Johnson awarded Muñoz Marín the Presidential Medal of Freedom with the above citation during a White House ceremony December 6, 1963. The medal was presented with the additional accolade "with distinction." Muñoz Marín had been selected as a medal recipient earlier in 1963 by President John F. Kennedy, who was assassinated shortly before the award ceremony.

Puerto Rico's first elected governor, Luis Muñoz Marín was born in San Juan, Puerto Rico, in 1898. His father, popularly known as the "George Washington of Puerto Rico," had sought independence from Spain and was disappointed when the United States took control of the islands after the Spanish-American War. Nevertheless, he became Puerto Rico's resident commissioner in Washington, D.C., eventually winning U.S. citizenship for Puerto Ricans, as well as the right to an elected legislature.

The young Muñoz Marín grew up with this family background and yet spent most of his youth in the United States. Educated in the United States, he proved an indifferent student, though he enjoyed some success as a freelance writer, poet, and translator of poetry (he translated Walt Whitman, Carl Sandburg, and others into Spanish). Muñoz Marín also published two books in the United States, *Borrones* and *Madre Haraposa* (both 1917) and two years later married Muna Lee, a Mississippi-born poet.

After some years of shuttling back and forth between Puerto Rico and the New York literary scene, Muñoz Marín settled in his homeland (1926) and became a newspaper editor for *La Democracia,* which his father had founded. Siding with the more radical Liberal Party, Muñoz Marín next won a seat in the Puerto Rican Senate in 1932. Six years later he broke with the Liberals and founded the Popular Democratic Party, leading it to a surprise election victory two years later. Muñoz Marín thus became president of the Puerto Rican Senate, retaining that post until 1948. Meanwhile, he divorced his first wife and in 1948 married Inéz Mendoza, a onetime schoolteacher.

When the U.S. Congress made the Puerto Rican governorship an elective office in 1948, Muñoz Marín won it in an overwhelming victory and was reelected to three more consecutive terms in 1952. Over the years he won considerable financial aid from the United States and used it to build roads, schools, hospitals, and public housing. But Puerto Rico was a land stricken by poverty when he took office, and drastic measures were needed to build the island's economy.

Responding to that desperate need, Muñoz Marín created Operation Bootstrap, which offered tax breaks to U.S. companies willing to open factories on the island. Considered one of his two major achievements, the program led to the opening of 600 new plants in Puerto Rico by 1960.

Perhaps his greatest accomplishment was winning commonwealth status for Puerto Rico in 1952. In granting the special status, the U.S. Congress allowed the island to have its own constitution while also making it eligible for all federal grant programs. (Puerto Ricans do not pay federal income taxes but also do not vote for the president and do not have a vote in Congress.) Muñoz Marín sought the status as the best compromise between the economic benefits of continued U.S. control and the risks of complete independence.

In 1964 Muñoz Marín refused to run for governor again and returned to the Puerto Rican Senate. Some years later in 1978, when a movement to request U.S. statehood was gaining momentum, he briefly campaigned for keeping the commonwealth status. Ill health forced him to withdraw from the fight, though, and he died in 1980. He was eighty-two years old.

Pope John XXIII

His Holiness Pope John XXIII, dedicated servant of God. He brought to all citizens of the planet a heightened sense of the dignity of the individual, of the brotherhood of man, and of the common duty to build an environment of peace for all human kind.

★ ★ ★

President Lyndon B. Johnson awarded Pope John XXIII a posthumous Presidential Medal of Freedom with the above citation during a White House ceremony December 6, 1963.

During his brief tenure from 1958 until his death in 1963, John XXIII became the first pope since the Reformation to call for the reform and spiritual renewal of Roman Catholicism. He infused the church with a new spirit of openness to other religions and convoked the Second Vatican Council, whose many reforms sought to modernize the church. John's personal warmth and humility also helped make him one of the most popular of all popes.

One of thirteen children, Pope John XXIII was born Angelo Roncalli on his family's farm near Bergamo, Italy, in 1881. Roncalli decided on the priesthood while still a child and entered the seminary at age eleven. Eventually sent to Rome for further theological studies, he was ordained in 1904, at age twenty-two. Soon after, Roncalli became secretary to the new bishop of Bergamo, an Italian nobleman, and from 1925 served in the Vatican diplomatic corps. Though elevated to archbishop, he at first held relatively obscure posts in Bulgaria (1925–1935) and Greece and Turkey (simultaneously, 1935–1944).

His appointment as papal nuncio to France in 1944 marked a sudden change in his fortunes, however. The situation was delicate there, because church officials had cooperated with the Nazi-dominated Vichy government during World War II and because younger French clergymen had fallen prey to radicalism. He not only managed to resolve the crisis but also proved highly popular with French Catholics. His success in France was capped with his being named cardinal in 1953 and his appointment as patriarch of Venice.

Nearly seventy-seven years old when Pope Pius XII died in 1958, Roncalli was elected the new pope on the twelfth ballot. A compromise candidate who, because of his advanced age, was expected to serve only as an "interim" pope, Roncalli chose the name John XXIII and became an unexpectedly vigorous church leader. Instead of continuing his predecessor's conservative policies, he announced his plan to "bring the church up to date" and set about fostering greater unity among the various Christian churches. Despite considerable opposition within the church, Pope John XXIII succeeded in convening the Second Vatican Council in 1962 to reassess church dogma and doctrines.

He also sought to promote world peace during some particularly difficult years of the Cold War. His 1963 encyclical *Peace on Earth* announced that peaceful coexistence between Western nations and the Communist bloc was necessary for the continued survival of mankind. Pope John XXIII died later in 1963, at the age of eighty-one. The work of the Second Vatican Council was continued under his successor, Pope Paul VI.

Clarence B. Randall

LEADER OF INDUSTRY, COUNSELOR TO PRESIDENTS, HE HAS BEEN A FORCEFUL AND ARTICULATE PHILOSOPHER OF THE ROLE OF BUSINESS IN A FREE SOCIETY.

★ ★ ★

President Lyndon B. Johnson awarded Randall the Presidential Medal of Freedom with the above citation during a White House ceremony December 6, 1963. Randall had been selected as a medal recipient earlier in 1963 by President John F. Kennedy, who was assassinated shortly before the award ceremony.

A longtime steel company executive and spokesman for the industry, Clarence B. Randall was born in Newark Valley, New York, in 1891. His father was a storekeeper, and the family later moved to Cambridge, Massachusetts, to enable the young Randall to attend Harvard on scholarship. He earned his bachelor's degree in 1912 and his law degree from Harvard Law School three years later.

Turning down an offer to work for a New York City law firm, Randall joined his cousin's law office in Ishpeming, Michigan, in 1915. He married Emily Fitch Phelps in 1917, and after two years in the army during World War I, he became a partner in an Ishpeming law firm.

In 1925 he joined the steel industry as an assistant vice president of the Inland Steel Company. The company moved him up to vice president in 1930 and then named him president in 1949. From 1953 to 1956 Randall was Inland's board chairman and chief executive officer.

As head of Inland, Randall expanded operations, moving the company up in the rankings from the eighth to the seventh-largest U.S. steel firm. He also gained a reputation as a proponent of corporate responsibility and collective bargaining.

Randall became a national celebrity in 1952 after President Harry

S. Truman ordered U.S. steel plants seized to prevent a strike that might interrupt production for the Korean War. Chosen as their spokesman by ninety-two steel companies, Randall bluntly denounced Truman's move in a nationwide radio address. Calling the seizure an "evil deed" and an "abuse of power," he accused the president of using the order to repay political debts to the Congress of Industrial Organizations (CIO). The Supreme Court later over-turned Truman's order as unconstitutional.

A conservative Republican and champion of free trade, Randall served on a variety of government commissions and councils. A member of the Commerce Department's Business Advisory Council from 1951 to 1957, he also was President Dwight D. Eisenhower's special assistant on foreign economic policy from 1956 to 1961. During the Kennedy administration, Randall headed an advisory group reviewing federal salary schedules.

Meanwhile, he also wrote books, including *Civil Liberties and Industrial Conflict* (1938, with Roger Baldwin), *A Creed for Free Enterprise* (1953), *The Folklore of Management* (1961), and *Making Good in Management* (1964). He also published two memoirs, *Over My Shoulder* (1956) and *Sixty-five Plus* (1963).

Randall died in 1967, at age seventy-six.

Rudolf Serkin

ARTIST AND TEACHER, HE HAS GIVEN THE CLASSICAL TRADITIONS OF THE PIANO NEW LIFE IN A DISORDERED AGE.

★ ★ ★

President Lyndon B. Johnson awarded Serkin the Presidential Medal of Freedom during a White House ceremony December 6, 1963. Serkin had been selected as a medal recipient in 1963 by President John F. Kennedy, who was assassinated shortly before the award ceremony.

Among the world's great pianists, Rudolf Serkin was born in Cheb, now in the Czech Republic, in 1903. His father, who had been a former singer in Russia, gave Serkin his first lessons on the piano and taught him to read music before he could read words. Serkin gave his first public performance at five and entered private study in Vienna in 1912. He debuted as a piano soloist with the Vienna Symphony Orchestra three years later. Meanwhile, he also studied composition under the famed composer Arnold Schonberg.

Impressed by Serkin's playing, violinist Adolf Busch invited him to tour with his musical company in 1920, thus beginning a lifelong friendship and professional association. Serkin made a triumphant appearance with Busch's chamber orchestra in Berlin, playing Bach's Brandenburg Concerto no. 5, and later toured Europe giving solo recitals and performing in Busch's chamber-music concerts. He moved in with Busch's family, living first in Germany, then in Switzerland, and then in the United States (from 1939). He married Busch's daughter Irene in 1935.

Serkin's U.S. concert debut at Carnegie Hall came in 1936, and the closing appearance of his U.S. tour that year marked the start of a fifty-year association with the New York Philharmonic Orchestra as one of its regular soloists. His playing of Brahms's D-minor Piano Concerto with the Philharmonic brought the Carnegie Hall audience to its feet.

Beginning in 1937 he toured the United States and Europe annually, generally performing the works of Bach, Mozart, Brahms, and Beethoven. His pianism, which proved immensely popular, mingled classical and romantic styles. His talent was not a natural gift, though. Rather, Serkin achieved worldwide recognition through almost monastic devotion to practice. He evolved a technique that was articulate and finely crafted, yet he could use it to dazzle his audience.

Serkin and the Buschs emigrated to the United States in 1939, and in addition to performing, Serkin that year began teaching piano at Philadelphia's Curtis Institute. As a teacher for the next several decades, Serkin had a significant impact on generations of young pianists. In 1949 he also became a cofounder of the Marlboro Festival in Vermont, an annual chamber-music festival that has since turned Marlboro into a summertime chamber-music mecca and helped promote interest in the musical genre.

From 1968 to 1975 Serkin served as director of the Curtis Institute. He performed at the White House twice (1966 and 1970) and recorded numerous albums. In 1986 he marked his fiftieth year as a guest soloist with the New York Philharmonic Orchestra at a special Carnegie Hall recital. He gave his last concert performance two years later. Serkin died in 1991, at age eighty-eight.

Edward Steichen

PHOTOGRAPHER AND COLLECTOR, HE HAS MADE THE CAMERA
THE INSTRUMENT OF AESTHETIC PERCEPTION AND THEREBY
TRANSFORMED A SCIENCE INTO AN ART.

★ ★ ★

*President Lyndon B. Johnson awarded Steichen the Presidential Medal
of Freedom with the above citation during a White House ceremony
December 6, 1963. Steichen had been selected as a medal recipient
earlier in 1963 by President John F. Kennedy, who was assassinated
shortly before the award ceremony.*

A pioneering American photographer, Edward Steichen was born in
Luxembourg in 1879 and emigrated to the United States with his
family in 1881. Raised in Hancock, Michigan, he took his first pictures
with a Kodak at age sixteen. Out of fifty exposures the young Steichen
shot, only one came back clear enough to print, but his mother
encouraged him by saying that the one good picture of his sister was
"so good and so wonderful that it was worth forty-nine failures."

Steichen left school in 1894 and worked for four years as an
apprentice lithographer. Later he studied painting and pursued his
interest in photography, while spending time in both the United
States and France. His photographs in this period tended to imitate
his painting style—impressionistic, soft-focus images with artificial
enhancements then popular among photographers. His first photographic exhibits were mounted in 1899 and 1900 in the United States,
and in the early 1900 Steichen gained a reputation for his portraits,
including those of Theodore Roosevelt and J. P. Morgan.

Joining with fellow photographer Alfred Stieglitz, Steichen
founded the Photo-Secession group in 1902 to promote photography
as an art form. That same year he opened the famous 291 gallery at
291 Fifth Avenue in New York City. The gallery exhibited works by
Steichen and other photographers and also showed paintings by such
artists as Pablo Picasso and Paul Cezanne for the first time in
America.

The great turning point in Steichen's career came shortly after his
service in World War I, in which he headed the U.S. Army air corps
photographic service. Convinced that photographic realism was an
art form in itself, he abandoned his impressionistic techniques and
began experimenting with a sharply realistic style that has dominated American photography ever since. In one case he pho-
tographed a white cup against a black velvet background over a
thousand times, testing the gradations of black, white, and gray for
the best possible combination. At the end of this experimental phase,
in 1923, he married his second wife, Dana Desboror Glover, having
divorced his first wife two years earlier.

In the 1920s and 1930s Steichen specialized in portraits and commercial photography, becoming a highly paid and widely known photographic artist. His portraits of the era's socialites and artistic personalities include such famous pictures as those of the veiled Gloria Swanson and a smiling Charlie Chaplin. He also worked as the chief photographer for the two high-profile magazines of the time, *Vogue* and *Vanity Fair*. In 1932 he pioneered the *photomural* with a mural of the George Washington Bridge.

He left commercial photography in 1938 and during World War II became an officer in the navy photographic corps. He prepared two important exhibitions, Road to Victory (1943) and Power in the Pacific (1944), that were shown at the Museum of Modern Art. After the war, as director of photography at the Museum of Modern Art (from 1947), he gave up taking photographs and instead focused on assembling exhibits. His most famous was the hugely popular Family of Man exhibit that opened at the museum in 1955 and eventually exhibited at other museums around the world. Seen by over nine million people, the exhibit focused on the universality of the human experience and was culled from photographs of people taken in over sixty-eight countries.

Steichen married Joanna Taub in 1960, three years after the death of his second wife, and retired from the Museum of Modern Art in 1962. He died in 1973, two days before his ninety-fourth birthday.

George W. Taylor

ECONOMIST AND ARBITRATOR, HE HAS BEEN THE VOICE OF REASON AND GOOD WILL IN THE INDUSTRIAL RELATIONS OF OUR SOCIETY, ENLISTING MANAGEMENT AND LABOR IN THE CAUSE OF INDUSTRIAL PEACE.

★ ★ ★

President Lyndon B. Johnson awarded Taylor the Presidential Medal of Freedom with the above citation during a White House ceremony December 6, 1963. Taylor had been selected as a medal recipient earlier in 1963 by President John F. Kennedy, who was assassinated shortly before the award ceremony.

A labor arbitrator who served five presidents, George W. Taylor was born in Philadelphia in 1901, the son of a hosiery mill superintendent. He proved an exceptional student and earned his bachelor's degree (1923), master of business administration degree (1926), and doctorate (1929) at the University of Pennsylvania. While pursuing his advanced degrees, Taylor also served as chairman of the Schuylkill College Department of Business Administration from 1924 to 1929 and, in 1924, married Edith Ayling, a high school classmate. He joined the faculty of the Wharton School in 1929 as an associate professor of labor relations.

Soon after, Taylor became one of the first academics to venture into mediation of labor-management disputes, gaining national attention by settling a 1929 strike at a hosiery mill. He went on to settle over two-thousand labor disputes during the next four decades. Taylor also served in a succession of government posts, beginning with President Franklin D. Roosevelt's New Deal program. He was a high official with the National Labor Relations Board, the National Fair Labor Standards Administration, and the National War Labor Board under Roosevelt. In 1942, with the United States suddenly in World War II, he designed the famous Little Steel award, in which union workers got job security in return for strict government regulation of wartime wages.

While continuing to teach at the Wharton School and act as an independent arbitrator in labor disputes, he served variously as chairman of the Office of War Mobilization and Reconversion under President Harry S. Truman (1946–1947), chairman of President Dwight D. Eisenhower's inquiry board for the steel strike (1959), and a member of the President's Advisory Committee on Labor-Management Policy during the Kennedy and Johnson administrations (1961–1969). He is perhaps best known for his work on New York State's Taylor Law (1967), which was named after him. The law imposed stiff fines for public-employee unions that went out on strike, but gave public employees the right to join unions and bargain collectively.

Taylor retired from teaching at the Wharton School in 1971 and died the following year, at age seventy-one.

Alan T. Waterman

Physicist and public servant, he has been the far-sighted advocate of Federal support of the sciences, using the resources of government to improve the quality and increase the thrust of basic research.

★ ★ ★

President Lyndon B. Johnson awarded Waterman the Presidential Medal of Freedom with the above citation during a White House ceremony December 6, 1963. Waterman had been selected as a medal recipient earlier in 1963 by President John F. Kennedy, who was assassinated shortly before the award ceremony.

The first director of the National Science Foundation, Alan T. Waterman was born in Cornwall, New York, in 1892. His father was a Smith College physics professor, but the young Waterman did not decide on a career in science until midway through his education at Princeton University. Remaining at Princeton, Waterman earned his bachelor's degree (1913), master's degree (1914), and doctorate (1916) in experimental physics. He married Mary Mallon in 1917, while teaching physics at the University of Cincinnati.

Waterman joined the Yale faculty in 1919, and during the next twenty-seven years he taught and did research on the conductivity of electricity in solids. He also served on the editorial board of the prestigious *American Journal of Science*, which was published by Yale.

When World War II broke out Waterman began his career as a scientific administrator. As a deputy at the Office of Scientific Research and Development, he was deeply involved in mobilizing American scientists and technologists for the war effort. He helped review the progress of such projects as those for developing guided missiles, electronic communications, and especially applications of the newly discovered radar. Eventually, some five thousand people were employed in developing war applications for radar alone.

Waterman became chief of the Office of Scientific Research in 1945 and in the postwar years helped put in place mechanisms that maintained the relationship between government and the country's research institutions and scientists. As deputy chief of the Office of Naval Research, for example, he helped devise a new system of navy contracts for scientific research projects at universities.

Named head of the newly created National Science Foundation (NSF) in 1951, Waterman became responsible for the foundation's missions of furthering basic scientific research, shaping the government's policies on science, and furthering scientific education. During his twelve-year tenure, he consistently backed basic scientific research over work on technological applications, set up a peer-review and panel system for selecting and overseeing research programs, and presided over a NSF budget that mushroomed from $400,000 to $500 million.

Waterman served as president of the American Association for the Advancement of Science in 1962 and the following year retired as head of the NSF. He died in 1967, at age seventy-five.

Mark S. Watson

SOLDIER IN THE FIRST WORLD WAR AND CORRESPONDENT IN THE SECOND, HE HAS GIVEN THE AMERICAN PEOPLE INFORMED, WIDE-RANGING AND INDEPENDENT COVERAGE OF THE NATION'S SECURITY AND DEFENSE.

★ ★ ★

President Lyndon B. Johnson awarded Watson the Presidential Medal of Freedom with the above citation during a White House ceremony December 6, 1963. Watson had been selected as a medal recipient earlier in 1963 by President John F. Kennedy, who was assassinated shortly before the award ceremony.

A veteran military correspondent for the *Baltimore Sun*, Mark S. Watson was born in Plattsburgh, New York, in 1887. He went on to graduate from New York's Union College in 1908. By that time he had already begun his career as a journalist, having worked during college vacations for his hometown newspaper, the *Plattsburgh Press*. Watson worked as a correspondent for the *Chicago Tribune* until 1917, when he enlisted in the army. He served in Europe as an intelligence officer during World War I.

Watson's long career with the *Baltimore Sun* began in 1920 when the newspaper hired him as assistant managing editor. A year later he married Susan Elizabeth Owens. The *Sun* named him editor of its Sunday edition in 1927.

With the outbreak of war in Europe in 1939, Watson began writing in-depth articles on military matters. His interest in reporting on the war grew, until he gave up his job as Sunday editor to become the *Sun's* full-time military correspondent. His insightful coverage of the war from both Washington and the European front (he was with U.S. troops entering Paris in 1944) won him a Pulitzer Prize for reporting in 1945.

Watson continued as the newspaper's military reporter after the war, covering such stories as the postwar demobilization, the Berlin airlift, the first hydrogen bomb test, the launching of the first nuclear-powered submarine, and the development of intercontinental ballistic missiles, as well as the Korean War. Over the years he developed an extensive network of contacts in the Pentagon and worked for the *Sun* until shortly before his death in 1966. He was seventy-eight years old.

Annie D. Wauneka

FIRST WOMAN ELECTED TO THE NAVAJO TRIBAL COUNCIL, BY
HER LONG CRUSADE FOR IMPROVED HEALTH PROGRAMS SHE HAS
HELPED DRAMATICALLY TO LESSEN THE MENACE OF DISEASE
AMONG HER PEOPLE AND TO IMPROVE THEIR WAY OF LIFE.

★ ★ ★

*President Lyndon B. Johnson awarded Wauneka the Presidential Medal
of Freedom with the above citation during a White House ceremony
December 6, 1963. Wauneka had been selected as a medal recipient
earlier in 1963 by President John F. Kennedy, who was assassinated
shortly before the award ceremony.*

Born Annie Dodge on the Navajo reservation near Sawmill, Arizona,
in 1910, Wauneka was the daughter of the first elected chairman of
the Navajo Tribal Council, created after the Navajos adopted a constitutional government in 1923. Wauneka was raised in a family that
regarded the traditional Navajo ways as important but that also was
receptive to ideas of modern society. Like her father, Wauneka
learned both Navajo and English, and she attended boarding schools
for native Americans until she was eighteen, having completed the
eleventh grade. She married George Wauneka a year later, in 1929,
and eventually raised six children.

Because living conditions on reservations were often less than
sanitary, and many Navajos distrusted modern medicine, tuberculosis and other infectious diseases were a common part of life
among the Navajos. While still in boarding school, Wauneka was
caught up in a devastating flu epidemic that killed a number of her
classmates. During the epidemic she assisted the school nurse and at
that time realized how important learning proper health care was for
her people. The realization would later prove important to her life
and that of the Navajo nation.

After her marriage, she accompanied her father to tribal council
meetings, and during the next two decades she helped him establish
programs for water-system development, conservation, and day-
schooling on the reservation. After her father's death in 1947, she
became secretary and interpreter for her local chapter of the tribal
council and in 1951 was elected the first woman delegate to the Navajo
Tribal Council itself. She continued serving for over two decades and
from the early 1950s was head of the council's Health and Welfare
Committee. She launched a highly successful drive to educate Navajos
in Western concepts of disease and medicine, beginning with an effort
to check the spread of tuberculosis on the reservation.

She earned her bachelor's degree in public health at the University of
Arizona in the mid–1950s and began making educational movies to
promote acceptance of better health care among Navajos. During the

1960s she hosted a radio program that discussed basic sanitation techniques and health care for her tribe. She also worked for improved education, scholarships, and better roads to make schools more accessible.

From the 1970s onward she also held a variety of posts at the state and national levels, including serving on the Surgeon General's Advisory Board and as a member of the National Tuberculosis Association.

E. B. White

AN ESSAYIST WHOSE CONCISE COMMENT ON MEN AND PLACES HAS REVEALED TO YET ANOTHER AGE THE VIGOR OF THE ENGLISH SENTENCE.

★ ★ ★

President Lyndon B. Johnson awarded White the Presidential Medal of Freedom with the above citation during a White House ceremony December 6, 1963. White was unable to attend because of an illness. He had been selected as a medal recipient earlier in 1963 by President John F. Kennedy, who was assassinated shortly before the award ceremony.

A longtime contributing editor to the *New Yorker* magazine and a coauthor of the classic text *The Elements of Style,* White was born Elwyn Brooks White in Mount Vernon, New York, in 1899. He went on to graduate from Cornell University in 1921 with a degree in English and for the next five years worked variously as a reporter and an advertising copywriter.

Soon after the *New Yorker* was founded in 1925, it began publishing White's stories, poems, and articles. A year later he joined the magazine's staff and there met his future wife, Katharine Sergeant Angell, who was the fiction editor. White and Angell were married in 1929. White spent his first twelve years at the *New Yorker* writing the "Notes and Comments" essays, as well as poems, articles, stories, and even filler items. Though he worked in a freelance capacity from 1937, White continued writing for the magazine throughout his career.

White teamed up with humorist James Thurber in 1929 to write his first book, *Is Sex Necessary?*, and that same year also published his first volume of poems, *The Lady is Cold.* Six years later White published one of his most enduring books, *The Elements of Style,* which he wrote by expanding and revising notes made in 1918 by William Strunk, his professor at Cornell. Strunk and White, as the book is familiarly known, became a classic text on writing style that has been used by writers, editors, and students for generations.

During the 1930s, 1940s, and 1950s, White continued writing books, essays, articles, and poems, but none achieved the lasting popularity of his three children's books. *Stuart Little* (1945), *Charlotte's Web* (1952), and *The Trumpet of the Swan* (1970) are considered classics.

Among his later works are *The Points of My Compass* (1962), the *Essays of E.B. White* (1977), and *Poems and Sketches of E.B. White* (1981). In 1978 White won a special Pulitzer Prize for his work. He suffered from Alzheimer's disease in his last years and died in 1985. He was eighty-six.

Thornton Wilder

ARTIST OF RARE GAIETY AND PENETRATION, HE HAS INSCRIBED A NOBLE VISION IN HIS BOOKS, MAKING THE COMMONPLACES OF LIFE YIELD THE WIT, THE WONDER AND THE STEADFASTNESS OF THE HUMAN ADVENTURE.

★ ★ ★

President Lyndon B. Johnson awarded Wilder the Presidential Medal of Freedom with the above citation during a White House ceremony December 6, 1963. Wilder had been selected as a medal recipient earlier in 1963 by President John F. Kennedy, who was assassinated shortly before the award ceremony.

A leading American playwright and novelist who wrote the famous play *Our Town*, Thornton Wilder was born in Madison, Wisconsin, in 1897. He was the son of a journalist who also spent time in the foreign service. Wilder graduated from Yale University in 1920 and then spent a year studying Latin and classical history in Rome. By chance he was in Rome when Luigi Pirandello's *Six Characters in Search of an Author* was first performed, and the play significantly influenced Wilder's later work as a dramatist.

Returning to the United States in 1921, he taught French at a prep school in Princeton, New Jersey, and wrote his first novel, *The Cabala*, which was published in 1926. Encouraged by favorable reviews, Wilder published his second novel two years later. *The Bridge of San Luis Rey* was a major success, established Wilder's international reputation as a writer, and won him his first Pulitzer Prize. That same year he also published a book of short plays, *That Troubled the Waters*.

While continuing to write novels, *Heaven's My Destination* (1934) among them, Wilder began to focus on drama. He wrote two screenplays, including *Shadow of a Doubt* (1942) for Alfred Hitchcock, and his dramatic masterpiece, the play *Our Town,* premiered in 1938.

An immediate hit on Broadway, the innovative, witty, and compelling drama garnered Wilder's second Pulitzer Prize and has become something akin to America's national play. Four years later Wilder again took Broadway by storm, with *The Skin of Our Teeth,* his second dramatic masterpiece. For it he won a third Pulitzer Prize.

During World War II Wilder served in the air corps as a strategic planning officer in the Mediterranean theater. After the war he wrote another novel, *The Ides of March,* in 1948, and in 1954 he returned to Broadway with a popular lighthearted farce, *The Matchmaker.* The play was made into a film and also inspired the smash hit musical *Hello, Dolly!* (1964).

Wilder's last major play, *The Alcestiad* (1955), was unsuccessful. He wrote the novel *The Eighth Day* in 1967 and six years later, at age seventy-five, published his last novel, *Theophilus North.* Wilder, who never married, died in 1975 at age seventy-eight.

Edmund Wilson

CRITIC AND HISTORIAN, HE HAS CONVERTED CRITICISM ITSELF INTO A CREATIVE ACT, WHILE SETTING FOR THE NATION A STERN AND UNCOMPROMISING STANDARD OF INDEPENDENT JUDGMENT.

★ ★ ★

President Lyndon B. Johnson awarded Wilson the Presidential Medal of Freedom with the above citation during a White House ceremony December 6, 1963. Wilson was unable to attend. He had been selected as a medal recipient earlier in 1963 by President John F. Kennedy, who was assassinated shortly before the award ceremony.

An essayist and the foremost literary critic of his day, Edmund Wilson was born in Red Bank, New Jersey, in 1895. His father was a trial lawyer and former New Jersey state attorney general. Wilson, interested in writing as a youth, went on to Princeton University, worked on the university's *Nassau Literary Magazine,* befriended fellow classmate F. Scott Fitzgerald, and graduated in 1916.

Wilson then tried newspaper reporting in New York, served in the army during World War I, and following the war worked briefly as the managing editor of *Vanity Fair* from 1920 to 1921. Meanwhile, he had also been writing stories, poems, and essays, and after 1921 he contributed articles on books and other subjects to the *New Republic* and other magazines. In 1926 he published *Discordant Encounters,* a collection of miscellaneous writings, and then spent the next five years as an associate editor at the *New Republic.*

His first major book was *Axel's Castle* (1931), a literary analysis considered a seminal work on symbolism. Other critical works, for which Wilson became famous, followed and included *The Wound and the Bow* (1941), about creativity and neurosis, *The Shores of Light* (1952), focusing on the 1920s and 1930s, and *Patriotic Gore* (1962), about Civil War-era literature. His two books on social history were *To the Finland Station* (1940), on revolutionary ideology, and *The American Earthquake* (1958), about the depression years.

Over the years Wilson's books and critical pieces in magazines established him as a leading critic, and his writings helped gain notice for such young American writers as Ernest Hemingway, William Faulkner, Fitzgerald, and John Dos Passos. Fitzgerald especially was a longtime friend, and his death in 1940 was a personal loss for Wilson. Wilson edited Fitzgerald's last, unfinished, novel, *The Last Tycoon* (1941) and his posthumous papers, which were published as *The Crack-Up* in 1945. The following year Wilson went through a marital crack-up, divorcing his third wife, the writer Mary McCarthy, and marrying Elena Mumm Thornton. This fourth marriage succeeded, however, and he remained with Elena until his death.

Among Wilson's later works are *The Scrolls from the Dead Sea* (1955), for which he learned Hebrew, *Apologies to the Iroquois* (1960), *O Canada: An American's Notes on Canadian Culture* (1965), and his autobiographical works, *A Piece of My Mind: Reflections at Sixty* (1956), *A Prelude* (1967), and *Upstate: Records and Recollections of Northern New York* (1971). He also wrote plays, poems, and one novel, and his magazine writings were collected in such books as *Classics and Commercials* (1950) and *The Bit Between My Teeth* (1965).

Highly regarded for his great intellect and breadth of learning, he was a distinguished and influential man of letters, as well as a literary and social critic. Wilson died in 1972, at age seventy-seven.

Andrew Wyeth

Painter of the American scene, he has in the great humanist tradition illuminated and clarified the verities and delights of everyday life.

★ ★ ★

President Lyndon B. Johnson awarded Wyeth the Presidential Medal of Freedom with the above citation during a White House ceremony December 6, 1963. Wyeth had been selected as a medal recipient earlier in 1963 by President John F. Kennedy, who was assassinated shortly before the award ceremony.

Among the great American painters of this century, Andrew Wyeth was born in 1917 at Chadds Ford, a picturesque farming town in Pennsylvania. His father, an illustrator of such children's classics as *Robin Hood* and a noted muralist as well, began training Wyeth as an artist at age fifteen. The younger Wyeth worked in watercolors, portrayed his subjects in a realistic manner, and learned quickly. Just five years later, in 1937, he had his first one-man show of watercolor landscapes, at New York City's William Macbeth Gallery. It was an immediate success and established him as an important artist. He married Betsy Merle James in 1940.

Despite his newfound popularity, Wyeth still was not satisfied with his work. He began concentrating on painting people and in 1941 also took up egg-tempera painting, which allowed him to heighten the effects of texture. But his father's death in an auto accident in 1945 marked perhaps the most important turning point in Wyeth's life. Recovering from the emotional shock, he decided to do "something serious" with his artistic talent. The result was twofold: his paintings revealed a marked increase in emotion, and he began regularly painting people, often portraits of a solitary figure with a thoughtful, unsmiling expression.

Wyeth's success was all the more unusual because he established himself as a realistic painter at a time when abstract expressionism had overtaken the art world. Wyeth's brand of naturalism was not merely photographic, however. Through his choice of subject matter and use of perspective, color (usually subdued earth tones), and emphasis, he managed to instill a scene with a deeper symbolism and emotion. His paintings may evoke loneliness, tranquility, nostalgia, or a sense of foreboding in the viewer.

He painted what is probably his most popular work, the hauntingly appealing *Christina's World*, in 1948. Among his other noted watercolor and tempera paintings are *Wind from the Sea* (1947), the portrait *Karl* (1948), *Trodden Weed* (1951), *Nicholas* (1955), *Groundhog Day* (1959), *Weather Side* (1965), and *Indian Summer* (1970).

Wyeth was the first painter chosen to receive the Presidential

Medal of Freedom. During the 1960s, 1970s, 1980s, and 1990s, his paintings continued to command both critical acclaim and some of the highest prices paid for works of a living artist. His exhibitions during the 1960s drew hundreds of thousands of people, and numerous museums here and abroad have exhibited his works over the past decades. He has been inducted to the French Academy of Fine Arts (1977), the Soviet Academy of the Arts (1978, honorary member), and Britain's Royal Academy (1980, the first living American artist so honored).

Dean Acheson

AN ARCHITECT OF THE DEFENSE AND GROWTH OF A FLOUR-
ISHING ATLANTIC COMMUNITY, HIS MORAL RESOLVE AND INTEL-
LECTUAL GRASP HAVE PLACED ALL MEN IN HIS DEBT.

★ ★ ★

President Lyndon B. Johnson awarded Acheson the Presidential Medal of Freedom with the above citation during a White House ceremony September 14, 1964. The medal was presented with the additional accolade "with distinction."

The secretary of state from 1949 to 1953 and an adviser to presidents, Dean Acheson was a guiding hand of U.S. foreign policy during the early years of the Cold War. He became the principal architect of the Cold War policy emphasizing containment of communism and worked to solidify the anticommunist alliance of Western nations through the North Atlantic Treaty Organization (NATO) and other means.

Born in Middletown, Connecticut, in 1893, Acheson was the son of the Episcopal bishop of Connecticut. After graduating from Yale (1915) and from Harvard Law School (1918), he clerked for Supreme Court Justice Louis D. Brandeis for two years and then joined a Washington law firm. In 1917 he married Alice Stanley, a Wellesley graduate.

A Democrat, Acheson entered government service in 1933 as undersecretary of the Treasury in the Roosevelt administration, but he left that post the same year over a policy disagreement. He was an early supporter of the president's policy of U.S. intervention in World War II, though. In 1941 he returned to the Roosevelt administration as assistant secretary of state for economic affairs. Acheson's work eventually included postwar economic planning, and he helped organize the International Monetary Fund and the World Bank. As President Harry S. Truman's under secretary of state from 1945 to

1947, Acheson became a staunch anticommunist and helped shape the Truman Doctrine and Marshall Plan.

President Truman appointed Acheson secretary of state in 1949. Acheson sought to contain the communist threat worldwide through foreign economic and military aid, while also seeking to preserve sufficient U.S. economic and military strength. He helped establish the NATO military alliance and urged further development of nuclear weapons to maintain U.S. superiority over the Soviet Union. When North Korean armies attacked South Korea, he advocated military intervention and helped win UN backing for the Korean War. But he seriously underestimated China's willingness to back North Korea, which prolonged the war and helped elect Dwight D. Eisenhower president in 1953. Acheson returned to private practice that year.

During the 1960s Acheson served as an adviser to President John F. Kennedy and remained in that capacity throughout both of President Johnson's terms. Between 1970 and 1971 he also advised President Richard Nixon. During his long career Acheson wrote six books, including a memoir, *Present at the Creation: My Years in the State Department* (1969), for which he won the 1970 Pulitzer Prize in history. He died suddenly in 1971 at age seventy-eight.

Detlev W. Bronk

SCIENTIST AND LEADER OF SCHOLARS, HIS VISION AND UNTIRING EFFORTS HAVE ADVANCED SCIENCE EDUCATION AND HELPED FORGE AN ENDURING LINK BETWEEN GOVERNMENT AND THE SCIENTIFIC COMMUNITY.

★ ★ ★

President Lyndon B. Johnson awarded Bronk the Presidential Medal of Freedom with the above citation during a White House ceremony September 14, 1964.

A presidential science adviser, university president, and pioneer researcher in biophysics, Detlev W. Bronk was born the son of a New York City Baptist minister in 1897. After receiving his bachelor of science degree from Swarthmore in 1920, Bronk began teaching physics (and later physiology) at the University of Michigan, while also continuing his graduate studies. He married Helen Alexander Ramsey in 1921 and earned his doctorate in physics and physiology from the University of Michigan five years later.

After teaching at Swarthmore for several years, Bronk joined the University of Pennsylvania Medical School in 1929, where he became director of the Johnson Foundation for Medical Physics. Continuing his research in the emerging field of biophysics, Bronk and collaborators investigated processes in human nerve cells (neurons), including heat production, recovery from electrical activity, and use of oxygen, as well as broader questions about how the sympathetic nervous system controls the cardiovascular system. (He pioneered the use of electromicroscopy in studying human nerve cells.)

During World War II he turned to war-related research at the University of Pennsylvania, serving as coordinator of research for the Office of the Air Surgeon and as special consultant to the Secretary of War. In 1946 Bronk became chairman of the National Research Council, which coordinated research by individual scientists.

After the war he focused on educational and administrative work. Named president of Johns Hopkins University in 1949, he instituted the *Hopkins* plan, promoting self-directed study, undergraduate participation in graduate studies, and greater social concern by scientists and other scholars. In 1953 he became the first president of the Rockefeller Medical Institute for Medical Research in New York, which he helped reorganize into Rockefeller University.

Bronk frequently spoke out on the importance of science in modern society and helped promote the founding of the National Science Foundation and the Presidential Science Advisory Committee. He served as president of the National Academy of Sciences from 1950 to 1962 and as chairman of the National Science Foundation from 1955 to 1964. In addition, he was science adviser to three presidents—Harry S. Truman, Dwight D. Eisenhower, and John F. Kennedy.

Bronk's work and his concern for promoting human values as well as science helped him gain an international reputation. He was made a foreign associate of Britain's Royal Society, the French National Academy of Science, and the Russian Academy. Bronk gave up his post at Rockefeller University in 1968 and died seven years later in New York City. He was seventy-eight years old.

Aaron Copland

MASTERFUL COMPOSER AND GIFTED TEACHER, HIS MUSIC ECHOES OUR AMERICAN EXPERIENCE AND SPEAKS EXPRESSIVELY TO AN INTERNATIONAL AUDIENCE.

* * *

President Lyndon B. Johnson awarded Copland the Presidential Medal of Freedom with the above citation during a White House ceremony September 14, 1964.

Called "the dean of American composers," Aaron Copland greatly influenced the development of modernist music in America—through his works, his teaching, and his writings. His compositions, characteristically modernist and often embracing American themes, cover a wide range of forms, including orchestral works, ballets, chamber music, theater music, and film scores. In addition to the Presidential Medal of Freedom, which recognized his lifetime achievements, other awards Copland won include the 1944 Pulitzer Prize in music (for his *Appalachian Spring* symphony) and an Academy Award in 1949 for best dramatic score (in the movie *The Heiress*).

Born in 1900, Copland was the son of Russian-Jewish immigrants living in Brooklyn, New York. His sister began teaching him the piano when he was eleven—formal lessons started two years later—and by age fifteen Copland had decided to become a composer. After high school he went to France to continue his music studies and between 1921 and 1924 studied composition under Nadia Boulanger, a brilliant teacher who influenced other American musicians as well. Soon after his return to the United States in 1924, Boulanger commissioned him to write *Symphony for Organ and Orchestra*, which was first performed by the New York Symphony in 1925 with Mme. Boulanger playing the organ. He introduced the jazz idiom in *Music for the Theater* that year and in *Piano Concerto* the next but turned to more dissonant, avant-garde forms of modernism in the late 1920s and early 1930s.

Copland entered a new phase in the mid-1930s and began the most productive period of his career. Seeking to simplify and broaden the appeal of modern music, he turned to American folk themes and composed scores that won him worldwide fame. Among them were three famous ballets—*Billy the Kid* (1938), *Rodeo* (1942), and *Appalachian Spring* (1944)—as well as *Lincoln Portrait* (1942) for speaker and chorus, *Letter from Home* (1944), and *Third Symphony* (1946). He also did a series of movie scores during this time, including for *Our Town* (1940) and *The Heiress* (1948).

During the late 1950s and 1960s, Copland experimented with the stark, dissonant twelve-tone style of Arnold Schoenberg. Works like *Connotations* (1962) and *Inscape* (1967) were not especially successful, and around 1970 Copland abandoned composition altogether for conducting and lecturing, which he continued into his eighties. Copland published books about music, among them *Copland on Music* (1960) as well as a two-volume autobiography, *Copland: 1900 Through 1942* (1984) and *Copland: Since 1943* (1989). He died at age ninety, a year after the second volume appeared.

Willem de Kooning

ARTIST AND TEACHER, HE HAS ADVENTURED INTO A NEW RANGE OF ARTISTIC VISION AND OPENED BOLD PATHWAYS TO OUR EXPERIENCE OF THE WORLD.

★ ★ ★

President Lyndon B. Johnson awarded de Kooning the Presidential Medal of Freedom with the above citation during a White House ceremony September 14, 1964.

A master abstract expressionist, Willem de Kooning was born in the Netherlands city of Rotterdam in 1904, the son of a wine distributor. At age twelve he was apprenticed to a team of commercial artists and in his free time studied art at the Rotterdam Academy of Fine Arts and Techniques. Between 1920 and 1924 de Kooning was employed by a department store art director, worked as a commercial artist, and traveled. Completing his studies at Rotterdam Academy in 1925, he left the Netherlands for the United States in 1926, arriving illegally as a stowaway aboard a ship.

De Kooning settled in New York City by 1927, working at odd jobs while continuing his study of art. Intent on exploring new styles, he investigated cubism and surrealist modes while gradually evolving his own artistic style.

The Federal Arts Project hired de Kooning in 1935, providing him with his first opportunity to paint full time. He first exhibited his own works the following year in a group show at New York's Museum of Modern Art. De Kooning was then commissioned to paint a mural for the 1939 New York World's Fair. Four years later he married Elaine Marie Fried, an artist and critic.

With his longtime friend Jackson Pollock and other young experimental artists, de Kooning helped create a movement of abstract expressionism during the 1940s called the New York School. But de Kooning was still relatively unknown when he gave his first one-man show in 1948. Already unconcerned about artistic conventions, he exhibited a collection of bold black-and-white abstract paintings. The works were well received, though, and some critics still consider them his finest work.

These and subsequent paintings, in which he introduced sweeping brush strokes, helped establish de Kooning's reputation as an abstract expressionist. He also became known for using especially large canvases, his largest being *Excavation* (1950), which measures over 6½ feet by more than 8 feet.

De Kooning secured his reputation as an artist in 1953 when he exhibited a controversial group of paintings entitled *Woman*. The blunt, heavily drawn, and sometimes explicit representations of female forms caused a sensation because of their violent imagery and because de Kooning, until then an abstract painter, had introduced representational forms to his work. *Woman* eventually became the most reproduced artwork from the 1950s.

Such bold experiments marked de Kooning's unwillingness to belong to any one artistic movement or style. After returning to abstraction for a time, he painted a series of urban and highway landscapes, such as *Montauk Highway* (1958), and during the mid–1960s he did a series in which female forms appeared in abstract landscapes. *Clam Diggers* (1964) was among these works. A series of untitled paintings featuring bold, brightly colored slashes of paint in the 1970s set the stage for his shift during the 1980s to lighter, more lyrical works, again devoted to female forms.

A U.S. citizen since 1961, de Kooning has painted works that are now part of the permanent collections of the Metropolitan Museum of Art, the National Gallery, and various other noted institutions. His painting *Two Women* (1955) brought $1.2 million at a 1982 art auction, then the largest sum paid for any living American artist's work.

Walt Disney

ARTIST AND IMPRESARIO, IN THE COURSE OF ENTERTAINING AN AGE, HE HAS CREATED AN AMERICAN FOLKLORE.

★ ★ ★

President Lyndon B. Johnson awarded Disney the Presidential Medal of Freedom with the above citation during a White House ceremony September 14, 1964.

A pioneer in cartoon animation, Walt Disney used his imagination and vision to create an entertainment empire that amused and delighted generations of Americans. Cartoon characters like Mickey Mouse and Donald Duck, animated features like *Peter Pan* and *Cinderella,* live action films like *20,000 Leagues Under the Sea* and *Mary Poppins,* not to mention the Mouseketeers and the Disneyland fantasy world amusement park—all Disney creations—have touched the lives of almost every American who has grown up since World War II.

Walter Elias Disney was born in Chicago in 1901, one of five children. His family moved to a Missouri farm when he was four, and Walt and his older brother Roy handled many of the chores. The time they spent together helped them build a close bond that would last a lifetime and also play a key role in the success of Disney's entertainment ventures. But farm life had another important effect on Walt's life—it was there he discovered an interest in drawing and painting.

Though under age, Disney served as a Red Cross ambulance driver during World War I, passing his off-duty time by drawing. Still in his teens when he returned to the United States in 1919, Disney nevertheless decided on a career as a commercial artist. After working for a company that made short animated advertisements for Kansas City movie houses, Disney and a talented Dutch artist named Ub Iwerks decided to start an animation business of their own. Animation was still in its infancy, but Disney successfully produced some short animated films and in 1923 moved the business to Hollywood. With brother Roy as administrator, the struggling company grew and produced two series, *Alice Comedies* and *Oswald the Lucky Rabbit*. In 1925 Disney married Lillian Bounds, who worked at the company.

Disney's first cartoons featuring Mickey Mouse appeared in 1928, and the stunning success of the character provided the foundation for all that was to come. Though Disney stopped doing any actual drawing in 1924, he kept a close watch on the production process while also focusing on developing the business. The 1930s brought a host of new Disney characters—Donald Duck, Daisy Duck, Goofy, and Pluto—all of them immensely popular with children.

Bolstered by the success of his cartoons, Disney in 1937 produced the first feature-length animated movie, *Snow White and the Seven Dwarfs*. The movie struck a resonant chord and its enormous popularity led to a series of now-classic Disney animated movies based on children's stories. Appearing during the 1940s and 1950s, they included *Pinocchio*, *Fantasia*, *Bambi*, *Cinderella*, *Peter Pan*, and *Sleeping Beauty*.

The 1950s and 1960s brought documentaries and highly successful live-action movies from Disney's studios. *Treasure Island* (1950) was the first all live-action film, but many others followed, including *20,000 Leagues Under the Sea* (1954), *Pollyanna* (1960), and *Mary Poppins* (1964). Meanwhile, Disney broke into the rapidly growing television market with his show "Disneyland," which aired from 1954.

The 1950s also saw what was perhaps his most ambitious undertaking, Disneyland, a family amusement park in Anaheim, California. Developed at a cost of over $17 million, Disneyland was part fantasy world, part carnival, and part technological wonder. Millions flocked to the park, and its success encouraged Disney to begin working on similar theme parks elsewhere.

By the close of the 1950s Disney was among the most beloved and influential leaders of the entertainment world, but he was not without his critics. While he almost universally enthralled children with his lovable characters, magical fantasies, and happy endings, some adults complained about his creations. Critics especially took aim at what they saw as his sentimentality and unrealistically upbeat outlook, his use of stereotyping and sometimes violent elements, and his commercialization of children's fantasies.

Disney's popularity far outweighed the criticisms, however. In his last years he had begun work on his second theme park, The Walt Disney World Resort in Florida, but he did not live to see it completed. Disney died in 1966, at age sixty-five.

J. Frank Dobie

FOLKLORIST, TEACHER, WRITER, HE HAS RECAPTURED THE TREASURE OF OUR RICH REGIONAL HERITAGE IN THE SOUTHWEST FROM THE CONQUISTADORES TO THE COWBOYS.

★ ★ ★

President Lyndon B. Johnson awarded Dobie the Presidential Medal of Freedom with the above citation during a White House ceremony September 14, 1964.

Probably the leading writer of his day on the culture of the Southwest, J. Frank Dobie was born in rural Oak County, Texas, in 1888. The son of a cattle rancher, Dobie supplemented his schoolwork with reading lists supplied by his mother and later lived with his grandparents so that he could attend high school in Alice, Texas. A degree from Southwestern University in Texas followed in 1906, and he earned his master's degree from Columbia University in 1914 after a stint at teaching in public schools.

Returning to Texas, Dobie began what became a long and sometimes stormy teaching career at the University of Texas at Austin. By 1921 Dobie was teaching what was called the university's most popular course, "Life and Literature of the Southwest," and he subsequently established himself as a well-known folklorist. But his frequent leaves of absence and a bitter dispute with the university administration finally ended with his dismissal in 1947.

Two other events important to his life and writing career occurred at about the time he began teaching. In 1916 Dobie married Bertha McKee, on whom he came to rely as his editor and assistant. That same year his developing interest in folklore led him to join the Texas Folklore Society. Not long after, the society named him editor of its publications, a post he held for twenty-one years.

Dobie's first book received only limited notice but it marked the beginning of forty years as an author during which he produced a book about every year and a half. He established his reputation as a folklorist with *A Vaquero of the Brush Country* (1929) and *Coronado's Children* (1930), both collections of folktales about treasure hunting. Dobie won the Literary Guild Award in 1931 for *Coronado's Children* and received a Guggenheim grant.

Other books followed, eventually garnering him a national reputation as an author and folklorist. Among the later books were *Guide to Life and Literature of the Southwest* (1943) and a series on animals native to the Southwest, which began in 1941 with *The Longhorns* and ended with the posthumously published *The Rattlesnakes* (1965). *A Texan in England* (1945) dealt with his experiences as a visiting professor of American history at Cambridge University during World War II. One of the last volumes published during his lifetime was *Cow People*, a retrospective.

President Johnson, himself a native Texan, awarded Dobie the Presidential Medal of Freedom just four days before the writer's death on September 18, 1964. Dobie was nearly seventy-six years old.

Lena F. Edwards

PHYSICIAN AND HUMANITARIAN, SHE HAS APPLIED HER MEDICAL
SKILLS AND COMPASSIONATE UNDERSTANDING TO THE WOMEN
AND CHILDREN OF OUR MIGRATORY WORK FORCE.

★ ★ ★

President Lyndon B. Johnson awarded Edwards the Presidential Medal of Freedom with the above citation during a White House ceremony September 14, 1964.

One of the first black women certified in obstetrics and gynecology in this country, Lena Edwards was born in Washington, D.C., in 1900. She excelled in high school, graduating as class valedictorian in 1917, and entered Howard University's medical program. There she met and later married a classmate, Keith Madison, and in 1924 completed her studies for her medical degree.

By 1925 she and her husband had set up practices in Jersey City. She gained a reputation locally for her work in obstetrics, and when Jersey City's Margaret Hague Maternity Hospital opened in 1931, Edwards joined its staff as assistant gynecologist. While continuing to practice at Hague Hospital, she began studying obstetrics and gynecology in the 1940s, soon after such specialized medical training was first opened to blacks and women. She was certified in the specialty in 1948.

Leaving Hague Hospital in 1954, she spent the next five years teaching obstetrics and gynecology at Howard University. That proved only an interim step, however, and in 1959 Edwards, a Roman Catholic, began the work that would win her the Presidential Medal of Freedom. That year she left Howard University to help found the Our Lady of Guadeloupe Maternity Clinic in Hereford, Texas.

Between 1960 and 1965 she dedicated herself to providing medical care to migrant workers who came to the Texas clinic while also helping to raise funds for it. President Johnson recognized her efforts in behalf of the migrant workers shortly before her return to New Jersey in 1965.

She was then almost sixty-five years old but continued working to provide medical care to needy women. In 1973 she won recognition for helping to introduce the use of the Pap smear, a test for cervical cancer, among low-income women. In her final years she endowed a scholarship fund for medical students at Howard University, and in 1984 the school's medical alumni association honored the pioneering black physician as a "Living Legend." She died two years later in 1986, at age eighty-six.

Thomas Stearns Eliot

POET AND CRITIC, HE HAS FUSED INTELLIGENCE AND IMAGIN-
ATION, TRADITION AND INNOVATION, BRINGING TO THE WORLD
A NEW SENSE OF THE POSSIBILITIES FOR ORDER IN A REVOLU-
TIONARY TIME.

★ ★ ★

President Lyndon B. Johnson awarded Eliot the Presidential Medal of Freedom with the above citation during a White House ceremony September 14, 1964.

Among the century's most outstanding poets, T. S. Eliot revolutionized English poetry with such renowned works as *The Waste Land* and *Four Quartets* and was a leading voice of the modernist movement. Eliot was born in Saint Louis, Missouri, in 1888, the son of a brick manufacturer and a volunteer social worker. Raised in comfortable circumstances, he attended Smith Academy, where he wrote poems for the literary magazine.

Eliot graduated from Harvard College in 1909 after only three years and began his postgraduate studies soon after. By this time he had discovered the medieval Italian poet Dante Alighieri, whose clear visual images and precise diction, Eliot later said, had the greatest influence on his own poetry. While studying at the Sorbonne in France from 1910 to 1911, Elio wrote "The Love Song of J. Alfred Prufrock," generally regarded as his first great work in the modernist vein. In the poem Eliot wrote about the sterility and hopelessness of modern life and, breaking with poets of the past century, created verse rhythms based on those of contemporary speech.

Between 1911 and 1914 he largely abandoned poetry for the study of philosophy, and, after completing the required course work for his doctorate at Harvard, Eliot went to England to write his dissertation. There he met the American poet Ezra Pound, who was taken by "Prufrock" and urged Eliot to focus on writing poetry. The following year Eliot married his first wife, Vivien Haigh-Wood, the daughter of a British artist. An intelligent but frail and neurotic woman, she was mentally ill by 1935 and died in 1947.

Eliot completed his dissertation but because of World War I could not return to Harvard for his oral examination and so never completed his doctorate. During this period Eliot took up teaching and contributed many essays and reviews to philosophical journals. By 1917 his poetry and other writings had won him attention in British literary circles, and he befriended Leonard and Virginia Woolf, who published his next book of verse.

Nevertheless, the financial pressure of supporting his ailing wife forced him to take a job at Lloyd's Bank in 1917. The demands of the job and his writing strained Eliot's health, until, in 1921, he spent six weeks in a Swiss psychiatric institution. Ironically, it was there that he drafted his next great work *The Waste Land*, a poem he had been thinking about for several years.

The subject of violent controversy when it was published in 1922, the poem employed modernist verses that broke sharply with conventional poetic forms. Eliot used his poem to contrast the despair and spiritual stagnation of modern times with myths of the past that had once provided a source of spiritual regeneration. The poem's powerful evocation of the profound disillusionment following World War I nevertheless made it a key work of literary modernism and won Eliot an international reputation.

Tied to Britain by his ailing wife, Eliot renounced his U.S. citizenship and become a British citizen in 1926. That year he also announced his conversion to Catholicism, and religion became a recurrent theme in the poetic dramas he wrote during the 1930s, including *The Rock, Murder in the Cathedral, The Family Reunion,* and others. Meanwhile, Eliot left his job at Lloyd's and began working as an editor at a British publishing house, a position he held until his death.

Eliot's masterpiece, *Four Quartets*, was published as a book in 1943. Consisting of four previously published poems, the elaborately constructed *Four Quartets* concerns time and eternity and is invested with a complex of symbols, recurrent images, and historical, literary, and Christian references. Critically acclaimed, the work won the 1948 Nobel Prize in literature.

Eliot married his second wife, Esme Valerie Fletcher, in 1957. She had been his private secretary since 1949.

During his long career as a poet, editor, critic, and dramatist, Eliot won numerous awards besides the Nobel Prize. Among the last was the Presidential Medal of Freedom. Eliot died in London four months later in January 1965. He was seventy-six years old.

John W. Gardner

GUARDIAN AND CRITIC OF AMERICAN EDUCATION, HE HAS
INSPIRED OUR SCHOOLS AND COLLEGES TOWARD HIS OWN GOAL
OF INCREASING EXCELLENCE.

★ ★ ★

*President Lyndon B. Johnson awarded Gardner the Presidential Medal
of Freedom with the above citation during a White House ceremony
September 14, 1964.*

The president of the Carnegie Corporation and a long-time consultant
to the government on education, John W. Gardner became President
Lyndon Johnson's secretary of Health, Education and Welfare (HEW)
in 1965, less than a year after receiving the Presidential Medal of
Freedom. Gardner served as secretary during the height of Johnson's
Great Society program for social welfare reforms. In subsequent years
he remained in the nation's capital and founded such proactivist
groups as the National Urban Coalition and Common Cause.

Born in Los Angeles in 1912, Gardner was raised in Beverly Hills
and graduated from Stanford University with a psychology degree in
1935. After earning his doctorate at the University of California,
Berkeley, he taught psychology first at Connecticut College and then
at Mount Holyoke over the next four years. While still at Stanford in
1934, Gardner married Aida Marroquin.

An officer in the Office of Strategic Services (OSS) during World
War II, he joined the staff of the Carnegie Corporation foundation in
1946, after his release from active duty. Rising quickly, Gardner became
acting president of the philanthropic fund in 1950 and president in
1955. At Carnegie he oversaw distribution of research and education
grants. Among the many proposed programs he funded were the "new
math" program and a seminal study of high schools in the United
States by James B. Conant. *(See also the entry for Conant, p. 53.)*

Gardner became nationally known for his work in education and
served as a White House education consultant during the
Eisenhower, Kennedy, and Johnson administrations. That led to his
first (and only) government post, as secretary of HEW under
President Johnson. Serving from 1965 to 1968, he oversaw the
founding of Medicare and various other social welfare programs.

Soon after leaving HEW, Gardner formed the National Urban
Coalition in 1968. The group hoped to halt the urban decay then
being blamed for the rioting in America's major cities. But Gardner
and others grew to believe that the government itself also needed
reform. To that end he founded the now-famous organization,
Common Cause in 1970. As its director, he sought to make government more responsive to the public interest. Meanwhile, Gardner
also founded Independent Sector, a group promoting voluntarism.

Gardner retired from public service in 1989 and returned to California to teach at Stanford University. He is the author of several books on education and social reform, including *Self-Renewal: The Individual and the Innovative Society* (1964) and *The Rediscovery of Confidence* (1970).

Theodore M. Hesburgh

EDUCATOR AND HUMANITARIAN, HE HAS INSPIRED A GEN-
ERATION OF STUDENTS AND GIVEN OF HIS WISDOM IN THE
STRUGGLE FOR THE RIGHTS OF MAN.

★ ★ ★

President Lyndon B. Johnson awarded Hesburg the Presidential Medal of Freedom with the above citation during a White House ceremony September 14, 1964.

A Roman Catholic priest and widely respected educator, Theodore M. Hesburgh served as president of the University of Notre Dame for over three decades. During that time he implemented an ambitious plan to raise the university's academic standing by adding new faculty and programs as well as by greatly enlarging the university's physical plant. He also achieved national recognition for his work with such public-service organizations as the U.S. Civil Rights Commission, the American Council on Education, and the National Science Foundation.

The son of a Pittsburgh Plate Glass Company executive, Hesburgh was born in Syracuse, New York, in 1917. He planned to enter the priesthood from as early as age four and after being educated in Catholic schools in Syracuse, he went to the University of Notre Dame in 1934. Completing his bachelor's degree at Italy's Gregorian University in 1940, Hesburgh went on to graduate studies at Holy Cross seminary and Catholic University in Washington, D.C. He was ordained in 1943 and earned his doctorate in theology from Catholic University in 1945.

Assigned to teach religion at Notre Dame, Hesburgh developed close ties with the students while also rising quickly in the administration. Named a department head in 1948, he was promoted to executive vice-president the following year, at age thirty-two. Three years later, in 1952, the university made him its president.

Hesburgh wasted no time embarking on his program of change. Up till then Notre Dame had been a small, undergraduate liberal arts school with a rigorously regulated student body. Hesburgh shook up the university administration and in 1954 introduced a new liberal arts curriculum. In addition to promoting academic freedom, he also eliminated many campus regulations, such as midnight dormitory curfews, that had been alienating the student body. Years later he gained national attention for his firm stand against campus violence, as well as for his opposition to the Vietnam War.

Meanwhile, Hesburgh's highly successful fund-raising campaigns financed the construction of over twenty new university buildings during his tenure as president, including the world's largest college library building, a computer center, and a radiation research center. Money also went to expanding the faculty, adding a new psychology department, enlarging engineering and science colleges, founding the Graduate School of Business and Public Administration, and funding various other special programs.

Public service was Hesburgh's second vocation. Beginning with the National Science Foundation board of directors (from 1954), he served with a long list of prestigious groups, including the Rockefeller Foundation, the Carnegie Commission on the Future of Higher Education, the American Council on Education, the United Negro College Fund, and even the International Atomic Energy Commission. Appointed to the U.S. Civil Rights Commission in 1957 by President Dwight D. Eisenhower, Hesburgh chaired the organization from 1969 to 1972, when he resigned over disagreements with the Nixon administration. Under President Jimmy Carter, he chaired the Overseas Development Council.

The president emeritus of Notre Dame since his retirement in 1987, Hesburgh has published numerous books, many of them collections of addresses, including *Patterns for Educational Growth* (1958), *Thoughts for Our Times* (1962), and *The Humane Imperative: Challenge for the Year* 2000 (1974). In addition to the Presidential Medal of Freedom, he has received numerous other awards and honors.

Clarence L. "Kelly" Johnson

AERONAUTICAL ENGINEER, HIS GENIUS FOR CONCEIVING UNIQUE AIRFRAMES AND HIS TECHNICAL MANAGEMENT SKILLS CONTRIBUTE MIGHTILY TO THE NATION'S SECURITY BY CREATING AIRCRAFT OF DARING DESIGN WITH UNMATCHED RAPIDITY AND EFFECTIVENESS.

★ ★ ★

President Lyndon B. Johnson awarded Johnson the Presidential Medal of Freedom with the above citation during a White House ceremony September 14, 1964.

Clarence L. Johnson was among the country's best aircraft designers, helping the United States maintain its lead as a producer of ever-faster and more technically advanced planes. During his fifty-year career as an aircraft designer and administrator of advanced development projects, he helped develop over forty aircraft. They included the P-38 Lightning, a famous World War II fighter; the F-80 Shooting Star, America's first jet fighter; the Constellation and Super-constellation airliners; the F-104 Star-Fighter; and the U-2 spy plane and its successor, the SR-71 Blackbird.

Johnson was born in Ishpeming, Michigan, in 1910. Fascinated as a youth by the newly invented airplanes, he took to heart some advice a barnstorming pilot once gave him: "Don't grow up to be an airport bum like me. Learn to build airplanes." Johnson collected newspaper and magazine articles on aircraft design as a teenager and then studied aeronautical engineering at the University of Michigan.

But Lockheed refused to hire him as an engineer after he graduated with his bachelor of science degree in 1932; so Johnson went back to Michigan and got his master's degree the following year. Before reapplying to Lockheed in 1933, however, he took the initiative by developing his own design improvements for Lockheed's racing planes. Company officials saw his plans and immediately put him to work as a junior engineer at their Burbank, California, facility.

Johnson remained at Lockheed for the rest of his life, eventually becoming a senior vice president. By 1937 he had won the first of his many aeronautical industry awards for improved designs, and the following year, as chief research engineer, he began work on what became the P-38 Lightning. Johnson organized and headed the development team for the P-38, establishing a pattern for developing new aircraft in record time. His group, nicknamed the "skunk works" after the Li'l Abner comic strip, set a record by designing and producing the F-80 jet fighter in just 143 days during 1943.

Perhaps Johnson's strongest asset was his skill as a problem solver. After World War II, as jets pushed into the realm of supersonic speeds, aircraft designers were stymied by the problem of high heat produced by air friction. Johnson solved the so-called thermal thicket by developing aerodynamically sleek fuselages and building them from titanium. These and other design breakthroughs went into the high-speed SR-71 spy plane and the A-11 jet interceptor, which Lockheed began producing in 1964. That same year Johnson received the Presidential Medal of Freedom for his outstanding work in aircraft design.

Though he retired from Lockheed in 1975, he stayed on as a member of the board of directors until 1980. Johnson continued as a senior adviser at Lockheed until his death in 1990. He was eighty years old.

Frederick Kappel

A CREATIVE LEADER OF BUSINESS, HE SYNTHESIZES THE SKILLS OF
MANAGEMENT WITH A FARSIGHTED APPRECIATION OF HOW TECH-
NOLOGY AND COMMUNICATIONS MAY BETTER SERVE OUR COUNTRY.

★ ★ ★

President Lyndon B. Johnson awarded Kappel the Presidential Medal
of Freedom with the above citation during a White House ceremony
September 14, 1964.

A former head of AT&T Corporation and the chairman of the U.S.
Postal Service during the Nixon administration, Frederick Kappel was
born at Albert Lea, Minnesota, in 1902. His father ran a local barbershop, and as a youth Kappel worked at odd jobs to earn extra
money. Later he worked his way through the University of Minnesota
at Minneapolis, graduating in 1924 with an engineering degree. Three
years later he married a former college classmate, Ruth Carolyn Ihm.

The year he graduated, Kappel began what became a forty-three-
year career with AT&T. He started at the bottom rung of the corporate ladder—digging holes for telephone poles at the Minnesota
regional subsidiary. Moving up steadily, Kappel became area plant
engineer for Nebraska and South Dakota in 1934 and eventually vice
president in charge of operations at Omaha in 1942. Seven years later
he was transferred to AT&T in New York City, becoming vice
president of operations and engineering for the company's long-
distance division. He spent five years in this top technical post before
being named president of Western Electric Company, Bell
Telephone's largest subsidiary and, then, the manufacturer of all
telephone apparatus for the telephone company.

Regarded as a top-flight administrator at Western Electric, he
spent only two years there before being elected AT&T president in
1956. (At that time AT&T was the parent company for all regional
telephone companies in the United States, Western Electric, and other
subsidiaries.) During Kappel's eleven years as president, AT&T grew
at a stunning pace, adding 60 percent more telephones to the system,
which by the time he retired in 1967 served eighty million telephones.

Still only sixty-five years old and seeking new challenges, Kappel
accepted the chairmanships of various presidential commissions
during the Johnson administration, including the Commission on
Postal Organization. President Richard Nixon named him a U.S.
Postal Service governor, and between 1972 and 1974 Kappel was the
postal service chairman. Meanwhile, in addition to being a director
of other major corporations, he also was a top executive at the
International Paper Company.

Kappel's first wife died in 1974, and four years later he remarried.
He died in 1994, at age ninety-two.

Helen Keller

AN EXAMPLE OF COURAGE TO ALL MANKIND, SHE HAS DEVOTED
HER LIFE TO ILLUMINATING THE DARK WORLD OF THE BLIND
AND THE HANDICAPPED.

★ ★ ★

*President Lyndon B. Johnson awarded Keller the Presidential Medal of
Freedom with the above citation during a White House ceremony
September 14, 1964.*

A world-renowned crusader for the handicapped as well as an author
and lecturer, Helen Keller overcame phenomenal handicaps as a
child to become a symbol of the indomitable human spirit. Born in
Tuscumbia, Alabama, in 1880, Keller suffered an unidentified fever
(possibly scarlet fever) the following year that left her blind, deaf, and
unable to speak. Trapped inside a world without sight or sound,
Keller grew into a frightened, temperamental young deaf-mute who
only dimly understood the world around her.

When she was nearly seven, her parents arranged for a live-in
tutor, Anne Sullivan, who was a recent graduate of the Perkins
School for the Blind. Improvising on the Perkins Institute system—
communicating by spelling words on the hand—she began teaching
the young Keller to communicate with the world around her.

Keller never forgot learning her first word. Sullivan took her to
the well-house, and, holding Keller's hand under the cool stream
gushing from the pump spout, spelled out w-a-t-e-r on Keller's other
hand. "That living word awakened my soul," she later recalled, "gave
it light, hope, joy, set it free."

With Sullivan as her teacher, interpreter, and constant companion, Keller went on to a life of extraordinary accomplishment at a
time when deaf-mutes were expected to learn little more than a few
rudimentary skills. She conquered the crushing limitations of her
affliction with courage and sheer determination. Keller not only
learned to communicate by touch, but also to read and write in
braille and raised letters, to talk passably, and even to dance a waltz.
Keller never married, though in 1916 her parents broke up a planned
wedding to a younger man they deemed unsuitable.

A celebrity while still a child because of her accomplishments, she
went on to graduate cum laude from Radcliffe College in 1904, learned
French, German, Italian, Greek, and Latin, and became a prolific writer
who published hundreds of newspaper and magazine articles as well as
a number of books. While still at Radcliffe she published *The Story of
My Life* (1903), the first of her five books of personal reminiscences.

For many years after graduating, Keller raised money for living
expenses while also promoting better treatment of the blind and other
handicapped persons. In addition to writing, she appeared in a

Hollywood film about her life (*Deliverance*, 1918), gave lectures (with the aid of an interpreter), and even demonstrated her skills in a successful vaudeville act for four years (1919 to 1923). Her radical political views—she actively supported socialism and communism—proved unpopular with her audiences, though, finally forcing her out of vaudeville. In 1924 she became a staff fund-raiser for the American Foundation for the Blind, work that, along with writing and lecturing, she continued for the rest of her life.

Among her other books were *Helen Keller's Journal* (1938) and *Teacher* (1955), a biography of Anne Sullivan. A Pulitzer Prize-winning play about Keller and Sullivan, *The Miracle Worker*, became a Broadway hit in 1959 and, along with the movie version, helped ensure Keller's enduring fame for generations to come. She died in 1968 at age eighty-seven.

John L. Lewis

ELOQUENT SPOKESMAN OF LABOR, HE HAS GIVEN VOICE TO THE ASPIRATIONS OF THE INDUSTRIAL WORKERS OF THE COUNTRY AND LED THE CAUSE OF FREE TRADE UNIONS WITHIN A HEALTHY SYSTEM OF FREE ENTERPRISE.

★ ★ ★

President Lyndon B. Johnson awarded Lewis the Presidential Medal of Freedom with the above citation during a White House ceremony September 14, 1964.

The longtime president of the United Mine Workers and the founder of the Congress of Industrial Organizations, John L. Lewis was born in the coal-mining town of Cleveland, Ohio, in 1880. His parents were Welsh immigrants, and his father was a sometime coal miner, farm laborer, and policeman. Lewis left high school a year before graduation and in 1897 became a coal miner. Over the next ten years he worked at various jobs, traveled out West, and ran a grain business that failed during the financial panic of 1907. That same year he married Myrta Edith Bell.

Lewis began his career as a union organizer in 1908 after moving to Panama, a coal-mining town in Illinois. There he organized a local union that became one of Illinois's largest, and his success started him on his way up the ranks of the United Mine Workers (UMW) organization. Meanwhile, he also worked as an organizer for the American Federation of Labor (AFL).

After years of organizational work in Pennsylvania, West Virginia, and Ohio, Lewis was made UMW statistician and editor of the union's journal in 1917. A year later he became the union's acting vice president and in 1919 the acting president. Lewis called a nationwide coal-miners' strike soon after, and then skillfully negotiated a compromise with government officials. That impressed the union's 400,000 members, who elected him president in 1920. Miners reelected him to consecutive terms for the next four decades.

Lewis's career as a union leader proved erratic, however. During the 1920s he allied himself with the Republicans, who held the White House then, and critics charged him with being a conventional labor boss. But even as he consolidated his hold over the organization in the 1920s, his union was shrinking. Unemployment due to overproduction of coal and extensive mining in the nonunion South was to blame and membership dipped to 100,000 in the late 1920s, even before the depression hit.

During the 1930s Lewis transformed himself from labor boss to resourceful labor leader and led his union's fight for better wages, mine safety, and other benefits. Having embraced the Democrats and President Franklin D. Roosevelt's New Deal, he took advantage of New Deal labor reforms to win many new collective bargaining contracts for the UMW, even in the nonunion South. By early 1934 UMW membership was back up to 350,000, and Lewis was eyeing the millions of largely unskilled, nonunion workers in America's mass-production factories.

Risking all the financial resources of the UMW, he organized what became the Congress of Industrial Organizations (CIO) in 1935, eventually adding millions of these unskilled workers to the labor movement. Again relying on New Deal reforms, he managed to negotiate collective bargaining agreements with United States Steel and General Motors, two of the country's foremost nonunion companies. By late 1937, he could claim a larger membership than that of the AFL.

As president of the UMW and CIO, Lewis reached the peak of his power in 1937, but events soon turned against him. The recession of 1937–1938 brought industrial unemployment, cutting deeply into CIO membership rolls and encouraging manufacturers to resist any new union organizing efforts. Meanwhile, Lewis also broke with President Roosevelt to back isolationists who wanted to stay out of World War II. Lewis feared union interests would be quickly forgotten in a wartime atmosphere, and in 1940 threw his support behind Republican presidential challenger Wendell Willkie. Having promised to step down as CIO president if Roosevelt won, Lewis kept his word by resigning in 1940.

Now considerably less powerful in the labor movement, Lewis nevertheless led the UMW in a series of nationwide strikes during World War II and for the rest of the 1940s. The labor unrest benefited coal miners but aroused public opinion against strikers and unions generally, and Lewis called his last strike in 1949.

The 1950s saw the emergence of Lewis the "labor statesman," who succeeded in reaching cooperative agreements with coal companies and maintaining labor peace. At least part of the reason Lewis changed tactics was that he again faced production declines and a shrinking membership. Overproduction of coal and increased competition from other fuels during the decade meant fewer jobs and fewer UMW members. But Lewis's new philosophy of "cooperative capitalism" secured high wages, better working conditions, and good benefits for members who did find jobs.

Lewis retired from the UMW in 1960 and died nine years later. He was eighty-nine years old.

Walter Lippmann

PROFOUND INTERPRETER OF HIS COUNTRY AND THE AFFAIRS OF THE WORLD, HE HAS ENLARGED THE HORIZONS OF PUBLIC THINKING FOR MORE THAN FIVE DECADES THROUGH THE POWER OF MEASURED REASON AND DETACHED PERSPECTIVE.

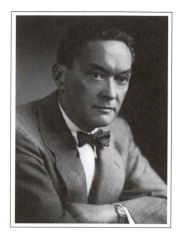

★ ★ ★

President Lyndon B. Johnson awarded Lippmann the Presidential Medal of Freedom with the above citation during a White House ceremony September 14, 1964.

Walter Lippman was among this century's most influential journalists, with a career that spanned sixty years. Born in New York City in 1889, he grew up in an affluent household and, as a youth, attended the best schools. While at Harvard he counted William James and George Santayana among his mentors. During his time at Harvard, he also spent a year as Lincoln Steffens's assistant at the reformist weekly *Boston Common*.

After graduating in 1910, Lippmann worked briefly for a magazine and then for a socialist mayor in upstate New York before taking a summer off in 1912 to write his first book, *A Preface to Politics*. The book was a critical success the following year and helped land him a job at the *New Republic*, which was then being organized as a journal of liberal commentary.

Unlike many liberals at that time, Lippmann supported U.S. intervention in World War I and in 1917 went to work for President Woodrow Wilson's administration. He married Faye Albertson the same year and spent the next eight months working on a secret commission, called simply the Inquiry, whose recommendations gave rise to a number of the famous "Fourteen Points" President Wilson proposed at the Versailles peace conference.

Again working at the *New Republic* after the war, Lippmann found time to write *Public Opinion* (1922), the book that firmly established him as one of the country's leading political philosophers. In his characteristically well-reasoned, lucid prose, Lippmann argued that modern democratic societies too often require their citizens to decide issues without adequately informing them.

He went on to write several other books dealing with similarly broad concerns in political and social philosophy, including *A Preface to Morals* (1929), *U.S. Foreign Policy* (1943), and *The Public Philosophy* (1955).

Following the success of *Public Opinion*, which ranks among his best works, Lippmann moved to the liberal *New York World* newspaper and in 1924 became director of its editorial page. In 1931 he joined the *New York Herald Tribune* and there began writing his highly influential syndicated column, "Today and Tomorrow," which eventually appeared in over two hundred newspapers. Through his newspaper column especially, Lippmann gained his reputation as a tough-minded critic of U.S. foreign policy, and he won Pulitzer Prizes in 1958 and 1962 for his commentary.

Meanwhile, in 1938, Lippmann married Helen Byrne Armstrong, having been divorced from his first wife the previous year. Intellectually, he was changing at this time, moving steadily away from his earlier liberalism to an increasingly conservative, though decidedly independent, viewpoint—especially in his books on the workings of the democratic system. During the 1960s Lippmann actively supported President Johnson and the Great Society reforms, but he eventually turned against Johnson for expanding the Vietnam War.

Lippmann, who had moved to the *Washington Post* in 1963, retired from writing "Today and Tomorrow" in 1967 and from a column in *Newsweek* in 1971. He died three years later, at age eighty-five.

Alfred Lunt and Lynn Fontanne

A LUMINOUS PARTNERSHIP OF ARTISTIC TALENTS AND PERSONAL DEVOTION, THEY HAVE BRILLIANTLY ENLIVENED AND ENRICHED THE AMERICAN STAGE.

★ ★ ★

President Lyndon B. Johnson awarded Lunt and Fontanne the Presidential Medal of Freedom during a White House ceremony September 14, 1964.

Called the greatest husband-and-wife acting team in theater history, Alfred Lunt and Lynn Fontanne appeared together in twenty-seven plays during their nearly forty years on the American stage. Their seemingly effortless performances and almost magical rapport on stage (and off) thrilled audiences, packing theaters wherever they played. A 1929 ballad by humorist Ring Lardner highlighted what was by then a Broadway axiom:

"You want to pack 'em in out front? / Hire Lynn Fontanne and Alfred Lunt."

Born in Milwaukee, Wisconsin, in 1892, Lunt put on his first play at home when he was just eight, and his interest in theater was encouraged by his mother, and later, his stepfather. He attended Wisconsin's Carroll College and Harvard University, but he went into acting full time before graduating. Lunt made his professional stage debut in Boston in 1912.

Fontanne was born Lillie Louise Fontanne in Essex, England, in 1887, five years before her future husband. An aspiring performer, she was introduced to the British actress Ellen Terry, who helped her get a part in a 1905 stage production. She spent the next nine years doing bit parts before establishing herself as a success in London theater with a major role in *Milestones*, by Arnold Bennett. Her reputation growing, Fontanne made her New York debut in 1916.

Lunt appeared on Broadway for the first time a year later in the romantic comedy *Romance and Arabella*. He soon after impressed playwright Booth Tarkington with his style and personality and Tarkington decided to write the title role of *Clarence* specifically for him. During the summer of 1919, though, Lunt was to make an impression of an entirely different kind on first meeting his future wife at a New York theater. He fell for her on the spot—literally. Standing on an iron staircase backstage, Lunt slipped when he bent forward to shake hands with her and wound up flat on his face. A long courtship followed.

Lunt's performance that September in *Clarence* was a smash hit on Broadway, establishing him as a star, and two years later Fontanne's role as a talkative young woman in *Dulcy* did the same for her. They were married in the spring of 1922 and appeared on stage together in *Sweet Nell of Old Drury* the following year. Their performance was a success, but not nearly the smash hit they enjoyed in the 1924 play *The Guardsmen*.

Lunt and Fontanne performed together for the next four decades as the reigning husband-and-wife team of the theatrical world. Except for a few rare occasions they never appeared alone in productions and both repeatedly insisted that they performed better together. That may have stemmed in part from their habit of rehearsing together. They usually sat face-to-face on two chairs, with knees interlocked, while reciting their lines. When one of them would knock their knees together it meant that something seemed wrong, and they would begin the lines over again.

Their effortless performing style and onstage rapport sustained them as leading stars on Broadway during the 1920s, 1930s, and 1940s. They starred in many Noël Coward plays, including one he wrote especially for them, *Design for Living* (1933). But their biggest hit was *O Mistress Mine* (1946), which ran for 451 performances on Broadway and toured for three years after that. Their last performance together was the 1958 hit *The Visit.*

While the couple subsequently made occasional movie and television appearances, they were for the most part retired from show business and spent increasingly more time at Ten Chimneys, their farm outside Milwaukee. Lunt died in 1977, at age eighty-four. Fontanne died at Ten Chimneys six years later. She was ninety-five years old.

Ralph McGill

EDITOR AND JOURNALIST, HE HAS COURAGEOUSLY SOUNDED THE VOICE OF REASON, MODERATION, AND PROGRESS DURING A PERIOD OF CONTEMPORARY REVOLUTION.

★ ★ ★

President Lyndon B. Johnson awarded McGill the Presidential Medal of Freedom with the above citation during a White House ceremony September 14, 1964.

Ralph McGill was the Pulitzer Prize-winning editor of the *Atlanta Constitution* who courageously spoke out for the rights of blacks during the 1950s and 1960s. Called the "conscience of the New South," he was a southerner who deeply cared about the South but who also believed that it was time to end segregation and other forms of discrimination against blacks.

Born at Igou's Ferry, Tennessee, in 1898, McGill was the son of a sometime farmer, coal miner, and clerk. He wrote for the *Nashville Banner* to help pay his expenses at Vanderbilt University and interrupted his college education to serve in the marines during World War I. McGill then returned to Vanderbilt, but he was expelled in 1922, his senior year, for a fraternity prank. The *Banner* immediately hired him as a full-time reporter.

During the 1920s he established himself as nationally known journalist through his stories about Floyd Collins, a man trapped in a cave. The incident became one of the decade's most sensational news items. Meanwhile, McGill also wrote a syndicated column and gained a reputation as a sportswriter, leading to his being hired by the *Atlanta Constitution* in 1929 as an assistant sports editor. McGill married Mary Elizabeth Leonard the same year.

Working his way up at the *Constitution*, McGill became its editor in chief in 1942 and, through his editorials, also established himself as a spokesman for the South. He used his daily front-page column to celebrate southern rural life, but from the 1950s onward also called for an end to discrimination against blacks. Despite the anger and outright violence aroused by the civil rights movement in his native South, he courageously supported most aspects of it, including the 1954 Supreme Court decision in *Brown v. Board of Education*, protests against segregated facilities, the freedom riders, the forced integration of universities, and demonstrations for voting rights for blacks.

McGill's editorial about a bombing attack on an Atlanta synagogue won him the 1959 Pulitzer Prize. Five years later President Johnson, a fellow southerner, rewarded his crusading efforts in behalf of integration with a Presidential Medal of Freedom. Meanwhile, McGill became publisher of the *Constitution* in 1960 and in 1963 wrote the largely autobiographical *The South and the Southerner*. He died in 1969, just two days before his seventy-first birthday.

Samuel Eliot Morison

SCHOLAR AND SAILOR, THIS AMPHIBIOUS HISTORIAN HAS COMBINED A LIFE OF ACTION AND LITERARY CRAFTSMANSHIP TO LEAD TWO GENERATIONS OF AMERICANS ON COUNTLESS VOYAGES OF DISCOVERY.

★ ★ ★

President Lyndon B. Johnson awarded Morison the Presidential Medal of Freedom with the above citation during a White House ceremony September 14, 1964.

A master of narrative history and the "dean of American historians" of his day, Morison was born in Boston, Massachusetts, in 1887. He was the grandson of Samuel Eliot, an educator and historian and the builder of the Boston house where the young Morison was born. Morison went off to Harvard fully intending to major in mathematics, but, as a junior, chanced to take a course from Professor Albert Bushnell Hart, a noted historian.

Hart's assignment, to write a paper on a famous American who meant something to him personally, captured Morison's imagination. Thoughts about a mathematics major evaporated as he wrote about his great-great grandfather, Harrison Gray Otis, a Federalist leader whose papers lay in the basement of his family's house. Morison graduated from Harvard cum laude in 1908 and went on to get his doctorate there in 1913. His dissertation, *The Life and Letters of Harrison Gray Otis, Federalist,* expanded on the theme of Hart's had assignment and became Morison's first published book, in 1913.

Morison began his long teaching career at Harvard in 1915 as an instructor. A few years later he pulled together material from one of his courses on the history of Massachusetts and wrote *The Maritime History of Massachusetts* (1921). The book, a happy combination of his interests in history, New England, and sailing, became one of his most successful.

A professor of American history at Oxford University from 1922 to 1925, he then returned to Harvard as a full professor. A few years later Morison wrote what would become a classic American history textbook with coauthor Henry Steele Commager, *The Growth of the American Republic* (1930). Then in 1936, as the official historian of Harvard, he completed a multivolume work on the university to commemorate its 300th anniversary.

Morison's greatest successes lay in his narrative histories, though. *Admiral of the Ocean Sea: A Life of Christopher Columbus* (1942) grew out of his several crossings of the Atlantic in sailing vessels to retrace Columbus's actual route. His meticulous scholarship, skill as a narrative historian, and enthusiasm for stories of the sea worked together to create what became the Pulitzer Prize winning biography for 1943.

The book's early success in 1942 opened President Franklin D. Roosevelt's door to Morison, who proposed to write a full and accurate history of the U.S. Navy's role in World War II. Granted a commission as a reserve officer, Morison spent the next three years observing almost all of the major naval operations of the war, serving aboard a dozen ships and winning seven Battle Stars. The first volume of his monumental fifteen-volume *History of United States Naval Operations in World War II* appeared in 1947, and for the next thirteen years he produced about a volume each year. Morison married his second wife, Priscilla Barton, in 1949, his first wife having died four years earlier.

Meanwhile, Morison, who had resumed teaching at Harvard, retired from the navy as a rear admiral in 1951. Four years later he retired from teaching, but he continued writing his histories at a prodigious rate for the next two decades. Among them was his second Pulitzer Prize–winning biography, *John Paul Jones: Sailor's Biography* (1959); his *The Oxford History of the American People* (1965), which he called his legacy to his country; *Old Bruin: Commodore Matthew C. Perry* (1967); and *The European Discovery of America: The Southern Voyages* (1974).

Morison wrote his autobiographical *One Boy's Boston* in 1962, when he was seventy-five and still very much an active writer. He continued writing until shortly before his death in 1976. He was eighty-eight years old.

Lewis Mumford

IN THE NAME OF SANITY, HE HAS CONSTANTLY WORKED TO RESCUE
AND EXTEND THE QUALITIES OF URBAN LIFE THAT WILL PRESERVE
AND STIMULATE THE HUMANE SPIRIT OF WESTERN CIVILIZATION.

★ ★ ★

*President Lyndon B. Johnson awarded Mumford the Presidential Medal
of Freedom with the above citation during a White House ceremony
September 14, 1964.*

A cultural historian, social philosopher, and internationally known
expert on architecture and city planning, Lewis Mumford was born in
Flushing, New York, in 1895. He was an only child and grew up in New
York City. Deciding to become a writer while in high school, he studied
variously at City College of New York, Columbia University, and the
New School for Social Research. Mumford never actually received his
bachelor's degree but did accumulate enough credits to graduate.

While pursuing his college studies, Mumford also tried his hand
at writing. Published sporadically in magazines from 1914 onward, he
finally landed a job as an associate editor at *Dial*, a prestigious
literary magazine, in 1919. Meanwhile, in about 1915, Mumford first
encountered the writings of Patrick Geddes, a pioneer in modern
urban planning who was to have a deep influence on his later work.

Mumford's first book, *The Story of Utopias* (1922), was a study of
classic utopias throughout history. His second book, however, more
clearly established his intellectual territory: the study of architecture,
urban life, and other aspects of culture within the larger social
context. The book, *Sticks and Stones: Study of American Architecture
and Civilization* (1924), gave an insightful historical account of
American architecture within a social context. Mumford established
himself as an authority on architecture and urban planning through
additional books and numerous articles during the 1920s.
Meanwhile, he married Sophia Wittenberg in 1921.

During the 1930s he wrote a column about architecture for the
New Yorker and regularly contributed to *Harper's*, the *New Republic*
and other well-known magazines. But it was while on a Guggenheim
Fellowship in Europe in 1932 that he developed the idea for his four-
volume series called *Renewal of Life*. Published over the next two
decades, the books trace the evolution of modern technological
society and criticize its dehumanizing tendencies. The first volume,
Technics and Civilization, appeared in 1934. Four years later *The
Culture of Cities* appeared and not only won Mumford an international reputation but also influenced the development of city
planning in Europe. Two other volumes, *The Condition of Man*
(1944) and *The Conduct of Life* (1951), completed the series.

A decade later Mumford wrote one of his most important works,

The City in History (1961). A critical study of cities and their impact on human civilization throughout history, the book won him the 1962 National Book Award. Later in the 1960s Mumford returned to the themes of technology and society in a two-volume work entitled *The Myth of the Machine* (1967, 1970). His later works especially reflected a growing concern with technological society and with the threat of nuclear war.

From the 1930s onward Mumford variously held research positions and taught as a visiting professor at a number of universities, including Columbia University, the University of Pennsylvania, Stanford University, the University of California at Berkeley, and the Massachusetts Institute of Technology. Among the more than thirty books he wrote during his lifetime were several autobiographical works, of which *Sketches from Life: the Autobiography of Lewis Mumford* (1982) is one.

Mumford died in 1990, at ninety-four.

Edward R. Murrow

A PIONEER IN EDUCATION THROUGH MASS COMMUNICATION, HE HAS BROUGHT TO ALL HIS ENDEAVORS THE CONVICTION THAT TRUTH AND PERSONAL INTEGRITY ARE THE ULTIMATE PER- SUADERS OF MEN AND NATIONS.

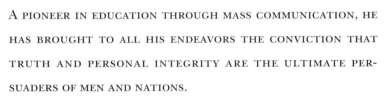

★ ★ ★

President Lyndon B. Johnson awarded Murrow the Presidential Medal of Freedom with the above citation during a White House ceremony September 14, 1964. The medal was awarded with the additional accolade "with distinction for government service."

The most highly regarded and influential broadcaster during the formative years of American broadcast journalism, Edward R. Murrow was born Egbert Roscow Murrow in 1908 on a farm near Greensboro, North Carolina. Raised in Blanchard, Washington, Murrow was exposed to the rough frontierism of the West and even spent a year working in the lumber camps after finishing high school. At Washington State College (now University), Murrow changed his first name to Edward, enrolled in the country's first college course in radio broadcasting, and became involved in the student movement. He graduated in 1930 with a bachelor's degree in speech.

Elected president of the National Student Federation, he spent the next two years traveling to various college campuses and arranging student exchanges with foreign universities. He moved to the

Institute of International Education in 1932 and as assistant director helped about three hundred German scholars fleeing Nazism immigrate to the United States.

Murrow married Janet Huntington Brewster in 1934 and the following year began his career in broadcasting as "director of talks" for the CBS network. Sent to London in 1935 to report on newsworthy events, his first big story was the Nazi invasion of Austria in 1938. He got to Vienna just in time to give live radio coverage of Nazi troops marching into the city. Broadcast in the United States, the report made Murrow famous and marked the arrival of radio as a source of up-to-the-minute news. Murrow also arranged the first news roundup for this famous broadcast, using live transmissions from London, Berlin, Washington, and other capitals.

While Murrow was on hand for other events early in World War II, his eyewitness coverage of the Battle of Britain produced some of his most memorable broadcasts. With anti-aircraft guns, air-raid sirens, and exploding bombs as a backdrop, Murrow broadcast his reports on the London blitz from the rooftops. The work had its risks; once a BBC studio where he was broadcasting was hit by a bomb.

He went on to give many other dramatic eyewitness radio reports during World War II, and on his return to the United States in 1946, became a CBS vice president. A year later Murrow was back on radio, though, as host of a weekly news digest, *Hear It Now*. He moved to television in 1951 with *See It Now*. The show proved both informative and controversial, based on the technique of using "the little picture" to serve as a microcosm of much larger stories. While many listeners believed the show was the conscience of broadcasting, critics charged Murrow with encouraging dissent and dismissed him as "old gloom and doom."

Murrow's other shows during the 1950s were far less controversial. *Person to Person*, a weekly celebrity-interview show, aired from 1953 to 1959, and *Small World* closed out the last two years of the 1950s. But television's increasing concern with entertainment programming and the cancellation of *See It Now* in 1958 led him to publicly accuse the networks of promoting "decadence" and "escapism."

In 1961 he left broadcasting to become director of the U.S. Information Agency under President John F. Kennedy. Three years later lung cancer forced his retirement, and Murrow died in 1965. He was fifty-seven years old.

Reinhold Niebuhr

THEOLOGIAN, TEACHER, SOCIAL PHILOSOPHER, HE HAS INVOKED
THE ANCIENT INSIGHTS OF CHRISTIANITY TO ILLUMINATE THE
EXPERIENCE AND FORTIFY THE WILL OF THE MODERN AGE.

★ ★ ★

*President Lyndon B. Johnson awarded Niebuhr the Presidential Medal
of Freedom with the above citation during a White House ceremony
September 14, 1964.*

Among this century's most influential theologians, Reinhold Niebuhr
also has been called the greatest political philosopher of his time.
Born in Wright City, Missouri, in 1892, he was the son of a minister
belonging to a Lutheran sect known as the Evangelical Synod.
Niebuhr was raised in a devoutly religious atmosphere and, like two
of his brothers, entered religious studies in college. He graduated
from Elmhurst College in Illinois (1910), Eden Theological Seminary
in Missouri (1913), and Yale Divinity School (1915). Niebuhr was
ordained a minister in the Evangelical Synod in 1915 and that year
became pastor of the Bethel Evangelical Church in Detroit.

Niebuhr's experiences in Detroit played a significant role in his later
career. At the time, Henry Ford was expanding his automobile
company, which was opening up new jobs and contributing to the
rapid growth in Detroit's population. But instead of praising Ford,
Niebuhr attacked him for the conditions his workers had to accept,
including lack of job security, no insurance or retirement benefits, and
the monotonous, physically exhausting work on the assembly lines.

While criticizing Ford and capitalism in general, Niebuhr actively
supported the labor movement and the need for economic justice. By
the end of the 1920s his prolabor sympathies led him to join the
Socialist Party, and in 1929 he published *Leaves from the Notebook of a
Tamed Cynic*, which recounted his years in Detroit. Meanwhile, in 1928
he began teaching Christian ethics at New York's Union Theological
Seminary, a post he held until retiring in 1960. In 1931 he married
Ursula Keppel-Compton, who taught religion at Barnard College.

The following year Niebuhr published one of his most influential
books, *Moral Man and Immoral Society*, which set forth his ideas on
the philosophical school that he founded, Christian Realism. Pride,
self-centeredness, self-righteousness, hypocrisy—these were the
enduring sources of evil Niebuhr saw in people and their society.
Destructive pride, he believed, was the sin of many besides those who
commit obvious crimes. It was all the more dangerous among people
who believed themselves good, he thought, and the tendency toward
it was especially strong among those claiming perfection, whether in
the realm of politics, business, or even religion.

He stung many intellectuals of his day by attacking liberals for their optimistic belief in the steady improvement of society and radicals for their utopian dreams. But in many respects it was criticism from within the fold. Niebuhr, while not an optimist, believed that by overcoming their pretensions people could achieve good. He also maintained that sin could never fully destroy the image of God that resides in all men.

Popular with his students and in demand as a speaker, he delivered what became his famous "Serenity Prayer" in 1934 while preaching at a Massachusetts church. In it one can find the seeds of Niebuhr's thought, at once insightful and filled with paradox:

> *O God, give us*
> *serenity to accept what cannot be changed*
> *courage to change what should be changed*
> *and wisdom to distinguish the one from the other*

The prayer gained wide circulation in print and was adopted by various groups, including Alcoholics Anonymous.

After flirting with Marxist ideas, Niebuhr began turning away from both Marxist absolutism and socialism. In the late 1930s he broke with the Socialist Party because of its pacifistic stand against U.S. intervention in the war against Hitler. Becoming a left-wing Democrat and anticommunist, he helped found and headed the Americans for Democratic Action (ADA), which among other things sought better government and to influence its policy. *(See also the entry on Joseph Rauh, p. 492.)* He also did much to convince Christian pacifists of the need to fight the Nazis.

Niebuhr's great theological work was the two-volume *The Nature and Destiny of Man* (1941, 1943). Furthering his thesis of Christian Realism, he compared biblical and other views on the nature and destiny of man. He expressed faith in the "indeterminate possibilities" for the human race but warned against being deceived by absolute solutions to historical problems.

After World War II Niebuhr influenced U.S. foreign policy planners then developing Cold War strategies to resist Soviet expansionism. Meanwhile, he founded and edited the journal *Christianity and Crisis*, continued to teach, and wrote books. His *The Irony of American History* (1952) criticized American claims to special virtue, as well as the American people's penchant for self-righteous crusades. Among Niebuhr's other books—he wrote nearly twenty— were *The Self and the Dramas of History* (1955), *Pious and Secular America* (1958), and *The Structure of Nations and Empires* (1959). Niebuhr died in 1971, at age seventy-eight.

Leontyne Price

A VOICE OF STIRRING POWER AND RARE BEAUTY, HER SINGING
HAS BROUGHT DELIGHT TO HER LAND AND TO ALL THOSE WHO
TREASURE MUSICAL VALUES.

★ ★ ★

*President Lyndon B. Johnson awarded Price the Presidential Medal of
Freedom with the above citation during a White House ceremony
September 14, 1964.*

Among the few black Americans to achieve worldwide fame as an
opera singer, Price was born Mary Violet Leontyne Price in Laurel,
Mississippi, in 1927. Her parents sang in the church choir and
encouraged their daughter's early interest in music. During her
school years, Price sang at school, church, and community programs,
but it was a concert by the black opera singer Marian Anderson that
provided Price with a lasting inspiration to pursue singing. Anderson
was "a vision of elegance and nobility," Price later remembered. *(See
also the entry for Anderson, p. 47.)*

After graduating from Central State University in Wilberforce,
Ohio, with her bachelor's degree in 1946, Price spent the next four
years studying at the prestigious Julliard School of music in New
York. Her singing debut came two years later, in 1952, in Virgil
Thompson's Broadway revival of *Four Saints in Three Acts.* That same
year she landed the part of Bess in Ira Gershwin's revival of *Porgy
and Bess,* which enjoyed a two-year run and toured both the United
States and Europe. The role established her as a singer and revealed
her exceptional ability for interpreting modern compositions. She
married *Porgy and Bess* co-star William C. Warfield in 1952, but the
marriage ended in a long separation and divorce in 1973.

Price, a lyric soprano, in 1955 became the first black opera singer
to perform on television, appearing on NBC in the starring role of
Puccini's *Tosca.* She gained wide exposure through her acclaimed
performance and appeared in a number of other NBC television
opera productions in the 1950s and 1960s.

With her fame growing, Price made her operatic stage debut at
the San Francisco Opera in 1957 in *Dialogue's of the Carmelites* by
Poulenc. Next came widely acclaimed performances in Vienna,
Austria (1959), and at Milan's La Scala opera house (1960), establishing her reputation in Europe and setting the stage for her debut
at New York's Metropolitan Opera in 1961. With her hit performance
at the Metropolitan as Leonora in *Il Trovatore,* Price became one of
America's most sought-after lyric sopranos and continued singing
with the Metropolitan during the 1960s and 1970s. Among her
notable performances was a starring role in Samuel Barber's *Antony
and Cleopatra* (1966). The performance opened the Metropolitan's

new quarters at Lincoln Center that year. She also sang at the White House in 1978.

In her later years, Price increasingly focused her energies on giving recitals. During her long singing career, she has made numerous recordings of operas by Verdi, Puccini, Mozart, and others, as well as hymns and spirituals, popular tunes, and art songs. She has won twenty Grammy awards for her records.

A. Philip Randolph

TRADE UNIONIST AND CITIZEN, THROUGH FOUR DECADES OF CHALLENGE AND ACHIEVEMENT HE HAS LED HIS PEOPLE AND HIS NATION IN THE GREAT FORWARD MARCH OF FREEDOM.

★ ★ ★

President Lyndon B. Johnson awarded Randolph the Presidential Medal of Freedom with the above citation during a White House ceremony September 14, 1964.

One of the great civil rights leaders of this century, A. Philip Randolph was born near Jacksonville, Florida, in 1889. The son of a minister in the African Methodist Episcopal Church, he was raised with a respect for learning. After graduating from a Methodist missionary school in Jacksonville (1907), he worked at odd jobs for three years before moving to Harlem, New York.

Randolph studied sociology and English literature at City College of New York night school, supporting himself by working days at various menial jobs. While at City College he became a socialist and also made friends with a Columbia University law student named Chandler Owen. The pair launched an unsuccessful attempt to organize black workers in 1912 through an employment agency called the Brotherhood of Labor. Randolph also took to the streets, speaking in black sections of cities across the country. Meanwhile, he married Lucille Green, a former schoolteacher, in 1913.

In 1917, with the United States involved in World War I, Randolph and Owen started a magazine called the *Messenger,* which among other things called on President Woodrow Wilson to put more blacks in the military and to get them more jobs in the burgeoning war industries.

After the war Randolph continued his efforts to organize black workers and in 1925 founded the Brotherhood of Sleeping Car Porters. This organization became the country's first successful black union, despite years of stiff opposition from the Pullman Company and all-white unions opposed to organizing blacks. Randolph's first great victory came in 1937 when the Pullman Company finally agreed to a union contract. The success made Randolph the labor movement's leading black spokesman.

He also grew bolder in his fight against discrimination. In 1941 he threatened a mass march on Washington if President Franklin D. Roosevelt did not end discrimination in federal bureaus and the defense industries. President Roosevelt resisted at first but that summer signed Executive Order 8802, opening the jobs to black workers and creating the Fair Employment Practices Committee.

After the war Randolph formed the League for Nonviolent Civil Disobedience Against Military Segregation and in 1948 started a civil disobedience campaign that finally forced President Harry S. Truman to issue Executive Order 9981, banning segregation in the armed forces. Meanwhile, Randolph remained president of his porters' union, and when the American Federation of Labor (AFL) and the Congress of Industrial Organizations (CIO) joined in 1955, he became an AFL-CIO vice president. From 1960 to 1966 he headed the Negro American Labor Council, which sought to end discrimination in the AFL-CIO.

His last great effort in the civil rights movement came in 1963, when the aging Randolph helped organize the March on Washington. Some 200,000 people demonstrated nonviolently in support of civil rights legislation that summer. Two years later Randolph founded the A. Philip Randolph Institute to study the causes of poverty.

Randolph resigned as president of the Sleeping Car Porters union in 1968 and retired from public life. He died in 1979, at age ninety.

Carl Sandburg

SON OF THE PRAIRIE, HE HAS HELPED THE NATION AND THE WORLD TO COMPREHEND AND SHARE IN THE GREAT AFFIRMATION OF AMERICAN LIFE, ASSERTING ALWAYS, AND IN THE FACE OF DISASTER NO LESS THAN TRIUMPH, THE PEOPLE.

★ ★ ★

President Lyndon B. Johnson awarded Sandburg the Presidential Medal of Freedom with the above citation during a White House ceremony September 14, 1964.

A poet, biographer, and folklorist whose works celebrated American life, Carl Sandburg was born in the Illinois prairie town of Galesburg in 1878. His father was a Swedish immigrant and blacksmith for the railroad. From age eleven Sandburg worked at various odd jobs, and he left school after the eighth grade. As a teenager he rode boxcars for a time, taking menial jobs when he could find them. When the Spanish-American War broke out in 1898, he enlisted and was sent to Puerto Rico. Sandburg saw no combat, but his letters to the *Galesburg Evening Mail* became his first published works.

Back in Illinois, he spent four years at the tiny Lombard College, leaving before graduating to once again ride the rails. In Milwaukee, Wisconsin, then a center of liberal social ferment, Sandburg found work as a newspaper reporter and editorial writer. Meanwhile, sympathizing with the plight of the worker, he became an active member of the Social Democratic Party and there met his future wife, a fellow party worker named Lillian Paula Steichen, sister of the photographer Edward Steichen. The Sandburgs were married in 1908.

Sandburg was secretary to Milwaukee's Socialist mayor from 1910 to 1912. In the latter year he went to Chicago, where he worked for various newspapers and magazines. Beginning in 1914 his free-verse poems began appearing in *Poetry: A Magazine of Verse,* and two years later he published *Chicago Poems,* containing two of his best-known poems, "Chicago" ("City of the Big Shoulders") and "Fog" ("The fog comes on little cat feet"). This book and the collected poems that followed established Sandburg as an important free-verse poet with a keen eye for the American scene. He went on to produce three other collections, *Cornhuskers* (1918), *Smoke and Steel* (1920), and *Slabs of the Sunburnt West* (1922), which contain many of the most memorable of the thousand or so poems he wrote during his lifetime.

In 1926 Sandburg published the first two volumes of his monumental biography of Abraham Lincoln, *Abraham Lincoln: The Prairie Years,* which proved a popular and critical success. He published the biography *Steichen the Photographer* in 1929 and seven years later another notable collection of poems, *The People, Yes.* But his crowning achievement was the final four volumes of his Lincoln biography, *Abraham Lincoln: The War Years.* Widely praised when it appeared in 1939, the work won the Pulitzer Prize for biography.

Sandburg also wrote a novel, *Remembrance Rock* (1948), which was not a critical success, and another book of collected poems, *Complete Poems* (1950), which won him his second Pulitzer Prize. He published his memoirs, *Always the Young Strangers,* in 1953. Sandburg died in 1967 at age eighty-nine.

John Steinbeck

A WRITER OF WORLDWIDE INFLUENCE, HE HAS HELPED AMERICA
TO UNDERSTAND HERSELF BY FINDING UNIVERSAL THEMES IN
THE EXPERIENCE OF MEN AND WOMEN EVERYWHERE.

★ ★ ★

*President Lyndon B. Johnson awarded Steinbeck the Presidential Medal
of Freedom with the above citation during a White House ceremony
September 14, 1964.*

The great American novelist, John Steinbeck was born in Salinas
County, California, in 1902. He began writing short stories at age
fifteen and during the 1920s variously attended Stanford University
(from which he did not graduate), worked at menial jobs, and wrote.
In 1930 Steinbeck married Carol Henning, a woman he had met
while working at a Tahoe fish hatchery.

His first novel, *Cup of Gold* (1929), and the two that followed were
not successful, but his popular book about Mexican-Americans, *Tortilla
Flat* (1935), established him as a writer. Steinbeck followed in quick succession with two more successful books, *In Dubious Battle* (1936) and
Of Mice and Men (1937). Meanwhile, he wrote a seven-part newspaper
series for the *San Francisco News* on the plight of Okies who had
migrated from the dust bowl and who were being exploited as low-paid
migrant laborers in California. The series provided the basis for what
became his most famous novel, *The Grapes of Wrath* (1939), which won
the Pulitzer Prize and established him as a major American novelist.

Steinbeck was uncomfortable with the notoriety, though, and
went on an extended trip to escape the attention. Soon after
achieving his sudden fame he divorced his wife to marry singer
Gwendolyn Conger. During World War II Steinbeck worked for
various government agencies. Also, as a newspaper reporter, he went
on secret missions in the Mediterranean with a commando unit.

Despite being deeply disturbed by those wartime experiences,
Steinbeck went back to writing fiction after World War II, producing
Cannery Row (1945), *The Pearl* (1947), and *The Wayward Bus* (1947).
But in 1948 Steinbeck suffered a series of setbacks. His close friend Ed
Ricketts was killed in an accident and then his second wife abruptly
left him. Emotionally overwhelmed, he suffered a nervous
breakdown. Pulling himself back together, Steinbeck wrote first
Burning Bright (1950) and then *East of Eden* (1952), his most
ambitious novel after *The Grapes of Wrath*. Meanwhile, he married
Elaine Scott, a divorcée, in 1950 and for the next several years experimented unsuccessfully with becoming a playwright.

These failures and the lighter journalistic pieces he wrote at this
time contributed to what critics saw as his declining reputation. In 1961
Steinbeck produced the more-ambitious *The Winter of Our Discontent*,

which examined the moral decline of America, but the following year was genuinely stunned when he won the Nobel Prize in Literature. The shock turned to a deep wound following the mean-spirited abuse he received from what he called the eastern literary establishment, which regarded him as a popular writer unsuitable for the award. Though Steinbeck continued writing, he never wrote fiction again.

Steinbeck, a determined supporter of U.S. involvement in Vietnam in the 1960s, also became a friend and adviser to President Lyndon B. Johnson, which helped further alienate him from the literary world. He went to Vietnam in 1966 as a war correspondent for *Newsday* and died two years later after undergoing back surgery. Steinbeck was sixty-six years old.

Helen B. Taussig

PHYSICIAN, PHYSIOLOGIST, AND EMBRYOLOGIST, HER FUNDA-
MENTAL CONCEPTS HAVE MADE POSSIBLE THE MODERN SURGERY
OF THE HEART WHICH ENABLES COUNTLESS CHILDREN TO LEAD
PRODUCTIVE LIVES.

★ ★ ★

President Lyndon B. Johnson awarded Taussig the Presidential Medal of Freedom with the above citation during a White House ceremony September 14, 1964.

The founder of pediatric cardiology and codeveloper of the first successful operation for blue babies, Helen B. Taussig was born in Cambridge, Massachusetts, in 1898. Her father was a Harvard economics professor and her mother, who died while she was still a young girl, had been among the first students at Radcliffe College. Taussig, who studied for a time at Radcliffe, graduated from the University of California at Berkeley in 1921. While pursuing her medical studies, she decided to specialize in heart research, and she won her degree from Johns Hopkins Medical School in 1927.

After completing her internship, Taussig in 1930 became head of the Johns Hopkins Hospital children's heart clinic, a post she held until retiring in 1963. At the clinic she focused her attention on blue babies, so-called because their skin turned blue for lack of oxygen in their blood. Taussig traced the cause of the usually fatal abnormality to congenital defects in the babies' hearts. Teaming up with Dr. Alfred Blalock, professor of surgery at Johns Hopkins Hospital, she and Blalock developed the first successful operation to correct the defect. They published their results in 1945 after performing three operations on blue babies, and since then doctors around the world have used the procedure to save thousands of lives.

The following year she became an associate professor of pediatrics at Johns Hopkins Medical School. Continuing her pioneering studies of the heart and heart defects, she published her findings in the book *Congenital Malformations of the Heart* (1947). Her work led to the development of numerous other procedures for heart disorders.

In 1959 she became the first woman appointed a full professor at Johns Hopkins, and in 1965 she was the first woman elected president of the American Heart Association. Meanwhile, Taussig also was the first American doctor to investigate birth defects related to the use of the tranquilizer thalidomide; and by her prompt action in alerting U.S. Food and Drug Administration authorities, she kept the drug from being released in the United States.

Taussig, who never married, continued her research work after retiring in 1963. She was killed in an auto accident in 1986, at age eighty-seven.

Carl Vinson

MASTER LEGISLATIVE CAPTAIN, HELMSMAN, AND NAVIGATOR, HIS FIXED STAR HAS ALWAYS BEEN THE NATIONAL INTEREST.

★ ★ ★

President Lyndon B. Johnson awarded Vinson the Presidential Medal of Freedom with the above citation during a White House ceremony September 14, 1964. The medal came with the additional accolade "with distinction for government service."

A Georgia Democrat who served fifty years in the House of Representatives, Carl Vinson was born in the Georgia farm town of Milledgeville in 1883. He attended Georgia Military College and following his graduation earned his law degree at Georgia's Mercer University (1902). After some years in private practice in Milledgeville, he began his career in public service as a local court solicitor in 1906 and went on to serve as a Georgia state legislator (1910–1912) and county court judge (1912–1914).

After running successfully for the U.S. House of Representatives in 1914, Vinson was reelected every two years for the next fifty years. When he finally retired in 1965, at age eighty-one Vinson held the record for the longest-serving House member. That record has since been surpassed, though, by Mississippi Democrat Jamie L. Whitten, who served fifty-two years before retiring early in 1995. Whitten died later that year.

Not long after taking his seat in the House, Vinson became a member of the House Naval Affairs Committee and soon established himself as a staunch supporter of the navy and of a strong military generally. Named committee chairman in 1932, Vinson initiated a shipbuilding program to enlarge and modernize the U.S. Navy, which at the time was less than popular. But he persevered, and by 1941 the navy was in a position to rebound fairly quickly from the disastrous attack on Pearl Harbor.

Already a powerful House member, Vinson became even more influential after World War II when his Naval Affairs Committee was enlarged to include oversight of all military branches, becoming the House Armed Services Committee. Vinson, of course, retained his chairmanship of the new committee and over the decades both tightened his hold on the military and consistently backed a strong defense. During the 1960s especially, he wielded immense power over the military and its many multimillion-dollar weapons development programs.

His influence was such that in 1973 the navy broke tradition and for the first time named a ship after someone who was still living— the nuclear-powered aircraft carrier USS *Carl Vinson*. Vinson lived for another eight years before succumbing to heart problems. He was ninety-seven.

Thomas J. Watson, Jr.

A BUSINESS STATESMAN WHO COMBINED DISTINCTION IN PRIVATE LIFE WITH A CHEERFUL ACCEPTANCE OF COUNTLESS PUBLIC DUTIES PLACED ON HIM BY A GRATEFUL GOVERNMENT.

★ ★ ★

President Lyndon B. Johnson awarded Watson the Presidential Medal of Freedom with the above citation during a White House ceremony September 14, 1964.

The business executive who transformed IBM into one of the world's biggest corporations, Thomas J. Watson, Jr., was born in Dayton, Ohio, in 1914. His father was president of IBM and Watson grew up in comfortable circumstances. He graduated from Brown University in 1937 and joined his father's company as a salesman. His flair for marketing helped him double the sales quota for his district; and, after serving as an air force pilot during World War II, Watson returned to the company as a top executive. He married Olive Field Cawley in 1941.

By the late 1940s academic researchers had assembled a mass of wires and vacuum tubes into one of the first big electronic computers, called Eniac, and Watson early on realized the importance electronics would someday have in the business world. At the time IBM was just a medium-size company producing business machines operated by electric motors, levers, and punch cards, but Watson steered the company toward electronics.

After his father's death in 1952, Watson became IBM president and as head of the company continued to work toward developing computers and other electronic equipment for use by businesses. Thanks to the early start in electronics, IBM was far ahead of rival companies like RCA and Honeywell when computers became big business in the late 1950s and early 1960s. The technological edge that IBM had, especially in the large mainframe computers used by business and government, spurred the company's tremendous growth surge during the 1960s.

But IBM did not become a major international corporation by technology alone. Watson's concern for sound management and his flair for aggressive marketing also played an important role. One of Watson's key management innovations, for example, was the "contention system." Watson's system exploited internal competition among managers by allowing them to challenge each other's decisions and force an explanation of the thinking behind it. (While the system worked well during the rapid expansion of the company, it fell into disuse after Watson retired and was later abandoned.) Meanwhile, Watson himself regularly worked from twelve hours to fourteen hours daily while building the company into a corporate giant.

After retiring as IBM board chairman in 1971, Watson became more involved in public affairs and regularly spoke out for nuclear arms reduction. President Jimmy Carter named him ambassador to the Soviet Union in 1979, a post Watson held until 1981.

He published his memoirs, *Father, Son, & Co.*, in 1990. Watson died four years later, at age seventy-nine.

Paul Dudley White

PHYSICIAN, HUMANIST, AND TEACHER, HE HAS LED THE WAY TOWARD A GREATER KNOWLEDGE OF HEART DISEASE AND THE PROMOTION OF INTERNATIONAL UNDERSTANDING THROUGH SCIENTIFIC MEDICINE.

★ ★ ★

President Lyndon B. Johnson awarded White the Presidential Medal of Freedom with the above citation during a White House ceremony September 14, 1964.

A pioneer in the study of heart disease and an outspoken proponent of preventing heart and circulatory problems through proper diet and regular exercise, Paul Dudley White was born in 1886 in Roxbury, Massachusetts. His father was a doctor, and at first White did not plan to study medicine. After entering Harvard University, though, he pursued his medical degree, which the university granted him in 1911. That same year he began his lifelong association with Massachusetts General Hospital, as an intern.

After serving as a medical officer during World War I, White in 1920 became chief of the Massachusetts General Outpatient Department and the following year joined the Harvard University faculty as a clinical instructor. By this time he had already become interested in diseases of the heart and circulatory system and had been among the first (in 1914) to use the electrocardiograph to diagnose heart problems. His study of over twenty-thousand electro-cardiograms between 1914 and 1931, as well as case histories on thousands of heart patients, provided the data for his thousand-page *Heart Disease,* which became a standard reference soon after its publication in 1931 and helped lay the foundation for much of what followed in the field of cardiology.

White's studies convinced him of the relationship between heart ailments and poor diet and lack of exercise. He urged Americans to stay healthy by eating and drinking in moderation, avoiding cigarettes, and exercising daily. This was especially important for patients recovering from coronary problems and for people over forty. White took his own advice as well, and walked or bicycled daily into his mid–seventies.

Active in promoting the study of cardiology, White helped found the American Heart Association in 1924. Later, he resigned from Massachusetts General in 1948 to help found the National Heart Institute and served as its chief consultant from 1948 to 1955. White also was influential in organizing the International Association of Cardiology, the International Cardiology Foundation, and other organizations.

White gained national media exposure in 1955 when he became President Dwight D. Eisenhower's cardiologist after the president's heart attack, but by this time he had already been recognized as a leading heart specialist. But he used his newfound fame to promote his recommendations for good health and once even walked from Washington National Airport to a meeting with President Eisenhower at the White House.

During his later years especially, White devoted considerable effort to winning government support for medical research. He died of a stroke in 1973. He was eighty-seven years old.

Ellsworth Bunker

FOR EXTRAORDINARY LEADERSHIP AND DIPLOMATIC SERVICE UNDER ARDUOUS AND TAXING CIRCUMSTANCES.

AMBASSADOR BUNKER WAS AWARDED THE MEDAL OF FREEDOM WITH SPECIAL DISTINCTION IN DECEMBER OF 1963. THIS AWARD WAS IN RECOGNITION OF HIS SERVICE OVER THE YEARS AS AMBASSADOR TO ARGENTINA, ITALY, INDIA, AND NEPAL, HIS SERVICE AS PRESIDENT OF THE AMERICAN RED CROSS, AND A NUMBER OF SPECIAL AND IMPORTANT MISSIONS PERFORMED AS A CONSULTANT FOR THE DEPARTMENT OF STATE IN THE PERIOD FROM 1962 ONWARD. A SECOND MEDAL OF FREEDOM WITH SPECIAL DISTINCTION IS HEREBY CONFERRED UPON ELLSWORTH BUNKER OF VERMONT. THIS SECOND AWARD—THE FIRST OF ITS KIND—RECOGNIZES AMBASSADOR BUNKER'S SERVICE AS AMBASSADOR TO THE ORGANIZATION OF AMERICAN STATES FROM 1964–1965. IT FURTHER RECOGNIZES THE CRUCIAL ROLE HE PLAYED UNDER THE MOST DIFFICULT CONDITIONS, IN THE RESTORATION OF DEMOCRATIC PROCESSES IN THE DOMINICAN REPUBLIC IN 1965–1966.

IN PARTICULAR IT RECOGNIZES THE ROCK-LIKE DEVOTION TO DUTY WHICH LED AMBASSADOR BUNKER TO ACCEPT THE MOST DIFFICULT AND DEMANDING PRESENT POSITION IN THE UNITED STATES DIPLOMATIC SERVICE OVERSEAS, THAT OF AMBASSADOR TO THE REPUBLIC OF VIETNAM, AT THE AGE OF NEARLY 73. IN THAT POSITION, AMBASSADOR BUNKER HAS ONCE AGAIN DEMON-STRATED EXTRAORDINARY DIPLOMATIC SKILL, AS WELL AS DEEP SYMPATHY AND UNDERSTANDING FOR THE ASPIRATIONS AND EFFORTS OF THE PEOPLE AND GOVERNMENT OF SOUTH VIETNAM. HIS QUIET AND EFFECTIVE LEADERSHIP OF ALL AMERICAN ACTIVITIES IN VIETNAM HAVE MADE AN IMMEASURABLE CONTRI-BUTION TO THE PROGRESS OF OUR EFFORTS TO ASSIST THAT COUNTRY TO DETERMINE ITS OWN FUTURE WITHOUT EXTERNAL INTERFERENCE.

THROUGH THIS AWARD, A GRATEFUL NATION ONCE AGAIN PAYS TRIBUTE TO ONE OF ITS MOST DISTINGUISHED CITIZENS AND PUBLIC SERVANTS.

★ ★ ★

President Lyndon B. Johnson awarded Bunker a second Presidential Medal of Freedom with the above citation during a ceremony at Cam Ranh Bay, Vietnam, December 23, 1967. The medal was accompanied by the accolade "with distinction." (For the biography of Bunker and his first Presidential Medal of Freedom citation, see p. 49.)

Robert W. Komer

HIS LONG RECORD OF GOVERNMENT SERVICE HAS BEEN IN POSTS WITH A HIGH DEGREE OF SENSITIVITY, INVOLVING OFTEN THE MOST CONFIDENTIAL RELATIONSHIP WITH HIS SUPERVISORS AND WITH THE OFFICE OF THE PRESIDENT. HE HAS BROUGHT TO THESE ASSIGNMENTS A TRAINED AND DISCIPLINED MIND, HIGH INTELLIGENCE, UNFLAGGING ZEAL, AND AN UNUSUAL ABILITY TO MASTER A WIDE RANGE OF PROBLEMS. THE EXCELLENCE OF HIS PERFORMANCE, AND THE DEPTH OF HIS KNOWLEDGE OF THE EXCEEDINGLY COMPLEX AND DIFFICULT PROBLEMS WITH WHICH OUR GOVERNMENT IS FACED IN VIETNAM CAUSED THE PRESIDENT TO APPOINT HIM TO THE POST OF DEPUTY TO GENERAL WESTMORELAND WITH THE RANK OF AMBASSADOR, WITH RESPON-SIBILITY FOR CIVIL OPERATIONS AND REVOLUTIONARY DEVEL-OPMENT SUPPORT. TAKING OVER HIS POST AT A TIME WHEN THE ORGANIZATION OF OUR SUPPORTING ROLE WAS UNDERGOING MAJOR CHANGES HE HAS EXHIBITED IMMENSE DEDICATION, DRIVE, IMAGINATION, ORGANIZING ABILITY AND SKILL. HE HAS CON-TRIBUTED GREATLY TO THE EFFECTIVENESS OF OUR SUPPORTING ROLE AND TO THE STEADY PROGRESS BEING MADE IN THE CRUCIAL AREA OF PACIFICATION. HE HAS THUS MADE AN OUTSTANDING CONTRIBUTION TO THE UNITED STATES EFFORT IN VIETNAM.

★ ★ ★

President Lyndon B. Johnson awarded Komer the Presidential Medal of Freedom during a ceremony at Cam Ranh Bay, South Vietnam, December 23, 1967. The above citation was presented later in 1968.

Born in Chicago in 1922, Robert W. Komer proved a strong student in his youth and graduated magna cum laude from Harvard in 1942.

After serving in the army during World War II, he earned his business degree at Harvard in 1947 and worked with the Central Intelligence Agency at the Directorate of Intelligence and the Office of National Estimates from 1947 to 1960.

During the Kennedy-Johnson years, Komer became a high-level adviser, with positions as a senior staff member of the president's National Security Council (1961–1965) and as a special assistant to President Johnson (1966–1967). He took on his duties in the Vietnam pacification program in 1967 and served there until 1968. During the last months of the Johnson administration, Komer was ambassador to Turkey.

While the Republicans were in the White House, Komer worked for the Rand Corporation, a think tank. He returned to public service when President Jimmy Carter took office, serving as the defense secretary's adviser for North Atlantic Treaty Organization affairs from 1977 to 1979. Promoted to Defense Department undersecretary for policy in 1979, he remained in that post until Carter left office in 1981.

Komer taught at George Washington University from 1981 to 1984 and in 1982 rejoined the Rand Corporation as a consultant, a position he continues to hold. He also wrote two books, *Maritime Strategy or Coalition Defense?* (1984) and *Bureaucracy at War* (1986).

Eugene Murphy Locke

A DISTINGUISHED CITIZEN OF TEXAS, HE WAS APPOINTED BY PRESIDENT JOHNSON TO BE AMBASSADOR TO PAKISTAN IN 1966. HE SERVED WITH ENORMOUS SKILL IN THIS IMPORTANT POST AT A TIME OF DIFFICULTIES IN U.S.-PAKISTAN RELATIONS AND WHEN RELATIONS BETWEEN THE TWO GREAT COUNTRIES OF THE SUB-CONTINENT, BOTH GOOD FRIENDS OF THE UNITED STATES, WERE UNDER CONSIDERABLE STRAIN. HE MADE A SIGNIFICANT CONTRI-BUTION TO THE IMPROVEMENT OF U.S.-PAKISTAN RELATIONS. HIS ABILITY TO GRASP PROBLEMS QUICKLY, AND THE QUALITIES OF FIRMNESS, TACT, AND POLITICAL INSIGHT HE BROUGHT TO BEAR ON THE ISSUES WITH WHICH HE WAS CONFRONTED THERE LED PRESIDENT JOHNSON TO NAME HIM AS DEPUTY AMBASSADOR TO THE REPUBLIC OF VIETNAM. TO THIS VITAL POST AMBASSADOR LOCKE HAS BROUGHT IMPRESSIVE ENERGY, HIGH INTELLIGENCE, INTEGRITY, UNDERSTANDING AND WISDOM, QUALITIES WHICH HAVE WON FOR HIM THE ESTEEM AND RESPECT OF HIS COL-

LEAGUES AND OF VIETNAMESE IN OFFICIAL AND UNOFFICIAL
CIRCLES. IN THIS MOST DIFFICULT AND COMPLEX SITUATION
AMBASSADOR LOCKE HAS ACTED WITH SINGLE-MINDED DEVOTION
IN CARRYING FORWARD THE CRUCIAL TASK IN WHICH THE
UNITED STATES IS ENGAGED ON THE SOIL OF VIETNAM.

★ ★ ★

*President Lyndon B. Johnson awarded Locke the Presidential Medal of
Freedom with the above citation during a ceremony held at Cam Ranh
Bay, South Vietnam, December 23, 1967. Locke, unable to attend,
received the award in early 1968.*

A lawyer's son, Eugene Murphy Locke was born in Dallas, Texas, in
1918. He graduated from the University of Texas in 1937 and earned
his law degree at Yale University in 1940. Locke spent the next two
years working at the federal Office of Price Administration before
joining the navy. He served aboard an attack transport in the Pacific
during World War II. He married Adele Neely in 1941.

Returning to Dallas after the war, Locke entered private practice
and some years later began moving up in the business world. He
eventually served as head of a major real estate development firm and
a steel company in Dallas, and acquired a twenty-five-thousand-acre
cattle ranch. A friend of Lyndon B. Johnson and John Connally, he
also was active in the Democratic Party, serving as head of the Texas
Democratic executive committee for a time. In 1962 Locke set up and
ran John Connally's successful gubernatorial campaign in Texas.

President Johnson sent Locke abroad in 1966, naming him U.S.
ambassador to Pakistan. Taking office a year after the border war
between India and Pakistan, Locke successfully handled a challenging
assignment there. Then in 1967 President Johnson sent him to South
Vietnam as a trouble-shooter. Deputy ambassador Locke coordinated various activities related to the U.S. mission in Vietnam and
dealt with bureaucratic red tape to expedite projects amid the chaos
of the Vietnam War. He spent nine months there before resigning to
return to Texas.

Locke mounted an unsuccessful campaign for the Democratic
nomination for governor of Texas in 1968. Three years later he
underwent surgery for a brain tumor and died the following year, in
1972. Locke was fifty-four years old.

Robert S. McNamara

FOR SEVEN YEARS, YOU HAVE ADMINISTERED OUR COMPLEX
DEFENSE ESTABLISHMENT—UNIFYING OUR STRENGTH SO THAT
WE MAY RESPOND EFFECTIVELY WHEREVER THE SECURITY OF
OUR FREE WORLD WAS CHALLENGED. A BRILLIANT ANALYST AND
MODERN ADMINISTRATOR, YOU HAVE BROUGHT A NEW
DIMENSION TO DEFENSE PLANNING AND DECISION-MAKING. YOU
HAVE GRASPED THE URGENT SOCIAL CRISIS OF OUR TIME—THE
AWAKENING OF HOPE AMONG THE WORLD'S POOR. YOU HAVE
UNDERSTOOD THAT WHILE FREEDOM DEPENDS ON STRENGTH,
STRENGTH ITSELF DEPENDS ON THE DETERMINATION OF FREE
PEOPLE. YOUR SEVEN LONG YEARS OF UNSHAKEABLE LOYALTY TO
THE REPUBLIC, TO THE PRESIDENT, AND TO ALL WHO SERVED
BESIDE AND UNDER YOU IN THE SERVICES, IS AN EXAMPLE FOR
THE PUBLIC SERVANT AND AN INSPIRATION FOR YOUR COUN-
TRYMEN. MAY YOUR SELFLESS SERVICE—SPENT IN DEFENDING
FREEDOM—BRING EVEN GREATER REWARDS IN THE LARGER
WORK YOU NOW UNDERTAKE TO PROMOTE FREEDOM THROUGH-
OUT THE WORLD.

★ ★ ★

*President Lyndon B. Johnson awarded McNamara the Presidential
Medal of Freedom with the above citation during a White House
ceremony February 28, 1968.*

Robert S. McNamara was born in San Francisco, California, in 1916.
His father was in the wholesale shoe business. A bright student, he
graduated with honors from the University of California at Berkeley
in 1937 and earned his business degree at Harvard two years later. He
married Margaret Craig in 1940. *(See also the entry for Margaret Craig
McNamara, p. 288.)*

When the United States entered World War II, he was teaching
accounting at Harvard. After being rejected by the military for near-
sightedness, he became a consultant to the air corps instead.
McNamara helped set up statistical systems to manage the flow of
supplies, war materiel, and personnel to the far-flung air corps bases
and from 1943 was stationed in England to develop and control
logistical systems for the massive bombing raids against Nazi
Germany and occupied enemy territory.

McNamara's genius for developing accounting and control
systems won him a position at the ailing Ford Company after the
war. One of the "Whiz Kids" who revamped the company and saved

it from bankruptcy, he introduced cost-accounting practices and reformed the administrative structure. Remaining at Ford, he rose quickly through the upper echelons of the company during the 1950s and in 1960 became its president—the first person outside the Ford family to hold the top job.

A month later he left Ford, however, to become secretary of defense in the new Kennedy administration. With characteristic energy and vision, he took control of the military bureaucracy. McNamara restructured the budgeting system, cut costs, eliminated wasteful procurement practices and obsolete weapons systems, and changed the country's basic military strategy from massive nuclear retaliation to one of "flexible response." While maintaining a "second strike" nuclear capability, McNamara's flexible-response strategy meant creating a mobile military force trained to fight either a guerrilla insurgency or a conventional war.

McNamara oversaw the naval blockade of Cuba in the 1962 missile crisis during the Kennedy administration. He was also an early advocate of military involvement in Vietnam and helped formulate the U.S. strategy in the Vietnam War. At the time, he believed U.S. combat troops could prop up the Saigon regime. Continuing as secretary of defense under President Johnson, McNamara joined other top advisers in recommending intensive bombing of North Vietnam in 1965. As U.S. involvement in Vietnam escalated dramatically, McNamara increasingly became the administration spokesman for the war and a focus of antiwar protests.

At the same time, though, he was privately having second thoughts about the effectiveness of bombing North Vietnam and even began questioning the wisdom of continued U.S. involvement in South Vietnam. He ordered the study of American involvement that eventually was published as *The Pentagon Papers* and in 1968, after advising President Johnson to stop the bombing and turn the combat over to South Vietnamese troops, left the Pentagon to become president of the World Bank.

McNamara spent the next thirteen years at the World Bank and during that time changed its basic strategy for investing in underdeveloped countries. Instead of granting loans for large projects such as dams and power plants, the World Bank began to focus on small projects to help improve facilities and meet basic needs in rural villages of third world countries. Meanwhile, he also increased loans to developing countries for opening up new oil, gas, and coal deposits.

Retiring from the World Bank in 1981, McNamara continued working with such organizations as the Brookings Institution, the Ford Foundation, and the Overseas Development Council. He also wrote several books, including *Blundering Into Disaster* (1986), *Out of the Cold* (1989), and, most recently, his controversial *In Retrospect: the Tragedy and Lessons of Vietnam* (1995), in which he publicly criticized U.S. involvement in Vietnam as a "mistake" for the first time. McNamara listed eleven key reasons why the United States failed in

Vietnam, including underestimating the determination of the North to win, overestimating the determination of the South, failing to recognize the limits of a high-tech military in a guerrilla war, and exaggerating the dangers of the fall of South Vietnam to U.S. security.

James E. Webb

A MOST DISTINGUISHED PUBLIC ADMINISTRATOR, HE HAS BEEN A FARSIGHTED AND FORCEFUL LEADER OF THIS NATION IN THE PIONEER EXPLORATION OF OUTER SPACE, OPENING NEW FRONTIERS OF DISCOVERY AND PROGRESS FOR THE AMERICAN PEOPLE.

★ ★ ★

President Lyndon B. Johnson awarded Webb the Presidential Medal of Freedom with the above citation during a White House ceremony honoring members of the space program December 9, 1968.

James E. Webb was born in 1906 in Tally Ho, North Carolina. His father was superintendent of the county school system, and Webb went on to graduate from the University of North Carolina with a bachelor's degree in education in 1928. He worked his way through George Washington University Law School, graduating in 1936, and spent the next seven years as an executive of Sperry Gyroscope Corporation, which manufactured hi-tech equipment for the military. In 1938 he married Patsy Aiken Douglas.

After serving as a marine aviator during World War II, Webb went into government service in 1946 as an assistant to the undersecretary of the treasury, but within months he became President Harry S. Truman's director of the Bureau of the Budget. Three years later President Truman named him under secretary of state. Meanwhile, Webb also served as deputy governor of the World Bank and of the International Monetary Fund. In 1952, he returned to the business world, eventually becoming an oil company executive.

When in 1957 the Soviet Union launched *Sputnik*, the first space satellite, American government officials became deeply concerned about recovering the U.S. lead in the areas of science and technology. Then, in 1961, President John F. Kennedy announced the centerpiece of the strategy, to land an American astronaut on the moon before the end of the 1960s. Kennedy tapped Webb to be head of the National Aeronautics and Space Administration (NASA), because of Webb's reputation as an outstanding administrator.

In fact, Webb's managerial abilities played a key role in the tremendously complex Apollo moon-landing program, which involved creating the space craft, training and adapting astronauts to the inhospitable world of space, and then getting them to the moon and back. With Webb as director, NASA orchestrated the first U.S. manned space flight (by Alan B. Shepard, Jr., aboard a Mercury space capsule), the first space walk (by John Glenn outside his Gemini capsule), and other notable firsts.

Meanwhile, NASA scientists and technicians also were developing the Apollo spacecraft, which would carry American astronauts to the moon and back. Preliminary testing in the Apollo program was well under way when a launching-pad fire in 1967 resulted in the only serious accident during Webb's term as director. The fire killed three astronauts aboard the *Apollo 1* rocket. Webb resigned as director in 1968, but by late that year a preliminary Apollo flight (*Apollo 8*) had already orbited the moon. His work had brought NASA to the final stages of the moon-landing program, and in mid–1969 *Apollo 11* marked the crowning success. *(See also entries for the* Apollo 11 *crew: Edwin Aldrin, p. 172, Neil Armstrong, p. 173, and Michael Collins, p. 175.)*

At one time or another Webb served on the boards of McDonnell Aircraft Corporation, the Oak Ridge Institute of Nuclear Studies, the Federal National Advisory Cancer Council, the Transportation Research Foundation, and other groups. He died in 1992.

Dean Rusk

FOR EIGHT YEARS HE SERVED HIS COUNTRY AS SECRETARY OF STATE. HE BROUGHT TO THAT OFFICE A BRILLIANT MIND, A WIDE KNOWLEDGE OF THE WORLD, A PROFOUND HISTORICAL PER-SPECTIVE AND A RICH EXPERIENCE IN INTERNATIONAL AFFAIRS. HE GAVE TO THAT OFFICE A TIRELESS DEVOTION TO HIS COUNTRY'S INTEREST, AND TO THE ORGANIZATION OF A DURABLE PEACE. HE BECAME, FOR MILLIONS OF HIS FELLOW CITIZENS AND FOR COUNTLESS MILLIONS THROUGHOUT THE WORLD, A SYMBOL OF MAN'S DAUNTLESS QUEST TO BE FREE. HE KNEW THAT FREEDOM REQUIRED A WILLINGNESS TO SACRIFICE IN ITS BEHALF. BUT HE ALSO KNEW THAT RESOLUTION IN THE FACE OF AGGRESSION WAS NOT ENOUGH—THAT MEN MUST SEARCH FOR AREAS OF COMMON INTEREST, AND COOPERATIVE ENDEAVORS TO REDUCE THE THREAT OF A THIRD WORLD WAR. THIS HE DID. HE DID IT WITH STEADY DETERMINATION, WITH COOL REASONING

AND ALWAYS WITH UNFAILING COMPASSION. DISCIPLINED AND RESTRAINED IN THE FACE OF CALUMNY, BRAVE AND SURE IN THE TIME OF CRISIS, HE EARNED THE ENDURING RESPECT OF ALL WHO SERVED WITH HIM. SELFLESS PATRIOT, STALWART FIGHTER FOR HUMAN RIGHTS, GUARDIAN OF HIS NATION'S WELFARE AND SERVANT OF MANKIND, HISTORY WILL RANK HIM HIGH AMONG THOSE WHO DESERVE TO BE CALLED STATESMEN.

★ ★ ★

President Johnson awarded Rusk the Presidential Medal of Freedom with the above citation during a ceremony at the Department of State on January 16, 1969.

Dean Rusk was born in Cherokee County, Georgia, in 1909. Having learned to read from his brothers' schoolbooks, he started school in the second grade and maintained nearly straight As through grammar school and high school. After graduating from Davidson College in North Carolina magna cum laude in 1931, he attended Oxford University on a Rhodes scholarship and there earned bachelor's (1933) and master's (1934) degrees.

Returning to the United States, Rusk taught political science at Mills College in Oakland, California, from 1934 to 1940. An army officer from 1940 to 1945, he saw action in Southeast Asia. After 1945 he held senior posts in the State Department and as assistant secretary of state for Far Eastern affairs (1950–1952) was involved in Korean War policy making.

After serving as the Rockefeller Foundation president from 1952 to 1960, Rusk became secretary of state in 1961. President John F. Kennedy relegated him to a reduced role in foreign policy matters, though, often consulting other officials or keeping his own counsel. Nevertheless, Rusk took part in a formidable series of crises during the Kennedy years, including those in Cuba, Indochina, and Berlin. During the Cuban Missile Crisis he and Defense Secretary Robert S. McNamara recommended what became Kennedy's successful course of action—the partial naval blockade of Cuba. President Johnson kept Rusk as secretary of state and, as Kennedy had not, sought his advice on foreign policy. Rusk, who had serious doubts about U.S. involvement in South Vietnam as early as 1961, eventually became convinced that the United States had to make an aggressive stand against communist expansionism in Southeast Asia. From 1964 to 1969, he consistently defended the Vietnam War and became a target for considerable antiwar sentiment.

Rusk retired from politics in 1969, having served as secretary of state for eight years. He taught international law at the University of Georgia from 1970 and published his memoirs, *As I Saw It,* in 1990. Rusk died in 1994, at age eighty-five.

Eugene R. Black

EUGENE BLACK HAS SERVED THE PEOPLE OF THE WORLD WITH A DEDICATION KNOWN TO FEW MEN IN PUBLIC SERVICE. ONE OF THE GREAT FINANCIAL MINDS OF OUR TIME, WITH A COMPASSION UNSURPASSED, HE HAS DEVOTED HIS ENERGY AND TALENTS TO THE BETTERMENT OF THE HUMAN CONDITION. WHEREVER ON EARTH PEOPLE STRIVE FOR DEVELOPMENT—WHEREVER WANT AND HUNGER EXIST, HE FINDS HIS TALENTS. AN OUTSTANDING AMERICAN, HE IS AN OUTSTANDING CITIZEN OF THE WORLD AS WELL. AND PEOPLE THE WORLD OVER ARE IN HIS DEBT, AS IS HIS PRESIDENT.

★ ★ ★

President Lyndon B. Johnson awarded Black the Presidential Medal of Freedom with the above citation on the last day of his presidency, January 20, 1969. The medal was accompanied by the additional accolade "with distinction" and was delivered by mail at a later date.

Eugene Black was born in 1898, the oldest child of an Atlanta, Georgia, bank president who later became a governor of the Federal Reserve Board. Black graduated cum laude from the University of Georgia in 1917 and, after serving during World War I, joined the Atlanta office of a New York financial firm. In 1930 he married his second wife, Suzette Heath, his first wife having died in 1928.

Eventually recognized in financial circles as a bond expert, he became a second vice president at New York's Chase National Bank in 1933. Four years later he moved up to senior vice president. Assignments at Chase dealing with overseas accounts in the years immediately after World War II gave him valuable experience in international finance, and when Chase president John J. McCloy became president of the recently formed World Bank in 1947, Black became the World Bank executive director representing the United States. *(See also the entry for McCloy, p. 68.)* Two years later Black became the World Bank president.

As president between 1949 and his retirement in 1962, Black increased the World Bank's membership from forty-eight nations to eighty and its capital from $8.3 billion to $20.5 billion. The bank made over three hundred loans—primarily to third world nations—for industrial, agricultural, and power generating projects. Black was described as both charming and "hard as nails" when evaluating projects being considered for World Bank loans. Usually he looked for projects that would stimulate the private sector of a borrowing nation, to help raise the standard of living, create new opportunities for investment, and create the income needed to pay off the loan.

After retiring from the World Bank in 1962, he served on the boards of various banking, business, educational, and philanthropic institutions, including Chase Manhattan Bank, Equitable Life Assurance Society, International Telephone and Telegraph Company, American Express Company, Royal Dutch Petroleum, Johns Hopkins University, the Ford Foundation, and the John F. Kennedy Library. Black retired from most of these positions during the late 1960s and early 1970s. Black spent the next two decades largely in retirement. He died in 1992.

McGeorge Bundy

McGeorge Bundy brought to America's security and the cause of freedom in the world a passion for excellence never surpassed in the ranks of American public servants. A man of wisdom and soundness, of complete loyalty and exceptional intelligence, he helped to shape the course on which America could honor its solemn commitments and keep freedom alive when it was grievously threatened. He has answered every call his country has made. He is an architect of that stable world free men seek to build.

★ ★ ★

President Lyndon B. Johnson awarded Bundy the Presidential Medal of Freedom with the above citation January 20, 1969, the last day of his presidency. The medal was sent to Bundy at a later date.

McGeorge Bundy was born in 1919, one of five children in a prominent Boston family. His father later served as assistant secretary of state under Henry Stimson in the Hoover administration and as a special assistant to Stimson in the War Department during World War II. Bundy, who at one point in his early schooling was a classmate of John F. Kennedy, graduated from Yale in 1940 with a mathematics degree. As an intelligence officer during World War II, he took part in planning both the Sicily and Normandy invasions. After the war he coauthored Secretary Stimson's memoirs, *On Active Service in Peace and War,* which was published in 1948. Mary Buckminster Lothrop became his wife in 1950.

Bundy joined the Harvard faculty as a lecturer on government in 1949 and by 1953 had been appointed dean of arts and sciences. He was then just thirty-four years old. Some years later he and John F. Kennedy met in connection with business at Harvard, and during the 1960 election, impressed by Bundy, President Kennedy made him part of his inner circle of advisers after taking office in 1961.

As Kennedy's special assistant for national security, Bundy directed the National Security Council staff and played a key role in major foreign policy matters, including the disastrous Bay of Pigs invasion, the Cuban Missile Crisis, and the sending of troops to Vietnam. President Johnson kept Bundy as his national security adviser, and Bundy advocated increased U.S. military involvement in Vietnam, backed the bombing of North Vietnam, and in 1965 went to the Dominican Republic to resolve the crisis there.

From 1966 to 1979 Bundy served as the Ford Foundation's president. From 1979 to 1989 he was a professor of history at New York University. He chaired the Carnegie Corporation committee on reducing the nuclear danger from 1990 to 1993 and remains at Carnegie as a scholar in residence. In addition to coauthoring Stimson's memoirs, he has written several books, including *The Strength of Government* (1968) and *Danger and Survival* (1988).

Clark McAdams Clifford

CLARK CLIFFORD IS A MAN OF ACTION AND COMPASSION, A COUNSELOR OF PRESIDENTS AND A SERVANT OF THE PEOPLE WITH WISE AND COOL JUDGEMENT, A FORCEFUL AND BRILLIANT LEADER. DETACHED, STRONG, SOUND, UNSWAYED BY THE PASSIONS OF THE DAY, HE HAS SEARCHED WITH CLEAR VISION INTO THE URGENT PROBLEMS OF OUR NATION AND THE COMMUNITY OF MANKIND. AMERICA AND THE WORLD WILL ALWAYS BE THE BETTER FOR HIS SERVICE.

★ ★ ★

President Lyndon B. Johnson awarded Clifford the Presidential Medal of Freedom with the above citation on the last day of his presidency, January 20, 1969. The medal was accompanied by the additional accolade "with distinction" and was delivered by mail at a later date.

A stunningly successful Washington lawyer as well as a presidential adviser, Clark Clifford was born at Fort Scott, Kansas, in 1906. His father was a railroad official and his mother a children's book author. The family moved to Saint Louis, and he went to public school and college there, getting his law degree from Washington University in 1928. That year he joined a Saint Louis law firm and eventually became a successful lawyer specializing in corporate, labor, and trial cases. He married Margery Pepperell Kimball in 1931.

A navy supply officer during World War II, Clifford became President Harry S. Truman's naval aide in 1946. Truman was impressed with Clifford and soon made him a special counsel and an intimate adviser. Among Clifford's high-level tasks were preparing a 1946 memorandum that influenced America's toughening postwar stance toward the Soviet Union, assisting in the formulation of the Truman Doctrine and Marshall Plan, helping to orchestrate Truman's surprise election victory in 1948 (including the successful cross-country whistle-stop campaign), and participating in the postwar reorganization of the War Department (creating the Defense Department, Central Intelligence Agency, and National Security Council).

In 1950 Clifford returned to private practice and formed a law firm in Washington, D.C., which made him one of the city's wealthiest and most respected corporate lawyers. By 1961 he was back in government, having advised John F. Kennedy during his election campaign. President Kennedy named him to the President's Foreign Intelligence Advisory Board in 1961 and from early 1963 to 1968 Clifford served as its chairman. After Kennedy's assassination, President Lyndon B. Johnson relied on Clifford as a close adviser and sent him on fact-finding missions to Southeast Asia.

Following the 1968 Tet Offensive in Vietnam, President Johnson named him secretary of defense, replacing Robert McNamara. Though Clifford had supported U.S. involvement in Vietnam, he reportedly advised Johnson in 1968 to seek a negotiated settlement and to halt bombing of North Vietnam, advice that Johnson acted upon that same year. When President Johnson left office, Clifford returned to private practice.

An influential member of the Democratic Party in subsequent years, he served as an informal adviser to President Jimmy Carter and in 1991 published his memoirs, *Counsel to the President.* His long, highly successful career was marred though, when he was indicted in connection with the Bank of Credit and Commerce International financial scandal in 1992. The charges were later dropped.

Michael De Bakey

MODERN AMERICAN PIONEER, SURGEON OF WORLD RENOWN, DR. MICHAEL DE BAKEY HAS LED DOCTORS THROUGHOUT THE WORLD TO NEW FRONTIERS IN SURGERY OF THE HEART. HIS RESEARCH AND METHODS HAVE CONQUERED INFIRMITIES CONSIDERED HOPELESS ONLY A FEW YEARS AGO. HE HAS BROUGHT

NEW HOPE AND LONGER LIFE TO MILLIONS FOR THEMSELVES AND THEIR POSTERITY. HE HAS INSPIRED HIS COUNTRY TO DO MORE TO IMPROVE PEOPLE'S HEALTH THE WORLD OVER. HE WILL HIMSELF LIVE IN THE HISTORY OF SCIENCE'S NEVER-ENDING EXPLORATIONS FOR THE PROLONGATION OF LIFE.

★ ★ ★

President Lyndon B. Johnson awarded De Bakey the Presidential Medal of Freedom with the above citation on January 20, 1969, the last day of his presidency. The medal was delivered by mail at a later date.

Michael De Bakey was born in Lake Charles, Louisiana in 1908, the son of a Lebanese immigrant businessman. One of five children, he showed an early interest in biology and in 1930 graduated from Tulane University as a science major. Deciding on a medical career, he earned his medical degree from Tulane Medical School in 1932. Residencies in the United States, France, and Germany followed before De Bakey joined the faculty of Tulane Medical School in 1937. A year earlier he had married Diana Cooper, a nurse.

By this time De Bakey was already known for his interest in innovative approaches to medical problems. The *roller pump* he invented in 1932 would became a key component of heart-lung machines used in open-heart surgery, though both the machine and the surgical procedures were still decades away. He was among the earliest proponents of blood banks and transfusions and wrote about their importance. In 1936 he and Dr. Alton Ochsner, one of De Bakey's mentors from his days as a Tulane medical student, were among the first physicians to warn the public about the link between cigarette smoking and lung cancer. During World War II De Bakey joined the army and, as director of the surgical consultants division, investigated various aspects of war-related surgery.

After the war, in 1948, De Bakey became chairman of the Department of Surgery at Baylor University. He continued performing surgery, however, and experimenting with new procedures. For example, he tackled the problem of correcting an aortic aneurysm, a bubble, or blow-out, in the blood vessel's wall that is often fatal. De Bakey's procedure involved grafting in a new section of blood vessel, the replacement section having been frozen until needed. Later, he used flexible plastic tubing as the replacement material for aneurysms in aortas. De Bakey was among the first surgeons involved in open-heart surgery and in 1963 led a team that implanted a mechanical device to help a patient's diseased heart pump blood.

De Bakey gave up his chairmanship of the surgery department at Baylor in 1993 but continues to teach and, since 1978, has served as the school's chancellor. He is associated with numerous other institutions and organizations and has received various awards besides the Presidential Medal of Freedom.

David Dubinsky

DAVID DUBINSKY IS A NATIONAL LEADER OF FORESIGHT AND COMPASSION. HE HAS ADVANCED THE CAUSE OF THE WORK-INGMAN IN AMERICA — AND THE BROADER CAUSE OF SOCIAL JUSTICE IN THE WORLD, WITH UNFAILING SKILL AND UNCOMMON DISTINCTION. THE AMERICAN PEOPLE ARE RICHER FOR THE SERVICE HE HAS GIVEN THEM.

★ ★ ★

President Lyndon B. Johnson awarded Dubinsky the Presidential Medal of Freedom with the above citation on January 20, 1969, the last day of his presidency. The medal was delivered by mail at a later date.

The International Ladies' Garment Workers' Union (ILGWU) president for thirty-four years, David Dubinsky was born in 1892 in Brest Litovsk, then a Polish city controlled by Russia. He attended school until age eleven, when he went to work in his father's bakery. Dubinsky learned the trade quickly, joined the local bakers' union, and by age sixteen had become its secretary. That same year, though, Russian authorities arrested him as a labor agitator and packed him off to Siberia. Young Dubinsky managed to escape and return to Poland under an assumed name, but he did not stay long in Brest Litovsk. Instead, he and a brother fled Russia for the United States.

Arriving in New York City by 1911, Dubinsky became a cloth cutter and joined the ILGWU, then a struggling union in a sweatshop industry employing mainly low-paid workers. After marrying Emma Goldberg in 1915, he began climbing through the ranks of his union, and in 1922 the ILGWU made him a vice president. Then a disastrous strike by Communist members in the late 1920s crippled the ILGWU, and officials turned to Dubinsky to help rebuild the union, first making him secretary-treasurer and then, in 1932, president.

By the time Dubinsky came to power, union membership had fallen to 40,000 out of the 300,000 garment workers employed in the industry, and the union was $2 million in debt. An astute financial manager, Dubinsky cut the debt in half by 1932, but President Franklin D. Roosevelt's National Industrial Recovery Act of 1933 provided the ILGWU with an unexpected windfall. The law made collective bargaining mandatory, and Dubinsky quickly took advantage of that leverage to organize the garment industry. By 1935, when the Supreme Court overturned the law, Dubinsky had increased union membership to 200,000 workers and amassed $850,000 in union assets.

While continuing as ILGWU president, Dubinsky became a vice president of the American Federation of Labor (AFL) in 1935 and with

John L. Lewis helped organize what became the Congress of Industrial Organizations (CIO). *(See also the entry for Lewis, p. 109.)* Dubinsky resigned from the AFL briefly during a dispute over the CIO, but in 1940 he led the ILGWU into its affiliation with the AFL. From 1945 onward he was a high-level official in the AFL, as well as ILGWU president.

During his long tenure, ILGWU president Dubinsky built a strong union—it had assets of $500 million and some 450,000 members at its peak. He also helped improve working conditions for the garment workers. Among his most important achievements was winning a thirty-five-hour workweek in what had once been a sweatshop industry. He also pioneered such benefit programs as health centers and pension plans, promoted anti-racketeering initiatives in the ILGWU and AFL-CIO, and prodded unions into being more socially responsible, particularly in terms of integration.

Dubinsky retired in 1966 and in 1977 published his autobiography, *David Dubinsky: A Life with Labor.* He died in 1982, at the age of ninety.

Ralph Ellison

RALPH ELLISON IS A WRITER WHO HAS COMBINED SOCIAL AWARENESS, GREAT ARTISTRY, AND COMPASSIONATE UNDERSTANDING. HE HAS GIVEN HIS FELLOW CITIZENS NEW INSIGHT INTO THE PLIGHT OF THE AMERICAN NEGRO. HE HAS INSPIRED THE WHITE AMERICAN NOT JUST TO UNDERSTAND THE BLACK AMERICAN'S PROBLEMS, BUT TO STAND UP AND FIGHT TO ELIMINATE THEM. HIS VISION OF OUR DEMOCRACY HAS HELPED AMERICANS TO A NEW DETERMINATION TO BRING EQUALITY TO THE LIVES OF ALL OUR PEOPLE.

★ ★ ★

President Lyndon B. Johnson awarded Ellison the Presidential Medal of Freedom with the above citation on January 20, 1969, the last day of his presidency. The medal was delivered by mail at a later date.

Author of the classic *Invisible Man,* about a black man's search for identity, Ralph Waldo Ellison was born in Oklahoma City, Oklahoma, in 1914. Named for the nineteenth-century philosopher Emerson, he was only three when his father died. His mother supported the family, and the magazines she brought home from her work as a domestic gave Ellison his first glimpses of the world outside his native Oklahoma.

In school, Ellison read voraciously, but his earliest ambition was to become a musician. He took private lessons and eventually won a scholarship to study music at Tuskegee Institute in Alabama. From 1933 Ellison studied classical music there, but he was greatly influenced by jazz as well. He traveled to New York City's Harlem in 1937 after his junior year, and there met the novelist Richard Wright.

Wright changed the direction of Ellison's life by asking him to write first a book review and then a short story for a new magazine Wright was editing. Fascinated by the work, Ellison decided to stay in New York and continue writing. The New York City Federal Writers' Project employed him from 1938 until 1942, and he served as managing editor of the *Negro Quarterly*, which was published for only a year in 1943.

With the United States fighting in World War II, Ellison served in the merchant marine until 1945. During this time he published several short stories, including the frequently republished "King of the Bingo Game" (1944). He married Fanny McConnell in 1946.

Ellison began writing his now-famous novel, *Invisible Man* in 1945, while visiting a friend in Vermont. The book was seven years in the writing, but when finally published in 1952, it became an immediate bestseller. Critics hailed Ellison's first novel as an American classic.

Ellison wrote of a young black man's journey from the South, the theme being one of social invisibility and the search for one's true, inner identity in a world concerned only with superficial characteristics. The novel won the 1953 National Book Award, an unusual honor for a first novel, and it has been ranked with works by Albert Camus and existentialist John-Paul Sartre.

Ellison's fans waited patiently for a second novel, making do with published excerpts from a work in progress. In the years after *Invisible Man*, Ellison published two books of essays, *Shadow and Act* (1964) and *Going to the Territory* (1986). He also was a frequent lecturer, and from 1958 onward taught at various universities, including Yale, the University of California at Los Angeles, and New York University. He became a professor emeritus at NYU in 1979.

Ellison died in 1994, at age eighty, without having completed the long-awaited second novel. The following year, however, an English professor at Oregon's Lewis and Clark College began work on organizing the manuscript for eventual publication.

Henry Ford II

HENRY FORD II SYMBOLIZES THE CONCERNED AND ENLIGHTENED BUSINESS LEADER WHO HOLDS MUCH OF THE HOPE OF OUR NATION'S FUTURE. HE HAS COMMITTED HIMSELF AND HIS FORMIDABLE ABILITIES TO LEADING THE EFFORT TO FIND A PLACE AT INDUSTRY'S WORKBENCH FOR EVERY AMERICAN, AND HE HAS SUCCEEDED IN AROUSING HIS FELLOW INDUSTRIALISTS TO THAT CAUSE. IN HIM, THE GENIUS OF AMERICAN ENTERPRISE MEETS A DEVOTION TO THE CAUSE OF OUR COUNTRY, SETTING A STANDARD OF ENLIGHTENED SERVICE WHICH WILL INSPIRE BUSINESS LEADERSHIP FOR GENERATIONS TO COME.

★ ★ ★

President Lyndon B. Johnson awarded Ford the Presidential Medal of Freedom with the above citation on January 20, 1969, the last day of his presidency. The medal was delivered by mail at a later date.

A grandson and the namesake of the founder of the Ford Motor Company, Henry Ford II was born in Detroit, Michigan, in 1917. As Edsel Ford's eldest son, he grew up in the privileged society of the very rich and was assured of a career in the family-run company. Schoolwork never especially interested him, though, and he wound up leaving Yale in his senior year without graduating.

During World War II Henry Ford II served in the navy. But by 1943 the pressing needs of the family business, and the country's desperate need for the war materiel it produced, far outweighed the importance of his work as a navy officer. That year the navy released him from active duty to take charge of Ford Motor Company.

The immediate problem was that Ford's father, Edsel, the unassertive president of the company, had died unexpectedly in 1943, and the eighty-year-old Henry senior had largely lost control over the firm, relying increasingly on his unpopular security chief, Harry Bennett. But the company had been dying for some years already—besides losing millions each year, it was by the early 1940s producing only about 20 percent of all American cars. Something had to be done, and with the backing of his mother and grandmother (both major shareholders), the younger Henry was named executive vice president in late 1943. He ranked second only to Henry senior himself. Two years later Henry II won complete control when his grandfather again bowed to pressure from stockholders and company executives.

Henry II knew very little about running the business, but he learned quickly and made the right decisions. He immediately fired Bennett and set about improving relations with the United Automobile Workers union, finding new managerial talent, and modernizing the company. He brought in many new top executives, among them a group of former air force officers dubbed the "Whiz Kids," to help reorganize the company. *(See also the entry for Robert S. McNamara, p. 134.)* He also began a major expansion program that included thirteen new manufacturing plants. By 1953 Henry II had performed a near miracle—he had turned the failing company around and made it the country's second-leading auto manufacturer.

As head of the Ford Motor Company, he approved the Edsel, the company's disastrous attempt to break into the medium priced car market in 1957. But during his tenure Ford also introduced the now-classic Thunderbird and Mustang models with stunning success. The Falcon, the first compact manufactured by a Big Three automaker, also proved successful, as did Ford's later low-priced cars like the Maverick. Perhaps even more important, though, was his decision in the 1960s to aggressively expand the company into foreign markets, especially Europe. The move turned Ford Motor Company into a highly profitable international corporation.

With the company back on sound footing Henry II increasingly became identified with the jet set of wealthy socialites. In 1980 he married his third wife, Kathleen DuRoss, his two previous marriages having ended in divorce. However, he also was a sometimes outspoken critic on social issues and became known for his commitment to integration in the workplace and his efforts to revitalize the city of Detroit. A board member of the Ford Foundation, among the country's largest philanthropic institutions, Henry II helped modernize the organization. He supported even its most controversial social programs, including community organizing in poor neighborhoods, until he resigned during a dispute in 1977.

In 1979 Henry II resigned as chief executive of Ford Motor Company and the following year gave up his post as board chairman. He retained a measure of control, however, by keeping his seat as chairman of the finance committee of the board of directors. One of the country's most powerful industrialists and among its richest men, Henry II died in 1987 at age seventy.

W. Averell Harriman

AVERELL HARRIMAN, IN A CAREER OF SERVICE THAT SPANS A GENERATION, HAS SCALED THE HEIGHTS OF PATRIOTISM AS FEW MEN IN OUR HISTORY HAVE. HE IS A MAN OF SINGULAR GRACE AND FORCEFUL SPIRIT, WHO HAS ANSWERED HIS COUNTRY'S CALL IN CRISIS AND CALM ALIKE, NEVER HESITATING TO PUT HIS

ABUNDANT ENERGY AND MANIFOLD TALENTS TO THE TASKS AT
HAND. THE PEACE FOR WHICH THE WORLD HUNGERS WILL, WHEN
IT COMES, BEAR HIS PRINT FOREVER.

★ ★ ★

*President Lyndon B. Johnson awarded Harriman the Presidential
Medal of Freedom with the above citation on the last day of his presidency, January 20, 1969. The medal was accompanied by the added
accolade "with distinction" and was delivered by mail at a later date.*

The son of a multimillionaire financier and railroad magnate, W.
Averell Harriman was born in New York City in 1891. While a student
at Yale, the young Harriman spent his summers working in low-level
jobs for the Union Pacific Railroad and, after graduating in 1913,
began rising quickly through the corporate ranks. He soon showed
his gift for getting things done. By the early 1930s he not only had
become the Union Pacific board chairman, but also had run a successful shipbuilding company, founded a bank, and started development of what became the famous Sun Valley resort.

During the 1930s Harriman began his long career in government
service with a high-level post in President Franklin D. Roosevelt's
National Recovery Administration and a three-year stint as the
president's Business Advisory Council chairman. With the outbreak of
World War II in Europe, President Roosevelt tapped Harriman for the
important task of arranging crucial lend-lease aid to Britain (from
1941) and the Soviet Union, a program by which the United States sent
Allied nations badly needed military hardware and supplies to help in
the fight against the Nazis. In 1943 Roosevelt named him U.S.
ambassador to the Soviet Union. During the war years Harriman met
regularly with both Winston Churchill and Joseph Stalin and played an
important role in developing Soviet-American relations.

Under President Harry S. Truman, Harriman served variously as
U.S. ambassador to Great Britain (1946), secretary of commerce
(1946–1948), and a special representative in Europe for the Marshall
Plan. He also served Truman as a national security affairs special
assistant and as director of the Mutual Security Agency, which oversaw
foreign aid. During the Eisenhower administration, Harriman served
one term as governor of New York (1955–1959) and lost two bids for
the Democratic presidential nomination (1952 and 1956).

Returning to the government with the Democrats in 1961,
Harriman served as a high-level State Department official in the
Kennedy administration. He negotiated the 1962 agreement ending the
Laotian civil war and the 1963 Nuclear Test Ban Treaty. He also helped
bring about the overthrow of South Vietnamese dictator Diem in 1963.

Though Harriman disagreed with President Lyndon B. Johnson's
decision to escalate the war in Vietnam, he served as ambassador at
large and became increasingly involved in seeking a negotiated set-

tlement. He led the U.S. delegation to the Paris peace talks in 1968, retiring when Republican President Richard Nixon took office in 1969.

Harriman's wife of forty years, Marie Norton, died the following year. He married Pamela Digby Hayward in 1971.

Recalling his wartime diplomatic service, Harriman wrote *America and Russia in a Changing World* (1971) and *Special Envoy to Churchill and Stalin, 1941⁸1946* (1975). In his later years, he remained an unofficial spokesman in foreign affairs, calling for nuclear disarmament. Harriman died in 1986, just a few years before the collapse of the Soviet Union and the end of the Cold War. He was ninety-four years old.

Bob Hope

OVER THE SPAN OF A GENERATION, BOB HOPE HAS LIGHTENED AMERICA'S HEART. HE HAS BROUGHT LAUGHTER INTO THE LIVES OF MILLIONS. HE HAS GIVEN UNSTINTINGLY OF HIMSELF, HIS TIME, AND HIS TALENTS IN SUPPORT OF A HOST OF WORTHY CAUSES ON BEHALF OF HIS COUNTRY. HE HAS BROUGHT HAPPINESS AND PLEASURE TO AMERICAN FIGHTING MEN ON THE BATTLEFRONTS OF THREE WARS. WITH HIS GIFTS OF JOY TO ALL THE AMERICAN PEOPLE, HE HAS WRITTEN HIS NAME LARGELY IN THE HISTORY OF OUR TIMES.

★ ★ ★

President Lyndon B. Johnson awarded Hope the Presidential Medal of Freedom with the above citation on the last day of his presidency, January 20, 1969. The medal was delivered by mail at a later date.

The son of an English stonemason and a former Welsh concert singer, Leslie Townes Hope was born in Eltham, England, in 1903. His family moved to Cleveland, Ohio, four years later, and when Hope was just ten years old his flair for performing won him an award in a Charlie Chaplin imitation contest. After graduating from high school, Hope and a friend put together a song-and-dance routine that landed them in vaudeville. By 1927 they also were appearing in Broadway shows. The following year Hope delivered his first monologue at a Newcastle, Indiana, performance, and its success convinced him to go it alone as a comic, using the name Bob Hope.

Engagements proved hard to find for the young comedian, though. Hope was nearly destitute when a friend introduced him to an agent, who quickly landed him a much-needed vaudeville performance in Chicago. That was the turning point in Hope's career, and within a few years his talent as a comic vaulted him to stardom. By 1932 he had appeared in his first Broadway musical, *Ballyhoo*, and two years later the singer Dolores Reade became his wife.

Hope's radio debut came in 1935. His comedy routines were so successful with radio audiences that he landed his own radio show in 1938. That same year he also appeared in his first movie, *The Big Broadcast of 1938*, in which he sang "Thanks for the Memory." Hope, who later used "Thanks for the Memory" as his theme song, went on to make six other movies before starring with Bing Crosby in the hit *The Road to Singapore* (1940). Hope and Crosby did seven highly popular "Road" movies together, the last being *The Road to Hong Kong*, in 1962. Meanwhile, Hope also starred in other movie comedies, including *The Paleface* (1948), *Fancy Pants* (1950), *Paris Holiday* (1958), *Call Me Bwana* (1963), *Cancel My Reservation* (1972), and *Spies Like Us* (1985).

Hope began touring Allied military bases overseas with a troupe of performers during World War II and continued making annual United Service Organizations (USO) Christmas tours to entertain U.S. soldiers for decades afterward. Because of these and other benefit performances, Hope has received four special Oscars for humanitarian service, as well as distinguished service awards from every branch of the U.S. military. President John F. Kennedy awarded him the Congressional Gold Medal, and, in addition to the Presidential Medal of Freedom, Hope has received numerous other awards.

Already a top-rated comedian on radio and in the movies during the 1940s, he made his first appearance on television in 1950, when television audiences were just beginning to mushroom. For the next forty years he regularly hosted television specials, including the more recent *Bob Hope Christmas Special* (1987) and *Hope: A 90th Birthday Celebration* (1993). He also has published ten books, the most recent being *Don't Shoot, It's Only Me* (1990).

Edgar Kaiser

EDGAR KAISER IS A PIONEER WHOSE LEADERSHIP HAS HELPED THE NATION BEGIN TO MAKE GOOD ON ITS PLEDGE OF A DECENT HOME FOR EVERY AMERICAN. HE HAS BROUGHT HIS LONG EXPERIENCE AND HIS BUSINESS SKILLS TO THE PROBLEM OF BUILDING HOUSES WITHIN THE REACH OF ALL OUR PEOPLE. THE AMERICA OF THE FUTURE WILL BE BUILT ON FOUNDATIONS HE HAS HELPED TO LAY.

★ ★ ★

President Lyndon B. Johnson awarded Kaiser the Presidential Medal of Freedom with the above citation on the last day of his presidency, January 20, 1969. The medal was delivered by mail at a later date.

Edgar Kaiser literally grew up with the construction company founded by his father, Henry J. Kaiser, and from the 1940s onward played an important role in expanding and diversifying it into a billion-dollar international industrial empire. Capitalizing on such massive construction projects as the Boulder and Grand Coulee dams, the Kaisers built their California-based construction company into a corporate giant that included the Kaiser Aluminum and Chemical Corporation, Kaiser Steel, Kaiser Cement, and the Kaiser Foundation Medical Care Program, as well as numerous other subsidiaries. Edgar Kaiser, meanwhile, also devoted considerable time and energy to civic work during the 1950s and 1960s. He served in four presidential administrations and was awarded the Presidential Medal of Freedom for his efforts to expand the existing stock of low- and moderate-income housing in the United States.

Born in Seattle, Washington, in 1908, Edgar Kaiser traveled with his family from one construction site to another during his youth, often living in rough construction camps. From age twelve he worked variously as a water carrier, messenger, and clerk, but on entering the University of California, Kaiser majored in economics instead of engineering. With his father's approval, he left college in 1930—just two months before graduating—to take a job as a construction superintendent on a natural-gas pipeline being built by his father's company. Two years later he married Susan Mead, the daughter of a family friend.

Progressively more responsible jobs followed during the 1930s, and from 1941 to 1945 he was vice president and general manager of Kaiser shipyards. Kaiser played a major role in the rapid expansion of the family's newly acquired shipbuilding interests on the Pacific Coast, which by 1945 included seven shipyards. The shipbuilding company made a vital contribution to the U.S. war effort by producing about a third of all "Liberty ships," the workhorse of the U.S. merchant marine during World War II.

After serving as president of the family's unsuccessful venture in manufacturing passenger cars, Edgar Kaiser gradually took over control of the family enterprises from his father. In 1956 he became president of Kaiser Industries Corporation, the controlling company for all Kaiser businesses, and by 1967, when his father died, Edgar Kaiser was in full control. By that time Kaiser Industries had companies or major construction projects in Latin America, Europe, Asia, Africa, and Australia, as well as in North America.

Kaiser, known for his innovative approaches to labor problems, served on President John F. Kennedy's Missile Sites Labor Commission and the Committee on Equal Employment Opportunities. President Lyndon B. Johnson, appointed him to the committees on Urban Housing and Labor-Management Policy. President Gerald R. Ford gave him a post on the Advisory Committee on Refugees, while President Jimmy Carter named him to the National Health Insurance Issues Council. The Kaiser Foundation Medical Care Program, the country's largest private, prepaid medical plan, sprang from a program Edgar Kaiser set up in the 1930s for Kaiser employees building the Bonneville Dam in Washington.

Kaiser's first wife died in 1974, and he married Nina McCormick in 1975. Kaiser died six years later after a long illness. He was seventy-three years old.

Mary Lasker

HUMANIST, PHILANTHROPIST, ACTIVIST—MARY LASKER HAS INSPIRED UNDERSTANDING AND PRODUCTIVE LEGISLATION WHICH IMPROVED THE LOT OF MANKIND. IN MEDICAL RESEARCH, IN ADDING GRACE AND BEAUTY TO THE ENVIRONMENT, AND IN EXHORTING HER FELLOW CITIZENS TO RALLY TO THE CAUSE OF PROGRESS, SHE HAS MADE A LASTING IMPRINT ON THE QUALITY OF LIFE IN THIS COUNTRY. SHE HAS LED HER PRESIDENT AND THE CONGRESS TO GREATER HEIGHTS FOR JUSTICE FOR HER PEOPLE AND BEAUTY FOR HER LAND.

★ ★ ★

President B. Johnson awarded Lasker the Presidential Medal of Freedom with the above citation on the last day of his presidency, January 20, 1969. The medal was delivered by mail at a later date.

A philanthropist who successfully lobbied the federal government to increase research spending on cancer and other diseases, Lasker was born Mary Woodard in Watertown, Wisconsin, in 1900. Often sick as a child, she was nevertheless a good student and, studying art and history, graduated cum laude from Radcliffe College in 1923. She spent seven years as an art dealer, but, following an unsuccessful marriage to a gallery owner, left the art world in 1932 to set up her own business. Her Hollywood Patterns, which manufactured paper patterns for making clothing in the home, thrived despite the depression, and she later sold the business to a large company.

Mary and Albert Lasker married in 1940, and, remembering her own childhood experiences with sickness, Mary convinced her husband to join her in a career to promote research and education in public health issues, particularly heart disease, cancer, and mental illness. Her husband, a multimillionaire and owner of a highly successful advertising agency, retired in 1942, and the couple founded the Albert and Mary Lasker Foundation to encourage medical research. The annual monetary awards given by the foundation to medical researchers were soon regarded as a high honor in the medical field. By the mid–1990s fifty-one researchers who got the Lasker Award later received Nobel Prizes. The Laskers also focused money and promotional efforts on what later became the American Cancer Society and worked for greater public awareness of the disease.

Lasker continued these efforts after her husband died of colon cancer in 1952, and she formed the National Health Education Committee to publish informative books on various diseases. But perhaps her most important contribution was as a Washington lobbyist. For decades she worked to promote greater government funding for medical research, and she recorded some important successes.

Lasker was instrumental in transforming the National Institutes of Health from a loose collection of government laboratories with a $2.4 million budget in 1945 to a highly sophisticated research agency that received $5.5 billion in federal funds in 1986. She lobbied intensively for her idea of a separate federal authority on cancer, and it became a reality with the 1971 National Cancer Act and President Richard Nixon's "war on cancer."

An energetic woman, Lasker in later years also promoted public awareness of, and government involvement in, research for various other diseases, including AIDS and growth and endocrine disorders. She also contributed to environmental and beautification projects, notably one of Lady Bird Johnson's highway beautification projects—Lasker helped fund the planting of a million daffodil bulbs along Washington parkways.

Although slowed by a stroke in 1981, she continued her work as a lobbyist during the 1980s. She died of pneumonia in 1994, at age ninety-three.

John Macy

JOHN MACY RECRUITED MORE TALENT OF PROVEN ABILITY INTO GOVERNMENT SERVICE THAN ANY OTHER MAN OF OUR TIME. IN DEMANDING ONLY THE BEST—AND IN SEEKING IT OUT—HE SET A STANDARD OF EXCELLENCE THAT WILL SERVE AS A BENCHMARK FOR MANY YEARS TO COME. OUR GOVERNMENT IS STRONGER

TODAY FROM TOP TO BOTTOM BECAUSE OF HIS EFFORTS. THE GOVERNMENT IS FAIRER, TOO, BECAUSE JOHN MACY INSISTED THAT EQUAL EMPLOYMENT OPPORTUNITY MEANT WHAT IT SAYS. HE INSISTED ONLY ON ABILITY AND CHARACTER, WITHOUT REGARD TO RELIGION OR RACE OR COLOR OR SECTION.

★ ★ ★

President Lyndon B. Johnson awarded Macy the Presidential Medal of Freedom with the above citation on the last day of his presidency, January 20, 1969. The medal was delivered by mail at a later date.

A former executive director and chairman of the U.S. Civil Service Commission, John Macy was born in Chicago in 1917 and was raised in Winnetka, Illinois. He majored in government at Wesleyan University in Connecticut and received his bachelor's degree in 1934. Macy's government career began later that summer when he interned at the National Institute of Public Affairs.

A series of administrative and managerial positions followed, including work for the Social Security Board and the War Department. Macy served in the air force during World War II and in 1944 married Joyce Hagen. After the war he worked for the Atomic Energy Commission—as an administrative executive of atomic testing in Nevada—and later served as a special assistant to the army's undersecretary.

Macy became executive director of the Civil Service Commission in 1953 during President Dwight D. Eisenhower's first term. Among the many reforms Macy instituted over the next five years were improved fringe benefits for government workers, a revitalized college recruiting system for prospective employees, and incentive systems for job performance and innovations. He eventually resigned in 1958, though, amid some speculation that he was unhappy with Eisenhower administration policies.

After a three-year stint as executive vice president of Wesleyan University, Macy was named chairman of the Civil Service Commission by President John F. Kennedy. Macy remained chairman throughout the Kennedy-Johnson years (1961–1969) and was successful in his efforts to draw more talented people into government work. Macy was a favorite of President Johnson, who called the chairman his "talent scout" and relied on him to provide suggestions for high-level appointments. Macy retired from the commission at the end of Johnson's term in 1969.

President Kennedy also appointed Macy in 1963 to the Distinguished Civilian Service Awards Board, which was responsible for providing the president with lists of proposed Presidential Medal of Freedom nominees. Macy served as executive secretary of the board and was instrumental in reviving the award during the Johnson administration.

In 1969 Macy became president of the newly organized Corporation for Public Broadcasting. Policy disagreements with the Nixon administration forced him out of that job in 1972, however, and it was not until President Jimmy Carter took office that Macy returned to public service. Appointed director of the Federal Emergency Management Agency, he served in that post until the Carter administration left office in 1981.

Macy remained in the Washington area as a consultant and in 1983 wrote *America's Unelected Government.* He died two years later, at age sixty-nine.

Gregory Peck

AN ARTIST WHO HAS BROUGHT NEW DIGNITY TO THE ACTOR'S PROFESSION, GREGORY PECK HAS ENRICHED THE LIVES OF MILLIONS. HE HAS GIVEN HIS ENERGIES, HIS TALENTS, AND HIS DEVOTION TO CAUSES WHICH HAVE IMPROVED THE LIVES OF PEOPLE. HE IS A HUMANITARIAN TO WHOM AMERICANS ARE DEEPLY INDEBTED.

★ ★ ★

President Lyndon B. Johnson awarded Peck the Presidential Medal of Freedom with the above citation on the last day of his presidency, January 20, 1969. The medal was delivered by mail at a later date.

Among Hollywood's biggest stars from the late 1940s to the mid–1960s, Peck was born Eldred Gregory Peck in the southern California town of La Jolla in 1916. His parents separated when he was very young, and he lived variously with his mother and father while growing up. After working a year driving trucks, Peck settled down to his studies as a premed student at the University of California at Berkeley. His first acting experience came at the Little Theater in Berkeley when the theater director needed someone tall (Peck was six-foot-three by age seventeen).

The experience changed Peck's life. He switched majors to English literature and, after acting in several more college plays, decided on an acting career. Two years of study at the Neighborhood Playhouse School of Theater in New York followed his graduation from Berkeley, and in 1942 Peck made his first Broadway appearance, in *The Morning Star.* He used the name Gregory Peck.

Appearances in several other plays led to a starring role in a war film, *Days of Glory* (1944), produced by a small Hollywood studio.

The film, not among Hollywood's more memorable efforts, nevertheless got the big studios interested in Peck, and the following year his role as a missionary priest in *The Keys of the Kingdom* won him the first of his several Oscar nominations. That same year he starred in Alfred Hitchcock's *Spellbound* and in 1947 made one of his most important films, *Gentleman's Agreement*.

Peck, who stubbornly insisted on choosing his own roles—a rare feat in the heyday of the big studios—emerged as one of Hollywood's most popular male actors in the late 1940 s and early 1950s. The war film *12 O'Clock High* (1949) won him another Oscar nomination, but his performance as an aging gunfighter in *The Gunfighter* (1950) established him as a formidable actor. Peck married Veronique Passani in 1955, having divorced his first wife the year before.

Other successful films in the 1950s and early 1960s included *The Snows of Kilimanjaro* (1952), *Roman Holiday* (1953), *Pork Chop Hill* (1959), and *The Guns of Navarone* (1961). They helped cement his fame, but it was his performance as a small-town southern lawyer in *To Kill a Mockingbird* (1963) that finally won him an Oscar for best actor. The role was in many respects tailor-made for Peck, who is a lifelong liberal and whose movie roles had so often featured a decent, honest man who is tested and responds in a moral fashion.

Among his other successful films since then were *Arabesque* (1966), *The Omen* (1976), *MacArthur* (1977), *The Boys From Brazil* (1978), *The Sea Wolves* (1981), and, more recently, *Other People's Money* (1991), in which he costarred with Danny DeVito. During the 1970s and 1980s Peck also produced some of the movies in which he appeared. He played Abraham Lincoln in the successful television miniseries *The Blue and the Gray* (1982).

Laurance Rockefeller

LAURANCE ROCKEFELLER, CITIZEN, PHILANTHROPIST, AND CONSERVATION LEADER, HAS WITH EXTRAORDINARY VISION AND LEADERSHIP, FOCUSED THE SIGHTS OF HIS COUNTRYMEN ON THE QUALITY OF THEIR PHYSICAL ENVIRONMENT—NOT JUST FOR TODAY, BUT FOR COUNTLESS TOMORROWS. QUIET, PATIENT, AND PERSISTENT SERVANT OF THE PEOPLE, HE HAS RECALLED THE WILDERNESS AND ENRICHED THE LANDSCAPE AND THE LIVES OF PEOPLE. HE IS A WORTHY MEMBER OF A WORTHY FAMILY WHICH HAS SET AN EXAMPLE FOR PUBLIC SERVICE TO THE COUNTRY.

★ ★ ★

President Lyndon B. Johnson awarded Rockefeller the Presidential Medal of Freedom with the above citation on the last day of his presidency, January 20, 1969. The medal was delivered by mail at a later date.

A grandson of oil magnate John D. Rockefeller and the third son of John D. Rockefeller, Jr., Laurance was born in New York City in 1910. Raised as an heir to one of the country's richest men, he took an early interest in both aviation and conservation and later earned his bachelor's degree in philosophy at Princeton University (1932). Nevertheless, he went on to become the most business-oriented of his brothers.

Married to Mary French in 1934, Rockefeller became a director of the family-owned business and entertainment facility, New York City's Rockefeller Center, in 1936. (Later, in the 1950s, he became its chairman.) He also pursued his interest in aeronautics by helping found Eastern Airlines during the 1930s and soon after acquired the majority of the company stock. Rockefeller served as a director of McDonnell Aircraft Corporation in the early 1940s and was director of the National Aeronautics Association from 1942 to 1944. During World War II he served in the navy's bureau of aeronautics and was a trouble-shooter concerned with airplane production problems.

Returning to civilian life, Rockefeller became president of the family's venture-capital firm, Rockefeller Brothers, in 1946. He invested in a wide range of areas, including hotels, equipment for nuclear reactors, planes and missiles, and computers. Among the many specific projects Rockefeller backed financially were the development of the Viking rocket and a twelve-hundred-acre Dorado Beach resort in Puerto Rico.

Meanwhile, in his later years especially, Rockefeller pursued his interest in conservation, eventually becoming president of the Jackson Hole Preserve, a foundation to conserve scenic areas. In 1951 he donated land encompassing Donderberg Mountain along the Hudson River to the Palisades Interstate Park and five years later gave the land needed to create the Virgin Islands National Park. More recently, in 1990, he pledged $21 million to create a Center for Human Values at his alma mater, Princeton University.

He has supported numerous conservation groups and served on various commissions, and he has chaired the Citizens Advisory Committee on Environmental Quality (1969–1973) and the New York Zoological Society, among others. Rockefeller also has been active in groups concerned with cancer research.

Walt Whitman Rostow

OF WALT WHITMAN ROSTOW IT CAN BE SAID IN TRUTH THAT HE
ADVANCED THE CAUSE OF FREEDOM AS FEW MEN DID IN HIS TIME.
PATIENT AND INFORMED, FAIR AND JUST, WITH SUPPORTERS AND
CRITICS ALIKE, HE IS A MAN OF WISE JUDGEMENT AND SOUND
COUNSEL. HE HAS SERVED THE PRESIDENT OF THE UNITED
STATES, THE CITIZENS OF HIS COUNTRY, AND ALL WHO PRIZE
FREEDOM, TIRELESSLY, WITH UNREMITTING EFFORT, AND WITH
THE HIGHEST DISTINCTION.

★ ★ ★

*President Lyndon B. Johnson awarded Rostow the Presidential Medal
of Freedom with the above citation during a special ceremony held in
Bethesda, Maryland, January 20, 1969, the last day of Johnson's
presidency. The medal was presented with the additional accolade "with
distinction."*

A noted economic historian and high-level official during the Kennedy
and Johnson administrations, Walt Whitman Rostow was born in New
York City in 1916. He went on to earn both his bachelor's degree (1936)
and his doctorate (1940) from Yale University. He studied at Oxford
University from 1936 to 1938 on a Rhodes scholarship and taught economics at Columbia University from 1940 to 1941.

Rostow served with the Office of Strategic Services during World
War II and afterward held his first government posts, as assistant
chief of the German-Austrian economics division at the State
Department (1945–1946) and then as assistant to the executive secretary of the Economic Commission for Europe (1947–1949). He also
taught American history at Oxford University (1946–1947) and at
Cambridge University (1949–1950). Meanwhile, he married Elspeth
Vaughan Davies in 1947 and published his first book, *British Economy
of the Nineteenth Century: Essays,* the following year.

Returning to the United States, Rostow in 1950 joined the faculty
of the Massachusetts Institute of Technology as a professor of
economic history, a post he held for the next ten years, and from 1951
to 1960 was a staff member at the Center for International Studies.
During the 1950s he also collaborated on various books, including
The Process of Economic Growth (1952) and *A Proposal: Key to an
Effective Foreign Policy* (1957).

Rostow joined the circle of advisers to Sen. John F. Kennedy in
1957, and after Kennedy became president, he was named deputy
special assistant to the president for national security affairs. Between
1961 and 1966 Rostow served as chairman of the policy planning
council at the State Department and, as a holdover during the
Johnson administration, was the U.S. representative to the Inter-

American Committee of the Alliance for Progress from 1964 to 1966.

Leaving government service, Rostow returned to writing books and teaching. Among his later works were *East-West Relations: Is Détente Possible?* (1969), *The World Economy: History and Prospect* (1978), *History, Policy, and Economic Theory* (1989), and *Theorists of Economic Growth from David Hume to the Present* (1990).

He is currently a professor of political economy at the University of Texas, Austin, and since 1982 has been board chairman of the Austin Project, an urban revitalization program.

Merriman Smith

FOR A QUARTER OF A CENTURY, THE STORY OF THE AMERICAN PRESIDENCY HAS BEEN WRITTEN MOST FREQUENTLY UNDER A FAMOUS BY-LINE, "MERRIMAN SMITH." THE DEAN OF THE WHITE HOUSE CORRESPONDENTS HAS BROUGHT TO HIS REPORTING THE DISPASSIONATE PRESENTATION OF THE FACTS AND THE REALISTIC PERSPECTIVE IN THE BEST TRADITION OF JOURNALISM. FIVE PRESIDENTS HAVE RECEIVED FROM HIM AN OBJECTIVITY NOT UNIVERSAL IN HIS PROFESSION. MILLIONS KNOW AND UNDERSTAND AMERICA BETTER BECAUSE OF HIS PATRIOTIC AND DEDICATED SERVICE.

★ ★ ★

President Lyndon B. Johnson awarded Smith the Presidential Medal of Freedom with the above citation on the last day of his presidency, January 20, 1969. The medal was delivered by mail at a later date.

The United Press International (UPI) White House correspondent through six presidential administrations, Merriman Smith was born in Savannah, Georgia, in 1913. He spent three years at Oglethorpe University before taking a job as a sportswriter for the *Atlanta Georgian*. In 1936 he became a reporter for the UPI Atlanta bureau, covering news events in the South.

Smith was transferred to Washington, D.C., in 1941 and there began covering the White House during the Roosevelt administration. A conscientious and aggressive reporter, he served as White House correspondent for nearly the next thirty years. In addition he wrote a weekly syndicated column, "Backstairs at the White House."

A facile writer who regularly dictated news stories over the telephone with nothing more than his notes as a guide, Smith won a

National Headliner Award for his coverage of President Franklin D. Roosevelt's death in 1945. Almost two decades later he won a Pulitzer Prize for his stories on President John F. Kennedy's assassination in Dallas, Texas. Smith had been riding in the press pool car of the presidential motorcade that fateful November day in 1963, and within seconds of the shooting he began dictating the first news story on the tragedy over the car telephone.

An accomplished speaker as well as news writer, Smith often appeared on television news shows and as a guest on late-night talk shows. He wrote five books about his White House experiences, among them *Thank You, Mr. President* (1946), *A President's Odyssey* (1961), and *The Good New Days* (1962).

Divorced in 1966, he later married his second wife, Gailey L. Johnson. Smith was hospitalized in 1968 but was back covering the White House within a few weeks. After a short stay in the hospital for an undisclosed illness in 1970, he was found dead in his home with an apparent self-inflicted gunshot wound. Smith was fifty-seven years old.

Cyrus Vance

CYRUS VANCE HAS BROUGHT A NEW DIMENSION TO THE WORD "TROUBLE-SHOOTER." AN ADMINISTRATOR OF TESTED AND PROVEN ABILITIES, HE HAS SERVED HIS NATION WITH HIGH DISTINCTION—IN THE EXECUTIVE BRANCH, AND ON SPECIAL MISSIONS IN THE NATION'S INTEREST AND THE CAUSE OF WORLD PEACE. IN EVERY TASK, HE HAS EXEMPLIFIED THE HIGHEST STANDARDS OF DEDICATED PUBLIC SERVICE.

★ ★ ★

President Lyndon B. Johnson awarded Vance the Presidential Medal of Freedom with the above citation at a special ceremony in Bethesda, Maryland, January 20, 1969, the last day of Johnson's presidency. Vance's medal was presented with the added accolade "with distinction."

A high-level diplomatic official in the Johnson administration and President Jimmy Carter's secretary of state, Cyrus Vance was born in Clarksburg, West Virginia, in 1917. His father died of pneumonia when he was just three. Vance went on to Yale University, where he majored in economics and graduated in 1939. He took his law degree at Yale in 1942 and afterward served as a navy gunnery officer aboard destroyers in the Pacific theater during World War II.

After the war Vance joined a Wall Street law firm, becoming a

partner in 1956. In the 1950s he served as counsel to Senate investigative committees and this led to his appointment in 1960 as the
Department of Defense general counsel. Moving rapidly up the
ranks at defense, he became army secretary under President John F.
Kennedy (1962–1963) and deputy secretary of defense under
President Lyndon B. Johnson (1964–1967). Originally a staunch supporter of the war in Vietnam, Vance had come to oppose it by the
time he resigned in 1967. In 1968 he called on President Johnson to
institute a cease-fire in South Vietnam and soon afterward Johnson
named him deputy chief delegate to the Paris peace talks. Vance was
deeply involved in negotiations with the North Vietnamese until the
close of the Johnson administration in 1969.

Vance returned to private practice until President Jimmy Carter
took office when he appointed Vance secretary of state. He promoted
the Carter administration's human-rights policies, played a key role in
securing the Strategic Arms Limitation Talks II treaty (which the
Senate refused to ratify), and saw his efforts at Middle East diplomacy
bear fruit with the Camp David accords of 1978. Deeply involved in
efforts to free U.S. hostages being held in Iran, Vance resigned in 1980
over his opposition to the failed commando mission to rescue them.

In private practice since then, Vance has nevertheless found time to
serve on various corporate and foundation boards, including those of
Yale University (1968–1978, 1980–1987) and the Federal Reserve Bank
of New York (1989–1993). He also has been involved in foreign affairs,
acting as the UN secretary-general's envoy on the Yugoslavian crisis
(1991–1992), and on South Africa and Nagorno-Karabakh in the
former Soviet Union (1992). He also was cochairman of a UN-
sponsored conference on the former Yugoslavia (1992–1993).

William S. White

WILLIAM S. WHITE HAS BROUGHT TO HIS LONG DOCUMENTATION
OF THE CONTINUING CHRONICLE OF AMERICA A WISDOM, COM-
PASSION, AND AN INSIGHT WHICH HAVE HELPED THE AMERICAN
PEOPLE UNDERSTAND AND APPRECIATE THEIR HISTORY AND THE
LEGACY OF THEIR DEMOCRATIC HERITAGE. AMERICA'S STORY IS
BETTER TOLD BECAUSE HE WAS HERE TO TELL IT.

★ ★ ★

*President Lyndon B. Johnson awarded White the Presidential Medal of
Freedom with the above citation on the last day of his presidency,
January 20, 1969. The medal was delivered by mail at a later date.*

A *New York Times* reporter and Pulitzer Prize-winning biographer, William S. White was born at De Leon, Texas, in 1906. He went on to study at the University of Texas at Austin and began working as a reporter for the *Austin Statesman* while still a student. The Associated Press (AP) hired him as a correspondent for its Austin office in 1926, his junior year at the University of Texas.

White moved to the AP bureau in Washington, D.C., in 1933 and three years later became a news editor for the AP photo service in New York. During World War II he served as an infantry officer but was discharged within a year after suffering spinal meningitis. Determined to be a part of the war effort, White went overseas to Europe as an AP war correspondent, covering some of the major military operations of the war. He landed on the French coast with Allied troops on D-Day, was with French troops who liberated Paris, and joined the Third Armored Division as it pushed into Germany for the first time.

On returning to the United States in 1945, White moved to the *New York Times*, where he became the newspaper's chief congressional correspondent. During that time he got to know Sen. Robert A. Taft of Ohio, a noted Republican member of Congress and an unsuccessful presidential candidate in 1952. Taft died the following year, prompting the book publisher Harper & Brothers to ask White to write Taft's biography. White took just two months off from the *Times* to to write the book, which appeared in 1954 and won him the 1955 Pulitzer Prize for biography.

Despite his newfound fame as a book author, White remained with the *Times* until 1958. Between then and his retirement in 1973 he devoted himself to writing his syndicated column, which at one time was carried in 175 newspapers. White also wrote two other books, *Citadel* (1957), about his days as a Capitol Hill reporter, and *The Making of a Journalist*, (1986), his memoirs.

White, who was married to the former June McConnell, died in 1994. He was eighty-eight years old.

Roy Wilkins

ROY WILKINS—ONE OF OUR GENERATION'S EARLY CIVIL RIGHTS LEADERS—REMAINS ONE OF THE NATION'S GREAT CIVIL RIGHTS LEADERS. IN HIS LONG DEVOTION TO THE CAUSE OF THE AMERICAN NEGRO, HE HAS ADVANCED THE CAUSE OF ALL THE AMERICAN PEOPLE. WITH COURAGE, HE HAS SERVED BOTH BLACK AND WHITE AND HELPED HIS PRESIDENT TO BE JUST TO BOTH. NO ONE KNOWS BETTER THAN HE THE ANGER BORN OF INJUSTICE. BUT HE ALSO KNOWS THAT ANGER ALONE NEVER FREED A HUMAN SOUL. AND SO HE HAS STIRRED THE NATION'S CONSCIENCE AND MOBILIZED ITS COMMITMENT TO MAKE GOOD THE CENTURY-OLD PROMISE OF EMANCIPATION. IN SO DOING, HE HAS HELPED MAKE OUR DEMOCRATIC DREAM A LIVING REALITY.

★ ★ ★

President Lyndon B. Johnson awarded Wilkins the Presidential Medal of Freedom with the above citation on the last day of his presidency, January 20, 1969. The medal was delivered by mail at a later date.

The head of the National Association for the Advancement of Colored People (NAACP) for over twenty years, Roy Wilkins was born in Saint Louis, Missouri, in 1901. Raised by his aunt and uncle in Saint Paul after his mother died, he attended integrated schools and graduated from the University of Minnesota in 1923, having studied sociology and journalism. The lynching of a black man in Duluth, Minnesota, while Wilkins was still in college aroused his determination to advance civil rights for blacks.

In 1923 he became a reporter for the *Kansas City Call*, an influential black weekly. He married Aminda Ann Bandeau in 1929. The following year, as the paper's managing editor, he orchestrated a drive to block the reelection of a Kansas senator accused of being a militant racist.

That campaign brought him an offer to work for the NAACP and in 1931 Wilkins became chief assistant to NAACP leader Walter White. By 1934 Wilkins had been arrested for leading a demonstration against lynching at the U.S. attorney general's office and had also taken on the editorship of the NAACP magazine, *The Crisis*. He became administrator of internal affairs at the NAACP in 1950 and was a chief architect of the group's legal attack on school segregation. The resulting landmark Supreme Court ruling, *Brown v. Board of Education* (1954), overturned the long-standing doctrine of separate but equal facilities for blacks and whites.

The following year Wilkins was named overall director of the NAACP and remained in that post for the next twenty-two years, including some of the most tumultuous and productive years of the civil rights movement. As NAACP director he focused the organization's efforts on nonviolent methods to end segregation, using legislation and the courts to achieve equality for blacks. During the 1960s especially, with Wilkins exerting his influence as a civil rights statesman, remarkable progress on civil rights legislation was made.

From the mid–1960s onward, though, Wilkins's policy of working patiently within the system came under fire from black militants and separatists. Eventually, Wilkins himself was forced to take a more militant stance and approved NAACP involvement in direct, albeit nonviolent, action to advance civil rights. The sudden loss of momentum in the civil rights movement in the late 1960s and early 1970s fueled a sometimes acrimonious debate within the NAACP over Wilkins's leadership and policies.

Wilkins finally resigned in 1977, becoming the NAACP director emeritus. He died four years later, at the age of eighty.

Whitney M. Young, Jr.

WHITNEY M. YOUNG, JR., HAS LIVED HIS LIFE TO REDEEM THE PROMISE OF HIS COUNTRY—EQUALITY FOR ALL AMERICANS. A FIGHTER TO MAKE HIS DREAMS COME TRUE, A MAN OF ACTION WHO HAS LABORED TO ACHIEVE HIS IDEALS, HIS ENTIRE CAREER HAS BEEN AN AFFIRMATION OF WHAT ONE MAN'S DEDICATION TO THE GOAL OF THE BETTER, MORE JUST AMERICA CAN ACCOMPLISH. THE PRESIDENT AND THE CONGRESS, AS WELL AS ALL THE PEOPLE, HAVE BEEN THE BENEFICIARIES OF HIS COMPASSION AND CONCERN.

★ ★ ★

President Lyndon B. Johnson awarded Young the Presidential Medal of Freedom with the above citation on the last day of his presidency, January 20, 1969. The medal was delivered by mail at a later date.

The head of the National Urban League during the 1960s, Whitney M. Young, Jr., was born at Lincoln Ridge, Kentucky, in 1921. His father was the president of a private boarding school for blacks, and his mother was a teacher. A strong student, Young finished high school at the age of fifteen and went on to get his bachelor's degree from Kentucky State Industrial College, then the leading higher education facility for blacks in Kentucky. Young graduated first in his class in 1941.

While serving in the army during World War II, Young married Margaret Buckner and also decided on a career in social work. He earned his master's degree in that discipline at the University of Minnesota in 1947 and that same year joined the Saint Paul Urban League staff. He soon began focusing, with substantial success, on increasing job opportunities for blacks in Saint Paul. That led to his being hired as director of the Omaha, Nebraska, Urban League in 1950. There he worked on desegregating public housing and increasing the number of black teachers in the public schools, as well as on opening up employment for blacks.

Later he served as dean of the Atlanta University School of Social Work (1954–1960) and as an organizer of the Atlanta Committee for Cooperative Action. He was on fellowship at Harvard University when the National Urban League named him its director in 1961.

The next ten years were both chaotic and crucial to the civil rights movement. Meanwhile, under Young's leadership, the Urban League grew substantially, in size, in the number of professional staffers (up fourfold), and in its budget (up tenfold). The organization became a key nongovernment force in the civil rights movement, directed toward getting blacks into jobs.

Young made the Urban League a cosponsor of the 1963 March on Washington and played a role in organizing the protest. He also proved singularly able to get the corporate establishment to support the civil rights movement and his goal of more jobs for blacks. Young repeatedly urged a domestic "Marshall Plan" for America as a solution to race problems, an idea that found expression in President Johnson's War on Poverty.

Young, who worked closely with President Johnson, served on seven presidential commissions and also wrote two books, *To Be Equal* (1964) and *Beyond Racism* (1969). He died unexpectedly in 1971 of an apparent cerebral hemorrhage. Young was just forty-nine years old.

Richard Nixon

RICHARD NIXON, A REPUBLICAN, WAS ELECTED TO SERVE
TWO TERMS (1969–1973, 1973–1977) IN OFFICE. HE
RESIGNED THE PRESIDENCY ON AUGUST 9, 1974.

MEDAL
CEREMONIES

APRIL 29, 1969 *The White House East Room*

AUGUST 13, 1969 *Century Plaza Hotel, Los Angeles*

JANUARY 24, 1970 *Philadelphia Academy of Music*

APRIL 18, 1970 *Houston, Texas; Honolulu, Hawaii*

APRIL 22, 1970 *The White House East Room*

MARCH 27, 1971 *Beverly Hills, California*

JUNE 2, 1971 *The White House*

SEPTEMBER 29, 1971 *The White House East Room*

JANUARY 28, 1972 *The White House East Room*

JUNE 16, 1972 *The White House*

MARCH 31, 1973 *Beverly Hills, California*

OCTOBER 15, 1973 *The White House East Room*

MARCH 26, 1974 *The White House East Room*

JUNE 21, 1974 *New York, New York*

JULY 27, 1974 *San Clemente, California*

Duke Ellington

Edward Kennedy Ellington, pianist, composer, and orchestra leader, has long enhanced American music with his unique style, his intelligence, his impeccable taste. For more than 40 years he has helped to expand the frontiers of jazz, while at the same time retaining in his music the individuality and freedom of expression that are the soul of jazz. In the royalty of American music, no man swings more or stands higher than the Duke.

★ ★ ★

President Richard Nixon awarded Ellington the Presidential Medal of Freedom with the above citation during a White House ceremony April 29, 1969.

Probably the most important and prolific jazz composer of all time, Duke Ellington wrote some two-thousand works, among them hit songs, instrumentals, orchestral suites, musical comedies, and film scores. He was born Edward Kennedy Ellington in Washington, D.C., in 1899. Nicknamed "Duke" by a grade school classmate because of his formal manner, Ellington started piano lessons at age seven.

For a time he was more interested in sports and in art, which he studied at Armstrong High School in Washington. But while still in high school, Ellington attended performances by local pianists and suddenly began studying music more seriously. It was during these years that he first performed professionally, as a solo ragtime pianist at the Washington True Reformers Hall.

By 1914 he was a substitute pianist at the Poodle Dog Cafe and that year composed his first song, "Soda Fountain Rag." Soon after came his first composition with lyrics: "What Are You Going to do When the Bed Breaks Down?" Stints at local hotels and theaters and with area bands brought Ellington into contact with many contemporary jazz musicians, and he formed his first group, the Duke's Serenaders, in 1918. That same year he married Edna Thompson.

By the early 1920s he had established his reputation as a ragtime musician and in 1923 moved from Washington to New York City. Three years later his band made its first significant recording, "East St. Louis Toodle-oo." With his popularity growing, he and his group played Harlem's famous Cotton Club between 1927 and 1931. Radio broadcasts of these performances and the success of his recordings soon brought Ellington and his orchestra nationwide fame. Meanwhile, he separated from his wife in 1930.

The 1930s and early 1940s marked Ellington's most creative period. He established a popular musical "jungle style" and with his band enlarged to fourteen musicians recorded some of his best songs, including "Mood Indigo" (1930), "Sophisticated Lady" (1932), "In a Sentimental Mood" (1935), "Black and Tan Fantasy" (1938), and "Take the 'A' Train" (1941). "Take the 'A' Train" eventually became his band's theme song. These and his other songs were marked by the so-called Ellington effect, his gift for working with unusual instrumental groupings, and tonal effects. As a serious composer, Ellington also extended the accepted boundaries of jazz compositions, such as in "Reminiscing in Tempo" (1935) and "Black, Brown, and Beige" (1943).

Ellington began touring regularly in the 1930s, traveling to Europe in 1933 and 1939. In addition to his prolific career as a songwriter and orchestra leader, Ellington also composed scores for musicals, television, and ballet. During the 1960s he began writing religious music.

Ellington published his autobiography, *Music Is My Mistress,* in 1973 and died the following year. He was seventy-five years old.

Edwin E. "Buzz" Aldrin

As a member of the crew of the United States spacecraft Apollo Eleven, he participated directly in a unique and profoundly important adventure. The accumulated scientific knowledge and technological ability of mankind made man's first step on the moon practicable; the courage and skill of men like Buzz Aldrin made it possible. His contribution to this great undertaking will be remembered so long as men wander and dream and search for truth on this planet and among the stars.

★ ★ ★

(Note: The same wording was used in medal citations presented to Neil Armstrong and Michael Collins.) President Richard Nixon awarded Aldrin the Presidential Medal of Freedom with the above citation during a ceremony at the Century Plaza Hotel in Los Angeles on August 13, 1969. The medal was accompanied by the additional accolade "with distinction."

The second man to walk on the moon, Buzz Aldrin was born in Montclair, New Jersey, in 1930. He graduated third in his class from West Point in 1951, and after becoming an air force fighter pilot, he flew combat missions during the Korean War. The air force awarded him its Distinguished Flying Cross for his combat service.

Aldrin was selected for the astronaut program in 1963 after

earning his doctorate in astronautics from Massachusetts Institute of Technology. His first trip into outer space was the four-day *Gemini 12* mission in November 1966. He set a record by successfully completing a five-and-one-half-hour spacewalk during the flight and piloted his spacecraft during a successful docking exercise. But his crowning achievement came as a member of the three-man *Apollo 11* mission that put the first men on the moon.

Aldrin, flight commander Neil Armstrong, and fellow astronaut Michael Collins took off for the moon aboard the *Apollo 11* spacecraft July 16, 1969. Four days later they achieved moon orbit. While Collins remained in the orbiting mothership, Aldrin and Armstrong took the lunar lander down to the moon on July 20. Aldrin piloted the lander to a soft landing and Armstrong became the first man to walk on the moon. Nineteen minutes later though, Aldrin joined him on the moon's surface, observing the moonscape was one of "magnificent desolation." After about two hours of walking about, collecting samples, and performing other chores, the two astronauts clambered back aboard the lunar lander and returned to the orbiting spacecraft. Aldrin, Collins, and Armstrong returned safely to earth July 24, 1969, completing the historic first flight to the moon. *(See also entries for Armstrong, below, and Collins, p. 175.)*

Aldrin retired from the space program in 1971 and from the air force in 1972. Adjustment to life outside the space program proved difficult for Aldrin, who later successfully underwent therapy for severe depression and alcoholism. Since then he has been involved in business and has worked as an aerospace consultant. He married his third wife, the former Beverly Van Zile, in 1988. His two earlier marriages had ended in divorce. Aldrin has collaborated on books about the space program, including the recent *Men from Earth,* published in 1989.

Neil Alden Armstrong

For citation, see Edwin E. "Buzz" Aldrin, *p. 172.*

★ ★ ★

The first to man walk on the moon, Neil Armstrong led the three-man *Apollo 11* crew on its history-making trip to the moon and back in 1969. Armstrong and his fellow astronauts will always be remembered as the first explorers who traveled to another heavenly body beyond earth, but in fact they also collected important scientific data while on the moon, including soil and rock samples that shed light on the moon's origins.

Neil Alden Armstrong was born in 1930 on a farm near Wapakoneta, Ohio. Armstrong developed an early interest in aviation.

He took his first airplane ride at age six, started taking flying lessons at fourteen, and earned his pilot's license at sixteen. During the Korean War Armstrong flew seventy-eight combat missions and was awarded three Air Medals. After graduating from Purdue University with an aeronautical engineering degree in 1955, he married Janet Shearon.

Armstrong became a civilian research pilot in 1955, test flying various supersonic fighter jets and the experimental X–15 rocket-plane. Then in 1962 the National Aeronautics and Space Administration (NASA) selected him for the astronaut program.

Armstrong commanded the *Gemini 8* mission in March 1966 and during the flight performed the first-ever manual docking maneuver in space with another orbiting craft (an Agena rocket). After the maneuver a malfunctioning thruster rocket sent the docked *Gemini* craft into a dangerously erratic spin, but Armstrong managed to safely undock his craft, stabilize it, and bring it safely back to earth for an emergency landing.

His greatest achievement remains the *Apollo 11* moon mission, however. With astronauts Buzz Aldrin and Michael Collins, he left earth aboard the rocket ship on July 16, 1969. Their spacecraft soon reached moon orbit, and on July 20 Armstrong and Aldrin went down to the moon's surface aboard *Eagle*, the lunar lander, while Collins remained behind in the orbiting spacecraft. Armstrong and Aldrin landed on the moon at 4:17 P.M. Eastern Daylight Time. Almost seven hours later, while millions of people on earth watched via a live satellite television broadcast, Armstrong became the first man to set foot on the moon. As the boot of his spacesuit sank into the moon's dusty surface, he spoke the now famous words, "That's one small step for man, one giant leap for mankind." Joined soon after by Aldrin, the two explored the surface, before taking *Eagle* back up to the orbiting mothership.

They returned to a hero's welcome on earth, splashing down in the Pacific on July 24.

President Richard Nixon, who greeted them aboard the recovery ship, also arranged to award Armstrong, Aldrin, and Collins Medals of Freedom after their postflight processing. Armstrong left NASA in 1971 and for the next eight years taught aerospace engineering at the University of Cincinnati. Between 1979 and 1992 he served as a corporate board chairman. *(See also entries for Aldrin, p. 172, and Collins, p. 175.)*

Michael Collins

For citation, see Edwin E. "Buzz" Aldrin, *p. 172.*

★ ★ ★

Michael Collins was born in 1930 in Rome, Italy, where his father, a U.S. Army general, was serving as a military attaché. His family moved back to the United States during his youth, relocating several times before settling in Washington, D.C. After graduating from West Point in 1952, Collins joined the air force and eventually became a test pilot at Edwards Air Force Base. He married Patricia M. Finnegan in 1957. Five years later NASA accepted him for its astronaut training program.

The three-day *Gemini 10* mission in July 1966 marked his first flight into space, and Collins completed two spacewalks before returning to earth. His second spaceflight, aboard *Apollo 11*, was by far his most memorable achievement in space.

Collins never actually set foot on the moon. While fellow astronauts Neil Armstrong and Buzz Aldrin maneuvered down to the moon's surface aboard the lunar lander, he remained in command of the spaceship *Columbia*, which stayed in moon orbit until time came for the trip back to earth. They received a hero's welcome after splashdown in the Pacific. President Nixon, who greeted them aboard the recovery ship USS *Hornet* arranged to award all three Presidential Medals of Freedom after their postflight processing. *(See also entries for Aldrin, p. 172, and Armstrong, p. 173.)*

Like Armstrong and Aldrin, Collins left NASA soon after the *Apollo 11* mission and for two years served as assistant secretary of state for public affairs. Between 1971 and 1980 he was an administrator at the Smithsonian Institution in Washington, D.C., and from 1980 to 1985 worked as a vice president for an aerospace company. Since then he has been an aerospace consultant. Collins has published four books about his NASA experiences and space exploration, including his autobiography *Carrying the Fire* (1974), *Liftoff* (1988), and *Mission to Mars* (1990).

Eugene Ormandy

FROM EARLY CHILDHOOD HE HAS POSSESSED SUPERB MUSICAL GIFTS. FOR THIRTY-FOUR YEARS HE HAS BROUGHT THESE GIFTS TO THE CONDUCTING OF THE PHILADELPHIA ORCHESTRA, A NAME SYNONYMOUS WITH EXCELLENCE IN MUSIC. YET HE BRINGS TO EACH PERFORMANCE SOMETHING MORE PRECIOUS THAN HIS GREAT GIFTS; HE BRINGS HIMSELF. FROM THE RICH EXPERIENCES OF HIS LIFE IN MUSIC HE HAS FASHIONED A UNIQUE AND UNFORGETTABLE ORCHESTRAL SOUND, THE SOUND OF ORMANDY. HE HAS REMINDED AUDIENCES HERE IN HIS ADOPTED COUNTRY AND ALL OVER THE WORLD THAT THE HEART OF MUSIC IS A HUMAN HEART AND THAT THE GLORY OF MUSIC REFLECTS AND SUSTAINS THE TRUE GLORY OF THE HUMAN SPIRIT.

★ ★ ★

President Richard Nixon awarded Ormandy the Presidential Medal of Freedom with the above citation during a ceremony at the Philadelphia Academy of Music on January 24, 1970.

A child prodigy on the violin, Ormandy was born Jeno Ormandy Blau in Budapest, Hungary, in 1899. His father had already decided that if the baby turned out to be a boy he would be named after the famed Hungarian violinist Jeno (Eugene) Hubay. While still a toddler, Ormandy played a one-eighth-sized fiddle his parents had made for him, and at age five, he became the youngest pupil at the Royal Academy of Music in Budapest.

The boy gave his first public performance at age seven and, after studying under Hubay, earned his master's degree from the Royal Academy at age fourteen. Ormandy continued his studies and three years later became a professor of music. Meanwhile, the violin virtuoso also gave performances on tours in Germany and Austria.

Lured to the United States in 1920 with promises of a lucrative concert tour that did not materialize, Ormandy found himself stranded in New York City. Stories have it that the twenty-one-year-old virtuoso had only one nickel left when he applied for a job playing violin in a movie orchestra at the Capitol Theater. Luckily, he got the position and spent the next nine years with the orchestra, which provided accompaniment for silent films.

Ironically, the years at the Capitol Theater proved fruitful for Ormandy. There he met Stephanie Goldner, a harpist in the orchestra, whom he married in 1922. Three years later Ormandy got his start as a conductor at the Capitol Theater as well. Because of an emergency, managers asked him to conduct Tchaikovsky's Fourth

Symphony, giving him just a few minutes' notice. Ormandy rose to the occasion and afterward decided conducting was his true calling. The orchestra, he had discovered, was an instrument "richer and more responsive than the violin."

Ormandy, who became a U.S. citizen in 1925, had ample opportunity to develop his talents as a conductor in the ensuing years. Between 1925 and 1929 he conducted the Capitol Theater's movie orchestra in four or five performances daily, often repeating the same work twenty times a week. Ultimately, he performed the better part of all symphonic music while at the Capitol Theater and, at the same time, also began conducting classical music on radio and at summer concerts.

Having conducted the New York Philharmonic for a concert the previous year, Ormandy in 1931 got his big break. The great Italian conductor Arturo Toscanini had fallen ill and could not conduct the Philadelphia Orchestra as planned during a series of concerts. Ormandy once again stepped in on short notice, and his performance landed him a contract as conductor of the Minneapolis Symphony Orchestra.

He began his long association with the Philadelphia Orchestra in 1936, starting out as a codirector alongside the famed conductor Leopold Stokowski. The Philadelphia Orchestra was then among the world's great ensembles, and over the next two years Ormandy gradually assumed control. In 1938 he became the orchestra's sole director and from then until his retirement in 1980 maintained its international reputation for instrumental virtuosity and perfection of ensemble. But Ormandy, a masterful orchestra technician who achieved a remarkable homogeneity of tone, also injected his personal stamp on the orchestra, creating what became the orchestra's trademark lush, velvety string sound—the so-called Ormandy sound.

Ormandy led the Philadelphia Orchestra on numerous tours of the United States, Europe, and Latin America. He also conducted the orchestra on a historic tour of China in 1973. The orchestra made hundreds of recordings under his direction as well, including many symphonic classics and albums with the Mormon Tabernacle Choir. Meanwhile, in 1950 he married his second wife, Margaret Frances Hitch, having divorced his first wife in 1947.

In 1984, four years after his retirement, he led the Philadelphia Orchestra in his last concert, a performance at Carnegie Hall featuring works by Beethoven and Bartók. He died the following year, at age eighty-five.

Apollo 13 Mission Operations Team

WE OFTEN SPEAK OF SCIENTIFIC "MIRACLES"—FORGETTING THAT THESE ARE NOT MIRACULOUS HAPPENINGS AT ALL, BUT RATHER THE PRODUCT OF HARD WORK, LONG HOURS AND DISCIPLINED INTELLIGENCE. THE MEN AND WOMEN OF THE APOLLO 13 MISSION OPERATIONS TEAM PERFORMED SUCH A MIRACLE, TRANSFORMING POTENTIAL TRAGEDY INTO ONE OF THE MOST DRAMATIC RESCUES OF ALL TIME. YEARS OF INTENSE PREPARATION MADE THIS RESCUE POSSIBLE. THE SKILL, COORDINATION AND PERFORMANCE UNDER PRESSURE OF THE MISSION OPERATIONS TEAM MADE IT HAPPEN. THREE BRAVE ASTRONAUTS ARE ALIVE AND ON EARTH BECAUSE OF THEIR DEDICATION, AND BECAUSE AT THE CRITICAL MOMENTS THE PEOPLE OF THAT TEAM WERE WISE ENOUGH AND SELF-POSSESSED ENOUGH TO MAKE THE RIGHT DECISIONS. THEIR EXTRAORDINARY FEAT IS A TRIBUTE TO MAN'S INGENUITY, TO HIS RESOURCEFULNESS AND TO HIS COURAGE.

★ ★ ★

President Richard Nixon the awarded Apollo 13 *mission operations team the Presidential Medal of Freedom with the above citation during a ceremony in Houston, Texas, April 18, 1970. He then flew on to Hawaii, where he awarded the* Apollo 13 *astronauts with their own Medals of Freedom.*

Apollo 13, the third United States manned moon landing mission, had nearly completed a seemingly routine flight from the earth to the moon when on April 13, 1970, an explosion and massive power failure suddenly put the astronauts' lives in jeopardy. An oxygen tank in the spacecraft's service module had burst, blowing out the side of the module. Though the command capsule and attached lunar lander remained intact, the rupture cut oxygen supplies to the astronauts and to the fuel cells, which were used for generating electrical power.

Nearly 205,000 miles from earth and still hurtling toward the moon, astronauts James A. Lovell, Jr., Fred W. Haise, Jr., and John L. Swigert, Jr., suddenly found themselves with severely limited reserves of electrical power and oxygen. While ground controllers desperately worked out the quickest way to bring *Apollo 13* safely back to earth, the astronauts scrambled to conserve power by shutting down systems and then crawled into the lunar lander module, which had its own oxygen supply.

Tense days followed as the astronauts used an orbit around the moon to send their craft speeding back to earth. Fortunately, the rockets and systems for controlling them still functioned, and mid-course firings brought the damaged spacecraft into the proper reentry course. Freeing the command capsule from the lunar lander and wrecked service module remained a nagging question, however. Reentry with them still attached would have almost certainly ended in disaster. But as earth loomed before the spacecraft on the crucial day of April 17, the astronauts sealed themselves inside the command capsule with a small supply of oxygen and safely jettisoned both the service module and the lunar lander. Soon after, the command capsule streaked through earth's atmosphere to a safe splashdown in the Pacific Ocean.

A day later President Nixon awarded the *Apollo 13* mission operations team the Medal of Freedom for its impressive display of ingenuity and resourcefulness during the crisis. While recognizing the role thousands of other ground personnel played in getting the astronauts safely back to earth, President Nixon presented the medal to Sigurd A. Sjoberg, director of flight operations, and the other members of the *Apollo 13* mission operations team: Glynn Lunney, Milt Windler, Gerald Griffin, and Gene Kranz. The ceremony was held at the Manned Spacecraft Center in Houston, Texas. *(See also entries for Haise, below, Lovell, p. 181, and Swigert, p. 182.)*

Fred Wallace Haise, Jr.

ADVERSITY BRINGS OUT THE CHARACTER OF A MAN. CONFRONTED SUDDENLY AND UNEXPECTEDLY WITH GRAVE PERIL IN THE FAR REACHES OF SPACE, HE DEMONSTRATED A CALM COURAGE AND QUIET HEROISM THAT STAND AS AN EXAMPLE TO MEN EVERYWHERE. HIS SAFE RETURN IS A TRIUMPH OF THE HUMAN SPIRIT—OF THOSE SPECIAL QUALITIES OF MAN HIMSELF WE RELY ON WHEN MACHINES FAIL, AND THAT WE RELY ON ALSO FOR THOSE THINGS THAT MACHINES CANNOT DO. FROM THE START, THE EXPLORATION OF SPACE HAS BEEN HAZARDOUS ADVENTURE. THE VOYAGE OF APOLLO 13 DRA-MATIZED ITS RISKS. THE MEN OF APOLLO 13, BY THEIR POISE AND SKILL UNDER THE MOST INTENSE KIND OF PRESSURE, EPIT-OMIZED THE CHARACTER THAT ACCEPTS DANGER AND SUR-MOUNTS IT. THEIRS IS THE SPIRIT THAT BUILT AMERICA. WITH

GRATITUDE AND ADMIRATION, AMERICA SALUTES THEIR SPIRIT
AND ACHIEVEMENT.

★ ★ ★

*(Note: The same wording was used in medal citations presented to
James A. Lovell, Jr., and John Leonard Swigert, Jr.) President Richard
Nixon awarded Haise the Presidential Medal of Freedom with the above
citation during a ceremony in Honolulu, Hawaii, April 18, 1970.*

Born in Biloxi, Mississippi, in 1933, Fred Haise had had extensive
training as a military pilot even though he was a civilian when he
became an astronaut. A naval-aviation cadet from 1952 to 1954, he
served as a marine corps fighter pilot between 1954 and 1956 and was
a member of the air national guard from 1957 to 1963. He married
Mary Griffin Grant in 1954.

Though he again served briefly in the military, this time as an Air
Force captain (1961–1962), Haise worked mainly as a research pilot
for NASA from 1959 onward, and in 1966 NASA selected him for its
astronaut program. Haise had never been in space before when he
became a last-minute replacement for an *Apollo 13* crewman who had
come down with measles.

Joining fellow astronaut John L. Swigert and mission commander
James A. Lovell, Haise blasted off from earth on April 11, 1970, on
what seemed a routine flight to the moon. But just minutes after a
regular communication with Houston ground control—ironically on
April 13—the Apollo spacecraft was shaken by an explosion that
wrecked part of the service module.

With *Apollo 13* almost 205,000 miles from earth and still hurtling
toward the moon, Haise radioed Houston with the ominously under-
stated message, "We've got a problem." In fact, the spacecraft's air and
electrical supply were sharply reduced by the blast, but Haise and his
fellow astronauts managed to bring *Apollo 13* safely back to earth on
April 17, arriving to a hero's welcome. *(See also entries for the Apollo 13
Operations Mission Team, p. 178, Lovell, p. 181, and Swigert, p. 182.)*

Haise stayed on with NASA until 1979, serving as a backup com-
mander for *Apollo 16* in 1972 and as commander of the space shuttle
Orbiter crew from 1977 to 1979. An executive at Grumman Aerospace
Corporation since 1979, he is now president of Grumman Technical
Services, a Grumman division located in Titusville, Florida.

James A. Lovell, Jr.

For citation, see FRED WALLACE HAISE, JR., *p. 179.*

★ ★ ★

An astronaut with both the Gemini and Apollo space programs, James Lovell was born in Cleveland, Ohio, in 1928. He was an only child, as were nearly all the astronauts selected early in the U.S. space program, and grew up in Milwaukee, Wisconsin. After completing two years at the University of Wisconsin, Lovell entered the U.S. Naval Academy, from which he graduated in 1952 with a bachelor's degree. He married high school classmate Marilyn Gerlach the day he graduated.

For the next several years Lovell served as a navy test pilot and flight instructor, logging over four-thousand hours of flying time. NASA selected him for the astronaut program in 1962 and three years later launched him on his first spaceflight, aboard *Gemini 7*. With fellow astronaut Frank Borman, Lovell stayed aloft for what was then a record-making fourteen-day spaceflight. During the flight they rendezvoused with another space capsule, the first such meeting in space of two U.S. manned vehicles and only the second space rendezvous in history. Lovell went up into space again for four days in 1966 aboard *Gemini 12*, the last flight in the Gemini series.

Two years later he joined Borman and William Anders on the *Apollo 8* flight, the first of three flights leading up to an actual manned moon landing. On December 24, 1968, Lovell and his fellow astronauts became the first men in history to orbit the moon and to see firsthand the moon's dark side. *Apollo 8* orbited the moon ten times before returning safely to earth.

The 1970 *Apollo 13* mission, with Lovell as commander and astronauts Fred Haise and John Swigert aboard, was to be the third U.S. manned moon landing. Everything appeared to be going smoothly after the launch, but about 205,000 miles from earth an explosion rocked the *Apollo 13* spacecraft's service module. With their oxygen and electrical power reserves dangerously reduced, the *Apollo 13* crew faced the frightening possibility they might not be able to get back to earth.

But with NASA ground control feeding them information and instructions, Lovell and his fellow crewmen calmly maneuvered the spacecraft to swing around the moon and head back to earth. Four days later, Lovell, Haise, and Swigert endured tense moments during reentry before arriving safely on earth to a hero's welcome. *(See also entries for the Apollo 13 Operations Mission Team, p. 178, Haise, p. 179, and Swigert, p. 182.)*

Lovell spent the next two years as deputy director of the Johnson Space Center in Houston. Retiring from the space program and the navy in 1973, he became a corporate executive. In 1994 he wrote *Lost Moon: The Perilous Voyage of Apollo 13* with Jeffrey Kluger. The book was adapted into a hit movie.

John Leonard Swigert, Jr.

For citation, see FRED WALLACE HAISE, JR., *p. 179.*

★ ★ ★

The command module pilot for the *Apollo 13* mission, John Swigert was born in Denver, Colorado, in 1931. He went on to graduate from the University of Colorado in 1953 with a bachelor of science degree in mechanical engineering and served the next three years in the air force as a fighter pilot. Swigert saw combat during the Korean War and once narrowly escaped being killed when his jet crashed.

Leaving the air force, Swigert became a civilian test pilot for North American Aviation in 1956. In 1965 he earned his master's degree in aerospace science at Rensselaer Polytechnic Institute and two years later got his business degree from the University of Hartford. Meanwhile, NASA selected him for astronaut training in 1966. Two years later he served as a support crew member for the *Apollo 7* mission, one of the several test flights leading up to the *Apollo 11* moon landing the following year.

Originally designated as a backup crewman, Swigert had became command module pilot for the *Apollo 13* lead crew by the time the mission was launched in 1970. It was to be the third manned moon mission. With flight commander James Lovell, fellow astronaut Fred Haise, and Swigert aboard, *Apollo 13* was heading toward the moon two days later when an oxygen tank in the spacecraft's service module exploded.

The astronauts were unharmed, but their electric power and oxygen supplies had been reduced to dangerously low levels. While ground controllers desperately worked out the quickest way to bring *Apollo 13* back to earth, the astronauts scrambled to conserve power by shutting down all but the most necessary lunar lander module, which had its own oxygen supply.

Eventually, Swigert and his fellow astronauts used an orbit around the moon to hurtle *Apollo 13* back to earth. They received a hero's welcome upon their safe landing four days later. *(See also entries for the Apollo 13 Operations Mission Team, p. 178, Lovell, p. 181, and Haise, p. 179.)*

Three years after the return to earth of *Apollo 13* Swigert left NASA to become the executive director of the House Science and Technology Committee staff, a post he held until 1979. He then worked as a corporate executive in private business and in 1980 won a seat in the U.S. House of Representatives as a Republican from Colorado. Swigert, a lifelong bachelor, had been undergoing treatment for cancer, however. Just one week before his congressional term was to begin in early 1981, he succumbed to the disease. Swigert was forty-nine years old.

Earl C. Behrens

THROUGH ALMOST FIFTY YEARS AS A REPORTER, HE HAS SHOWN THAT A GREAT NEWSPAPERMAN IS ONE WHO COMBINES INEXHAUSTIBLE ENERGY WITH INSATIABLE CURIOSITY AND IMPECCABLE JUDGMENT. HE HAS BECOME A LEGEND AMONG POLITICAL REPORTERS NOT ONLY FOR HIS GREAT SKILL BUT ALSO FOR FAIRNESS, UNFAILING GOOD HUMOR AND CONSISTENT GOOD SENSE. IT HAS BEEN WRITTEN OF HIM THAT HIS "MIND AND HEART HAVE BEEN CLOSE TO POLITICS AND POLITICAL PEOPLE." HIS SOURCES AND HIS READERS HAVE LONG RECOGNIZED THAT HIS MIND AND HIS HEART HAVE ALSO BEEN DEVOTED TO TRUTH, TO INTEGRITY, AND PROFESSIONALISM OF THE HIGHEST ORDER.

★ ★ ★

President Richard Nixon awarded Behrens the Presidential Medal of Freedom with the above citation during a White House ceremony April 22, 1970.

The *San Francisco Chronicle* political editor for over fifty years, Earl Behrens was born in 1892, the son of a merchant and Wells Fargo agent in Shasta, California. Called "Squire" during high school—a nickname that stayed with him for the rest of his life—Behrens graduated from Stanford University in 1914. World War I interrupted his graduate studies at the University of California in Berkeley, and Behrens was seriously wounded by a land mine during his tour with the U.S. Expeditionary Force in Siberia.

His career as a journalist began in 1921 at the now-defunct *San Francisco Journal,* but by 1923 he had moved to the *Chronicle,* where he remained for the rest of his career. At the *Chronicle* Behrens covered every major national political convention between 1924 and 1972 and gained a nationwide reputation for his skilled political reporting. His sense of fairness and courtesy also won him many friends among the politicians he covered. He married the fashion consultant Bernice Woodard in 1963, his first wife having died in 1954.

President Nixon chose Behrens to be one of eight outstanding American journalists to receive the Presidential Medal of Freedom in 1970. Four years later, at age eighty-two, Behrens finally decided to retire from the *Chronicle.*

During his long career, he wrote numerous magazine articles and the "Political Primer for Americans," which in 1948 won the American Heritage Foundation Award. Squire Behrens died in 1985, at age ninety-three.

Edward T. Folliard

BORN IN WASHINGTON, D.C., THE NATION'S CAPITAL HAS BEEN HIS WORKING BASE THROUGHOUT A LONG AND DISTINGUISHED PROFESSIONAL CAREER. HIS KEEN INSIGHTS INTO THE LIFE AND POLITICS OF THE NATION'S CAPITAL HAVE BEEN MATCHED BY A PERCEPTIVE UNDERSTANDING OF THE BROADER AMERICAN SCENE, AND OF INTERNATIONAL AFFAIRS. COMBINING A DETERMINED CURIOSITY WITH ENERGY, INTEGRITY AND SKILL, HE HAS WON THE ADMIRATION OF HIS COLLEAGUES AND CONTRIBUTED GREATLY TO THE ENLIGHTENMENT OF THREE GENERATIONS OF READERS.

★ ★ ★

President Richard Nixon awarded Folliard the Presidential Medal of Freedom with the above citation during a White House ceremony April 22, 1970.

A Pulitzer Prize-winning reporter for the *Washington Post,* Edward T. Folliard was born in 1899 in Georgetown, a Washington, D.C., neighborhood. The son of Irish immigrant parents, he was raised in Washington and had his first brush with journalism as a copy boy for International News Service's Washington bureau from 1916 to 1917. During World War I he served in the navy, survived the sinking of his ship in the English Channel, and wrote some articles for the armed services newspaper, *Stars and Stripes.*

Returning to civilian life Folliard landed his first job as a reporter in 1922 with the Washington *Herald,* even though he had not attended college. A year later he moved to the *Washington Post,* where he remained for the rest of his newspaper career. Working his way up from the *Post*'s police beat reporter, he eventually did local, national, and international reporting. As a White House reporter for the *Post,* he covered the presidents from Calvin Coolidge to Lyndon B. Johnson, as well as political conventions and presidential election campaigns.

Once, when an interviewer asked about his qualifications for his demanding job at the *Post,* he quipped that he had "a natural Irish curiosity, two long wiry legs, and a firm resolve never to write a story the boys back in Foggy Bottom couldn't understand." Folliard had in fact taken some classes at George Washington University during the 1920s, but he never completed his degree. Nevertheless, he learned to write effectively on a wide range of subjects. He covered crime stories like the 1936 electrocution of Bruno Hauptman in the Lindbergh kidnapping case; reported on the national political scene; interviewed the likes of Winston Churchill, Madame Chiang Kai-shek, and the future Pope Pius XII; and gave firsthand reports from the European front during World War II.

Folliard's story about the U.S. Marines' heroic stand against Japanese attacks on Wake Island shortly after Pearl Harbor was praised widely and broadcast around the world. But it was his 1946 series about an Atlanta, Georgia, hate group—the Columbians—that won him the 1947 Pulitzer Prize for reporting. His articles attacked the white supremacists' ideology of hate and eventually helped put the group's founders behind bars.

Folliard, who married Helen Liston in 1933, reported for the *Post* for over four decades. He retired in 1966 and died ten years later, at age seventy-seven.

William M. Henry

HE PROUDLY CLAIMED BUT ONE TITLE: REPORTER. THE MANY THOUSANDS WHO READ HIS COLUMN, AND LISTENED TO HIS BROADCASTS KNEW THAT HE WAS ONE OF THE BEST REPORTERS, AND MORE. A NEWSPAPERMAN SINCE 1911, AND A PIONEER OF BROADCAST JOURNALISM NEARLY HALF A CENTURY AGO, HE COVERED SPORTS, POLITICS AND ALL THE RICH VARIETY OF HUMAN ACTIVITY THAT IS NEWS. HIS COLUMN "BY THE WAY" BECAME AN INSTITUTION AMONG CALIFORNIANS. HE BROUGHT TO HIS WORK A UNIQUE TALENT, A WARM LOVE OF HUMANITY, AN UNFAILING FAIRNESS, AND A DEVOTED PROFESSIONAL'S RESPECT FOR HIS CRAFT.

★ ★ ★

President Richard Nixon awarded Henry a posthumous Presidential Medal of Freedom with the above citation during a White House ceremony April 22, 1970. Henry's grandson, Robert McHargue, accepted the medal on his behalf.

The son of a traveling Baptist evangelist, Bill Henry was born in San Francisco in 1890. He grew up attending various schools as his father traveled around the country (and occasionally to Europe) and graduated from Occidental College in 1911. While still in college, he began writing articles for the *Los Angeles Times* and after graduating became a staff sportswriter. Henry married Corinne Stanton in 1914.

He soon branched out to cover other areas for the *Times* besides sports, including aviation, music, drama, and motion pictures. He was among the first movie columnists, and he became the first Sunday editor of the *Times*. Named sports editor in 1933, he began writing a regular sports column, "Bill Henry Says," and also started doing news broadcasts for a radio station opened by the *Times*.

While continuing with the *Times*, Henry was involved in other work as well. He helped organize the Douglas Aircraft Company after World War I and also had a hand in setting up Western Air Express, an early airline. In 1932 he served as technical director and announcer for the Olympic Games at Los Angeles.

His best known work was his column on the Washington political scene, "By the Way," which he began writing in 1939. For the next thirty years he wrote three columns a week, and his plainspoken, nonpartisan approach made it one of the most widely read features in the *Times*. Meanwhile, Henry continued working as a radio newscaster and later as a television news commentator, eventually doing work for three major networks. There were times when Henry provided newspaper coverage and also recorded television and radio material all in the same day—as happened at the 1952 nominating conventions for the presidential election.

Illness forced Henry to cut back his column from three times a week to once weekly in 1969. The following year he received word from President Nixon that he had been chosen to receive the Presidential Medal of Freedom. Sadly, he died about a week before the White House ceremony. Henry was seventy-nine years old.

Arthur Krock

FROM THE POLICE BEAT IN LOUISVILLE TO A POSITION OF THE HIGHEST EMINENCE AMONG THE WORLD'S JOURNALISTS, HE BUILT A REPUTATION THAT MADE HIS NAME SYNONYMOUS WITH EXCELLENCE AND INTEGRITY. HIS INCISIVE REPORTING, PERCEPTIVE ANALYSIS, SOUND JUDGMENT AND SUBTLE HUMOR HAVE MADE A UNIQUE CONTRIBUTION TO THE UNDERSTANDING OF THE AMERICAN PROCESS BOTH AT HOME AND ABROAD. IN THE ALL-TIME ROSTER OF GREAT WASHINGTON CORRESPONDENTS—AND IN THE HISTORY OF POLITICAL REPORTING—HIS COLLEAGUES, HIS COMPETITORS, HIS READERS, AND THOSE WHOSE DEEDS HE HAS CHRONICLED, ALL WOULD PLACE HIM IN THE VERY FIRST RANK.

★ ★ ★

President Richard Nixon awarded Krock the Presidential Medal of Freedom with the above citation during a White House ceremony April 22, 1970.

A long-time Washington bureau chief and editorial columnist for the *New York Times*, Arthur Krock was born in the Kentucky town of Glasgow in 1886. The son of a bookkeeper, he proved a good student and in 1904 entered Princeton University. But family financial problems forced him to drop out midway through his first year, and two years later he earned an associate's degree at Lewis Institute in Chicago. Krock landed his first newspaper reporting job with the *Louisville Herald* in 1907 and by 1919 had become editor in chief of the *Louisville Times*. That same year he traveled to Europe to cover the Versailles peace conference ending World War I.

After four years as an editorial writer at Ralph Pulitzer's *New York World*, Krock moved to the *New York Times*, where he would spend the rest of his career. The *Times* named him head of its Washington bureau in 1932, and from that time forward Krock became the dominant figure in the paper's coverage of the federal government as well as one of the most influential Washington insiders from the administration of Franklin D. Roosevelt to that of Lyndon B. Johnson. In addition to administering the bureau, he also wrote lead news stories and from 1933 to 1966 wrote his regular column of commentary, "In the Nation." In 1939 he married his second wife, Martha Granger Blair, his first wife having died the year before.

Krock, a conservative who scrupulously guarded against partisanship in news stories, won his first Pulitzer Prize in 1935 for his coverage of the New Deal. His exclusive interview with President Roosevelt in 1937 broke the story of Roosevelt's ill-fated plan to pack the Supreme Court and won him his second Pulitzer. Another exclusive interview, this time with President Harry S. Truman, won him a citation from the Pulitzer committee (Krock refused an outright award because he was a member of the committee). He won an unprecedented fourth Pulitzer award in 1955, a special citation for distinguished correspondence from Washington.

After retiring from the *Times* in 1966, Krock published several books, including his bestselling *Memoirs: Sixty Years on the Firing Line* (1968), *The Consent of the Governed, and Other Deceits* (1971), and *Myself When Young: Growing Up in the 1890s* (1973). He died in 1974, at age eighty-seven.

David Lawrence

WRITER OF THE FIRST WASHINGTON DISPATCH TO BE SYN-
DICATED NATIONALLY BY WIRE, HE HAS SERVED HIS PROFESSION,
HIS NATION AND HIS AUDIENCES FOR MORE THAN 60 YEARS AS
REPORTER, CORRESPONDENT, NEWS COMMENTATOR, COLUMNIST,
EDITOR AND AUTHOR. SINCE THE DAYS OF WOODROW WILSON'S
PRESIDENCY, HE HAS BEEN RECOGNIZED AS A DISTINGUISHED
INTERPRETER OF THE AMERICAN POLITICAL SCENE. HE HAS WON
AND HELD THE RESPECT OF MILLIONS FOR HIS PERCEPTION, HIS
JUDGEMENT, HIS FAIRNESS, AND HIS DEVOTION TO THE PRIN-
CIPLES ON WHICH AMERICA WAS FOUNDED.

★ ★ ★

*President Richard Nixon awarded Lawrence the Presidential Medal of
Freedom with the above citation during a White House ceremony
April 22, 1970.*

The founder of *U.S. News & World Report,* David Lawrence was born
in Philadelphia on Christmas Day of 1888 and grew up in Buffalo,
New York. He was the son of an immigrant tailor and while still in
high school used his own initiative to gain a foothold in the
newspaper business. After selling photographs of some local sports
heroes to the *Buffalo Express,* he convinced the editors to let him write
general news items during school vacations. Later, at Princeton
University, he helped pay for his education by working for the
Associated Press (AP) wire service as a campus correspondent.

Lawrence got his first big scoop while he was still at Princeton. He
had become friends with Mrs. Grover Cleveland while covering her
husband's illness in early 1908, and when the former president finally
died that summer, she immediately telegraphed Lawrence. He tele-
phoned the AP, which broke the story of Cleveland's death and
rewarded Lawrence with a job during his time off from college.

After graduating from Princeton in 1910, Lawrence went to work
at the AP Washington bureau. He moved to the *New York Evening
Post* in 1916 and became the first Washington correspondent to have
his dispatches syndicated nationally over the wire services. Two years
later he married Ellanor Campbell Hayes.

In 1919 Lawrence formed his first business, the Consolidated Press
Association, which sent out sports, financial, and other information
over the wire services. Then in 1926 he founded the *United States
Daily,* a newspaper that carried national news and analysis. Lawrence
founded the *World Report,* which covered international news, in
1946, and he merged the two into the now-famous *U.S. News &
World Report* in 1947. He served as the editor of the magazine until

his death and built up its circulation into the millions. Meanwhile, he continued writing syndicated columns on world and national affairs that appeared in more than three-hundred U.S. daily newspapers.

A lifelong conservative, Lawrence generally supported business interests and opposed government growth. Though he often criticized President Franklin D. Roosevelt and the New Deal in his columns, he was concerned about the needs of his employees and organized *U.S. News* so that they were eventually able to take over ownership. He also gave considerable financial support to medical, educational, civic, and religious groups.

In addition to writing for magazines and newspapers, Lawrence published nine books, including *Beyond the New Deal* (1934), *Supreme Court or Political Puppets?* (1937), and *Diary of a Washington Correspondent* (1942). He died in 1973, at age eighty-four.

G. Gould Lincoln

A JOURNALIST SINCE 1902, HE HAS BEEN A PERCEPTIVE PROFESSIONAL WITNESS TO THE EVENTS OF THE TWENTIETH CENTURY ALMOST FROM THE DAY OF ITS BEGINNING. HE HAS REPORTED THOSE EVENTS WITH GREAT INTEGRITY, UNFAILING SKILL AND UNCOMPROMISING PROFESSIONALISM. HIS CONSISTENTLY EXCELLENT REPORTING OF HISTORY-IN-THE-MAKING FROM HIS NATIVE WASHINGTON, D.C., HAS BEEN, THROUGH THESE YEARS OF SWEEPING CHANGE, ONE OF THE MOST ADMIRED ACHIEVEMENTS IN ALL OF AMERICAN JOURNALISM.

★ ★ ★

President Richard Nixon awarded Lincoln the Presidential Medal of Freedom with the above citation during a White House ceremony April 22, 1970.

A veteran political reporter for the *Washington Star-News,* George Gould Lincoln was born in 1880 just a few blocks from the White House he would eventually cover. His father was a Union Army surgeon during the Civil War, and though he knew President Abraham Lincoln, the two were not related. G. Gould Lincoln, as he came to be known, graduated from Yale University in 1902 and a year later began working for the *Washington Times.* By 1909 he had moved to the *Washington Evening Star,* which later became the *Star-News,* and remained there for nearly sixty years.

Eventually specializing in political reporting, Lincoln wrote stories about every president from Theodore Roosevelt to Gerald R. Ford during his long career as a journalist. He covered his first national political convention in 1920 for the *Washington Times* and reported on every one afterward for the next forty years.

Called the dean of Washington political reporters, Lincoln was so consistently objective and fair in his reporting that he had top sources in both political parties. He said he guarded his integrity as a White House journalist by always remembering that his role there was not to advise the president but to be a reporter.

Lincoln formally retired from the *Star-News* in 1964 but continued to write a weekly column for the paper for another decade. His third wife (of twenty-four years), the former Delia Hazeltine Pynchon, died in 1971. Lincoln died at few years later, in 1974. He was ninety-four years old.

Raymond Moley

IT HAS BEEN SAID OF HIM THAT HE IS "A MASTER OF SCIENTIFIC ANALYSIS APPLIED TO POLITICS." HIS EXCEPTIONAL ABILITY AS A POLITICAL ANALYST IS MATCHED BY A DEEP LOVE OF HIS COUNTRY, AND OF THE PRINCIPLES OF DEMOCRATIC GOVERNMENT. HIS LONG CAREER AS A GOVERNMENT OFFICIAL, SCHOLAR, LECTURER, HISTORIAN AND POLITICAL COMMENTATOR HAS BEEN AS RICH IN DISTINCTION AS IT HAS IN VARIETY. A MAN OF THOUGHT AND A MAN OF ACTION, HE HAS NOT ONLY STUDIED AND ANALYZED THE HISTORY OF OUR TIMES, BUT ALSO HELPED TO MAKE IT.

★ ★ ★

President Richard Nixon awarded Moley the Presidential Medal of Freedom with the above citation during a White House ceremony April 22, 1970.

The onetime leader of President Franklin D. Roosevelt's "Brain Trust" and a key figure in shaping New Deal policies, Raymond Moley was born in Berea, Ohio, in 1886. After graduating from Baldwin-Wallace College in 1906, he worked variously as a superintendent of schools, a high school history teacher, and a college teacher. Meanwhile, he earned his master's degree at Oberlin College (1913) and his doctorate in political science at Columbia University (1918). Moley married Eva Dall in 1916 and three years later was named director of the Cleveland Foundation, a community trust that promoted civic reform.

Moley's civic work, especially in the field of criminal justice reform, helped him secure a post as an associate professor of government at Columbia University in 1923 and caught the attention of Louis Howe, an associate of Franklin D. Roosevelt. During Roosevelt's governorship, Moley served on the New York State Commission on Administration of Justice (1931–1933). Meanwhile, he also published two highly regarded books on criminal justice, *Politics and Criminal Prosecution* (1929) and *Our Criminal Courts* (1930). But it was not until Roosevelt began organizing his presidential campaign in early 1932 that Moley came into his own in the political arena.

At the time the nation was sinking into the depths of the Great Depression. The economy was in chaos—national income had fallen by one-half during the past four years, 25 percent of all workers had lost their jobs, and the country faced the possibility of mass starvation and even open revolt. Roosevelt's campaign advisers recommended that he call in some university professors to act as consultants on these difficult issues, and thus the Brain Trust was born.

With Moley as its leader, the Brain Trust convinced Roosevelt to make an important break with tradition with regard to the economy. In the past the government had followed either a conservative hands-off approach toward business or a reformist philosophy based on trust-busting and the belief that business was inherently exploitative. The trust advised Roosevelt to adopt the (then) radical policy of directing government and business to work together to rebuild the country's shattered economy. In fact, Roosevelt stayed with that approach throughout most of his first term before concluding that business was just unwilling to cooperate with government economic planning.

During the campaign of 1932 and through the hectic first "Hundred Days" of Roosevelt's first term, Moley ranked as Roosevelt's most influential adviser. Moley wrote many of Roosevelt's speeches and coined the terms "the Forgotten Man" and the "New Deal." On taking office, Roosevelt appointed him assistant secretary of state with the understanding that Moley would be the president's special assistant.

In fact, Moley became a central figure in the White House during the Hundred Days and served as the administration's key liaison with Congress as it passed a flood of Roosevelt's New Deal legislation.

Moley's meteoric rise in national government circles ended as quickly as it had begun, though, following a well-publicized policy disagreement with President Roosevelt in mid–1933. Moley left the Roosevelt administration soon afterward and became editor of a new public affairs magazine, *Today*, which was merged with *Newsweek* in 1937. During the late 1930s he became disenchanted with the increasingly antibusiness policies of the New Deal and openly broke with Roosevelt in 1939 with publication of his book *After Seven Years*, a critical account of the president's policies. Thereafter, Moley consistently backed Republican presidential candidates but remained outside the government.

Instead he wrote a weekly column for *Newsweek* and published several other books, including *The Republican Opportunity in 1964* and *The First New Deal* (1966, with Elliot A. Rosen). Moley continued as a contributing editor at *Newsweek* until 1968. He died seven years later, in 1975. He was eighty-eight years old.

Moley's memoirs of his early years were published posthumously in 1980 as the book *Realities and Illusions, 1886–1931*.

Adela Rogers St. Johns

REPORTER, FEATURE WRITER, AUTHOR, SHE HAS ENHANCED EVERY FIELD SHE HAS ENTERED. BEGINNING HER CAREER WHEN WOMEN REPORTERS WERE FEW, SHE HAS BROUGHT ENTERTAINMENT AND INFORMATION TO MILLIONS WITH THE ENERGY, VIGOR AND GRACE CHARACTERISTIC OF BOTH HER STYLE AND HER PERSONALITY. DEMONSTRATING AN EXCEPTIONAL ABILITY TO REVEAL THE HUMAN STORY BEHIND THE NEWS, SHE HAS BROUGHT TO HER WRITING AN EXCITEMENT AND WARMTH THAT FOR MANY YEARS HAVE EARNED HER THE HIGH ESTEEM OF HER PROFESSION AND OF HER PUBLIC.

★ ★ ★

President Richard Nixon awarded St. Johns the Presidential Medal of Freedom with the above citation during a White House ceremony April 22, 1970.

A veteran reporter for Hearst publications and other newspapers, Adela Rogers St. Johns was born Adela Rogers in Los Angeles in 1894. She was raised largely by her father, a noted criminal lawyer, and spent much of her childhood in his office and at the courthouse. Though she did not complete high school, she was a voracious reader and showed an early talent for writing. Later, in 1913, her father introduced her to William Randolph Hearst, who put the nineteen-year-old to work as a cub reporter for the *San Francisco Examiner*.

She eventually worked for several Hearst papers as well as its International News Service. In 1914, while working at Hearst's Los Angeles *Herald* she married William St. Johns, the paper's copy editor. Four years later she left the paper to raise a family, but she continued to be an occasional contributor to Hearst newspapers and magazines. Meanwhile, she began writing profiles of Hollywood stars for *Photoplay* magazine, and her frank portrayals of such celebrities as Rudolf Valentino, Tom Mix, Greta Garbo, and Gloria Swanson earned her the title "Mother Confessor of Hollywood."

St. Johns also began publishing fiction in 1918, her first short story being "The Black Cat." Her first novel, *The Sky Rocket*, was published in 1923 and she followed with the novels *A Free Soul* (1924) and *A Single Standard* (1925). All three books were made into movies.

Longing for the excitement of newspaper reporting, St. Johns went back to work for the Hearst papers in the 1920s and over the next two decades covered such notable events as the trial of the Lindbergh baby kidnapper and the abdication of Edward VIII. She also wrote short stories and several screenplays. Meanwhile, she divorced her first husband in 1929 and eventually married two more times, with both of these marriages also ending in divorce.

After retiring as a journalist in 1948, she continued writing books, including *Final Verdict* (1962), a biography of her father; *Tell No Man* (1966), a bestselling novel; *The Honeycomb* (1969), her memoirs; and *Some Are Born Great* (1974). St. Johns died in 1988, at age ninety-four.

Samuel Goldwyn

HIS CAREER AS A PRODUCER OF DISTINGUISHED MOTION PICTURES SPANS THE ENTIRE HISTORY OF THE AMERICAN FILM INDUSTRY. SINCE 1913 HE HAS EXERCISED FORCEFUL, CREATIVE LEADERSHIP IN HELPING THE MEDIUM OF FILM TO REALIZE ITS GREAT TWOFOLD POTENTIAL IN TWENTIETH CENTURY LIFE: GOLDWYN MOVIES HAVE NOT ONLY ENTERTAINED AND DELIGHTED MILLIONS — THEY HAVE ALSO BROADENED THE DIMENSIONS OF DRAMATIC ART. PROFESSIONALLY, HE HAS BUILT A BODY OF WORK WHOSE EXCELLENCE IS UNEQUALED; PERSONALLY, HE STANDS AS A WELL-LOVED AND WIDELY RESPECTED GIANT ON THE HOLLYWOOD SCENE. THE HALLMARKS OF HIS LIFE AND WORK ARE FIERCE INDEPENDENCE, DEEP RESPECT FOR QUALITY, STRICT ETHICS, AND UNCOMPROMISING INTEGRITY. FOR THESE, GENERATIONS OF FILM ARTISTS AND A NATION OF MOVIEGOERS ARE IN HIS DEBT.

* * *

President Richard Nixon awarded Goldwyn the Presidential Medal of Freedom with the above citation at the Goldwyn residence in Beverly Hills, California, on March 27, 1971.

The son of a poor Jewish merchant, Samuel Goldwyn was born Schmuel Gelbfisz in Warsaw, Poland, in 1879. At sixteen he left home, going first to Germany, then to England (where he became Samuel Goldfish), and finally, in 1899, to the United States. There he joined a community of Jewish immigrants who had made Gloversville, New York, a glove manufacturing center. After becoming a U.S. citizen in 1904, he took up selling gloves and quickly became a star salesman, with earnings upward of $15,000 a year.

Fascinated by what was then the emerging movie business, the future Samuel Goldwyn talked his brother-in-law Jesse Lasky into forming the Jesse L. Lasky Feature Play Company. With a then-unheard-of director named Cecil B. DeMille, the company shot a feature-length Western in an unremarkable little town called Hollywood just outside Los Angeles, California. *The Squaw Man* became the first feature-length movie filmed in Hollywood and proved an instant success when released in 1914.

Among the first big producers in the rough-and-tumble movie world, Goldwyn eventually played an important role in building the film industry. He also quickly established personal traits that followed him throughout his long filmmaking career—he paid lavishly for talented people and scripts, he sought (but did not always produce) feature films with a literary flavor, and he could be combative, authoritarian, and fiercely independent in business dealings.

That determination to do things on his own terms brought about his ouster from two companies he had built—from Famous Players-Lasky in 1916 and from Goldwyn Pictures in 1923. (Still known as Goldfish when he cofounded Goldwyn Pictures in 1916, he changed his name to Goldwyn in 1919 before being forced out.) Resolved to operate independently from that time forward, Goldwyn formed Samuel Goldwyn Pictures with his own money in 1923 and for the next thirty-six years produced films entirely on his own. Two years after forming his company, he married his second wife and longtime business confidante, the actress Frances Howard McLaughlin.

Over the years, Goldwyn discovered or promoted such screen stars as Eddie Cantor, David Niven, Paulette Goddard, Lucille Ball, Danny Kaye, and Gary Cooper. Among the more than seventy films he produced were such literary efforts as *Arrowsmith* (1931) and *Wuthering Heights* (1939), as well as more entertainment-oriented films like *Roman Scandals* (1933) and *Guys and Dolls* (1955). *The Best Years of Our Lives* (1946) is generally considered one of his best films.

Goldwyn's last picture was the controversial *Porgy and Bess* (1959). By then in his eighties and discouraged by a lack of promising projects, he gave up making movies and rented out his studios for television production. He died in 1974, at age ninety-four.

William J. Hopkins

DURING HIS FORTY YEARS IN THE WHITE HOUSE, UNDER SEVEN PRESIDENTS, WILLIAM J. HOPKINS HAS WRITTEN A RECORD OF SKILLED AND DEVOTED SERVICE UNIQUE IN THE ANNALS OF THE PRESIDENCY. NOT ONLY HAS HE BORNE HEAVY RESPONSIBILITIES WITH GREAT EFFICIENCY AND UNCOMMON GOOD SENSE, BUT EACH NEW PRESIDENT IN TURN HAS LEARNED TO RELY ON HIM AS A FOUNT OF WISDOM, A RESERVOIR OF EXPERIENCE AND A ROCK OF LOYALTY. GUIDING EACH NEW ADMINISTRATION THROUGH ITS NEW INITIAL STEPS, STANDING AS A STAUNCH FRIEND TO ALL, HE HAS BEEN, IN THE BEST SENSE, A SELFLESS PARTISAN OF THE PRESIDENCY, AND OF THE NATION THAT THESE SEVEN PRESIDENTS HAVE BEEN ABLE TO SERVE BETTER BECAUSE OF THE HELP HE GAVE.

★ ★ ★

President Richard Nixon awarded Hopkins the Presidential Medal of Freedom with the above citation during a White House ceremony June 2, 1971.

Born in Netawaka, Kansas, in 1910, William J. Hopkins took his first job with the government in 1929, the year of the stock market crash. He began as a clerk/typist in the Bureau of Naturalization, but two years later, while Herbert Hoover was still president, Hopkins moved over to the White House Correspondence Section.

While moving up through the ranks of the White House administrative staff, Hopkins in 1938 earned his law degree from Southeastern University. Though admitted to the bar in the U.S. District Court and Court of Appeals for Washington, D.C., he chose to stay with the White House staff. Presidents came and went, but Hopkins remained, eventually becoming in 1948 the White House executive clerk and thereafter serving as a discreet, trusted assistant of the president in office at the time. As executive clerk, he supervised all the White House clerical and administrative functions, including correspondence, filing, accounts, and communications equipment and services.

Dwight D. Eisenhower became the first president to officially recognize the value of Hopkins's work when, in 1960, he presented Hopkins with the President's Award for Distinguished Federal Service. Six years later President Lyndon B. Johnson gave him a special award and changed his title to executive assistant to the president. In 1971, having reached age seventy, Hopkins retired. Richard Nixon, the seventh president served by Hopkins, marked the retirement with a special Rose Garden ceremony.

Manlio Giovanni Brosio

A DISTINGUISHED DIPLOMAT, HE HAS NOBLY SERVED FREEDOM
IN THE WORLD AS SECRETARY GENERAL OF THE NORTH
ATLANTIC TREATY ORGANIZATION. HE HAS WON THE HIGHEST
RESPECT IN HIS UNTIRING WORK FOR BOTH DEFENSE AND
DÉTENTE, AND HE HAS PERFORMED HIS TASK WITH EXCEPTIONAL
SKILL, PERSEVERANCE, AND FAIRNESS. IN HIS DEDICATION TO
THE CAUSE OF COMITY AMONG NATIONS, MANLIO BROSIO HAS
DEMONSTRATED THAT THOSE WHO WORK TO KEEP THE PEACE
ARE AS BLESSED AS THE PEACEMAKERS.

★ ★ ★

*President Nixon awarded Brosio the Presidential Medal of Freedom with
the above citation during a White House ceremony September 29, 1971.*

Born in 1897, Manlio Giovanni Brosio was raised in Turin, a major
industrial center in northern Italy. After distinguished service during
World War I, he earned his law degree from the University of Turin
in 1920 and practiced law as a corporate lawyer for the next twenty-
two years. In 1936 he married a cousin, Clotilde Brosio.

A member of the underground opposition to the Fascists in Italy
during World War II, he held various posts in the postwar governments. From 1947 to 1964 Brosio acquired a strong background in
international affairs by winning a string of appointments as the
Italian ambassador to key nations of the postwar world, including
the Soviet Union (1947–1952), Great Britain (1952–1954), the United
States (1955–1961), and France (1961–1964). In 1964 he became secretary-general of the North Atlantic Treaty Organization (NATO), a
post he held until retiring in 1971.

A crucial military alliance among the United States and Western
European nations, NATO was an important defensive bulwark
against the threat posed by the Communist bloc during the Cold
War. But the first crisis Brosio faced as NATO's chief political officer
was an internal one. In 1964 France withdrew from its longstanding
membership in NATO, forcing Brosio to negotiate the transfer of
NATO headquarters to Belgium. In 1967 he used his diplomatic skills
to help avert a war between NATO members Greece and Turkey over
a crisis in Cyprus. During his last years, when détente between the
United States and the Soviet Union had begun to flower, Brosio also
handled the delicate task of exploring improved relations with the
Soviet Union.

In 1971 President Richard M. Nixon selected the retiring NATO
chief as the first non-American Medal of Freedom recipient named
during his administration. Brosio returned to Italy and served briefly

as a member of the Italian senate. He lived out the remainder of the 1970s in his native Italy. Brosio was eighty-three years old when he died in 1980.

DeWitt and Lila Wallace

THE CO-FOUNDER WITH LILA ACHESON WALLACE OF READER'S DIGEST AND PARTNER IN ITS DIRECTION FOR HALF A CENTURY, HE HAS MADE A TOWERING CONTRIBUTION TO THAT FREEDOM OF THE MIND FROM WHICH SPRING ALL OUR OTHER LIBERTIES. THIS MAGAZINE HAS BECOME A MONTHLY UNIVERSITY IN PRINT, TEACHING 100 MILLION READERS WORLDWIDE THE WONDER OF COMMON LIFE AND THE SCOPE OF MAN'S POTENTIAL. IN DEWITT WALLACE, AMERICA HAS A SON TO BE DEEPLY PROUD OF—ONE WHOSE LIFEWORK SHOWS AMERICAN ENTERPRISE AT ITS CREATIVE BEST, AND THE AMERICAN ETHIC IN ITS FULLEST FLOWER. CO-FOUNDER WITH DEWITT WALLACE OF READER'S DIGEST HALF A CENTURY AGO AND PARTNER WITH HIM IN ITS DIRECTION EVER SINCE, LILA WALLACE HAS HELPED MAKE ALL AMERICA BETTER READ. HER VISION AND DRIVE HAVE GIVEN WINGS TO THE WORKHORSE PRINTED WORD, FASHIONING A PEGASUS OF A MAGAZINE THAT CARRIES AMERICAN INSIGHTS TO 100 MILLION READERS WORLDWIDE. HER GRACIOUS TOUCH AT PLEASANTVILLE HAS SHOWN THE WAY TO INFUSING INDUSTRIAL SETTINGS WITH CULTURE AND THE JOY OF WORK.

★ ★ ★

President Richard Nixon awarded the Wallaces the Presidential Medal of Freedom with the above citations during a White House ceremony January 28, 1972.

DeWitt Wallace was born in Saint Paul, Minnesota, in 1889. His father was a professor at, and eventually the president of, the Presbyterian Macalester College in Saint Paul. DeWitt later attended both Macalester and the University of California at Berkeley before dropping out in 1912 to sell agricultural textbooks for the Webb Publishing Company in Saint Paul. While working at Webb, he published on his own a 120-page booklet on agriculture based on condensations of government publications, eventually marketing over 100,000 copies to banks and stores for sale to farmers. From that success came his idea of condensing general-interest magazine articles, but World War I intervened before he could act on it.

Lila Acheson was born in Virden, Manitoba, Canada, in 1889. She was the daughter of a Presbyterian minister who became a U.S. citizen soon after her birth. She earned her bachelor's degree from the University of Oregon (1917) in just two-and-a-half years, taught high school for two years, and then began doing social-service work for the Young Women's Christian Association (YWCA). She first met DeWitt in 1911, and they again saw each other years later after he was wounded during World War I.

By late 1919 DeWitt had prepared and mailed out a sample issue of the *Reader's Digest,* only to have it turned down by every publisher on his list. Lila, by now engaged to DeWitt, then encouraged him to try publishing the magazine on his own. He sold some 5,000 subscriptions by mail order, and in 1921 DeWitt and Lila published the first issue of the *Reader's Digest.* The two were married later that year.

The monthly magazine proved extremely popular with readers and became an astounding commercial success. By 1926 the Wallaces had 30,000 subscribers, and by 1929 that had mushroomed to 290,000. Eventually, the *Digest* reached a circulation of some 30 million worldwide, with editions in seventeen languages. From 1934 the Wallaces also began publishing condensed books. For each issue of the magazine the Wallaces sought a pleasing mix of articles on such subjects as self-improvement, inspiration, science, humor, and sex and strove to keep the overall tone positive. Many criticized the *Digest* as too middlebrow, but the Wallaces had found a popular formula that over the years made them multimillionaires.

In their later years, the Wallaces donated large sums of money to charity and other causes, including the preservation of Egyptian temples and restoration work on the house of the famous French painter Claude Monet.. DeWitt died in 1981, at age ninety-one. Lila died three years later, at age ninety-four.

John Paul Vann

SOLDIER OF PEACE AND PATRIOT OF TWO NATIONS, THE NAME OF JOHN PAUL VANN WILL BE HONORED AS LONG AS FREE MEN REMEMBER THE STRUGGLE TO PRESERVE THE INDEPENDENCE OF SOUTH VIETNAM. HIS MILITARY AND CIVILIAN SERVICE IN VIETNAM SPANNED A DECADE, MARKED THROUGHOUT BY RESOURCEFULNESS, PROFESSIONAL EXCELLENCE AND UNSUR-

PASSED COURAGE; BY SUPREME DEDICATION AND PERSONAL SAC-
RIFICE. A TRULY NOBLE AMERICAN, A SUPERB LEADER, HE
STANDS WITH LAFAYETTE IN THAT GALLERY OF HEROES WHO
HAVE MADE ANOTHER BRAVE PEOPLE'S CAUSE THEIR OWN.

★ ★ ★

*President Richard Nixon awarded Vann a posthumous Presidential
Medal of Freedom with the above citation during a White House
ceremony June 16, 1972. John Allen Vann accepted the medal on his
father's behalf.*

An influential and often controversial figure during the Vietnam War
years, John Paul Vann was born in Roanoke, Virginia, in 1924. He
enlisted in the army air force during World War II and saw combat as
a navigator aboard a B–29 bomber. Remaining in the military after
the war, he became an army paratrooper and in 1950 led the first
airborne ranger unit into combat during the Korean War. His experiences behind enemy lines with this unit sparked what became a
lifelong fascination with guerrilla warfare.

Following the Korean War, in 1954, Vann earned his bachelor of
science degree from Rutgers University (1954) and meanwhile also
taught courses in military science and tactics for the ROTC program
there. While continuing his career in the air force, he earned a master's
degree in business administration from Syracuse University. By the
early 1960s he also had advanced to the rank of lieutenant colonel.

South Vietnam became Vann's passion soon after he volunteered
to go there in 1962. Assigned as a military adviser to South
Vietnamese soldiers fighting Vietcong guerrilla forces in the Mekong
Delta region, he made a point of getting to know the countryside,
often taking personal risks the Vietnamese regarded as foolhardy.
Vann had many close calls with Vietcong patrols but gained an
intimate knowledge of the battlefield and the soldiers on both sides.
He also began making controversial observations about the conduct
of the war that challenged his overly optimistic army commanders.

Early in the Vietnam War, for example, the South Vietnamese
were fighting what was essentially a grassroots rebellion supported
by Communists in the North. At this stage, Vann argued, the heli-
copters, bombs, artillery, and other heavy weaponry that the United
States was then sending to South Vietnam were counterproductive
for the simple reason that many innocent civilians were being killed
along with the few Vietcong in their midst. This type of political war
had to be fought aggressively one-on-one, with rifles and knives, he
believed. Vann also prepared a controversial report blaming the
failure of the pacification program on South Vietnam's lack of
determined effort and on corruption in its government.

When Vann returned to the United States in 1963, he found no
interest in his criticisms at the Pentagon, which was awash in glowing

reports on the war. Resigning that year, he found work with a Denver aircraft company and served as a campaign organizer in Colorado for the unsuccessful 1964 presidential primary bid of Henry Cabot Lodge, Jr. But early the next year he returned to South Vietnam as an Agency for International Development employee. In 1966, with Lodge now the U.S. ambassador in South Vietnam, Vann was named a regional head of civilian operations. In 1971 he became director of all civilian operations in the Second Regional Assistance Group (the Central Highlands), an area where the pacification program had been failing.

Vann formed close friendships with South Vietnamese people and even as a civilian risked his life on various occasions during his years there. He was by the early 1970s both a near legend among the South Vietnamese and one of the most influential American civilians in the country. Vann was killed in 1972 while flying into a city besieged by a division of North Vietnamese regulars, who apparently shot down his helicopter. He was forty-seven years old.

John Ford

IN THE ANNALS OF AMERICAN FILM, NO NAME SHINES MORE BRIGHTLY THAN THAT OF JOHN FORD. DIRECTOR AND FILM MAKER FOR MORE THAN HALF A CENTURY, HE STANDS PRE-EMINENT IN THE CROWD, NOT ONLY AS A CREATOR OF INDI-VIDUAL FILMS OF SURPASSING EXCELLENCE, BUT AS A MASTER AMONG THOSE WHO TRANSFORMED THE EARLY MOTION PICTURES INTO A NEW ART FORM THAT DEVELOPED IN AMERICA AND SWEPT THE WORLD. AS AN INTERPRETER OF THE NATION'S HERITAGE, HE LEFT HIS PERSONAL STAMP INDELIBLY IMPRINTED ON THE CON-SCIOUSNESS OF WHOLE GENERATIONS, BOTH HERE AND ABROAD. IN HIS LIFE AND IN HIS WORK, JOHN FORD REPRESENTS THE BEST IN AMERICAN FILMS, AND THE VERY BEST IN AMERICA.

★ ★ ★

President Richard Nixon awarded Ford the Presidential Medal of Freedom with the above citation during the first annual awards dinner of the American Film Institute in Beverly Hills, California, on March 31, 1973.

A five-time winner of the Academy Award, John Ford was born John Martin Feeney in Cape Elizabeth, Maine, in 1895. The son of a saloonkeeper, he became fascinated with nickelodeons in his youth, spending every penny he had on the flickering movies. Meanwhile, Ford's older brother Francis suddenly disappeared for ten years, finally resurfacing in California as Francis Ford, a motion picture star, director, and head of his own company at Universal Studios. Francis would eventually provide his younger brother with a start in the movie business.

In fact, when John graduated from Portland High School in 1914, he immediately set out for Hollywood and there was promptly hired as an actor and assistant director. He continued acting regularly during his first years in Hollywood and in 1917 directed his first film, *The Tornado*. His early directorial style probably was most influenced by his brother and by director D. W. Griffith. In any event he had ample opportunity to practice his craft over the next six years. When he left Universal Studios in 1923, he had already directed thirty-nine films. He married Mary MacBride Smith in 1920.

After joining Fox Studios, he began using the name John Ford. Then in 1924 his film *The Iron Horse*, a movie of giant proportions about the transcontinental railroad, won him international recognition as a director. Ford used some five-thousand extras, ten-thousand cattle, and thirteen-hundred buffalo to make the film. Among the most profitable movies of the 1920s, it grossed over $2 million.

The advent of talking pictures created an even broader canvas on which the talented director could work. His first sound picture was *The Black Watch* (1929). *Arrowsmith*, an adaptation of Sinclair Lewis's novel, appeared in 1931 and garnered four Academy Award nominations. Ford's production of *The Informer* (1935) ranks among the best films of all time, while four years later his *Stagecoach* won two Academy Awards and incidentally also made a star of John Wayne. *(See also the entry for Wayne, p. 274.)*

During World War II Ford worked for the Office of Strategic Services as head of the Field Photographic Branch. Under Ford's direction, his photographers produced numerous award-winning documentaries, including the *Battle of the Midway* (1942), which won him an Academy Award for best documentary. Caught in the middle of the fighting at Midway, Ford himself shot some of the footage.

Ford returned to Hollywood and in the postwar years became known especially for his Westerns. Among them were *My Darling Clementine* (1946), *Fort Apache* (1948), *Wagonmaster* (1950), and *How the West Was Won* (1962). But he did other films as well and won Academy Awards for best direction with *Grapes of Wrath* (1940), *How Green Was My Valley* (1941), and *The Quiet Man* (1952).

He was awarded the first American Film Institute Life Achievement Award in 1973. During the same ceremony President Nixon awarded him the Presidential Medal of Freedom. Ford died later in 1973, at age seventy-eight.

William P. Rogers

PROSECUTOR, CONGRESSIONAL INVESTIGATOR, AND CABINET
LEADER UNDER TWO PRESIDENTS, HIS BRILLIANT CAREER OF
PUBLIC SERVICE HAS SPANNED MORE THAN A THIRD OF A
CENTURY AND TOUCHED ALL THREE BRANCHES OF
GOVERNMENT. AS THE 63RD ATTORNEY GENERAL OF THE
UNITED STATES, HE PIONEERED IN THE BATTLE FOR EQUAL
RIGHTS. AS THE NATION'S 55TH SECRETARY OF STATE, HE
PLAYED AN INDISPENSABLE ROLE IN ENDING OUR LONGEST WAR
AND IN STARTING TO BUILD A NEW STRUCTURE OF PEACE.
THROUGH THESE EFFORTS, THE DECENCY AND INTEGRITY THAT
ARE WILLIAM ROGERS' PERSONAL STAMP ARE NOW FELT MORE
STRONGLY AMONG ALL PEOPLE AND NATIONS. NO MAN COULD
SEEK A GREATER MONUMENT.

★ ★ ★

*President Richard Nixon awarded Rogers the Presidential Medal of
Freedom with the above citation during a White House ceremony October
15, 1973.*

William P. Rogers was born in the mill town of Norfolk, New York, in
1913. His mother died in 1926 when he was just thirteen, and his father, a
once-prosperous executive, was reduced by the depression to running a
small insurance business. Rogers proved a bright, industrious student,
though, and after working his way through Colgate University (1934),
he earned his law degree from Cornell Law School in 1937. The editor of
the *Cornell Law Review* from 1935 to 1937, he graduated fifth in his class.
Meanwhile, he married Adele Langston, a law school classmate, in 1936.

During his early career, Rogers worked as an assistant district
attorney in New York, served aboard the aircraft carrier *Intrepid*
during World War II, and, in the late 1940s, served as counsel to
various Senate committees. During this period he befriended Sen.
Richard Nixon and advised him to pursue the controversial Alger
Hiss case, which helped launch Nixon in national politics.

After a brief stint in private practice from 1950 to 1952, Rogers
became deputy attorney general, and then attorney general (from
1957), in the Eisenhower administration. He became the first attorney
general to actively pursue prosecution of voting-rights cases, insisted
on enforcing school desegregation, and opened the federal government's campaign against organized crime. Returning to private
practice during the Kennedy and Johnson administrations, he nevertheless served on the President's Commission on Law Enforcement
and Administration from 1965 to 1967.

When President Nixon took office in 1969, he surprised many observers by naming Rogers his secretary of state. Though Rogers lacked foreign affairs experience, Nixon chose him because of his negotiating ability. More importantly, as a longtime friend, Rogers could be trusted to let Nixon run foreign policy from the White House, which was what the president wanted. As secretary of state, Rogers had little to do with the Strategic Arms Limitation Talks (SALT) or the Vietnamese peace negotiations—the most important foreign policy concerns of the day—but did push for more restrained use of U.S. military might and successfully negotiated a cease-fire agreement between Egypt and Israel in 1970. Ultimately, President Nixon's national security adviser, Henry Kissinger, came to dominate U.S. foreign policy. In 1973 Rogers left office at President Nixon's request to allow Kissinger to become secretary of state. *(See also the entry for Kissinger, p. 247.)*

Since then he has practiced law and directed the government commission investigating the space shuttle *Challenger* disaster. In 1992 he was named U.S. Olympic Committee Ethics Committee chairman.

Melvin R. Laird

FEW MEN HAVE SERVED AMERICA BETTER THAN MELVIN R. LAIRD. AS A PROMISING YOUNG STATE SENATOR, AS AN OUTSTANDING MEMBER OF THE UNITED STATES CONGRESS FOR SIXTEEN YEARS, AS SECRETARY OF DEFENSE AND AS PRESIDENTIAL COUNSELOR FOR DOMESTIC AFFAIRS, HE HAS SUPERBLY DEMONSTRATED A LOVE OF COUNTRY, A STRONG CAPABILITY FOR LEADERSHIP AND A BRILLIANT UNDERSTANDING OF PEOPLE AND IDEAS. LAWMAKER, ADMINISTRATOR, THEORIST AND MASTER OF THE AMERICAN POLITICAL PROCESS, MELVIN LAIRD HAS HELPED TO PRESERVE A STRONG, FREE UNITED STATES AND HAS LEFT AN INDELIBLE MARK ON THE HISTORY OF OUR TIMES.

★ ★ ★

President Richard Nixon awarded Laird the Presidential Medal of Freedom during a White House ceremony March 26, 1974.

Melvin R. Laird was born in Omaha, Nebraska, in 1922, and was raised in Marshfield, Wisconsin. His father was a Presbyterian minister who became a Wisconsin state senator in the late 1930s, and his mother, herself active in the Republican Party, was the daughter of a former lieutenant governor. Laird graduated with a bachelor's degree from

Minnesota's Carleton College in 1942 and spent the next two years in the navy, seeing action in five battles. He was wounded in action twice, and in 1945 married Barbara Masters, a former college classmate.

Laird entered politics in 1946 when he was elected to the Wisconsin state senate seat left vacant by his father's death. He served as a Republican state senator from 1947 to 1952 and from 1953 to 1969 represented his state in the U.S. House of Representatives. A member of the Appropriations Committee for nearly all his years in the House, Laird supported the country's nuclear defense strategy and backed big budgets for the military. His support for the Polaris missile submarine in 1958 helped speed development of a key element in the U.S. nuclear defense system. During this time Laird also outlined his views on military strategy and foreign policy in *A House Divided: America's Strategy Gap* (1962).

Named secretary of defense in 1969 by President Nixon, Laird served at time when pressure for withdrawal of U.S. troops from the Vietnam War was reaching its peak. He implemented the Nixon administration policy of using bombing to force North Vietnam to the bargaining table, of widening the war into Cambodia and Laos, and turning over the combat role to the South Vietnamese (Vietnamization). Laird resigned just days before the signing of the Paris peace settlement in 1973 ended U.S. involvement in Vietnam. He then served as the president's domestic adviser for the duration of Nixon's term.

After Nixon was forced to resign in 1974, Laird joined the *Reader's Digest* as a senior counselor on national and international affairs, a post he continues to hold. A trustee of the Kennedy Center, he has served as a board member for various other organizations and businesses, including Metropolitan Life Insurance Company, Northwest Airlines, and Communications Satellite Corporation (Comsat). He became board chairman of Comsat in 1992.

Paul G. Hoffman

INDUSTRIALIST, PHILANTHROPIST, AND TOWERING INTERNATIONAL STATESMAN, PAUL HOFFMAN HAS ALWAYS EXEMPLIFIED WHAT IS BEST ABOUT AMERICA. HIS GENEROUS HUMANITARIAN SPIRIT AND HIS GENIUS FOR ADMINISTRATIVE CHALLENGES HAVE MADE A PROFOUND IMPACT FOR GOOD WITHIN OUR OWN COUNTRY AND THROUGHOUT THE PLANET. PAUL HOFFMAN PLAYED A CENTRAL ROLE IN MOVING THE WORLD OUT OF THE DEVASTATION OF WORLD WAR II AND THROUGH A DIFFICULT PERIOD OF DECOLONIZATION AND EMERGENT NATIONHOOD. HE

WAS A BOLD PIONEER IN THE FIELD OF INTERNATIONAL DEVEL-
OPMENT ASSISTANCE. THE FORCE OF HIS DEEDS AND THE POWER
OF HIS EXAMPLE HAVE MADE A UNIQUE AND MONUMENTAL CON-
TRIBUTION TO WORLD PEACE AND PROGRESS.

★ ★ ★

*President Richard Nixon awarded Hoffman the Presidential Medal of
Freedom with the above citation. The medal was presented in New York
City by special arrangement on June 21, 1974.*

The son of an inventor, Paul G. Hoffman was born in Chicago in 1891
and was raised in nearby Western Springs, Illinois. Fascinated by cars
as a youth, he dropped out of college in 1909 after a year at the
University of Chicago and became a car salesman. The business was
then in its infancy, and soon after moving to Los Angeles in 1911
Hoffman began selling Studebaker cars. He married Dorothy Brown
four years later.

Hoffman rose quickly from star salesman to district sales
manager, and after serving in World War I, he became a wholesale
distributor of Studebakers. By 1925 Hoffman had made his first
million, but his long and varied career was only just beginning. That
year he became vice president of sales for the Studebaker
Corporation, and when the company went bankrupt during the
depression the court appointed him one of two receivers to run it.
He got the company back on its feet by 1935 and then became its
president, a post he held until 1948.

Because of Hoffman's business experience and outspoken support
of foreign aid programs, President Harry S. Truman named him
chief administrator of the Marshall Plan, the massive U.S. aid
program designed to help countries in Europe and elsewhere rebuild
after World War II. The highly successful program distributed $10
billion under his supervision and provided the foundation for the
economic recovery of postwar Europe. Awarded the Presidential
Medal of Freedom years later for his outstanding work on the
Marshall Plan, Hoffman at the time also gained valuable experience
in working closely with foreign leaders.

Hoffman tried to retire in 1950, but before long he became
president of the Ford Foundation (1951–1953) and then took over as
chairman of the ailing Studebaker Corporation. He arranged the
merger of Studebaker with Packard before returning to public service
as a member of the U.S. delegation to the United Nations in 1956.
Two years later his deep interest in international development won
him an appointment as director of the UN Development Program.

Then already sixty-seven, the car salesman turned economic
visionary took over the job of providing underdeveloped nations
with technical aid designed to stimulate investment and economic
development. For the next thirteen years Hoffman traveled widely,

raising some $250 million a year for the program from member nations and overseeing such aid projects as identifying mineral deposits in various countries, surveying a dam site in Nigeria, and eradicating locust plagues in Africa and Asia.

Meanwhile, in 1967, he married his second wife, Anna M. Rosenberg, his first wife having died six years earlier. He also found time to publish *World Without Want* (1962), one of several books he wrote during his lifetime. Hoffman remained with the UN Development Program until he retired in 1972. Unable to travel to the White House due to ill health, he received the Presidential Medal of Freedom during a ceremony at his home in New York City. John A. Scali, the U.S. representative to the United Nations, presented the award on behalf of President Nixon. Hoffman died later that year, at age eighty-three.

Charles LeRoy Lowman

A PIONEER IN MEDICINE, A PHYSICIAN OF SURPASSING SKILL, AND A GREAT HUMANITARIAN, DR. CHARLES LEROY LOWMAN HAS DEVOTED HIS LIFE TO THE SERVICE OF HIS FELLOW MAN. HIS GOOD WORKS HAVE ENRICHED THE LIVES OF THOUSANDS OF PATIENTS, BUT NONE MORE SO THAN THE GENERATIONS OF HANDICAPPED CHILDREN WHO HAVE BEEN TREATED AT THE HOSPITAL THAT HE FOUNDED IN LOS ANGELES EARLY IN THIS CENTURY. THE WORLD WILL LONG BE INDEBTED TO THIS DISTIN-GUISHED AND NOBLE AMERICAN.

★ ★ ★

President Richard Nixon awarded Lowman the Presidential Medal of Freedom with the above citation during a ceremony at San Clemente, California, on July 27, 1974.

Born in 1880 and raised in Park Ridge, Illinois, Charles LeRoy Lowman graduated from the University of Southern California Medical School in 1907. He studied orthopedic surgery—which is concerned with correcting diseases and deformities of the bones, joints, and muscles—at Massachusetts General Hospital in Boston and at Boston Children's Hospital. Elizabeth Arnold became his wife in 1909.

Returning to California, Lowman founded the Los Angeles Orthopedic Hospital in 1913. At the time, orthopedic surgery had not yet been formally recognized as a medical specialty, and his hospital was one of the first devoted to it.

Lowman was soon recognized as an authority in the field and eventually wrote eight medical textbooks. He also devised training programs for surgeons learning orthopedic surgery. Over the years he researched therapeutic pool treatments for polio victims and developed a surgical procedure to restore some muscle function for polio patients.

Active in the community, he gave considerable time to needy children. Between 1909 and 1972 he conducted a regular outpatient clinic for Los Angeles-area children and frequently donated his time to work with handicapped children at an orthopedic clinic in Calexico, Mexico. Lowman was instrumental in the passage of a 1927 California state law mandating state-supported education for handicapped children in hospitals and at home. For five decades he also served the Los Angeles Board of Education as an orthopedic consultant.

After 1945 Lowman served as chief of staff emeritus and director of education at his hospital, allowing him to focus on training young orthopedic surgeons. He continued his work with handicapped children in Mexico and remained active at the hospital until his last years. Lowman died in 1977, at age ninety-seven.

Gerald R. Ford

VICE PRESIDENT GERALD R. FORD, A REPUBLICAN, BECAME
PRESIDENT AUGUST 9, 1974, FOLLOWING THE RESIGNATION
OF PRESIDENT RICHARD NIXON. FORD COMPLETED THE
REMAINDER OF NIXON'S TERM (1974–1977).

MEDAL
CEREMONIES

FEBRUARY 10, 1976 *The White House Cabinet Room*

APRIL 1, 1976 *The White House East Room*

AUGUST 5, 1976 *The White House East Garden*

OCTOBER 14, 1976 *The White House State Dining Room*

JANUARY 10, 1977 *The White House East Room*

JANUARY 13, 1977 *Pan American Union*

JANUARY 19, 1977 *The White House Oval Office*

David Kirkpatrick Bruce

As a diplomat and scholar, he has distinguished himself and brought great honor to his country. With wisdom, courage, discipline, dedication to principle and unerring fidelity to the best interests of the United States, he has brilliantly discharged an array of diplomatic assignments—to France, Germany, Great Britain, the People's Republic of China and the North Atlantic Treaty Organization—unmatched in modern American history. David K. E. Bruce has truly earned the title Ambassador Extraordinary.

★ ★ ★

President Gerald R. Ford awarded Bruce the Presidential Medal of Freedom with the above citation during a White House ceremony February 10, 1976. The medal was accompanied by the added accolade "with distinction."

The first American diplomat to hold all three of the most prestigious ambassadorships in Europe—those to France, Germany, and Great Britain—David Kirkpatrick Bruce was born to a prominent Baltimore family in 1898. His father, William Cabell Bruce, was a Pulitzer Prize-winning biographer and a senator from Maryland. After seeing combat in World War I, David Bruce attended law schools at the University of Virginia and the University of Maryland and in 1921 began practicing law in Baltimore.

His first post with the foreign service came in 1925 as vice-consul in Rome, but his marriage in 1926 to Ailsa Mellon, daughter of financier and (then) Treasury Secretary Andrew W. Mellon, soon ended this first brush with diplomacy. Entering the world of finance in 1927, Bruce worked first for Bankers Trust Company and then with W. A. Harriman and Company Inc. At one point twenty-five corporations counted him on their boards of directors, yet he also found time to oversee his 500-acre tobacco plantation and a parachute manufacturing company and to write *Revolution to Reconstruction*, published in 1939.

With the U.S. entry into World War II, Bruce helped organize the Office of Strategic Services (OSS) and from 1943 to 1945 was chief of the intelligence corps' European division. By 1945 his first marriage had ended in divorce, and that year he married Evangeline Bell.

A civilian again after the war, he first helped administer the Marshall Plan in France and then in 1949 became U.S. ambassador to France. Between 1953 and 1955 Bruce was assigned the task of arranging for military and economic integration of Western European nations, a policy initiative that failed at that time.

Bruce next served the Eisenhower administration as ambassador to West Germany from 1957 to 1959. A popular and highly regarded diplomat, Bruce then capped an already impressive career with a long and highly successful appointment as U.S. ambassador to Great Britain from 1961 to 1969.

His first retirement from the State Department came in 1969, after having served Presidents Harry S. Truman, Dwight D. Eisenhower, John F. Kennedy, and Lyndon B. Johnson. But before long President Richard Nixon brought him back to handle the vexing Paris peace talks on ending the Vietnam War, an assignment that Bruce relinquished in 1971 with the talks still deadlocked. In 1973, however, he became the first head of the U.S. liaison in China. Then, in 1974, President Ford named him U.S. delegate to the North Atlantic Treaty Organization (NATO).

President Ford awarded the Presidential Medal of Freedom to Bruce upon his retirement from NATO in 1976. Bruce died less than two years later, at age seventy-nine.

Arthur Rubinstein

MUSICIAN, GENTLEMAN, AND BON VIVANT, ARTHUR RUBINSTEIN HAS SHARED HIS SINGULAR AND DEEPLY PERSONAL MASTERY OF THE PIANO THROUGHOUT THE WORLD. FOR OVER SEVEN DECADES HIS CEASELESS VITALITY, HIS LUMINOUS SPIRIT AND HIS PROFOUND DEPTH OF MIND HAVE BROUGHT A FRESH SPARKLE TO THE LIVES OF PEOPLE EVERYWHERE. HIS AUDIENCES LOVE HIM; HIS COLLEAGUES AND FRIENDS REVERE HIM; AND HIS COUNTRY, THE UNITED STATES OF AMERICA, IS PROUD TO PROCLAIM HIM AS A GIANT AMONG ARTISTS AND MEN.

★ ★ ★

President Gerald R. Ford awarded Rubinstein the Presidential Medal of Freedom with the above citation during a White House ceremony April 1, 1976.

Among the foremost pianists of this century, Arthur Rubinstein was born in Lodz, Poland, in 1887. His musical career began remarkably early; at age three he began taking piano lessons and the following year gave his first public performances as "Artur the Great Piano Virtuoso." After studying at the Warsaw Conservatory of Music until age eight, Rubinstein went to Germany, becoming a student of the famed violinist and friend of Brahms and Schumann, Joseph Joachim.

Rubinstein gave his Berlin debut at age twelve and during the next few years success in Europe continued to come easily. But music critics gave him a cool reception during his American debut at Carnegie Hall in 1906, and the discouraged young virtuoso stopped giving concerts for the next four years. When Rubinstein returned to the concert stage, he established himself as one of Europe's leading pianists.

His ability to improvise had much to do with his popularity in Europe, though, and when he returned to Carnegie Hall in 1919, critics again were unimpressed. Rubinstein was disappointed, but this time he continued playing, diverting himself with his playboy lifestyle as a member of Europe's international set.

The late 1920s became an important crossroads in Rubinstein's life. About this time he met and fell in love with fifteen-year-old Aniela Mlynarski, a conductor's daughter, while also reassessing himself as a musical artist. Abandoning his dissolute lifestyle, he began a period of intensive study and long, daily practice sessions, bringing a new discipline and intelligence to what had become his characteristic "grand manner" on the piano. Meanwhile, he also started making recordings, which helped spread his fame. In 1932 he married the nineteen-year-old Aniela.

The third time at Carnegie Hall proved to be the charm for Rubinstein. His performance in 1937 was hailed by critics—they called him a genius and established his lasting popularity in America. During World War II he moved his family to the United States and became a U.S. citizen in 1946.

After the war Rubinstein continued making recordings and giving concerts throughout much of the world. He eventually completed some two-hundred record albums during his career. While he regularly played pieces by Beethoven, Mozart, Ravel, Stravinsky, and others throughout the 1950s and 1960s, Rubinstein in his later years especially became acknowledged as the world master of Chopin.

Rubinstein played into the 1970s, when age and failing eyesight forced him to stop. He published his two-volume autobiography, *My Young Years* (1973) and *My Many Years* (1980). Rubinstein died in 1982, at age ninety-five.

Jesse Owens

ATHLETE, HUMANITARIAN, SPEAKER, AUTHOR—A MASTER OF THE SPIRIT AS WELL AS THE MECHANICS OF SPORT. HE IS A WINNER WHO KNOWS THAT WINNING IS NOT EVERYTHING. HE HAS SHARED WITH OTHERS HIS COURAGE, HIS DEDICATION TO THE HIGHEST IDEALS OF SPORTSMANSHIP. HIS ACHIEVEMENTS

HAVE SHOWN US ALL THE PROMISE OF AMERICA AND HIS FAITH
IN AMERICA HAS INSPIRED COUNTLESS OTHERS TO DO THEIR
BEST FOR THEMSELVES AND FOR THEIR COUNTRY.

★ ★ ★

*President Gerald R. Ford, a former athlete himself, awarded Owens the
Presidential Medal of Freedom with the above citation during a White
House ceremony August 5, 1976. The medal was accompanied with
the added accolade "with distinction."*

A black sharecropper's son and the grandson of slaves, Jesse Owens was
born in Danville, Alabama, in 1913. He picked cotton until moving to
Cleveland, Ohio, with his family at age nine and ran his first race four
years later. While still in high school he gained a national reputation as
a sprinter by winning three events at the 1933 National Interscholastic
Championships. Owens went on to Ohio State University, working his
way through because he did not have an athletic scholarship. He made
the track team in 1934, his sophomore year.

Though his feats at the 1936 Berlin Olympic Games were
undoubtedly his best known, some consider his performance the
year before at the Big Ten intercollegiate championships the best day
in track history. Just days before that meet Owens seriously wrenched
his back while wrestling playfully with a fraternity brother. He could
not practice before the meet and was in such pain that he needed
help getting out of the car at the track. But Owens steadfastly refused
to drop out of the running, courageously telling his coaches he
wanted to try and would see how it went one event at a time.

By any yardstick it was a stunning performance. In just forty-five
minutes Owens shattered a host of track and field records despite, or
perhaps because of, his injured back. He broke world records for the
long jump, the 220-yard dash, and the 220-yard low hurdles, and
equaled the world record for the 100-yard dash. Owens's record for
the long jump, an astounding twenty-six feet and eight and one-
quarter inches, stood for twenty-five years.

The United States almost did not send a track team to the 1936
Olympics at Berlin because of Nazi racial policies, but in the end
sixty-six Americans, including ten blacks, went. Nazi dictator Adolf
Hitler had been touting the superiority of the Aryan race before the
Olympics and was present when Owens snatched four Olympic gold
medals, with two record-breaking performances (the 200-meter
dash, and the long jump). Owens also tied the 100-meter dash record
and helped the United States win the gold in the 100-meter relay. An
embarrassed Hitler was relegated to congratulating Aryan athletes
who had come in second to the supposedly racially inferior black.

When Owens returned to the United States he set about capitalizing on his new-found fame with what were initially mixed
results. Ending his career as an amateur, he announced his plan to

become a professional entertainer. Over the next several years he stumped for Republican presidential candidate Alf Landon, ran races against horses and cars, and toured with a band, basketball teams, and baseball teams. He made money, but in 1939 stock market losses and the failure of his laundry company sent Owens into bankruptcy.

Never one to give up, he recovered financially during the 1940s and began to prosper as the owner of a marketing and public relations firm. Eventually earning over $100,000 a year, Owens toured the country making two or three speeches a week to primarily white audiences at sales meetings and conventions. He proved an extremely popular speaker, with an old-fashioned, spellbinding delivery in which he talked about patriotism, fair play, and clean living.

Long an inspiration for American black athletes, Owens was diagnosed with advanced lung cancer in 1979. He died the following year, at age sixty-six.

Martha Graham

DANCER, TEACHER, AND CHOREOGRAPHER, MARTHA GRAHAM HAS CAPTIVATED THE WORLD WITH HER MAGIC AND HAS LEFT A LEGACY OF IMAGINATION WITH ALL WHO HAVE WITNESSED HER TALENT. HER ENERGY, CREATIVITY AND DARING HAVE OPENED NEW DOORS OF EXPRESSION IN DANCE. HER FOLLOWERS AND FRIENDS ADORE HER, AND HER COUNTRY, THE UNITED STATES OF AMERICA, IS PROUD TO PROCLAIM HER A BRILLIANT STAR AND A NATIONAL TREASURE.

★ ★ ★

President Gerald R. Ford awarded Graham the Presidential Medal of Freedom with the above citation during a White House ceremony October 14, 1976.

A pioneer who helped create modern dance as the first enduring dance form outside ballet, Graham was born in Allegheny, Pennsylvania, in 1894. Her father was a physician and her mother was descended from the pilgrim Miles Standish who came to America aboard the *Mayflower*. Graham took up dancing in 1916 shortly after her father died, joining the Denishawn school in Los Angeles to learn the company's exotic "art" dance style. Eventually disenchanted with exoticism, she one day saw an abstract painting by the Russian artist Wassily Kandinsky and immediately decided to "dance like that."

Breaking with Denishawn, Graham went to New York in 1923 and there began developing her dance version of abstract, nonrepresentational art—a stark, sparing, angular style marked by tension and frank eroticism. Graham organized her first dance company in the mid–1920s, and she founded the Martha Graham School of Contemporary Dance some years later that became a training ground for a generation of modern dancers and a showcase for the works she choreographed. Also during the 1920s she began her longtime collaboration with Louis Horst, her accompanist.

Originally acclaimed as a dancer, she continued to pioneer her powerful, abstract style in the works she choreographed and usually produced with her own company. During the 1930s she was known especially for creating dances on American themes, such as *Appalachian Spring* and *Salem Shore*. From 1946 onward though she explored themes from Greek mythology and the Bible, including *Errand Into the Maze*, *Judith*, and *The Witch of Endor*. In 1948 she married Erick Hawkins, a modern dance choreographer, but the marriage ended in divorce within a few years.

Graham danced featured roles in her works for decades, only reluctantly retiring from the stage in 1969 when she was in her late sixties. Seven years later she became the first person from the world of dance to receive the Presidential Medal of Freedom when President Gerald Ford awarded it to her at the White House. Meanwhile, she continued choreographing and directing her company. The last of over 180 works she choreographed during her lifetime—*Maple Leaf Rag*—premiered just months before her death in 1991. She was ninety-six years old.

Iorwith Wilbur Abel

STEELWORKER, SOCIAL REFORMER, UNION ORGANIZER, AND LABOR STATESMAN, I. W. ABEL HAS FORGED A DISTINGUISHED RECORD OF WISE AND FIRM LEADERSHIP THAT EXEMPLIFIES THE VERY BEST TRADITIONS OF THE AMERICAN LABOR MOVEMENT. HIS MANY ACHIEVEMENTS AND HIS UNFAILING CONCERN FOR PEOPLE HAVE EARNED HIM NOT ONLY THE GRATITUDE, BUT THE ESTEEM AND RESPECT OF FELLOW CITIZENS.

★ ★ ★

President Gerald R. Ford awarded Abel the Presidential Medal of Freedom with the above citation during a White House ceremony January 10, 1977. The medal was accompanied by the added accolade "with distinction."

Iorwith Wilbur Abel, popularly known as Abe among rank-and-file steelworkers, was a pioneer union organizer in the 1930s who went on to become one of America's most influential labor leaders. A blacksmith's son, Abel was born in Magnolia, Ohio, in 1908. He got his first job as a steelworker at a Canton, Ohio, steel mill in 1925 after graduating from high school. For a time Abel found steady work and married Bernice N. Joseph in 1930.

Jobs at the steel mills became scarce during the depression, though, and at one point Abel took a brickyard worker's job paying just seven dollars a week. That job, he later said, straightened out his social thinking. In 1936, while working at the Timken Roller Bearing Company, he began what became a career in labor organization by helping form Local Union 1123 of the Steel Workers Organizing Committee (SWOC), which was then unionizing the steel industry. The next year the SWOC made him its staff representative.

Convinced a strong labor movement was needed, he became a militant unionist, in one year leading forty-two strikes. When the SWOC reorganized as the United Steelworkers of America (USW) in 1942, Abel was named district director for the Canton area. Ten years later the union selected him as its secretary-treasurer, making him the international union's second in command. Abel remained largely behind the scenes though, meeting with members of union locals and listening to their grievances. His affable manner won him a wide following, and in 1965 the USW elected him president.

His twelve years as president proved productive for the union and secured his reputation as a top labor leader. Abel won increased wages and benefits for steelworkers, added half a million members to the USW, negotiated productivity agreements, and initiated separate bargaining procedures for aluminum and other metal unions. He also lobbied the federal government for laws protecting employee pensions and promoting health and safety in the workplace. No longer the militant unionist of years past, Abel now believed the labor movement had progressed far enough that the interests of workers, employers, and the public had become intertwined. While calling collective bargaining a crisis business, he cautioned the need for patience. A strike, he said, was an act of last resort, a worker's right that was best used with good judgment. To that end he signed a historic negotiating agreement with steel companies in 1973, barring a strike during contract talks and submitting any unresolved differences to binding arbitration. The agreement produced a contract in 1974 without work stoppages, a major accomplishment in the strike-prone steel industry. The agreement was repeated in 1977.

That year Abel retired as USW president. He remarried after his first wife died in 1982 but succumbed to cancer a few years later. He died in 1987, just one day before his seventy-ninth birthday.

John Bardeen

A PHYSICIST OF GENIUS, JOHN BARDEEN HAS COMBINED FORMIDABLE AND UNIQUE SCIENTIFIC INSIGHTS WITH THE MATHEMATICAL ABILITY TO CARRY THEM THROUGH. HIS DISCOVERIES HAVE REVOLUTIONIZED ELECTRONICS AND COMMUNICATIONS CHANGING EACH OF OUR LIVES FOR THE BETTER. WE ARE PROUD TO HONOR HIM AS A CREATIVE MASTER IN THE FINEST TRADITIONS OF SCIENCE AND TECHNOLOGY.

★ ★ ★

President Gerald R. Ford awarded Bardeen the Presidential Medal of Freedom with the above citation during a White House ceremony January 10, 1977. The medal was accompanied by the added accolade "with distinction" and was accepted by Bardeen's son William.

Born in Madison, Wisconsin, in 1908, John Bardeen was the son of the dean of the University of Wisconsin medical school. His mother died when he was just twelve, and the boy suffered a congenital disorder that caused his hands to tremble. Nevertheless, the young Bardeen became a champion swimmer and graduated from the University of Wisconsin with a degree in electrical engineering in 1928. He won his master's degree at Wisconsin the following year, and in 1936 earned his doctorate at Princeton, having focused his dissertation on the forces holding electrons within metals. From 1935 to 1938 he held a research fellowship at Harvard and in the latter year married Jane Maxwell.

After working for the Naval Ordinance Laboratory during World War II, Bardeen went to Bell Telephone Laboratories as a research physicist. William Shockley and Walter H. Brattain had already begun work there on semiconductors, materials such as silicon with more electrical resistance than a metal but less than an insulator. They hoped to build a semiconductor device to replace vacuum tubes, which wasted large amounts of power and were fragile, bulky, and short-lived. Bardeen joined the effort in 1945, and when the semiconductor device designed by Shockley failed to perform as expected, Bardeen came up with the crucial explanation why—a layer of electrons trapped on the semiconductor's surface was interfering with its normal operation.

With Dr. Brattain leading the actual physical experimentation, the researchers thoroughly investigated the problem and by 1948 announced they had built the first working transistor. Within a few years transistors produced a revolution in electronics, making components smaller, more durable, and more efficient. Meanwhile, the innovation was further refined to produce miniaturized clusters of transistors on a single silicon chip, making the revolution in computers possible. For their work, Bardeen, Shockley, and Brattain shared the 1956 Nobel Prize in physics.

Bardeen next turned his attention to superconductivity and other properties of matter at low temperatures, after becoming professor of physics and electrical engineering at the University of Illinois in 1951. With two of his students, Leon N. Cooper and J. Robert Schrieffer, Bardeen studied superconductivity phenomena, in which metals at very low temperatures conduct electricity with no resistance. By 1957 the three had developed a theory to successfully explain superconductivity, marking an important advance in theoretical physics. Bardeen shared the 1972 Nobel Prize in physics with his coworkers for the achievement.

During his long career, Bardeen won a number of other awards besides the Nobel and the Presidential Medal of Freedom, including the National Science Foundation's National Medal of Science (1965). He lived until 1991, reaching the age of eighty-two.

Irving Berlin

MUSICIAN, COMPOSER, HUMANITARIAN, AND PATRIOT, IRVING
BERLIN HAS CAPTURED THE FONDEST DREAMS AND DEEPEST
EMOTIONS OF THE AMERICAN PEOPLE IN THE FORM OF POPULAR
MUSIC. HIS ENORMOUS TALENT, TIRELESS ENTHUSIASM, AND
BOUNDLESS COMPASSION HAVE INSPIRED GENERATIONS OF HIS
COUNTRYMEN. HIS SONGS WILL INSPIRE GENERATIONS MORE. IN
HIS LIFE—IN HIS WORK—WE HAVE TRULY SEEN GOD BLESS
AMERICA.

★ ★ ★

*President Gerald R. Ford awarded Berlin the Presidential Medal of
Freedom with the above citation during a White House ceremony
January 10, 1977. The medal was accompanied by the added accolade
"with distinction." Neither Berlin nor a representative was able to
attend the presentation.*

A Russian-born immigrant, Irving Berlin rose from the tenements of
New York's Lower East Side to become one of America's best-known
and prolific composers of popular songs. His "Alexander's Ragtime
Band," "God Bless America," and "White Christmas" are among the
most enduring of the approximately 1,500 songs he wrote during his
lifetime. He also composed the scores for nineteen Broadway
musicals, including the 1946 smash hit *Annie Get Your Gun,* and
eighteen films, including *Top Hat* and *White Christmas.*

Hardship was almost a way of life for the young Berlin, who was
born Israel Baline in a Russian village in 1888. His father served as an
official at the town synagogue, and in 1893 persecution of Jews in
Russia forced his family to emigrate to the United States. Berlin's
father died three years after they settled in New York's rough-and-
tumble Lower East Side, leaving an eight-year-old Berlin to find work
on the city streets to help support the family. In those first years he
hawked newspapers and served as a guide for a blind, singing beggar
known as "Blind Sol," but by age seventeen he had become a singing
waiter at a Chinatown cafe.

Berlin published his first song, "Marie from Sunny Italy," in 1907
while at the restaurant and in 1909 started working as a staff lyricist
for a music publisher. At about that time he began writing tunes in
ragtime, a jazz style with a highly syncopated melody just then
becoming popular. His smash hit "Alexander's Ragtime Band" (1911)
turned ragtime into a national craze, sold over one million copies in
sheet music, and won him an international reputation. But Berlin's
marriage two years later ended in tragedy after just five months. His
new wife died of typhoid fever contracted while on their honeymoon.

Despite his personal loss he continued writing songs and next set his sights on Broadway. Berlin composed the score for his first complete Broadway musical, *Watch Your Step,* in 1914 and, after serving in World War I, built the off-Broadway Music Box Theater. His musical revues there rivaled Ziegfeld productions during the 1920s. In 1926 he married again in a highly publicized wedding, and his second wife, Ellin Mackay, inspired his popular love song "Always."

The 1929 stock market crash and the depression hit Berlin hard financially, forcing him to rely again on writing songs for a living. His light revues being inappropriate in the dark days of the depression, he turned for a time to musicals concerning social awareness, such as *Face the Music* (1932). In 1935 he completed his first motion picture musical, *Top Hat,* the first of a series of successful films he made during the 1930s and 1940s. It proved a fertile period, in which he produced some of his best-known songs, including "God Bless America" (1938), "White Christmas" (1942), and "There's No Business Like Show Business" (1946).

The Broadway musical *Annie Get Your Gun* (1946) marked Berlin's return to stage productions after World War II, and in 1950 he wrote the highly successful *Call Me Madam.* He wrote the score for the 1954 film musical *White Christmas* and then retired that year. Berlin made one last Broadway musical in 1962, *Mr. President.*

Certainly among the most successful and durable popular song writers of this century, Berlin died in 1989. He was 101 years old.

Norman Borlaug

REVOLUTIONARY SCIENTIST AND ELOQUENT PROPHET, HE PERFORMED MIRACLES WITH GRAIN AND SAVED UNTOLD MILLIONS FROM STARVATION. HIS WORK HAS PUSHED BACK THE SHADOW OF HUNGER ON THIS PLANET AND GIVEN US PRECIOUS TIME TO FORCE ITS FINAL RETREAT.

★ ★ ★

President Gerald R. Ford awarded Borlaug the Presidential Medal of Freedom with the above citation during a White House ceremony January 10, 1977. The medal was accompanied by the added accolade "with distinction."

A key figure in the creation of the high-yield crops that produced the 1960s Green Revolution, Norman Borlaug was born in 1914, the son of Norwegian immigrants who had settled in the Midwest. He grew up on a farm near Cresco, Iowa, and graduated from the University of Minnesota with a forestry degree in 1937. That year he also married Margaret Gibson. Continuing his academic studies at the University of Minnesota, he won his doctorate in plant pathology in 1942 and then went to work for DuPont as a researcher in charge of investigating bactericides, fungicides, and preservatives.

Meanwhile, severe crop failures in Mexico threatened food supplies in a nation already importing 50 percent of its wheat. The country needed a more disease-resistant strain of wheat bred specifically for local conditions, and the Mexican government turned to the United States for help. The Rockefeller Foundation agreed to supply technical assistance, and in 1944 Borlaug joined a team of agricultural scientists sent to Mexico. Borlaug took charge of organizing and directing the Cooperative Wheat Research and Production Program there.

He and his research team worked with Mexican agricultural scientists to develop high-yield, disease-resistant strains suited to the local conditions. The results were dramatic. By 1948 new strains had already made Mexico self-supporting in wheat production, and a dwarf strain produced by Borlaug's team in 1954 doubled Mexico's wheat yields again when it was distributed to farmers in 1961.

Other developing countries soon became interested in Borlaug's work at what was now known as the International Center for Maize and Wheat Improvement. The Green Revolution, which drastically increased food production around the world, soon began to get under way. Meanwhile, scientists in the Philippines adapted to rice Borlaug's idea of developing high-yield dwarf strains, thus spreading the Green Revolution to rice production.

His success at sharply increasing food production in developing nations dramatically cut world hunger and won him the 1970 Nobel Peace Prize. Borlaug retired as director of the International Center for Maize and Wheat Improvement in 1979 but continued as associate director of the Rockefeller Foundation, a position he had assumed in 1964. The author of several books, he has been a professor at Texas A&M University since 1984.

Omar N. Bradley

MILITARY HERO, COURAGEOUS IN BATTLE, AND GENTLE IN
SPIRIT, FRIEND OF THE COMMON SOLDIER, GENERAL OF THE
ARMY, FIRST CHAIRMAN OF THE JOINT CHIEFS OF STAFF, HE
EMBODIES THE BEST OF THE AMERICAN MILITARY TRADITION
WITH DIGNITY, HUMANITY, AND HONOR.

★ ★ ★

*President Gerald R. Ford awarded Bradley the Presidential Medal of
Freedom with the above citation during a White House ceremony
January 10, 1977. The medal was accompanied by the added accolade
"with distinction."*

Called the "GI's General" because of his concern for the individual foot
soldier, Omar N. Bradley became a leading U.S. general in the
European theater during World War II. From the earliest campaigns
involving U.S. troops in North Africa and Italy to the final Allied drive
into Nazi Germany, General Bradley demonstrated his superior ability
for organizing and directing his armies to victory in battle. He was
widely recognized as both a skilled planner and a master tactician.

Bradley was born in Clark, Missouri, in 1893. When he was just
thirteen his father died, and a few years later Bradley found his
calling in the army. Graduating from the U.S. Military Academy at
West Point in 1915, he served in various posts during the 1920s and
1930s, including two stints as an instructor at West Point. He married
Mary Elizabeth Quayle in 1916.

During the years leading up to the U.S. entry into World War II,
Bradley served with the War Department staff in Washington, D.C.,
and won his promotion to brigadier general. In 1943, when U.S.
troops went into battle in North Africa, Bradley was there, first as a
reconnaissance officer for General Dwight D. Eisenhower and then as
commander of the Second U.S. Corps in northern Tunisia. Aided by
British forces, Bradley's troops captured Bizerte and Tunis to split the
German armies and force their surrender in North Africa. Promoted
to lieutenant general soon after, he led the Second U.S. Corps to
victory in Sicily as well.

His greatest victories were still to come, though. After helping
plan the Normandy invasion, he commanded all U.S. ground forces
for the cross-channel attack. Once the beachhead was firmly established, he became Twelfth Army Group commander and orchestrated
the breakout from the beachhead that began pushing the Nazis
eastward toward Germany. Bradley's Twelfth Army Group soon grew
to thirty-four divisions—at some 1,400,000 combat troops, the
biggest field command in U.S. history—and became the main Allied
force driving into Germany. Despite the Nazis' last-gasp offensive

(the Battle of the Bulge), Bradley's Twelfth Army pushed deep into Germany and finally linked up with Soviet armies driving westward.

Promoted to a four-star general after the German surrender in 1945, he became army chief of staff in 1948 and the first chairman of the Joint Chiefs of Staff upon reorganization of the armed forces command the following year. A five-star general in that post, he retired in 1953 at the close of the Korean War.

For Bradley's many years of service to the country in both war and peacetime, President Ford awarded him a Presidential Medal of Freedom in 1977. Among Bradley's many military honors were the Distinguished Service Medal with oak leaf cluster, the Legion of Merit with oak leaf cluster, the Silver Star, the Bronze Star, the Navy Distinguished Service Medal, and several foreign decorations. The GI's General died in 1981 at age eighty-eight.

Arleigh "Thirty-one Knot" Burke

COMBAT COMMANDER, INNOVATIVE NAVAL STRATEGIST AND TACTICIAN, INSPIRING LEADER, FIRST THREE TERM CHIEF OF NAVAL OPERATIONS, HE MADE THE SEA A PLACE OF VICTORY IN WAR, A MIGHTY FORTRESS IN PEACE.

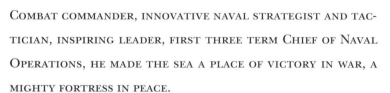

★ ★ ★

President Gerald R. Ford awarded Burke the Presidential Medal of Freedom with the above citation in a White House ceremony January 10, 1977. The medal was accompanied by the added accolade "with distinction."

A highly decorated combat commander and leading naval strategist, Arleigh Burke was born in Boulder, Colorado, in 1901. Raised on a farm, he nevertheless decided on the navy early in his life and graduated from the U.S. Naval Academy in 1923. That same year he married Roberta Gorsuch. After serving aboard the battleship *Arizona* and elsewhere, he won a master's degree in engineering at the University of Michigan in 1931. As a naval ordnance specialist, Burke was assigned to the navy's Bureau of Ordnance between sea duty tours on various ships during the 1930s and early 1940s.

In 1943 the navy granted his request for a combat role and made him commander of Destroyer Squadron 23 in the South Pacific. At Bougainville, Empress Augusta Bay, and other naval actions in the Solomons, Burke quickly became known for his daring high-speed combat tactics and the devastating precision of his gun crews.

Impressed by Burke's high-speed attacks against the Japanese, Admiral William F. Halsey dubbed him "Thirty-one Knot Burke" later in 1943. In all, Burke commanded his squadron during twenty-two combat missions between 1943 and 1944.

By 1945 Burke was rapidly moving up the chain of command. He served as Admiral Marc Mitscher's chief of staff in 1945, as chief of staff to the Atlantic Fleet from 1945 to 1947, and as a member of the navy's nuclear weapons development program in the office of the chief of naval operations from 1947 to 1949. Promoted to rear admiral in 1950, Burke saw action as a cruiser division commander during the Korean War and also sat on the armistice commission during 1951.

Back in Washington again, he directed the Navy Department's strategic plans division from 1952 to 1954. Then in 1955 President Dwight D. Eisenhower appointed Burke chief of naval operations, passing over some ninety, more senior, officers to choose him. Burke remained in the post for six years, longer than any previous appointee, until his retirement in 1961. During his tenure he fostered the adoption of new technology, including the widespread use of missiles and the accelerated building of nuclear-powered submarines and surface ships. He oversaw the development of the Polaris submarine missile program, the first submarine-launched nuclear missiles, and promoted many other technological innovations as well. But of still greater importance was his role in readying the navy for future defense needs. Burke correctly foresaw limited wars as the navy's primary task of the future and strove to maintain a versatile fleet to meet that need.

After retiring in 1961, Burke held several directorships of large corporations. Retired from his business interests in the 1970s, Burke died in December 1995, at the age of ninety-four.

Alexander Calder

Sculptor, painter, artistic genius and gentleman, Alexander Calder breathed new life into the ancient art of sculpture and added spirit and vitality to his country even as he did to his work. His wit and imagination graced a broad range of disciplines and created a truly public art. The face of America is richer and more beautiful for the many examples of his imagination which cover it.

★ ★ ★

President Gerald R. Ford awarded Calder a posthumous Presidential Medal of Freedom with the above citation during a White House ceremony January 10, 1977. The medal was accompanied by the added accolade, "with distinction." No representative for Calder was able to attend, and the medal was delivered at a later date.

An artist who worked comfortably in many different mediums, Alexander Calder was born in Lawnton, Pennsylvania, in 1898. He was truly a child of the art world—his father was a noted sculptor, his mother was a painter, and his grandfather had sculpted the statue of William Penn adorning the top of Philadelphia's city hall. Though his first playground was his parents' art studio, Calder's initial choice of a career turned out to be engineering. He graduated from Stevens Institute of Technology in Hoboken, New Jersey, with a master's degree in engineering in 1919 but he worked only briefly as an engineer. In 1923 he began following in his parents' footsteps by studying art at the Art Students League in New York. About this time he also found work as an illustrator for the *National Police Gazette.*

Three years later, in 1926, he began establishing his reputation as an artist. In addition to having his paintings exhibited at a New York gallery, Calder also published a book, *Animal Sketches,* and saw his fanciful re-creation of a miniature circus fashioned from pieces of wire, cork, and wood become the rage in Paris. (Calder added to the circus over the years, and it is now on permanent display at New York's Whitney Museum of American Art.) But from an artistic standpoint, 1930 proved an even more important turning point. That year Calder abandoned his representational style for abstract designs and soon after exhibited his abstract sculpture, *Universe,* in France.

In 1932 he added the crucial element of motion to his art, creating the first mobiles, the art form for which he became famous. His earliest works used motors and pulleys to move the discs, globes, and other abstract geometric shapes, but Calder soon turned to balancing the moving parts so that a breeze or a light touch by an admirer set the whole in motion. The parts moving in relation to one another thus presented spontaneous and often playfully varying patterns not possible with stationary art.

Calder created mobiles large and small, incorporating imaginative designs that won him world fame. Among the outdoor mobiles for which he is known are the water mobile at the New York World's Fair (1939–1940), the *Water Ballet* mobile at a General Motors center in Detroit (1954), and the *Four Elements* mobile in Stockholm (1962). He also created mobile-stabiles, so called because they combine parts that move with others that remain stationary. Among these are *The Spiral* (1958) in Paris, and *Five Rudders* (1964) in Saint Louis, Missouri.

Considered one of the century's most versatile artists, he also made oil paintings, drawings, lithographs, toys, jewelry, and tapestries. His autobiography, *An Autobiography with Pictures,* was published in 1966. Calder died in 1976, at age seventy-eight.

Bruce Catton

MAN OF LETTERS, PREEMINENT HISTORIAN OF THE WAR
BETWEEN THE STATES, HE MADE US HEAR THE SOUNDS OF
BATTLE AND CHERISH PEACE. HE MADE US SEE THE BLEEDING
WOUND OF SLAVERY AND HOLD MAN'S FREEDOM DEAR.

★ ★ ★

*President Gerald R. Ford awarded Catton the Presidential Medal of
Freedom with the above citation during a White House ceremony
January 10, 1977. The medal was accompanied by the added accolade
"with distinction."*

The son of a Congregational minister, Bruce Catton was born in 1899
and grew up in a small Michigan lumber town named Benzonia. His
religious upbringing certainly influenced his later writings, and so too
did his boyhood fascination with the war stories he heard from local
Civil War veterans. He entered Oberlin College in 1916, but interrupted
his studies to serve in the navy during World War I. Then, following
his junior year, he left school for good to became a newspaper reporter.

Between 1920 and 1926 he wrote for the *Cleveland News, Cleveland
Plain Dealer,* and the *Boston American.* Catton married Hazel Cherry
in 1925, and the following year began writing for the Newspaper
Enterprise Association. He remained there until 1943, when he became
information director of the War Production Board in Washington,
D.C. Similar jobs followed in the Commerce and Interior departments
until 1948. That year he published *The War Lords of Washington,* which
had been inspired by his War Production Board experiences, and
decided to devote himself to writing history full time.

Catton's now famous first trilogy grew out of a commission to
write a centennial history of the Civil War, and today it ranks among
his best works. Written in his characteristic journalistic style, the three
books focused on the Army of the Potomac and drew heavily on the
observations of the soldiers themselves. The first two volumes, *Mr.
Lincoln's Army* (1951) and *Glory Road* (1952), did well enough, but
Catton's third volume secured his reputation as a leading Civil War
historian. That volume, *A Stillness at Appomattox,* appeared in 1953
and won both the Pulitzer Prize and the National Book Award.

Catton became editor of *American Heritage* magazine in 1954 and
helped revitalize the struggling publication. Though he remained a
senior editor on the magazine until his death, he began devoting more
time to his own writing after 1959. A second Civil War trilogy appeared
in the 1960s—*The Coming Fury* (1961), *Terrible Swift Sword* (1963), and
Never Call Retreat (1965)—as well as two books about Ulysses S. Grant,
Grant Moves South (1960) and *Grant Takes Command* (1969).

In his later years, he worked with his son William on *The Bold and
Magnificent Dream: America's Founding Years, 1492–1815.* The book

was the last he published during his lifetime; Catton died in 1978, the year it appeared in print. He was seventy-eight years old.

Joe DiMaggio

Superb athlete, coach, author and businessman, Joe DiMaggio stands tall among the ranks of genuine American heroes. Known and revered around the world as the "Yankee Clipper," he contributed many years of style and splendid ability to the sport which has come to be known as our national pastime. His character and grace both on and off the playing field have been a continuing source of inspiration to Americans of all ages.

★ ★ ★

President Gerald R. Ford awarded DiMaggio the Presidential Medal of Freedom with the above citation during a White House ceremony January 10, 1977. The medal was accompanied by the added accolade "with distinction" and was accepted by Dominic DiMaggio on his brother's behalf.

A leading hitter and one of baseball's all-time best outfielders, Joe DiMaggio was born in Martinez, California, in 1914. The son of Italian immigrant parents and one of nine children, DiMaggio was raised in San Francisco. Two of his older brothers also played baseball professionally: Dominic became a star player for the Boston Red Sox, and Vince played center field for the San Francisco Seals, a minor league team. But Joe got his start in baseball the way millions of youngsters have, by playing informal games in neighborhood sand lots. As a teenager he played in the Boys Club league and often skipped school to watch his brother Vince play.

It was Vince who finally got Joe, a seventeen-year-old hopeful, his big break. Vince talked the Seals into taking on his little brother as shortstop for the last few games of the 1932 season, and in Joe's first game he won a spot on the team by scoring a double and a triple. He also made a few wild throws at shortstop and was promptly moved to the outfield, where he played for the rest of his baseball career.

DiMaggio played just three seasons in the minor leagues before joining the New York Yankees in 1936. Already known as a hitter, the highly publicized rookie amazed fans with his seemingly effortless grace. He batted .323 for his first season, and posted more assists than any other outfielder. Chosen for the all-star team every year he played, the "Yankee Clipper" quickly became an inspiration to his teammates, not only for his athletic ability but also because he often played despite painful injuries. Before DiMaggio, the Yankees had lost in the playoffs several years running. With him, the Yankees won the World Series in 1936, and he helped them take it eight more times during his career.

Except for his stint in the army (1943–1945), DiMaggio played for the Yankees every year from 1936 until his retirement in 1951. He posted various records during that time, but perhaps the most important was his major-league record of hitting safely in fifty-six consecutive games, in 1941.

After his retirement DiMaggio became a public relations executive and also made appearances on television. His five-year marriage to his first wife had ended in divorce in 1944, and in 1954 he married the film star Marilyn Monroe. The highly publicized marriage lasted only nine months, however.

DiMaggio published two books, *Lucky To Be A Yankee* (1946) and *Baseball for Everyone* (1948), and was inducted into the Baseball Hall of Fame in 1955. The Baseball Writers' Association in 1969 named him the Greatest Living All-Time Baseball Player.

Will and Ariel Durant

WRITER, HISTORIAN AND PHILOSOPHER, WILL DURANT HAS PROVIDED AN OPEN WINDOW INTO THE LIVES AND THOUGHTS OF PAST AGES. WITH THE COLLABORATION OF HIS WIFE, ARIEL, HE HAS HELPED LEAD US THROUGH THE PAST TO THE MEANING OF THE PRESENT. AN ELOQUENT APOSTLE OF SOCIAL ORDER AND INDIVIDUAL FREEDOM, HE IS AN ENEMY OF CHAOS, A FRIEND AND AN INVALUABLE GUIDE TO THE MILLIONS OF GRATEFUL READERS.

WRITER, HISTORIAN AND PHILOSOPHER, ARIEL DURANT HAS COMBINED A SENSITIVE AND SWEEPING VISION WITH UNIQUE LITERARY TALENTS. HER LIFELONG COLLABORATION WITH HER HUSBAND, WILL, HAS HELPED MAKE HISTORY ACCESSIBLE, POPU-LARIZING BUT NEVER CHEAPENING ITS LESSONS. THE STYLE AND SUBSTANCE OF HER WRITING HAVE MADE THE PAST MORE VIVID AND ENRICHED OUR LIVES IN THE PRESENT.

★ ★ ★

President Gerald R. Ford awarded Will and Ariel separate Presidential Medals of Freedom with the above citations during a White House

*ceremony January 10, 1977. The medals were accompanied by the
added accolade "with distinction."*

Will and Ariel Durant were best known for their *The Story of
Civilization,* an eleven-volume work tracing world history from its
origins to the nineteenth century. Written as a popular history for
the average reader, the series sought to convey a broader sense of past
civilizations, and so included material on their art and literature,
science, manners, and morals, as well as their governments. The
series proved an enormous success, establishing the Durants among
the most widely read writers of popular history.

William James Durant was born in North Adams, Massachusetts,
in 1885. A son of French-Canadian parents and one of eleven
children in a devoutly Catholic family, Will grew up in Massachusetts
and New Jersey. After graduating from Saint Peter's College in 1907,
he worked briefly as a newspaper reporter before deciding to enter
the priesthood. His religious zeal lasted only until 1911, however,
when he suffered a loss of faith and left the seminary.

Two years later, while teaching at the anarchist-sponsored Ferrer
Modern School in New York City, he met and married a fifteen-year-
old student, Ada Kaufman. Ada, who legally changed her name to
Ariel after husband Will began calling her that, was born in Prosurov,
Russia, in 1898 and came to the United States with her parents in
1900. Years afterward she fondly recalled her wedding day in 1913,
when she roller-skated to New York's City Hall to marry her twenty-
eight-year-old husband-to-be.

A year after the marriage, Will became director of an adult education center in New York City, a position he held until 1927.
Meanwhile, in 1917 he earned his doctorate in philosophy from
Columbia University and published his dissertation as his first book,
Philosophy and the Social Problem. His second book, *The Story of
Philosophy: The Lives and Opinions of the Greatest Philosophers,*
appeared in 1926 and became a huge success. A popular and highly
readable treatment, the book eventually sold more than two million
copies and allowed Will to devote himself to writing full time.

The following year Will and Ariel began work on *The Story of
Civilization,* a popular history he had conceived years earlier in 1912
while recuperating from an attack of dysentery in Damascus, Syria.
The idea sprang from the work of the British historian Henry
Thomas Buckle, who had written an introduction to a history of civilization but who had died in Damascus before writing the history
itself. Ariel contributed to *The Story of Civilization* from the very
beginning, and the first volume appeared in 1935.

Will formally recognized the great importance of his wife's continuing contribution to the series by listing her as coauthor on the
seventh volume, *The Age of Reason,* which was published in 1961. She
was coauthor on every succeeding volume, including the tenth,
Rousseau and Revolution, which won a Pulitzer Prize in 1968. The

Durants' published the eleventh and last volume, *The Age of Napoleon*, in 1975.

They wrote their joint autobiography, *Will and Ariel: A Dual Autobiography*, in 1977. Four years later Ariel died at age eighty-three. Her husband and longtime writing partner died just thirteen days after her. He was ninety-six.

Arthur Fiedler

VIOLINIST, CONDUCTOR AND MUSICAL INNOVATOR, MAESTRO FIEDLER HAS BRIDGED THE GAP BETWEEN POPULAR AND CLASSICAL MUSIC AND GIVEN MILLIONS AROUND THE WORLD A GREATER APPRECIATION OF AMERICA'S RICH CULTURAL HERITAGE. HIS SPIRIT AND ZEST FOR LIVING HAVE MADE AN IMMEASURABLE CONTRIBUTION TO THE QUALITY OF AMERICAN LIFE.

★ ★ ★

President Gerald R. Ford awarded Fiedler the Presidential Medal of Freedom with the above citation during a White House ceremony January 10, 1977. The medal was accompanied by the added accolade "with distinction."

The Boston Pops Orchestra leader for nearly fifty years, Arthur Fiedler was born in Boston, Massachusetts, in 1894, to a very musical family. His mother was an amateur pianist and his father played in the first violin section of the Boston Symphony Orchestra, and there had been so many previous generations of musicians that his family had long ago acquired the surname Fiedler, from the German for *fiddler*. Young Arthur was named after a family friend who had conducted the Boston Symphony for many years.

Fiedler took violin lessons as a child. When he was sixteen, his family went to Vienna, and Fiedler continued his musical training at the exclusive Royal Academy of Music in Berlin, studying under Ernst von Dohnanyi, the Hungarian composer, Willy Hess, a former Boston Symphony conductor, and others. Fiedler made his conducting debut when he was only seventeen and also performed as a musician with his father's group, the Berlin String Quartet, and at nearby theaters and cafes.

With the outbreak of World War I Fiedler returned to the United States and in 1915 made his first appearance with the Boston Symphony Orchestra, playing second violin. Rejected by the U.S. Army when he tried to enlist in 1918, Fiedler returned to the Boston

Symphony, this time playing the viola. From time to time he was switched to other instruments, playing the piano, organ, violin, celesta, and percussion. His shifting among instruments eventually led fellow musicians to nickname him the orchestra's "floating kidney."

Despite his skill as a musician, Fiedler's great ambition was conducting. In 1924 he gathered twenty-two of Boston's finest musicians to form the Boston Sinfoniatta, a chamber orchestra that performed many seldom-heard compositions and toured Massachusetts and nearby states. Fiedler's reputation was on the rise, but in 1926 he nevertheless lost an opportunity to conduct the Boston Pops Orchestra when the organization bypassed him for an established Italian conductor. Deeply disappointed, Fiedler took over the directorship of Boston University's student orchestra.

He refused to give up, however, and the following year he organized free open-air concerts of symphonic music, personally overseeing construction of a wooden concert shell along Boston's Charles River and enlisting forty-six members of the Boston Symphony Orchestra for the project. Fiedler's Esplanade concerts were an immediate success and became a popular summertime tradition in Boston. (Fiedler began morning Esplanade concerts for children, featuring young musicians, in 1938.)

Largely because of his enormously popular summer concerts, Fiedler finally realized his dream of becoming an established conductor—he was named conductor of the Boston Pops in 1930. Holding that position for forty-nine years, he became the nation's longest-reigning symphony orchestra conductor. During his long tenure Fiedler became known as "Mr. Pops" and was one of the best-known musicians in the country. Twelve years after taking over the Boston Pops, he married Ellen Bottomley.

Fiedler's enormous popularity stemmed from his knack for understanding his audiences. He frequently combined popular tunes (show music, pop songs) with semiclassical and more serious classical fare. Varying this wide-ranging repertoire from season to season, Fiedler enjoyed introducing new music by American composers as well as recent hits and surprise selections, such as songs from the children's television program "Sesame Street." His was the first symphony orchestra to perform rock-and-roll music in a live concert.

Under Fiedler's direction the Boston Pops also enjoyed great success in the record market. From 1935, when the Pops began recording its music, to the early 1970s, it had sales totaling some fifty-million records. In 1953 Fiedler created the Boston Pops Tour Orchestra and traveled with them throughout the United States and to Europe in 1971. Fiedler frequently appeared as guest conductor with other orchestras throughout the world.

Fiedler never retired from his beloved Boston Pops, continuing as its conductor until he died in 1979. He was eighty-four years old.

Henry J. Friendly

HONORED STUDENT AND SERVANT OF THE LAW, MAN OF INTELLECT
AND WISDOM, HE BROUGHT A BRILLIANCE AND A SENSE OF PRE-
CISION TO AMERICAN JURISPRUDENCE, SHARPENING ITS FOCUS AND
STRENGTHENING ITS COMMITMENT TO THE HIGH GOAL OF EQUAL
AND EXACT JUSTICE FOR EVERY AMERICAN CITIZEN.

★ ★ ★

*President Gerald R. Ford awarded Friendly the Presidential Medal of
Freedom with the above citation during a White House ceremony
January 10, 1977. The medal was accompanied by the added accolade
"with distinction."*

A federal appeals court judge for twenty-seven years, Henry J.
Friendly was born in Elmira, New York, in 1903. He proved an exceptional student. Graduating summa cum laude from Harvard in 1923,
he earned his law degree there four years later. After clerking for
Supreme Court Justice Louis D. Brandeis from 1927 to 1928, Friendly
joined a New York City law firm and there gained expertise in
railroad reorganizations. He married Sophie S. Stern in 1930.

Pan American World Airways made him a vice president and
general counsel in 1946, and Friendly played an important role in
securing new routes for the airline. Then, in 1959, President Dwight
D. Eisenhower appointed him to the U.S. Court of Appeals for the
Second Circuit, a busy and influential court handling cases arising
from New York, Connecticut, and Vermont.

In his post as federal judge, Friendly gained a reputation for producing especially lucid, scholarly legal opinions dealing with a wide
variety of cases. A conservative Republican, he joined the debate over
Fifth Amendment rights, arguing that criminals were using protections to shield themselves from the law and that police should
have the power to question suspects before arresting them.

Friendly served as chief judge of the second circuit court between
1971 and 1973 but later in the 1970s went into semiretirement. He continued hearing cases even after receiving the Presidential Medal of
Freedom, but the death of his wife in 1985 affected him deeply. His
health and eyesight failing, he died the following year, at age eighty-two.

Lady Bird Johnson

ONE OF AMERICA'S GREAT FIRST LADIES, SHE CLAIMED HER OWN
PLACE IN THE HEARTS AND HISTORY OF THE AMERICAN PEOPLE.
IN COUNCILS OF POWER OR IN HOMES OF THE POOR, SHE MADE
GOVERNMENT HUMAN WITH HER UNIQUE COMPASSION AND HER
GRACE, WARMTH AND WISDOM. HER LEADERSHIP TRANSFORMED
THE AMERICAN LANDSCAPE AND PRESERVED ITS NATURAL
BEAUTY AS A NATIONAL TREASURE.

★ ★ ★

*President Gerald R. Ford awarded Johnson the Presidential Medal of
Freedom with the above citation during a White House ceremony
January 10, 1977. The medal was accompanied by the added accolade
"with distinction."*

A celebrated hostess and successful businesswoman in her own right,
Lady Bird Johnson was born Claudia Alta Taylor in the tiny north-
eastern Texas town of Karnack in 1912. Her father was a prosperous
merchant and landowner, and her mother, a cultured woman,
believed in such humanitarian causes as integration and women's
suffrage. She acquired her nickname at age two after her nursemaid
remarked she was "pretty as a lady bird." A good student, Taylor
graduated high school at age fifteen and earned two degrees from the
University of Texas at Austin—a bachelor of arts degree in 1933 and a
second bachelor's degree in journalism in 1934.

Introduced to her future husband Lyndon B. Johnson soon after
graduating, she later summed up the encounter with, "I knew I'd met
something remarkable, but I didn't know quite what." She remained
understandably cautious when he proposed to her the next day, but
Lyndon Johnson, then executive secretary to a member of Congress
from Texas, was not to be denied. After a whirlwind courtship lasting
just a few months, he convinced her to marry him.

The marriage proved a lasting and fulfilling partnership that
brought them to the White House three decades later. From the very
beginning she helped further his political career, and he helped her
overcome her shyness. During his years as a member of the U.S.
House of Representatives (1937–1949), she mastered the art of being a
Washington hostess. Then, while her husband was in the navy, she
managed his congressional office and from that experience gained
the confidence to try her hand at business. In 1943 the Johnsons
bought a failing Austin, Texas, radio station, and she took over its
management. Within a year it began to show a profit, and from that
one station the Johnsons eventually built a multimillion-dollar radio
and television corporation.

Lady Bird began campaigning actively for her husband during his successful Senate race in 1948. When he was the 1960 Democratic vice-presidential candidate, she traveled extensively, making television appearances, holding press conferences, and giving hundreds of speeches. For the next three years her husband served as vice president, while she turned out their Washington home and the LBJ Ranch in Texas to entertain visiting foreign dignitaries. But then in late 1963 the tragic assassination of President John F. Kennedy thrust the Johnsons into the White House.

As the nation's first lady, however, she soon revealed herself as an influential force in the White House, as well as a graceful and tactful hostess. By early 1964 she was touring Appalachia to focus attention on poverty, and she later traveled through the Deep South promoting the administration's commitment to integration. But among her most lasting and visible successes were the Highway Beautification bill, which she initiated, and the national Head Start education program, which she actively supported and of which she was honorary chairman (1963–1968). Meanwhile, her two daughters, Lynda Bird and Luci Baines, were both married during the White House years.

Just four years after the Johnsons left Washington and returned to their Texas ranch, the former president died. Lady Bird has since remained active in conservation and beautification organizations and still oversees the Johnson cattle ranches. She served on the University of Texas board of regents from 1971 to 1977 and in 1982 founded the National Wildflower Research Center in Austin. Johnson published a book of memoirs, *A White House Diary,* in 1970. *(See also the entry for Lyndon B. Johnson, p. 266.)*

Archibald MacLeish

POET AND PLAYWRIGHT, TEACHER AND STATESMAN, ARCHIBALD MACLEISH HAS COMBINED THE VOCATION OF MAN OF LETTERS WITH THAT OF PUBLIC SPOKESMAN. A POET OF REALITIES AS WELL AS DREAMS, HIS ELOQUENT WORDS ARE MATCHED BY HIS SENSITIVE SOCIAL CONSCIENCE. HE SEEKS TRUTH INSPIRED BY LOVE OF HIS FELLOW MEN AND OF HIS COUNTRY. WE ARE PROUD TO RECOGNIZE HIS STATURE AS A HUMANIST, AN ARTIST, AND AN AMERICAN.

* * *

President Gerald R. Ford awarded MacLeish the Presidential Medal of Freedom with the above citation during a White House ceremony January 10, 1977. The medal was accompanied by the added accolade "with distinction" and was accepted by Roderick MacLeish on his uncle's behalf.

A Chicago department store magnate's son, Archibald MacLeish was born in Glencoe, Illinois, in 1892. He was raised in comfortable circumstances, and by the time he graduated from Yale in 1915 he had decided to write poetry. After marrying his childhood sweetheart in 1916, however, MacLeish entered Harvard Law School with the idea of supporting both his wife and his poetry by working as a lawyer. Meanwhile, Yale University Press published a collection of his poems, *Tower of Ivory,* in 1917.

After interrupting his studies to serve as an officer in the field artillery during World War I, MacLeish graduated from Harvard at the top of his class in 1919. He joined a Boston law firm and practiced law for just three years before he could stand no more of the legal profession. Packing up his wife and two children, he abruptly left for Europe and became part of the so-called "lost generation" of expatriate American writers and artists—T. S. Eliot, Gertrude Stein, Ezra Pound, and Ernest Hemingway among them.

MacLeish's major work from this period, *The Hamlet of A. MacLeish,* was published in 1928, the year he and his family returned to the United States. Critics praised the long poem, but MacLeish's reputation as a major poet was established by his next work, *Conquistador* (1932), an epic poem narrating the Spanish conquest of Mexico. The work won him his first Pulitzer Prize in 1932, but MacLeish continued working for Henry Luce's *Fortune* magazine throughout most of the 1930s.

During the 1930s and 1940s especially, MacLeish's works became increasingly concerned with social and political problems. Among his verse plays, for example, *Panic* (1935) involved the banking crisis and the depression, and *The Fall of the City* (1937) concerned the rise of fascism.

From 1939 until the mid–1940s MacLeish devoted much of his time to public service. President Franklin D. Roosevelt appointed him librarian of Congress in 1939, and during the next six years MacLeish reorganized the library, set up a permanent film collection, and began a collection of Slavic works. Meanwhile, he also aided the war effort as director of the Office of Facts and Figures and as assistant director of the Office of War Information. As assistant secretary of state between 1944 and 1945, MacLeish helped plan the UN Educational, Scientific and Cultural Organization (UNESCO) and in 1946 led the U.S. delegation to UNESCO's first session.

Leaving Washington in 1949, he became a professor of creative writing and English literature at Harvard and published his *Collected Poems, 1917–1952* three years later. MacLeish won his second Pulitzer Prize for the book and got a third for *J. B.: A Play in Verse,* which became a bestseller in 1958.

By the time he retired from Harvard in 1962, MacLeish also had written verse plays for radio and television. Later he contributed to the Academy Award-winning movie *The Eleanor Roosevelt Story* (1966), wrote *The Wild Old Wicked Man, and Other Poems* (1968), and published the collected essays *Riders on the Earth* (1978). MacLeish died in 1982, at age eighty-nine.

James Albert Michener

AUTHOR, TEACHER AND POPULAR HISTORIAN, JAMES MICHENER HAS ENTRANCED A GENERATION WITH HIS COMPELLING ESSAYS AND NOVELS. FROM TALES OF THE SOUTH PACIFIC, TO CENTENNIAL, THE PROLIFIC WRITINGS OF THIS MASTER STORY-TELLER HAVE EXPANDED THE KNOWLEDGE AND ENRICHED THE LIVES OF MILLION[S].

★ ★ ★

President Gerald R. Ford awarded Michener the Presidential Medal of Freedom with the above citation during a White House ceremony January 10, 1977. The medal was accompanied by the added accolade "with distinction."

A foundling born in New York City in 1907, James A. Michener was later adopted in Pennsylvania by Quakers. His adoptive father was a farmer and his adoptive mother a laundress. Michener read widely even as a child and proved a restive, adventurous youth. He ran away for a time during his teens, hitchhiking across the country and working at odd jobs. But he also showed early promise as a writer, having begun to write a sports column for the newspaper in Doylestown, Pennsylvania, at age fifteen. Swarthmore College gave him a scholarship, and, despite some disciplinary problems along the way, Michener graduated summa cum laude in 1929 with a major in English.

During the 1930s he variously taught at private schools, studied abroad, earned his master's degree at the University of Northern Colorado (1937), and taught at his alma mater as an associate professor (1937–1941). His writing at this time consisted of numerous scholarly articles for professional journals, though he was becoming increasingly interested in history.

After a stint as a visiting professor of history at Harvard University (1940–1941), he went to work at Macmillan publishing company as an associate editor of education books. Then, despite his Quaker upbringing, Michener enlisted in the navy during World War II. As a record keeper for maintenance of naval aircraft in the Pacific theater, he traveled widely and later also became the navy's chief historical officer for the South Pacific.

Michener's wartime experiences provided the basis for his first popular book, *Tales of the South Pacific* (1947), a collection of eighteen stories. The book was an immediate success and won him the 1948 Pulitzer Prize for fiction. Rodgers and Hammerstein's smash hit musical *South Pacific* was adapted from the book, and *Tales of the South Pacific* became the first of several Michener books that have been made into movies.

Michener published both fiction and nonfiction books during the

1950s, including *Sayonara* (1954), a novel about an American's ill-fated love affair during the Korean War, and *The Bridge at Andau* (1957), an account of the plight of thousands of Hungarian refugees who managed to escape the country after the Soviets quashed the 1956 revolution. But he did not establish what became the characteristic formula for his novels—epic works of massive scope weaving together fiction, history, and abundant factual detail—until he published *Hawaii* in 1959. Seven years in the writing, the book traced the evolution of the islands from the beginning of their geologic history and followed the arrival of various peoples who settled there.

His books on this basic plan proved hugely successful, selling millions of copies, and Michener continued to produce them over the next thirty-plus years. Among his other epics were *The Source* (1965), *Centennial* (1974), *Chesapeake* (1978), *Texas* (1985), *Alaska* (1988), and *Mexico* (1992). He also wrote nonfiction works, including *The Floating World* (1954, a history of Japanese art prints), *Kent State: What Happened and Why* (1971), and more recently *Literary Reflections* (1993).

Michener married his third wife in 1955, having divorced his two previous wives. He became active in politics for a time and made an unsuccessful bid for a seat in the U.S. House of Representatives in 1962. He also has served on government commissions, including the State Department advisory commission on the arts (1957) and the National Aeronautics and Space Administration advisory committee (1980–1983).

Georgia O'Keeffe

PAINTER, TEACHER, AUTHOR, AND ARTISTIC PIONEER, GEORGIA O'KEEFFE HELPED TO SHAPE AND DEFINE THE HISTORY OF MODERN ART IN AMERICA. FOR OVER SIX DECADES HER SENSITIVITY AND SKILL PRODUCED WORKS OF STRIKING BEAUTY THAT SPAN A BROAD RANGE OF CONTEMPORARY STYLES. HER COUNTRY IS PROUD TO RECOGNIZE HER AS AN AMERICAN OF SPECIAL DISTINCTION.

★ ★ ★

President Gerald R. Ford awarded O'Keeffe the Presidential Medal of Freedom with the above citation during a White House ceremony January 10, 1977. The medal was accompanied by the added accolade "with distinction." O'Keeffe was unable to attend and received the medal at a later date.

Among the leading American painters of this century and a pioneer in the field of modern art, Georgia O'Keeffe was born in the town of Sun

Prairie, Wisconsin, in 1887. She was raised on her father's farm and decided to become a painter before reaching age twelve. After graduating from high school in 1904, she spent a year studying at the Art Institute of Chicago and another at the Art Students League in New York.

While still at the Art Students League, she became discouraged and from 1909 to 1915 abandoned painting for work, first as a commercial freelance artist and then as a teacher. She moved to Texas and supervised the art program in Amarillo public schools from 1913 to 1916. But, while spending the Summer of 1915 studying art at Columbia University Teachers College, she rediscovered her desire to paint. Returning to Texas, she began developing her characteristic approaches to color and composition.

O'Keeffe's career as an artist was launched almost accidentally a year later. She and a classmate at Columbia Teachers College had kept in touch by letter, and one day in 1916 O'Keeffe sent her some charcoal sketches to demonstrate how her work was progressing. Ignoring O'Keeffe's request not to show anyone else the sketches, the woman took them to the noted photographer Alfred Stieglitz, who was immediately impressed. "Finally, a woman on paper!" he blurted out and soon after displayed O'Keeffe's work at his famous New York gallery, 291.

Stieglitz, who had been instrumental in promoting other young modern artists of the day, actively promoted her work from that time forward. O'Keeffe was initially upset at the unauthorized showing and at the symbolism some critics read into her works, but Stieglitz managed to mollify her. Accepting her unexpected success, she continued painting and in 1918 moved to New York to devote herself to painting full time. Stieglitz sponsored O'Keeffe's first one-artist show in 1923 (and every year thereafter to 1946) and the following year married her.

O'Keeffe's most widely known works were painted from the 1920s to the 1940s and were noted for the artist's remarkable originality and power, her use of color, her precision and use of suggestive imagery, and her ability to bring out an abstract beauty in the natural forms she painted. A prolific artist, she often painted skulls and assorted other animal bones, shells, flowers, rocks, feathers, leaves, and other natural objects.

After spending the summer of 1929 in New Mexico, O'Keeffe was taken by the desert landscapes. She returned nearly every summer until her husband died in 1946 and then moved there permanently. Her works from the late 1940s onward often featured the stark beauty of New Mexico's desert.

Almost forgotten for a time by the art world, O'Keeffe enjoyed a revival in 1970 when New York's Whitney Museum of American Art gave her a retrospective exhibition. She published her autobiography, *Georgia O'Keeffe,* six years later and participated in a television film about her life and artwork in 1977.

Meanwhile, O'Keeffe continued painting into the 1980s. She died in 1986, at age ninety-eight.

Nelson A. Rockefeller

PATRIOT, PHILANTHROPIST, PATRON OF THE ARTS, DIPLOMAT, GOVERNOR OF NEW YORK, VICE PRESIDENT OF THE UNITED STATES, HIS LONG YEARS OF SERVICE TO HIS COUNTRY HAVE YIELDED GOVERNMENTAL, ECONOMIC, SOCIAL AND CULTURAL CONTRIBUTIONS BEYOND MEASURES.

★ ★ ★

President Gerald R. Ford awarded Rockefeller the Presidential Medal of Freedom with the above citation during a White House ceremony January 10, 1977. The medal was accompanied by the added accolade "with distinction."

The forty-first vice president of the United States, Nelson A. Rockefeller was born in Bar Harbor, Maine, in 1908. His grandfather was John D. Rockefeller, founder of Standard Oil, and the young Rockefeller was among the heirs to the family's huge fortune. Rockefeller graduated from Dartmouth College in New Hampshire with an economics degree in 1930 and married Mary Todhunter Clark that same year. For the next ten years he worked for family-owned companies, including Chase National Bank and Rockefeller Center.

Rockefeller's interest in Latin America, where his family had large oil holdings, landed him his first government job in 1940, as the State Department coordinator of inter-American affairs. By 1944 he had been promoted to assistant secretary of state for the American republics and later held posts in the Truman and Eisenhower administrations, including as undersecretary of Health, Education and Welfare (1953–1955).

A liberal Republican, Rockefeller won his first term as New York State governor by a comfortable margin in 1958. He went on to win reelection to four terms as governor and served from 1959 to 1973, longer than any previous New York governor except George Clinton (who served twenty-one years). During that time he instituted programs that drastically changed the economic, political, and cultural life of the state. He vastly expanded the state university system, adding more than forty new campuses and increasing enrollment from 38,000 to 246,000. Among the big-ticket development projects he backed was the construction of the $1-billion Albany Mall. He also nearly doubled the state workforce and quadrupled the state budget.

Rockefeller made three unsuccessful attempts to gain the Republican presidential nod (in 1960, 1964, and 1968), and after leaving the New York governorship in 1973, one year before the end of his term, he intended to retire from politics. But when Vice President Ford succeeded Richard Nixon as president in 1974, Rockefeller accepted the appointment as vice president, becoming only the second appointed under the Twenty-fifth Amendment (Ford was the first). Sworn in December 19, Rockefeller served just over two years with the Ford administration and campaigned with the president in his unsuccessful 1976 bid for an elected term.

When the Ford administration left office in 1977, Rockefeller retired from politics to devote time to his vast art collection and to writing books on art. He died two years later, at age seventy.

Norman Rockwell

ARTIST, ILLUSTRATOR AND AUTHOR, NORMAN ROCKWELL HAS PORTRAYED THE AMERICAN SCENE WITH UNRIVALED FRESHNESS AND CLARITY. INSIGHT, OPTIMISM AND GOOD HUMOR ARE THE HALLMARKS OF HIS ARTISTIC STYLE. HIS VIVID AND AFFECTIONATE PORTRAITS OF OUR COUNTRY AND OURSELVES HAVE BECOME A BELOVED PART OF THE AMERICAN TRADITION.

★ ★ ★

President Gerald R. Ford awarded Rockwell the Presidential Medal of Freedom with the above citation during a White House ceremony January 10, 1977. The medal was accompanied by the added accolade "with distinction" and was accepted by Jarvis Rockwell on his father's behalf.

Probably the country's most popular artist for over half a century, Norman Rockwell was born in New York City in 1894. His father was an amateur artist and his grandfather was an English portrait painter who trained his twelve children to paint landscapes using the assembly-line system. Rockwell developed an interest in drawing during his childhood and began taking lessons at age thirteen. At sixteen he left high school to study at the Art Students League.

Rockwell's talent developed quickly and the following year he landed his first freelance assignments for Conde Nast magazines. For the next few years he worked full time providing illustrations for various magazines, notably for *Boy's Life,* the Boy Scouts of America magazine.

Then in 1916 a friend convinced him to try submitting a cover to the *Saturday Evening Post.* The friend rejected Rockwell's first try, a sketch of a gracious woman. Rockwell, who freely admitted his women invariably became the homey type, no matter what type he intended to draw, turned to his "kid stuff." The result was a disconsolate-looking boy pushing a baby carriage while his laughing friends desert him for a game of baseball. The *Saturday Evening Post* snapped it up along with three others and in the spring of 1916 featured the boy and the baby carriage on its cover. That one illustration launched his career, and soon after he was making $40,000 a year doing magazine covers and advertisements.

Rockwell drew about ten covers a year for the *Post* during the next four decades, some 317 up to 1963 when the magazine published his last. He also had a long-standing tie with the Boy Scouts and illustrated the official Boy Scout Calendar from 1926 to 1976.

His nostalgic visions of small towns and family life, of boys fishing from logs and other similarly idealized scenes, won him widespread and enduring popularity. He also was unquestionably a careful craftsman with excellent technique and an artist who took great pains to find genuine models and artifacts for his paintings. But art critics generally dismissed Rockwell as a mere illustrator whose works lacked artistic merit and genuine social insight.

He rarely responded to his critics and was well aware of his limitations, perhaps too much so. He entitled his autobiography *Norman Rockwell: My Adventures as an Illustrator* (1960) and made a few tentative efforts at relevant social criticism in his paintings during the early 1960s. But the mood of the country was rapidly changing, and in 1963 he stopped doing covers for the *Post* altogether. Five years later the first formal retrospective exhibition of Rockwell's paintings at a Madison Avenue gallery in New York proved a popular event, and another exhibit at the Brooklyn Museum in 1972 was similarly successful.

Rockwell married his third wife, Mary L. Punderson, in 1961, his second wife having died two years earlier. In failing health after 1976, he died two years later, at age eighty-four.

Catherine Filene Shouse

CATHERINE FILENE SHOUSE HAS GIVEN HER COUNTRY HALF A CENTURY OF INVALUABLE VOLUNTEER SERVICE. A PIONEER IN JOB TRAINING FOR WOMEN, SHE HERSELF IS AN OUTSTANDING EXAMPLE OF WHAT GOOD TASTE AND INTELLIGENCE, PRAGMATISM AND PERSISTENCE CAN ACCOMPLISH. A WORKING PATRON OF THE ARTS AS WELL AS A GIVING ONE, HER KEEN INTEREST AND INVOLVEMENT HAVE ENRICHED IMMEASURABLY OUR NATION'S CULTURAL LIFE.

★ ★ ★

President Gerald R. Ford awarded Shouse the Presidential Medal of Freedom with the above citation during a White House ceremony January 10, 1977.

The founder of the Wolf Trap Farm Park for the Performing Arts outside Washington, D.C., Shouse was born Catherine Filene in Boston in 1896. She was heir to a family fortune made in retailing; her grandfather had founded Filene's department store chain and her father, the Federated Department Stores company. After graduating from Wheaton College in Massachusetts (1918), she studied education at Harvard University and obtained her masters' degree in 1923.

Meanwhile, in 1919 the Democratic National Committee named her the first woman to serve in its ranks, and two years later she married businessman Alvin E. Dodd. In the mid 1920s she became chairwoman of the country's first federal prison for women and set up a pioneering program of rehabilitation and job training for the inmates. In 1932 she married her second husband, Democratic National Executive Committee Chairman Jouett Shouse. She had divorced her first husband two years earlier.

A lifelong patron of the performing arts, Shouse was a board member of the National Symphony Orchestra from 1949 and was the orchestra's vice president for nearly two decades, from 1951 to 1968.

From 1959 she also served on the board of the National Cultural Center, the forerunner of the John F. Kennedy Center for the Performing Arts.

Shouse founded Wolf Trap in 1966 as a national park for the performing arts and donated one-hundred acres from her farm just west of Washington, D.C., for the project. She also created the Wolf Trap Foundation to administer the park under the auspices of the U.S. Interior Department and to raise funds for its operation. Since 1971, when the park opened, Wolf Trap has become a noted arts center, featuring performances by singers, dancers, musicians, and others.

Her husband died in 1967, but Shouse remained active into her nineties. She died in 1994, at age ninety-eight.

Lowell Thomas

PIONEER RADIO AND TELEVISION COMMENTATOR, WAR CORRE-
SPONDENT, AUTHOR AND EXPLORER, LOWELL THOMAS HAS
LIVED AND FULFILLED MANY DREAMS. HIS ELOQUENT VOICE, HIS
ZEST FOR LIVING, HIS SUPERB PROFESSIONALISM AND
PATRIOTISM HAVE LEFT A LEGACY OF EXCELLENCE WITH THE
MILLIONS WHO HAVE SEEN AND HEARD HIM OVER THE YEARS.

★ ★ ★

*President Gerald R. Ford awarded Thomas the Presidential Medal of
Freedom with this citation during a White House ceremony
January 10, 1977.*

A famous radio newscaster for over fifty years, Lowell Thomas was
born in Woodington, Ohio, in 1892. His father was a doctor who
instilled in his son a belief in the importance of learning, and the
young Thomas graduated from Indiana's Valparaiso University in
1911 after just two years. He later earned another bachelor's degree
and his master's degree from the University of Denver in just one
year, 1912, and got a second master's degree from Princeton
University in 1916. The following year he married Frances Ryan.

Meanwhile he worked as a journalist for a time and in 1914 took
time out to photograph movies of the Klondike and other parts of
Alaska. During his time at Princeton, Thomas began giving what
became extremely popular public "presentations," combining his Alaska
film footage with a talk. His success led eventually to an unofficial U.S.
government commission to cover World War I, and after touring the
western front in Europe, Thomas visited British forces in Egypt.

There he met Thomas Edward Lawrence (Lawrence of Arabia),
who became the subject of his highly romanticized and extremely
popular presentation *The Last Crusade.* His "show," as he called it,
included film footage of Lawrence and packed theaters in Britain and
the United States in 1919. Thomas also published a popular book
about his experiences, *With Lawrence in Arabia* (1924). Earnings from
this and a subsequent book, *Beyond Khyber Pass,* made him a millionaire, and he amassed a considerable fortune from his many enterprises over the next decades. (He eventually wrote fifty books in all.)

Thomas, who had a stentorian voice, made perhaps his most lasting
success on radio, however. Having worked for the pioneering radio
station KDKA in Pittsburgh in the 1920s, he became a CBS radio newscaster in 1930 and for the next forty-six years delivered newscasts for
one or another radio network. In 1935 Movietone News hired him to
narrate its newsreels, and for seventeen years Thomas's voice was
heard at movie theaters across the country as well as on radio.

The new medium of television also drew on Thomas's talents, and in 1939 he broadcast the first television newscast, on NBC. He also appeared in the first daily television program, covered political conventions during the 1950s, and hosted the television program "High Adventure With Lowell Thomas" from 1957 to 1958. Radio remained his primary medium, though, and he delivered his nightly newscast until 1976, when CBS finally took it off the air.

In 1976 and 1977 he published his two-volume autobiography, *Good Evening, Everybody* and *So Long Until Tomorrow*. Meanwhile, in 1977 he married his second wife, Marianna Munn, his first wife having died two years earlier. Thomas died in 1981, at age eighty-nine.

James D. Watson

SCHOLAR, TEACHER, AUTHOR AND SCIENTIFIC PIONEER, JAMES D. WATSON HAS CHALLENGED THE MYSTERIES OF LIFE ITSELF AND CHARTED A NEW PATH IN MANKIND'S ENDLESS SEARCH FOR TRUTH. HIS INTELLECTUAL COURAGE AND RELENTLESS PURSUIT OF SCIENTIFIC KNOWLEDGE HAVE EARNED HIM THE RESPECT AND ADMIRATION OF HIS COUNTRY AND A PERMANENT PLACE AS ONE OF THE GREAT EXPLORERS OF THE 20TH CENTURY.

★ ★ ★

President Gerald R. Ford awarded Watson the Presidential Medal of Freedom with the above citation during a White House ceremony January 10, 1977. The medal was accompanied by the added accolade "with distinction."

The codiscoverer of the structure of DNA, among the greatest scientific findings of this century, James D. Watson was born in a poor section of Chicago in 1928. His father, a debt collector, was a voracious reader, and even as a child the younger Watson himself could read five-hundred words a minute. Finishing high school at age fifteen, he won a scholarship to the University of Chicago and in 1947 earned his bachelor's degree in zoology. He began focusing on genetics, the study of heredity, while working toward his doctorate at Indiana University.

After earning his degree in 1950, Watson got a fellowship to the University of Copenhagen to study DNA, a microscopic substance that scientists knew was important when cells divided to reproduce themselves. Many researchers thought it played a key role in heredity, but they had no idea what it looked like or how it worked. Watson believed that solving the riddle of DNA's molecular structure also would reveal how it worked, but in 1950 there was no way to get a look at something as small as DNA.

The following year Watson moved to the Cavendish Laboratory at Cambridge University, where he met Francis Crick, a physicist turned microbiologist. Both believed the key to understanding cell replication and genetics lay in unlocking the secret of DNA structure. It took them two years to unravel it, but in 1953 they constructed a three-dimensional model of DNA, the now-famous double-helix, which looked like a gently spiraling staircase.

Their discovery not only revealed the secret of the mechanics of genetics, but also opened the way for the revolutionary technology of genetic engineering that was developed in subsequent decades. Watson, Crick, and another British researcher who helped them, Maurice Wilkins, shared the 1962 Nobel Prize in medicine for the discovery of the DNA structure. Meanwhile, Watson continued his research in microbiology first at the California Institute of Technology and then at Harvard (from 1956), and wrote the influential textbook *Molecular Biology of the Cell.*

The year 1968 was something of a watershed in Watson's life. He married Elizabeth Lewis that year and published his frank and controversial book about the discovery of the DNA structure, *The Double Helix.* The book, which revealed the little-known human side of scientific research, became a bestseller. That year he also became director of Cold Spring Harbor Laboratory on Long Island, New York, a research facility that had fallen on hard times. Watson, who left Harvard in 1976 to devote himself full time to running Cold Spring Harbor, transformed it into a leading cancer research center.

Watson became director of the multibillion-dollar, federally funded Human Genome Project in 1989. A vast research project established to map the tens of thousands of genes found in human beings, it was scheduled to continue for about fifteen years. Watson resigned from his post in 1992, though, and since 1994 has served as president of Cold Spring Harbor Laboratory.

Henry A. Kissinger

SCHOLAR, STATESMAN AND PUBLIC SERVANT. BY HIS EXTRAORDINARY ACHIEVEMENTS HE HAS EARNED A PLACE IN THE FIRST RANK OF AMERICAN PATRIOTS. A PRINCIPAL ARCHITECT OF AMERICA'S DIPLOMACY UNDER TWO PRESIDENTS, HE GUIDED THE NATION IN MEETING THE RESPONSIBILITIES OF WORLD LEADERSHIP. A BRILLIANT NEGOTIATOR, HE WIELDED AMERICA'S GREAT POWER WITH WISDOM AND COMPASSION IN THE SERVICE OF PEACE. HE IS HONORED BY A GRATEFUL PRESIDENT AND NATION IN THE EXPECTATION THAT THE PAST IS BUT A PROLOGUE.

★ ★ ★

President Gerald R. Ford awarded Kissinger the Presidential Medal of Freedom with the above citation during a ceremony at the Pan American Union January 13, 1977.

The dominant figure in U.S. foreign policy during much of the 1970s, Henry A. Kissinger was born in Fürth, Germany, in 1923. He was raised in a middle-class Jewish family and along with his family suffered increasing persecution after the Nazis came to power in Germany. The Kissingers finally fled to the United States in 1938 and settled in New York City. The young Kissinger was drafted into the U.S. Army during World War II. In addition to seeing combat at the Battle of the Bulge, Kissinger also served in the Counter-Intelligence Corps.

After the war Kissinger, a naturalized citizen since 1943, graduated from Harvard summa cum laude in 1950 and four years later earned his doctorate there as well. Meanwhile, he already had begun part-time consulting work for the Eisenhower administration, while also serving as an instructor at Harvard. But it was his book *Nuclear Weapons and Foreign Policy* (1957) that first gained him an international reputation as a defense expert and opened doors to high-level advisory work in government. In it he argued for a flexible response strategy, instead of the (then) current strategy of massive retaliation. Strategy should direct weapons technology, Kissinger said, instead of letting available weapons direct strategy.

While continuing to teach at Harvard and publish books on foreign policy, Kissinger took on steadily more important defense and foreign policy work for the government during the 1960s. A consultant to the National Security Council during the Kennedy administration, he served in various capacities during the presidency of Lyndon B. Johnson. In one case he acted as President Johnson's special emissary at secret meetings with the North Vietnamese to arrange the 1968 Paris peace talks.

As President Richard Nixon's national security adviser (1969–1973), Kissinger effectively circumvented the State Department and concentrated the making of foreign policy in the White House itself. He also made himself the most powerful and controversial diplomat since World War II. Through his secret negotiations he engineered a short-lived détente with the Soviets, opened relations with Communist China, and extracted the United States from the Vietnam War with the Paris Peace accords, a feat that won him the Nobel Peace Prize in 1973. Kissinger married his second wife, Nancy Maginnes, in 1974, having divorced his first wife ten years earlier.

President Nixon named him secretary of state in 1973, and in that capacity Kissinger conducted his "shuttle diplomacy" between Israel, Egypt, and Syria after the 1973 Arab-Israeli War. President Ford kept him in office as secretary of state, and though Kissinger achieved a cease-fire and disengagement of troops after the Mideast war, a lasting Mideast peace agreement eluded him.

After leaving office with the Ford administration in 1977, Kissinger largely devoted himself to writing. Among other books he has since published are *White House Years* (1979), *Years of Upheaval* (1982), and *Diplomacy* (1994).

Donald Rumsfeld

DONALD RUMSFELD HAS SERVED HIS COUNTRY WITH RARE DISTINCTION AS A NAVAL OFFICER, LEGISLATOR, DIPLOMAT, COUNSELLOR TO THE PRESIDENT, AND THE SECRETARY OF DEFENSE. AS UNITED STATES AMBASSADOR TO NATO, HE BROUGHT A NEW LEVEL OF UNDERSTANDING AND COOPERATION TO OUR RELATIONS WITH OUR OLDEST ALLIES. UNDER HIS SUPERB LEADERSHIP AS SECRETARY OF DEFENSE, THE SECURITY OF THE UNITED STATES WAS PRESERVED AND STRENGTHENED. IN EACH OF THESE ENDEAVORS, DONALD RUMSFELD HAS CONTRIBUTED IMMEASURABLY TO THE SECURITY OF THE UNITED STATES AND TO THE CONTINUED STRENGTH OF THE FREE WORLD.

★ ★ ★

President Gerald R. Ford awarded Rumsfeld the Presidential Medal of Freedom with the above citation during a White House ceremony January 19, 1977. The medal was accompanied by the added accolade "with distinction."

Born in Evanston, Illinois, in 1932, Donald Rumsfeld was raised in nearby Winnetka. His father was a successful Chicago real estate agent. The young Rumsfeld went on to graduate from Princeton University in 1954 with his bachelor's degree in political science. He married Joyce Pierson that same year. After serving as a navy pilot from 1954 to 1957, he spent two years in Washington, D.C., as a congressional administrative assistant and then returned to Chicago to work as an investment broker.

In 1962 he won election to Congress as a Republican representative from Illinois and eventually was reelected to three additional terms. A conservative, he opposed much of the Kennedy-Johnson social legislation of the 1960s but joined reformers attacking the House seniority system and calling for public reporting of campaign funds. He also favored what became the Nixon administration policy of "Vietnamization"—letting South Vietnamese troops take responsibility for fighting the war in Vietnam.

Rumsfeld campaigned actively for Richard Nixon in the 1968 presidential election and in 1969 was rewarded with the difficult task of heading the embattled Office of Economic Opportunity. At the same time he also served as a presidential assistant, though, and in 1970 President Nixon made him a full-time White House counselor. Among his other duties, Rumsfeld served as director of the economic stabilization program (1971–1972) and as U.S. ambassador and representative to the United Nations (1973–1974).

When Gerald R. Ford succeeded to the presidency after the Watergate scandal, he named Rumsfeld his White House chief of staff. Rumsfeld served from mid–1974 to late 1975, a difficult time for the country generally and for the presidency as well. Among the problems facing the Ford administration then were the Watergate aftermath, the final withdrawal of Americans from Saigon, concerns about oil shortages, and a steadily worsening economy. From late 1975 to the end of the Ford administration in 1977, Rumsfeld held the cabinet post of secretary of defense.

Returning to the business world, Rumsfeld headed companies in Chicago and served on the boards of several major corporations, including the Rand Corporation and Sears Roebuck. He did serve as President Ronald Reagan's special envoy to the Mideast from 1983 to 1984, however. From 1990 to 1993 Rumsfeld was chairman and chief executive officer of the General Instrument Corporation in Chicago.

Jimmy Carter

JIMMY CARTER, A DEMOCRAT, BECAME PRESIDENT ON
JANUARY 20, 1977, AND SERVED ONE TERM (1977–1981).

MEDAL
CEREMONIES

JULY 11, 1977 *Old Executive Office Building*

JULY 26, 1978 *The White House Rose Garden*

JANUARY 20, 1979 *New York, New York*

JUNE 9, 1980 *The White House*

DECEMBER 8, 1980 *Van Nuys, California*

JANUARY 16, 1981 *The White House*

Martin Luther King, Jr.

MARTIN LUTHER KING, JR., WAS THE CONSCIENCE OF HIS GEN-
ERATION. HE GAZED UPON THE GREAT WALL OF SEGREGATION
AND SAW THAT THE POWER OF LOVE COULD BRING IT DOWN.
FROM THE PAIN AND EXHAUSTION OF HIS FIGHT TO FULFILL THE
PROMISES OF OUR FOUNDING FATHERS FOR OUR HUMBLEST
CITIZENS, HE WRUNG HIS ELOQUENT STATEMENT OF HIS DREAM
FOR AMERICA. HE MADE OUR NATION STRONGER BECAUSE HE
MADE IT BETTER. HIS DREAM SUSTAINS US YET.

★ ★ ★

*President Jimmy Carter awarded King a posthumous Presidential
Medal of Freedom with the above citation during a ceremony at the Old
Executive Office Building July 11, 1977. King's wife, Coretta, and his
father, Dr. Martin Luther King, Sr., accepted the award on his behalf.*

A pillar of the civil rights movement, Martin Luther King, Jr., was
born in Atlanta, Georgia, in 1929. He was a Baptist minister's son and
proved an exceptional child—he recited biblical passages from
memory as early as age five. But the young King could not escape the
same humiliating racial slurs suffered by other black youths in segregated Atlanta, and there was a time when he seethed with a deep
racial hatred for all whites. During college, contacts with sympathetic
whites helped diminish that hatred, and King eventually managed to
focus it on the underlying cause, segregation itself.

Skipping grades through Atlanta's segregated school system, he
entered Morehouse College in Atlanta at age fifteen with an idea of
becoming a doctor or lawyer. But before graduating, King decided on
the ministry and was ordained in 1947. The following year he earned
his bachelor's degree in sociology and went on to the racially integrated Crozer Theological Seminary in Pennsylvania. There he
became a dedicated follower of Gandhi's teachings about redemptive
love and nonviolent resistance, which he would later apply with such
success against segregation in the South. After graduating from
Crozer with his bachelor's degree, King went on to get his doctorate
in theology at Boston University in 1955. Meanwhile, he met and
married Coretta Scott, a music student.

King was a young new pastor at a Baptist church in Montgomery,
Alabama, in late 1955 when Rosa Parks, an elderly black woman,
refused to move to segregated seating on a city bus. Seizing the
moment, Montgomery blacks launched a boycott against the city bus
line. With King as their leader, they mounted a successful nonviolent
campaign that aroused national attention and in 1956 sparked a
Supreme Court ruling overturning Alabama laws segregating buses.

Segregationists dynamited King's house the following year (no one was injured), but King had found his calling and would not be deterred. Already a powerful orator, he wanted to lead the moral crusade for black civil rights. In 1957 King became a founder and president of the Southern Christian Leadership Conference (SCLC), which began organizing blacks for the fight against segregation. The following year he published *Stride Toward Freedom: The Montgomery Story*.

By 1960 King had moved back to Atlanta and there helped black college students organize the Student Nonviolent Coordinating Committee (SNCC), which would eventually turn against him as the civil rights movement split between militant and nonviolent factions. Later that year he was arrested with college students at a sit-in against segregated department store lunch counters, but even then relations with SNCC activists were becoming strained. Meanwhile, Democratic presidential candidate John F. Kennedy used his influence to get King released and by doing so won black votes that helped him win the election.

Later, King tried to pressure President Kennedy into backing a major civil rights bill, organizing mass civil rights protests throughout the South in the early 1960s for that purpose. Among the most memorable was the 1963 demonstration in Birmingham, Alabama, where police attacked peaceful marchers with fire-hoses and police dogs. Broadcast nationwide on television, the images shocked the nation and boosted support for a massive march on Washington that summer. Some 250,000 people participated in the event. King delivered his famous "I Have a Dream" speech during the demonstration and the following year won the Nobel Peace Prize. But even more important to King was passage of the 1964 Civil Rights Act, which desegregated public facilities and ended legal discrimination.

A year later, the country was again shocked by attacks on marchers calling for voting rights in Selma, Alabama. King organized a follow-up mass march on Montgomery by some 25,000 demonstrators. Congress, meanwhile, responded by passing the 1965 Voting Rights Act, which reshaped southern politics by ensuring blacks the opportunity to vote.

Change was not happening rapidly enough for the radical militant wing of the civil rights movement, though. Following the 1965 riots in Watts, a black section of Los Angeles, militants openly denounced King's nonviolent teachings in favor of black power. Racial rioting soon became a regular feature of the American urban landscape, blunting the moral force of the civil rights movement.

Now under attack by militants, King also alienated the Johnson administration by openly opposing the Vietnam War as a drain on funds needed to help the poor. By early 1968 he had announced his Poor People's Campaign, what he believed would become an interracial class movement to reform American society. But that spring an escaped convict named James Earl Ray shot and killed King at a Memphis, Tennessee, motel.

Ray was caught and sentenced to life in prison for the murder.

King, meanwhile, continues to be remembered as a martyr of the civil rights movement he had helped found. His birthday (January 15) was made a federal holiday in 1986.

Jonas E. Salk

BECAUSE OF DR. JONAS E. SALK, OUR COUNTRY IS FREE FROM THE CRUEL EPIDEMICS OF POLIOMYELITIS THAT ONCE STRUCK ALMOST YEARLY. BECAUSE OF HIS TIRELESS WORK, UNTOLD HUNDREDS OF THOUSANDS WHO MIGHT HAVE BEEN CRIPPLED ARE SOUND IN BODY TODAY. THESE ARE DOCTOR SALK'S TRUE HONORS, AND THERE IS NO WAY TO ADD TO THEM. THIS MEDAL OF FREEDOM CAN ONLY EXPRESS OUR GRATITUDE, AND OUR DEEPEST THANKS.

★ ★ ★

President Jimmy Carter awarded Salk the Presidential Medal of Freedom with the above citation during a ceremony at the Old Executive Office Building on July 11, 1977.

Jonas E. Salk, who developed the first effective vaccine against polio, was born in New York City in 1914. A voracious reader and strong student, he went on to graduate with his bachelor of science degree from City College in New York in 1934. He earned his medical degree from New York University in 1939 and interned at New York's Mount Sinai Hospital.

Salk entered biomedical research in 1942, when he joined a research team at the University of Michigan School of Public Health. The group was investigating the use of killed viruses as a way to immunize people against influenza, an approach that would later prove important to the development of Salk's polio vaccine. The Michigan researchers' idea was to inject a healthy patient with a vaccine made of killed viruses, which could not possibly cause influenza but which would stimulate production of antibodies by the patient's immune system.

Salk became director of the University of Pittsburgh Virus Research Laboratory in 1947 and there began his search for an effective, killed-virus polio vaccine. First he participated in a study by researchers at four universities showing that three strains of virus were responsible for polio outbreaks in the United States. But there was still the initial problem of culturing enough of the virus to make a vaccine. In 1949, using a technique developed by Dr. John Enders, Salk found the way to grow sufficient quantities of the polio virus in the laboratory. *(See also the entry for Enders, p. 54.)* He used monkey kidney tissue and killed the resulting virus with formaldehyde.

A final problem remained, though: how to make the killed polio virus potent enough to stimulate the body into producing antibodies. For that, Dr. Salk turned to a technique developed by a New York City Health Department researcher in 1942: he boosted the vaccine potency by adding a tiny amount of specially prepared mineral oil and whipping the mix into a creamy emulsion. Salk tested the resulting vaccine on over one-hundred patients and in 1953 reported his success in developing an effective polio vaccine, which became known as the Salk vaccine. Further tests were conducted, and Salk's vaccine gained final approval in 1955. *(See also the entry for Albert Sabin, p. 384.)*

Salk became the director of the Salk Institute of Biological Studies in 1963, a position he held until 1975, and remained with the institute in various capacities. In the 1980s Salk began work on developing a vaccine for the AIDS virus. He died in 1995, at age eighty.

Arthur J. Goldberg

ARTHUR J. GOLDBERG, SECRETARY OF LABOR, ASSOCIATE JUSTICE OF THE SUPREME COURT OF THE UNITED STATES, UNITED STATES REPRESENTATIVE TO THE UNITED NATIONS, AMBASSADOR AT LARGE AND SOLDIER IN WORLD WAR II. DURING AN EMINENT CAREER OF ALMOST FIFTY YEARS, ARTHUR GOLDBERG HAS SHOWN HIS DEEP COMMITMENT TO INDIVIDUAL HUMAN DIGNITY, TO PEACE AND TO THE CAUSE OF HUMAN RIGHTS. AS A PRACTICING ATTORNEY AND COUNSEL FOR THE LABOR MOVEMENT, A LEGAL SCHOLAR, EDUCATOR AND A PUBLIC SERVANT, HE HAS DISPLAYED AN EXTRAORDINARY CAPACITY TO BRING PEOPLE TOGETHER, MEDIATE DIFFERENCES, AND TO HELP SOLVE THE PRESSING PROBLEMS OF OUR AGE. BY COMBINING IDEALISM AND VISION WITH WISDOM AND COMMON SENSE, ARTHUR GOLDBERG HAS SERVED HIS COUNTRY WELL.

★ ★ ★

President Jimmy Carter awarded Goldberg the Presidential Medal of Freedom with the above citation during a White House ceremony July 26, 1978.

A leading labor negotiator of the 1950s, Arthur J. Goldberg was the son of Jewish immigrants from Russia. He was born in Chicago in 1908, the youngest of eight children. The family was poor, and he began working at age twelve while also attending school. Later, Goldberg worked his way through law school at Northwestern University. He earned his law degree in 1930, finishing first in his class.

Goldberg worked with Chicago law firms between 1929 and 1933 and then opened his own practice. Within a few years he took on his first union cases and by 1938 was representing the United Steelworkers, the Congress of Industrial Organizations (CIO), and other labor organizations. After serving in the Office of Strategic Services during World War II, Goldberg returned to private practice.

The CIO and United Steelworkers both named him their general counsel in 1948, securing Goldberg's ties to labor, and in 1949 he won a historic court decision that put pensions among legitimate collective-bargaining issues. He was a key figure in arranging the 1955 merger of the CIO with the American Federation of Labor (he even suggested the name AFL-CIO) and became its special counsel afterward.

President John F. Kennedy named Goldberg secretary of labor in 1961 and in 1962 appointed him to the Supreme Court when a seat became vacant. On the high court, Goldberg provided a crucial fifth vote for a judicially activist majority. His two most important opinions came in *Escobedo v. Illinois* (1964), which helped pave the way for the controversial *Miranda* decision on police interrogation, and in *Griswold v. Connecticut* (1965), which protected married couples' right to use contraceptives and became a major precedent for the 1973 abortion rights ruling *Roe v. Wade*.

President Lyndon B. Johnson, eager to appoint Abe Fortas to the Court, pressured Goldberg into stepping down in 1965 after only two years on the bench. Convinced by President Johnson that his negotiating skills could end the unpopular war in Vietnam, Goldberg left the Court to become U.S. Ambassador to the United Nations. After three years of unsuccessful diplomatic efforts to end the war, he quit and returned to private practice.

During the late 1960s and early 1970s, Goldberg taught at various universities and in 1970 ran unsuccessfully for governor of New York. He also served as ambassador at large during the Carter administration. The author of three books, *AFL-CIO: Labor United* (1956), *Defenses of Freedom* (1966), and *Equal Justice: The Warren Era of the Supreme Court* (1972), he died in 1990, at age eighty-one.

Margaret Mead

MARGARET MEAD WAS BOTH A STUDENT OF CIVILIZATION AND AN EXEMPLAR OF IT. TO A PUBLIC OF MILLIONS, SHE BROUGHT THE CENTRAL INSIGHT OF CULTURAL ANTHROPOLOGY: THAT VARYING CULTURAL PATTERNS EXPRESS AN UNDERLYING HUMAN UNITY. SHE MASTERED HER DISCIPLINE, BUT SHE ALSO TRANSCENDED IT. INTREPID, INDEPENDENT, PLAIN-SPOKEN, FEARLESS, SHE REMAINS A MODEL FOR THE YOUNG AND A TEACHER FROM WHOM ALL MAY LEARN.

★ ★ ★

President Jimmy Carter awarded Mead a posthumous Presidential Medal of Freedom with the above citation. UN Ambassador Andrew Young presented the award to Mead's daughter, Dr. Catherine Bateson, at the American Museum of Natural History in New York City January 20, 1979.

A pioneering social anthropologist and celebrity scientist, Margaret Mead was born in Philadelphia in 1901. Her father was an economics professor, and her mother was a sociologist and feminist. Mead had already become deeply interested in anthropology by the time she graduated from Barnard College in 1923, and during her graduate studies at Columbia University she was strongly influenced by her mentors, the anthropologists Franz Boas and Ruth Benedict. She earned her master's degree in 1924 and her doctorate in 1929.

The first of Mead's studies of primitive cultures in the South Pacific—for which she became famous—was the result of an extended field trip to Samoa in 1925–1926, while she was still a graduate student. Prospects of so prolonged an absence resulted in a separation from her first husband, a seminarian named Louis Cressman.

In her Samoa study, Mead abandoned the statistical approach then favored by anthropologists, adopting instead one of direct observation and psychological interpretation. She sought to determine from studying a primitive culture what part of human behavior is natural and what part is induced by society, particularly Western society. The first of her twenty-three books, *Coming of Age in Samoa* (1928), was both controversial and a lasting success. In the book she noted the relative ease with which Samoan children matured sexually and concluded that lingering Victorian sexual repression made growing up in Western society needlessly difficult.

Ultimately, she went on extended expeditions to study primitive cultures in New Guinea, Bali, and elsewhere in the South Pacific. She published her observations in such works as *Growing Up in New Guinea* (1930), *Balinese Character* (1942), and *New Lives For Old* (1956). At the same time, she expanded on her theories about human behavior in *Sex and Temperament* (1935), concluding that social convention entirely determines how humans behave. Fourteen years later, however, she modified her position on this idea of cultural determinism somewhat in *Male and Female*.

Meanwhile, Mead's personal life defied the conventions of her own time concerning marriage and family life. By 1928 she had divorced her first husband and married fellow anthropologist Reo Fortune, whom she met on her way to Samoa. That marriage lasted until 1936, when she married a British anthropologist, Gregory Bateson. She bore her only child, a daughter, during her marriage to Bateson. They divorced in the 1950s, and Mead did not remarry.

Though Mead's work was often controversial and was sometimes criticized as being more like impressionistic journalism than rigorous science, it nevertheless helped popularize the field of anthropology and made her famous as well. By all accounts a remarkably energetic woman, she used her fame to publicize her views on a wide range of issues outside the field of anthropology. She lectured and wrote on such concerns as nuclear proliferation, world hunger, drug abuse, mental health, race relations, and population control. During her later years, she increasingly spoke out in behalf of feminist causes.

Mead wrote the largely autobiographical *Blackberry Winter* in 1972 and remained active into her last years. She died in 1978, at age seventy-six.

Ansel Adams

AT ONE WITH THE POWER OF THE AMERICAN LANDSCAPE, AND RENOWNED FOR THE PATIENT SKILL AND TIMELESS BEAUTY OF HIS WORK, PHOTOGRAPHER ANSEL ADAMS HAS BEEN VISIONARY IN HIS EFFORTS TO PRESERVE THIS COUNTRY'S WILD AND SCENIC AREAS, BOTH ON FILM AND ON EARTH. DRAWN TO THE BEAUTY OF NATURE'S MONUMENTS, HE IS REGARDED BY ENVIRONMENTALISTS AS A MONUMENT HIMSELF, AND BY PHOTOGRAPHERS AS A NATIONAL INSTITUTION. IT IS THROUGH HIS FORESIGHT AND FORTITUDE THAT SO MUCH OF AMERICA HAS BEEN SAVED FOR FUTURE AMERICANS.

★ ★ ★

President Jimmy Carter awarded Adams the Presidential Medal of Freedom with the above citation during a White House ceremony June 9, 1980.

Ansel Adams was born in 1902 and was raised in San Francisco, California, a short trip from the Sierra Nevada celebrated in his earliest landscapes. In fact, a fourteen-year-old Adams took his first photograph during a family trip to Yosemite National Park in the Sierra Nevada. Soon after, he became an apprentice at a San Francisco photofinishing company, where he began learning the secrets of photographic developing techniques. He returned to Yosemite during the summers and in 1919 joined the Sierra Club, beginning his long association with the conservation movement. He married Virginia Best in 1928.

Until about 1930 Adams wanted most to be a concert pianist, regarding photography as only a hobby. But the concern for technical perfection he learned from music affected his photographic work as well, and in 1927 and 1930 he published limited edition portfolios of his photographs. The technical mastery for which Adams became famous was already evident.

The year 1930 also saw a fundamental shift in Adams's artistic style. Until then his photographs were in the fashionable pictorial style, a soft-focus, impressionistic approach. Then he met Paul Strand, a noted photographer who worked in the so-called straight photography style. The clarity, sharpness of detail, and beauty of tone made possible by this approach immediately won over Adams, and in 1932 he cofounded Group f/64 to promote straight photography. The group had a significant impact on American photography, even though it lasted only until 1934.

The M. H. de Young Memorial Museum in San Francisco presented Adams's first important one-man show in 1932, and four years later renowned photographer Alfred Stieglitz gave Adams a one-man show at his New York gallery. In 1935 Adams successfully published the first of several photography manuals, *Making a Photograph.*

To promote photography as a fine art, Adams and others organized the New York Museum of Modern Art collection of photographs in 1940, the first such collection at any museum in the world. Six years later he set up the first academic department of photography, at the California School of Fine Arts in San Francisco. At about this time he also developed the *zone system,* making it possible to predetermine the tone of each part of a scene in a finished print.

During his long career Adams was known particularly for his dramatic landscapes of the American West, but his subjects varied widely, including still lifes, architectural studies, and portraits of people. In all he published seven portfolios and thirty books, a number of them aimed at promoting environmental causes.

Adams, a director of the Sierra Club from 1936 to 1971, died in 1984, at age eighty-two.

Rachel Louise Carson

NEVER SILENT HERSELF IN THE FACE OF DESTRUCTIVE TRENDS, RACHEL CARSON FED A SPRING OF AWARENESS ACROSS AMERICA AND BEYOND. A BIOLOGIST WITH A GENTLE, CLEAR VOICE, SHE WELCOMED HER AUDIENCES TO HER LOVE OF THE SEA, WHILE WITH AN EQUALLY CLEAR DETERMINED VOICE SHE WARNED AMERICANS OF THE DANGERS HUMAN BEINGS THEMSELVES POSE FOR THEIR OWN ENVIRONMENT. ALWAYS CONCERNED, ALWAYS ELOQUENT, SHE CREATED A TIDE OF ENVIRONMENTAL CON-SCIOUSNESS THAT HAS NOT EBBED.

★ ★ ★

President Jimmy Carter awarded Carson a posthumous Presidential Medal of Freedom during a White House ceremony June 9, 1980. Roger Christy, Carson's nephew and adopted son, accepted the award on her behalf.

Rachel Carson's book *Silent Spring*, now a classic of environmental literature, culminated a lifetime of devotion to two passions—nature and writing. Born in 1907, Carson was raised on a sixty-five acre farm in Parnassus, Pennsylvania, and there, with her mother's encour-agement, learned her love of nature. She also showed an early talent for writing, and on entering Pennsylvania College for Women she first majored in English. But a biology teacher awakened her interest in science, and Carson graduated in 1929 with a zoology degree. A master's degree from Johns Hopkins followed three years later.

During the next five years her job on the University of Maryland zoology department staff allowed her to spend several summers at the Woods Hole, Massachusetts, Marine Biological Laboratory, and there Carson formed a lifelong attachment to the sea and the marine environment it harbored. In 1936 she became a staff writer for the Bureau of Fisheries (later the Fish and Wildlife Service), working her way up to editor in chief by 1949. She also wrote articles at this time as well as her first book, *Under the Sea-Wind* (1941), an unusual blend of science and literature about the sea. Though the book was a critical success, it did not sell well.

Carson, who never married, kept writing, however. She wrote magazine articles to help support her mother and her deceased sister's two children, while also working on her next book. Published in 1951, *The Sea Around Us* proved an instant bestseller. Her new publisher reissued *Under the Sea-Wind* and that too hit the bestseller list. Financially secure, Carson left the Fish and Wildlife Service in 1952 and three years later pub-lished *The Edge of the Sea*. But it was her last book that won her lasting fame and helped set in motion the environmental movement.

The controversy over environmental pollution was just beginning when *Silent Spring* appeared in 1962, but Carson's book brought it home forcefully to the public at large. *Silent Spring* painted in stark terms the dangers of DDT, then a widely used insecticide that persisted in the environment long after its intended use. Eventually DDT and many other pesticides were banned as a result of the environmental awareness sparked by Carson's book, and the environmental movement has since attacked many different forms of pollution.

Carson died in 1964, just a few weeks before her fifty-seventh birthday.

Lucia Chase

BALLERINA LUCIA CHASE HAS BEEN A ONE-WOMAN SHOW, DEVOTING HER LIFEWORK TO SUSTAINING THE VITALITY OF AMERICAN DANCE. A DANCER AND BALLET DIRECTOR BOTH, SHE HAS INTERPRETED ROLES AND CREATED THEM, AND IN EVERY INSTANCE SHE HAS SERVED TO INSPIRE THE YOUNG, ENTERTAIN THE OLD AND WIN FOR AMERICAN TALENT ITS RIGHTFUL PLACE ON THE INTERNATIONAL STAGE OF DANCE.

★ ★ ★

President Jimmy Carter awarded Chase the Presidential Medal of Freedom with the above citation during a White House ceremony June 9, 1980.

Though interested in the theater from an early age, and a student of acting, dance, and voice for many years, Lucia Chase did not begin her career as a professional dancer until after her husband died unexpectedly in 1933. Soon after the tragedy she immersed herself in the study of ballet under former Bolshoi Ballet master Mikhail Mordkin. She proved a talented dance-actor, and when Mordkin organized his U.S. ballet company in 1937, Chase made her professional debut. Within the year she was being featured as one of his leading dancers.

The daughter of socially prominent parents, Chase was born in Waterbury, Connecticut, in 1897. As a young girl she often performed in children's plays, and after receiving her education at Bryn Mawr College she studied acting at New York City's Theatre Guild School. She took lessons in voice, piano, and ballet as well. Then in 1926 Chase married Thomas Ewing, Jr., a well-to-do business executive and an avid polo player. She gave birth to two sons, and while the demands of family life kept her from actively pursuing a performing career, she did continue her studies.

Ewing's death from pneumonia in 1933 changed her life. Using dance to help overcome her loss, she drew on her past training and soon became an innovative, internationally known dramatic ballet dancer. She performed actively in ballet theater productions from the late 1930s until her retirement in 1960. But her devotion to ballet went well beyond her onstage performances. In 1940 the American Ballet Theater was organized in New York City around the nucleus of the Mordkin Ballet, and Chase not only performed as a lead dancer for the new group, but also stepped forward as a chief financial backer. She had inherited some seven million dollars from her husband's estate and now actively supported the ballet theater group to which she had become devoted.

While continuing her dancing, Chase in 1945 also became codirector of the American Ballet Theater sharing the management responsibilities with stage designer Oliver Smith. They were dedicated to developing talented American dancers and showcased both classical and contemporary works on American themes. The ballet group eventually built a repertoire of over one hundred ballets, including works by Jerome Robbins, Agnes de Mille, Antony Tudor, and George Balanchine. By 1968 the American Ballet Theater had a worldwide reputation, having performed in fifty-five countries during fifteen international tours. That year the group became the official ballet company for the Kennedy Center for the Performing Arts in Washington, D.C.

Both Chase and Smith stepped down as codirectors of the ballet group in 1980, ending their thirty-five-year stewardship. Chase died in 1986, at age eighty-eight.

Hubert H. Humphrey

HUBERT H. HUMPHREY AWED US WITH THE SCOPE OF HIS KNOWLEDGE; HE INSPIRED US WITH THE DEPTH OF HIS SYMPATHY; HE MOVED US WITH HIS PASSION FOR SOCIAL JUSTICE; HE DELIGHTED US WITH HIS JOYOUS LOVE OF HIS FELLOW HUMAN BEINGS. HE BROUGHT HONOR AND ENTHUSIASM TO EVERYTHING HE DID. HE ENNOBLED THE POLITICAL PROCESS.

★ ★ ★

President Jimmy Carter awarded Humphrey the Presidential Medal of Freedom with the above citation during a White House ceremony June 9, 1980.

The thirty-eighth vice president of the United States, Hubert H. Humphrey was born in a South Dakota prairie town called Wallace in 1911. Raised in Doland, South Dakota, where his father ran the local drugstore, Humphrey excelled in school and during the 1930s worked as a pharmacist. A political science major at the University of Minnesota intent on entering politics, he graduated magna cum laude in 1939 and the following year earned his master's degree at Louisiana State University. Meanwhile, Humphrey married Muriel Fay Buck in 1936.

He held various jobs during the early 1940s, including teaching some college courses and working as a radio news broadcaster, before running President Franklin D. Roosevelt's reelection campaign in Minnesota. Humphrey also played a key role in merging the Farmer-Labor Party with the Democratic Party in Minnesota. In 1945 he won the first of two terms as mayor of Minneapolis and while in office set up the country's first municipal fair employment practices commission.

He next won election to the U.S. Senate in 1948, the first Democrat Minnesota voters ever sent to the Senate. During his next sixteen years in the Senate (1949–1964), Humphrey became known as a champion of liberal programs, including those mandating greater government support for the poor, expanded Social Security and unemployment benefits, and increased civil rights protections. In fact, the first bill he put before the Senate would have established a medical insurance plan for the aged (the bill failed).

With the help of Texas Sen. Lyndon B. Johnson, who became a close friend and ally, Humphrey became a skilled legislator and by the 1960s ranked among the most influential Senate leaders of his time. Among his most notable legislative feats were winning bipartisan support for the 1963 Nuclear Test Ban Treaty and the 1964 Civil Rights Act.

President Johnson chose Humphrey, who had lost a bid for the presidential nod in 1960, as his vice-presidential running mate for the 1964 election. The Johnson-Humphrey ticket won by a landslide, and Humphrey spent the next four years as chairman of the Civil Rights Council, coordinator of antipoverty programs, and staunch supporter of expanded U.S. involvement in the Vietnam War.

By 1968, when President Johnson declined to run again, the Democratic Party was badly split over the Vietnam War. In a convention marred by rioting, Democrats nominated Humphrey their presidential candidate, leaving him to deal with a divided party, as well as Republican challenger Richard Nixon. Despite a determined campaign in 1968, Humphrey lost by a narrow margin.

Reelected to the Senate in 1970, he lost another bid for the Democratic presidential nomination two years later. Still a highly regarded and effective legislator, Humphrey accepted his role as an elder statesman in the Senate and won reelection for the last time in 1976. He died of cancer two years later, at age sixty-six.

Archbishop Iakovos

GREEK ORTHODOX ARCHBISHOP IAKOVOS HAS LONG PUT INTO
PRACTICE WHAT HE HAS PREACHED. AS A PROGRESSIVE
RELIGIOUS LEADER CONCERNED WITH HUMAN RIGHTS AND THE
ECUMENICAL MOVEMENT, HE HAS MARCHED WITH DR. MARTIN
LUTHER KING, JR., AND HAS MET WITH THE POPE. AS THE
PRIMATE OF THE GREEK ORTHODOX CHURCH OF NORTH AND
SOUTH AMERICA CONCERNED WITH HIS CONGREGATION, HE HAS
GIVEN GUIDANCE TO MILLIONS.

★ ★ ★

*President Jimmy Carter awarded Iakovos the Presidential Medal of
Freedom with the above citation during a White House ceremony
June 9, 1980.*

The future Archbishop Iakovos was born Demetrios Coucouzis on
Imroz Island, Turkey, in 1911, the son of a storekeeper. While still a
youth, he decided to teach and at sixteen began his studies at the
Orthodox Halki Theological School. After graduating with honors in
1934, he spent the next five years as an archdeacon in Turkey.
(Clergymen in the Eastern Orthodox Church are ranked in three
major orders—deacon, priest, and bishop.)

He became archdeacon of the Greek Archdiocese of North and
South America in 1939 and as part of his duties began teaching at Holy
Cross Seminary in Massachusetts. Ordained an Orthodox priest in
1940, he followed church custom by adopting the name Iakovos, which
is Greek for James. He served as priest in various churches over the next
years and while in Boston earned a master of sacred theology degree
from Harvard Divinity School (1945). Iakovos then became dean of the
Holy Cross Seminary in 1947, a post he held for seven years.

In 1954 he was elevated to bishop, the church's highest order, and
made bishop of Malta. But his responsibilities expanded dramatically
the following year when he became a representative for his church at
the World Council of Churches, an international and interdenomi-
national fellowship of 173 Christian churches. He served as
copresident of the ecumenical group from 1959 to 1968 and during
that time visited Pope John XXIII on behalf of the Eastern Orthodox
Church, the first official contact between the two churches in
hundreds of years.

Named archbishop of North and South America in 1959, Iakovos
succeeded the late Archbishop Michael as head of the largest Orthodox
archdiocese on these two continents. He continued his interest in the
worldwide ecumenical movement and also sought greater unity among
the various Orthodox Eastern churches in America. To that end he
played an important role in founding the Standing Conference of

Canonical Orthodox Bishops in 1960. Meanwhile, he also gained a reputation outside the church during the 1960s by appearing in civil rights marches with Martin Luther King, Jr.

During the next decades Archbishop Iakovos also worked to bring what was once an immigrant ethnic church into the American mainstream. Now in his eighties, he remains active as the archbishop and leader of Eastern Orthodox Christians in the Western Hemisphere.

Lyndon B. Johnson

LYNDON B. JOHNSON CARED DEEPLY ABOUT OUR COUNTRY, ITS CITIZENS, AND THE CONDITION OF THEIR LIVES. HE KNEW WELL HOW TO TRANSLATE CONCERN INTO ACTION, AND ACTION INTO A NATIONAL AGENDA. HE DID MORE THAN ANY AMERICAN OF HIS TIME TO BREAK THE CHAINS OF INJUSTICE, ILLITERACY, POVERTY AND SICKNESS. WE ARE A GREATER SOCIETY BECAUSE PRESIDENT JOHNSON LIVED AMONG US AND WORKED FOR US.

★ ★ ★

President Jimmy Carter awarded Johnson a posthumous Presidential Medal of Freedom with the above citation during a White House ceremony June 9, 1980. Lady Bird Johnson accepted the medal on her late husband's behalf.

Lyndon B. Johnson was born on a farm near Stonewall, a southwest Texas town, in 1908. His father, a businessman and state legislator, moved the family to Johnson City, Texas, five years later, and for a time the family prospered. But young Lyndon was deeply affected when his father fell on hard times in the 1920s. After graduating from high school in 1924, he spent three years hitchhiking around the country before enrolling in Southwest Texas State Teachers College.

The long-delayed college education proved an important turning point in Johnson's life, though. His experience in campus politics helped him decide on a political career, while he also learned the value of education. Perhaps even more important for a politician in the segregated South, Johnson learned firsthand about the plight of poor Mexicans through an early teaching job. He was deeply affected, and his concern for the disadvantaged and for minority groups not only shaped his early political career as a New Deal Democrat, but also became a hallmark of his presidency.

Johnson arrived in Washington, D.C., for the first time in 1931 as a legislative assistant to a member of congress from Texas. Energetic and ambitious, Johnson became an ardent New Deal supporter and quickly learned the ins and outs of life on Capitol Hill. Three years later he met and married Claudia Alta "Lady Bird" Taylor in a whirlwind courtship, and between 1935 and 1937 he served as the National Youth Administration director for Texas. *(See also the entry for Lady Bird Johnson, p. 234.)*

Elected to the U.S. House of Representatives in 1937, Johnson served until 1949 as a loyal supporter of President Franklin D. Roosevelt's New Deal policies. Meanwhile, during the early 1940s, he and Lady Bird began building a media empire that would eventually help make them wealthy. He also suffered his first defeats while running for the Senate because of conservative Democrats' opposition. Finally, in 1948 Johnson narrowly won the Democratic Senate primary by just an eighty-seven-vote margin. Allegations of voting fraud during the primary were never proved, and Johnson gamely referred to himself as "Landslide Lyndon" after defeating his Republican opponent that fall.

Johnson fared well in the Senate's clubby atmosphere, though. His drive, legislative skills, and talent for intimate personal contact helped make him one of the Senate's most powerful leaders during the 1950s. Sometimes ruthless, sometimes tactful, he refined the art of consensus politics and as Senate majority leader from 1955 to 1961 acquired an almost legendary reputation as a legislative wheeler-dealer. In 1957 and again in 1960 he even managed to steer the first civil rights bills of the century past determined segregationist opposition in the Senate.

His own bid for the 1960 Democratic presidential nomination overwhelmed by John F. Kennedy's primary campaign, Johnson accepted the vice-presidential slot and campaigned hard for the Democratic ticket. Though he had provided valuable support in Kennedy's narrow victory over Richard Nixon, the tall, folksy Johnson did not fit in with the Ivy-League, eastern-establishment types who dominated the Kennedy administration. Johnson's years as vice president proved difficult, but he faced far greater personal trials following the assassination of President Kennedy. Because Kennedy was killed in Johnson's home state of Texas, there were suspicions, and eventually even farfetched allegations, that he had something to do with it.

Johnson calmed a distraught nation after Kennedy's death and, upon succeeding to the presidency, launched into an ambitious legislative program that included many bills Kennedy had been unable to get through Congress. With characteristic energy and legislative skill, President Johnson won passage of the landmark 1964 Civil Rights Act, declared his "war on poverty" (1964), and won a tax cut as well. During 1964 he also articulated his Great Society program to provide help for the aged, rebuild the nation's cities, and protect the environment. In following years, a host of reform legislation cleared Congress, much of it benefiting blacks and other minorities. Among Johnson's many reforms were the landmark Voting Rights Act of 1965, Medicare, Medicaid, the job corps, and community action, education, and urban renewal programs.

Despite his best efforts, President Johnson's far-reaching reform program was eventually jeopardized by his involving the United States in Vietnam. After winning election to a full term as president in 1964, Johnson set about systematically increasing U.S. forces in South Vietnam to prevent a Communist takeover. The war proved both unpopular and a costly drain on the government's finances, especially when coupled with the expensive Great Society programs Johnson had put in place.

President Johnson's term after 1964 was marred by increasing opposition to the Vietnam War, and by mass civil rights protests and outright rioting by blacks demanding better treatment in white-dominated American society. Unable to find a way to extricate the United States from Vietnam, and with unrest sweeping the country, President Johnson announced he would not run for office in 1968.

After leaving Washington in 1969, Johnson returned to his ranch in Texas and wrote his memoirs, *The Vantage Point* (1971). He died in 1973, just days before the signing of an agreement ending U.S. involvement in Vietnam. He was sixty-four years old.

Clarence M. Mitchell, Jr.

CLARENCE M. MITCHELL, JR., FOR DECADES WAGED IN THE HALLS OF CONGRESS A STUBBORN, RESOURCEFUL AND HISTORIC CAMPAIGN FOR SOCIAL JUSTICE. THE INTEGRITY OF THIS "101ST SENATOR" EARNED HIM THE RESPECT OF FRIENDS AND ADVERSARIES ALIKE. HIS BRILLIANT ADVOCACY HELPED TRANSLATE INTO LAW THE PROTESTS AND ASPIRATIONS OF MILLIONS CONSIGNED TOO LONG TO SECOND-CLASS CITIZENSHIP. THE HARD-WON FRUITS OF HIS LABORS HAVE MADE AMERICA A BETTER AND STRONGER NATION.

★ ★ ★

President Jimmy Carter awarded Mitchell the Presidential Medal of Freedom with the above citation during a White House ceremony June 9, 1980.

Born in Baltimore, Maryland, in 1911, Clarence M. Mitchell, Jr., was the son of a chef at a popular Annapolis, Maryland, restaurant. He got his bachelor's degree from Lincoln College in Pennsylvania and later earned his law degree at the University of Maryland. After additional graduate study and a stint at reporting for the Baltimore *Afro-American,* Mitchell joined the Saint Paul, Minnesota, Urban League office in 1937 as executive secretary.

He served on various government boards and commissions during World War II, including the War Manpower Commission, the Fair Employment Commission, and the War Production Board, and in 1945 began his long association with the National Association for the Advancement of Colored People (NAACP). Starting out as the national labor secretary in the NAACP Washington office, Mitchell eventually moved up to become head of the Washington office and the chief Washington lobbyist in 1950. He also was chief lobbyist for the Leadership Conference on Civil Rights, an umbrella organization for 115 groups concerned with advancing civil rights.

A veteran of many legislative battles on Capitol Hill, Mitchell maintained good relations with both Democrats and Republicans in Congress, and his influence was such that he earned the nickname "the 101st senator." He consulted with every president from Harry S. Truman to Jimmy Carter and had a hand in passage of all the groundbreaking civil rights legislation of the 1960s. He played a key role in winning the Fair Housing Act of 1968 and helped lead the successful fight against President Richard Nixon's Supreme Court nominees G. Harrold Carswell and Clement F. Haynsworth.

Mitchell retired as a lobbyist in 1978 and went into private practice, but he continued as a consultant for the NAACP. In addition to receiving the Presidential Medal of Freedom in 1980, he also received the NAACP Spingarn Medal in 1969. Mitchell died in 1984, at age seventy-three.

Roger Tory Peterson

ROGER TORY PETERSON HAS ACHIEVED DISTINCTION AS A CONSUMMATE PAINTER, WRITER, TEACHER AND SCIENTIST. AS AN UNABASHED LOVER OF BIRDS AND A DISTINGUISHED ORNITHOLOGIST, HE HAS FURTHERED THE STUDY, APPRECIATION AND PROTECTION OF BIRDS THE WORLD OVER. AND HE HAS DONE MORE. HE HAS IMPASSIONED THOUSANDS OF AMERICANS, AND HE HAS AWAKENED IN MILLIONS ACROSS THIS LAND, A FONDNESS FOR NATURE'S OTHER TWO-LEGGED CREATURES.

★ ★ ★

President Jimmy Carter awarded Peterson the Presidential Medal of Freedom with the above citation during a White House ceremony June 9, 1980.

The originator of *Peterson's Field Guide* series, Roger Tory Peterson was born in Jamestown, New York, in 1908. A troublesome youth in grammar school, he became fascinated with birds when his seventh-grade science teacher organized an Audubon Junior Club. He began making bird-watching field trips, and drawing the birds he saw stimulated his interest in art as well. Leaving high school, Peterson studied art at New York City's Art Students League from 1927 to 1928 and at the National Academy of Design from 1929 to 1931.

The depression forced him to find work, though, and from 1931 to 1934 he taught art and science at a private school in Massachusetts. Meanwhile, he continued studying birds and bird identification. He also completed the text and illustrations for his first field guide, the *A Field Guide to the Birds; Giving Field Marks of All Species Found in Eastern North America*. Houghton Mifflin published the book in 1934, and it quickly became a popular success.

By providing a workable system of bird identification, Peterson's book helped popularize bird-watching. The success of the book also landed Peterson a job as art director for *Audubon Magazine* (1934–1943) and led to a second field guide, *A Field Guide to Western Birds* (1941).

After serving in World War II, Peterson devoted himself full time to writing articles and books and lecturing for the Audubon Screen Tour. Since 1946 he has been the editor of the Houghton Mifflin Field Guide series, while also writing and illustrating books dealing with more general subject matter as well. Among his later books are *Birds Over America* (1948), *Wild America* (1955, coauthor), *Field Guide to Wildflowers* (1968, coauthor), *Peterson First Guide to Birds of North America* (1986, coauthor), and *The Field Guide Art of Roger Tory Peterson* (1990).

Hyman Rickover

ADMIRAL RICKOVER EXEMPLIFIES THE AMERICAN BELIEF THAT FREEDOM AND RESPONSIBILITY ARE INSEPARABLE; THE DUTY OF THE CITIZEN IS TO CONTRIBUTE HIS BEST TO THE NATION'S WELFARE AND DEFENSE. HIS SUCCESSFUL DEVELOPMENT AND APPLICATION OF NUCLEAR PROPULSION REVOLUTIONIZED NAVAL WARFARE. THE PERFORMANCE OF OUR NUCLEAR FLEET OVER MORE THAN A QUARTER OF A CENTURY IS PROOF OF HIS WELL-KNOWN COMMITMENT TO EXCELLENCE. THIS NATION'S FIRST CIVILIAN ELECTRIC UTILITY REACTOR, WHICH HE DESIGNED AND DEVELOPED IN THE 1950'S IS THE TECHNOLOGICAL FORERUNNER OF NEARLY ALL UTILITY REACTORS SUBSEQUENTLY BUILT IN THIS COUNTRY. A KEEN OBSERVER OF MANKIND, HE HAS NOT HES-

ITATED TO MEASURE PUBLICLY THE ACTIONS OF GOVERNMENT,
INDUSTRY, THE PROFESSIONS, AND OUR SCHOOLS AGAINST THE
STANDARD OF RESPONSIBILITY.

★ ★ ★

*President Jimmy Carter awarded Rickover the Presidential Medal of
Freedom with the above citation during a White House ceremony
June 9, 1980.*

The father of the nuclear navy, Hyman Rickover was born in Russia
in 1900 and emigrated to the United States with his family four years
later. Raised in Chicago, where his father worked as a tailor, Rickover
was a strong student and eventually graduated from the U.S. Naval
Academy in 1922. After five years spent on sea duty, Rickover was
assigned by the navy to postgraduate study in electrical engineering,
and in 1929 he earned his master's degree at Columbia University.

During the 1930s Rickover spent three years on submarine duty
and commanded a minesweeper (1937–1939) before being assigned as
head of the Electrical Section of the Bureau of Ships. He spent the
war at the bureau and oversaw the production of electrical lighting
and power equipment for navy ships. Other posts followed after the
war, but his assignment to the Oak Ridge nuclear development
facility proved crucial. While there, Rickover became convinced that
a nuclear reactor could be used to power a submarine.

When navy officials refused to consider the idea, he went around the
chain of command and, appealing directly to Chief of Naval Operations
Chester Nimitz, finally won approval for development of a nuclear submarine in 1949. Appointed head of the newly formed Nuclear Power
Division of the Bureau of Ships, Rickover also got himself named chief
of the Atomic Energy Commission Naval Reactors Branch in its Reactor
Development Division. With that bureaucratic maneuver, Rickover got
full control of the program to develop a nuclear submarine.

He worked wonders. Through adroit management, hard work,
and a novel approach (Rickover had the reactor and the submarine
designed and built simultaneously), he built the world's first nuclear
submarine in less than four years. The navy launched the USS
Nautilus in early 1954, the first of what became a fleet of 150 nuclear-
powered submarines, aircraft carriers, and other warships.

Promoted to rear admiral in 1953, he also developed the country's
first large-scale nuclear-powered electrical generating plant, which
became the model for U.S. nuclear power plants. The reactor, at
Shippingport, Pennsylvania, was completed in 1957 and supplied
power to Pittsburgh.

Rickover was promoted to admiral in 1973 and thanks to an act of
Congress remained on active duty well past the mandatory
retirement age. He finally retired in 1982, having served a record
sixty-three years as a navy officer. He died in 1986, at age eighty-six.

Beverly Sills

BEVERLY SILLS HAS CAPTURED WITH HER VOICE EVERY NOTE OF HUMAN FEELING, AND WITH HER SUPERB DRAMATIC TALENT PROJECTED THEM OUT TO US WITH RINGING CLARITY. THROUGH HER MANY AND DIVERSE ROLES, SHE TELLS AND RETELLS OPERA'S INTENSELY HEIGHTENED STORIES OF HUMAN FOLLY, GOODNESS, PAIN AND TRIUMPH. SHE HAS TOUCHED AND DELIGHTED AUDIENCES THROUGHOUT THE WORLD AS A PERFORMER, AS A RECORDING ARTIST, AND NOW AS A PRODUCER—AND OF ALL HER ARTS SHE IS A MASTER.

★ ★ ★

President Jimmy Carter awarded Sills the Presidential Medal of Freedom with the above citation during a White House ceremony June 9, 1980.

Among the world's great coloratura sopranos, Beverly Sills was born Belle Miriam Silverman in Brooklyn, New York, in 1929. Her parents were Eastern European immigrants. From age three Sills performed as a singer on the radio and she began serious vocal lessons at age eleven. The following year she retired from performing to concentrate on her schoolwork and her study of operatic roles. Two years in musical theater (1945–1946) were followed by her opera debut with the Philadelphia Civic Opera in 1947.

Slowly, sometimes almost painfully so in the following years, she advanced her career. Her first appearance at the San Francisco Opera in 1953 proved a great success, but she had to endure three years of unsuccessful auditions before the New York City Opera at last made her a member of the company in 1955. Sills married Peter Buckeley Greenough the following year.

The discovery that one of her young sons was deaf and the other was retarded nearly ended Sills's singing career in the early 1960s. But when she finally recovered from the shock and bitterness, she was noticeably more assured, both as an operatic singer and a skilled interpreter of her roles. Her memorable performance as Cleopatra in Handel's *Julius Caesar* in 1966 at last established Sills as an operatic star of international fame, and during the next few years she debuted at major European opera houses. Final certification of her fame came in 1975 when she at last had her New York Metropolitan Opera debut.

Sills continued performing until 1980, but in 1979 her career took another turn—she became director of the New York City Opera. She performed well in the world of opera administration, too, and served as president of the opera's board of directors from 1989 to 1990. Sills then moved to the Metropolitan Opera, where she has been the managing director since 1991.

Sills has served as a board member for a number of major corporations, including American Express and Time-Warner, and has published two books, *Bubbles—A Self Portrait* (1976) and *Beverly* (1987). She has received two Emmy Awards (in 1976 and in 1978) for television appearances and has recorded numerous albums.

Robert Penn Warren

ROBERT PENN WARREN EXCELS AS A POET, NOVELIST, LITERARY CRITIC, AND TEACHER. HIS TEXTBOOKS, WRITTEN WITH CLEANTH BROOKS, TRANSFORMED THE TEACHING OF LITERATURE AND WRITING IN THE UNITED STATES. AS A LITERARY CRAFTSMAN AND A COMMITTED HUMANIST ROBERT PENN WARREN HAS UNDERTAKEN A LIFELONG QUEST FOR SELF-KNOWLEDGE AND MORAL VISION WHICH HAS ESTABLISHED HIM AS ONE OF AMERICA'S GREATEST MEN OF LETTERS OF THE 20TH CENTURY.

★ ★ ★

President Jimmy Carter awarded Warren the Presidential Medal of Freedom with the above citation during a White House ceremony June 9, 1980.

A noted American novelist and the country's first poet laureate, Robert Penn Warren was born in 1905 in the small town of Guthrie, Kentucky, a center for tobacco marketing. Warren enjoyed reading poetry as a youth and while studying at Vanderbilt University joined an influential group of poets. Completing his undergraduate studies at Vanderbilt (1925), he earned his master's degree at the University of California at Berkeley (1927), studied at Yale, and attended Oxford as a Rhodes scholar.

While teaching at Vanderbilt and other colleges between 1930 and 1950, Warren cofounded and edited (with his friend Cleanth Brooks) the *Southern Review* (1935–1942). Until the magazine was disbanded, it ranked among the most influential literary magazines in the country. At about this time he and Cleanth Brooks also published *Understanding Poetry* (1938) and *Understanding Fiction* (1943), two widely used college textbooks.

In 1939 Warren also published his first novel, *Night Rider,* based on the war between growers and powerful tobacco companies at the turn of the century. Seven years later came one of his masterworks, *All the King's Men,* a powerful novel based on the life of Louisiana politician Huey Long. Awarded the Pulitzer Prize in 1947, the novel also was made into an Academy Award-winning film. Among

Warren's later novels are *World Enough and Time* (1950), *Band of Angels* (1955), and *The Cave* (1959). His highly praised book of short stories, *The Circus in the Attic,* was published in 1948.

In 1952, having recently divorced his first wife, Warren married the author Eleanor Clark, and the following year he published *Brother to Dragons,* a narrative poem. In his later years especially, he focused his energies on writing poetry and twice won Pulitzer Prizes for this work (in 1958 and 1979). Warren's books of collected poems include *Promises: Poems, 1954–1956, Audubon: A Vision* (1969), *Poems 1976–1978, Chief Joseph* (1983), and *New and Selected Poems, 1923–1985.*

Named the first American poet laureate in 1986, he served in that post until 1988. Warren died the following year, at age eighty-four.

John Wayne

JOHN WAYNE WAS BOTH AN EXAMPLE AND A SYMBOL OF TRUE AMERICAN GRIT AND DETERMINATION. THROUGH HIS COUNTLESS FILM ROLES, "THE DUKE" STILL LEADS MILLIONS ON HEROIC ADVENTURES ON BEHALF OF FAIRNESS AND JUSTICE. HE EMBODIES THE ENDURING AMERICAN VALUES OF INDIVIDUALISM, RELENTLESS BRAVERY AND PERSEVERANCE IN PURSUIT OF WHAT IS RIGHT. HE WAS THE QUINTESSENTIAL PATRIOT, AND WILL ESPECIALLY BE REMEMBERED WHENEVER OUR NATION FACES A CHALLENGE CALLING FOR STEADFAST COURAGE.

★ ★ ★

President Jimmy Carter awarded Wayne a posthumous Presidential Medal of Freedom with the above citation during a White House ceremony June 9, 1980. Wayne's wife, Pilar, accepted the award on his behalf.

An American folk figure and one of the biggest box office attractions in Hollywood history, John Wayne was born Marion Michael Morrison in Winterset, Iowa, in 1907. His father, a druggist, moved the family to Glendale, California, where Wayne acquired the nickname "Duke" and played football in high school. While attending the University of Southern California on a football scholarship, Wayne worked summers as a prop boy for director John Ford and from 1928 began getting bit parts in Ford's movies. Meanwhile, he dropped out of college after breaking his ankle in a football game.

With no formal training in acting, Wayne realized he needed some sort of gimmick to appeal to movie audiences and so developed his characteristic John Wayne style—the drawl, the menacing squint, and the way of moving that suggested he was ready to fight if needed. He practiced his virile good-guy mannerism in front of a mirror and used the same basic style for the rest of his movie career.

Wayne's first starring role, in *The Big Trail* (1930), also was his first under the name John Wayne. Director Raoul Walsh had insisted on the change, believing the name Marion was too sissified for a cowboy hero. The movie failed because it required special projectors at a time when theater owners were reluctant to spend money, but Wayne went on to star in eighty low-budget movies over the next eight years, about half of them Westerns. Then in 1939 Wayne appeared in Ford's Western classic *Stagecoach,* which legitimized the Western genre and helped establish Wayne's reputation as an actor. *(See also the entry for Ford, p. 200.)*

Another success the following year, in Ford's *The Long Voyage Home,* completed Wayne's rise as a Hollywood star and led to a string of starring roles that lasted for the next four decades and included over 250 films. He starred in a host of action and war movies, including *They Were Expendable* (1945), *The Sands of Iwo Jima* (1949), and *The Wings of Eagles* (1957), but Westerns remained his strongest suit. Among his best were *Red River* (1948), *Fort Apache* (1948), *She Wore a Yellow Ribbon* (1949), *The Searchers* (1956), *Rio Bravo* (1959), *The Man Who Shot Liberty Valence* (1962), *How the West Was Won* (1963), and *True Grit* (1969). Wayne won his first and only Oscar for his performance in *True Grit. Rooster Cogburn* (1975) and *The Shootist* (1976) were among his later Westerns.

Meanwhile, in 1954 Wayne married his third wife, a Peruvian named Pilar Palette, having divorced two previous wives. He also became involved in making movies, investing $1.2 million of his own money in the 1960 film *The Alamo.* The movie was a critical and commercial failure, but his later effort, as co-director and star of *The Green Berets* (1968), was a box office success. In 1970 he starred in the television special, "Swing Out, Sweet Land," an unabashedly patriotic show entirely in keeping with Wayne's outspoken Americanism. He was in fact a conservative Republican whose stands on issues at times aroused considerable controversy.

Wayne lost his left lung to cancer in 1964 but refused to let it halt his film career. He remained free of cancer for almost fifteen years before the disease reappeared in his intestine and stomach. Wayne died of cancer in 1979. He was seventy-two years old.

Eudora Welty

EUDORA WELTY'S FICTION, WITH ITS STRONG SENSE OF PLACE
AND TRIUMPHANT COMIC SPIRIT, ILLUMINATES THE HUMAN
CONDITION. HER PHOTOGRAPHS OF THE SOUTH DURING THE
DEPRESSION REVEAL A RARE ARTISTIC SENSIBILITY. HER
CRITICAL ESSAYS EXPLORE MIND AND HEART, LITERARY AND
ORAL TRADITION, LANGUAGE AND LIFE WITH UNSURPASSED
BEAUTY. THROUGH PHOTOGRAPHY, ESSAYS AND FICTION,
EUDORA WELTY HAS ENRICHED OUR LIVES AND SHOWN US THE
WONDER OF HUMAN EXPERIENCE.

★ ★ ★

*President Jimmy Carter awarded Welty the Presidential Medal of Freedom
with the above citation during a White House ceremony June 9, 1980.*

A distinguished American short-story writer and novelist whose
works center on the people inhabiting a small Mississippi town,
Eudora Welty was born in 1909 in what was then the small town of
Jackson, Mississippi. She was the daughter of an insurance company
president and at first wanted to become a painter, but by the time she
reached college, she had become interested in writing. After graduating from the University of Wisconsin in 1929 and doing some
postgraduate work at Columbia University, she worked briefly in
advertising, society newswriting, and radio broadcast writing before
devoting herself exclusively to fiction.

The literary magazine *Manuscript* was first to publish one of her
short stories ("The Death of a Travelling Salesman" 1936), but over
the next five years her work appeared in such magazines as *Harper's
Bazaar* and *Atlantic Monthly*. Welty finally arrived on the literary
scene in the early 1940s: she published her first book of collected
short stories, *A Curtain of Green*, in 1941 and won the first of three O.
Henry awards for her short stories (1942, 1943, 1968).

Welty, who never married, continued writing short stories for
various magazines during her long career. During the 1940s, however,
she also began writing novels about life in the South, including *Delta
Wedding* (1946), *The Ponder Heart* (1954), *The Shoe Bird* (1964), and
Losing Battles (1970). *The Optimist's Daughter* (1972) won her a
Pulitzer Prize in 1973. Meanwhile, she also published collections of
short stories, a book of essays called *The Eye of the Story* (1978), her
autobiographical *One Writer's Beginnings* (1984), and *Eudora Welty:
Photographs* (1989).

Noted for perceptive, richly descriptive character portraits in both
her short stories and novels, Welty successfully invested small-town
Mississippi Delta life with a universal reality. While tracing the

intricate relationships between her characters, she explored broader themes, such as the virtue in people that lies beneath the veneer of social conventions and the "separateness" of individuals.

Tennessee Williams

Tennessee Williams has shaped the history of modern American theater through plays which range from passionate tragedies to lyrical comedies. His masterpieces dramatize the eternal conflicts between body and soul, youth and death, love and despair through the unity of reality and poetry. Tennessee Williams shows us that the truly heroic in life or art is human compassion.

★ ★ ★

President Jimmy Carter awarded Williams the Presidential Medal of Freedom with the above citation during a White House ceremony June 9, 1980.

Among the best American playwrights of this century, Tennessee Williams was born Thomas Lanier Williams in Columbus, Mississippi, in 1911. Unhappy in his childhood, Williams began writing and making up stories. He dropped out of the University of Mississippi, and while working days at a shoe company, he drove himself to write plays, stories, and poems during the nights. Williams suffered his first nervous breakdown because of the strain of this regimen. After recovering, he got his degree from the University of Iowa in 1938.

Having returned to writing plays, he had some success in 1939 with a group of one-act plays called *American Blues*. That same year he adopted the name "Tennessee" in place of Thomas. Soon after, he went to Hollywood as a scriptwriter and there began working on what would become *The Glass Menagerie*. The play, about the escapist dreams of a southern woman who has fallen into poverty, premiered on Broadway in 1944 and became an instant success. Established as a major playwright, Williams followed with the second of his greatest plays, *A Streetcar Named Desire,* in 1947. Here, as in most of his plays, Williams focused on fragile individuals trapped in desperate circumstances. For *Streetcar* he created Blanche Du Bois, another southern woman fallen on hard times, and won his first Pulitzer Prize.

Williams won another Pulitzer Prize for his next big success, *Cat on a Hot Tin Roof* in 1955 and six years later wrote another hit, *The Night of the Iguana.* Suffering a creative crisis in the early 1960s, Williams changed his techniques and soon fell out of favor with critics and audiences alike. Meanwhile, his heavy drinking and addiction to sleeping pills also caught up with him, and, in poor health, he suffered a mental and physical collapse in 1969. He wrote more plays in the 1970s but was unable to rediscover his earlier successes.

Though Williams's fame rests largely on *The Glass Menagerie* and *A Streetcar Named Desire,* he wrote over seventy plays. Among his others were *Suddenly Last Summer* (1958), *Sweet Bird of Youth* (1959), and his less successful later plays, *Vieux Carré* (1977), *A Lovely Sunday for Creve Coeur* (1978), and *Clothes for a Summer Hotel* (1980). He also wrote two novels, *The Roman Spring of Mrs. Stone* (1950) and *Moise and the World of Reason* (1975), as well as his *Memoirs* (1975).

Williams, who never married, died at his New York City hotel suite in 1983. He was seventy-one years old.

Horace Marden Albright

A LIVING MONUMENT, LIKE THE GRAND TETONS HE FOUGHT SO HARD TO PRESERVE, HORACE M. ALBRIGHT HAS BEEN A DRIVING FORCE FOR CONSERVATION IN THIS COUNTRY DURING MOST OF THE 20TH CENTURY. A FOUNDING FATHER OF THE NATIONAL PARK SERVICE, HE IS A CHAMPION OF NATURE'S CAUSE AND A DEFENDER OF AMERICA'S MOST PRECIOUS INHERITANCE.

★ ★ ★

President Jimmy Carter awarded Albright the Presidential Medal of Freedom with the above citation on December 8, 1980. The medal was presented by special arrangement in Van Nuys, California.

A cofounder of the National Park Service and its second director, Horace Marden Albright was born in 1890 and raised in Bishop, California, a town surrounded by mountain vistas and unspoiled countryside. The natural beauty of his childhood surroundings left its mark on him, and after graduating from the University of California in 1912 he joined the staff of the Interior Department secretary. The National Park Service did not yet exist, but by 1915 a wealthy businessman and conservationist named Stephen T. Mather had volunteered to help administer national parks for the Interior Department. That same year Albright became Mather's special assistant, and the two cofounded the National Park Service. First they helped write the National Park Service Act of 1916 and shepherded it through Congress. Then, with Mather as director of the newly created park service and Albright as assistant director, the two established the organization's administrative and conservation policies.

Albright served as superintendent of Yellowstone National Park after 1919 and then succeeded Mather as park service director in 1929. During his tenure, he oversaw the establishment of the Grand Teton (Wyoming), Carlsbad Caverns (New Mexico), and Great Smoky Mountains (Tennessee and North Carolina) National Parks, and the beginning of a new historic preservation program. When President Franklin D. Roosevelt came to office, Albright helped found the Civilian Conservation Corps as part of Roosevelt's New Deal program.

Albright retired from the park service to become vice president of the United States Potash Company in 1933. Though he continued with the mining company until he retired as its president in 1956, Albright also managed to stay involved with the park service and the conservation movement. The restoration of Colonial Williamsburg was just one of the projects to which he donated his spare time.

An Interior Department official presented the Presidential Medal of Freedom to Albright, then ninety years old, in Van Nuys, California. He died seven years later.

Roger Nash Baldwin

FOUNDER OF THE AMERICAN CIVIL LIBERTIES UNION AND THE INTERNATIONAL LEAGUE FOR HUMAN RIGHTS, ROGER NASH BALDWIN IS A LEGEND IN THE FIELD OF CIVIL LIBERTIES. HE IS A NATIONAL RESOURCE, AND AN INTERNATIONAL ONE AS WELL, AN INSPIRATION TO THOSE OF US WHO HAVE FOUGHT FOR HUMAN RIGHTS, A SAINT TO THOSE FOR WHOM HE HAS GAINED THEM.

★ ★ ★

President Jimmy Carter awarded Baldwin the Presidential Medal of Freedom with the above citation on January 16, 1981. The medal was presented at a hospital in New Jersey by special arrangement.

Roger Nash Baldwin's ideals helped shape the American Civil Liberties Union (ACLU). As founder and its director for decades, he fought to ensure that the fundamental constitutional guarantees applied equally to all no matter how unpopular the cause might be. At various times, communists, Nazis, Ku Klux Klansmen, and members of many other groups across the spectrum benefited from the nonpartisan legal defense provided by the ACLU. So too did many decidedly nonpolitical individuals whose rights were denied.

Baldwin, the son of a well-to-do shoe manufacturer, was born in 1884 and was raised in the Boston suburb of Wellesley, Massachusetts. A graduate of Harvard in 1904, he also received his master's degree in anthropology there the following year. He then began teaching and doing social work in Saint Louis, and his book on probation, *Juvenile Courts and Probation* (1912, written with Bernard Flexner), became a standard text.

Baldwin credited a 1909 lecture by the anarchist Emma Goldman with having molded his libertarian belief in unrestricted freedom of thought and speech, and from 1910 he worked for a Saint Louis reform group. After World War I broke out, Baldwin went to New York to head the Civil Liberties Bureau of the American Union Against Militarism. In 1920, Baldwin and two lawyers reorganized that group to form the ACLU. With Baldwin as its director and with a corps of volunteer lawyers, the ACLU eventually built an international reputation by defending clients of every stripe. Among the most highly publicized cases with which the ACLU became involved were the Scopes "Monkey Trial," concerning the teaching of evolution, the Sacco-Vanzetti murder case, and the lifting of the ban on publication of James Joyce's *Ulysses*.

Already in his mid–sixties, Baldwin retired from the ACLU in 1950, though he remained active in the International League for the Rights of Man for many more years. His second wife, Evelyn Preston, whom he married in 1936, died in 1962.

Baldwin could not attend the White House ceremony to receive his Presidential Medal of Freedom in 1981 because medical problems confined him to a New Jersey hospital. President Carter made special arrangements, however, and the deputy U.S. ambassador to the United Nations presented Baldwin's medal at the hospital at the same time the award ceremony began in Washington. Baldwin died seven months later, at age ninety-seven.

Harold Brown

FROM THE GOVERNMENT OF SCIENCE TO THE SCIENCE OF GOV-
ERNMENT, HAROLD BROWN HAS SERVED HIS COUNTRY FIRST
AND HIS PRINCIPLES ALWAYS. AS AN ADVISOR TO PRESIDENTS,
AND A PRESIDENT OF A COMMUNITY OF SCHOLARS, HE HAS
HELPED BRIDGE THE GAP BETWEEN THE WORLD OF THEORY AND
THE WORLD OF REALITY. ADEPT AT TRANSLATING FROM THE
LANGUAGE OF SCIENCE TO THE LANGUAGE OF STATECRAFT, HE
EXCELS IN TRANSLATING PURPOSE INTO ACTION.

★ ★ ★

*President Jimmy Carter awarded Brown the Presidential Medal of
Freedom with the above citation during a White House ceremony
January 16, 1981.*

The first scientist to hold the top civilian job at the Pentagon, Harold
Brown was secretary of defense during the Carter administration. A
brilliant physicist who for many years worked on improving nuclear
weapons, he also proved an exceptionally effective administrator.

Brown advocated the idea of getting "more bang for the buck,"
and as defense secretary earned the nickname "Dr. No" because he
ruled against various weapons development projects as impractical
and too costly. Among the most controversial of them was the B–1
Bomber program. His term as secretary, lasting from 1977 to 1981,
came at a time of military cutbacks, increasing terrorism and insta-
bility abroad, and, from 1980, a freeze in relations with the Soviet
Union over its invasion of Afghanistan.

Brown's keen mind showed itself early. Born in New York City in
1927, he graduated from the Bronx High School of Science at age
fifteen with a 99.52 average. He took just two years to graduate from
Columbia University with honors in physics in 1945 and won his doctorate in physics from Columbia in 1949. Next he began working at the
University of California Lawrence Radiation Laboratory as a research
scientist, and in 1952 he moved to the center for weapons research, the
Lawrence Livermore laboratories. While there he helped develop the
Polaris missile warhead and in 1960 succeeded Dr. Edward Teller as
director. He married Colene Dunning McDowell in 1953.

President John F. Kennedy named Brown director of research and
engineering for the Defense Department in 1961, making him the third-
ranking civilian in the department. As secretary of the air force under
President Lyndon B. Johnson from 1965 to 1969, Brown frequently
advocated limited bombing of North Vietnam during the Vietnam War.

Returning to the academic world, he served as president of the
California Institute of Technology from 1969 to 1977. From 1969 to
1977 he also was a U.S. delegate to the Strategic Arms Limitation

Talks (SALT) with the Soviet Union, helping secure the historic SALT I arms reduction agreement in 1972. Brown returned to public office in 1977 as President Carter's secretary of defense and remained in that post until the end of Carter's term.

Again leaving the world of government, Brown became chairman of the Johns Hopkins Foreign Policy Institute (1984–1992), worked as a consultant, and held positions on various corporate boards of directors. He wrote the book *Thinking About National Security: Defense and Foreign Policy in a Dangerous World* (1983) and has served as a counselor at the Center for Strategic and International Studies since 1992.

Zbigniew Brzezinski

ZBIGNIEW BRZEZINSKI SERVED HIS COUNTRY AND THE WORLD. AN AUTHOR AND ARCHITECT OF WORLD AFFAIRS, HIS STRATEGIC VISION OF AMERICA'S PURPOSE FUSED PRINCIPLE WITH STRENGTH. HIS LEADERSHIP HAS BEEN INSTRUMENTAL IN BUILDING PEACE AND ENDING THE ESTRANGEMENT OF THE CHINESE AND AMERICAN PEOPLE. BUT ABOVE ALL, HE HELPED SET OUR NATION IRREVOCABLY ON A COURSE THAT HONORS AMERICA'S ABIDING COMMITMENT TO HUMAN RIGHTS.

★ ★ ★

President Jimmy Carter awarded Brzezinski the Presidential Medal of Freedom with the above citation during a White House ceremony January 16, 1981.

A noted expert on communism and the Communist world, Zbigniew Brzezinski was born in Warsaw, Poland, in 1928. The son of a Polish diplomat, he lived outside Poland virtually all of his childhood. When World War II broke out in Europe, his father was working at the Polish embassy in Canada, and the family settled there permanently after the Communists took over Poland. Brzezinski graduated from Canada's McGill University in 1949 and obtained his master's degree in political science the following year.

Harvard University awarded him his doctorate in 1953 and kept him on as an instructor in government and then as an assistant professor. In 1955 he married Emilie Beneö, a sculptor and grandniece of former Czech president Edvard Beneö. By then Brzezinski had developed his special interest in the Communist world, and in 1956 his doctoral thesis was published as *The Permanent Purge—Politics in Soviet Totalitarianism*. That same year he published (as a coauthor)

Totalitarian Dictatorship and Autocracy, which, along with numerous journal articles, helped establish him in academic circles.

After becoming a naturalized U.S. citizen in 1958, Brzezinski joined the Columbia University faculty as an associate professor in 1960 (full professor, 1962), and in 1961 became director of the university's new Institute on Communist Affairs. Meanwhile, he continued to publish works on the Communist world and foreign affairs including *The Soviet Bloc—Unity and Conflict* (1960), *Ideology and Power in Soviet Politics* (1962), and *Alternative to Partition* (1965). By the mid–1960s his outspoken support for U.S. involvement in Vietnam also had earned him a government post. He served on the State Department's Policy Planning Council from 1966 to 1968, during the Johnson administration.

Later, Brzezinski served as assistant to the president for national security affairs during the Carter administration. While he was a White House adviser, the United States established full diplomatic relations with Communist China, adopted sanctions against the Soviet Union for its invasion of Afghanistan, and monitored the beginning of Poland's Solidarity movement. When Carter left office in 1981, Brzezinski became a counselor to the Center for Strategic and International Studies, a post he continues to hold, and also returned to teaching at Columbia.

Back in government between 1987 and 1991, Brzezinski served as a member of the President's Foreign Intelligence Advisory Board during the Reagan and Bush administrations. In 1989 he left Columbia to become a professor at the Johns Hopkins School for Advanced International Studies. Meanwhile, he continued publishing books on foreign affairs, including *The Grand Failure: The Birth and Death of Communism in the Twentieth Century* (1989) and his most recent, *Out of Control: Global Turmoil on the Eve of the Twenty-first Century* (1993).

Warren Minor Christopher

WARREN CHRISTOPHER HAS THE TACT OF A TRUE DIPLOMAT, THE TACTICAL SKILLS OF A GREAT SOLDIER, THE ANALYTICAL ABILITY OF A FINE LAWYER, AND THE SELFLESS DEDICATION OF A CITIZEN-STATESMAN. HIS PERSEVERANCE AND LOYALTY, JUDGMENT AND SKILL HAVE WON FOR HIS COUNTRY NEW RESPECT AROUND THE WORLD AND NEW REGARD FOR THE STATE DEPARTMENT AT HOME.

★ ★ ★

President Jimmy Carter awarded Christopher the Presidential Medal of Freedom with the above citation during a White House ceremony

January 16, 1981. Christopher, then in Algiers conducting round-the-clock negotiations to free American hostages in Iran, could not attend. He did, however, listen to the ceremony over an open telephone line.

Few crises in recent years have affected the American public as deeply as the prolonged ordeal of fifty-two American hostages seized by Iranian Islamic fundamentalists in late 1979. At once causing widespread concern for the hostages' safety and intense frustration at the Carter administration's inability to end the prolonged standoff, the crisis became a symbol of the government's weakness in coping with terrorism, especially after a commando-style rescue attempt failed in 1980. Soon after the botched raid, then-Deputy Secretary of State Warren Christopher took over efforts to negotiate the hostages' release.

By late 1980 Christopher had enlisted Algerian officials as intermediaries in secret talks on Iran's four conditions for the hostages' release. In the tough bargaining that ensued, the Iranians balked at American offers, but Christopher advised them to act before recently elected Ronald Reagan took office. Reagan had successfully campaigned in 1980 on a hard line against terrorists. But on December 21, 1980, the Iranians stunned Christopher by suddenly asking for $24 billion.

Christopher continued negotiating, however, and by January 19, 1981, had whittled down Iranian demands to under $3 billion in net gains. Agreements were signed simultaneously in Algeria and Tehran that day, and it seemed the outgoing President Carter had won a surprising eleventh-hour victory. But within hours the Iranians discovered a mixup in an obscure provision involving Iranian bank deposits in the United States, and the last-minute wrangling delayed the hostages' release until the following afternoon, the day President Reagan took office.

Known as a tough, self-controlled negotiator well before the Iranian crisis, Warren Christopher was born in 1925, the son of a Scranton, North Dakota, banker. His father died while he was a child and his family moved to Los Angeles during the 1930s. After graduating from the University of Southern California magna cum laude in 1945 and from Stanford Law School in 1949, Christopher clerked for Supreme Court Justice William O. Douglas from 1949 to 1950. Entering private practice that year, he became a partner in a Los Angeles law firm by 1958. During breaks in his public service he has returned to work there ever since.

A Democrat, he served as a State Department consultant on international talks concerning the textile trade from 1961 to 1965, and from 1967 to 1969 was deputy attorney general in the Johnson administration. When President Carter took office, he named Christopher deputy secretary of state. Christopher served as a spokesman and diplomatic trouble-shooter during the Carter administration, propping up support for the Panama Canal Treaty, negotiating a new relationship with Taiwan after the United States formally recognized China, and coordinating opposition to the

Soviet invasion of Afghanistan. But by far his most highly publicized achievement during the Carter years was in negotiating the American hostages' release.

When Democratic President Bill Clinton took office in 1993, he named Christopher secretary of state. But with administration priorities initially focused on domestic issues, U.S. foreign policy occupied a much lower profile than in past administrations. The United States withdrew forces sent to Somalia for humanitarian purposes by the Bush administration and, after considerable deliberation, finally sent troops to Haiti as part of its effort to force a return to democratic government there. More recently, U.S. involvement in the ongoing war in Bosnia and trade negotiations with Japan, as well as disagreements with China over U.S. policy toward Taiwan and other issues, have dominated U.S. foreign policy. By far the administration's biggest foreign policy successes to date came in late 1995. The Israelis signed an agreement at the White House giving Palestinians control of Palestinian cities and enclaves in the West Bank. Soon after, the United States helped arrange a peace settlement in Bosnia.

Walter Cronkite

FOR THOUSANDS OF NIGHTS, THE EYES AND EARS OF MILLIONS OF AMERICANS HAVE BEEN TUNED IN TO THE EYES AND EARS OF WALTER CRONKITE. HE HAS REPORTED AND COMMENTED ON THE EVENTS OF THE LAST TWO DECADES WITH A SKILL AND INSIGHT WHICH STANDS OUT IN THE NEWS WORLD, IN A WAY WHICH HAS MADE THE NEWS OF THE WORLD STAND OUT FOR ALL OF US.

★ ★ ★

President Jimmy Carter awarded Cronkite the Presidential Medal of Freedom with the above citation during a White House ceremony January 16, 1981.

The CBS television news anchorman for almost twenty years, Walter Cronkite ranks among the most popular and highly regarded broadcast journalists of modern times. Born in Saint Joseph, Missouri, in 1916, Walter Leland Cronkite, Jr., had decided to become a journalist as early as in junior high school. At the University of Texas he studied journalism, political science, and other subjects while working part time as a student correspondent for the *Houston Post*, as a sportscaster for a local radio show, and as a reporter for Scripps-Howard newspapers.

Preferring journalism to his college studies, Cronkite dropped out after his junior year and in 1936 began working full time for the *Post*. The early years of his career saw Cronkite in a variety of journalistic posts, including news and sports editor at radio KCMO in Kansas City, football announcer for WKV in Oklahoma City, and finally as a United Press (UP) correspondent. In 1940 he married Mary Maxwell, a news columnist.

During World War II Cronkite was among the first American journalists to accompany U.S. troops into battle, reporting on many combat missions firsthand. He flew on the first Flying Fortress bombing raids over Germany, went ashore with Allied troops during the Normandy invasion, and covered the Allied victory at the Battle of the Bulge, which turned back the Nazis' last major offensive in World War II.

Following the war Cronkite remained in Europe and reestablished the UP news bureaus in Belgium, the Netherlands, and Luxembourg. After covering the Nuremberg war crimes trials in Germany for UP, he became UP's bureau chief in Moscow. Back in the United States in 1948, Cronkite reported briefly for a group of Midwestern radio stations before joining CBS News in July 1950.

Remaining with CBS for the next four decades, Cronkite rose from appearances on such public affairs programs as "Man of the Week" to become the country's leading broadcast journalist. In 1952 Cronkite covered the nominating conventions for the first nationally televised presidential campaigns and went on to cover nearly every national political convention and election until his retirement.

In April 1962 he delivered the first broadcast of the "CBS Evening News with Walter Cronkite." Cronkite's clear, objective, and thoroughly professional delivery eventually made the show an enormous success, and during his two decades as its anchorman he became one of America's most trusted broadcast journalists. The name Cronkite became a household word in America, and his nightly sign off, "And that's the way it is," was a mark of his striving for a balanced, objective delivery of the news.

Cronkite believed his position as a journalist was one of an impartial observer with a duty to deliver the facts, not to be an analyst or participant. He wrote and edited his stories carefully and thoughtfully to be objective, fair, and straightforward. "I feel no compulsion to be a pundit," he once told an interviewer.

In his career as an anchorman, Cronkite covered every imaginable type of story, from natural disasters, wars, space missions, and assassinations, to history-making interviews with the likes of President John F. Kennedy (and all other U.S. presidents of his time), Anwar Sadat, Archibald Cox, and Aleksandr Solzhenitsyn. In 1981, nineteen years after becoming the CBS News anchorman, he relinquished the position to Dan Rather.

Cronkite, then sixty-five, was named to the CBS board of directors, a post he retained until 1990. He also continued as a CBS special correspondent, has since appeared on news specials, and has hosted television series.

Kirk Douglas

ACCLAIMED AS A SCREEN ACTOR AND DIRECTOR HERE AT HOME,
KIRK DOUGLAS HAS OFTEN PLAYED A DIFFERENT ROLE ABROAD.
ACTING AS AN AMBASSADOR OF GOOD WILL BEYOND OUR
SHORES, HE HAS TRAVELED AROUND THE WORLD FOR OUR STATE
DEPARTMENT AND THE UNITED STATES INFORMATION AGENCY.
THE SON OF RUSSIAN IMMIGRANTS, HE TRAVELS, TOO, FOR THE
OPPORTUNITY TO SHARE WITH OTHER PEOPLES HIS LOVE OF
FILM, AND COUNTRY.

★ ★ ★

*President Jimmy Carter awarded Douglas the Presidential Medal of
Freedom with the above citation during a White House ceremony
January 16, 1981.*

Ranked among the twentieth century's best actors, Kirk Douglas was
born in Amsterdam, New York, in 1916. Issur Danielovitch Demsky,
as he was originally named, actively participated in high school
dramatic productions. A star wrestler, class president, and president
of the dramatic group at Saint Lawrence University, he earned his
bachelor's degree in 1939 and then enrolled at the American Academy
of Dramatic Arts in New York City.

Douglas spent two years at the academy while also acting in
summer stock theaters, working as a dramatics coach, and waiting
tables. At the academy he met Lauren Bacall, a fellow student who
later helped him start his movie career by introducing him to
Hollywood producer Hal Wallis. There, Douglas also met Diana Dill,
whom he married in 1943. (Divorced in 1950, he married his second
wife, Anne Buydens, four years later.)

His Broadway debut came in 1941 with a minor role as a messenger delivering singing telegrams. Though his wartime service in
the navy intervened, Douglas returned to New York in 1944 and
quickly began making the right connections. He appeared in
Broadway plays and on radio programs, and a year later producer
Hal Wallis signed him for his first movie, a nonstarring role in *The
Strange Love of Martha Ivers.*

Several other small parts followed before Douglas created a sensation with the lead in the low-budget, hit movie *Champion* (1949).
Douglas, who played a dishonest, ambitious prizefighter, trained for
months with a retired boxer before making the movie. That thorough
preparation paid off. His hit performance established him as a star
and won him a seven-year movie contract with Warner Brothers.

Many memorable film roles followed, among them his portrayal of
a jazz trumpet player in *Young Man with a Horn* (1950), the hardened
and unscrupulous New York City journalist in *Ace in the Hole* (1951),

and the troubled artist Vincent Van Gogh in *Lust for Life* (1956). He also starred in the ever-popular Westerns (as Doc Holliday in the 1957 film *Gunfight at the O.K. Corral* and others) and in adventure films like *20,000 Leagues Under the Sea* (1954) and *Spartacus* (1960).

While continuing to appear in films and on television during the 1970s and 1980s, Douglas headed his own motion picture production company and also directed movies. A three-time Academy Award nominee, he has won the New York Film Critics Award (1956) and the American Film Institute Lifetime Achievement Award (1991), among other honors.

In addition to performing, Douglas has served as a goodwill ambassador for the United States, touring overseas on behalf of the United States Information Agency and the State Department. He has also written books, including his autobiography, *Ragman's Son* (1988) and the novel *Last Tango in Brooklyn* (1994).

Margaret Craig McNamara

MARGARET CRAIG MCNAMARA SAW A NEED IN OUR SOCIETY, AND FILLED IT. BY CREATING THE READING IS FUNDAMENTAL PROGRAM, WHICH HAS PROVIDED YOUNGSTERS ALL OVER THIS COUNTRY WITH MILLIONS OF BOOKS, SHE HAS OPENED NEW DOORS IN THE MINDS OF YOUNG PEOPLE AND HAS GIVEN FRESH MEANING TO THE LIVES OF THE PARENTS, TEACHERS AND VOL-UNTEERS WHO HAVE JOINED HER PROGRAM.

★ ★ ★

President Jimmy Carter awarded McNamara the Presidential Medal of Freedom with the above citation during a White House ceremony January 16, 1981.

Born Margaret Craig in 1916, she was raised in the San Francisco area and graduated from the University of California at Berkeley. After college she worked as a biology and health education teacher until 1940, when she married Robert S. McNamara. *(See also the entry for Robert McNamara, p. 134.)*

While her husband moved up from assistant professor at Harvard business school to Ford Company "Whiz Kid" to the presidency of Ford itself, McNamara raised three children and remained active in community affairs. Her record of civic work prompted President Lyndon B. Johnson to appoint her to a national advisory council on antipoverty programs in 1965, four years after her husband had become secretary of defense. Meanwhile, she also continued her work among poor children in Washington, D.C.

The inspiration for her Reading is FUNdamental program came out of that volunteer work in 1966, when she was teaching poor children who were slow readers. One boy asked if he could take home a book by Jules Verne that she had brought to class. She let him, and a few months later he was reading voraciously.

Realizing that neither the children she was teaching nor their parents owned any books, she suddenly saw a way to make the children more enthusiastic about reading: let them pick out books to read and keep them as their own. At the time, she was on the executive committee of D.C. Citizens for Better Public Education, and through the group she started her Reading is FUNdamental program for children in Washington.

The program proved so successful that major contributions came from the Ford Foundation and other groups, and such celebrities as Arthur Ashe and Carol Burnett supported the idea. By 1980 local sponsors in some 13,000 places throughout the United States were distributing books to over three-million children. By 1981 some thirty-seven million books had been distributed to needy children through McNamara's program.

Already suffering from advanced stages of cancer when President Carter selected her for the Presidential Medal of Freedom in 1981, McNamara went to the White House in a wheelchair to receive her award. She died just over two weeks later. She was sixty-five years old.

Karl Menninger

KARL MENNINGER HAS TAUGHT US MUCH ABOUT OURSELVES AND OUR BEHAVIOR. AN ACUTE OBSERVER AND SOCIAL CRITIC, HE HAS PUT INTO ACTION WHAT HE HAS PUT ONTO PAPER. AS AN AUTHOR AND DOCTOR, HIS WORKS RANGE FROM POPULAR, WRITTEN ACCOUNTS OF PSYCHIATRY TO STUDIES DONE IN HIS OWN HOSPITAL, FROM CREATING HOMES FOR PARENTLESS CHILDREN TO REFORMING THE PENAL SYSTEM. WITH THE WISDOM OF HIS YEARS, HE TRULY DOES REPRESENT THE IDEAS OF ANOTHER GENERATION — ONE OF THE FUTURE, RATHER THAN OF THE PAST.

★ ★ ★

President Jimmy Carter awarded Menninger the Presidential Medal of Freedom with the above citation during a White House ceremony January 16, 1981.

A founder of the internationally famous Menninger Clinic and the writer of widely read books on psychiatry, Karl Menninger was born in Topeka, Kansas, in 1893. His father, a country doctor and professor at a small Kansas college, was a firm believer in group medical practice and planned to someday organize one. The young Menninger graduated from the University of Wisconsin in 1914. Deciding to follow his father into medicine, he earned his medical degree cum laude from Harvard Medical School three years later.

After his internship and service in World War I, Menninger spent the years 1918 and 1919 working under his friend and mentor, Dr. Ernest Southard, at the Boston Psychopathic Hospital. He also taught neuropathology at Harvard Medical School while in Boston and only decided to leave when Southard died in early 1920.

Returning to Kansas that same year, Menninger joined his father in founding the Menninger Clinic for treating psychiatric patients. They began with an old farmhouse that accommodated just thirteen patients but offered what was then a radical approach to psychotherapy. In the past, psychiatrists had treated patients one-on-one over a period of years. Menninger and his father provided a "total environment" for patients, though, including a family atmosphere, a healthy regime, and specialists from various disciplines to provide medical care.

Soon after, the youngest Menninger son also joined the group. Together they organized the Southard School for treating children and years later, in 1941, they also formed the Menninger Foundation for research, training of psychiatric professionals, and public education. The Menninger Clinic, which became an internationally famous teaching center and served as a model for many other psychiatric hospitals, expanded steadily until, by the 1990s, it consisted of two campuses with thirty-nine buildings and a staff of nine-hundred people.

Meanwhile, Menninger also made a name for himself and for the hospital by writing books about the (then) emerging field of psychiatry. His first book, *The Human Mind* (1930), provided a clear discussion of the field and was widely read by people outside professional circles. Other books followed, including *Man Against Himself* (1938), *Love Against Hate* (1942), *The Crime of Punishment* (1968), and *Whatever Became of Sin?* (1988). *Love Against Hate* was written with his second wife, the former Jeanetta Lyle, whom he married in 1941. He had divorced his first wife earlier in 1941.

While based on Freudian principles, Menninger's method of treatment did not rely on any one form of therapy. Instead, he remained elastic in his approach to treating what he saw as an emotional illness resulting from a serious conflict in the patient's mind. He placed great importance on the role of the parents in the emotional development of their children and in his later years especially came to regard society as a chief cause of mental illness.

Menninger largely removed himself from daily activities at the Menninger Foundation but remained as chairman of its board of trustees. He died in 1990, at age ninety-six.

Edmund S. Muskie

As Senator and Secretary of State, candidate and citizen, Edmund S. Muskie has captured for himself a place in the public eye and the public's heart. Devoted to his nation and our ideals, he has performed heroically in a time of great challenge, with great fortitude in an era of change.

★ ★ ★

President Jimmy Carter awarded Muskie the Presidential Medal of Freedom with the above citation during a White House ceremony January 16, 1981.

An elder statesman of the Democratic Party, Muskie was born in 1914 in Rumford, Maine, one of the many textile mill towns dotting the New England landscape. His father was a Polish immigrant and his mother a Polish American, and Muskie had a Roman Catholic upbringing. He worked his way through Maine's Bates College as a history major, graduating cum laude in 1936. Cornell University awarded him his law degree three years later.

Interrupting his newly formed private practice in Waterville, Maine, Muskie joined the navy in 1941 and spent the next four years serving aboard destroyer escorts in the Atlantic and Pacific. Returning to law practice in 1946, he became active in the Democratic Party and was elected to the Maine state legislature. He was a state representative for three terms before winning the governorship—Maine's first Democratic governor in twenty years—and serving two terms (1954–1958). Meanwhile he married a Waterville native, Jane Frances Gray, in 1948.

Muskie won his bid for a U.S. Senate seat in 1958, becoming the first popularly elected Democratic senator from the state of Maine. Over the next twenty-one years he earned a reputation as a skilled and resourceful legislator. A liberal and loyal Democrat, he chaired the Senate Budget Committee, the Subcommittee on Air and Water Pollution, and the Subcommittee on Arms Control, among other committee assignments. He was the chief sponsor of important environmental legislation, including the Clear Air Act (1963) and the Water Quality Act (1965), and was instrumental in passage of the model cities program.

His ability to work with Southern Democrats in the Senate and his ethnic background helped win him the nod as Hubert Humphrey's vice-presidential running mate in 1968. But the deep divisions in the Democratic Party over the Vietnam War contributed to the ticket's narrow loss to Republicans Richard Nixon and Spiro Agnew. Muskie launched an abortive bid for the Democratic presidential nomination in 1972, but when that failed, he did not seek the presidency again.

Muskie joined the Carter administration as secretary of state (1980–1981). He ran the State Department in the troubled final months of President Carter's term, overseeing the protracted negotiations with the Iranians for release of fifty-two American hostages.

After the Carter administration left office, Muskie became a partner in a Washington law firm. Later, he was a member of the Tower Commission, which investigated the Reagan administration's involvement in the Iran-contra affair. While continuing his Washington law practice into the 1990s, he also served as chairman of the Center for National Policy, the Democratic think tank. He died in 1996.

Esther Peterson

ONCE GOVERNMENT'S HIGHEST RANKING WOMAN, ESTHER PETERSON STILL RANKS HIGHEST AMONG CONSUMER ADVOCATES. SHE HAS ADVISED PRESIDENTS AND THE PUBLIC, AND HAS WORKED FOR LABOR AND BUSINESS ALIKE, ALWAYS KEEPING THE RIGHTS OF ALL AMERICANS TO KNOW AND TO BE TREATED FAIRLY AS HER HIGHEST PRIORITY. EVEN HER STAUNCHEST FOES RESPECT HER INTEGRITY AND ARE WARMED BY HER GRACE AND SINCERE CONCERN.

★ ★ ★

President Jimmy Carter awarded Peterson the Presidential Medal of Freedom with the above citation during a White House ceremony January 16, 1981.

The granddaughter of Mormons who crossed the Great Plains from Omaha to the Mormon center at Salt Lake City, Utah, Esther Peterson was born Esther Eggersten in Provo, Utah, in 1906. Her father was a school superintendent, and she went on to graduate from Brigham Young University in 1927. Pursuing her graduate studies, she earned her master's degree in physical education at Columbia University Teachers College three years later. Meanwhile, she also met her future husband, sociology student Oliver Peterson, and married him in 1932.

While teaching at a Boston college prep school for girls (1930–1936), Peterson also did volunteer teaching at the industrial department of the local Young Women's Christian Association (YWCA). There she gained her first experience with strikes when some of her students went out on strike against a clothing manufacturer who employed them as seamstresses. During the summers afterward, from 1932 to 1939, she worked as an assistant in economics at the Bryn Mawr Summer School for Women Workers.

That position led to an opportunity to work directly for the union movement. Amalgamated Clothing Workers of America made her its assistant director of education in 1939, and in 1945 she became the union's Washington lobbyist. In 1948, however, she left the post to move to Sweden, where her husband had been posted as labor attaché to the U.S. embassy in Stockholm. Peterson remained active in the labor movement while overseas, working for the Swedish Confederation of Trade Unions from 1948 to 1952. When her husband was sent to Brussels, Belgium, with the anticommunist International Confederation of Free Trade Unions (ICFTU) from 1952 to 1957, she helped found its school for working women.

Returning to the United States with her husband in 1957, she served as a lobbyist for the American Federation of Labor and Congress of Industrial Organizations (AFL-CIO) from 1958 to 1961. Peterson then began a long career in government service, first in the area of labor and then in consumer affairs. She served as the Women's Bureau director from 1961 to 1964 and as assistant secretary of labor for labor standards from 1961 to 1969. President Lyndon B. Johnson also made her his special assistant for consumer affairs (1964–1967) and chairwoman of the President's Commission on Consumer Interests.

When President Johnson left office, Peterson again worked as a lobbyist for the Amalgamated Clothing Workers of America (1969–1970) and then worked as a consumer affairs adviser for the Giant Food Corporation. She returned to government service in 1977 when the Carter administration took office. She was Carter's special assistant for consumer affairs from 1977 to 1980 and chairwoman of the Consumer Affairs Council from 1979 to 1980. Since then she has been active in the Democratic Party and as a consumer affairs advocate.

Gerard C. Smith

GERARD C. SMITH HAS REPRESENTED OUR COUNTRY IN MANY CAPACITIES — AS THE FIRST U.S. CHAIRMAN OF THE TRILATERAL COMMISSION, AS CHIEF U.S. DELEGATE TO THE STRATEGIC ARMS LIMITATION TALKS IN 1969. IN HELPING FORMULATE OUR NATIONAL SECURITY POLICY, IN PROMOTING A BETTER UNDERSTANDING OF FOREIGN RELATIONS, HE HAS HELPED US ALL TO PERCEIVE THAT IN THIS NUCLEAR AGE SECURITY AND PEACE ARE

INDIVISIBLE.

★ ★ ★

President Jimmy Carter awarded Smith the Presidential Medal of Freedom with the above citation during a White House ceremony January 16, 1981.

A top arms-control negotiator during the Nixon and Carter administrations, Gerard C. Smith was born in New York City in 1914. His father was chief counsel for General Motors, and Smith grew up in comfortable circumstances. He graduated from Yale University with his bachelor's degree in 1935 and from Yale Law School in 1938. The following year General Motors hired him for its legal staff.

After serving in the navy during World War II, Smith went into private law practice in New York, building up a lucrative business by the end of the 1940s. He felt a personal commitment to public service, though, and in 1950 left his practice to became a special assistant to the Atomic Energy Commission chairman. Having gained an expertise in nuclear weaponry, Smith moved to the State Department in 1954, serving first as Secretary of State John Foster Dulles's assistant for atomic affairs and then as a policy planner in both the Eisenhower and Kennedy administrations. He had an important role in President Eisenhower's proposals for regional arms control and for a permanent UN peacekeeping force. Leaving the State Department in 1961, he continued as a high-level State Department policy consultant. Smith was credited with suggesting the idea of the "hotline" communications system, which was set up between President John F. Kennedy and Soviet leader Nikita Khrushchev after the Cuban Missile Crisis.

As chief of the U.S. Arms Control and Disarmament Agency from 1969 to 1973, Smith directed the U.S. negotiating team at the Strategic Arms Limitation Talks (SALT) with the Soviet Union. Smith succeeded in negotiating the Antiballistic Missile (ABM) Treaty, which was signed by President Richard Nixon in 1972.

Smith next helped David Rockefeller found the nongovernmental Trilateral Commission to promote policy discussion between leaders in North America, Europe, and Japan. He remained as head of the U.S. delegation to the commission from 1973 to 1979, when President Jimmy Carter made him ambassador at large for nuclear nonproliferation. In this post he sought to discourage nonnuclear countries like South Africa, Argentina, and Brazil from acquiring nuclear weapons.

When Smith retired from government service in 1981, President Carter awarded him the Presidential Medal of Freedom for his three decades of public service. That same year Smith formed Consultants International Group. In addition to writing articles about the subject, nuclear affairs, and testifying before Congress, Smith wrote a history of the SALT negotiations, *Double-talk* (1985). He died in 1994, at age eighty.

Robert S. Strauss

FOR AMERICANS POLITICS IS THE ART OF THE POSSIBLE.
THROUGH INTELLIGENCE, ABILITY, AND THE MANY FRIENDSHIPS
EARNED DURING HIS SERVICE AS THE LEADER OF HIS PARTY AND
HIS NATION, ROBERT S. STRAUSS HAS REFINED THAT ART INTO A
SCIENCE. WITH DILIGENCE, PERSISTENCE, AND WIT, HE SUC-
CESSFULLY CONCLUDED THE MULTILATERAL TRADE NEGOTIATIONS
AT A TIME WHEN MANY BELIEVED THAT THEY WERE DOOMED FOR
FAILURE. FOR STRENGTHENING THE SYSTEM OF TRADE WHICH
LINKS THE NATIONS OF OUR INCREASINGLY INTERDEPENDENT
WORLD HE HAS EARNED OUR GRATITUDE AND RESPECT.

★ ★ ★

*President Jimmy Carter awarded Strauss the Presidential Medal of
Freedom with the above citation during a White House ceremony
January 16, 1981.*

A consummate Washington insider who thoroughly enjoyed the
game of politics, Robert S. Strauss was born in Lockhart, Texas, in
1918. He was the son of Jewish parents who settled in Stamford,
Texas, where they ran a dry-goods store and raised their family.
Strauss worked his way through college at the University of Texas at
Austin, where he became friends with two future nationally known
politicians, John Connally and Lloyd Bentsen. Strauss completed
both his bachelor's and law degrees at the University of Texas by 1941
and that same year married Helen Jacobs.

After spending World War II working as a special agent for the
Federal Bureau of Investigation, Strauss opened a law practice that
grew into one of the country's richest law firms, Akin, Gump,
Strauss, Hauer, & Feld. Meanwhile, he successfully invested in real
estate, broadcasting, and other ventures that eventually made him a
multimillionaire.

Strauss also began moving up the ranks of the Democratic Party,
beginning as chief fund-raiser for John Connally's 1962 Texas gubernatorial campaign. After serving as Democratic national committeeman from 1968 to 1972, he became a member of the national
executive committee (1969–1977), treasurer of the Democratic
National Committee (1970–1972), and finally the DNC chairman
(1972–1977). As chairman he sought to end factional infighting and to
undo the strict quota system, imposed after the disastrous 1968 convention, that seated women and minorities in large numbers at the
1972 convention but froze out party regulars.

Having helped unify the party behind Jimmy Carter's successful presidential bid in 1976, Strauss became President Carter's chief inflation

fighter (1977–1978) and special representative for trade negotiations with Japan (1977–1979). In protracted trade talks he tried to eliminate quotas and tariffs on imported food products and in 1978 succeeded in wresting an agreement from the stubborn Japanese. But the agreement was in fact expected to have little actual effect on trade with Japan. Strauss also served briefly as ambassador to the Mideast in 1979 before becoming head of Carter's unsuccessful 1980 reelection campaign.

Strauss returned to his lucrative law partnership in 1981, working out of his Washington office and becoming one of President Ronald Reagan's unofficial advisers. He likewise served President George Bush in a behind-the-scenes capacity to help line up Democratic support for the Persian Gulf War. In 1991 his good relations with President Bush landed him a surprise appointment as U.S. ambassador to the Soviet Union. When the Soviet Union collapsed a few months later, Strauss became ambassador to Russia and remained in that post until the Bush administration left office in 1993. He then returned to his law practice.

Elbert Tuttle

ELBERT TUTTLE IS A TRUE JUDICIAL HERO. AT A TIME WHEN IT WAS UNPOPULAR TO DO SO, HE CARRIED OUT THE MANDATE OF SUPREME COURT DECISIONS AND CONGRESSIONAL LEGISLATION TO END RACIAL DISCRIMINATION IN THE DEEP SOUTH. WITH STEADFAST COURAGE AND A DEEP LOVE AND UNDERSTANDING OF THE REGION, HE HAS HELPED TO MAKE THE CONSTITUTIONAL PRINCIPLE OF EQUAL PROTECTION A REALITY OF AMERICAN LIFE.

★ ★ ★

President Jimmy Carter awarded Tuttle the Presidential Medal of Freedom with the above citation during a White House ceremony January 16, 1981.

A federal appeals court judge for over forty years, Elbert Tuttle was born in Pasadena, California, in 1897. He earned his bachelor's degree (1918) and his law degree (1923) at Cornell University in New York. Sarah Sutherland became his wife in 1919.

After graduating from Cornell, Tuttle went into private practice in Atlanta, Georgia. He became a senior partner in the firm of Sutherland, Tuttle & Brennan, with offices in both Atlanta and Washington, D.C. His public career began thirty years later, in 1953, with a brief stint as a general counsel to the Treasury Department.

The following year President Dwight D. Eisenhower appointed him a judge on the Fifth Circuit Court of Appeals. The Fifth Circuit covered much of the Deep South, including Mississippi, Louisiana, and Texas.

That same year the Supreme Court handed down its landmark decision ending school segregation, *Brown v. Board of Education,* and over the next decade legal challenges to the Supreme Court's desegregation order, as well as other civil rights decisions, began flooding into the appeals court system. As a judge, and from 1960 the Fifth Circuit's chief justice, Tuttle played a key role in implementing desegregation in the Deep South. Supreme Court Chief Justice Earl Warren once praised his work, calling Tuttle "one of the great judges of this era."

Tuttle remained on the bench as the Fifth Circuit's chief justice until 1968, when he went into semiretirement as a senior judge. When the Fifth Circuit was divided in 1981, he accepted appointment as senior judge for the new Eleventh Circuit, which embraced his native Georgia, Alabama, and Florida. Now in his nineties, Tuttle remained active a senior judge into the mid–1990s.

Also noted for his skill as a judicial administrator, Tuttle served as chairman of two Judicial Conference of the United States advisory committees, one on judicial activities (1969–1977) and the other on civil rules (1972–1978).

Earl Warren

EARL WARREN LED A UNANIMOUS COURT THAT IN TURN LED THE NATION IN REVERSING A CENTURY OF JUDICIAL AND SOCIAL HISTORY. BY AFFIRMING THAT SEPARATE IS NOT EQUAL, HE AND HIS COURT REAFFIRMED THE TRUTH OF THE WORDS CARVED IN STONE AT THE ENTRANCE TO THE SUPREME COURT: "EQUAL JUSTICE FOR ALL." AS GOVERNOR, PRESIDENTIAL CANDIDATE AND CHIEF JUSTICE, HE HAS TRULY BEEN A CITIZEN FOR ALL SEASONS.

★ ★ ★

President Jimmy Carter awarded Warren a posthumous Presidential Medal of Freedom with the above citation during a White House ceremony January 16, 1981. Nina Warren accepted the medal on her late husband's behalf.

The chief justice who led the Supreme Court during a period of sweeping judicial activism, Earl Warren was born in Los Angeles, California, in 1891. His father was a railroad worker, and Warren spent his summers working for the railroad. He went on to graduate from the University of California at Berkeley (1912) and to get his law degree there (1914). After practicing with a private law firm and serving in the army during World War I, Warren began his long career in public office as a member of the Alameda County district attorney's staff (1920). He married Nina Palmquist Meyers, a widow, in 1925.

Warren served in a succession of California county and state government posts over the next decades, including county district attorney (1925–1939), state attorney general (1939–1943), and state governor (1943–1953). He gained a national reputation as a tough district attorney and as governor he modernized California's state government. During World War II he also supported the internment of Japanese Americans living in California, an action that was later roundly criticized.

A Republican, Warren lost two bids for his party's nomination for national office, for vice president in 1948 and for president in 1952. With his own presidential primary campaign failing in 1952, Warren threw his support behind Dwight D. Eisenhower's candidacy at the Republican National Convention that year. Eisenhower went on to win the presidency, and when Chief Justice Fred Vinson died unexpectedly in 1953, Eisenhower repaid the political debt by naming Warren to fill the vacancy. Warren's years as attorney general gave him a greater practical knowledge of the law than other justices on the Court, but his greatest asset was his ability to forge majorities on the Court to support major decisions.

For his first important decision, Warren won a unanimous vote of the on ending segregation, an issue that had split the Court 4–4. The landmark *Brown v. Board of Education* ruling in 1954 reversed the Court's long-held doctrine of "separate but equal" facilities for blacks and began the long-delayed integration of all schools and public facilities. It also marked the beginning of a judicial revolution that resulted in sweeping social changes in the 1950s and 1960s.

Warren believed the Court should take a more activist role in government, and completing a shift away from property rights begun in the late 1930s, the Warren Court now gave a clear constitutional preference to civil liberties. One major (and controversial) area of the resulting "due process" revolution greatly expanded criminals' rights. Among these important cases were *Mapp v. Ohio* (1961), forbidding the use in court of illegally seized evidence, and *Gideon v. Wainwright* (1963), guaranteeing legal counsel for indigent criminal defendants. But probably the best known case was *Miranda v. State of Arizona* (1966). The decision resulted in the Miranda warnings, in which police are compelled to advise suspects of their rights before questioning them. Meanwhile, the Court also expanded individual civil liberties in a series of controversial decisions, ruling against a Connecticut ban on the use of contraceptives by married couples, state and local loyalty oaths, a Virginia law against interracial marriages, prayer in public schools, and other matters the Court deemed a part of the individual's right of privacy.

Another landmark decision of the Warren Court was *Baker v. Carr* (1962), in which the Court established that it had the authority to rule on legislative apportionment. Later cases, including *Reynolds v. Sims*, established the principle that the "one man, one vote" rule must be applied when drawing state legislative districts. Virtually every state was forced to reapportion its election districts, which in places drastically rearranged the political landscape. And in yet another landmark case, *New York Times Co. v. Sullivan* (1964), the Court sharply limited the right of public figures to sue newspapers for libel.

Warren, who also headed the Warren Commission investigation into President John F. Kennedy's assassination, retired from the Court in 1969. One of the great chief justices of the United States, he died five years later, in 1974. He was eighty-three years old.

Andrew Young

ANDREW YOUNG BROUGHT TO DIPLOMATIC SERVICE A LIFETIME OF DEDICATION TO HUMAN RIGHTS. HE HELPED RESTORE TRUST IN THE UNITED STATES AMONG THIRD WORLD NATIONS, ESPECIALLY IN AFRICA, DEMONSTRATING TO THEM THAT AMERICAN FOREIGN POLICY WAS BASED ON OUR FIRM BELIEF IN JUSTICE, FREEDOM, MAJORITY RULE, AND OPPORTUNITY FOR ALL PEOPLE.

★ ★ ★

President Jimmy Carter awarded Young the Presidential Medal of Freedom with the above citation during a White House ceremony January 16, 1981.

A civil rights activist and U.S. ambassador to the United Nations, Andrew Young was born in New Orleans in 1932. The son of a prosperous black dentist, he was educated in segregated schools and graduated from the traditionally black Howard University in 1951. He then studied at the Hartford Theological Seminary in Connecticut, and after earning his bachelor of divinity degree in 1955, he was ordained a minister in the United Church of Christ. He married Jean Childs in 1954.

A pastor at black churches in Alabama and Georgia, he organized community action groups and voter registration drives during the 1950s and by the late 1950s had gotten to know fellow civil rights activist Dr. Martin Luther King, Jr. Young joined King's Southern Christian Leadership Conference (SCLC) in 1961 and was promoted to executive director in 1964. He oversaw the 1963 Birmingham, Alabama, civil rights protest in which television cameras showed police using fire-hoses and dogs against the peaceful marchers and which aroused a wave of sympathy for the civil rights movement. Later he had a hand in drafting the 1964 Civil Rights Act and the 1965 Voting Rights Act, and he conducted behind-the-scenes negotiations for desegregation programs in southern cities. As SCLC executive vice president (1967–1970), Young took part in planning the 1968 poor people's march on Washington.

Resigning from the SCLC to run for a seat in the U.S. House of Representatives, Young lost his election bid in 1970 but won two years later to become Georgia's first black congressman since the Reconstruction era. Reelected to two more terms, he served on the House Banking and Currency Committee and supported such social spending programs as food stamps, federally funded day care, Medicaid payments for abortions, and a federal public service jobs program. He also supported school busing for integration and simplified registration for voting.

Young supported Jimmy Carter's 1976 presidential bid and the following year was appointed ambassador to the United Nations. He forged links with many third world countries, but his statements about trouble spots in Africa and elsewhere got him into hot water with Carter's State Department. Finally, in 1979, revelations that he had met with a Palestine Liberation Organization representative caused a furor and forced his resignation.

Three years later he was elected mayor of Atlanta, Georgia. Young served two terms (1982–1989). Soon afterward he returned to the SCLC and now serves as a member of its board of directors.

Ronald Reagan

RONALD REAGAN, A REPUBLICAN, WAS SWORN INTO OFFICE
ON JANUARY 20, 1981, AND COMPLETED TWO TERMS AS
PRESIDENT (1981–1985, 1985–1989).

MEDAL
CEREMONIES

OCTOBER 9, 1981 *The White House East Room*

SEPTEMBER 7, 1982 *The White House East Room*

OCTOBER 26, 1982 *Raleigh Civic Center, North Carolina*

FEBRUARY 23, 1983 *The White House East Room*

JANUARY 12, 1984 *Manila, Philippines*

MARCH 26, 1984 *The White House East Room*

APRIL 5, 1984 *New York Hilton*

MAY 30, 1984 *The White House State Dining Room*

JUNE 26, 1984 *The White House Rose Garden*

MAY 23, 1985 *The White House East Room*

JUNE 20, 1985 *The White House Rose Garden*

NOVEMBER 7, 1985 *The White House East Room*

MAY 12, 1986 *The White House East Room*

JULY 28, 1986 *The White House East Room*

JUNE 23, 1987 *The White House East Room*

OCTOBER 7, 1987 *The White House Roosevelt Room*

NOVEMBER 17, 1987 *The Pentagon*

JANUARY 13, 1988 *Four Seasons Hotel, Washington, D.C.*

MAY 10, 1988 *The White House Roosevelt Room*

OCTOBER 17, 1988 *The White House East Room*

JANUARY 19, 1989 *The White House State Dining Room*

James Hubert "Eubie" Blake

Last of the great ragtime composers and pianists, the son of slaves, and a pioneer crusader for Black Americans in the world of arts and entertainment, Eubie Blake is a national treasure. As pianist, showman and, above all, as composer, he has added immeasurably to America's musical heritage and helped to clear the way for succeeding generations of talented artists who, but for his example, might have been denied access to the artistic mainstream.

★ ★ ★

President Ronald Reagan awarded Blake the Presidential Medal of Freedom with the above citation during a White House ceremony October 9, 1981.

Born in 1883—about the time ragtime began emerging as a new form of music—James Hubert Blake was the son of former slaves who had settled in Baltimore, Maryland. He was the only one of eleven children to live beyond infancy. At age six he already displayed a talent for music. His mother arranged piano lessons for him, and he studied classical music until he was about twelve, when he learned to play his first ragtime tunes.

Out of school and in need of work, Blake began his career as a performer in 1898 with a job as a pianist at a Baltimore bordello. The following year he wrote his first ragtime song, "Charleston Rag," which was not published until 1919. Within a few years he was playing ragtime piano music to steady bookings at hotels and clubs, and in 1919 he teamed up with fellow black performer and musician Noble Sissle. Billed as The Dixie Duo, they proved a hit on the vaudeville circuit.

The two also collaborated on songs (Blake wrote the music, Sissle the lyrics), and in 1921 they joined forces with two other black vaudevillians to produce the pioneering all-black hit Broadway musical *Shuffle Along.* The show also made a hit of Blake's now classic "I'm Just Wild About Harry." (President Harry S. Truman later adopted it for his 1948 campaign.)

Blake collaborated on five other musical comedies in the 1920s and 1930s including *Blackbirds of 1930.* During World War II, he served as a musical conductor for United Services Organization (USO) shows touring military installations, and in 1945 met and married his second wife, Marion Grant. His first wife had died in 1939.

In 1946, at age sixty-three, Blake retired from performing to study the Schillinger system of musical composition at New York

University. He then spent his time composing songs and recording on paper the tunes he had committed to memory in his early days.

The late 1960s brought a ragtime revival, and as one of the last surviving ragtime pioneers, Blake suddenly found himself in demand. The album *Eighty-Six Years of Eubie Blake* was released in 1969, and Blake began playing at jazz concerts and festivals, as well as making frequent appearances on television shows. Additional recordings followed, and he started teaching music courses at Yale and other universities.

In recognition of Blake's many contributions to American music, President Reagan presented him with the Presidential Medal of Freedom in 1981. Blake provided a musical finale for the White House ceremony by playing a rendition of his popular ragtime tune "Memories of You" on a piano provided for the occasion.

Blake gave his last public appearance the following year at New York's Lincoln Center at the age of ninety-nine. He died in 1983 shortly after his one-hundredth birthday.

Ella T. Grasso

LONG BEFORE THE WOMEN'S MOVEMENT HAD GAINED PROMINENCE, ELLA GRASSO HAD ALREADY BEGUN THE LONG, HARD ASCENT TO DISTINCTION AS AN ELECTED PUBLIC SERVANT. A FOND WIFE AND MOTHER, SHE PROVED THAT IT IS POSSIBLE TO RECONCILE A FULL FAMILY LIFE WITH A LONG AND EVENTFUL POLITICAL CAREER. AS A CHAMPION OF MORAL AS WELL AS POLITICAL PRINCIPLE, MRS. GRASSO WON THE RESPECT OF FELLOW CITIZENS OF BOTH PARTIES AND SERVED AS THE FIRST WOMAN GOVERNOR TO BE ELECTED TO OFFICE IN HER OWN RIGHT. TIRELESS IN THE PURSUIT OF DUTY AND COURAGEOUS IN THE FACE OF ILLNESS, ELLA GRASSO HAS EARNED THE ADMIRATION OF ALL AMERICANS AS A LEGISLATOR, A GOVERNOR AND A WOMAN OF OUTSTANDING CHARACTER AND ACHIEVEMENT.

★ ★ ★

President Ronald Reagan awarded Grasso a posthumous Presidential Medal of Freedom with the above citation during a White House ceremony October 9, 1981. Dr. Thomas A. Grasso accepted the medal on his late wife's behalf.

The only child of Italian immigrant parents, Ella Rosa Giovanna Oliva Tambussi was born in 1919 and raised in an old Connecticut mill town called Windsor Locks. She excelled in school and graduated from Mount Holyoke College magna cum laude in 1940 after majoring in sociology and economics. Two years later she earned her master's degree at Mount Holyoke and married Thomas A. Grasso, a schoolteacher. They had two children, a boy and a girl.

Her interest in politics dated from 1943 when she joined the League of Women Voters. A Democrat, Grasso became the protégé of John Bailey, Connecticut's Democratic party chairman, and eventually was elected to two terms as a state representative (1953–1957). For the next twelve years she served as Connecticut's secretary of state, a post traditionally held by a woman. Turning her office into a "people's lobby" for hearing grievances and advising constituents, Grasso became one of Connecticut's most popular politicians and consistently won reelection by wide margins.

Elected to two terms in the U.S. House of Representatives (1971–1975), Grasso voted with liberal Democrats for an array of social programs and spending packages to stimulate the economy. A veteran party politician by then, she did not identify herself with women's groups and was not well liked by them because of her firm opposition to abortion. Also, working in Washington severely disrupted her family life, and in 1974 she decided to run for the Connecticut governorship.

Grasso won by a comfortable margin that fall, thereby becoming the first woman elected a state governor in her own right and not as a former governor's wife. Unlike during her days in Congress, she proved a frugal governor, cutting back travel by state employees and limiting state spending in such areas as welfare, education, and aid to cities. By doing so she avoided imposing a state income tax, then a highly controversial issue in Connecticut. Meanwhile, she won important reforms, such as new campaign financing laws, rules for financial disclosure by public officials, and "sunshine" laws granting public access to state agency records and meetings.

Voters elected her to a second term in 1978, and by this time Connecticut's popular woman governor was gaining a national reputation as well. But midway through her second term she was diagnosed with cancer. She resigned in late 1980 following surgery and died just over a month later in 1981. She was sixty-one years old.

Bryce N. Harlow

COUNSELOR TO PRESIDENTS AND SAGE OBSERVER OF NEARLY HALF A CENTURY OF WASHINGTON HISTORY, BRYCE HARLOW'S VISION, INTEGRITY AND PERSUASIVENESS HAVE HELPED TO SHAPE THIS NATION'S DESTINY AS LEADER OF THE FREE WORLD. NEVER A CANDIDATE FOR ELECTED OFFICE HIMSELF, HIS EXPERIENCE AND ADVICE HAVE HELPED BRING OUT THE BEST IN COUNTLESS PUBLIC SERVANTS OF BOTH PARTIES, IN THE WHITE HOUSE, IN THE CONGRESS AND ACROSS THE NATION. BRYCE HARLOW IS A STERLING EXAMPLE OF THE POSITIVE SIDE OF POLITICS—A LIFE SPENT RECONCILING DIVERGENT INTERESTS, SERVING HIGH MORAL PRINCIPLES, AND CHANNELING THE FORCES OF PUBLIC POLICY TOWARD THE PUBLIC GOOD.

★ ★ ★

President Ronald Reagan awarded Harlow the Presidential Medal of Freedom with the above citation during a White House ceremony October 9, 1981.

An important figure in both the Eisenhower and Nixon administrations, Bryce N. Harlow was born in Oklahoma City in 1916. He studied political science at the University of Oklahoma and after graduating in 1936 found work in Washington, D.C., as an assistant librarian in the House of Representatives.

Harlow served as an army officer during World War II and on returning to civilian life became a staff assistant on the House Armed Services Committee. A few years later he rose to chief clerk for the committee.

During the Eisenhower administration, Harlow, a Republican, moved from Capitol Hill to the White House, beginning as an administrative assistant. Also a speechwriter for President Eisenhower, he became known as the president's "meat and potatoes man" because he wrote good basic speeches that people had no trouble understanding. But thanks to his previous experience on Capitol Hill, Harlow also knew the inner workings of Congress and was able to help promote Eisenhower's legislative agenda. By the close of the Eisenhower administration's second term, Harlow had risen to deputy assistant for legislative affairs.

After John F. Kennedy's election victory, Harlow became a Washington lobbyist, representing Procter and Gamble. When Richard Nixon won the 1968 presidential election, he made Harlow his presidential counselor and assigned him the tasks of handling relations with the Democratic Congress and developing the president's domestic agenda. But Harlow left the Nixon administration after only a year, returning to lobbying for Procter and Gamble.

The Watergate scandal in 1973 forced a purge of high-level White House staffers, and Nixon called Harlow back to the White House to help fill the void. Harlow served until Nixon's resignation in 1974 and after four more years as a lobbyist retired from Procter and Gamble.

Harlow's first wife, Betty, died in 1982, and a year later he married Sarah Jane Studebaker. Suffering from a chronic lung disease, Harlow died in 1987, at age seventy.

Walter H. Judd

LEGISLATOR, PHYSICIAN, MISSIONARY AND ORATOR, WALTER JUDD HAS SERVED HIS NATION AND MANKIND WITH UNFAILING COURAGE AND DISTINCTION—AS A YOUTHFUL MEDICAL MISSIONARY IN CHINA, AS A HIGHLY RESPECTED MEMBER OF CONGRESS FOR TWO DECADES, AND AS A LIFELONG FOE OF TYRANNY AND FRIEND OF FREEDOM BOTH AT HOME AND ABROAD. THE SKILLS OF A HEALER, THE ELOQUENCE OF A GREAT COMMUNICATOR, AND HIS FIRM GRASP OF DOMESTIC AND INTERNATIONAL AFFAIRS HAVE MADE WALTER JUDD AN ARTICULATE SPOKESMAN FOR ALL THOSE WHO CHERISH LIBERTY AND A MODEL FOR ALL AMERICANS WHO ASPIRE TO SERVE MANKIND AS PHYSICIANS, SPIRITUAL LEADERS AND STATESMEN.

★ ★ ★

President Ronald Reagan awarded Judd the Presidential Medal of Freedom with the above citation during a White House ceremony October 9, 1981.

Born in Rising City, Nebraska, in 1898, Walter H. Judd decided to become a medical missionary while still in his youth. Years later he worked his way through the University of Nebraska Medical School, earning his medical degree in 1923. Two years after that he realized his childhood dream by traveling to China as a medical missionary for the Congregational Church Board of Foreign Missions.

Judd spent the next five years treating needy Chinese in malaria-infested Fukien province before his forty-sixth attack of malaria forced him back to the United States in 1931. Married the following year to Mary Lou Carpenter, he became a hospital director in a malaria-free province of China in 1935. However, that assignment lasted only until the Japanese, who had invaded China, captured the hospital in 1937.

Using his own savings, Judd spent the next two years traveling the United States to make some fourteen-hundred speeches warning Americans about the danger of Japanese aggression. After Japan attacked Pearl Harbor, he was elected to the House of Representatives from Minnesota. A Republican, he ultimately spent the next twenty years as a House member (1943–1963).

Recognized as an expert on the Far East, Judd became a leader of the so-called China Lobby supporting Chiang Kai-shek's Nationalist Chinese, even after Chinese Communists had driven the Nationalists off the mainland to Taiwan. An outspoken critic of the Communist Chinese during the 1950s, he also worked to reform laws regulating the immigration of Chinese and other Asians to the United States. He was a longtime member of the House Foreign Affairs Committee and also served as a delegate to the UN General Assembly in 1957.

Judd remained active in politics after leaving Congress in 1963 and was nominated as a favorite-son candidate for president in 1964 and 1980. He died in 1994, at the age of ninety-five.

Morris I. Leibman

ATTORNEY, TEACHER, SCHOLAR AND PHILANTHROPIST, MORRIS LEIBMAN IS LIVING PROOF THAT A FULL CAREER IN THE PRIVATE SECTOR CAN FLOURISH HAND IN HAND WITH CIVIC AND HUMANI-TARIAN DUTIES. AS A GENEROUS PATRON OF THE ARTS AND CHARITIES, AS A LEGAL SCHOLAR AS WELL AS PRACTITIONER, AS A FOUNDING MEMBER OF THE GEORGETOWN UNIVERSITY CENTER FOR STRATEGIC AND INTERNATIONAL STUDIES AND AS CHAIRMAN OF THE AMERICAN BAR ASSOCIATION'S STANDING COMMITTEE ON LAW AND NATIONAL SECURITY, MORRIS LEIBMAN HAS SERVED SELFLESSLY TO MAKE A JUST, HEALTHY SOCIETY WITHIN AND A STRONG, SECURE NATION WITHOUT.

★ ★ ★

President Ronald Reagan awarded Leibman the Presidential Medal of Freedom with the above citation during a White House ceremony October 9, 1981.

Born in New York City in 1911, Morris I. Leibman was president of his class as a high school senior and later worked his way through the University of Chicago Law School. After earning his law degree in 1933, he was admitted to the bar and became a founding member of Leibman,

Williams, Bennett, Baird & Minow. Leibman and his firm prospered over the succeeding decades, and its merger with Sidley & Austin in 1972 helped make the resulting firm one of the country's largest.

An outspoken believer in America, Leibman actively promoted an awareness of the advantages that the democratic system offers. He once told an interviewer, "We are that one percent that have the privileges of kings—individual liberty, freedom of expression, complete access to the wonders of the world, and the right to achieve whatever we want." But he also firmly believed in doing his civic duty. For example, he served as chairman of the National Advisory Council on Economic Opportunity during the Johnson administration and was a civilian aide at large to the secretary of the army between 1964 and 1979.

During his long career as an attorney, Leibman also sought to promote the broader education of attorneys. He served as chairman of the American Bar Association Standing Committee on Law and National Security and frequently lectured on college campuses about domestic and international affairs.

He remained active even in his advancing years, helping found the United States Institute for Peace in 1986. Among several international strategy organizations he helped found were the Georgetown University Center for Strategic and International Studies and the National Strategy Forum, which brought high-level foreign dignitaries to the United States to speak during the late 1980s.

Leibman died in 1992, at age eighty-one.

Charles B. Thornton

INDUSTRIALIST, WARRIOR AND HUMANITARIAN, TEX THORNTON'S LIFE HAS EMBODIED ALL THAT IS BEST IN THE WORLDS OF COMMERCE, MILITARY SERVICE AND CIVIC DUTY. IN ALL THREE REALMS, TEX THORNTON HAS NEVER FAILED TO GIVE GENEROUSLY OF HIS BOUNDLESS ENERGY, HIS UNFAILING COURAGE, AND HIS DEEP LOVE OF COUNTRY. IN WAR AND PEACE, IN PUBLIC SERVICE AND THE PRIVATE SECTOR, TEX THORNTON HAS EARNED THE ESTEEM OF ALL AMERICANS WHO VALUE PATRIOTISM, ENTERPRISE AND COMPASSION AS CORNERSTONES OF OUR NATION'S GREATNESS.

★ ★ ★

President Ronald Reagan awarded Thornton the Presidential Medal of Freedom during a White House ceremony October 9, 1981. Charles B. Thornton, Jr., accepted the medal on his ailing father's behalf.

The head of the "Whiz Kid" management team that saved Ford Motor Company and a founder of Litton Industries, Charles B. Thornton was born in Haskell, Texas, in 1913. Raised in a household where initiative and responsibility were emphasized, he worked in his spare time after school, and at age nineteen, he and a friend opened a combined gas station and auto dealership. A few months later, though, Thornton entered Texas Technological College to study business administration. Leaving for Washington, D.C., in his junior year, he began working as a clerk at the Interior Department while attending classes at night. George Washington University awarded him his bachelor's degree in commercial science in 1937.

Ironically, Thornton's job as a clerk played the biggest part in launching his career. A report he compiled on financing low-cost federal housing caught the eye of Robert A. Lovett, assistant secretary of war for air. *(See also the entry for Lovett, p. 65.)* Impressed by Thornton's talent for culling key information and presenting it in a clear, straightforward fashion, Lovett brought him into the army air force and put him to work setting up a statistical control service. Thornton then brought together a team of bright young managers and with them created a sophisticated accounting system to keep track of war matériel and where it would be needed in the far-flung system of air force bases.

After the war Thornton took his management team to the ailing Ford Motor Company. Within a few years, Thornton's team—now dubbed the Whiz Kids—had reorganized Ford's antiquated management system and helped bring Ford back from the brink of bankruptcy to a profit-making state. *(See also the entry for Henry Ford II, p. 148.)* Thornton, meanwhile, went on to become vice president and general manager of Hughes Aircraft Company in 1948. Thornton reorganized that company and boosted sales by a third, to $200 million, in just five years. But in 1953 he decided to strike out on his own.

With another of his former air force staffers, Roy L. Ash, Thornton arranged $1.5 million in financing and bought a small electronics firm in 1953. At the time, he planned to build it into a blue-chip conglomerate designed to thrive in the emerging scientific and technological sector. The corporation was eventually to encompass engineering, manufacturing, financial, and other types of businesses. Under Thornton's leadership the new company, Litton Industries, went from $3 million to $100 million in sales in just three years, and thanks to an aggressive strategy of diversified acquisitions, sales passed $1 billion in 1966. By that time Litton Industries produced some five thousand products ranging from submarines to trading stamps.

Thornton served as the sprawling conglomerate's chairman and chief executive from its founding in 1953 until 1981, when cancer forced him to relinquish his post as chief executive. He received the Presidential Medal of Freedom just six weeks before his death in 1981. Thornton was sixty-eight years old.

Philip C. Habib

As the President's Special Emissary, Ambassador Philip C. Habib came out of retirement in 1981 to serve his country in the pursuit of peace and justice in the Middle East. His successful negotiation of the cease-fire in Lebanon and the resolution of the West Beirut crisis stands out as one of the unique feats of diplomacy in modern times. Ambassador Habib's efforts conducted in the most difficult and trying of circumstances over a period of months, not only brought honor and respect to the United States but also won for him world-wide admiration. Of the greatest importance, Philip Habib's mission saved the City of Beirut and thousands of innocent lives and brought us one step closer to a peaceful resolution to the Arab-Israeli conflict.

★ ★ ★

President Ronald Reagan awarded Habib the Presidential Medal of Freedom with the above citation during a White House ceremony September 7, 1982.

A career diplomat experienced in both Asian and Mideast affairs, Philip C. Habib was born in New York City in 1920. The son of Lebanese-American parents, he was raised in Brooklyn, New York and had at first planned a career as a forest ranger. After graduating from the University of Idaho College of Forestry (1942), Habib was studying for his doctorate when he noticed the State Department was testing prospective applicants. Accepted into the foreign service soon after, he became third secretary to the U.S. embassy in Canada, serving from 1949 to 1952. By this time he also had married Marjorie W. Slightam (1942), and had completed his doctorate (1952).

After a series of relatively obscure diplomatic posts, Habib joined the U.S. embassy in Saigon and by 1966 had become ambassador Henry Cabot Lodge's chief political adviser. Soon Habib was regarded as the State Department's leading expert on Southeast Asia.

Habib's behind-the-scenes reports and assessments reportedly helped President Lyndon B. Johnson decide to negotiate an end to the Vietnam War in 1968, and Habib served as acting head of the U.S. delegation from 1969 to 1970.

After serving as U.S ambassador to South Korea (1971–1974), he was appointed undersecretary of state for political affairs by the Ford administration. The high-level post gave Habib the opportunity to score his first big diplomatic success a few years later. Under

President Jimmy Carter, Habib helped arrange the historic Camp David peace accords between Egypt and Israel in 1977. But while continuing to press for further Mideast breakthroughs, he was forced to retire in 1978 after a major heart attack.

In 1981 President Ronald Reagan called Habib out of retirement to act as a diplomatic trouble-shooter in the Lebanese crisis. Fighting had broken out between Syrians and Christian militia in Lebanon, and with the Israelis becoming involved, the situation reached serious proportions. Habib, of Lebanese Christian descent, won a shaky cease-fire in mid–1981. But Israel, provoked by Palestine Liberation Organization (PLO) terrorist attacks, launched an all-out invasion of Lebanon in mid–1982. With the PLO soon bottled up in Beirut, Lebanon's capital, Habib negotiated the agreement by which PLO troops were allowed to withdraw from Lebanon by boat, thus averting a potentially explosive Mideast crisis.

Habib refused any further government assignments after 1987, but worked as a senior research fellow at Stanford University's Hoover Institution. He died of a heart attack in 1992, at the age of seventy-two.

Kate Smith

THE VOICE OF KATE SMITH IS KNOWN AND LOVED BY MILLIONS OF AMERICANS, YOUNG AND OLD. IN WAR AND PEACE, IT HAS BEEN AN INSPIRATION. THOSE SIMPLE BUT DEEPLY MOVING WORDS, "GOD BLESS AMERICA," HAVE TAKEN ON ADDED MEANING FOR ALL OF US BECAUSE OF THE WAY KATE SMITH SANG THEM. THANKS TO HER THEY HAVE BECOME A CHERISHED PART OF ALL OUR LIVES, AN UNDYING REMINDER OF THE BEAUTY, THE COURAGE AND THE HEART OF THIS GREAT LAND OF OURS. IN GIVING US A MAGNIFICENT, SELFLESS TALENT LIKE KATE SMITH, GOD HAS TRULY BLESSED AMERICA.

President Ronald Reagan awarded Smith the Presidential Medal of Freedom with the above citation at the Raleigh Civic Center in North Carolina on October 26, 1982.

A show business legend who reached the height of her singing career in the 1930s and 1940s, Kate Smith was born in Greenville, Virginia, in 1909. She first sang in public when she was four, as part of a Washington, D.C., church choir. Though she had no formal training, she continued singing in church and at community functions. At age seventeen she finally went to New York City to break into show business.

Her Broadway debut came soon after, in a musical comedy that ran for almost two years from 1926. But in this and two subsequent musical comedy roles, the overweight Smith was expected to endure fat-girl jokes as well as to sing. Then one evening in 1930 Ted Collins, an artists' representative for Columbia Records, missed his train and decided to take in the Broadway show starring Smith. After hearing her sing, he sent a note backstage asking her to meet with him.

Collins convinced her to forget comedy and became her manager, a business relationship that lasted until his death in 1964. Soon after she signed with him, Collins booked her as a singer at the top vaudeville house of the day, and she was on her way. The following year Smith debuted on radio and adopted her trademark opening, "Hello Everybody," as well as her theme song, "When the Moon Comes Over the Mountain." By the end of the year she had a lucrative contract for regular radio appearances and throughout the 1930s sang on her own radio shows, toured the vaudeville circuit, and even starred in a movie, *Hello, Everybody!* (1933).

During the late 1930s she also had a popular daytime talk show for women, "Kate Smith Speaks." But she is best remembered for premiering the song "God Bless America" (1938), written for her by Irving Berlin. For a time she had exclusive rights to sing the song, but she relinquished them because of the overwhelming popularity and patriotic message of the song. Berlin and Smith turned over all royalties from the song to the Boy Scouts of America. *(See also the entry for Berlin, p. 220.)*

Smith devoted herself to patriotic causes during World War II, entertaining the troops and mounting highly successful war-bond drives. During a series of marathon radio shows, she raised $600 million in war bonds, more than any other individual American. Mindful of Smith's patriotic image, President Franklin D. Roosevelt once introduced her to King George VI of England, saying "This is Kate Smith. Miss Smith is America."

Smith moved to television in 1950 with "The Kate Smith Hour," the first major daytime television program (1950–1954), and in 1952 also had a weekly nighttime show. Throughout the 1950s she made regular guest appearances on television and starred in another musical variety show that aired for six months in 1960.

During her long career Smith made almost three-thousand recordings (six-hundred hits) and popularized such songs as "The Music Goes Round and Round," "I'll Walk Alone," "Thanks for the Memory," and "White Cliffs of Dover." She also published two autobiographies, *Living in a Great Big Way* (1938) and *Upon My Lips a Song* (1960). Smith, who never married, died in 1986, at age seventy-seven.

George Balanchine

THE GENIUS OF GEORGE BALANCHINE HAS ENRICHED THE LIVES
OF ALL AMERICANS WHO LOVE THE DANCE. SINCE HE ARRIVED IN
AMERICA AS A YOUNG MAN IN 1933, HE HAS ENTERTAINED AND
INSPIRED MILLIONS WITH HIS STAGE AND FILM CHOREOGRAPHY.
MAJOR AMONG HIS GREATEST CONTRIBUTIONS AS A BALLET
MASTER ARE THE FOUNDING OF THE FIRST AMERICAN CLASSICAL
BALLET COMPANY, THE GREAT NEW YORK CITY BALLET, AND
THE SCHOOL OF AMERICAN BALLET. THROUGHOUT HIS CAREER
MR. BALANCHINE HAS ENTERTAINED, CAPTIVATED AND AMAZED
OUR DIVERSE POPULATION, LIFTING OUR SPIRITS AND
BROADENING OUR HORIZONS THROUGH HIS TALENT AND ART.

* * *

*President Ronald Reagan awarded Balanchine the Presidential Medal
of Freedom with the above citation during a White House ceremony
February 23, 1983. Suzanne Farrell, Balanchine's student and the
principal dancer of the New York City Ballet, accepted the medal on
his behalf.*

The greatest ballet choreographer of this century, Balanchine was
born Georgi Melitonovitch Balanchivadze in Saint Petersburg,
Russia, in 1904. In 1914, his mother enrolled him in the Imperial
Ballet School, which became a state-operated school after the
Communists seized power. Balanchine graduated in 1921, and while
touring Europe with the Soviet State Dancers in 1924, he defected to
the West. He joined the French dance company Ballets Russes and
there rapidly developed his impressive talent for choreography.

In 1933 the wealthy art patron Lincoln Kirstein invited
Balanchine to found the first ballet company in America. (*See also
the entry for Kirstein, p. 343.*) The enterprise began in 1934 with the
opening of the School of American Ballet, which soon became
America's most influential dance academy and remains so today.
Balanchine trained many outstanding ballet dancers through the
school, creating a technique that is now generally associated with
American ballet. It is characterized by speed and definition, particularly in leg and foot movements.

Meanwhile, Balanchine also choreographed ballets, as well as stage
and movie productions, and composed many original ballets. When
at last the first American ballet company, New York City Ballet, was
formed under Balanchine's direction in 1948, he was able to showcase
both his own compositions and dancers he had trained. The
company proved a great success and helped establish Balanchine's
international reputation.

Though Balanchine's 1954 ballet *The Nutcracker* enjoys an enduring popularity with audiences at Christmastime, his greatest works are generally abstract, modernist performances without a story line, narrative, or scenery. Instead they create meaning through the dancers' movements. Among the 200 original ballets he created during his career were *Symphony in C* (1948), *Agon* (1957), *Episodes* (1959), and *Don Quixote* (1965).

Balanchine, who had married and divorced a number of ballerinas during his lifetime, died in 1983, just two months after receiving the Presidential Medal of Freedom. He was seventy-nine.

Paul William "Bear" Bryant

IN MANY WAYS, AMERICAN SPORTS EMBODY THE BEST IN OUR NATIONAL CHARACTER—DEDICATION, TEAMWORK, HONOR AND FRIENDSHIP. PAUL "BEAR" BRYANT EMBODIED FOOTBALL. THE WINNER OF MORE GAMES THAN ANY OTHER COACH IN HISTORY, BEAR BRYANT WAS A TRUE AMERICAN HERO. A HARD BUT BELOVED TASKMASTER HE PUSHED ORDINARY PEOPLE TO PERFORM EXTRAORDINARY FEATS. PATRIOTIC TO THE CORE, DEVOTED TO HIS PLAYERS AND INSPIRED BY A WINNING SPIRIT THAT NEVER QUIT, BEAR BRYANT GAVE HIS COUNTRY THE GIFT OF A LEGEND. IN MAKING THE IMPOSSIBLE SEEM EASY, HE LIVED WHAT WE ALL STRIVE TO BE.

★ ★ ★

President Ronald Reagan awarded Bryant a posthumous Presidential Medal of Freedom with the above citation during a White House ceremony February 23, 1983. Bryant's daughter, Mary Harmon Tyson, accepted the medal on his behalf.

Bear Bryant, his name virtually synonymous with Alabama's Crimson Tide, coached teams at four universities during his thirty-five year career and only once posted a losing season. A colorful and sometimes controversial figure, he had an acknowledged obsession for winning, though he brought more than rock-solid determination and innovative onfield strategies to the game. A tough but respected disciplinarian, Bryant also was widely regarded as a shrewd recruiter and motivator of his players. As an Alabama quarterback once admitted, there was something about coach Bryant "that makes you want to run through a wall."

One of twelve children, Bryant was born in 1913 and grew up on his family's farm at Moro Bottom, Arkansas. Tall and husky in his teenage years, he won his nickname by getting into a ring to wrestle a bear, though by his own admission he did not stay there very long. Better suited to football, he won all-state honors as a high school tackle and played right end at the University of Alabama. He married his college sweetheart, Mary Harmon Black, in 1934. After graduating in 1936, he worked as assistant coach at Alabama and at Vanderbilt University. His first job as head coach was at the University of Maryland in 1945.

Bryant resigned after just one season when the university president reinstated a player Bryant had let go for breaking training. The following year found him at the University of Kentucky, where he remained for eight seasons and posted sixty wins, twenty-three losses, and five ties—including three bowl games and the school's first Southeastern Conference championship. Moving to Texas A&M in 1954, he suffered his only losing season that year. But in his next three seasons Texas A&M lost only four games altogether.

Alabama, which had suffered four straight losing seasons, hired him as head coach in 1958. Remaining at Alabama for the rest of his coaching career, Bryant quickly turned Alabama's football program around. He led the Crimson Tide to twenty-five consecutive winning seasons and twenty-four straight bowl games. Six of Bryant's Alabama teams were ranked first in the nation (the first in 1961), and during his career he coached such football greats as Joe Namath, Ken Stabler, and Ray Perkins. Many of his players later went into coaching, for both college and professional teams.

Bryant broke the national record for most wins by a football coach, with 315 career victories, after defeating Auburn on November 28, 1981. His last game before retiring, the 1982 Liberty Bowl, also was his last win and gave him a record 323 wins, 85 losses, and 17 ties. The country's winningest coach died just a few weeks after his last game. He was sixty-nine years old.

James Burnham

As a scholar, writer, historian and philosopher, James Burnham has profoundly affected the way America views itself and the world. Since the 1930s, Mr. Burnham has shaped the thinking of world leaders. His observations have changed society and his writings have become guiding lights in mankind's quest for truth. Freedom,

REASON AND DECENCY HAVE HAD FEW GREATER CHAMPIONS IN
THIS CENTURY THAN JAMES BURNHAM.

★ ★ ★

*President Ronald Reagan awarded Burnham the Presidential Medal of
Freedom with the above citation during a White House ceremony
February 23, 1983.*

A founding editor of the conservative journal, the *National Review,*
James Burnham was born in 1905, the son of a Chicago business
executive. Burnham graduated summa cum laude from Princeton
University in 1927 and earned his master's degree at Oxford
University in 1929. The latter year he joined the New York University
philosophy department, remaining there as an instructor until 1953.
Marcia Lightner became his wife in 1934.

During the 1930s Burnham became a prominent figure in the
Communist faction led by Leon Trotsky. He edited Marxist and
Trotskyite journals and frequently wrote articles for various radical
left-wing publications. But in 1940 he had a falling out with
Trotskyites and thereafter broke completely with the leftist
movement. Marxism, he came to believe, was false and in practice led
only to "totalitarian despotism."

While continuing his teaching, Burnham began writing books
and soon gained national attention as an author. His two works
about the perils of communism and the coming East-West competition, *The Struggle for the World* (1947) and *The Coming Defeat of
Communism* (1950), both became major successes, and in 1953
Burnham gave up his teaching post. After working for the Central
Intelligence Agency in Washington, D.C., he became a founding
editor of William F. Buckley's *National Review* in 1955. *(See also the
entry for Buckley, p. 445.)* As an editor and regular columnist for the
next two decades, Burnham helped establish the journal as a widely
respected forum for conservative thought and became an important
figure in the American conservative movement. He continued
editing and writing for *National Review* until 1977, when he went
into semiretirement.

Burnham died in 1987 at the age of eighty-two.

James Edward Cheek

As the president of one of our country's greatest institutions of higher learning, and as an outstanding black American scholar, James Cheek embodies the spirit of excellence in education. Dr. Cheek's distinguished career and community work are impressive testimony to his commitment to his calling and his country. His efforts have helped to build a better life for black Americans and a better country for us all.

★ ★ ★

President Ronald Reagan awarded Cheek the Presidential Medal of Freedom with the above citation during a White House ceremony February 23, 1983.

The president of predominantly black Howard University for twenty years, Cheek was born in Roanoke Rapids, North Carolina, in 1932. In 1953, while attending Shaw University in North Carolina, he married Celestine Juanita Williams. Cheek graduated with a bachelor's degree from Shaw two years later and went on to the Colgate-Rochester Divinity School, where he received another bachelor's degree in 1958. While pursuing his doctorate at Drew University in New Jersey, he taught at Drew Theological School (1959–1960), Union Junior College (1959–1960), and Virginia Union University (1960–1963). Cheek won his doctorate from Drew in 1962.

The following year he became president of Shaw University, traditionally a black institution. After serving in that post throughout much of the 1960s, he became president of Howard University in Washington, D.C., in 1969. A year later, President Richard Nixon named him to the President's Commission on Campus Unrest. Cheek also served as the president's special consultant on black colleges and universities. In addition, he gave his time to a host of black educational organizations, advisory boards, and various other civic groups, including the National Council for Black Studies, the American Foundation for Negro Affairs, and the National Committee for Full Employment. Cheek remained president of Howard University until retiring in 1989, at age fifty-six.

Richard Buckminster Fuller, Jr.

A TRUE RENAISSANCE MAN, AND ONE OF THE GREATEST MINDS OF OUR TIMES, RICHARD BUCKMINSTER FULLER'S CONTRIBUTIONS AS A GEOMETRICIAN, EDUCATOR, AND ARCHITECT-DESIGNER ARE BENCHMARKS OF ACCOMPLISHMENT IN THEIR FIELDS. AMONG HIS MOST NOTABLE INVENTIONS AND DISCOVERIES ARE SYNERGETIC GEOMETRY, GEODESIC STRUCTURES AND TENSEGRITY STRUCTURES. MR. FULLER REMINDS US ALL THAT AMERICA IS A LAND OF PIONEERS, HAVEN FOR INNOVATIVE THINKING AND FREE EXPRESSION OF IDEAS.

★ ★ ★

President Ronald Reagan awarded Fuller the Presidential Medal of Freedom with the above citation during a White House ceremony February 23, 1983.

An engineer, inventor, and world planner, Richard Buckminster Fuller, Jr., is probably most famous for the revolutionary geodesic dome he invented in 1947. Born in Milton, Massachusetts, in 1895, he was but one in a family of nonconformists that included his great-aunt, the feminist and social reformer Margaret Fuller. She cofounded the noted transcendentalist publication *The Dial*.

At age six, Fuller used toothpicks and dried peas in his kindergarten class to build his first tetrahedron creation, which hinted at the basic structure he would eventually use in his geodesic dome. Later he studied mathematics and science at Milton Academy, though he resisted the formal structure of education. His nonconformity came to a head at Harvard, and after being expelled twice, Fuller ended his formal education in 1915.

After working at odd jobs, Fuller joined the navy in 1917 and during his two-year tour completed his first two practical inventions—both devices for helping rescue downed pilots from the water. About the time he entered the navy he also married Anne Hewlett, and some years after returning to civilian life he went into the home construction business with his father-in-law. An architect, his father-in-law had invented a modular construction system using a fibrous building block, and Fuller supervised the building of hundreds of houses. Fuller was struck by the waste involved in home construction, though.

When financial difficulties hit the company in 1927, Fuller was left without a job. Distraught over this and grief lingering from the death of his first daughter five years earlier, Fuller began to drink heavily and reached a critical low point in his life. Deciding to make a "blind date with principle," he pulled himself together and vowed to spend the rest of his life designing patterns that would make the most efficient use of energy and resources for the betterment of society.

Hundreds of inventions and discoveries followed, including the Dymaxion house (1927). Factory assembled, the house had entirely self-contained utilities. In 1928, to complement his autonomous house, he designed an omni-directional vehicle, the Dymaxion car, which could cross rough terrain, reach the speed of 120 miles an hour, and make unbelievably quick, 180-degree turns. Manufactured in 1933, it was never commercially produced. Later he invented a system of cartography that depicted the world's land masses without significant distortion, and in 1938 he published *Nine Chains to the Moon,* which discussed his strategies for maximizing the use of energy resources for social good.

While working at various jobs during the 1930s and 1940s, Fuller continued his quest. Then in 1947 he hit on a system of geometry that he called "energetic-synergetic geometry," whose basic unit, the tetrahedron, could be combined to form the structure that made him famous, the geodesic dome. Fuller claimed that the domes, having no limiting dimensions, could be used to cover entire cities and even to provide sheltered environments in places like Antarctica. Perhaps the best known of Fuller's geodesic domes was built for the U.S. pavilion at Montreal's Expo '67.

Fuller joined the faculty at Southern Illinois University at Carbondale in 1959 and taught until becoming professor emeritus in 1975. Ultimately, he had over two-thousand patents to his credit, but he also was a prolific writer. Among his books are *No More Secondhand God* (1963), *Operating Manual for Spaceship Earth* (1969), *Synergetics: Explorations in the Geometry of Thinking* (1975, with E. J. Applewhite), and *Critical Path* (1981).

One of the century's most original thinkers, Fuller died in 1983, at age eighty-seven.

Billy Graham

REVEREND WILLIAM "BILLY" GRAHAM'S UNTIRING EVANGELISM HAS SPREAD THE WORD OF GOD TO EVERY CORNER OF THE GLOBE, AND MADE HIM ONE OF THE MOST INSPIRATIONAL SPIRITUAL LEADERS OF THE TWENTIETH CENTURY. AS A DEEPLY COMMITTED CHRISTIAN, HIS CHALLENGE TO ACCEPT JESUS CHRIST HAS LIFTED THE HEARTS, ASSUAGED THE SORROWS AND RENEWED THE HOPES OF MILLIONS. BILLY GRAHAM IS AN AMERICAN WHO LIVES FIRST AND ALWAYS FOR HIS FELLOW

CITIZENS. IN HONORING HIM, WE GIVE THANKS FOR GOD'S
GREATEST SPIRITUAL GIFTS — FAITH, HOPE, AND LOVE.

★ ★ ★

*President Ronald Reagan awarded Graham the Presidential Medal of
Freedom with the above citation during a White House ceremony
February 23, 1983.*

Probably the best-known and most widely respected evangelist
preacher in America today, William Franklin Graham, Jr., was born
in 1918 on his family's dairy farm near Charlotte, North Carolina. His
parents were Reformed Presbyterians, and his mother often read
devotional works to the family. Young Billy Graham showed more
interest in baseball and reading history, though, until he attended a
revival meeting in Charlotte when he was sixteen.

That day in 1934 Graham unexpectedly experienced a conversion
and made his "decision for Christ." After graduating from high
school in 1936, Graham went first to the fundamentalist Bob Jones
University and then transferred to the Florida Bible Institute, where
he became a Southern Baptist and decided that preaching was his
vocation. Ordained in 1939, he graduated from the Bible Institute the
following year and then went on to Wheaton College in Illinois,
where, in 1943, he earned his bachelor's degree in anthropology. He
married Ruth McCue Bell that summer.

Graham's first ministry after college was at the First Baptist
Church in Western Springs, Illinois, and between 1943 and 1945 he
also led a Sunday evening devotional radio broadcast in the Chicago
area. He took to the "sawdust trail" in 1945 as the featured preacher at
Youth for Christ rallies held across North America and in Great
Britain. For the first four years Graham met with disappointment,
but in 1949 his "canvas cathedral" in Los Angeles proved a major
success and won him attention in the national press.

Continuing his evangelical work on his own, Graham has since
mounted highly successful crusades that have won millions of converts
and have taken him to cities across the United States, Europe, Asia,
South America, Africa, and Australia. In addition to his well-organized
crusades, which include advance work and follow-up contacts with
converts, Graham also reaches out to his followers through periodic
crusade television broadcasts, his weekly radio program "Hour of
Decision" (since 1950), and a newspaper column (since 1952). He has
also published over a dozen books, including *Peace with God* (1953),
World Aflame (1965), *The Holy Spirit* (1978), *Approaching Hoofbeats*
(1985), and, most recently, *Storm Warning* (1992).

By 1957 Graham was able to pack Madison Square Garden for a
four-month New York City crusade, winning many more converts and
establishing his reputation as one of the country's leading evangelists.
His well-publicized relationships with U.S. presidents (beginning with

Truman) have earned him some criticism, though he has generally avoided politics. He also has been attacked by more militant fundamentalists for willingly cooperating with all denominations of Protestant clergy when conducting his crusades. But the overwhelming success of his worldwide crusades, which continued into the mid–1990s, has largely dampened such criticisms, and his sincere devotion to his mission of spreading the Christian faith has earned him a reputation as an elder statesman of American evangelicalism.

Eric Hoffer

THE SON OF IMMIGRANT PARENTS, ERIC HOFFER IS AN EXAMPLE OF BOTH THE OPPORTUNITY AND THE VITALITY OF THE AMERICAN WAY OF LIFE. AFTER OVERCOMING HIS LOSS OF SIGHT AS A CHILD, ERIC HOFFER EDUCATED HIMSELF IN OUR PUBLIC LIBRARIES. AS AN ADULT HE HAS RELISHED HARD WORK AND BELIEVED IN ITS DIGNITY, SPENDING 23 YEARS IN JOBS RANGING FROM LUMBERJACK TO DOCKWORKER. AS AMERICA'S LONGSHOREMAN PHILOSOPHER, HIS BOOKS ON PHILOSOPHY HAVE BECOME CLASSICS. MR. HOFFER'S SPIRIT, SELF-RELIANCE AND GREAT ACCOMPLISHMENTS REMIND US ALL THAT THE UNITED STATES REMAINS A LAND WHERE EACH OF US IS FREE TO ACHIEVE THE BEST THAT LIES WITHIN US.

★ ★ ★

President Ronald Reagan awarded Hoffer a posthumous Presidential Medal of Freedom with the above citation during a White House ceremony February 23, 1983. Lili Osborne accepted the award on Hoffer's behalf.

Family hardships and an intense love of reading dominated Hoffer's early life. The only child of German immigrant parents, he was born in New York City in 1902 and early on showed he had an active mind. By age five he could read in both English and German, but two years later an accidental fall left him partially blind. At about this time his mother died, and a German housekeeper took over the responsibility for raising him. Hoffer never attended school, but when his sight inexplicably returned at age fifteen, he became a voracious reader.

When his father died in 1920, Hoffer was still in his teens and was suddenly forced to support himself. For the next twenty-three years he moved from place to place in California, taking transient jobs—

dishwasher, lumberjack, migrant farmworker, whatever was available. All the while he continued reading books, satisfying his consuming passion for the written word and also providing himself with the education he never had.

By the late 1930s Hoffer began writing, and in 1943 he settled in San Francisco, where his job as a longshoreman paid well enough to support him on just two or three days of work a week. Hoffer devoted the rest of his time to writing and reading, and by 1951 had published *The True Believer*. A perceptive analysis of mass movements and their fanatical followers, the book proved an instant success and established Hoffer as one of the country's few self-educated scholars.

Despite the fame, Hoffer refused to give up his work as a longshoreman until 1967, when he reached the mandatory retirement age. Largely retaining his bare-bones lifestyle—he never married and disdained material possessions—the longshoreman-philosopher continued reading and writing books for the rest of his life, becoming something of a folk hero in the process. Among his other books are *The Passionate State of Mind* (1955), *The Ordeal of Change* (1963), and *Reflections on the Human Condition* (1972).

Hoffer stepped out of the limelight as determinedly as he had entered it, declaring in 1970 that he did not want to be a spokesman or public person. In stopping his appearances on public television, his newspaper column, and his lectures at the University of California, Hoffer said "Any man can ride a train. Only a wise man knows when to get off." He continued writing, though, and the book *Before the Sabbath* (1979) was among his last works. Hoffer died in 1983, at age eighty.

Jacob K. Javits

IN AN OUTSTANDING PUBLIC CAREER OF NEARLY 34 YEARS JACOB JAVITS HAS DISTINGUISHED HIMSELF AS A NEW YORK STATE ATTORNEY GENERAL, UNITED STATES REPRESENTATIVE AND UNITED STATES SENATOR. HE HAS ABLY REPRESENTED THE PEOPLE OF NEW YORK IN THE CONGRESS AND ALL AMERICANS TO THE WORLD. WITH LEADERSHIP AND WISDOM HE GUIDED AMERICA THROUGH HISTORIC TURNING POINTS, STRIVING ALWAYS FOR JUSTICE AT HOME AND PEACE IN THE WORLD.

★ ★ ★

President Ronald Reagan awarded Javits the Presidential Medal of Freedom with the above citation during a White House ceremony February 23, 1983.

Born an immigrant janitor's son in New York City in 1904, Jacob K. Javits was raised in the tenements of Manhattan's Lower East Side. "In New York State," he told a reporter many years later, "that is like being born in a log cabin." While growing up, neither he nor his friends believed they were trapped in a ghetto. Instead Javits later said they felt "the gates were open and that there was a way out, that nothing hemmed us in except the limitations of our own abilities, our own good fortune."

For Javits, education provided the way out. He worked his way through New York University Law School, and after being admitted to the New York State Bar in 1927, he became a partner in his brother's law firm. During World War II he served with the army Chemical Warfare Service and in 1947 married his second wife, Marion Ann Borris. His first marriage had ended in divorce ten years earlier.

Meanwhile, Javits had become more active in politics and in 1946 won his first election as a Republican member of the U.S. House of Representatives. After four terms in Congress, Javits further proved himself as a vote-getter by defeating Franklin D. Roosevelt's son in the 1954 race for New York State attorney general. That won him Republican backing for his successful U.S. Senate bid in 1956, when he handily defeated Robert F. Wagner, then New York City's mayor.

Javits went on to serve twenty-four years in the Senate, earning a reputation for his energy, intelligence, and effectiveness. A liberal Republican, he helped shape landmark legislation in the areas of civil rights, foreign affairs, and labor, even though his party was often in the minority. Javits himself counted three bills he had helped pass as being among the most significant of his career: the War Powers Act limiting presidential war-making powers; the ERISA Act guaranteeing private pensions; and legislation establishing the National Endowment for the Arts and the National Endowment for the Humanities.

By the late 1970s Javits was in his seventies and had begun suffering the effects of Lou Gehrig's disease, a degenerative disease of the nervous system that affects the muscles but leaves the mind alert. After losing Republican backing for another Senate term in 1980, Javits ran unsuccessfully on the Liberal party ticket. It was his last race and the only election he ever lost.

He published his autobiography, *Javits: The Autobiography of a Public Man* in 1981, the same year he left the Senate. Remaining active within the limits of his worsening condition, he continued to speak, write, and even testify before Congress on various issues. Javits died of a heart attack in 1986. He was eighty-one years old.

Clare Boothe Luce

A NOVELIST, PLAYWRIGHT, POLITICIAN, DIPLOMAT, AND ADVISOR TO PRESIDENTS, CLARE BOOTHE LUCE HAS SERVED AND ENRICHED HER COUNTRY IN MANY FIELDS. HER BRILLIANCE OF MIND, GRACIOUS WARMTH AND GREAT FORTITUDE HAVE PROPELLED HER TO EXCEPTIONAL HEIGHTS OF ACCOMPLISHMENT. AS A CONGRESSWOMAN, AMBASSADOR, AND MEMBER OF THE PRESIDENT'S FOREIGN INTELLIGENCE ADVISORY BOARD, CLARE BOOTHE LUCE HAS BEEN A PERSISTENT AND EFFECTIVE ADVOCATE OF FREEDOM, BOTH AT HOME AND ABROAD. SHE HAS EARNED THE RESPECT OF PEOPLE FROM ALL OVER THE WORLD, AND THE LOVE OF HER FELLOW AMERICANS.

★　★　★

President Ronald Reagan awarded Luce the Presidential Medal of Freedom with the above citation during a White House ceremony February 23, 1983.

The strong-minded, outspoken wife of publishing magnate Henry Luce, Clare Boothe Luce was the first woman ever posted as U.S. ambassador to a major nation. She was born Clare Boothe in New York City in 1903 to a father who was a sometime orchestra violinist and a mother who was a former dancer. Her parents separated when she was eight, and her mother later married a prominent Connecticut physician. Meanwhile, the young Boothe was educated privately and grew into a successful young socialite, who in 1923 married a millionaire playboy. The marriage ended in a divorce settlement six years later, and she then began her first career, as an editor and writer.

Boothe persuaded a society friend and publisher of *Vogue* magazine to hire her as an associate editor in 1930. A year later, as associate editor at *Vanity Fair*, she wrote satirical sketches about high society for the magazine. These were republished as a book under the title *Stuffed Shirts* (1931). From 1933 to 1934 she served as managing editor at *Vanity Fair*. Boothe also kept up her ties with the social set and through them met the millionaire publisher of *Time* and *Fortune* magazines, Henry Luce.

After resigning from *Vanity Fair*, Boothe began her career as a Broadway playwright with a dismal flop in 1935, *Abide with Me*. Soon afterward she married Henry Luce. Refusing to accept failure on Broadway, she enjoyed a stunning success the following year with *The Women*. Two other plays, *Kiss the Boys Goodbye* (1939) and *Margin for Error* (1940), also became Broadway hits and all three were made into movies.

Luce became active in politics during the early 1940s and won election from Connecticut as a Republican member of the U.S. House of Representatives in 1943. She served two terms, gaining a reputation for stirring controversy, as well as for her hard-line anti-communist views. Among the various bills she introduced was a resolution calling for creation of a UN agency to promote nuclear arms control and limitation agreements.

Retiring from the House in 1946, she remained influential in the Republican party and in 1950 actively campaigned for Dwight D. Eisenhower in the presidential election. With President Eisenhower in the White House, Luce accepted the appointment as U.S. ambassador to Italy, becoming only the second woman ambassador in U.S. history and the first posted to a major nation. She served from 1953 until 1957 and, while maintaining a tough stance on communism, nevertheless helped set up international talks on the disputed territory of Trieste that averted a war between Italy and communist-controlled Yugoslavia.

Following an unsuccessful bid for a Senate seat in 1964, Luce retired from politics. Her husband died in 1967, and for many years afterward she lived in Hawaii. Luce returned to politics as a member of President Reagan's Foreign Intelligence Advisory Board (from 1983). She died in 1987, at age eighty-four.

Dumas Malone

As one of the foremost historians, authors, and scholars of this century, Dumas Malone has recounted the birth of our nation and the ideals of our Founding Fathers. Among Dr. Malone's most notable accomplishments is his biography of Thomas Jefferson, now regarded as the most authoritative work of its kind. Dr. Malone's contributions to our national lore will remain invaluable to succeeding generations as each takes up responsibility for the heritage of freedom so eloquently described in his articles and books.

* * *

President Ronald Reagan awarded Malone a posthumous Presidential Medal of Freedom with the above citation during a White House ceremony February 23, 1983. Malone's son Gifford accepted the award on his father's behalf.

A minister's son, Dumas Malone was born in the small Mississippi town of Coldwater in 1892. Taught at home by his mother, he learned the importance of both education and religion and later earned his bachelor's degree from Emory College (1910). After serving in World War I, he took his doctorate in history at Yale University (1923) and then taught at the University of Virginia, in Charlottesville, until 1929.

The University of Virginia, as it happened, was founded by Thomas Jefferson and was overlooked by Jefferson's mansion, Monticello—circumstances that probably contributed to Malone's interest in the country's third president. Meanwhile, Malone married Elisabeth Gifford in 1925 and saw his Yale dissertation published as *The Public Life of Thomas Cooper* the following year.

Malone worked as an editor on the landmark reference, *The Dictionary of American Biography* from 1929 to 1931 and was its editor in chief from 1931 to 1936. While seeing the monumental work to completion, he also wrote seventeen of the many biographical sketches it contained, most notably the one on Jefferson, who later became the subject of his masterwork. Malone then served as editor in chief of Harvard University Press from 1936 until 1943.

Returning to Charlottesville, he began work on his six-volume biography of Jefferson. Though Malone moved on to teach at Columbia University in 1945, he continued working on the project and published the first volume, *Jefferson the Virginian*, three years later. Five other volumes in the series, titled *Jefferson and His Time*, appeared at intervals over the next thirty-three years, ending with *The Sage of Monticello* in 1981. From the publication of the first volume, Malone's work was recognized as an important scholarly endeavor and as other books in the series were published, he came to be regarded as the foremost authority on Jefferson's life. He won the Pulitzer Prize for history in 1975 for the biography.

Malone went back to the University of Virginia as the Thomas Jefferson Foundation Professor of History in 1960 and in 1962 retired to become the Thomas Jefferson Foundation biographer in residence. He completed the final two volumes of his series between 1962 and 1981, despite failing eyesight that left him nearly blind from 1977 onward. Malone died five years after completing his monumental work. He was ninety-four years old.

Mabel Mercer

MABEL MERCER HAS BEEN CALLED A LIVING TESTAMENT TO THE ARTFULNESS OF THE AMERICAN SONG, AND A LEGEND IF THERE EVER WAS ONE. HER TALENT, HER ELEGANCE AND HER UNIQUE WAY WITH A LYRIC HAVE GATHERED A DEVOTED FOLLOWING ALL OVER THE WORLD. HER SPECIAL STYLE HAS INFLUENCED SOME OF AMERICA'S MOST FAMOUS PERFORMERS, EARNING HER THE REPUTATION OF A SINGER'S SINGER. MISS MERCER'S CAREER HAS SPANNED MORE THAN 60 YEARS AND SHE CONTINUES TO DELIGHT AUDIENCES AND CRITICS ALIKE. WITH HER INCOMPARABLE TALENT SHE HAS HELPED SHAPE AND ENRICH AMERICAN MUSIC.

★ ★ ★

President Ronald Reagan awarded Mercer the Presidential Medal of Freedom with the above citation during a White House ceremony February 23, 1983.

A singer who made her name playing intimate supper clubs, Mabel Mercer was born in Burton-on-Trent, England, in 1900. Her father, who died before her birth, was a black American jazz musician, and her mother was a white English vaudeville singer. Extremely self-conscious and shy as a child, Mercer overcame these handicaps to join her mother and stepfather in the family's vaudeville act. Then only fourteen, she went to Paris on her own after World War I, singing in various cafés before beginning a seven-year engagement at Bricktops (1931–1938), a famous Paris café.

At Bricktops, a cabaret popular with American expatriates in Paris—the so-called lost generation of F. Scott Fitzgerald, Ernest Hemingway, and others—Mercer adopted her signature style of singing while seated in a high-backed armchair. Sitting with her hands folded in her lap, she focused her performance on presenting the story contained in the song's lyrics. Her style, which she perfected over the years, was especially suited to the intimate atmosphere of bistros and supper clubs, and Mercer, who became known as a singer's singer, developed a devoted following.

Forced to leave France by the coming of World War II, Mercer first performed in the United States in 1938, playing in various New York supper clubs and cafés during the 1940s. During this time she was briefly married to jazz musician Kelsey Pharr, and in 1952 Mercer became a U.S. citizen. She began giving theater and concert hall performances in the 1950s, and a concert the following decade produced one of her most popular record albums, *Mabel Mercer and Bobby Short at Town Hall* (1968). She appeared at Carnegie Hall in 1977 and that same year did a five-part BBC documentary titled *Miss Mercer in Mayfair*.

By 1960 Mercer was sixty years old and had lost much of her range as a singer, yet she continued to perform successfully for two decades more. To compensate for her failing soprano voice, she worked on her phrasing and other techniques and gave still greater emphasis to the emotions and the story in the song's lyrics. Over the years her techniques influenced many famous singers, including the likes of Nat King Cole, Frank Sinatra, Johnny Mathis, Tony Bennett, Lena Horne, and Barbra Streisand.

Mercer retired in 1979 but returned to the stage to give her last performances in 1982 and 1983. She died in 1984, a year after receiving the Presidential Medal of Freedom. Mercer was eighty-four years old.

Simon Ramo

As an engineer, businessman, physicist and defense and aerospace pioneer, Simon Ramo's career has been on the forefront of American technology, development and growth. The son of a storekeeper in Salt Lake City, Dr. Ramo built his business from a one-room office to a nationwide network of production plants. A shining symbol of American ingenuity and innovativeness, Dr. Ramo was also a distinguished author, philanthropist and civic leader. His life's work has strengthened America's freedom and protected our peace.

★ ★ ★

President Ronald Reagan awarded Ramo the Presidential Medal of Freedom with the above citation during a White House ceremony February 23, 1983.

A codeveloper of U.S. defense missiles in the 1950s, Simon Ramo was born in Salt Lake City, Utah, in 1913. He was a strong student who skipped grades in elementary school and graduated from the University of Utah in 1933 with top honors. Three years later he earned his doctorate magna cum laude in electrical engineering at Pasadena's California Institute of Technology. He married Virginia May Smith in 1937.

Ramo spent the ten years between 1936 and 1946 working at General Electric in Schenectady, New York, before becoming director of electronics research at the Hughes Aircraft Company in Culver City, California. At Hughes, he and staff engineer Dean E. Wooldridge devised what became the Air Force's standard fire control system and supervised development of the Falcon family of missiles, air-to-air missiles first used during the Korean War. He also worked on navigation, radar, computer, and various other aircraft electronic systems.

Deciding to strike out on their own, Ramo and Wooldridge left the Hughes Company in 1953 to form the Ramo-Wooldridge Corporation. The pair started out with nothing more than a one-room office and an established reputation as weapons-systems developers. By the following year they had started work on a huge defense contract to provide systems engineering and technical direction for development of the intercontinental ballistic missiles (ICBMs). Between 1954 and 1958, Ramo-Wooldridge played the primary role in creating the Atlas, Titan, and Minuteman missiles, among others, which were used for the defense and space exploration programs.

When Ramo-Wooldridge merged with Thompson Products in 1958 to become TRW (Thompson Ramo-Wooldridge), Ramo became a director and executive vice president. Three years later he was named vice chairman of the board, a post he held until 1978. He has remained a consultant to TRW since then.

Meanwhile, Ramo has been active in other business ventures, most recently as board chairman of Allenwood Ventures (since 1987). He has published various books on science, engineering, and management, including *The Business of Science* (1988), and has taught at various universities. He also has served on numerous government committees and commissions, such as the White House Energy Research and Development Advisory Council (1973–1975) and the President's Committee on Science and Technology (1976–1977).

Carlos P. Romulo

As parliamentarian, soldier, educator, U.N. Charter signatory, diplomat, and foreign minister, Carlos P. Romulo's statesmanship and promotion of international accord add up to a remarkable record of achievement. His more than fifty years of public service embody the warm relationship between the United States and the Philippines from the colonial period through the Commonwealth, wartime, and independence to the present.

★ ★ ★

President Ronald Reagan awarded Romulo the Presidential Medal of Freedom with the above citation. U.S. Ambassador Michael Armacost pre-

sented the medal to Romulo during a ceremony in Manila, Philippines, on January 12, 1984.

A signer of the United Nations charter, Carlos P. Romulo was born in the Philippines in 1899. He graduated with a bachelor's degree from the University of the Philippines in 1918 and three years later obtained his master's degree in English at Columbia University in the United States. Returning to the Philippines, he became a newspaper editor in 1922 and taught English at the University of the Philippines from 1923 to 1928.

Moving up quickly in the newspaper world, he served as editor in chief of a Philippine newspaper combine after 1931. In 1937 he became the publisher of another combine and in 1941 won a Pulitzer Prize for stories he wrote warning of the Japanese threat to Southeast Asia.

During World War II, Romulo became an aide to General Douglas MacArthur and eventually rose to the rank of brigadier general. He later came into world prominence as a signer of the UN charter (1945), after succeeding in having the document call for the independence of colonized countries (the United States granted the Philippines independence the following year). While serving as the Philippines' chief UN delegate from 1945 to 1954, Romulo also headed the UN General Assembly in 1949 and 1950, and from 1956 to 1957 he served as the Philippine delegate to the UN Security Council. During these early years at the United Nations, he became a leading spokesman for the emerging third world countries.

Meanwhile, he served as the Philippine ambassador to the United States from 1952 to 1953 and from 1955 to 1962. After a stint as president of the University of the Philippines (1962–1968), Romulo returned to government service under President Ferdinand Marcos, first as secretary of education (1966–1968), then as secretary of foreign affairs (1968–1978), and finally as minister of foreign affairs (1978–1984). In 1979 he married his second wife, Beth Day, his first wife having died eleven years earlier.

Romulo retired in 1984. He wrote over a dozen books during his long career, including *Crusade in Asia; Philippine Victory* (1955), and his autobiography, *I Walked with Heroes* (1961). Romulo died in 1985, at age eighty-six.

Howard Henry Baker, Jr.

As a Member of the United States Senate, one of the country's most powerful and influential citizens, and an individual whose character shines brightly as an

EXAMPLE TO OTHERS, HOWARD BAKER HAS BEEN A FORCE FOR
RESPONSIBILITY AND CIVILITY ON A GENERATION OF AMERICANS.
IN HIS ALMOST 20 YEARS OF SERVICE, HE HAS EARNED THE
RESPECT AND ADMIRATION OF HIS FELLOW CITIZENS REGARDLESS
OF THEIR POLITICAL PERSUASION. AS MAJORITY LEADER OF THE
SENATE, HIS QUIET COOPERATIVE STYLE AND KEEN LEGISLATIVE
SKILLS HAVE HONORED AMERICA'S FINEST TRADITIONS OF
ENLIGHTENED POLITICAL LEADERSHIP AND STATESMANSHIP.

★ ★ ★

*President Ronald Reagan awarded Baker the Presidential Medal of
Freedom with the above citation during a White House ceremony
March 26, 1984.*

The first Republican ever popularly elected to the Senate from
Tennessee, Howard Henry Baker, Jr., was born in 1925 to a pros-
perous and politically powerful family in Huntsville. His father
preceded him in Congress, having been a representative from
Tennessee between 1951 and 1964. After serving in the navy during
World War II, Baker earned his law degree from the University of
Tennessee in 1949. He practiced law and through shrewd investments
also managed to add considerably to his inherited wealth. In 1951 he
married Joy Dirksen, daughter of Illinois Republican Sen. Everett
McKinley Dirksen.

Entering politics in 1964, Baker won his first term as a senator
from Tennessee in 1966. A fiscal conservative, he was a moderate-to-
liberal Republican on other issues and during his Senate terms
became especially well known for his skill at arranging compromises
between competing factions. His role as ranking Republican on the
Senate Watergate investigating committee gave him national
exposure, and from 1977 to 1981 he served as Senate minority leader.
When Republicans gained the majority in the Senate in 1981, they
named Baker majority leader, a post he held until returning to
private practice in 1985.

While serving in the Senate, Baker tried unsuccessfully for higher
office. In 1976 Gerald R. Ford passed over him for the vice-presidential slot on the Republican ticket. Then he lost his primary bid for
the Republican presidential nomination in 1980, and that year opposition to his moderate views also ruined his chances of being named
the vice-presidential candidate on the Reagan ticket.

Baker's retirement from politics in 1985 lasted only until 1987.
Coming under heavy fire from the Iran-contra scandal, President
Reagan asked Baker to take over as White House chief of staff. Baker
agreed, serving from 1987 to 1988, though it effectively prevented him
from contending for the presidency in 1988. He has remained in
private practice since then.

James Francis Cagney

AS A GIANT IN THE WORLD OF ENTERTAINMENT, JAMES CAGNEY HAS LEFT HIS MARK NOT ONLY ON THE FILM INDUSTRY BUT ON THE HEARTS OF ALL HIS FELLOW AMERICANS. IN SOME 60 YEARS IN ENTERTAINMENT, PERFORMING ON STAGE AND SCREEN, HE MASTERED DRAMA AND ACTION ADVENTURE, AS WELL AS MUSIC AND DANCE. ONE OF HIS MOST REMEMBERED PERFORMANCES, AS GEORGE M. COHAN IN "YANKEE DOODLE DANDY," WAS A WHIRLWIND SINGING AND DANCING FILM THAT INSPIRED A NATION AT WAR WHEN IT SORELY NEEDED A LIFT IN SPIRIT. JAMES CAGNEY'S PROFESSIONAL AND PERSONAL LIFE HAS BROUGHT GREAT CREDIT TO HIM AND LEFT UNFORGETTABLE MEMORIES WITH MILLIONS WHO HAVE FOLLOWED HIS CAREER.

★ ★ ★

President Ronald Reagan awarded Cagney the Presidential Medal of Freedom with the above citation during a White House ceremony March 26, 1984.

James Cagney's famous tough guy mannerisms and his hard-nosed delivery of lines like "You dirty rat" have supplied legions of nightclub entertainers with instantly recognizable material for their impressions of him. He actually sought out such colorful touches for his tough-guy character roles, but he was a versatile actor who could and did play a song-and-dance man as easily as a gangster.

Born the second of five children in 1904, Cagney was raised in New York City. His father, a saloonkeeper in a rough neighborhood, died while Cagney was still young. Cagney worked after hours during high school and went on to attend Columbia University until family problems forced him to leave school and seek work. That proved an important turning point, because he decided to try acting, even though he had no training.

Unlike many actors who struggled for their first part, Cagney landed one on his first try—as a chorus boy in the musical comedy *Pitter Patter.* For seven years during the 1920s he worked the vaudeville circuit while also getting occasional parts in plays. Then two back-to-back hit plays in which Cagney starred opposite Joan Blondell caught the attention of executives at Warner Brothers movie studio.

Cagney's star rose quickly after that. In 1930 he played the lead opposite Blondell in his first movie, *Sinner's Holiday.* The following year his performance in *The Public Enemy,* his first gangster movie, cinched his reputation as an outstanding movie actor. A succession of tough-guy movies followed, with Cagney starring as a sadistic gangster or cynical, belligerent male who invariably roughed up a woman along the way. Among the films were *G-Men* (1935), *Ceiling Zero* (1935), *Angels with Dirty Faces* (1938), *The Roaring Twenties* (1939), and *The Fighting 69th* (1940).

With World War II looming in Europe, publicity surrounding charges he had associated with Communists hurt Cagney's image, but in 1940 he cleared himself by testifying before the House Special Committee to Investigate Un-American Activities and Propaganda. His role as superpatriot George M. Cohan in the 1942 hit movie *Yankee Doodle Dandy* helped erase any lingering public doubts and boosted Americans' morale following Japan's devastating sneak attack on Pearl Harbor. The movie also won Cagney an Academy Award.

Cagney continued making movies after the war, including *White Heat* (1949) and *Man of a Thousand Faces* (1957). He retired after making the 1961 film *One, Two, Three* and did not appear on screen again for two decades, when he made his last film, *Ragtime*. Cagney played a police inspector in the 1981 movie. The veteran performer died five years later, at age eighty-one.

Whittaker Chambers

AT A CRITICAL MOMENT IN OUR NATION'S HISTORY, WHITTAKER CHAMBERS STOOD ALONE AGAINST THE BROODING TERRORS OF OUR AGE. CONSUMMATE INTELLECTUAL, WRITER OF MOVING MAJESTIC PROSE, AND WITNESS TO THE TRUTH, HE BECAME THE FOCUS OF A MOMENTOUS CONTROVERSY IN AMERICAN HISTORY THAT SYMBOLIZED OUR CENTURY'S EPIC STRUGGLE BETWEEN FREEDOM AND TOTALITARIANISM, A CONTROVERSY IN WHICH THE SOLITARY FIGURE OF WHITTAKER CHAMBERS PERSONIFIED THE MYSTERY OF HUMAN REDEMPTION IN THE FACE OF EVIL AND SUFFERING. AS LONG AS HUMANITY SPEAKS OF FREEDOM AND DREAMS OF FREEDOM, THE LIFE AND WRITINGS OF WHITTAKER CHAMBERS WILL ENNOBLE AND INSPIRE. THE WORDS OF ARTHUR KOESTLER ARE HIS EPITAPH: "THE WITNESS IS GONE; THE TESTIMONY WILL STAND."

* * *

President Ronald Reagan awarded Chambers a posthumous Presidential Medal of Freedom with the above citation during a White

House ceremony March 26, 1984. Chambers's son John accepted the medal on his father's behalf.

A journalist whose spying for the Soviet Union thrust him into the midst of America's post–World War II anticommunist scare, Whittaker Chambers was born in 1901, the son of a commercial artist and a former actress. Chambers's given name was Jay Vivian Chambers, but he used various aliases during his lifetime, most notably his mother's surname before marriage, Whittaker. As a student at Columbia University in the early 1920s his potential to become a major writer was soon recognized, and his youthful conservatism gave way to the liberal influences of the academic atmosphere, including the views of such friends as Langston Hughes and Lionel Trilling.

Finally lured by the revolutionary leftist ideals of communism, Chambers dropped out of Columbia in 1925 and joined the Communist Party. He became famous as a proletarian writer through publication of his pieces for the *Daily Worker* and the *New Masses* and in 1931 married a socialist artist Esther Shemitz. He was named editor of the *New Masses* in 1931 and began spying for the Soviets in 1932, eventually becoming a courier for classified documents stolen from Washington.

This was no youthful flirtation with subterfuge; Chambers also served as a recruiter and spy-ring organizer and was decorated as a Red Army officer. But Stalin's bloody purges in 1937 and an ominous order recalling him to the Soviet Union finally turned him against communism. In 1939 he began writing for *Time* magazine, where he became known for his adamant anticommunist stance. About that time he also reported what he knew about Soviet spy operations to the State Department, but by 1941 the Soviet Union had joined the Allies in the fight against Hitler.

After the war was another matter, though. By the late 1940s Chambers had become *Time*'s foreign news editor and one of its top writers, while in Washington the House Un-American Activities Committee raised a furor over the threat of Communist subversives working in the government. Subpoenaed to testify, Chambers charged that many officials in the government had been Communist sympathizers or outright party members. Among those he identified was Alger Hiss, a former high-ranking State Department official and then president of the Carnegie Endowment for World Peace.

Hiss vehemently denied the charges and sued Chambers for libel. In the escalating, highly publicized battle Chambers produced the so-called pumpkin papers, microfilmed State Department documents he said Hiss had supplied him. The bitter controversy tended to divide observers along liberal/conservative lines, with Hiss supporters angrily questioning Chambers's truthfulness (some called him a pathological liar) and warning of the dangers of the hysteria over Communist subversives. Chambers's supporters, on the other hand, countered that Hiss was lying to protect himself and that Communist sympathizers had to be rooted out, by whatever means necessary.

Whether Hiss had indeed been a spy for the Soviet Union was never fully resolved. A grand jury indicted him, but his first trial in 1949 ended in a hung jury. With the statute of limitations on espionage passed, Hiss was tried in 1950 on perjury charges. Convicted this time, he served about four years in prison.

Chambers meanwhile retired to recover from the emotional strain of the protracted controversy and to write his autobiography, *Witness* (1952). His stand, however, had made him a hero to the emerging intellectual right, and from 1957 to 1959 he worked as an editor on the conservative *National Review*, newly founded by William F. Buckley, Jr. Chambers died in 1961 at the age of sixty.

The controversy was not easily forgotten, however, and President Reagan's decision to award Chambers the Presidential Medal of Freedom opened old wounds, even some thirty years after Hiss's conviction. Though liberal and conservative intellectuals had been among recipients named by past presidents, Chambers's selection drew protests from the intellectual left and revived questions about his testimony.

Leo Cherne

ALTHOUGH HE HAS NEVER HELD ELECTED OFFICE, LEO CHERNE HAS HAD MORE INFLUENCE ON GOVERNMENTAL POLICY THAN MANY MEMBERS OF CONGRESS. SINCE THE LATE 1930S, LEO CHERNE HAS STEPPED FORWARD WITH BRILLIANCE, ENERGY, AND MORAL PASSION HELPING THIS NATION OVERCOME COUNTLESS CHALLENGES. HIS LIFETIME DEVOTION TO AIDING HIS COUNTRY AND TO SERVING THE CAUSE OF HUMAN FREEDOM, ESPECIALLY THROUGH HIS WORK ON BEHALF OF REFUGEES, REFLECTS THE STRONG AND GENEROUS CHARACTER OF A MAN WHO DESERVES THE RESPECT AND GRATITUDE OF ALL AMERICANS.

★ ★ ★

President Ronald Reagan awarded Cherne the Presidential Medal of Freedom with the above citation during a White House ceremony March 26, 1984.

A man of unusually varied talents—an author, strategic and foreign policy adviser, and sculptor—Leo Cherne was born in Bronx, New York, in 1912. He went on to graduate from New York University in

1931 and earned his law degree from New York Law School three years later. In 1936, after working briefly in private practice, he became an editor for a publisher of business and law reference books. Cherne soon gained a reputation for putting together publications aimed at telling businessmen how the flood of recently passed New Deal legislation affected their businesses. Meanwhile, in 1936 he married Julia Rodriquez Lopez.

Cherne published his first book as an author in 1939, the controversial *Adjusting Your Business to War,* which discussed the impact that America's entering World War II would have on business. The book caused a sensation in the nation's capital, because it foresaw the creation of a vast war production industry and because at the time there was considerable sentiment in Congress, and the country at large, against taking part in what was believed a European problem. A year later Cherne published *M-Day and What It Means to You,* which was aimed at a broader audience and discussed how American life would be changed by war. His third and last book appeared in 1944 as *The Rest of Your Life.*

Turning from his career as an author-editor, Cherne taught at the New School for Social Research from 1946 to 1952. At about this time he also began his long association with the New York-based Freedom House, as chairman of the executive committee from 1946 to 1977 and as a board member and honorary chairman into the mid–1990s. During that time the group engaged in a wide range of activities, including promoting political rights and civil liberties worldwide, the strengthening of democratic institutions at home and abroad, and the active involvement of the United States in world affairs. During Cherne's long tenure as chairman, Freedom House became involved in such diverse issues as McCarthyism, nuclear disarmament, desegregation, the 1956 Hungarian revolt, and the wars in Vietnam and Afghanistan.

Cherne also became chairman of the International Rescue Committee in 1951, a post he held into the 1980s; a member of the Select Commission on Western Hemisphere Immigration from 1967 to 1968; and chairman of the Citizens Commission on Indochinese Refugees, from 1978 into the 1980s. His work at Freedom House also led to increasingly important government advisory roles during the 1970s and 1980s, as a member of the U.S. Advisory Commission on International Educational and Cultural Affairs and the President's Foreign Intelligence Advisory Board. He also was a member of the advisory board of the Center for Strategic and International Studies.

Cherne also found time to become a sculptor and completed bronze busts of such noted figures as Presidents John F. Kennedy, Lyndon B. Johnson, and Abraham Lincoln. His works are displayed in museums around the world. Though largely retired by the mid–1990s, he remains involved with the Freedom House and other groups.

Denton Arthur Cooley

IN AN OUTSTANDING PROFESSIONAL CAREER, DR. DENTON
COOLEY HAS DISTINGUISHED HIMSELF TIME AND AGAIN IN THE
FIELD OF MEDICINE. AS ONE OF THIS COUNTRY'S LEADING HEART
SURGEONS, HE HAS CHARTED NEW TERRITORY IN HIS SEARCH
FOR WAYS TO PROLONG AND ENRICH HUMAN LIFE. HIS EFFORTS
HAVE SAVED THE LIVES NOT ONLY OF HIS OWN PATIENTS, BUT
THOSE OF MANY OTHER DOCTORS WHO HAVE STUDIED AND
MASTERED TECHNIQUES DEVELOPED BY HIM.

★ ★ ★

*President Ronald Reagan awarded Dr. Cooley the Presidential Medal of
Freedom with the above citation during a White House ceremony
March 26, 1984.*

Three months after finishing medical school, Dr. Denton Cooley
assisted in the first-ever blue-baby operation, an experience that convinced him to specialize in heart surgery. In following years he
became a leading heart surgeon, pioneered techniques for replacing
heart valves, helped develop the heart-lung bypass machine used
during open-heart surgery, and devised improved procedures for
transplanting hearts. He also was the first surgeon to implant a
mechanical heart in a human. *(See also the entry for pediatric surgeon
Helen B. Taussig, p. 127.)*

Born in 1920, Cooley was the son of a Houston dentist. After
earning his bachelor's degree at the University of Texas, he entered
medical school there, but he finished his medical studies at Johns
Hopkins in 1944. In 1949 he married Louise Goldsborough Thomas.
Completing his residency, Cooley returned to Houston in 1951 to
teach at Baylor University Medical School and to begin collaborating
with Dr. Michael De Bakey, a noted heart surgeon. Together they
developed surgical techniques and the heart-lung machine, but by
1960 personal differences had ended their collaboration.

During the 1960s Dr. Cooley gained a wide reputation for his
work with infants and others suffering from congenital heart disease
and for his improvements in techniques for implanting heart valves.
He joined other surgeons in performing heart transplants soon after
the first was performed in late 1967 and one year performed twenty-
two in all. His implanting of the first artificial heart in a patient in
1969 proved controversial, however. While the patient survived for
sixty-five hours with the artificial heart, he died of complications
soon after receiving a transplanted human heart.

In the ensuing furor Dr. Cooley resigned from Baylor University
Medical School and became surgeon in chief of the Texas Heart
Institute, which he had founded in 1962 and which was part of the

Texas Medical Center, a leading health-care facility. He became a leading practitioner of coronary bypass procedures during the 1970s.

Since 1975 Cooley has been a professor at the University of Texas Medical School, as well as surgeon in chief at the Heart Institute.

Tennessee Ernie Ford

THROUGH HIS MUSICAL TALENTS, WARM PERSONALITY, AND QUICK "DOWN-HOME" WIT TENNESSEE ERNIE FORD WON THE HEARTS OF THE AMERICAN PEOPLE. FORD'S MUSIC, WHICH REVEALED HIS CHARACTER AND SOUL TO ALL WHO LISTENED, INSPIRED AS WELL AS ENTERTAINED HIS AUDIENCES. HIS RESPECT FOR TRADITIONAL VALUES, HIS STRONG FAITH IN GOD, AND HIS UNLIMITED CAPACITY FOR HUMAN KINDNESS HAVE GREATLY ENDEARED HIM TO HIS FELLOW COUNTRYMEN. AMERICA IS A NATION RICHER IN SPIRIT BECAUSE OF TENNESSEE ERNIE FORD.

★ ★ ★

President Ronald Reagan awarded Ford the Presidential Medal of Freedom with the above citation during a White House ceremony March 26, 1984.

A country and gospel recording star turned television host during the 1950s and 1960s, Tennessee Ernie Ford is probably best remembered for his hit song "Sixteen Tons." He was born in Bristol, Tennessee, in 1919, the son of a postal worker. As a youth he sang at family gatherings and later studied music at Virginia Intermount College in Bristol, Virginia, from 1937 to 1938.

Ford landed his first paid work as a disc jockey and announcer for a radio station while still at college and then used the money he saved to study briefly at the Cincinnati Conservatory of Music in 1939. Soon after, Ford moved on to radio stations in Atlanta, Georgia, and then Knoxville, Tennessee. He married Betty Heminger in 1942.

Ford served in the army air force during World War II and worked for several California radio stations after being discharged. His career as a singer skyrocketed after 1948, when he became a soloist on the hillbilly radio show, "Hometown Jamboree," and also landed a Capitol Records recording contract. Ford recorded his first hit, "I'll Never be Free" in 1949 and during the next six years had eleven hit singles on the country music chart. His biggest was "Sixteen Tons"

(1955), which sold two-million copies soon after its release and eventually sold some twenty million worldwide. Among his other notable recordings are "River of No Return," "Mule Train," and "The Ballad of Davy Crockett."

Ford's growing popularity led to television appearances during the early 1950s, and in 1956 he starred as the host of "The Ford Show," a prime-time variety program sponsored by the Ford Motor Company. Ford proved popular with viewers because of his southern drawl, charming wit, and relaxed, homespun country manner ("Bless your pea-pickin' hearts" was a favorite expression). The show quickly became one of the top ten rated programs, and he continued as its host until 1960.

From the late 1950s Ford sang mostly gospel music, and his *Hymns* (1956) became the first country music LP to top a million in sales. He wrote his autobiography, *This Is My Song, This Is My Story*, in 1963 and won a Grammy Award in 1964 for *Great Gospel Songs*. His later albums included *Spirituals* (1968) and *25th Anniversary* (1974).

Ford continued recording gospel music until the mid–1970s and appeared in concerts until the early 1980s. He died in 1991, at age seventy-two.

Hector Garcia

DR. HECTOR GARCIA'S PATRIOTISM AND COMMUNITY CONCERN EXEMPLIFY THE MEANING OF GOOD CITIZENSHIP. HIS MANY COMMUNITY-BUILDING ENDEAVORS INCLUDED HIS WORK AS A FOUNDER AND FIRST NATIONAL CHAIRMAN OF THE AMERICAN G.I. FORUM, A VETERANS' ORGANIZATION WHICH HAS DONE MUCH TO IMPROVE THE LOT OF AMERICANS OF MEXICAN DESCENT. OVER THE YEARS, HE HAS FAITHFULLY REPRESENTED OUR GOVERNMENT ON NUMEROUS OCCASIONS, OVERSEAS AND DOMESTICALLY. DR. HECTOR GARCIA IS A CREDIT TO HIS FAMILY AND COMMUNITY, AND TO ALL AMERICANS. THROUGH HIS EFFORTS, BASED ON A DEEP BELIEF IN TRADITIONAL AMERICAN IDEALS, HE HAS MADE THIS A BETTER COUNTRY.

★ ★ ★

President Ronald Reagan awarded Garcia the Presidential Medal of Freedom with the above citation during a White House ceremony March 26, 1984.

Hector Garcia's family moved from Mexico to south Texas after his birth in 1914, and he was raised in Texas. After graduating from the University of Texas in 1936, Garcia went on to get his medical degree there four years later and joined the army medical corps during World War II. He won the Bronze Star with six battle stars for his wartime service.

Soon after returning to civilian life, Garcia shifted his interest from practicing medicine to promoting Hispanic civil rights. In 1948 he founded and served as the first president of the American G.I. Forum, a pioneering group that organized Hispanics who had served in the U.S. military during World War II. Originally formed to promote both education and civil rights for Hispanics, the American G.I. Forum remains one of the most important Hispanic-rights groups in the country.

Garcia, who was active in another major Hispanic-rights group, the League of United Latin American Citizens (LULAC), also founded the Political Association of Spanish-Speaking Organizations (PASO) in 1960. A longtime member of the Democratic party, he campaigned for John F. Kennedy that year and served as an alternative ambassador to the United Nations in 1964. Four years later he represented Hispanic interests as a member of the U.S. Commission on Civil Rights.

Andrew Goodpaster

DURING HIS LONG SERVICE TO HIS COUNTRY, GENERAL ANDREW GOODPASTER SHOULDERED HEAVY RESPONSIBILITY AND WORKED TIRELESSLY WITH THE HIGHEST PROFESSIONAL STANDARDS. HIS ORGANIZATIONAL AND DIPLOMATIC SKILLS HELPED SHAPE THE NATO ALLIANCE AND DEVELOP AMERICAN MILITARY AND FOREIGN POLICY OVER THREE DECADES. AS SUPREME ALLIED COMMANDER OF THE NATO ALLIANCE, PRESIDENTIAL REPRE-SENTATIVE, AND SOLDIER, GENERAL GOODPASTER HAS EARNED A WELL-DESERVED REPUTATION AS A THOUGHTFUL AND DILIGENT PUBLIC SERVANT. HIS WORK HAS CONTRIBUTED IMMENSELY TO THE SECURITY AND FREEDOM OF HIS COUNTRY AND TO THE CAUSE OF PEACE.

★ ★ ★

President Ronald Reagan awarded Goodpaster the Presidential Medal of Freedom with the above citation during a White House ceremony March 26, 1984.

An adviser to Presidents Eisenhower, Johnson, and Nixon, Andrew Goodpaster was born in Granite City, Illinois, in 1915. Raised in Granite City, he attended McKendree College in nearby Lebanon, Illinois, for two years and then went to the United States Military Academy at West Point, where he graduated second in his class in 1939. He married Dorothy Andersen the same year.

Initially assigned to the army engineer corps, he saw combat during World War II as the Forty-eighth Engineer Battalion commander and won the Distinguished Service Cross for leading a reconnaissance mission through a minefield while under enemy fire. After the war the army sent him to Princeton University for advanced study. By 1950 Goodpaster had earned his doctorate in political science.

He served as the army's delegate on the Joint Chiefs of Staff Advanced Study Committee from 1950 to 1952, and for the next two years he was assistant to General Dwight D. Eisenhower's chief of staff at the military headquarters of the North Atlantic Treaty Organization (NATO) in Paris. During that time Goodpaster helped organize the newly formed NATO military command.

President Eisenhower recalled Goodpaster from Europe in 1954, making him White House staff secretary. Sometimes referred to in newspapers as "the man with the briefcase," he was a key White House official who oversaw all communications with the president as well as cabinet matters. He remained at the White House for the rest of Eisenhower's term and by 1957 had been promoted to brigadier general.

During the early 1960s, Goodpaster served as an assistant to the Joint Chiefs of Staff chairman, Gen. Maxwell Taylor, and as an adviser to President Lyndon B. Johnson. A member of the U.S. delegation to the Vietnam peace negotiations in 1968, he also saw duty in Vietnam that year and won promotion to full general. With the Nixon administration in office the following year, he returned to NATO as commander of the military arm. Goodpaster retired from the army in 1974 after nearly five years at NATO.

Following a major West Point cheating scandal, the army took the unprecedented step of calling Goodpaster out of retirement in 1977 to run the college. He stayed on at West Point until 1981, when he again retired. Remaining active during the 1980s, he presided over the Institute of Defense Analysis (1983–1985) and chaired the American Battle Monuments Commission (1985–1990). Goodpaster is the author of *For the Common Defense* (1977).

Lincoln Kirstein

LINCOLN KIRSTEIN IS AN AUTHOR AND ENTREPRENEUR WHO HAS HONORED AND DELIGHTED AMERICANS THROUGH HIS ENORMOUS CONTRIBUTION TO BALLET IN OUR COUNTRY. THROUGH HIS COMMITMENT, TWO MAJOR INSTITUTIONS OF AMERICAN DANCE, THE NEW YORK CITY BALLET AND THE SCHOOL OF AMERICAN BALLET, WERE CREATED AND FLOURISHED. DEVELOPING AND FOSTERING APPRECIATION FOR THE ARTS HAVE ALWAYS DEPENDED ON THE ENERGY, CREATIVITY, AND COMMITMENT OF INDIVIDUAL CITIZENS. LINCOLN KIRSTEIN STANDS TALL AS ONE OF A SELECT AND TREASURED FEW IN THE WORLD OF AMERICAN ART.

★ ★ ★

President Ronald Reagan awarded Kirstein the Presidential Medal of Freedom with the above citation during a White House ceremony March 26, 1984.

The son of wealthy parents, Lincoln Kirstein was born in Rochester, New York, in 1907, and was raised in an affluent section of Boston. Both his father and mother helped teach him an appreciation of the arts, though it was his mother who frequently took him to ballets and operas when he was growing up. His parents' lessons bore fruit while Kirstein was still a sophomore at Harvard, in 1927, when he founded a literary quarterly called *Hound & Horn*. During the seven-year life of the publication under Kirstein's editorship, it gained a national reputation and drew such noted contributors as T. S. Eliot, James Agee, and Katherine Anne Porter. Meanwhile, Kirstein also found time to organize the Harvard Society for Contemporary Art and to graduate in 1930.

He tried his hand at ballet dancing soon after graduating and eventually became interested in dance education. To that end he convinced the ballet dancer and choreographer George Balanchine to come to New York. Kirstein and others there formed the School of American Ballet in 1934 with Balanchine as director. *(See also the entry for Balanchine, p. 314.)*

Kirstein served as chief promoter and fund-raiser until 1936, when he formed Ballet Caravan. This new experimental group presented ballets based on American subjects and toured the United States until disbanding in 1941. Kirstein wrote librettos for a number of the ballets performed, including *Yankee Clipper, Filling Station,* and *Billy the Kid.* He married Fidelma Cadmus, an artist, in 1941.

Kirstein gained control of the School of American Ballet by buying up shares in 1940 and then reorganized it as a nonprofit institution under his leadership. As the school's president and director, he turned it into what he called "the West Point of the dance." Despite its demanding training program, the school flourished and by 1990 had five-hundred students.

With Balanchine, Kirstein also formed the New York City Ballet in 1948. Kirstein's second major and lasting contribution to American ballet, the group largely relies on students and graduates of the American School to produce its program of ballets.

Kirstein had a hand in other cultural pursuits as well. He helped found the American Shakespeare Festival and Academy in Stratford, Connecticut, and the American National Theater and Academy. He also published hundreds of books and articles about dance, art, literature, music, film, architecture, and photography. His autobiographical *Thirty Years: Lincoln Kirstein's the New York City Ballet* appeared in 1978, and his many books on dance include *Movement and Metaphor* (1970) and *Nijinsky Dancing* (1975). He died in 1996.

Louis L'Amour

THROUGH HIS WESTERN NOVELS, LOUIS L'AMOUR HAS PLAYED A LEADING ROLE IN SHAPING OUR NATIONAL IDENTITY. HIS WRITINGS PORTRAYED THE RUGGED INDIVIDUAL AND THE DEEP-SEATED VALUES OF THOSE WHO CONQUERED THE AMERICAN FRONTIER. STARTING OUT FROM HUMBLE BEGINNINGS, HE HAS LIVED A FULFILLING AND ADVENTUROUS LIFE. AN EMINENTLY SUCCESSFUL WRITER, MORE THAN 100 MILLION COPIES OF HIS NOVELS ARE IN PRINT, L'AMOUR'S DESCRIPTIONS OF AMERICA AND AMERICANS HAVE ADDED TO OUR UNDERSTANDING OF OUR PAST AND REAFFIRMED OUR POTENTIAL AS AN EXPLORING, PIONEERING, AND FREE PEOPLE.

★ ★ ★

President Ronald Reagan awarded L'Amour the Presidential Medal of Freedom with the above citation during a White House ceremony March 26, 1984.

The son of a veterinarian and the great-grandson of a settler who had been scalped by Apaches, Louis L'Amour was born in Jamestown, North Dakota, in 1908. He came from a long line of writers—thirty-three of his forebears had made a living through writing during the previous century—and family stories about settling the West fascinated him as a youth. But he did not start writing until he was in his thirties. Instead, the young L'Amour sought out a life of adventure, dropping out of school at age fifteen and drifting from job to job. He eventually spent time as a lumberjack, miner, elephant handler, cattle skinner, and deckhand on a schooner, among other jobs, and found his share of adventure. He survived a shipwreck in the West Indies, was stranded in the Mojave Desert, and for a time roamed the mountains of Tibet and western China with a bandit gang.

During the 1930s L'Amour fought as a professional light-heavyweight boxer and, in addition to posting thirty-four knockouts, also published his first book, a collection of poems called *Smoke from This Altar* (1939). Then, as an army officer during World War II, he entertained fellow soldiers with stories about his adventures and about the West. Taking the final, fateful step toward his writing career after the war, he started writing adventure stories for magazines. His first Western novel, *Hopalong Cassidy and the Riders of High Rock,* was published in 1951. *Hondo,* which became one of his most popular titles, appeared in 1953 and was made into a hit movie starring John Wayne the following year. L'Amour married Katherine Elizabeth Adams in 1956.

By 1955 L'Amour was under contract to write three Western novels a year, and a number were made into films. His Westerns were typically fast-paced adventures fleshed out with well-researched period detail. Law invariably wins out over lawlessness, but with surprisingly little violence, in L'Amour's novels.

In the 1970s, L'Amour began writing a series of novels tracing the lives of three families of settlers who left Europe and made their homes in the American West. *Treasure Mountain* (1972), *Sackett's Land* (1974), *The Man from Broken Hills* (1975), and *Fair Blows the Wind* (1978) were all from the family series.

Though largely ignored in literary circles, L'Amour published eighty-six novels and fourteen short-story collections in nearly four decades as a novelist. By the late 1980s all of his books were still in print, and an astounding two-hundred million copies were in circulation worldwide. "I guess I'm an industry," L'Amour once quipped.

In addition to receiving the Presidential Medal of Freedom, he also was the first novelist to receive the Congressional Gold Medal. L'Amour had just published his last novel, *The Haunted Mesa,* and was just proofreading his autobiography, *Education of a Wandering Man,* when he died in 1988. He was eighty years old.

Norman Vincent Peale

WITH A DEEP UNDERSTANDING OF HUMAN BEHAVIOR AND AN APPRECIATION FOR GOD'S ROLE IN OUR LIVES, DR. NORMAN VINCENT PEALE HELPED ORIGINATE A PHILOSOPHY OF HAPPINESS. THROUGH THE AMERICAN FOUNDATION OF RELIGION AND PSYCHIATRY AND HIS MANY BOOKS, DR. PEALE BECAME AN ADVOCATE OF THE JOY OF LIFE, HELPING MILLIONS FIND NEW MEANING IN THEIR LIVES. FEW AMERICANS HAVE CONTRIBUTED SO MUCH TO THE PERSONAL HAPPINESS OF THEIR FELLOW CITIZENS AS DR. NORMAN VINCENT PEALE.

★ ★ ★

President Ronald Reagan awarded Peale the Presidential Medal of Freedom with the above citation during a White House ceremony March 26, 1984.

Among the most influential religious figures of his day, Norman Vincent Peale was born in Bowersville, Ohio, in 1898. The son of a Methodist minister, he was shy and weak-willed as a youth, but he managed to overcome these traits in high school by becoming a star debater. After graduating from Ohio Wesleyan University (1920), he tried newspaper reporting for a year and then began theological studies at Boston University.

Peale was ordained a Methodist minister in 1922 and after earning his master's degree at Boston University (1924), was assigned variously to three Methodist churches in the 1920s, including the University Methodist Church in Syracuse, New York. He never forgot his father's advice that "the way to the human heart is through simplicity," and at each church his dynamic preaching style dramatically increased the congregation. What he later called his "obsession" with getting the Christian message out to everyone possible led him to take up preaching on the radio in 1927, making him one of the first American clerics to tap the power of the mass media. Three years later Peale married Loretta Ruth Stafford.

The prestigious Marble Collegiate Church in New York City became Peale's spiritual home in 1932. Founded in 1628 and regarded as the oldest continuous Protestant congregation in America, the church had lost the bulk of its members. Peale's preaching eventually brought them back in droves, however, with overflow crowds watching him on closed circuit television from the 1950s onward. Meanwhile, his Christian message and his fame spread rapidly. Peale began a weekly NBC radio program in 1935, *The Art of Living,* which by the mid–1950s reached an estimated five–million radio listeners. By that time his monthly magazine *Guideposts* also was growing rapidly.

Peale, meanwhile, became one of the first clerics to realize the potential benefit from a marriage of religion and psychiatry. As minister of Marble Collegiate Church, he worried about being unprepared to help members of his congregation in the early 1930s, especially those who had been devastated by the stock market crash of 1929. His wife, Ruth, suggested finding a psychiatrist to help them, leading Peale to a Freudian psychiatrist named Dr. Smiley Blanton. The two created a successful clinic at the church and in 1951 organized the nonprofit American Foundation of Religion and Psychiatry, which served hundreds of patients.

His biggest success, however, came with a book that applied simple Christian faith and some basic psychology to problems of everyday life. Peale's first effort in this direction was *The Art of Living*, a collection of short essays published in 1937. His fourth book, *A Guide to Confident Living* (1948), was his first to hit the bestseller list. But it was *The Power of Positive Thinking* (1952) that really struck a nerve. That book remained on the bestseller list for three straight years and established Peale and his message as a national phenomenon. Riding the wave of media attention, Peale hosted a television advice show called "What's Your Trouble?" (1952–1968), wrote a nationally syndicated newspaper column, and published dozens more books (forty-six during his lifetime). His life was the subject of a 1963 movie, *One Man's Way*.

Peale's fame also drew criticism, however, including charges that he too often oversimplified Christian doctrine and that his message was just a matter of moral pragmatism. Peale's political activities also created controversies from time to time. In one notable case he publicly opposed John F. Kennedy for president in 1960 because of concerns about Kennedy's Roman Catholicism. Later he drew fire for continuing to visit President Richard Nixon, his longtime friend and a congregant, throughout the Watergate scandal.

Peale, whose sundry enterprises and faith in the power of positive thought made him a wealthy man, continued preaching at Marble Collegiate well into the 1980s. His last book, *This Incredible Century*, was published in 1991 and brought total sales of his books to nearly twenty-million copies. Peale died at his estate in Pawling, New York, in 1993. He was ninety-five.

John Roosevelt "Jackie" Robinson

As an individual of courage and conviction, and as a skilled and dedicated athlete, Jackie Robinson stood tall among his peers. His courage opened the door of professional sports to all Americans when, in 1947, he became the first black baseball player in the major leagues. He bravely demonstrated to all that skill and sportsmanship, not race or ethnic background, are the qualities by which athletes should be judged. In doing so, he struck a mighty blow for equality, freedom, and the American way of life. Jackie Robinson was a good citizen, a great man, and a true American champion.

★ ★ ★

President Ronald Reagan awarded Robinson a posthumous Presidential Medal of Freedom with the above citation during a White House ceremony March 26, 1984. Robinson's wife, Rachel, accepted the award on her late husband's behalf.

A star player for the Brooklyn Dodgers, John Roosevelt Robinson was born in Cairo, Georgia, in 1919. He was raised in Pasadena, California, after his father, a farmworker, deserted the family. At Pasadena Junior College and later at the University of California at Los Angeles (UCLA), Robinson became an all-around athlete, starring in football, basketball, baseball, and track, as well as golf, swimming, and tennis. He left UCLA in his junior year, however, to help support his mother.

After playing the fall 1941 football season as a Honolulu Bears halfback, Robinson was drafted into the army and assigned to a cavalry post in Kansas. Helped by heavyweight boxing champ Joe Louis, Robinson got the ban on blacks lifted at the army officer candidate school and in 1943 earned his commission as a second lieutenant. He soon began protesting discriminatory practices in army life and even faced a court-martial rather than move to the back of a segregated army bus.

Though acquitted in the matter, Robinson was finally discharged in late 1944 for medical reasons relating to past football injuries. Some months later Robinson began playing shortstop for the Kansas City Monarchs, a baseball team in the Negro American League.

Brooklyn Dodgers co-owner Branch Rickey meanwhile had been looking for the right black athlete to break the color barrier and begin integration of the all-white major-league baseball teams.

Rickey settled on Robinson as the ideal candidate, signing him in October 1945 after getting his promise not to respond publicly to racial taunting. Robinson's signing generated widespread publicity, and his debut with the Dodgers farm team, the Montreal Royals, on April 18, 1946, could not have been a better demonstration of his athletic ability. In five at bats he hit three singles and a three-run homer. Robinson, known for his uncanny ability at base-stealing, also stole two bases and forced the pitcher to balk twice, thereby scoring four runs.

The Dodgers brought Robinson up from the farm team for the 1947 season, and that year he became the first black to play major league baseball in the twentieth century. By season's end he was voted the 1947 rookie of the year. Two years later he led the league with a .342 batting average and was named most valuable player. Ultimately, the second baseman played ten seasons with the Dodgers and helped them win six National League pennants.

After retiring from baseball in 1957, Robinson became involved in various business ventures and, as a role model for black athletes, also sought to widen employment opportunities for blacks. Robinson was elected to the Baseball Hall of Fame at Cooperstown, New York, in 1962 and a decade later published his autobiography, *I Never Had It Made*. He died in 1972, at age fifty-three.

Anwar el-Sādāt

PRESIDENT ANWAR EL-SĀDĀT, AS A SOLDIER, LED HIS COUNTRY IN WAR, BUT HIS GREATEST ACTS OF COURAGE CAME IN PURSUIT OF PEACE. HE CAPTURED THE IMAGINATION OF PEOPLE EVERYWHERE BY TAKING THE FIRST GREAT STEP TOWARD ACHIEVING A LASTING PEACE BETWEEN EGYPT AND ISRAEL. HIS HUMANITY AND SENSE OF RESPONSIBILITY, EVEN NOW THAT HE IS GONE, REMAIN A GIANT FORCE FOR PEACE AND STABILITY IN THE WORLD. ANWAR EL-SĀDĀT WAS A PEACEMAKER OF MONU-MENTAL WISDOM AND TENDERNESS WHO WILL REMAIN FOREVER A HERO IN THE HEARTS OF THE AMERICAN PEOPLE.

★ ★ ★

President Ronald Reagan awarded Sādāt a posthumous Presidential Medal of Freedom with the above citation during a White House ceremony March 26, 1984. Gamal el-Sādāt accepted the medal on his late father's behalf.

The Egyptian president who became the first Arab leader to sign a peace treaty with Israel, Anwar el-Sādāt was born in a Nile Delta village in 1918. His father was a clerk, and Sādāt, who wanted to become an army officer, graduated from the Abbassia Military Academy in 1938. At the academy he became close friends with Gamal Abdel Nasser, who would later overthrow the British-supported Egyptian monarchy, and in 1938 Sādāt, Nasser, and others formed a secret revolutionary group to liberate Egypt.

Sādāt was imprisoned twice during the 1940s for conspiring against the British but was restored as an army officer just a year after his last release in 1949, thanks to influential friends. In 1952 he joined Nasser in the bloodless coup that ousted the Egyptian monarchy and backed Nasser's bid for the presidency in 1956. For much of Nasser's long term of office, Sādāt held high-level but relatively unimportant posts. He did serve as vice president (1964–1966, 1969–1970), though, and after Nasser's death in 1970 he succeeded to the presidency.

President Sādāt proved an astute judge of the political climate and soon dismissed his chief rivals in the government, ousted the corps of Soviet military advisers in Egypt, and muzzled the unpopular secret police. Then in 1973 he led Egypt, allied with Syria, in a surprise attack on Israel that for a time had the formidable Israeli army on the defensive.

Even though Israel retook most of the Gaza Strip battleground, Sādāt gained considerable prestige in the Arab world as a result of the 1973 war. The United States also took a greater diplomatic interest in Egypt, and talks between Sādāt and U.S. Secretary of State Henry A. Kissinger led to limited Egyptian-Israeli accords in 1974 and 1975. The big breakthrough in the Mideast peace process came in 1977, though, when Sādāt made a historic first visit by an Arab leader to the Israeli parliament.

High-level peace talks between Egypt and Israel then began. President Jimmy Carter broke a serious deadlock in 1978 with the Camp David accords, which established a framework for peace. Sādāt and Israeli Prime Minister Menachem Begin won the Nobel Peace Prize that year and in 1979 finally concluded a historic peace treaty, ending thirty years of hostility between the two countries.

In the months following, Sādāt was hailed as a hero in the West and by many of his fellow Egyptians. But his Arab neighbors and Muslim extremists within his own country reviled him as a traitor for dealing with the hated Israelis. By 1981 he had to order a widespread crackdown against unruly Muslim militants in Egypt. Later that year the extremists struck back by assassinating him during a military review in Cairo.

Sādāt was sixty-two years old at his death. He was married to his second wife, Gehan, having divorced his previous wife. Sādāt published his memoirs, *In Search of Identity,* in 1978.

Eunice Kennedy Shriver

WITH ENORMOUS CONVICTION AND UNRELENTING EFFORT,
EUNICE KENNEDY SHRIVER HAS LABORED ON BEHALF OF
AMERICA'S LEAST POWERFUL PEOPLE, THE MENTALLY RETARDED.
OVER THE LAST TWO DECADES, SHE HAS BEEN ON THE
FOREFRONT OF NUMEROUS INITIATIVES ON THE BEHALF OF THE
MENTALLY RETARDED, FROM CREATING DAY CAMPS, TO ESTAB-
LISHING RESEARCH CENTERS, TO THE FOUNDING OF THE SPECIAL
OLYMPICS. HER DECENCY AND GOODNESS HAVE TOUCHED THE
LIVES OF MANY, AND EUNICE KENNEDY SHRIVER DESERVES
AMERICA'S PRAISE, GRATITUDE, AND LOVE.

★ ★ ★

*President Ronald Reagan awarded Shriver the Presidential Medal of
Freedom with the above citation during a White House ceremony
March 26, 1984.*

Eunice Kennedy Shriver was born Eunice Mary Kennedy in
Brookline, Massachusetts, in 1922. Her father was Joseph P. Kennedy,
a successful businessman who went on to become the U.S.
ambassador to Great Britain. She graduated from Stanford
University in 1943 with a bachelor's degree in sociology.

During the 1940s she worked in the special war problems division
of the State Department (1943–1945) and as secretary of the Justice
Department National Conference on the Prevention and Control of
Juvenile Delinquency. From 1951 to 1954 she was a social worker for
the Chicago Juvenile Court and for a charity house there. Meanwhile,
she married Robert Sargent Shriver in 1953 *(See also the entry for
Robert Sargent Shriver, p. 507.)*

The year she was married, Shriver convinced her father to focus
the Joseph P. Kennedy, Jr., Foundation on mental retardation,
because her older sister Rosemary was retarded. (Her father formed
the foundation in memory of her brother Joseph Jr., who had been
killed in World War II.) Shriver's husband became the director of the
foundation, and in 1956 she was named executive vice president.

She continued her social work during the late 1950s, but in the
early 1960s, with her brother John F. Kennedy in the White House,
Shriver found new opportunities to advance her work in behalf of
the mentally retarded. In 1961 she served as a consultant to President
Kennedy's Panel on Mental Retardation. That summer she also
founded a camp where retarded children could learn sports. Then,
the following year, she publicly revealed her sister Rosemary's condition in a magazine article, hoping to focus public attention on the
problems of mental retardation.

Convinced that athletics benefited the mentally retarded spiritually as well as physically, Shriver founded the Special Olympics for them in 1968. The program became a lasting success and by 1987 at the seventh International Special Olympics over 4500 disadvantaged children and adults were competing.

Shriver founded another organization, Community and Caring, in 1986 and in 1990 retired as head of the Special Olympics. That year she was named the Special Olympics honorary chairman.

Terence James Cooke

A SAINTLY MAN AND A GREAT SPIRITUAL LEADER, TERENCE CARDINAL COOKE INSPIRED HIS COUNTRYMEN WITH HIS DEDICATION TO HIS CHURCH, DEVOTION TO HIS FLOCK, AND SERVICE TO HIS COUNTRY. AS THE MILITARY VICAR TO OUR NATION'S ARMED FORCES, CARDINAL COOKE WORKED TIRELESSLY ON BEHALF OF THOSE WHO SERVE THEIR COUNTRY IN UNIFORM. AS A PATRIOT AND NATIONAL LEADER, HE PREACHED THE LOVE OF COUNTRY AND CHAMPIONED THE CAUSE OF HUMAN FREEDOM. HE WILL LIVE IN THE MEMORY OF HIS COUNTRYMEN AS A MAN OF COMPASSION, COURAGE, AND PERSONAL HOLINESS.

★ ★ ★

President Ronald Reagan awarded Cardinal Cooke a posthumous Presidential Medal of Freedom with the above citation. Archbishop O'Connor received the award on Cardinal Cooke's behalf during a New York State Federation of Catholic School Parents dinner held at the New York Hilton April 5, 1984.

The son of Irish immigrants, Terence James Cooke was born in New York City in 1921 and raised in a pious Catholic household. After his mother died in 1930, an aunt helped raise him, and during high school he decided on the priesthood. Completing his religious studies at Manhattan's Cathedral College and Saint Joseph's Seminary in Yonkers, New York, Cooke was ordained in 1945 and spent the next two years at Saint Athanasius Church in the Bronx. This would remain his only experience as a full-time parish priest.

Cooke earned his master's degree in social work from Catholic University of America in 1949 and later was assigned to Catholic Charities of New York. There he revealed a talent for fund-raising, and as bursar of Saint Joseph's Seminary (1954–1956), he proved an able handler of finances. But it was his close association with Cardinal Spellman, archbishop of New York and head of the Roman Catholic church in America, that led Cooke to the top of the church hierarchy. Cardinal Spellman was impressed by Cooke, his personal secretary starting in 1957, and moved him into positions of increasing importance. Eventually Spellman pressed Pope Paul VI to name Cooke as his successor.

In March 1968, three months after Cardinal Spellman's death, Pope Paul VI named Cooke archbishop of New York and Military Vicar of all Catholics in the U.S. armed forces. The following year Cooke became a cardinal. He was just forty-eight years old, which was unusually young.

Cooke took office at a time of great difficulty for the church and the country as a whole. Resistance to the Vietnam War, riots in black ghettos, the sexual revolution, the abortion-rights movement, and other bitterly divisive controversies wracked the country and challenged the church. Meanwhile, dissatisfaction with fundamental teachings of the church was mounting, and the church's pressing financial problems threatened to force cuts in social services it provided.

Cooke worked quietly and patiently to resolve the problems. He became famous for his reshaping of the archdiocese according to the principles of the Second Vatican Council, instituting a conciliar form of government to replace the old hierarchical system. He sought more welfare benefits for the poor, strengthened a program to recruit and train Spanish-speaking priests, shored up inner-city parochial schools by establishing an interparish program in which wealthier parishes helped poorer ones, and instituted a scholarship program to help minority students attend parochial schools. A moderate conservative who willingly listened to divergent views, he nevertheless took a firm stand on certain issues, most notably abortion, racism, and terrorism.

Highly regarded as a devoted, mild-mannered, and effective church leader, Cardinal Cooke died of leukemia in 1983. He was sixty-two.

Joseph M. A. H. Luns

On his retirement, after almost thirteen years at NATO's helm, I take immense pleasure in awarding Secretary General Joseph Luns the Presidential Medal of Freedom—America's highest civilian award—for his staunch defense of the transatlantic partnership; for his manifold initiatives to strengthen the Atlantic

ALLIANCE; FOR HIS VISION OF AND TIRELESS EFFORTS TOWARD BUILDING A MORE SECURE ATLANTIC COMMUNITY; AND FOR A CAREER OF UNCOMMON DEDICATION AND SINGULAR CONTRIBUTIONS TO PEACE AND THE ATLANTIC ALLIANCE.

★ ★ ★

President Ronald Reagan awarded Luns the Presidential Medal of Freedom with the above citation during a White House ceremony May 30, 1984.

A longtime affairs minister in the Dutch government, Joseph Marie Antoine Hubert Luns was born in Rotterdam, the Netherlands, in 1911. His father was an artist, teacher, and author of books on art, but Luns decided to study law in college. He received his doctor of jurisprudence from the University of Amsterdam in 1937 and began working as a diplomatic attaché at the Dutch Ministry of Foreign Affairs the following year. The Baroness Elisabeth Cornelia van Heemstra became his wife in 1939.

Luns was stationed with the Dutch diplomatic corps in Switzerland when Nazi German troops overran the Netherlands in 1940. Serving the Dutch government in exile, he was posted to London after 1943 and was first secretary of the Dutch embassy there from 1944 to 1949. His last post in the diplomatic corps was as a member of the Dutch United Nations delegation (1949–1952).

Appointed minister without portfolio for the Netherlands' Ministry of Foreign Affairs in 1952, Luns became minister for foreign affairs in 1956 and held onto the cabinet post continuously until 1971. During his many years in office, Luns was an outspoken advocate of greater unity among European nations and, acting on behalf of the Netherlands, signed the original agreement creating the European Economic Community. He later supported Britain's admission to the group despite objections from France and, supporting further integration of European nations, called their growing interdependence an "inescapable reality."

A well-known figure in European circles by the early 1970s, Luns was named to succeed Manlio Brosio as secretary-general of the North Atlantic Treaty Organization (NATO) in 1971. *(See also the entry for Brosio, p. 196.)* For the next thirteen years he presided over the political arm of NATO and confronted various crises involving NATO members, including Greece's withdrawal from NATO in 1974 to protest a Turkish invasion of Cyprus, and a dispute over coastal fishing rights between Britain and Iceland.

Despite considerable opposition, he backed the basing of U.S. intermediate-range nuclear missiles in Western Europe during the late 1970s to counter recently deployed Soviet SS-20 missiles. (The Netherlands government agreed to allow NATO missiles on its soil in 1979.) Luns also supported development of neutron warheads for missiles and otherwise sought to maintain NATO as an effective deterrent force. Meanwhile, he also worked toward improved relations with East European nations and the Soviets.

A staunch ally of the United States during his term as NATO secretary, he was awarded the Presidential Medal of Freedom when he retired from NATO in 1984.

Henry M. "Scoop" Jackson

REPRESENTATIVE AND SENATOR FOR MORE THAN FOUR DECADES, HENRY MARTIN JACKSON WAS ONE OF THE GREAT LAWMAKERS OF OUR CENTURY. HE HELPED TO BUILD THE COMMUNITY OF DEMOCRACIES AND WORKED TIRELESSLY TO KEEP IT VIGOROUS AND SECURE. HE PIONEERED IN THE PRESERVATION OF THE NATION'S NATURAL HERITAGE, AND HE EMBODIED INTEGRITY AND DECENCY IN THE PROFESSION OF POLITICS. FOR THOSE WHO MAKE FREEDOM THEIR CAUSE HENRY JACKSON WILL ALWAYS INSPIRE HONOR, COURAGE, AND HOPE.

★ ★ ★

President Ronald Reagan awarded Jackson a posthumous Presidential Medal of Freedom with the above citation during a White House ceremony June 26, 1984. Helen Jackson accepted the medal on her late husband's behalf.

Born in Everett, Washington, in 1912, Henry M. Jackson was the son of Norwegian immigrants and got the nickname "Scoop" while working as a newspaper delivery boy in Everett. Years later he worked his way through the University of Washington and, after earning his law degree there in 1935, entered private practice in Everett. At about that time he also became head of the local Democratic party organization.

Jackson moved quickly after that, winning election first as a county prosecutor and then, in 1940, as a member of the U.S. House of Representatives from Washington State. He kept his House seat while in the army during World War II and served in the House without further interruption until winning his Senate seat in 1952. Sometimes called the "Senator from Boeing" because the powerful defense contractor was located in Washington State, Jackson spent the next thirty years in the Senate and became one of the country's most influential lawmakers.

Soon after becoming a senator, he established a national reputation through his decisive cross-examination of Sen. Joseph R.

McCarthy during the televised Army-McCarthy hearings of 1954. In the years following, he served variously as chairman of the Senate Energy and Natural Resources Committee, the Government Operations Committee, and the Permanent Subcommittee on Investigations. Jackson also was a member of the Armed Services Committee, the Select Committee on Intelligence, and the Joint Congressional Committee on Atomic Energy. A liberal Democrat, he solidly supported organized labor, civil rights legislation, and environmental concerns, but he pushed for a strong military and a hard line against the Soviet bloc.

Jackson, who married Helen Hardin in 1961, was a firm supporter of U.S. involvement in Vietnam during the 1960s and became a key figure in passing the Environmental Protection Act. Distrustful of the Soviet Union, he forced changes in the SALT I arms reduction treaty and helped defeat SALT II. Meanwhile, he was considered a possible presidential candidate during the 1970s, but his bids for the Democratic nomination failed in 1972 and 1976.

Called "a pillar" of the Senate, Jackson died unexpectedly of a heart attack in 1983. He was seventy-one years old.

William "Count" Basie

FOR MORE THAN HALF A CENTURY, WILLIAM "COUNT" BASIE ENRAPTURED THE PEOPLE OF AMERICA WITH HIS BRILLIANT AND INNOVATIVE WORK IN THE FIELD OF JAZZ. IN THE 1930'S AND 40'S, THE COUNT BECAME PART OF THE FABRIC OF AMERICAN LIFE AS THE LEADER OF ONE OF THE GREATEST BANDS OF THE BIG BAND ERA. HIS SONGS, FROM "APRIL IN PARIS" TO "ONE O'CLOCK JUMP," ARE AMERICAN CLASSICS. COUNT BASIE CUT A NOTCH IN MUSICAL HISTORY AND FOUND A PLACE IN OUR HEARTS FOREVER. AMONG THE ROYALTY OF AMERICAN ARTS AND ENTERTAINMENT, THERE IS NO ONE MORE HONORED AND MORE BELOVED THAN THE COUNT.

★ ★ ★

President Ronald Reagan awarded Basie a posthumous Presidential Medal of Freedom with the above citation during a White House ceremony May 23, 1985. Basie's son, Aaron Woodward, accepted the medal on his behalf.

A top African American jazz pianist, composer, and big-band leader, Count Basie was born just plain William Basie in Red Bank, New Jersey, in 1904. Both his parents were talented amateur musicians, and Basie's mother gave him his first lessons on the piano. During the early 1920s he landed jobs playing in New York while also studying informally with jazz pianist Fats Waller and others in the Harlem music scene. By his twentieth birthday, he was touring the vaudeville circuit both as a performer and as a musical director for blues singers and dancers.

Lured by the booming jazz nightclub scene in Kansas City, he headed West in 1926. Ironically, Basie's first job in Kansas City—as a theater organist—provided him with both a paycheck and his nickname. It was there that his distinctive playing style and personal manner inspired the nickname "Count," and Basie used the name for the rest of his life.

An important break came in 1929 when he joined Bennie Moten's Kansas City Orchestra. Renowned in the Midwest, it was among the pioneering groups in big-band jazz and featured a driving rhythm section that became a hallmark of Kansas City bands of that era. When Moten died unexpectedly in 1935, Basie reorganized the group, landing both important performances nationally and a recording contract with Decca Record Company. By the late 1930s, the Count Basie Orchestra ranked among the top big bands of the swing era.

Basie's sparse, sparkling piano style blended especially well with the strong rhythm section that characterized his band. In fact, Basie early on became known as the "Jump King" because many of his tunes had such an irresistible rhythmic quality. While Count Basie wrote such famous original compositions as "One O'Clock Jump," he was foremost a jazz band leader and a pianist with remarkable durability. He directed his band from 1935 until his death in 1984, with only a brief break during 1950 and 1951. He was eighty years old when he died.

Jacques-Yves Cousteau

FOR DECADES, CAPTAIN JACQUES-YVES COUSTEAU HAS BEEN A CELEBRATED UNDERSEA EXPLORER. HIS JOURNEYS ABOARD THE *Calypso* HAVE BECOME KNOWN TO MILLIONS THROUGH HIS BOOKS AND FILMS. HIS MANNED, UNDERSEA COLONIES YIELDED [A] WEALTH OF RESEARCH AND DATA AND MADE IMPORTANT TECHNICAL ADVANCES. HIS AQUALUNG HAS MADE UNDERWATER DIVING AVAILABLE TO ALL. CAPTAIN COUSTEAU PERHAPS HAS DONE MORE THAN ANY OTHER INDIVIDUAL TO REVEAL THE MYSTERIES OF THE OCEANS THAT COVER MORE THAN TWO-THIRDS OF THE SURFACE OF OUR PLANET. IT IS, THEREFORE, LIKELY THAT HE WILL BE REMEMBERED NOT ONLY AS A PIONEER IN HIS TIME, BUT AS A DOMINANT FIGURE IN WORLD HISTORY.

★ ★ ★

President Ronald Reagan awarded Cousteau the Presidential Medal of Freedom with the above citation during a White House ceremony May 23, 1985.

A co-inventor of the aqualung, Jacques-Yves Cousteau was born in Saint-Andre-de-Cubzac, France, in 1910 and did not show any special interest in underwater exploits until 1936, six years after his graduation from the French Naval Academy. Having already been at sea aboard various navy ships as a gunnery officer, he chanced to go swimming one day while wearing diving goggles. Catching his first glimpse of undersea life, Costeau was suddenly fascinated by the strange world beneath the sea. He became an avid *goggle-diver* and spear fisherman.

Longing to spend more time underwater without being encumbered by the heavy diving helmets and airhoses then in use, Cousteau began working on an improved underwater breathing system. A re-breather he built failed (it caused convulsions), but by late 1942 he had designed a diving lung made of three tanks strapped to the diver's back. In Paris he met Emile Gagnan, who had designed an automatic air valve, and in 1943 the two built the world's first successful aqualung. Manufactured widely after the war, their aqualung enabled divers to remain underwater for an hour without bulky, expensive equipment and opened up the undersea world to widespread exploration.

Cousteau, who had been a member of the French underground during World War II, set up the Undersea Research Group in 1946 with French navy backing and headed it until 1956. With that, the first of several groups he organized over the years, he began a career of experimentation and research that continues to the present day. In the early days he was a pioneer in diving techniques, underwater color photography, and underwater television. But it was as an explorer of the vast and mysterious undersea world that he became world famous.

In 1950 he outfitted a surplus minesweeper as an oceanographic research vessel, dubbed it the *Calypso*, and with his crew began his decades-long exploration of the marine world, recording vast amounts of data and extensively photographing all of the strange and beautiful creatures he found. He published many books of undersea photographs, such as *The Silent World* (1953) and more recently *Jacques Cousteau: The Ocean World* (1985), and produced highly acclaimed films, including *The Silent World* (1956), *The Golden Fish* (1959), and *The Desert Whales* (1969). Several of his films have won Academy Awards, Emmys, and Cannes film festival awards. Cousteau is probably even better known for the over one-hundred films he produced for television, including such series as "The Undersea World of Jacques-Yves Cousteau" (1968–1976) and "The Cousteau Odyssey Series" (1977–1981). He was inducted into the Television Academy Hall of Fame in 1987.

Over the years Cousteau has been closely associated with the environmental movement and in 1982 helped develop a wind propulsion system for ships, the Turbosail. He became a member of the prestigious Académie Française in 1989.

Jerome Hartwell Holland

DR. JEROME HARTWELL HOLLAND, ONE OF THIRTEEN CHILDREN IN A SMALL-TOWN FAMILY IN NEW YORK STATE, ROSE FROM POVERTY TO BECOME A LEADING EDUCATOR, CIVIL RIGHTS ACTIVIST, AUTHOR AND DIPLOMAT. DR. HOLLAND DEDICATED HIS CAREER TO IMPROVING THE LIVES OF OTHERS, PARTICULARLY HIS FELLOW BLACK AMERICANS, AND TO WORKING FOR PEACE. A MAN OF VIGOR AND WISDOM, DR. HOLLAND LED A LIFE OF SERVICE, THE MEMORY OF WHICH TODAY SERVES AS AN INSPIRATION TO MILLIONS.

★ ★ ★

President Ronald Reagan awarded Holland a posthumous Presidential Medal of Freedom with the above citation during a White House ceremony 23, 1985. Laura Holland accepted the medal on her late husband's behalf.

A longtime advocate of education as the best means of advancement for African Americans, Jerome Hartwell Holland was born in Auburn, New York, in 1916. His father, a gardener-handyman, put him to work when he was just eight, and Holland soon decided that applying himself in school was the best way out of poverty. His efforts eventually were rewarded handsomely; he graduated from Cornell University with honors and left his mark on collegiate football as well. As an end on the Cornell team, he was twice selected for All-American football teams.

Furthering his education remained Holland's chief goal, though. He won his master's degree in sociology from Cornell in 1941 and his doctorate from the University of Pennsylvania in 1950. In 1953 he became president of the predominately black Delaware State College and in 1960 was named president of Hampton Institute, in Hampton, Virginia. As an educator, Holland encouraged students to work within the system by getting the education and training they needed to move into better-paying jobs. He wrote the book *Black Opportunity* to promote his ideas on the subject.

Holland remained at Hampton Institute until 1970, when President Richard Nixon appointed him U.S. ambassador to Sweden. After two years in the diplomatic post, he resigned to become the first black board member of the New York Stock Exchange. Holland also served on the boards of several important corporations, including American Telephone and Telegraph, General Foods, Union Carbide, Chrysler, and Manufacturers Hanover.

Holland was married to Laura Mitchell. He died of cancer in 1985, at the age of sixty-nine.

Sidney Hook

SCHOLAR, PHILOSOPHER, AND THINKER—SIDNEY HOOK STANDS AS ONE OF THE MOST EMINENT INTELLECTUAL FORCES OF OUR TIME. HIS COMMITMENT TO RATIONAL THOUGHT AND CIVIL DISCOURSE HAS MADE HIM AN ELOQUENT SPOKESMAN FOR FAIR PLAY IN PUBLIC LIFE. HIS DEVOTION TO FREEDOM MADE HIM ONE OF THE FIRST TO WARN THE INTELLECTUAL WORLD OF ITS MORAL OBLIGATIONS AND PERSONAL STAKE IN THE STRUGGLE BETWEEN FREEDOM AND TOTALITARIANISM. A MAN OF TRUTH, A MAN OF ACTION, SIDNEY HOOK'S LIFE AND WORK MAKE HIM ONE OF AMERICA'S GREATEST SCHOLARS, PATRIOTS, AND LOVERS OF LIBERTY.

★ ★ ★

President Ronald Reagan awarded Hook the Presidential Medal of Freedom with the above citation during a White House ceremony May 23, 1985.

Born in Brooklyn, New York, in 1902, Sidney Hook was raised in a poor section of the city. He pursued a college education, though, and after graduating from City College of New York in 1923, went on to get advanced degrees at Columbia University. A protégé of the noted educator and pragmatic philosopher John Dewey, Hook had earned his doctorate in philosophy by 1927.

Hook began teaching philosophy at New York University in 1927 and soon after spent two years studying abroad in Germany and the Soviet Union. Promoted to assistant professor in 1932, he became chairman of the philosophy department at New York University three years later. He remained chairman for thirty-four years, until retiring in 1969.

Like many young intellectuals of his time, Hook was taken by Marxist ideals and the promise of the newly formed communist society in the Soviet Union. But he shocked fellow left-wing intellectuals in 1933 with his first important book, *Towards the Understanding of Karl Marx: A Revolutionary Interpretation,* in which he pointed out the vast differences between Marx's humanistic ideals and the reality of Soviet society under Stalin's dictatorship. By the mid–1930s Hook had broken completely with the communist movement and, while calling himself a social democrat, became an ardent foe of totalitarianism.

A firm believer that there are no absolutes, Hook based his moral philosophy on pragmatism, secularism, and rationalism. Decisions on how to respond to situations should be made by examining problems in the light of reason, he believed, not by blindly following one's emotions or religious beliefs. He called the spirit of absolutism "the greatest enemy of a liberal civilization" and held that even freedom could never be absolute, because any one individual who demands complete freedom automatically deprives another of some measure of freedom.

During his long career Hook spoke out on various contemporary issues, at times even supporting such conservative causes as maintaining a strong military and opposing racial quotas in university admissions. He wrote hundreds of articles and over thirty-five books, including *From Hegel to Marx* (1936), *The Hero in History* (1943), and *Pragmatism and the Tragic Sense of Life* (1974). His autobiography, *Out of Step: An Unquiet Life in the 20th Century,* was published in 1986.

After retiring from New York University in 1969, Hook became a senior research fellow at the Hoover Institution on War, Revolution, and Peace at Stanford University in California. He remained with the institute until his death in 1989. He was eighty-six years old.

Jeane Kirkpatrick

FOR FOUR YEARS AS THE REPRESENTATIVE OF THE UNITED STATES TO THE UNITED NATIONS, AMBASSADOR JEANE KIRKPATRICK HELD HIGH THE FLAG OF OUR COUNTRY WITH COURAGE AND WISDOM. SHE IS AN ENDLESSLY ARTICULATE SPOKESWOMAN FOR THE MORAL AND PRACTICAL BENEFITS OF FREEDOM AND A TIRELESS DEFENDER OF THE DECENCY OF THE WEST. JEANE KIRKPATRICK IS A PATRIOT, AND THERE IS NO HONOR MORE APPROPRIATE FOR HER THAN ONE ENTITLED, "THE PRESIDENTIAL MEDAL OF FREEDOM." IT'S BESTOWED THIS DAY BY A NATION THAT KNOWS JEANE KIRKPATRICK'S WORK HAS ONLY JUST BEGUN.

★ ★ ★

President Ronald Reagan awarded Kirkpatrick the Presidential Medal of Freedom with the above citation during a White House ceremony May 23, 1985.

The daughter of a wildcat oil prospector, Jeane Kirkpatrick was born Jeane Jordan in Duncan, Oklahoma, in 1926. She earned her bachelor's degree from Barnard College in 1948 and her master's degree in political science from Columbia University two years later. After further studies and stints as a researcher, she married a fellow academic and political scientist, Evron M. Kirkpatrick, in 1955 and for the next seven years devoted most of her time to raising her three children.

Returning to academia in 1962, Kirkpatrick became an assistant professor at Trinity College in Washington, D.C., and five years later moved to Georgetown University as an associate professor of political science. In 1968 she completed her doctorate at Columbia and in 1973 was promoted to full professor at Georgetown, a position she continues to hold.

Meanwhile, Kirkpatrick also proved a prolific writer, and she contributed to such periodicals as *Commentary* and *American Political Science Review* and published books on both domestic politics and foreign policy with increasing frequency during the 1970s. Her *Political Woman* (1974) reached an audience outside academic circles, but Kirkpatrick's writings ranged far beyond the confines of feminist concerns. Among her other works were *Dismantling the Parties: Reflections on Party Reform and Party Decomposition* (1978), *Dictatorships and Double Standards* (1982), *Legitimacy and Force* (1988), and *The Withering Away of the Totalitarian State* (1990).

A longtime Democrat who had worked actively on the Democratic National Committee during the 1970s, she was a member of the so-called neoconservative wing, which opposed counterculture and antiwar elements in the party. Her views on foreign policy especially turned increasingly conservative, and in 1977 she became a resident scholar at the conservative think tank the American Enterprise Institute for Public Policy. Two years later she wrote an article in *Commentary* denouncing what she saw as a double standard in the Carter administration's foreign policy in which the threat from pro-Soviet dictatorships was ignored while right-wing autocracies friendly to the United States were undermined. Her hardline anticommunist views caught Ronald Reagan's attention, and, after meeting with him in 1980, Kirkpatrick became an energetic supporter.

Kirkpatrick did not formally become a Republican until 1985, but in 1981 President Reagan made her U.S. representative to the United Nations, a cabinet-rank position in his administration. During the next four years she sought to promote the Reagan administration's policy of supporting pro-Western regimes in Central America, Pakistan, and elsewhere while taking a hardline stance against the Soviets and their allies. She did not, however, have ambitions for higher office, and in the mid–1980s she quashed talk of her becoming a vice-presidential candidate.

Since leaving public office in 1985, Kirkpatrick has continued writing books and teaching, and she remains a senior fellow at the American Enterprise Institute. Since 1985 she also has written a syndicated newspaper column.

George M. Low

DURING HIS DISTINGUISHED PUBLIC SERVICE AT NASA, DR. GEORGE M. LOW HELPED LEAD THIS NATION'S SPACE PROGRAM TO ITS GREATEST ACHIEVEMENTS, DIRECTING THE FIRST MANNED LANDING ON THE MOON AND PLANNING THE SHUTTLE PROGRAM. AS PRESIDENT OF RENSSELAER POLYTECHNIC INSTITUTE, HE CONTINUED TO MAKE HIS MARK ON THE FUTURE, IMPROVING ACADEMIC EXCELLENCE AND LAUNCHING A PROGRAM TO SPUR TECHNOLOGICAL INNOVATION. OUR NATION WILL BE REAPING THE BENEFITS OF HIS WISDOM AND VISION FOR YEARS TO COME.

★ ★ ★

President Ronald Reagan awarded Low a posthumous Presidential Medal of Freedom with the above citation at a White House ceremony May 23, 1985. Mary Low accepted the award on her late husband's behalf.

Born in Vienna, Austria, in 1926, George M. Low moved to the United States with his family in 1940, shortly after the outbreak of World War II. After serving in the U.S. Army during the war, he became a U.S. citizen in 1946 and entered Rensselaer Polytechnic Institute. Low went on to get his master's degree in aeronautical engineering there and married Mary Ruth McNamara in 1949.

After graduating, Low began working for the National Advisory Committee for Aeronautics (NACA), the forerunner of the National Aeronautics and Space Administration (NASA). A specialist in problems of aerodynamic heating, he joined other NASA researchers in advising President John F. Kennedy that the United States could send astronauts to the moon by the end of the 1960s.

Spurred by Soviet successes in the "space race," President Kennedy committed the nation to just that goal in 1961. By the mid–sixties the space program was in high gear, and Low had risen to deputy director of Houston's Manned Spacecraft Center. But then tragedy struck in 1967; a fire in the *Apollo 1* space capsule killed three astronauts during a test, and the program came to a standstill while engineers redesigned the Apollo spacecraft.

Low became head of the Apollo program after the 1967 accident and oversaw the thousands of changes and tests that went into rebuilding the spacecraft. Two years later he celebrated with the thousands of Apollo program personnel—and the world—when the first manned moon landing went off without a hitch in July 1969. Low remained program head through all six Apollo moon landings in the late 1960s and early 1970s.

Named acting administrator of NASA in the 1970s, Low left the space program in 1976 to become president of Rensselaer Polytechnic Institute. He promoted a sharp increase in research at the college, pushing up the annual research volume from $20 million to $600 million in the span of just eight years. He also oversaw the development of a three-hundred-acre research park near the college.

Low died of cancer in 1984, fifteen years and one day after the *Apollo 11* spacecraft left earth for its historic moon landing. Low was fifty-eight years old.

Frank Reynolds

REPORTER AND ANCHORMAN, FAMILY MAN AND A PATRIOT, FRANK REYNOLDS'S LIFE EXEMPLIFIED THE HIGHEST STANDARDS OF HIS PROFESSION. HIS COMMITMENT TO THE TRUTH, HIS UNFAILING SENSE OF FAIRNESS, HIS LONG EXPERIENCE AS BOTH WITNESS AND PARTICIPANT IN THE GREAT EVENTS OF OUR TIME

EARNED HIM THE RESPECT OF HIS COLLEAGUES AND THE TRUST AND ADMIRATION OF THE AMERICAN PEOPLE. WE HONOR HIS MEMORY FOR HIS AGGRESSIVE BUT FAIR-MINDED REPORTING AND DEVOTION TO PROFESSION, TO FAMILY, AND TO COUNTRY.

★ ★ ★

President Ronald Reagan awarded Reynolds a posthumous Presidential Medal of Freedom with the above citation during a White House ceremony May 23, 1985. Reynolds's wife, Henrietta, accepted the award on her late husband's behalf.

The chief anchor of ABC "World News Tonight" from 1978 until 1983, Frank Reynolds was born in East Chicago, Illinois, in 1924. He attended Wabash College in Indiana and served in the army during World War II. After the war he entered the emerging television broadcast industry by way of station WJOB in Hammond, Indiana, in 1947 and spent fourteen years with various Chicago television stations before moving to ABC network news in 1965. He had anchored daily news programs for the ABC Chicago affiliate WBKB from 1963 to 1965.

ABC made Reynolds its first network news White House correspondent in 1965, and for the next three years he reported from Washington. Between 1968 and 1970 he was coanchor, with Howard K. Smith, of "ABC Evening News" but lost his position as anchor when Harry Reasoner left CBS for ABC. Reynolds remained with ABC, though, covering political campaigns, the space program, and other special events. In 1972 his coverage of President Richard Nixon's historic trip to China figured in the decision to award ABC an Emmy that year. (Reynolds himself won an Emmy in 1980 for his work on the ABC "Post Election Special Edition.")

Reynolds became chief anchor of ABC "World News Tonight" in 1978 and that year introduced ABC's mobile anchor concept during coverage of the Camp David talks between Egypt and Israel. He anchored the newscasts from Camp David and the White House while the talks were going on. The following year he anchored a late-night news special, "The Iran Crisis: America Held Hostage," which gave both a daily news recap and the latest updates on the hostage crisis in Iran. That popular show gave birth to ABC's long-running late-night favorite, "Nightline."

During his five years as chief anchor, he covered such major stories as space-shuttle missions, President Reagan's inauguration, and the assassination attempts against both Reagan and Pope John Paul II. But for those five years he kept his ongoing battle with bone cancer a tightly guarded secret. He worked until a few months before he died in 1983. Just fifty-nine years old, he was survived by his wife, the former Henrietta Mary Harpster.

S. Dillon Ripley

Upon becoming Secretary of the Smithsonian Institute, S. Dillon Ripley ordered the statue of Joseph Henry turned so that it faced not inward toward the castle, but outward toward the Mall, thereby signaling his intentions to open the Institution to the world. During the next 20 years, S. Dillon Ripley did just that, opening eight museums and doubling the number of visitors to the Institution. With dedication and tireless effort, S. Dillon Ripley made the Smithsonian one of the greatest museums and centers of learning on Earth.

★ ★ ★

President Ronald Reagan awarded Ripley the Presidential Medal of Freedom with the above citation during a White House ceremony May 23, 1985.

An ornithologist who became the Smithsonian Institution's longtime director, S. Dillon Ripley was born in New York City in 1913. His father was a stockbroker, and Ripley was raised in comfortable circumstances. He discovered his fascination for birds while still a teenager but honored his father's wishes and took pre-law classes while at Yale University, graduating with a bachelor's degree in 1936.

From that time forward, though, he pursued his interest in birds, joining zoological expeditions to New Guinea and Sumatra sponsored by the Philadelphia Academy of Natural Sciences. Having literally learned his zoology in the field, he spent a year in the late 1930s as a volunteer assistant at New York City's American Museum of Natural History and then went on to earn his doctorate from Harvard University in 1943. Meanwhile, he published an account of his adventures in New Guinea, *Trail of the Money Bird* (1942).

After serving with the Office of Strategic Services in the Far East during World War II, Ripley became a lecturer and associate curator of Yale University's Peabody Museum of Natural History. During the late 1940s he continued making zoological expeditions, including the first ever by Western naturalists to Nepal in 1948 (recounted in *Search for the Spiny Babbler,* 1952). Ripley married Mary Moncrieffe Livingston in 1949.

Yale named him director of the Peabody Museum in 1959, but Ripley spent only four years there before becoming the Smithsonian Institution's chief administrative officer in 1964. Taking over control of what is popularly regarded as "the nation's attic," he sought to make the museum a center for education and research, as well as a popular public attraction. Over the years he greatly enlarged the facility, adding the National Air and Space Museum, the Renwick Gallery, the National Portrait Gallery, and the Hirshhorn Museum and Sculpture Garden and making it the world's largest museum complex. He also sharply increased attendance (millions visit the museum each year) and spurred research by the museum's scholars.

Ripley retired in 1984, having served twenty years as head of the Smithsonian.

Frank Sinatra

FOR NEARLY 50 YEARS, AMERICANS HAVE BEEN PUTTING THEIR DREAMS AWAY AND LETTING ONE MAN TAKE THEIR PLACE IN OUR HEARTS. SINGER, ACTOR, HUMANITARIAN, PATRON OF ART AND MENTOR OF ARTISTS, FRANCIS ALBERT SINATRA AND HIS IMPACT ON AMERICA'S POPULAR CULTURE ARE WITHOUT PEER. HIS LOVE OF COUNTRY, HIS GENEROSITY TOWARD THOSE LESS FORTUNATE, HIS DISTINCTIVE ART, AND HIS WINNING AND PASSIONATE PERSONA MAKE HIM ONE OF OUR MOST REMARKABLE AND DISTIN-GUISHED AMERICANS, AND ONE WHO TRULY DID IT "HIS WAY."

* * *

President Ronald Reagan awarded Sinatra the Presidential Medal of Freedom with the above citation during a White House ceremony May 23, 1985.

Ranked among the greatest pop singers of this century, Frank Sinatra was born in Hoboken, New Jersey, in 1917. The son of Italian immigrants, he discovered an interest in music, especially singing, after his uncle gave him a ukulele. He did help organize his high school glee club but otherwise had no plans to become a singer until 1936, when a Bing Crosby concert he attended suddenly inspired him. With no formal musical training, Sinatra quit work and began singing with local groups.

He spent the better part of 1937 and 1938 singing at a northern New Jersey roadhouse called the Rustic Cabin, while doing occasional radio shows for free just to get the exposure. After marrying Nancy Barbato in 1939, Sinatra finally got his big break. He began touring with Harry James's band that same year. A few months later Sinatra broke his contract to join an even more famous band, Tommy Dorsey's. He stayed with Dorsey until 1942 and during this time developed his characteristic singing style, complete with his unusual phrasing, pauses, moans, and other distinctive techniques.

Striking out on his own in 1942, Sinatra landed an eight-week engagement at the Paramount Theater in New York. In 1942 and 1943 he became a phenomenon, idolized by hordes of hysterical teenage girls called bobby-soxers who squealed, shrieked, and swooned whenever he sang. His romantic ballads like "All or Nothing at All" and "In the Blue of the Evening" became smash hits in 1943, and from 1943 to 1945 Sinatra had a solo spot on the "Your Hit Parade" radio show. Meanwhile, he began making movies, beginning with *Higher and Higher* (1943). Most of them were light musicals like *Anchors Aweigh* (1945), but in 1945 he did a short film on racial tolerance called *The House I Live In*, which won a special Academy Award.

Having reached a peak of his popularity, Sinatra in the late 1940s suddenly hit the skids. He came under attack by McCarthyites as an alleged communist sympathizer, he had throat problems, his popularity and his movie contracts disappeared, and he had a highly publicized affair with Ava Gardner. Divorcing his first wife, Sinatra married Gardner in 1951, only to divorce her six years later. Meanwhile, though, he managed a stunning turnabout of his career with an impressive performance in the 1953 movie *From Here to Eternity*. Sinatra won an Oscar for best supporting actor, and the film captured six other Oscars as well.

Sinatra went on to make thirty-one more films, including *Guys and Dolls* (1955), *The Man with the Golden Arm* (1955), *Pal Joey* (1957), *The Manchurian Candidate* (1962), *Von Ryan's Express* (1966), and *The Detective* (1968). Meanwhile, he also regained his popularity as a singer, becoming a popular music institution during the 1950s and 1960s. Among his many hit singles of this period were "Love and Marriage" (1955), "Chicago" (1957), "High Hopes" (1959), "It Was a Very Good Year" (1965), "Strangers in the Night" (1966), and "My Way" (1969), his signature song. He won Grammy Awards in 1959, 1965, and 1966. As a star attraction, he made numerous television appearances and during the 1950s hosted his own television shows (1950–1952, 1957–1958).

Though the 1950s and 1960s proved to be Sinatra's most creative, they also marked an especially tumultuous period in his personal life. There were highly publicized incidents at nightclubs and another marriage, to Mia Farrow, that ended in divorce. Sinatra largely took himself out of the public eye by retiring in 1971, and in 1976, married his current wife, Barbara Marx.

Widely known for helping his friends and promoting the careers of many fellow performers, Sinatra published his autobiography, *A Man and His Art*, in 1990.

James M. Stewart

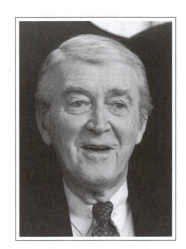

JAMES MAITLAND STEWART ARRIVED IN HOLLYWOOD IN 1935, AND TODAY, HALF A CENTURY LATER, HIS CREDITS INCLUDE MORE THAN 70 PICTURES, INCLUDING SUCH CLASSICS AS MR. SMITH GOES TO WASHINGTON, THE PHILADELPHIA STORY, AND IT'S A WONDERFUL LIFE. A PATRIOT, MR. STEWART SERVED WITH DISTINCTION AS A PILOT DURING WORLD WAR II, RISING TO THE RANK OF COLONEL IN THE EIGHTH AIR FORCE. HIS TYPICALLY AMERICAN CHARACTERS—BOYISH, HONEST AND KIND—MIRROR THE JIMMY STEWART IN REAL LIFE—AN AMERICAN BOY WHO GREW TO A GLORIOUS MANHOOD, BUT NEVER LOST HIS SENSE OF WONDER OR HIS INNOCENCE.

★ ★ ★

President Ronald Reagan awarded Stewart the Presidential Medal of Freedom with the above citation during a White House ceremony May 23, 1985.

Born in Indiana, Pennsylvania, in 1908, James M. Stewart was raised in a devout Presbyterian household in which responsibility, frugality, and prudence were stressed. He went on to Princeton University, where he was an active member of the university theater group and graduated with a degree in architecture in 1932. His heart was in show business, though, and after a stint in summer theater, Stewart landed his first bit part on Broadway in the fall of 1932.

Other parts followed in the next three years before he decided to try Hollywood in 1935. His first movie performance, in *Murder Man*, left much to be desired, but numerous other movie roles followed and his boyishly naive, engaging screen personality proved popular with audiences. By the late 1930s Stewart had established himself as a star with hit movies like *You Can't Take It With You* (1938) and *Mr. Smith Goes to Washington* (1939). He won an Oscar for his starring role as a reporter in *Philadelphia Story* (1940).

During World War II Stewart served as a bomber pilot in the Eighth Air Force, and between 1943 and 1945 he flew twenty-five bombing missions as a squadron commander. His first film after the war was Frank Capra's *It's a Wonderful Life* (1946), now a perennial Christmas classic. After 1950 Stewart began consciously changing his screen image to a tougher, less boyish character. Some of his greatest movie performances date from this time, including the Alfred Hitchcock thrillers *Rear Window* (1954), *The Man Who Knew Too Much* (1956), and *Vertigo* (1958), and Otto Preminger's *Anatomy of a Murder* (1959). Meanwhile, he married Gloria Hatrick McLean in 1949.

Stewart made film biographies, *The Glenn Miller Story* (1953) and

The Spirit of St. Louis (1957) among them, and a number of adult Westerns, such as *How the West Was Won* (1962), *The Rare Breed* (1966), and *The Shootist* (1976). Among his other films were *The Strategic Air Command* (1955), and, more recently, *Airport '77* (1977) and *The Big Sleep* (1978). Stewart hosted the "Jimmy Stewart Show" (1971–1972), made other appearances on television, and in 1984 won a special Oscar for his outstanding film career.

Albert C. Wedemeyer

AS ONE OF AMERICA'S MOST DISTINGUISHED SOLDIERS AND PATRIOTS, ALBERT C. WEDEMEYER HAS EARNED THE GRATITUDE OF HIS COUNTRY AND THE ADMIRATION OF HIS COUNTRYMEN. IN THE FACE OF CRISIS AND CONTROVERSY, HIS INTEGRITY AND HIS OPPOSITION TO TOTALITARIANISM REMAINED UNSHAKEABLE. FOR HIS RESOLUTE DEFENSE OF LIBERTY AND HIS ABIDING SENSE OF PERSONAL HONOR, ALBERT C. WEDEMEYER HAS EARNED THE THANKS AND THE DEEP AFFECTION OF ALL WHO STRUGGLE FOR THE CAUSE OF HUMAN FREEDOM.

★ ★ ★

President Ronald Reagan awarded Wedemeyer the Presidential Medal of Freedom with the above citation during a White House ceremony May 23, 1985.

A World War II military planner and expert on China, Albert C. Wedemeyer was born in Omaha, Nebraska, in 1897. His father was an army bandmaster, and Wedemeyer eventually graduated from the United States Military Academy at West Point in 1918. He served in various posts with the army over the next two decades, including a stint in China during which he studied Mandarin Chinese and two years of special study at Germany's General Staff School in Berlin (1936–1938). He married Elizabeth Dade Embick in 1925.

Returning to the United States in 1938, he prepared an incisive report on the Nazi military machine from information gained while at the German staff school. By early 1941 he was serving under General Dwight D. Eisenhower as a member of the Plans Group of the War Department's War Plans Division. Wedemeyer played a key role in developing overall U.S. strategy during World War II, as well as the Allied strategy for the Mediterranean theater and for the massive Normandy invasion in 1944. A brigadier general by 1942, he accompanied General George Marshall, U.S. military chief of staff, on overseas trips to Allied conferences on the war.

Named deputy commander of the Allied Southeast Asian theater in 1943, Wedemeyer became commander of U.S. forces in China the following year. In this post he also served as the chief military adviser to Chiang Kai-shek, leader of the Chinese Nationalists. By war's end Wedemeyer advocated a policy of strong U.S. intervention in China to support the Nationalists in their war against Communist rebels. The Truman administration demurred, though, and Wedemeyer became the Pentagon's deputy chief of staff for plans and operations.

In 1947 he returned to China as part of a U.S. government mission to investigate the postwar turmoil in China and Korea. His secret, highly controversial report included a recommendation for creating a South Korea military under U.S. leadership that could meet the threat from Communist-controlled North Korea. The report put Wedemeyer out of favor with the Truman administration. Later transferred from his planning position at the Pentagon, Wedemeyer retired from the army in 1951 as a lieutenant general.

Wedemeyer went on to a successful career as a business executive and in 1958 wrote a book on his work at the Pentagon, *Wedemeyer Reports!* He died in 1989, at the age of ninety-two.

Chuck Yeager

A HERO IN WAR AND PEACE, CHARLES YEAGER HAS SERVED HIS COUNTRY WITH DEDICATION AND COURAGE BEYOND ORDINARY MEASURE. ON OCTOBER 14, 1947, IN A ROCKET PLANE WHICH HE NAMED "GLAMOROUS GLENNIS" AFTER HIS WIFE, CHUCK YEAGER BECAME THE FIRST HUMAN BEING TO TRAVEL FASTER THAN THE SPEED OF SOUND, AND IN DOING SO, SHOWED TO THE WORLD THE REAL MEANING OF "THE RIGHT STUFF."

★ ★ ★

President Ronald Reagan awarded Yeager the Presidential Medal of Freedom with the above citation during a White House ceremony May 23, 1985.

Chuck Yeager was born in Myra, West Virginia, in 1923. He was the son of a gas well driller. After graduating from high school, he enlisted in the army air corps. Commissioned as a flight officer during World War II, he became a fighter pilot attached to the Eighth Air Force in England in 1943.

A year later Yeager was shot down over Germany and, despite a leg wound, made his way into France and the care of the French underground. Disguised as a peasant and accompanied by French guides, Yeager crossed the Pyrenees on foot, only to be arrested when he entered Spain. Spanish police did not count on Yeager's determination, though, and before long he succeeded in escaping from the jail. The Royal Air Force finally flew him back to England, forty-five days after the escape.

Yeager eventually flew sixty-four missions over Nazi-held Europe, shot down thirteen enemy aircraft, and was awarded a barrage of medals, including the Silver Star, Distinguished Flying Cross, Bronze Star, Air Medal, and Purple Heart. After the war he married Glennis Faye Dickhouse and became a test pilot at Wright-Patterson Air Force Base in Ohio. In 1947 he was selected to fly the then-secret X-1 rocket plane, which had been designed to break the sound barrier.

No plane had ever flown faster than the speed of sound before, and researchers did not know whether a pilot could even control a plane at speeds of 600 to 700 miles per hour. The crucial test came on a clear day over Rogers Dry Lake in California on October 14, 1947. Riding aboard the X-1, not much more than a rocket engine, a cockpit, and a pair of small wings, Yeager ignited the X-1's powerful engine after being released from the belly of a B-29 bomber at 25,000 feet.

The sudden thrust slammed him back in his seat and hurled the X-1 upward at a forty-five degree angle until, at about 40,000 feet, Yeager saw the Mach needle slip past 1.0, or 662 miles per hour, the speed of sound at that altitude. Soon afterward, the plane's fuel tanks went dry, ending his pioneering supersonic flight as planned. Gliding his plane back to earth and into the record books, an ecstatic Yeager did rolls and wing-overs all the way to the landing strip.

Yeager's other ride into the record books, on February 22, 1954, was not nearly as smooth. Trying to break the world's speed record (1,327 miles per hour, as of 1953), he rocketed aloft in an X-1A rocket plane after being released at high altitude from a B-29 bomber. Once again he shot upward at a steep angle, finally reaching 70,000 feet and the then-record speed of 1,650 miles per hour. At just that moment though, Yeager noticed the plane's stubby wings buffeting and then suddenly lost control of the plane. The X-1A hurtled earthward, dropping about 50,000 feet before its intrepid pilot managed to pull out of the dive. Yeager, at that time being the world's fastest man, also may have been the luckiest. In 1963 he survived the crash of the experimental jet NF-104, which had gone out of control at an altitude of 104,000 feet.

In the years following, Yeager flew tactical bombers over Vietnam and held various staff assignments, including commandant of the Aerospace Research Pilot School at Edwards Air Force Base. He retired in 1975 with the rank of brigadier general and published two books, *Yeager: An Autobiography* (1985) and *Press On!* (1988). Yeager was a central character in Tom Wolfe's best-selling book about the early days of the space program, *The Right Stuff* (1979).

Mother Teresa

MOST OF US TALK ABOUT KINDNESS AND COMPASSION, BUT MOTHER TERESA, THE SAINT OF THE GUTTERS, LIVES IT. AS A TEENAGER, SHE WENT TO INDIA TO TEACH YOUNG GIRLS. IN TIME, MOTHER TERESA BEGAN TO WORK AMONG THE POOR AND DYING OF CALCUTTA. HER ORDER OF THE MISSIONARIES OF CHARITY HAS SPREAD THROUGHOUT THE WORLD, SERVING THE POOREST OF THE POOR. MOTHER TERESA IS A HEROINE OF OUR TIMES.

★ ★ ★

President Ronald Reagan awarded Mother Teresa the Presidential Medal of Freedom with the above citation during a White House ceremony June 20, 1985.

The Nobel Prize–winning founder of the Missionaries of Charity, Mother Teresa was born Agnes Gonxha Bojaxhiu in 1910 in the town of Skopje, in what became part of Yugoslavia. The daughter of Albanian parents, she decided on missionary work while still a schoolgirl and at age fifteen had already decided she wanted to devote herself to work in India. She left home in 1928, at age eighteen, to join the Sisters of Loretto, Irish nuns who did missionary work in Calcutta, India.

After training in Ireland and Darjeeling, India, Mother Teresa began teaching at St. Mary's High School in Calcutta. She remained there for years but could not help but be affected by the appalling poverty she saw in the city's slums. Finally, in 1946 she realized her calling to help the poor and, getting permission from the Vatican, began working among the most destitute in Calcutta's slums in 1948.

Her first effort was an open-air school for children of the slums, and she soon began to attract both volunteers and donors, who provided her with rudimentary facilities. The Missionaries of Charity was officially founded as a religious community within the Archdiocese of Calcutta in 1950. Dedicated to helping even the most destitute, Mother Teresa opened the Nirmal Hriday Home for Dying Destitutes two years later. As volunteers, donations, and facilities became available, Mother Teresa steadily opened new schools and centers to serve abandoned children and the blind, crippled, aged, and dying. When Pope Paul VI gave her his white limousine during a 1964 visit to India, Mother Teresa quickly raffled it off and used the money to help pay for a leper colony in West Bengal.

Mother Teresa's Missionaries of Charity was recognized as a pontifical congregation in 1965, putting it under the direct jurisdiction of the pope. Meanwhile, Mother Teresa continued opening new facilities, expanding first to other cities in India and then to places in other countries where her special brand of help was needed. By the 1970s some two hundred schools and other facilities were being operated in Sri Lanka, Tanzania, Jordan, Venezuela, Great Britain, Australia, and elsewhere, and the Missionaries of Charity counted more than one thousand nuns among its number.

Pope Paul VI honored her devotion to helping the poor in 1971 by awarding her the first Pope John XXIII Peace Prize. Further recognition outside the church came in 1979 when she won the Nobel Peace Prize and in 1985 when she was awarded the Presidential Medal of Freedom. In 1990 Mother Teresa, who had become an Indian citizen, formally resigned as head of the Missionaries of Charity, but she was quickly reelected that year.

Paul H. Nitze

IN A CAREER SPANNING NINE PRESIDENCIES, PAUL NITZE HAS MADE ENORMOUS CONTRIBUTIONS TO THE FREEDOM AND SECURITY OF HIS COUNTRY. PAUL NITZE EXEMPLIFIES THE POWERS OF MIND, COMMITMENT, AND CHARACTER NEEDED TO FULFILL AMERICA'S WORLD RESPONSIBILITIES. HE WAS PRESENT AT THE CREATION OF THE STRATEGY THAT HAS KEPT US AT PEACE FOR 40 YEARS. HIS DEEP UNDERSTANDING OF THE ISSUES OF WAR AND PEACE, HIS DISCHARGE OF HIGH PUBLIC ASSIGNMENTS, AND HIS ADVICE TO THOSE IN AUTHORITY HAVE BEEN INVALUABLE TO OUR NATIONAL WELL-BEING. HE REMAINS THE MOST RIGOROUS, DEMANDING, AND INDEPENDENT OF ANALYSTS AND THE WISEST OF COUNSELORS.

★ ★ ★

President Ronald Reagan awarded Nitze the Presidential Medal of Freedom with the above citation during a White House ceremony November 7, 1985.

A senior official in the State and Defense departments and an arms control negotiator, Paul H. Nitze was born in Amherst, Massachusetts, in 1907. His father was a noted philologist and college professor, and Nitze went on to graduate cum laude from Harvard University in 1928 after majoring in economics and finance. The New York investment banking firm of Dillon Read & Company made him a vice president soon after his graduation, and in 1932 he married Phyllis Pratt, an heiress whose grandfather had founded Pratt Institute.

Nitze remained at Dillon Read until 1938, when he formed a company of his own. In 1940 he decided to enter government service and worked in various high-level posts related to the U.S. war effort during the next years. Moving to the State Department Office of International Trade Policy in 1946, he played an important role in putting together the Marshall Plan.

President Harry S. Truman named him assistant secretary of state for economic affairs in 1948, and the following year Nitze became one of the country's top foreign policy advisers as the State Department's director of policy planning. He played a central role in developing the Truman administration's Cold War strategy of containment and oversaw the writing of a pivotal study, NSC–68, which cast the Cold War as a struggle between good and evil and contained the statement, "a defeat of free institutions anywhere is a defeat everywhere." He also helped shape the North Atlantic Treaty Organization and was involved in settling the oil dispute between Britain and Iran in 1952.

After the Truman administration left office, Nitze became president of the Foreign Service Educational Foundation in Washington, a post he held throughout President Dwight D. Eisenhower's two terms. During the Kennedy-Johnson years Nitze was back in government. He served as assistant secretary of defense for international security affairs (1961–1963), navy secretary (1963–1967), and finally deputy secretary of defense (1967–1969). He was variously a principal in policy debates concerning the Cuban Missile Crisis, the crisis over the building of the Berlin Wall, and the prolonged escalation of U.S. involvement in Vietnam.

Under President Richard Nixon Nitze became an arms control negotiator and as part of the U.S. delegation helped conclude the first agreement from the Strategic Arms Limitation Talks (SALT I), in 1972. The longtime cold warrior resigned two years later, though, over concerns that the United States was bargaining away its military strength to the Soviets in the name of détente.

Becoming a Washington activist, Nitze helped found the bipartisan Committee on the Present Danger in 1976. The group sought to publicize the decline in America's defenses and the fact that the Soviets were increasing their military strength. Nitze openly attacked the 1979 SALT II agreement and in 1980 served as a campaign adviser for presidential candidate Ronald Reagan, who made rebuilding U.S. military strength a campaign issue.

In 1981 President Reagan appointed Nitze chief U.S. negotiator at the arms control talks with the Soviets in Geneva, a post Nitze held until resigning three years later. Nitze remained a special adviser for arms control until the end of the Reagan administration.

In 1990 Nitze was the subject of a sometimes critical book, *Dangerous Capabilities,* which chronicled his long career as a top policy maker. But just a year later the aging cold warrior witnessed the collapse of the Soviet Union and no doubt welcomed, with many others, the long-awaited end of the Cold War. In 1994 the eighty-seven-year-old Nitze married Elisabeth Scott Porter, a divorcée thirty-five years his junior. His first wife had died seven years earlier.

Roberta and Albert Wohlstetter

Participants in the nuclear era's most momentous events, Roberta and Albert Wohlstetter have shaped the ideas and deeds of statesmen, and have helped create a safer world. Over four decades, they have marshaled logic, science, and history and enlarged our democracy's capacity to learn and act. Through their work, we have seen that mankind's safety need not rest on threats to the innocent, and that nuclear weapons need not spread inexorably. Their powers of thought and exposition are, in themselves, among the Free World's best defenses.

★ ★ ★

President Ronald Reagan awarded Roberta and Albert Wohlstetter separate Presidential Medals of Freedom, with the one citation above, during a White House ceremony November 7, 1985.

Little biographical information is generally available on the Wohlstetters, perhaps because of the sensitive nature of their work. The husband and wife have figured prominently in the field of strategic analysis and national security over the past decades. Roberta Wohlstetter, who has worked for the social science department of the Rand Corporation, has been involved in analyzing the problems of terrorism, intelligence, and warning for the government. Albert has helped with the design and deployment of the nation's strategic forces since the 1950s.

Albert's work has involved making American forces safer from attack and less destructive, as well as devising the means to restrain nuclear proliferation and making significant contributions to basic concepts concerning nuclear deterrence. During the mid–1980s, when he was director of research at PAN Heuristics, a defense consulting firm, he served as cochairman of the Commission on Integrated Long-Term Strategy, which reexamined and revised the overall U.S. national security strategy.

Albert also has served as president of the European-American Institute for Security Research. Roberta published *Pearl Harbor: Warning and Decision* in 1962.

Walter Hubert Annenberg

FOLLOWING A BRILLIANT CAREER IN PUBLISHING AND PIO-
NEERING THE USE OF TELEVISION FOR EDUCATIONAL PURPOSES,
WALTER HUBERT ANNENBERG WAS IN 1969 APPOINTED
AMBASSADOR TO THE COURT OF ST. JAMES, WHERE HE SERVED
WITH EXTRAORDINARY DILIGENCE, BRINGING THE GOV-
ERNMENTS AND PEOPLE OF THE UNITED STATES AND UNITED
KINGDOM CLOSER TOGETHER. SINCE RETURNING TO PRIVATE
LIFE, WALTER ANNENBERG HAS DEVOTED HIMSELF TO THE
DEVELOPMENT OF HIGHER EDUCATION AND HAS PROVIDED
SUPPORT TO COUNTLESS INSTITUTIONS. TODAY OUR NATION
REPAYS HIS LIFETIME OF ACHIEVEMENT WITH ITS GRATITUDE.

★ ★ ★

*President Ronald Reagan awarded Annenberg the Presidential Medal
of Freedom with the above citation during a White House ceremony
May 12, 1986.*

Walter Annenberg was born in 1908 in Milwaukee, Wisconsin, the
only son among nine children. His father, an immigrant from East
Prussia, had risen from an impoverished background to control
several publications, eventually including the *Philadelphia Inquirer*.
But young Annenberg and his sisters grew up knowing only the
comfort and security their father's wealth provided.

After a year at the University of Pennsylvania's Wharton School of
Finance, Annenberg in 1928 went to work for his father as an
assistant in the bookkeeping office. By the late 1930s he had become a
vice president. A devastating shock came in 1938 when his father was
sentenced to a prison term for income tax evasion. The elder
Annenberg served two years in prison and died in 1942, just one
month after being paroled.

Taking over as president of Triangle Publications, Annenberg
added considerably to his father's holdings, eventually creating a
publishing empire rivaling some of the country's largest media con-
glomerates. He founded the popular teen magazine *Seventeen* in 1944
and the hugely successful *TV Guide* in 1953. Soon after, he bought the
Philadelphia Daily News and also began acquiring radio and television stations. In 1951 he married his second wife, the former Mrs.
Leonore Rosenstiel. His first marriage had earlier ended in divorce.

In his role as editor and publisher of the *Inquirer*, Annenberg
drew criticism for his conservative views but also became known as a
generous philanthropist. He supported numerous charities and
endowed various educational and cultural institutions. Eventually he
founded graduate schools in communications at the University of

Pennsylvania and the University of Southern California, as well as the Albert Einstein College of Medicine in New York City.

Though Annenberg had no prior experience in diplomacy, President Richard Nixon named him to the prestigious post of U.S. ambassador to Great Britain in 1969. He served as ambassador until 1974, when he returned to his business and philanthropic ventures. Annenberg retired in 1988, at age eighty.

Earl "Red" Blaik

A SOLDIER OF THE GRIDIRON, COLONEL EARL "RED" BLAIK LED THE WEST POINT TEAM HE COACHED INTO THE PAGES OF THE HISTORY BOOKS. HE RALLIED THE BLACK KNIGHTS FROM A RECORD OF DEVASTATING DEFEATS AND CARRIED THEM ON TO SOME OF THEIR GREATEST VICTORIES, WINNING THE ESTEEM OF HIS CADET PLAYERS AND THE ADMIRATION OF HIS VANQUISHED RIVALS. ONE OF AMERICA'S GREAT COACHES, HE BROUGHT A WINNING SPIRIT TO HIS TEAM, HONOR TO HIS BRANCH OF SERVICE, AND PRIDE TO HIS NATION.

★ ★ ★

President Ronald Reagan awarded Blaik the Presidential Medal of Freedom with the above citation during a White House ceremony May 12, 1986.

When Earl Blaik became coach of the Army football team in 1941, the Black Knights had just completed another dismal losing season, capped by the most humiliating defeat that had ever been suffered by Army. Penn State punished Army in that November 1940 outing, winning 48 to 0. But Colonel Blaik, as he was known at Army, quickly turned the team around. He orchestrated back-to-back championship seasons in 1944 and 1945, and during his eighteen seasons as coach at West Point, he led his teams to winning seasons in all but one. Overall, Army compiled an impressive 121 wins, 33 defeats, and 10 ties under Blaik.

Blaik was born in Detroit, Michigan, in 1897 and graduated from Miami University of Ohio during World War I. Entering the U.S. Military Academy at West Point as an army cadet, he played football, basketball, and baseball and graduated as the top athlete of his class in 1920. He served another two years before retiring from the army and then worked for his father's business in Dayton, Ohio, from 1923 to 1934. Blaik married his childhood sweetheart, Merle McDowell, in 1924.

In 1926 he began coaching football part time, first at the

University of Wisconsin at Madison and then at West Point. He became head coach at Dartmouth in 1934 and took only two years to turn around Dartmouth's losing football team. While at Dartmouth he compiled a record of forty-five wins, fifteen losses, and four ties and would have remained there had not the superintendent of West Point prevailed upon him to take over the Army coaching job in 1941.

Blaik took a cerebral approach to football and proved remarkably effective at organizing his staff and the team. But he also had the determination to win and a strong loyalty to West Point, which was nowhere clearer than during the disastrous 1951 season. That year West Point dismissed ninety cadets for honor code violations. Among those dismissed were fifty-one football players, including Blaik's son, the starting quarterback. Blaik stayed on as Army's coach, however, and after posting his only losing season in 1951, rebuilt the football program in just three years.

He retired as Army's coach in 1958 to become executive committee chairman of both Avco Corporation and Blaik Oil Company. The National Football Hall of Fame inducted him as one of the all-time great coaches in 1959.

Blaik, who was eighty-nine years old when he received the Presidential Medal of Freedom in 1986, died three years later.

Barry Morris Goldwater

Soldier and statesman, Barry Morris Goldwater has stood at the center of American history. Respected by both ally and adversary, Barry Goldwater's celebrated candor and patriotism have made him an American legend. Hailed as a prophet before his time, selfless in the service of his nation, Barry Goldwater has earned the unbounded affection and admiration of his countrymen and the enduring gratitude of all future generations of Americans.

★ ★ ★

President Ronald Reagan awarded Goldwater the Presidential Medal of Freedom with the above citation during a White House ceremony May 12, 1986.

A longtime leader of conservative Republicans, Barry Morris Goldwater was born in Phoenix, Arizona, in 1909. His family owned what was then known as Goldwaters, an exclusive department store chain. As a youth Goldwater had little interest in schoolwork, and after spending just a year at the University of Arizona (1928), he dropped out to join the family business. While working his way up from store clerk, Goldwater married Margaret Johnson in 1934. Three years later he became the company's president and retained that post until 1953. Since then he has served as the firm's board chairman.

Early on, Goldwater also began actively pursuing other interests outside the family business, including getting his pilot's license. During World War II, the army air force rejected him (as overage and for medical reasons), but a determined Goldwater battled his way into the service and as an air force pilot ferried military cargo and fighter planes to overseas bases. After the war he entered politics at the local level, serving as a Phoenix city councillor from 1949 to 1952.

By 1952 Goldwater was ready to try for the U.S. Senate. Campaigning as a conservative Republican, he scored a narrow upset victory over his opponent, then the Democratic Senate majority leader. Goldwater ultimately spent thirty years in the Senate, from 1953 to 1965 and from 1969 to 1987.

During that time he frequently criticized excessive federal spending on domestic programs such as urban renewal, public housing, and job training. The federal government, he believed, was shouldering responsibilities better left to the states, churches, and private charities. He also opposed financing medical care for the aged through the Social Security system, contending it would eventually bankrupt the system. On foreign policy matters, he was a hardline anticommunist who supported a strong military and the use of nuclear weapons, should it become necessary.

Goldwater's moment in the national spotlight was as the Republican nominee during the 1964 presidential campaign. But his tough conservative and extreme anticommunist views only fed popular fears that he would be a war-mongering, trigger-happy president. His opponent, President Lyndon B. Johnson, adroitly played up such fears during the campaign and ultimately won the election by a huge landslide. Commenting later on how exaggerated his image had become by election day, Goldwater quipped, "In fact, if I hadn't known Goldwater, I'd have voted against the SOB myself."

Returning to the Senate in 1969, Goldwater loyally backed Republican President Richard Nixon and his policies on the Vietnam War, but during the Watergate scandal he led the delegation of Republican leaders who finally persuaded Nixon to resign. During Goldwater's remaining years in the Senate, he backed such conservative causes as anti-inflationary policies, less regulation of the economy, a balanced federal budget, and reduced federal spending on social programs.

The author of several books outlining his conservative views, he has published *The Conscience of a Conservative* (1960), *Where I Stand* (1964), and *The Coming Breakpoint* (1976). His autobiography, *Goldwater*, appeared the year after he left the Senate, in 1988. Goldwater married Susan McMurray Wechsler in 1992, his first wife having died in 1985.

Helen Hayes

MANY ARE ADMIRED, BUT FEW ARE BELOVED, AND FEWER STILL
ARE BOTH. BUT HELEN HAYES IS AND HAS BEEN FOR ALMOST
ALL THE YEARS OF THIS CENTURY BOTH. PEERLESS ACTRESS,
PEERLESS STAR, SHE HAS EXCELLED ON STAGE, SCREEN, AND
TELEVISION, PLAYING EVERYTHING FROM VIRTUOUS YOUNG
INGENUES TO VICTORIAN QUEENS. HELEN HAYES IS THAT RARE
THING—A TRUE ORIGINAL. SHE IS ALSO, DEMONSTRABLY, A
GREAT ACTRESS, A GREAT PATRIOT, AND A GREAT SOUL.

★ ★ ★

*President Ronald Reagan awarded Hayes the Presidential Medal of
Freedom with the above citation during a White House ceremony
May 12, 1986.*

Among the greatest actresses of the twentieth century, Helen Hayes
Brown was born in Washington, D.C., in 1900. Encouraged by her
mother, who was a sometime actress, Hayes made her professional
acting debut at age five. Three years later she landed her first
Broadway role, and by 1917, when she graduated from high school,
she had already established herself as an actress, using the name
Helen Hayes.

Though her first star billing was in the light comedy *Bab, the Sub-
Deb* (1920), Hayes revealed the extraordinary power and breadth of
her talent with a hit performance as the tragic heroine in *Coquette*
(1927). She married playwright Charles MacArthur the following
year and gave birth to a daughter in 1930. (She later adopted a son as
well.) Some of her most memorable Broadway performances
followed in the 1930s, including starring roles in such tremendous
hits as *Mary of Scotland* (1933) and *Victoria Regina* (1935). As Queen
Victoria in *Victoria Regina*, Hayes portrayed the monarch from
youth to old age and established herself as a truly brilliant actress.

She appeared in many other famous Broadway productions over
the next decades, including Thornton Wilder's *The Skin of Our Teeth*
(1955), Tennessee Williams's *The Glass Menagerie* (1956), and Eugene
O'Neill's *Long Day's Journey into Night* (1971). Hayes received two
Tony Awards during her Broadway acting career, for performances in
Happy Birthday (1946) and *Time Remembered* (1957).

Though she always preferred the theater, Hayes also appeared in
Hollywood films and on television. Among her motion pictures were
The Sin of Madelon Claudet (1931), which won her an Academy
Award, *A Farewell to Arms* (1932), and *Airport* (1970), which won her
a second Academy Award as best supporting actress. Hayes performed on television from the earliest days and won an Emmy Award
in 1952 for her dramatic roles.

Along with a lifetime of successes, however, came two deep personal tragedies. Her daughter died of polio in 1949, and seven years later her husband Charles died as well. Despite the losses, Hayes continued acting and did not finally retire from the stage until 1972. Often called the First Lady of the American Theater, she died twenty years later, at age ninety-two. The day she died Broadway honored her memory by dimming theater marquees for one minute.

Matthew B. Ridgway

WHEN A SOLDIER RISING, SWORD IN HAND, REACHES TO PROTECT AN IDEA—FREEDOM, LIBERTY, HUMAN KINDNESS—THE WORLD IS, FOR A MOMENT, HUSHED. GREATNESS IS OFTEN BORN IN QUIET, IN STILLNESS. AND SO IT WAS THAT NIGHT IN JUNE OF 1944 WHEN GENERAL MATTHEW B. RIDGWAY PRAYED THE WORDS GOD SPOKE TO JOSHUA: "I WILL NOT FAIL THEE, NOR FORSAKE THEE." D-DAY SAVED A CONTINENT, AND SO, A WORLD. AND RIDGWAY HELPED SAVE D-DAY. HEROES COME WHEN THEY'RE NEEDED; GREAT MEN STEP FORWARD WHEN COURAGE SEEMS IN SHORT SUPPLY. WORLD WAR II WAS SUCH A TIME. AND THERE WAS RIDGWAY.

★ ★ ★

President Ronald Reagan awarded Ridgway the Presidential Medal of Freedom with the above citation during a White House ceremony May 12, 1986.

Matthew B. Ridgway, the World War II commander of the first-ever U.S. airborne assault, was born at Fort Monroe, Virginia, in 1895. After graduating from West Point in 1917, he served in various staff posts over the next two decades. After World War II broke out, he was transferred to the War Plans Division of the War Department. Promoted to brigadier general in 1942, he became commander of the Eighty-second Infantry Division.

Ridgway oversaw the transition of his division to an airborne unit, one of the army's first two, and commanded it during the army's first airborne assault, which was part of the 1943 invasion of Sicily. On D-Day, June 6, 1944, the Eighty-second was among the airborne units that helped ensure the success of the Normandy invasion, and Ridgway parachuted in with his troops. Two months later he took command of the Eighteenth Airborne Corps and oversaw various offensives pushing eastward from France into Germany, including the Ardennes campaign, the Rhine crossing, and the historic linkup with Soviet troops at the Elbe River in 1945.

In 1946, as military adviser to the U.S. delegation to the United Nations Ridgway helped plan the establishment of the UN multinational military force. Four years later he was tapped to command UN forces in Korea. In short order he rallied the troops and turned back a massive Chinese Communist offensive that had nearly pushed UN forces off the Korean peninsula. He again stepped into the breach in 1951, becoming Allied commander of the Far East after General Douglas MacArthur lost a highly publicized dispute with President Harry S. Truman. Meanwhile, in 1947 Ridgway married Mary Anthony Long, having previously divorced his first two wives.

After a stint as supreme commander of Allied forces in Europe (1952), Ridgway began what should have been the crowning achievement of his military career: the post of army chief of staff. Instead he spent the next two years opposing the Eisenhower administration's new strategy of relying on the threat of massive nuclear attack to defend the country. Ridgway argued strenuously against cutting the army's budget and downplaying the foot soldier's role in future wars, but to no avail.

Retiring from the army in 1955, he published his memoirs, *Soldier*, the following year. He was awarded a Congressional Gold Medal in 1991 and died two years later, at age ninety-eight.

Vermont Connecticut Royster

FOR OVER HALF A CENTURY, AS A JOURNALIST, AUTHOR, AND TEACHER, VERMONT ROYSTER ILLUMINATED THE POLITICAL AND ECONOMIC LIFE OF OUR TIMES. HIS COMMON SENSE EXPLODED THE PRETENSIONS OF "EXPERT OPINION," AND HIS COMPELLING ELOQUENCE WARNED OF THE EVILS OF SOCIETY LOOSED FROM MOORINGS IN FAITH. THE VOICE OF THE AMERICAN PEOPLE CAN BE HEARD IN HIS PROSE—HONEST, OPEN, PROUD, AND FREE.

★ ★ ★

President Ronald Reagan awarded Royster the Presidential Medal of Freedom with the above citation during a White House ceremony May 12, 1986.

A longtime *Wall Street Journal* editor and Pulitzer Prize-winning commentator, Vermont Connecticut Royster was born in Raleigh, North Carolina, in 1914. He earned his bachelor's degree in English literature at the University of North Carolina in 1935 and began his lifelong association with the *Wall Street Journal* a year later. Frances Claypoole became his wife in 1937.

For the next several years he reported on Congress, the White House, and the Supreme Court for the *Journal.* When World War II broke out he joined the navy and saw action in the Pacific and Atlantic theaters. The *Journal* promoted him to head of its Washington bureau after the war, and he was soon writing editorials and a column. Royster won his first Pulitzer Prize in 1953 for the overall outstanding quality and insightfulness of his editorials.

Named senior associate editor in 1951, Royster moved up through the executive ranks and served as editor of the *Journal* from 1958 to 1971. He also was a senior vice president from 1960 to 1971. After 1971 he became a contributing editor and columnist, a post he continues to hold, and in 1984 won a Pulitzer Prize for his commentary. The *Journal* named Royster editor emeritus in 1993.

The editorials for which Royster became famous tended to bring out the underlying moral issues embedded in the events of the day. Stalin's death in 1953, for example, sparked an editorial that touched on a fundamental flaw of the communist revolution in Russia. Lenin, Stalin, and the rest proclaimed their intent to "slay" the inhumanities of the world around them. But unlike other revolutionaries, their aim was not to set people free. Instead, Royster wrote, "the communists came to remake the world into a world as they would have it be." Such visions of rebuilding the world, he said, inevitably come to evil, and eventually leaders like Stalin justify compulsion, enslavement, and murder to achieve their extravagant aims.

Royster wrote articles for numerous other periodicals and published five books, including *Journey Through the Soviet Union* (1962) and his memoirs, *My Own, My Country's Time* (1983).

Albert Bruce Sabin

When, as a boy, Albert Bruce Sabin came to the United States from Russia, no one could have known that he would number among the most prominent immigrants of our century. From an early age Sabin devoted his life to medicine and by the 1950s his research had resulted in a

BREAKTHROUGH. IN THE YEARS SINCE THE SABIN VACCINE HAS HELPED TO MAKE DRAMATIC ADVANCES AGAINST THE SCOURGE OF POLIO MYELITIS.

★ ★ ★

President Ronald Reagan awarded Sabin the Presidential Medal of Freedom with the above citation during a White House ceremony May 12, 1986.

Born in Bialystok, Poland, in 1906, Albert Bruce Sabin immigrated to the United States with his family in 1921. He went on to graduate from New York University in 1928 and, deciding on a career in medical research, earned his medical degree there in 1931. A polio epidemic in New York that same summer prompted his decision to focus on polio and other contagious diseases affecting the nervous system.

After four years of further medical training, Sabin became a researcher at the Rockefeller Institute for Medical Research and there discovered a way to cultivate the polio virus in human nerve tissue outside the human body. Then in 1939 the University of Cincinnati named him head of infectious disease research at its Childrens Hospital Research Foundation. While there he showed that polio enters the body through the digestive tract, not through the respiratory system as had been previously believed.

World War II interrupted Sabin's polio research, but during his work for the army, he found a means for preventing the sandfly fever afflicting soldiers in Africa and also developed vaccines for dengue fever and Japanese encephalitis. Returning to the Childrens Hospital in the mid–1940s, Sabin continued his polio research. He became convinced that a vaccine made from weakened, live polio virus would give longer immunity than a killed-virus vaccine, and by 1954 he had developed an effective, live-virus polio vaccine. Meanwhile, though, Jonas Salk had already successfully developed and tested a killed-virus polio vaccine, which was approved in 1955. *(See also the entry for Salk, p. 255.)*

Testing of Sabin's vaccine went forward in Mexico, the Netherlands, and the Soviet Union, and soon a heated rivalry developed between professionals who supported either the Salk or Sabin vaccine. Sabin himself believed his live-virus approach superior. His vaccine could be taken orally and provided lifetime immunity, while Salk's required an injection and periodic booster shots. Sabin's vaccine was approved in 1961 and eventually replaced Salk's vaccine as the preferred polio vaccine in the United States and throughout much of the world.

Sabin later served as president of Israel's Weizmann Institute of Sciences, from 1970 to 1972, and as a research professor at the University of South Carolina, from 1974 to 1982. In his later years he studied the relationship between viruses and cancer.

In 1972 he married his third wife, Heloisa Dunshee de Abranches, having divorced his second wife. His first wife died in 1966. Sabin died in 1993, at age eighty-six.

Vladimir Horowitz

HE HAS SAID THAT IT REMAINS THE PURPOSE OF HIS LIFE TO BRING MEANING TO MUSIC EACH TIME HE PLAYS. WITH MASTERFUL TECHNIQUE, CONSUMMATE MUSICIANSHIP, AND PROFOUND HUMANITY, VLADIMIR HOROWITZ BRINGS NOT ONLY MEANING TO MUSIC, BUT JOY AND BEAUTY AND MEANING TO ALL OUR LIVES. THIS ADOPTED SON OF AMERICA, THE LAST OF THE GREAT ROMANTICS AS HE IS SOMETIMES CALLED, IS MORE THAN A NATIONAL TREASURE, HE IS A TREASURE TO PEOPLE THE WORLD OVER.

★ ★ ★

President Ronald Reagan awarded Horowitz the Presidential Medal of Freedom with the above citation during a White House ceremony July 28, 1986.

Among the 20th century's most famous pianists, Vladimir Horowitz was born Vladimir Gorowitz in Kiev, Ukraine, in 1903. A talented piano player even as a young child, he began informally at age three and took regular lessons from age six. Later he studied at the Kiev Conservatory. He wanted to become a composer then, but the 1917 Russian Revolution stripped his family, which had been affluent, of almost everything they owned. To help feed and clothe them, he began giving concerts in 1922 and by the following year had established himself as a leading pianist within the Soviet Union. That one year he gave a series of twenty-three recitals in which he performed more than two-hundred different works.

While the impressive breadth of his repertoire gained him wide regard, it was his amazing playing technique that never failed to dazzle his audiences and won him worldwide acclaim. After taking Europe by storm during a two-year concert tour between 1925 and 1927, he created a sensation at his American debut with the New York Philharmonic in 1928 and firmly established his international reputation. Meanwhile, in 1926 he changed his name from Gorowitz to Horowitz and in 1933 he married Wanda Toscanini, daughter of the famed Italian conductor.

Horowitz's especially demanding concert schedule in 1935 brought on the first of several retreats from the concert circuit. Generally considered "high strung," Horowitz returned to the concert hall in 1938. In 1944, a few years after settling in the United States, he became a U.S. citizen. The immensely popular Horowitz had also managed to make himself the country's highest paid concert pianist by 1942.

Often called the last nineteenth-century romantic, Horowitz played with what he called the "grand manner." His object, he said, was to "transform the piano from a percussive instrument into a singing instrument." He was in fact capable of remarkable speed and force in playing and was not afraid to take chances, often improvising and reinterpreting during performances of works by Tchaikovsky, Liszt, Prokofiev, Scarlatti, Scriabin, Rachmaninoff, and other classical composers. While his extraordinary, highly personal style invariably electrified his audiences, some music critics strongly disapproved. One went as far as to call him a "master of distortion and exaggeration."

But for most concert-music lovers Horowitz's dazzling virtuosity transformed him into an almost mythical figure. During his subsequent retreats from concerts (1953–1965, 1968–1974, and 1983–1985), he was sorely missed, though he continued to make recordings during these periods. Among the most memorable concerts of his later years were his 1965 Carnegie Hall concert, which marked his first public performance in twelve years, and his 1986 concerts in Moscow and Leningrad (now Saint Petersburg), his first performances in Russia since 1925.

Horowitz toured extensively during the 1980s, giving his last concerts in Germany in 1987. He died two years later, at age eighty-six.

Anne Legendre Armstrong

SINCE HER EARLIEST DAYS IN GRASSROOTS POLITICS, ANNE ARMSTRONG HAS BEEN AN INTREPID FIGHTER FOR THE CAUSE OF FREEDOM AND LIBERTY, AND AGAINST THE INTRUSIONS OF BIG GOVERNMENT. HER GREAT TALENTS AND CAPACITY FOR WORK CATAPULTED HER ONTO THE NATIONAL POLITICAL SCENE, WHERE SHE HAS SERVED HER PARTY AND NATION WITH DISTINCTION, HOLDING HIGH OFFICES IN BOTH. HER GREAT SKILL AND UNSTINTING EFFORT IN THE SERVICE OF HER COUNTRY HAVE EARNED HER THE GRATITUDE OF OUR NATION.

★ ★ ★

President Ronald Reagan awarded Armstrong the Presidential Medal of Freedom with the above citation during a White House ceremony June 23, 1987.

A former U.S. ambassador to Great Britain, Anne Legendre Armstrong worked her way up through Republican party ranks to hold posts in the Nixon, Ford, and Reagan administrations. Born in 1927, she was the daughter of a New Orleans coffee importer who was a French Creole.

Armstrong graduated from Vassar in 1949 and a year later married Tobin Armstrong. Settling with him on his expansive Texas cattle ranch, she took an active part in ranch life while raising her five children. She also found time to become involved in local Texas politics.

Armstrong's first brush with politics had been as a volunteer worker for Harry S. Truman's presidential campaign in 1948, but she switched to the Republican party and in 1952 served as a local precinct worker in Texas for Dwight D. Eisenhower's successful presidential bid. Executive posts on the county and Texas state Republican committees followed in the 1950s and 1960s, along with Republican National Convention platform committee work in 1964 and 1968.

In 1971 she became the first woman cochairman of the Republican National Committee, and the next year she was the first woman ever to deliver the keynote address at a major political party convention. After his reelection, President Richard Nixon named her counselor to the president, a position with cabinet-level rank. While serving in the Nixon administration, she founded the first Office of Women's Programs, chaired the Federal Property Council, and served on various presidential councils. Armstrong steadfastly supported President Nixon during the Watergate scandal, until the White House tapes showing Nixon's involvement were released in 1974.

Remaining as presidential counselor under President Gerald R. Ford through 1974, she left politics briefly to attend to family matters. She returned in 1976 to become the U.S. ambassador to Great Britain, a post she held until 1977 when Democratic President Jimmy Carter took office. Ronald Reagan made her cochairman of his successful presidential campaign in 1980, and she served as chairman of the President's Foreign Intelligence Advisory Board from 1981 to 1990.

Armstrong is a member of the board of directors of General Motors, American Express, and other corporations, and is on the Smithsonian Institution's board of regents.

Justin Whitlock Dart

A LEADING ENTREPRENEUR, JUSTIN DART HAS MADE VITAL CONTRIBUTIONS TO AMERICA THAT WILL LONG BE REMEMBERED. CONSIDERED A REVOLUTIONARY BY HIS TRADE, HE WAS ALREADY HEAD OF THE LARGEST DRUG COMPANY IN THE WORLD BY THE AGE OF 35, AND HIS SURE HAND WOULD SOON TRANSFORM THE

BUSINESS. JUSTIN DART BECAME A LEADING FORCE IN POLITICS AND AN ADVISER TO THE PRESIDENT, VALUED NOT ONLY FOR HIS BUSINESS ACUMEN BUT HIS COURAGEOUS CHAMPIONING OF POLITICAL AND ECONOMIC LIBERTY. JUSTIN DART'S LIFE STANDS AS ELOQUENT TESTIMONY TO THE CREATIVE FORCE OF FREEDOM.

★ ★ ★

President Ronald Reagan awarded Dart the Presidential Medal of Freedom, with the above citation, posthumously. Dart's wife, Jane, accepted the medal on his behalf during a White House ceremony held June 23, 1987.

Dart was born in 1907 and raised in suburban Hinsdale, Illinois. The only one of three children to survive childhood, he excelled at track in prep school and trained for the sport by carrying a fifty-six-pound weight and a sixteen-pound hammer wherever he went. While at Northwestern University, he switched to football and not only became a star player, but also caught the eye of Ruth Walgreen, daughter of the Walgreen drugstore magnate. Dart graduated in 1929 with a degree in business administration and that same year married Ruth.

After spending his first year working as a $25-a-week stock clerk in a Walgreen's drug store, Dart moved up the corporate ladder quickly and by 1932 headed operations for the 375-store chain. Though his marriage had made the rapid rise possible, he quickly showed he knew how to make the most of an opportunity. He changed purchasing and distribution systems, redesigned stores to stimulate sales, and eliminated stores which performed poorly. Still in his early thirties, Dart was appointed Walgreen's general manager in 1939, but the year brought major upheavals in his personal life. His divorce from Ruth became final, his former father-in-law died on Christmas day, and he married his second wife, Jane O'Brien, on New Year's Eve. Though he had inherited a substantial share of Walgreen's, he resigned under pressure in 1941.

That year he became president of Liggett Drug Company, which owned the Rexall drug line and which was a struggling division of a larger, poorly organized conglomerate. By 1943, at the age of thirty-five, he moved up to the presidency of the parent company, United Drug, then the world's largest drug company. Once again he demonstrated his merchandising skill and quickly turned the company around. He renamed the business Rexall Drug in 1946, changing that to Dart Industries in 1969. After selling off his Rexall interests in 1977, he merged his company with Kraft Foods in 1980. He remained in control of Dart and Kraft, Inc.

Long a force in California politics, Dart became a friend to Ronald Reagan during the 1940s and an unofficial adviser during Reagan's years as California's governor. He was among President Reagan's informal advisers—Reagan's kitchen cabinet—until his death in 1984. Dart was seventy-six.

Danny Kaye

AN ENTERTAINER, HUMANITARIAN, AND AN INDIVIDUAL WHO
LIFTED THE SPIRIT OF HIS FELLOW COUNTRYMEN, HIS
ENTHUSIASM FOR LIFE INFECTED ALL WHO SAW HIM. HE SPREAD
LAUGHTER AND GOOD WILL, TOUCHING THE HEARTS OF PEOPLE
THROUGHOUT THE WORLD, ESPECIALLY YOUNG PEOPLE. HE WAS
A TRUE PROFESSIONAL, A STAR OF FILM, STAGE, TELEVISION, AND
RADIO. HIS DEDICATION TO HELPING LESS FORTUNATE
CHILDREN IS ALSO REMEMBERED. HE WAS A GOOD MAN, A PRO
WHO CARED, AN EXAMPLE OF THE BEST IN AMERICA'S SOUL. AND
HE WILL ALWAYS BE REMEMBERED ROUND THE WORLD BY
MILLIONS OF CHILDREN FOR HIS UNSELFISH WILLINGNESS TO
SERVE EVERY TIME THE U.N. CALLED UPON HIM TO DO SO.

★ ★ ★

*President Ronald Reagan awarded Kaye a posthumous Presidential
Medal of Freedom with the above citation during a White House
ceremony June 23, 1987. Dena Kaye accepted the medal on her late
father's behalf.*

A master of comic improvisation and exaggeration, Danny Kaye was
born David Daniel Kominski in Brooklyn, New York, in 1913. His
father and mother were Russian immigrants, and the young Kaye
grew up wanting to be a doctor. But by the time he reached high
school it was clear that his family could not afford college. As a child
he also had enjoyed making people laugh, however, and after quitting
high school during his senior year, he developed a song-and-dance
routine for private parties. Performances in Catskill Mountain
resorts in New York State and in vaudeville followed, and by 1933 he
had adopted his stage name, Danny Kaye.

Kaye's Broadway debut came in 1939, with parts in the *Straw Hat
Revue,* starring Imogene Coca. The following year he married Sylvia
Fine, a pianist and composer from Brooklyn. She eventually helped
make him an enduring success, both by writing material and by
serving as his coach and critic. But it was a tongue-twisting Ira
Gershwin tune called "Tchaikovsky" in the 1941 Broadway play *Lady
in the Dark* that first established Kaye as a hit comedian. Audiences
raved when he rattled off the song's fifty tongue-twisting names of
Russian composers in just thirty-nine seconds.

Given star billing for the 1941 Broadway musical *Let's Face It,* Kaye
interrupted his stage career the following year to help sell government war bonds and then entertained U.S. troops in the Pacific
theater during World War II. By 1944, though, he found time to make

his first Hollywood film, *Up in Arms,* and in the late 1940s and 1950s he starred in a succession of hit film comedies. Usually he played a meek character who after many comic mishaps finally triumphs. Among his most popular movies were *The Secret Life of Walter Mitty* (1947), *Hans Christian Andersen* (1952), and *The Court Jester* (1956). In 1954 he received a special Academy Award.

By the late 1950s, with his movie box office appeal slipping, Kaye switched to television and there had his own variety show from 1963 to 1967. Meanwhile, he had begun working for the United Nations in the 1950s, entertaining children in third world countries. Eventually designated a UNICEF ambassador at large, he devoted much of his time in the 1970s and 1980s to performing in comedy routines for children. Kaye also appeared in numerous benefit concerts for symphony orchestras, performing as a hapless guest conductor whose antics included using a flyswatter to conduct *The Flight of the Bumblebee* and dancing a tango while conducting *Bolero.*

After nearly five decades as one of the country's top comedians, Kaye died in 1987. He was seventy-four years old.

Lyman L. Lemnitzer

A BRAVE AND DEDICATED MILITARY OFFICER WHO SERVED OUR NATION IN PEACE AND WAR, GENERAL LEMNITZER'S SKILL AS A TACTICIAN, PLANNER, AND NEGOTIATOR WAS INSTRUMENTAL IN THE SECOND WORLD WAR. HE FOUGHT IN KOREA, HE SERVED AS U.S. COMMANDER-IN-CHIEF IN EUROPE, AND EVENTUALLY BECAME THE CHAIRMAN OF THE JOINT CHIEFS OF STAFF. HIS LIFE HAS BEEN ONE MARKED BY HIGH MILITARY SKILL AND UNSELFISH DEVOTION TO HIS COUNTRY.

★ ★ ★

President Ronald Reagan awarded Lemnitzer the Presidential Medal of Freedom with the above citation during a White House ceremony June 23, 1987.

Born in Honesdale, Pennsylvania, in 1899, Lyman L. Lemnitzer graduated from West Point in 1920. He spent the next six years as a member of the coast artillery and in 1923 married Katherine Mead Tryon. Between 1926 and 1939 he variously taught at military schools and pursued advanced military studies. During that time he graduated from the General Staff School at Fort Leavenworth and the Army War College in Washington, D.C.

A stint at the War Department War Plans Division in 1941 led to his promotion to brigadier general and an assignment as assistant chief of staff at General Dwight D. Eisenhower's Allied headquarters, in London, England. Just before the United States invaded North Africa in 1942, Lemnitzer accompanied General Mark Clark on a daring secret mission to Algeria. There they negotiated with French officers willing to defy France's Nazi puppet government and surrender their North African territories without a fight. Later, he commanded the Thirty-fourth Antiaircraft Brigade during the battles for German-held Tunisia and in the early part of the Allied invasion of Sicily.

While moving up to high-level positions at the Supreme Allied Command for the Mediterranean from 1943 to 1945, Lemnitzer went on additional secret missions, which involved negotiations for Italy's surrender (1943) and the surrender of German armies in Italy and Austria (1945).

Assigned to high-level posts in the Pentagon after the war, he played a key role in directing U.S. military aid to European nations to help bolster their defenses against the Soviet threat. Then, with the outbreak of the Korean War, Lemnitzer took command of the Seventh Infantry Division and saw action at Heartbreak Ridge, the Punch Bowl, and other battlefields in 1951 and 1952. Promoted to full general in 1955, he was named commander-in-chief of the U.S. Far East Command and of the UN Command.

Two years later he became one of the country's top military leaders as a member of the Joint Chiefs of Staff. Lemnitzer served at a time when technology was increasingly a part of military armament and when the Cold War was at its height. During his term as chairman of the Joint Chiefs (1960–1962), he oversaw the buildup of U.S. military strength in Europe in response to the crisis over the Berlin Wall and directed the organizing of the U.S. Central Command, a unified command of American ground and air tactical forces.

Lemnitzer left the Joint Chiefs to become Supreme Allied Commander in Europe in 1963 and remained in that post until retiring from the military six years later. He died in 1989, at age eighty-nine.

John A. McCone

As Director of Central Intelligence between 1961 and 1965, John A. McCone guided our nation's intelligence community through some of its most difficult hours. He strengthened the Nation's critical capacity for effective intelligence operations, maintained the intel-

LIGENCE COMMUNITY'S REPUTATION FOR UNBIASED ANALYSIS,
AND PLAYED AN ACTIVE ROLE IN POLICY DEBATES. INTEGRITY,
PATRIOTISM—THESE QUALITIES HAVE MARKED HIS LONG AND
DISTINGUISHED SERVICE TO OUR NATION.

★ ★ ★

*President Ronald Reagan awarded McCone the Presidential Medal of
Freedom with the above citation during a White House ceremony
June 23, 1987.*

A successful West Coast business executive before entering government service, John A. McCone was born in San Francisco in 1902. His family had been involved with machinery and manufacturing since the mid–1800s, and McCone graduated from the University of California at Berkeley with a degree in engineering in 1922. Starting out as a riveter at a Los Angeles ironworks, he rose steadily up the company ranks and was named its director and executive vice president in 1933.

Four years later he struck out on his own, forming Bechtel-McCone in partnership with Stephen Bechtel. The company designed and built power plants, refineries, and processing facilities in the United States and internationally. McCone also expanded into shipbuilding during World War II, becoming director of the California Shipbuilding Corporation and overseeing construction of over 450 ships for the war effort. Bechtel-McCone disbanded after the war, and McCone bought up the Joshua Hendy Corporation, which under his leadership operated cargo ships and tankers in the Pacific. By 1948 he also had been named chairman of a Pacific steamship line, Pacific Far East Inc.

Meanwhile, McCone began his government service with an appointment to President Harry S. Truman's Air Policy Commission in 1947. The following year, as Secretary James Forrestal's special deputy, he helped prepare the budget of the newly formed Department of Defense. Between 1950 and 1951 he was undersecretary of the Air Force and while in that office urged President Truman to create a program for building guided missiles. No action was taken, though, and when the Soviet Union surprised the world by launching *Sputnik* in 1957, critics pointed out that the "missile gap" between the United States and the Soviet Union probably would not have existed if McCone's recommendation had been followed.

In 1958 President Dwight D. Eisenhower named McCone to his next important government post—Atomic Energy Commission (AEC) chairman. McCone launched the AEC "Atoms for Peace" program and unsuccessfully sought a nuclear test ban agreement with the Soviet Union during his two years in office.

Soon after the Bay of Pigs fiasco in 1961, President John F. Kennedy named McCone director of the Central Intelligence Agency

(CIA). With the CIA demoralized and in disfavor with President Kennedy because of the bungled Cuban invasion, McCone de-emphasized the agency's covert activities in favor of intelligence gathering and analysis. As a result he was able to warn President Kennedy that the Soviet Union intended to base nuclear missiles in Cuba, information that gave rise to the Cuban Missile Crisis of 1962. McCone thus restored the CIA's credibility at a crucial time and went on to become one of the agency's strongest directors. Meanwhile, he married Thelline Pigott in 1962, his first wife having died the previous year.

Continuing as CIA director under President Lyndon B. Johnson, McCone remained in office until resigning in 1965. At the time, he warned President Johnson that a bombing campaign against North Vietnam would ultimately turn public sentiment against the United States and that all-out war might be necessary to win in Vietnam, though he personally was against the idea.

Returning to private business, he became chairman of the Hendy International Company. He also served as a director of International Telephone and Telegraph and various other corporations. McCone died in 1991, at age eighty-nine.

Frederick D. Patterson

FOR FIVE DECADES, AS PRESIDENT AND PRESIDENT EMERITUS OF TUSKEGEE INSTITUTE, DR. FREDERICK D. PATTERSON HAS BEEN ONE OF AMERICA'S OUTSTANDING EDUCATORS. HE IS ALSO THE FOUNDER OF THE UNITED NEGRO COLLEGE FUND AND THE COLLEGE ENDOWMENT FUNDING PLAN, AND THROUGH THESE, HE HAS HELPED FINANCE EXCELLENCE THROUGHOUT AMERICA'S COMMUNITY OF HISTORICALLY BLACK COLLEGES. BY HIS INSPIRING EXAMPLE OF PERSONAL EXCELLENCE AND UNSELFISH DEDICATION, HE HAS TAUGHT THE NATION THAT, IN THIS LAND OF FREEDOM, NO MIND SHOULD BE ALLOWED TO GO TO WASTE.

★ ★ ★

President Ronald Reagan awarded Patterson the Presidential Medal of Freedom with the above citation during a White House ceremony June 23, 1987.

Named after the black antislavery leader Frederick Douglass, Frederick Douglass Patterson was born in Washington, D.C., in 1901.

He was orphaned while still very young and his older sister, a school-teacher in Texas, raised him. Patterson went on to earn his doctorate in veterinary medicine from Iowa State College in 1923. Continuing his studies at Cornell University, he got a master's degree (1927) and a second doctorate (1932).

Meanwhile, Patterson taught veterinary medicine and chemistry at Virginia State College in Petersburg, Virginia, from 1923 to 1928 and in 1928 became head of the veterinary division at Alabama's all-black Tuskegee Institute. He also taught bacteriology there.

Patterson advanced rapidly at Tuskegee. Promoted to director of the institute's School of Agriculture in 1933, he succeeded Dr. Robert R. Moton as president of Tuskegee Institute two years later. Patterson married Catherine Elizabeth Moton that same year. While continuing as president of Tuskegee, Patterson turned his attention to the larger problem of raising funds for the country's all-black colleges. In 1943 he proposed what became the United Negro College Fund, a consortium of twenty-seven black colleges organized in 1944 to raise money for scholarships and other educational needs. Patterson became president of the fund, which by the 1980s had grown to include forty-two colleges and provided aid to forty-five-thousand students. The United Negro College Fund, now the largest independent source of funds for private black colleges, has adopted the slogan, "A mind is a terrible thing to waste."

Patterson left his post at Tuskegee to become president of the Phelps-Stokes Fund in 1953, a position he held for the next seventeen years. There he worked for the betterment of blacks in the United States and Africa, for improvements to low-income housing in New York City, and on other projects. In the mid–1970s, after having relinquished his post as president of Phelps-Stokes, Patterson organized yet another college fund, the College Endowment Funding Plan. This organization seeks endowment funds from private businesses to help keep small, independent colleges from becoming too dependent on federal funds.

Among the most prominent black Americans of his day, Patterson died in 1988. He was eighty-six years old.

Nathan Perlmutter

IN THE "DIARY OF A CANCER PATIENT," NATHAN PERLMUTTER WROTE: "FUNNY WHAT I FEEL I'VE ACCOMPLISHED. I MARRIED THE PRETTIEST GIRL. I MADE IT TO MARINE INFANTRY OFFICER, WROTE A FEW BOOKS, AND BECAME DIRECTOR OF THE ANTI-DEFAMATION LEAGUE." THAT CASUAL, SELF-DEPRECATING VOICE

IS THE VOICE OF A HERO. FOR MR. PERLMUTTER HAS MADE IT
HIS LIFE'S WORK TO CHAMPION HUMAN DIGNITY. HE IS A HERO
INDEED, A HERO OF THE HUMAN SPIRIT.

★ ★ ★

President Ronald Reagan awarded Perlmutter the Presidential Medal of
Freedom with the above citation during a White House ceremony June
23, 1987. Ruth Perlmutter accepted the medal on her husband's behalf.

Nathan Perlmutter, who spent most of his working life with the Anti-
Defamation League (ADL) of B'nai B'rith, was born in 1923 and was
raised in the Williamsburg section of Brooklyn, New York. The son
of Jewish immigrants from Poland, he attended Georgetown and
Villanova universities before enlisting in the marines during World
War II. After serving in China, Perlmutter returned to his studies and
earned his law degree from New York University in 1949.

He went to work for the ADL that same year and spent the next
fifteen years working in regional offices around the country.
Perlmutter moved to the American Jewish Committee in 1965,
serving as its associate national director for the next four years. Then,
between 1969 and 1973, he was a vice president at Brandeis University
in Massachusetts. Meanwhile, Perlmutter also published two books,
How to Win at the Races (1964) and *A Bias of Reflections* (1972).

Returning to the ADL in 1973 as assistant national director,
Perlmutter became the group's national director two years later. As
chief executive he served as a leading spokesman for Jews in America
and oversaw ADL activities in the New York headquarters office, the
thirty-one regional offices in the United States, and overseas offices
as well. Part of his work included speaking out against incidents of
anti-Semitism in America. Among his deepest concerns, though, was
a growing isolationism in America that he feared might eventually
deprive Israel of needed support. Meanwhile, he was coauthor, with
his wife, Ruth, of the book *The Real Anti-Semitism in America* (1982).

In 1985 Perlmutter was diagnosed with lung cancer, and for some
weeks kept a diary while adjusting to the news that he did not have
long to live. His *Diary of a Cancer Patient* was published in the *New
York Times* later that year.

Perlmutter died in 1987, at age sixty-four. President Ronald
Reagan awarded him the Presidential Medal of Freedom a month
before his death.

Mstislav Rostropovich

HE ONCE JOKINGLY ASKED HIS MOTHER WHY SHE HAD CARRIED HIM LONGER THAN THE USUAL 9 MONTHS. "SLAVA," SHE ANSWERED, "TO GIVE YOU SUCH BEAUTIFUL HANDS." PERFORMING, TEACHING, AND CONDUCTING, THE BEAUTIFUL HANDS OF MSTISLAV ROSTROPOVICH HAVE SHARED WITH MILLIONS HIS PASSION FOR MUSIC, ESPECIALLY THE MUSIC OF THE HOMELAND HE HAS NEVER CEASED TO LOVE. HE IS A VIRTUOSO NOT ONLY OF MUSIC BUT OF HEART AND MIND, AS WELL.

★ ★ ★

President Ronald Reagan awarded Rostropovich the Presidential Medal of Freedom with the above citation during a White House ceremony June 23, 1987.

Among this century's best-known cellists, Mstislav Rostropovich was born in 1927 in the former Soviet Republic of Azerbaijan. Music was in his blood; Rostropovich's grandfather was a pianist; his grandmother, the head of a music school; his father, a cellist; his mother, a pianist; and his sister, a violinist. Rostropovich taught himself the piano at age four and developed his talent for the cello at a school for the musically gifted.

During World War II Rostropovich contributed to the Soviet war effort by playing for the troops. Later, in 1943, he entered the Moscow Conservatory. While studying under the modernist composer Dimitry Shostakovich, he continued performing and during the 1940s extended his reputation throughout the Eastern bloc. Meanwhile, the Soviet government denounced modernist composers amid the heightened Cold War tensions of 1948. When Shostakovich was forced out of the conservatory, Rostropovich ignored the risks to his own career and quit in sympathy. Like everyone else, he said later, he had believed in the communist system. But the events of 1948 made him wonder if there was something wrong.

Nevertheless, his career as cellist flourished in the 1950s. In 1955 he married a Bolshoi Opera Company soprano, Galina Vishnevskaya, and the following year enjoyed an enormous success at his American debut at Carnegie Hall in New York. With his reputation established in the West, he was ranked with the famed Pablo Casals. *(See also the entry for Casals, p. 51.)*

He again risked official condemnation, however, by inviting the dissident Soviet writer Aleksandr Solzhenitsyn to live at his country home. Rostropovich's support for Solzhenitsyn finally resulted in his own official condemnation in 1970. The Soviet government canceled his foreign tours and forbade his playing with major orchestras.

Four years later, though, the authorities did allow Rostropovich and his wife to play in the United States. After their two-year tour ended in 1976, the couple decided to remain in the West.

In 1977 Rostropovich was named music director of the National Symphony Orchestra in Washington, D.C. The orchestra itself was not then among the best, and Rostropovich's conducting during his first years also was criticized. But by the late 1980s he had turned the National Symphony Orchestra into a world-class ensemble and had even won over some of his harshest critics. Rostropovich resigned as music director of the National Symphony Orchestra in 1994.

When performing on the cello, Rostropovich prefers playing modern compositions by Shostakovich, Benjamin Britten, and others. Numerous composers have written cello works for him, and by the late 1980s he had premiered seventy new cello pieces.

William B. Walsh

DR. WILLIAM B. WALSH HAS SPENT A LIFETIME GIVING HOPE TO OTHERS. FOR 14 YEARS, IN PORTS AROUND THE WORLD, MILLIONS CHEERED THE SHIP THAT DR. WALSH'S DREAMS LAUNCHED, THE SS HOPE. MEDICAL CARE AND TRAINING— THESE WERE THE HOPE'S CARGO, TOGETHER WITH A MESSAGE OF GOOD WILL FROM ALL AMERICANS. TODAY PROJECT HOPE HAS STEPPED ASHORE, AND DR. WALSH IS REACHING PEOPLE WHEREVER THERE IS NEED AND, AS ALWAYS, IS GIVING OF HIMSELF SO THAT OTHERS MIGHT FIND HOPE. HE IS A CREDIT TO HIS PROFESSION AND TO HIS COUNTRY.

★ ★ ★

President Ronald Reagan awarded Walsh the Presidential Medal of Freedom with the above citation during a White House ceremony June 23, 1987.

The founder of Project HOPE, William B. Walsh was born in Brooklyn, New York, in 1920. He went on to graduate from Saint John's University in New York in 1940 and earned his medical degree three years later at Georgetown University. He married Helen Rundvold that same year.

A medical officer aboard a navy destroyer during World War II, Walsh came up with the idea for the S.S. *Hope* after seeing the poor health conditions and lack of medical care among peoples of the

South Pacific. For some years after the war, he concentrated on his private practice as a Washington, D.C., heart specialist. Then, in 1958, he convinced President Dwight D. Eisenhower that a surplus navy hospital ship should be converted into the first-ever peacetime hospital ship. Walsh organized Project HOPE—Health Opportunity for People Everywhere—to administer the effort and served as its president, chief executive officer, and medical director.

The S.S. *Hope* outfitted and staffed, began its maiden voyage in 1960, visiting developing coastal nations and providing medical and dental care as well training for local health-care workers. S.S. *Hope* continued in operation for the next fourteen years, and Walsh wrote three books based on its voyages, *A Ship Called HOPE* (1964), about the maiden voyage to Asia; *Yanqui, Come Back!* (1966), about the mission to Peru; and *HOPE in the East: The Mission to Ceylon* (1970).

Project HOPE continued under Walsh's direction after S.S. *Hope* went out of service in 1974 and today provides health education and training programs both here and abroad. As of the mid–1990s, Project HOPE operated some seventy programs worldwide. Since 1981 the group also has produced a widely read journal called *Health Affairs,* of which Walsh is publisher.

Meanwhile, Walsh has served in a variety of other medical and health advisory capacities. He has been a clinical professor of internal medicine at Georgetown University since 1970, the chairman of Project Vietnam (1965–1966), a member of the President's Committee on Employment of the Handicapped (1977–1985), chairman of the President's Advisory Committee on Health (1979–1981), a U.S. delegate to the World Health Assembly (1986–1992), and a board member of various other groups.

Walsh retired from most of his posts related to Project HOPE in 1992, remaining as vice chairman of the organization's board of directors.

Meredith Willson

OUR COUNTRY KNOWS MEREDITH WILLSON AS THE COMPOSER-LYRICIST WHOSE MUSICALS AND SONGS CAPTURED THE JOY AND INNOCENCE OF AMERICA. MEREDITH WILLSON'S CAREER EMBRACED THE MUSICAL LIFE OF HIS NATION. HIS GREATEST HITS, "THE MUSIC MAN" AND "THE UNSINKABLE MOLLY BROWN," WILL FOREVER STAND AS LANDMARKS OF THE BROADWAY STAGE. AS ONE CRITIC SAID: "HIS MUSIC IS AS AMERICAN AS APPLE PIE AND A FOURTH OF JULY ORATION." HE

WILL ALWAYS BE REMEMBERED AFFECTIONATELY AND WITH
RESPECT FOR HIS VIRTUOSITY AS OUR MUSIC MAN.

★ ★ ★

President Ronald Reagan awarded Willson a posthumous Presidential Medal of Freedom with the above citation during a White House ceremony June 23, 1987. Rosemary Willson accepted the medal on her late husband's behalf.

Born in Mason City, Iowa, in 1902, Meredith Willson was raised in a musical family and had become an accomplished pianist and flutist by the time he finished high school in 1919. He then went to New York, attending what would become the prestigious Julliard School of music, and between 1921 and 1923 toured with John Philip Sousa's band. He married Elizabeth Wilson in 1920.

Willson's symphonic career began in 1924 when he became first flutist with the New York Philharmonic Symphony Orchestra, then under the direction of famed conductor Arturo Toscanini. Five years later Willson himself became a conductor, of the Seattle Symphony Orchestra, and simultaneously began working for NBC radio as a musical director for its West Coast operations. His first symphony, no. 1 in F Minor, was performed in San Francisco in 1936, and the following year he went to Hollywood to become musical director of the "Maxwell House Coffee Time" NBC radio show.

Striking out in a variety of musical directions, Willson composed the scores for the films *The Great Dictator* (1940) and *The Little Foxes* (1941); served as the music division head for Armed Forces Radio Service during World War II; hosted the "Meredith Willson Show" on television in 1949; starred on the radio program "Music Room" in the early 1950s; and wrote such hit songs as "Two in Love" (1941) and "May the Good Lord Bless and Keep You" (1951). He also wrote books, including *And There I Stood with My Piccolo* (1948) and *Eggs I Have Laid* (1955).

But Willson's most enduring successes came on the Broadway stage. He had been working on *The Music Man* since 1948, slogging through revision after revision until the show premiered on December 19, 1957. The show, which included now famous songs like "*76* Trombones," was an instant success and won the New York Drama Critics Circle Award for best musical show of 1957–1958. After *The Music Man,* Willson's next greatest Broadway hit was *The Unsinkable Molly Brown.* Both of these musicals were made into movies.

Willson wrote other popular musicals, such as *Here's Love,* but they did not achieve the success of his two most memorable hits. Willson died in 1984, at age eighty-two. He was survived by his third wife, Rosemary.

Irving R. Kaufman

IRVING ROBERT KAUFMAN BECAME AN ASSISTANT FEDERAL PROS-
ECUTOR AT THE AGE OF 25. MORE THAN FIVE DECADES LATER,
BOTH HIS ENERGY AND HIS DEVOTION TO THE RULE OF LAW
REMAIN UTTERLY UNFLAGGING. ASSISTANT FEDERAL PROS-
ECUTOR, SPECIAL ASSISTANT TO THE UNITED STATES ATTORNEY
GENERAL, DISTRICT COURT JUDGE, JUDGE ON THE UNITED
STATES COURT OF APPEALS FOR THE SECOND CIRCUIT, MEMBER
OF COUNTLESS PANELS AND COMMISSIONS, INCLUDING THE LEAD-
ERSHIP OF THE PRESIDENT'S COMMISSION ON ORGANIZED
CRIME—JUDGE KAUFMAN HAS BROUGHT TO EACH HIS PRACTICAL
SKILLS, HIS ZEAL FOR JUSTICE, AND AGAIN, THAT REMARKABLE
ENERGY. HE IS A DISTINGUISHED JURIST AND A GREAT AMERICAN.

★ ★ ★

President Ronald Reagan awarded Kaufman the Presidential Medal of
Freedom with the above citation during a White House ceremony
October 7, 1987.

Probably best remembered as the federal judge who in 1951 sentenced
Ethel and Julius Rosenberg to the electric chair for delivering atomic
secrets to the Soviets, Irving R. Kaufman was born in New York City
in 1910. The son of a manufacturer, he was an exceptional student,
graduating from Fordham University Law School in 1931 at age
twenty. Admitted to the bar in 1932, he practiced with a New York
City law firm for the next few years. Kaufman married Helen
Rosenberg (no relation to Ethel and Julius Rosenberg) in 1936.

Dubbed the "boy prosecutor" in the newspapers, the twenty-
something Kaufman became assistant U.S. attorney for the Southern
District of New York in 1936 and handled various high-profile fraud
cases. Returning to private practice in 1940, he was again called to the
Justice Department in 1947, this time to set up a division for investigating illegal lobbying. Then, in 1949, President Harry S. Truman
named the thirty-nine-year-old Kaufman a district court judge—
making him the country's youngest federal judge.

The Rosenberg spy case, the espionage case of the century, landed
in Kaufman's court in 1951. At the time, the Korean War was in full
fury and Senator Joseph McCarthy was stirring up fears about communist infiltrators within the government. Leftists, under fire for their
communist sympathies, meanwhile made the Rosenberg case a
rallying point, charging that the husband and wife were the victims of
anticommunist hysteria. But the Rosenbergs were found guilty of
passing atomic secrets to the Soviet Union during World War II, thus

enabling the Soviets to explode an atomic bomb five or ten years earlier than expected and ending the U.S. nuclear weapons monopoly.

To Judge Kaufman fell the decision on their sentence. Calling their crime worse than murder, he ordered the convicted husband and wife electrocuted, the only death sentence for espionage ever carried out by a civilian court in the United States. Judge Kaufman's decision ignited a much wider controversy over the sentence itself, earning him both an international reputation and the lingering hatred of some Rosenberg supporters. But despite numerous appeals, the Rosenbergs were finally executed in 1953.

President John F. Kennedy appointed Kaufman to the U.S. Court of Appeals for the Second Circuit in 1961, a seat he retained until retiring in 1987. During his long term on the bench, he wrote a number of landmark decisions, including opinions on First Amendment protections that expanded press freedoms, as well as on antitrust and civil rights cases. Judge Kaufman, who as a district judge handed down stiff sentences (later overturned) for Mafia leaders arrested in 1957 at the Appalachia underworld convention, also issued the first court-ordered desegregation of an elementary school in the North in 1961. During the Reagan administration, Judge Kaufman also served on the President's Commission on Organized Crime.

Designated a senior judge after his 1987 retirement, he remained active on the bench. Kaufman died in 1992, at age eighty-one.

Caspar Weinberger

MILITARY OFFICER, STATE LEGISLATOR, STATE CABINET MEMBER, FEDERAL REGULATORY AGENCY CHAIRMAN, AND THREE-TIME FEDERAL CABINET MEMBER, CASPAR (CAP) W. WEINBERGER HAS, IN THE TRADITION OF OUR FOUNDING FATHERS, DEDICATED HIS LIFE TO THE SERVICE OF HIS COUNTRY. HIS PROUDEST PUBLIC ACCOMPLISHMENT IS THE REBUILDING OF OUR COUNTRY'S NATIONAL DEFENSES SO THAT THE FREEDOM WE SO CHERISH MIGHT ENDURE. HIS LEGACY IS A STRONG AND FREE AMERICA—AND FOR THIS, AND FOR A LIFETIME OF SELFLESS SERVICE, A GRATEFUL NATION THANKS HIM.

President Ronald Reagan awarded Weinberger the Presidential Medal of Freedom with the above citation during a special ceremony at the

Pentagon November 17, 1987. The award was accompanied by the added accolade "with distinction."

The secretary of defense through most of President Ronald Reagan's two terms, Caspar Weinberger was born in San Francisco in 1917. A youth who read the *Congressional Record* for fun, he became involved in student politics in high school and went on to Harvard University, from which he earned his bachelor's degree magna cum laude in 1938 and his law degree in 1941. Weinberger joined the army during World War II and became a member of General Douglas MacArthur's intelligence staff. Meanwhile, he married Jane Dalton in 1942.

After the war he joined the San Francisco law firm of Heller, Ehrman, White & McAuliffe. Though Weinberger kept his ties with the firm until 1969, he had already embarked on his political career by 1952, when he was elected to the California state legislature. A Republican, he was reelected and served until 1958. He was a top official in the California Republican organization from 1960 to 1964 and spent two years as California's director of finance (1968–1969). His first federal post came in 1970, as chairman of the Federal Trade Commission under President Richard Nixon.

From there Weinberger moved quickly into Nixon's inner circle, serving first as deputy and then as director of the Office of Management and Budget (1970–1972, 1972–1973), as councilor to the president (1973), and finally as secretary of health, education, and welfare (1973). While at the budget office, Weinberger got the nickname "Cap the Knife" for his budget cutting skills, and as HEW secretary he proposed various spending cuts. The Democratic-controlled Congress effectively blocked social-spending reductions, however. Leaving government service in 1975, Weinberger spent the next five years as a top executive at the Bechtel Corporation.

With the Republicans back in power in 1981 under President Ronald Reagan, Weinberger was appointed secretary of defense. For the next seven years he presided over the nation's largest-ever peacetime military spending increase. He supported strengthening the country's nuclear arsenal and such controversial weapons systems as the MX missile, the B-1 bomber, and the "star wars" Strategic Defense Initiative (SDI). During his seven years in office, some $2 trillion was channeled into the Defense Department, a substantial part of it for modernizing and strengthening the U.S. military.

Weinberger returned to private practice early in 1988, this time as a member of the Washington, D.C., law firm of Rogers and Wells.

Facing a trial for allegedly withholding a diary in the Iran-contra probe, Weinberger was pardoned by President George Bush in late 1992. While remaining with the law firm until 1994, he also became chairman of *Forbes* magazine, a position he continues to hold. In 1990 he published his memoirs, *Fighting for Peace: Seven Critical Years in the Pentagon.*

Roger L. Stevens

"A QUARTER OF THE TIME, I HAVE BIG HITS; A QUARTER OF THE TIME, ARTISTIC SUCCESSES; A QUARTER OF THE TIME, THE CRITICS WERE CRAZY; AND A QUARTER OF THE TIME, I'M CRAZY. IT FIGURES OUT WELL THAT WAY." THAT HUMBLE ASSESSMENT IS BY ROGER L. STEVENS, CHAIRMAN OF THE JOHN F. KENNEDY CENTER FOR THE PERFORMING ARTS, REAL ESTATE GIANT, CHAIRMAN OF THE FIRST NATIONAL COUNCIL ON THE ARTS, AND PRODUCER OR COPRODUCER OF MORE THAN 200 PLAYS, INCLUDING SUCH AMERICAN CLASSICS AS "CAT ON A HOT TIN ROOF" AND "WEST SIDE STORY." ROGER STEVENS MAY BE HUMBLE, BUT HIS ACHIEVEMENTS HAVE ENRICHED OUR NATION'S CULTURE BEYOND MEASURE.

★ ★ ★

President Ronald Reagan awarded Stevens the Presidential Medal of Freedom with the above citation during a ceremony at Washington's Four Seasons Hotel January 13, 1988.

The son of a real estate broker, Roger L. Stevens was born in Detroit, Michigan, in 1910. He attended the University of Michigan for one year, leaving in 1930 during the height of the depression to work on an auto assembly line. Much of his spare time over the next five years was spent reading, and at this point in his life, he developed an interest in plays.

Stevens began working as a broker for a Detroit real estate firm in 1935. By 1938 he had accumulated about $50,000 from his ventures and that year married Christine Gesell. After serving in the navy during World War II, he set his sights on the theater world and went about earning the money he would need to produce plays.

Aggressively expanding his real estate investments, Stevens bought properties in Cleveland, Miami, and, after 1949, New York City, where he bought and sold a number of hotels and other high-profile buildings. In 1951 he headed the syndicate of investors who bought the Empire State Building, then the world's tallest, for over $51 million. He continued buying and selling investment properties until 1960, when he decided to devote himself full time to the theater and the arts.

Stevens had begun financing theatrical productions for the Detroit Theater Guild in the late 1940s and even helped bring a production of Shakespeare's *Twelfth Night* to Broadway in 1949. The following year he coproduced a Broadway revival of *Peter Pan*. In subsequent years he produced or coproduced some 200 plays, including *West Side Story, Cat on a Hot Tin Roof, Bus Stop, A Man for All Seasons, Deathtrap, Death of a Salesman,* and *A Few Good Men.*

Also active in theater and arts administration, he was a board chairman of the Kennedy Center (1961–1988), special assistant on the arts to President Lyndon B. Johnson (1964–1968), chairman of the National Council on the Arts (1965–1969), chairman of the American Film Institute (1969–1972), and chairman of the advisory committee for the National Book Award (1970–1975, 1988–1989). He is chairman of the Fund for New American Plays, a post he has held since 1986, and since 1982 he has been a member of the President's Committee on the Arts and Humanities.

Lord Peter Alexander Rupert Carington, Sixth Baron Carrington

Foreign Secretary, Defense Minister, Parliamentary leader, and tank commander, Peter Alexander Rupert Carington, the Sixth Baron Carrington, has proved himself the devoted servant of Her Majesty's government, a friend of the American people, and the faithful defender of human freedom. As Secretary General of the North Atlantic Treaty Organization, his tireless efforts have at a critical moment in history strengthened the cause of peace and freedom for all humanity. For his selfless service the American people honor him and extend to him their gratitude and warmest affection.

★ ★ ★

President Reagan awarded Carington the Presidential Medal of Freedom with the above citation during a White House ceremony May 10, 1988.

Born on the family estate in Buckinghamshire, England, in 1919, Lord Carrington was educated at the prestigious Eton preparatory school and the Royal Military College. He succeeded to his title as sixth baron upon his father's death in 1938 and in 1942 married Iona McClean. During World War II he served with distinction as a tank commander and was decorated for his bravery in combat. Returning to civilian life in 1946, he entered politics by taking his hereditary seat in the House of Lords.

Lord Carrington joined Prime Minister Winston Churchill's Conservative government as a junior minister in 1951 and five years later began a three-year term as British high commissioner to Australia. A change in government meanwhile brought Labour Prime Minister Harold Macmillan to power. Macmillan named Lord Carrington, then just forty years old, to the powerful post of Lord of the Admiralty. Serving from 1959 to 1963, Lord Carrington pushed for modernization of Britain's navy and presided over the launching of his country's first nuclear submarine.

Named Conservative Party leader in the House of Lords in 1963, Lord Carrington led the opposition when the Labour party held power between 1964 and 1970. With the Conservatives back in power under Prime Minister Edward Heath (1970–1974), Lord Carrington served first as defense secretary and then as energy secretary. Conservative Prime Minister Margaret Thatcher appointed him foreign secretary in 1979, and the next year he was widely praised for successfully negotiating an end to the bloody war in Rhodesia. But Lord Carrington misjudged Argentina's intentions in the 1982 Falkland Islands crisis and was forced to resign after Argentina invaded the British-held islands.

Appointed secretary-general of the North Atlantic Treaty Organization (NATO) in 1984, he emphasized the need for better East-West communication. But he also used his considerable diplomatic skills to maintain unity among the member nations during the crisis over siting medium-range nuclear missiles in Europe. U.S. President Ronald Reagan later said that NATO unity helped force the Soviet Union to sign the Intermediate Nuclear Forces Treaty (1987), eliminating medium-range missiles on both sides of the iron curtain. On Lord Carrington's retirement as NATO secretary-general in 1988, President Reagan awarded him the Presidential Medal of Freedom.

Pearl Bailey

As a girl, Pearl Bailey began singing in her father's church in Virginia and kept singing all the way to Broadway and into America's heart. Among the pre-eminent American entertainers of this century, she has dazzled audiences all over the world. She has also served the Nation as a Special Adviser to the United States Mission to the United Nations. And America loves Pearl Bailey, for her songs and for her soul.

★ ★ ★

President Ronald Reagan awarded Bailey the Presidential Medal of Freedom with the above citation during a White House ceremony October 17, 1988.

A singer as well as a stage and screen actress, Pearl Bailey was born in 1918 in Newport News, Virginia. She began singing and dancing in her father's church at age three, but did not decide on a show business career until she reached high school. Soon after winning an amateur night contest in Philadelphia in 1933, she dropped out of school and began working in nightclubs as a dancer and singer.

Eleven years later she made her debut as a soloist at a major New York nightclub, the Village Vanguard, and it was there that club owner Max Gordon told her to relax and be herself on stage. Bailey took the advice, creating her signature *throwaway* singing style with many casual asides and other devices. She secured her position as a top-ranking nightclub performer later in 1944 with a long engagement at Manhattan's exclusive Blue Angel nightclub and by making appearances with Cab Calloway's band.

Bailey debuted on stage in the all-black musical *St. Louis Woman* in 1946 and the following year sang in her first movie, *Variety Girl*. She performed in nightclubs and theaters during the 1950s and 1960s, while also making records and appearing in plays and movies, including the 1959 film version of *Porgy and Bess*. Bailey married jazz drummer Louis Bellson in 1952, having ended earlier unsuccessful marriages.

Continuing to work despite a chronic heart condition, she appeared for the first time at New York's Lincoln Center in 1966 and was widely acclaimed for her lead in the all-black version of the musical *Hello, Dolly!,* which opened on Broadway in 1967. Bailey won a special Tony Award for her performances.

Among the hit songs she recorded were "Toot Toot Tootsie (Goo'Bye)," "Takes Two to Tango," and "Tired." Bailey appeared on various television variety shows and her own show aired in 1970 and 1971. She also published two autobiographical books, *The Raw Pearl* (1968) and *Talking to Myself* (1971). Despite her health problems, she kept on working into the 1980s. The indefatigable singer died in 1990, at age seventy-two.

Malcolm Baldrige

COWBOY, BUSINESS EXECUTIVE, POLITICAL ACTIVIST, CABINET
SECRETARY—MAC BALDRIGE WAS ALL OF THESE AND MORE. TO
EVERY TASK AND ROLE, HE BROUGHT THE STRENGTH OF HIS
INTEGRITY AND THE POWER OF HIS VISION. IN SERVING HIS
COUNTRY, HE BECAME AN ARCHITECT OF OUR INTERNATIONAL
ECONOMIC POLICY. AND YET, THOUGH HE MOVED WITH
PRESIDENTS, PRIME MINISTERS, AND KINGS, HE WAS ALWAYS
HAPPIEST WITH THE KIND OF STRAIGHT-TALKING COWBOYS WHO
ELECTED HIM TO THE COWBOY HALL OF FAME. MALCOLM
BALDRIGE HAD UNCOMMON ACCOMPLISHMENTS AND CHARACTER.
HE WAS A TRUE EMBODIMENT OF THE AMERICAN SPIRIT.

★ ★ ★

*President Ronald Reagan awarded Baldrige a posthumous Presidential
Medal of Freedom with the above citation during a White House
ceremony October 17, 1988. Margaret Baldrige accepted the award on
her late husband's behalf.*

President Ronald Reagan's secretary of commerce, Malcolm Baldrige
was born in Omaha, Nebraska, in 1922. As a youth he spent his
summers working as a ranch hand on Nebraska cattle ranches and
began riding horses at age eight. He went on to graduate from Yale in
1944 and saw combat in the army during World War II.

After returning to civilian life, Baldrige landed a job in 1947 as a
foundry foreman for the Eastern Malleable Iron Company in
Connecticut. Rising quickly, he became a division manager in 1951
and president nine years later. He married Margaret Trowbridge
Murray in 1951.

In 1962, he was hired as president of Scovill Inc., a Connecticut
brass milling firm suffering from poor sales. Baldrige turned the
company around, eventually creating a fully diversified multinational
company with annual sales of about $1 billion.

A delegate to Republican conventions from 1964 onward, he
became part of George Bush's unsuccessful 1980 presidential primary
bid. But his work on the victorious Reagan-Bush campaign that year
put him in position for a high-level appointment, and President
Reagan named him commerce secretary in 1981.

Baldrige quickly took the reins at commerce, but probably his
biggest single task was finding a way to stem the tide of Japanese
imports. After various steps failed, including efforts at convincing the
Japanese to voluntarily limit their exports, he finally resorted to a
more drastic remedy. A longtime free-trade advocate, he reluctantly
became a key figure in the Reagan administration's decision to

impose punitive tariffs against Japanese electronics companies producing computer chips during 1986 and 1987.

By that time Baldrige was sixty-five years old and had shouldered many responsibilities, but he refused to give up his longtime hobby of rodeo riding. He had been named to the Cowboy Hall of Fame in 1984 and still competed in about two rodeos a year as a heeler-in, the rider who lassos a steer by the hind legs while a second man takes the horns. But the sport's inherent risks finally caught up with him at a July 1987 competition in California, when his horse stumbled and fell on top of him. Baldrige died of injuries sustained in the tragic accident.

Irving Brown

AS THE EUROPEAN REPRESENTATIVE OF THE AMERICAN FEDERATION OF LABOR IN THE LATE 1940S, IRVING BROWN PLAYED A CRUCIAL ROLE IN BREAKING THE HOLD OF INTERNATIONAL COMMUNISM OVER POSTWAR WESTERN EUROPE. BY DOING SO, HE CAN TRULY BE CALLED ONE OF THE ARCHITECTS OF WESTERN DEMOCRACY. HE HAS SHUNNED PUBLICITY, BELIEVING THE CAUSE OF FREEDOM IS FAR MORE IMPORTANT THAN THE PLEASURE OF FAME. BUT HIS MODESTY CANNOT OBSCURE THE SIZE OF HIS ACCOMPLISHMENTS, AND THEY HAVE EARNED IRVING BROWN THE GRATITUDE OF HIS COUNTRY.

★ ★ ★

President Ronald Reagan awarded Brown the Presidential Medal of Freedom with the above citation during a White House ceremony October 17, 1988.

An international affairs specialist for the American Federation of Labor and Congress of Industrial Organizations (AFL-CIO), Irving Brown was born in New York City in 1911, the son of a Teamsters labor leader. He joined the labor movement in 1934, after graduating from New York University with an economics degree in 1932 and attending Columbia University for two years. Also in 1934, he married Lillie Clara Smith.

His first union experience was in helping organize the auto industry, and from 1936 to 1942 he worked as a national labor organizer for the AFL. Opposition to unionization was still strong then, and in 1937 Brown and some other union leaders were attacked and beaten by anti-union thugs in Chicago.

When the United States entered World War II, Brown became a labor representative on the War Production Board and two years later, in 1944, was named deputy vice-chairman for labor. With the war over in 1945, the AFL made Brown its European representative, putting him in charge of providing aid to workers' groups and finding ways to counter communist domination of the labor movement in Western Europe. Among his most significant accomplishments was helping found the International Confederation of Free Trade Unions (ICFTU) in 1949, an organization of unions that broke away from the communist-dominated World Federation of Trade Unions.

After serving as the ICFTU representative to the United Nations from 1962 to 1965, he directed the AFL-CIO African-American Labor Center, which supported noncommunist unions in Africa. His extensive experience in the international labor movement won him the directorship of international affairs for the AFL-CIO European division in 1982, and Brown held that post until being named senior adviser to AFL-CIO head Lane Kirkland in 1986.

The longtime labor specialist died of cancer in 1988, just one month after receiving the Presidential Medal of Freedom. He was seventy-seven years old.

Warren Earl Burger

AS TEACHER, LAWYER, ASSISTANT ATTORNEY GENERAL OF THE UNITED STATES, AND JUDGE, WARREN BURGER PROVED HIS ABIDING LOVE OF THE LAW. FOR 17 YEARS, HE SERVED IN THE HIGHEST POST ON THE HIGHEST COURT IN THE LAND AS THE 15TH CHIEF JUSTICE OF THE UNITED STATES. CHIEF JUSTICE BURGER STEPPED DOWN FROM THE SUPREME COURT TO LEAD OUR COUNTRY IN A BICENTENNIAL CELEBRATION OF THE CONSTITUTION—ONE MORE ACT OF DEVOTION AND DISTINCTION BY WARREN EARL BURGER TO THE REPUBLIC HE LOVES AND SERVES SO WELL.

★ ★ ★

President Ronald Reagan awarded Burger the Presidential Medal of Freedom with the above citation during a White House ceremony held October 17, 1988.

A moderate conservative and advocate of judicial restraint, Warren Earl Burger was born in Saint Paul, Minnesota, in 1907. One of seven children, he sold newspapers as a boy to help with family finances, and though not an exceptional student, he was offered a scholarship to Princeton. Unable to meet the additional expenses required, Burger instead attended night school at the University of Minnesota while working as an insurance agent. He eventually graduated magna cum laude from the Saint Paul College of Law in 1931 and for the next twenty-two years practiced law while also teaching at his alma mater. He married Elvera Stromberg in 1933.

A Republican, Burger caught the attention of national party officials at the Republican conventions of 1948 and 1952 while working for Minnesota governor Harold Stassen's unsuccessful presidential campaigns. When Dwight D. Eisenhower won the presidency, Burger was named assistant attorney general for the Civil Division of the Justice Department. Then in 1956 President Eisenhower appointed him to the U.S. Court of Appeals for the District of Columbia, an influential position because the court handles cases concerning federal agencies and departments. Over the next thirteen years, Burger became known as an articulate conservative, a judicial moderate on many issues but firmly opposed to expanding criminals' rights.

President Richard Nixon, who had campaigned as a law-and-order candidate in 1968, selected Burger as chief justice to succeed the retiring Earl Warren in 1969. Under Burger, the Court gradually turned away from the liberal judicial activism of the Warren years and began a sometimes contentious transition toward a more conservative court. While the pace of change certainly slowed, the Court left intact the major liberal initiatives of the Warren years and even opened some new areas, including abortion rights, gender discrimination, and affirmative action—at times despite Burger's opposition.

Burger's most important decisions involved the issue of separation of powers. His opinion in *United States v. Nixon* (1974) recognized President Nixon's right to privileged conversations but nevertheless ordered him to turn over the Watergate tapes—ultimately leading to Nixon's resignation. In *Immigration and Naturalization Service v. Chadha* (1983) he wrote the majority opinion holding that Congress's legislative veto over certain executive branch decisions violated separation of powers. Then too, in *Bowsher v. Synar* (1986), he ruled that the so-called Gramm-Rudman-Hollings budget-cutting act was unconstitutional because it gave Congress control over executive branch functions.

Burger also was known for his work in reforming the federal court system. He retired in 1986 to become chairman of the Commission of the Bicentennial of the United States Constitution and was chancellor of the College of William and Mary in Virginia until mid–1993. At his death in 1995, Burger was eighty-seven.

Milton Friedman

TEACHER, SCHOLAR, AND THEORIST—MILTON FRIEDMAN
RESTORED COMMON SENSE TO THE WORLD OF ECONOMICS. A
WINNER OF THE NOBEL PRIZE, MILTON FRIEDMAN'S TECHNICAL
MASTERY OF HIS PROFESSION IS UNCHALLENGED. BUT MORE
CENTRAL TO HIS WORK IS ITS MORAL COMPONENT: AN IDEA OF
HUMAN FREEDOM IN WHICH MAN'S ECONOMIC RIGHTS ARE AS
VITAL AS HIS CIVIL AND HUMAN RIGHTS. IT IS FOR HIS CELE-
BRATION OF THE HUMAN SPIRIT AS WELL AS THE BRILLIANCE OF
HIS MIND THAT I BESTOW UPON MILTON FRIEDMAN THE
PRESIDENTIAL MEDAL OF FREEDOM.

★ ★ ★

*President Ronald Reagan awarded Friedman the Presidential Medal of
Freedom with the above citation during a White House ceremony
October 17, 1988.*

Among the leading conservative economists of the twentieth
century, Milton Friedman was born in Brooklyn, New York, in 1912.
The son of immigrants from Austria-Hungary, he was raised in
New Jersey and attended Rutgers University, where in 1932 he
earned a bachelor's degree in economics. That same year Friedman
began graduate studies at the University of Chicago, earning a
master's degree in 1933 and remaining at Chicago for a time as a
research assistant.

In 1935 Friedman moved to Washington, D.C., where he worked
as an economist, first for the National Resources Committee and
then for the National Bureau of Economic Research. He married
fellow economist Rose Director in 1938. While in Washington he also
helped compile the book *Consumer Expenditures in the United States*
(1939), and two years later became the principal economist at the
Treasury Department's tax research division.

Between 1943 and 1946, Friedman studied at Columbia
University and after earning his doctorate saw his thesis published
as his first book, *Income from Independent Professional Practice*
(1946). He joined the faculty at the University of Chicago the same
year and became a full professor in 1948. Friedman taught economics there for over three decades before becoming professor
emeritus in 1983.

As a leading laissez-faire economist, Friedman has argued against
government intervention in the economy, notably through spending
and taxing—key elements in the Keynesian economics that have
dominated federal government policy since the depression. He
believes that an ample money supply is a more important factor in

preventing recessions than increased government spending, and Friedman has done much to promote this monetarist policy through his writings, including *A Theory of the Consumption Function* (1957). Testifying before the Joint Congressional Economic Committee in 1959, Friedman even suggested that the Federal Reserve Board give up trying to control the economy by expanding and contracting the money supply and, instead, just steadily and consistently increase it.

Friedman's collected lectures, published under the title *Capitalism and Freedom* (1960), explained his radical "negative income tax" idea. In it, people earning less than their exemption deductions for federal income taxes would be paid the difference, in cash. The plan is sometimes also called a "guaranteed annual income," since everyone would get at least the minimum amount.

In 1963 Friedman and coauthor Anna Jacobson Schwartz published the eight-hundred page *A Monetary History of the United States, 1867–1960*, tracing the effect of money supply on economic events during the period. Three years later he became a columnist for *Newsweek* and continued writing for the magazine until 1984. Meanwhile, he also continued teaching and writing books on monetarist economics and by the 1970s was known worldwide. He won the Nobel Prize in economics in 1976.

As an established voice for conservative economics, Friedman has appeared on television and regularly advised Congress and the White House on economic issues. He served as an adviser to President Richard Nixon, and from 1981 to 1988, on President Ronald Reagan's Economic Policy Advisory Board.

Among Friedman's many other books are *There's No Such Thing As A Free Lunch* (1975), *Monetary Trends in the United States and United Kingdom* (1982, with Anna J. Schwartz), and *Money Mischief* (1992, with Thomas S. Szasz).

Jean Faircloth MacArthur

VIBRANT, CHARMING, BRAVE, AND EVER LOYAL—AS SHE ALWAYS PUTS IT—"TO MY GENERAL," JEAN MACARTHUR HAS WITNESSED THE GREAT CATACLYSMS OF OUR TIME, SURVIVED WAR AND PEACE, CONQUERED TRAGEDY, AND KNOWN TRIUMPH. WHETHER ON A PT BOAT EVADING ENEMY SHIPS IN THE SOUTH CHINA SEA OR BEING WELCOMED HOME BY ALL AMERICANS IN 1951, JEAN MACARTHUR WAS AND IS A SHINING EXAMPLE—A WOMAN OF SUBSTANCE AND CHARACTER; A LOYAL WIFE AND MOTHER; AND

LIKE HER GENERAL, A PATRIOT SELFLESS IN THE SERVICE OF OUR
COUNTRY AND THE CAUSE OF FREEDOM.

★ ★ ★

*President Ronald Reagan awarded MacArthur the Presidential Medal
of Freedom with the above citation during a White House ceremony
October 17, 1988.*

The wife of World War II hero General Douglas MacArthur, Jean
MacArthur was born Jean Faircloth in Murfreesboro, Tennessee. Her
parents divorced when she was still a young child, and her stepfather
was a well-to-do businessman. MacArthur was particularly proud of
her grandfather, who was a Confederate captain in the Civil War, and
was dubbed "the flagwavingest girl in Murfreesboro" for her outspoken patriotism.

In many ways she was ideally suited to become General
MacArthur's wife. His first marriage had ended in divorce in 1929
when his wife could not adjust to army life. The second Mrs.
MacArthur, on the other hand, had a high regard for the army, and
after their marriage in 1937, she proved a devoted wife who thoroughly enjoyed army life. She and her husband were virtually inseparable for the remainder of the general's life. She bore one child, a
son Arthur, in 1938.

During the remainder of General MacArthur's career, through
war and controversy, Jean MacArthur was at her husband's side.
Soon after their wedding, she went with him to the Philippines, and
she was there when the Japanese attacked and forced the general to
flee to Australia. She stayed with him in Australia, following him
back to the Philippines after U.S. forces recaptured the islands in
1944. She was with him in Tokyo, Japan, during the U.S. occupation
and in Korea until his dispute with President Harry S. Truman over
the war strategy cost him his job in 1951.

General MacArthur retired from the army that year and for over a
decade served as a board chairman, first for the Rand Corporation
and then for Sperry Rand. At his death in 1964, he left his wife a substantial estate. In subsequent years, Jean MacArthur has made
appearances at public functions from time to time.

J. Willard Marriott

THE SON OF A HUMBLE UTAH SHEEP RANCHER, J. WILLARD
MARRIOTT TURNED A SMALL ROOT BEER STAND IN THE NATION'S
CAPITAL INTO ONE OF AMERICA'S LARGEST AND MOST SUC-
CESSFUL BUSINESSES. KNOWN FOR HIS VISION, INGENUITY, AND
HARD WORK, J. WILLARD MARRIOTT WILL ALSO BE REMEMBERED
AS A MAN OF DEVOTION TO FAMILY, A LEADER IN HIS CHURCH, A
RESPECTED VOICE IN THE HALLS OF GOVERNMENT, AND AS A MAN
WHO IN HIS LIFE AND CAREER BROUGHT HONOR TO AMERICA.

★ ★ ★

*President Ronald Reagan awarded Marriott a posthumous
Presidential Medal of Freedom with the above citation during a White
House ceremony October 17, 1988. Marriott's wife, Alice, accepted the
medal on her late husband's behalf.*

J. Willard Marriott was born at the Mormon settlement of Marriott,
Utah, in 1900, and was raised on his father's sheep farm. Marriott's
grandfather, for whom the town was named, had been among the
first Mormon pioneers who migrated westward to Utah in 1847.
While growing up, Marriott learned the Mormon values of industry,
thrift, individualism, and social responsibility and at age eighteen he
set out on two years of missionary work in New England, which was
required of all young Mormons. He then worked his way through
college by teaching, managing a bookstore, and working as a
salesman, finally graduating from the University of Utah in 1926. The
following year he married his college sweetheart, Alice Sheets, and
together the young couple moved to Washington, D.C.

With $500 in savings and borrowed money, Marriott opened an
A & W root beer stand in downtown Washington. The business
thrived during the summer, but in fall the cool weather brought a big
drop in sales. Undaunted, Marriott outfitted his small shop with a
barbecue machine and stools to create his first Hot Shoppe. Working
eighteen hours a day—he once observed that "no person can get very
far in this life on forty hours a week"—Marriott expanded his
business to include seven Hot Shoppes in the Washington area by
1932. He had a simple formula for his success: offer good food at a
low price, a family atmosphere, and good service.

Then in 1933, with his business thriving despite the depression,
Marriott collapsed with a disease of the lymphatic system. Doctors told
him he had just two years to live, but after fishing, hunting, and riding in
Maine and Florida for six months, he went back to expanding his
restaurant chain—proving his doctors wrong. Marriott added an airline
catering division to his business in 1937, and by the end of World War II,
he had opened Hot Shoppes throughout the eastern United States.

Marriott made expansion the cornerstone of his business, doubling the size of his corporation every five years from its inception. He expanded into hotels in the 1950s, opening the first Marriott motel in 1957, and by the 1980s had parlayed his initial $500 investment into a lodging and food service empire generating $3.5 billion a year in sales. By that time, the Marriott Corporation, so named from 1967 onward, included 1,400 restaurants, 143 hotels and resorts, the airline catering division, and other businesses.

While remaining board chairman, Marriott began turning over the reins of power to his son, J. Willard, Jr., naming him president of Marriott Corporation in 1964 and chief executive officer in 1972. The senior Marriott, meanwhile, gained a reputation as a philanthropist, was a longtime supporter of the Republican party, and was a friend of Republican presidents. He chaired President Richard Nixon's inaugural committees in 1969 and 1973. Marriott died in 1985, at age eighty-four.

David Packard

ACCOMPLISHED BUSINESSMAN AND SKILLFUL MANAGER, NOTED PHILANTHROPIST AND PUBLIC SERVANT OF THE HIGHEST INTEGRITY—DAVID PACKARD HAS HAD A LEGENDARY LIFE AND CAREER. DEDICATED TO FURTHERING THE PURSUIT OF SCIENTIFIC, TECHNOLOGICAL, AND HUMAN PROGRESS, DEVOTED TO HIS COUNTRY AND THE CAUSE OF KEEPING HER STRONG IN A DANGEROUS WORLD, DAVID PACKARD HAS SERVED THE AMERICAN PEOPLE EFFECTIVELY, GENEROUSLY, AND PROUDLY.

★ ★ ★

President Ronald Reagan awarded Packard the Presidential Medal of Freedom with the above citation during a White House ceremony October 17, 1988.

The cofounder of the multimillion-dollar Hewlett-Packard electronics company, David Packard was born in Pueblo, Colorado, in 1912. A lawyer's son, Packard was raised in comfortable circumstances and earned his bachelor's degree as an electrical engineering major at Stanford University in California (1934). He spent three years working on vacuum tubes for the General Electric Company before returning to Stanford on a fellowship program for another electrical engineering degree, which he attained in 1939. Packard married fellow Stanford graduate Lucile Laura Salter in 1938.

Meanwhile, he and a fellow electrical engineering student, William R. Hewlett, set up shop in the Packard family garage and with initial capital of just $538 began inventing electronic devices. Their first fruits included a bowling alley foul-line warning device, an aid for weight-reduction, and a harmonica tuner. Walt Disney Studios became their first paying customer, purchasing some specialized electronic equipment for the *Fantasia* sound track.

The young entrepreneurs realized a net profit of just over $1,600 their first year, all of which was plowed back into the business. They decided early on to specialize in the field of electronic test and measuring instruments. As their business grew, they also were careful to keep their facility close to Stanford, so that they could keep in touch with current research and attract recent electrical engineering graduates as employees.

With Packard focusing on management and Hewlett on the engineering side, the Hewlett-Packard company grew rapidly throughout the 1950s and 1960s into a major American defense contractor and a leading international electronic equipment manufacturer. Packard served as president from 1947 to 1964. He was board chairman and chief executive officer from 1964 to 1968, with Hewlett serving as president from 1964.

A long-time Republican, Packard entered government service in 1969 during the difficult Vietnam years. The deputy secretary of defense under Melvin Laird, Packard served for two years at the Defense Department during the Nixon administration. Among his other tasks, Packard conducted a review of the longstanding U.S. policy of helping protect virtually any country under threat of Communist aggression, which had led to U.S. involvement in Vietnam in the first place.

After resigning in 1971, Packard returned to Hewlett-Packard as board chairman, a post he retained until his retirement in 1993. Meanwhile, he continued as a high-level presidential adviser on defense management and procurement for the next two decades. He also served on numerous councils and commissions, including the Trilateral Commission (1973–1981), the U.S.-U.S.S.R. Trade and Economic Council (1975–1982), the White House Science Council (1982–1988), and the President's Council of Advisors on Science and Technology (1990–1992). He also served on the boards of numerous nonprofit organizations, including educational, environmental, and public affairs groups.

Michael Joseph Mansfield

DURING WORLD WAR I, MIKE MANSFIELD, NOT YET 15, ENLISTED IN THE UNITED STATES NAVY, CROSSING THE ATLANTIC SEVEN TIMES BEFORE HE WAS DISCHARGED. HIS SERVICE TO COUNTRY WOULD SPAN SEVEN DECADES AND WOULD HELP SHAPE AMERICA'S DESTINY AS A PACIFIC POWER. THROUGH 34 YEARS IN CONGRESS—INCLUDING 16 AS SENATE MAJORITY LEADER—AND WITH MORE THAN A DECADE AS U.S. AMBASSADOR TO JAPAN, MIKE MANSFIELD HAS SET HIS INDELIBLE MARK UPON AMERICAN FOREIGN POLICY AND DIS-TINGUISHED HIMSELF AS A DEDICATED PUBLIC SERVANT AND LOYAL AMERICAN.

★ ★ ★

President Ronald Reagan awarded Mansfield the Presidential Medal of Freedom with the above citation during a White House ceremony January 19, 1989.

The longest-serving majority leader in Senate history, Michael Joseph Mansfield was born in New York City's Greenwich Village in 1903. His mother died when he was still very young, and an aunt and uncle raised him in Great Falls, Montana. Mansfield dropped out of school in the eighth grade and served in the navy during World War I. Eventually discharged for being underage, he spent a year in the army and two in the marines, serving for a time in the Philippines, China, and Siberia.

After 1922 he worked in Butte, Montana, copper mines and might have stayed there had his future wife, a teacher named Maureen Hayes, not talked him into returning to school. Mansfield entered the University of Montana at Missoula in 1930 as a special student. He married his wife in 1932 and earned both his high school diploma and his bachelor's degree in 1933. The following year Mansfield got his master's degree and became an instructor at the university, eventually becoming a full professor of Far Eastern and Latin American history.

Elected to the U.S. House of Representatives as a Democrat in 1942, he served five terms, 1943 through 1953, and established himself both as a solid liberal and as an expert on the Far East. In 1952 Mansfield won a narrow Senate race, overcoming Sen. Joseph McCarthy's charges that he was soft on communism. Taking his seat the following year, he soon joined the inner circle of Senate Democrats (Lyndon B. Johnson among them) and became a member of the Senate Foreign Relations Committee.

Moving up through party ranks in the Senate, the Montana

Democrat was named majority whip in 1957 and majority leader in 1961, when Lyndon Johnson became vice president. Mansfield's leadership style was considerably less forceful than Johnson's, though, and at times he even drew criticism for a lack of toughness with members. He also preferred to delegate considerable power to fellow members through the Democratic Policy Committee.

Meanwhile, his expertise in the Far East caused him to become concerned about U.S. involvement in Vietnam, probably the most troubling issue of his term as majority leader. He had warned Presidents Dwight D. Eisenhower and John F. Kennedy that the South Vietnamese dictatorship would ultimately fail if it did not have popular support and did not govern justly. During the 1960s Mansfield gradually became openly critical of America's escalating involvement in the Vietnam War, and during the Nixon administration he sponsored bills to end it.

He also was concerned about the growth of presidential powers, particularly in light of the Watergate scandal, and in 1973 supported the War Powers Act. Among other legislation he voted for during his long career in the Senate were the 1964 Civil Rights Act and the Equal Rights Amendment. He also supported bills to reduce the U.S. troop commitment in Europe, provide federal funding for abortion, create a consumer protection agency, fund presidential election campaigns, and return Okinawa to Japanese control.

Still the majority leader, Mansfield retired from the Senate in 1977, but soon after President Jimmy Carter named him U.S. ambassador to Japan. He took charge of America's largest single diplomatic mission and, considering the tremendous importance of trade between the two countries, probably one of the most sensitive posts in the foreign service. Continuing as ambassador through the Carter years and both of President Ronald Reagan's terms, Mansfield finally retired in 1989. President Reagan awarded him the Presidential Medal of Freedom on his retirement.

George Shultz

Unyieldingly dedicated to the protection of the American national interest, the advancement of freedom and human rights, the battle against tyranny, and reductions in nuclear arms, George P. Shultz has presided over the Department of State during one of the most critical periods in the history of this nation's foreign policy. For years of public service and his vital

PART IN INAUGURATING A NEW ERA OF HOPE IN FOREIGN POLICY,
HIS COUNTRYMEN HONOR HIM.

★ ★ ★

President Ronald Reagan awarded Shultz the Presidential Medal of
Freedom with the above citation during a White House ceremony
January 19, 1989.

The holder of four different cabinet posts during his long government career, George Shultz was born in New York City in 1920
and was raised in comfortable circumstances in suburban
Englewood Cliffs, New Jersey. After graduating cum laude from
Princeton University with a bachelor's degree in economics (1942),
he served as a marine artillery officer in the Pacific theater during
World War II. Shultz married Helena Maria O'Brien in 1946 and
three years later earned his doctorate in industrial economics at the
Massachusetts Institute of Technology (MIT).

During the 1950s Shultz taught at MIT, served on arbitration
panels for labor-management disputes, and acted as senior staff
economist to President Dwight D. Eisenhower's Council of
Economic Advisers (1955). In 1957 he became a professor of industrial
relations at the University of Chicago, a post he held until 1968, and
he also served as dean of the university's Graduate School of
Business from 1962 to 1968.

After serving in advisory roles to Presidents John F. Kennedy and
Lyndon B. Johnson, Shultz was appointed to his first cabinet post,
secretary of labor, by President Richard Nixon in 1969. Taking office
at a time of increasing labor militancy and worsening economic
problems, he opposed increasing the minimum wage, averted a
railroad strike, helped settle a strike by postal workers, and instituted
a program to increase minority employment.

Named head of President Nixon's new Office of Management and
Budget in 1970, he joined with other cabinet officials to impose
Nixon's New Economic Policy, which included a wage and price
freeze to combat inflation. Shultz then accepted his third cabinet
appointment in 1972, as Nixon's secretary of the Treasury, and in that
post focused on the problem of rising inflation. He also participated
in the 1973 international conference that introduced floating
currency exchange rates in place of the old fixed-rate system.

Back in the business world after resigning as Treasury secretary in
1974, Shultz became a vice president of Bechtel Corporation. A year
later he was named president, then corporate vice chairman in 1977,
and finally president of Bechtel Group in 1981. Meanwhile, he also
taught management and public policy at Stanford University
(1974–1982).

Shultz's last cabinet post, as secretary of state, came in the Reagan
administration. Appointed in 1982, he quickly became an adminis-

tration insider and remained in the post until the Reagan administration left office in 1989. Shultz helped shape U.S. policy in Central America and the Mideast, including the ill-fated U.S. military presence in Beirut, and was a strong advocate of direct action against terrorists. He established good relations early on with Soviet leader Mikhail Gorbachev and helped arrange the historic Intermediate Nuclear Forces Treaty in 1987.

After 1989 Shultz returned to teaching at Stanford, becoming professor emeritus in 1991, and has been a distinguished fellow at Stanford's Hoover Institution. He is a member of various corporate boards and in 1993 published his autobiography, *Turmoil and Triumph: My Years as Secretary of State.*

George Bush

GEORGE BUSH, A REPUBLICAN, WAS SWORN INTO OFFICE ON
JANUARY 20, 1989, AND SERVED ONE TERM (1989–1993).

MEDAL
CEREMONIES

MAY 25, 1989 *Walter Reed Hospital, Washington, D.C.*

JULY 6, 1989 *The White House East Room*

NOVEMBER 13, 1989 *The White House East Room*

MARCH 7, 1991 *The White House East Room*

JULY 3, 1991 *The White House East Room*

NOVEMBER 18, 1991 *The White House*

DECEMBER 12, 1991 *The White House*

MARCH 17, 1992 *Bentonville, Arkansas*

DECEMBER 11, 1992 *The White House East Room*

JANUARY 12, 1993 *The White House Oval Office*

JANUARY 13, 1993 *The White House Dining Room*

Claude D. Pepper

As champion of the most vulnerable among us, Claude Pepper has enhanced America's national character. Through his legislative efforts and personal example he has helped the disadvantaged and elderly gain self-respect and dignity. Through six decades of public service, Claude Pepper has built bridges that span the generations. For his efforts to make governments responsive and responsible and his lifetime devotion to the U.S. Senate and House of Representatives his countrymen salute a career dedicated to preserving the values that make America great.

★ ★ ★

President George Bush awarded Pepper the Presidential Medal of Freedom with the above citation during a special ceremony held at Walter Reed Hospital in Washington, D.C., on May 25, 1989.

Called a "fighting liberal" by President Franklin D. Roosevelt, Claude D. Pepper was born near Dudleyville, Alabama, in 1900. He was raised in a family of loyal Democrats and later worked his way through the University of Alabama at Tuscaloosa, earning his bachelor's degree with honors in 1921. Pursuing a law degree, Pepper graduated from Harvard Law School in 1924, finishing sixth in his class.

During the 1920s Pepper taught law at the University of Arkansas and then moved to Florida, where he entered private practice. Pepper's first political office was as a Florida state legislator, but he served only one term. His opposition to a censure resolution against President Herbert Hoover's wife, who had invited the black wife of a congressman to tea at the White House, angered segregationists and cost him his reelection.

Moving to Tallahassee, he narrowly lost his bid for a U.S. Senate seat in 1934. Refusing to give up, though, Pepper tried again and won a special election for a vacant Senate seat two years later. Twice reelected, Pepper spent the next fourteen years in the Senate, making a name for himself as a liberal and a strong supporter of President Roosevelt's New Deal policies. Meanwhile, he married Mildred Irene Webster in 1936.

Senator Pepper played an important role in passing a minimum wage law, the statute establishing an eight-hour workday, the Lend-Lease Act, and a measure establishing the National Cancer Institute. He was an early proponent of America's joining the war against Adolph Hitler but seriously misjudged Soviet dictator Joseph Stalin, publicly describing him as "a man Americans can trust" after visiting the Soviet Union in 1945. The remark came back to haunt him in an especially sordid Senate race in 1950. His opponents played on anti-communist fears and mounted a racial smear campaign as well to defeat him that year.

Back in private practice, Pepper had to wait until 1962 before making his political comeback. This time he won election to the U.S. House of Representatives, where he served for the next twenty-seven years and made his mark as a champion of the nation's elderly. A staunch supporter of the social legislation of the Kennedy-Johnson years, he was among the few southern representatives to vote for civil rights bills. Meanwhile, he joined the growing opposition to U.S. involvement in Vietnam in 1968.

A decade later he became chairman of the newly created House Select Committee on Aging and there focused national attention on the problems of the elderly. Among the many initiatives benefiting the aged that he sponsored or supported was the 1986 law ending mandatory retirement based on age. Known as "Mr. Social Security" for his efforts to prevent cuts in the Social Security and Medicare programs, Pepper became chairman of the powerful House Rules Committee in 1983.

He published his autobiography, *Pepper: Eyewitness to a Century*, in 1987. In 1989, at age eighty-eight, Pepper fell ill with cancer. By May he was confined to Walter Reed Hospital and his condition was rapidly worsening. Pepper had been selected to receive the Presidential Medal of Freedom in a ceremony to be held that July. But because of his deteriorating condition, President Bush presented him with the medal in a special ceremony at the hospital. After Pepper's death a week later, the House voted to have his body lie in state in the Capitol Rotunda, the first incumbent House member so honored since 1868.

Lucille Ball

A GIFTED COMEDIENNE KNOWN AND LOVED BY GENERATIONS OF AUDIENCES AROUND THE WORLD, LUCILLE BALL LEFT A LASTING IMPRESSION OF AMERICAN ENTERTAINMENT. FOR OVER 50 YEARS, SHE WARMED THE HEARTS OF MILLIONS WITH HER HUMOR, BOTH IN FILMS AND LATER ON TELEVISION, WHERE NO PROGRAM WAS BETTER NAMED THAN "I LOVE LUCY." AS PRESIDENT OF HER OWN PRODUCTION COMPANY, SHE SET AN EXAMPLE WITH HER COMMITMENT TO PROGRAMMING OF QUALITY FOR FAMILY ENJOYMENT. LUCY'S WORK CONTINUES TO BRING JOY AND

LAUGHTER INTO AMERICAN HOMES. AND A GRATEFUL NATION
REMEMBERS HER WITH LOVE AND APPRECIATION.

★ ★ ★

*President George Bush awarded Ball a posthumous Presidential Medal
of Freedom with the above citation during a White House ceremony July
6, 1989. Gary Morton accepted the award on his late wife's behalf.*

Offstage, the lovable, irrepressible redheaded Lucille Ball believed in
the "power of positive thought." Her stunningly successful career
stands as a testimony to that faith: despite failing as a New York City
dramatic school student, she persevered and eventually became an
internationally acclaimed comedian. Ultimately, Lucy starred in three
hit television sitcoms and appeared in over seventy films, as well as
proving herself a shrewd business executive.

Lucille Ball was born a blond in 1911 and grew up in a western
New York town named Celoron. With her mother's encouragement,
the young Lucy put on informal plays at home as a child and actively
participated in school theatrical productions. At fifteen she made the
ill-fated journey to the John Murray Anderson-Robert Milton drama
school in New York City—classmate Bette Davis shined but Lucy
lasted only six weeks. Lucy refused to give up, however, trying unsuccessfully for bit parts on Broadway during the late 1920s before
turning to modeling to support herself. Ironically, modeling led to
the long-sought chance to act. By 1933 Lucy had become nationally
known as the Chesterfield Cigarette Girl, and the exposure landed
her a contract for bit parts in ten films.

Her stock in the movie world rose painfully slowly, though. She
appeared in thirty-three films during the seven years between 1935
and 1942, moving up from bit parts to supporting roles and lead
parts. In 1940 she married the Cuban band leader Desi Arnaz,
beginning inconspicuously a marriage that would eventually become
a facet of American life.

Lucy's performance as a crippled nightclub singer opposite Henry
Fonda in *The Big Street* (1942) secured her both stardom and an MGM
contract. MGM dyed her hair red, created a new image for her, and gave
her starring roles in such movies as *Du Barry Was a Lady* (1943) and *Best
Foot Forward* (1943). While continuing to make movies, she also acted in
theatrical productions, and between 1947 and 1951 she played a banker's
featherbrained wife on the CBS radio show "My Favorite Husband."

The television series "I Love Lucy" cast her in a similar role as the
lovable but scatterbrained wife of a Cuban band leader played by Desi
Arnaz, and made Lucille Ball a household name. The show topped the
charts just six months after it premiered in 1951 and over the next six
years garnered five Emmys and about two-hundred other awards.
Seemingly inseparable on television, she and husband Desi divorced
in 1960. Lucy married comedian Gary Morton the following year.

Lucy finally had a Broadway hit with the 1960 musical comedy *Wildcat,* but her biggest successes continued to come on television—"The Lucy Show" (1962–1968) and "Here's Lucy" (1968–1974). Having bought out her husband, Lucy astutely managed their Desilu production company until 1967, when she sold it for $17 million. She formed Lucille Ball Productions the next year. Her last film was *Mame* (1974). The Television Academy inducted Lucy into its Hall of Fame in 1984. She died four years later.

Clarence Douglas Dillon

In a lifetime of responsible positions, C. Douglas Dillon has dedicated himself to bettering America and the world. By fostering European economic and military unity, he furthered the cause of democracy. Through his leadership on economic issues, he helped make possible the material advance of a generation. Through his dedication to the Alliance for Progress, he made real for a million America's determination to promote social development. For service to three Presidents and for commitment to his fellow man, America honors Mr. Dillon.

★ ★ ★

President George Bush awarded Dillon the Presidential Medal of Freedom with the above citation during a White House ceremony July 6, 1989.

The son of a prominent American investment banker, Clarence Douglas Dillon was born in Geneva, Switzerland, in 1909, while his parents were touring Europe. He had ample opportunity to learn about the world of finance during his youth. When Dillon was just seven, his father became president of the prestigious international investment banking firm William A. Read and Company, which was renamed Dillon, Read and Company in 1920.

After graduating from Harvard magna cum laude in 1931, the younger Dillon acquired a seat on the New York Stock Exchange and worked as a stock trader until 1936. Joining his father's company in 1937, he became director of two investment firms affiliated with Dillon, Read and Company—the United States and Foreign Securities Corporation and the International Securities Corporation. The following year he also was named a vice president and board member at Dillon, Read. Dillon served in the navy's air arm during

World War II, and on returning to civilian status secured his position as a leading American financier by becoming chairman of the board at Dillon, Read, a position he held from 1946 to 1953. Meanwhile, Dillon actively supported the Republican Party, working for Thomas E. Dewey's unsuccessful 1948 presidential campaign and for Dwight D. Eisenhower's successful presidential bid in 1952.

President Eisenhower rewarded Dillon by naming him U.S. ambassador to France, a post Dillon held until 1957. Next he became a high-level official in the State Department, rising to undersecretary of state in 1959. His government service continued during the Kennedy and Johnson administrations, this time as Treasury secretary from 1961 to 1965. While at the Treasury Department Dillon became involved in developing a new tax policy and helped found the Alliance for Progress, a Kennedy administration economic aid program for Latin America.

After 1965 Dillon served for over a decade as director of the Council on Foreign Relations. He also returned to a more active role in the investment business, serving as managing director of Dillon, Read from 1971 to 1983. During the 1970s and early 1980s, though, he gradually retired from his business and philanthropic activities. Among the latter were chairmanships of the Rockefeller Foundation (1971–1975) and of the Metropolitan Museum of Art (1977–1983).

James "Jimmy" H. Doolittle

Aviation pioneer and military hero, James H. Doolittle is a symbol of vision and courage. His numerous contributions to aeronautical science, often at great personal hazard, extend from the earliest achievements in long-distance flying to the age of rockets. In the uniform of his country, General Doolittle's heroic leadership inspired the American people during the darkest hours of the Second World War. In public service, he continued to foster American advances in aeronautics, the cause to which he devoted his life. For extraordinary service to country, the American people salute one of their foremost heroes.

★ ★ ★

President George Bush awarded Doolittle the Presidential Medal of Freedom with the above citation during a White House ceremony July 6, 1989.

The devastating blow of Japan's sneak attack on Pearl Harbor in 1941 left the country reeling. Thousands of U.S. military personnel had been killed in the early-morning raid. The U.S. Navy had been seriously weakened by the destruction of so many warships. And suddenly, irrevocably, America was at war. With Japan dominating the Pacific theater and Nazi Germany in control of Europe, the outlook for America and its World War II allies was truly bleak, and the American people knew it.

Soon after Pearl Harbor, U.S. military planners hatched a daring scheme they hoped would give American morale a much-needed shot in the arm. Jimmy Doolittle, an army air force officer and well-known test pilot, was called on to organize and lead a bombing raid against Tokyo, the heart of the Japanese empire. The operation was extremely risky. Long-range bombers did not exist then and the United States had no bases left in the Pacific close enough to strike Japan, forcing Doolittle to launch his B-25 bombers from aircraft carriers off the Japanese coast.

Doolittle hastily assembled his team, and in the early-morning hours of April 18, 1942, the carrier USS *Hornet* steamed as close to Japan as it dared. With Doolittle flying the lead plane, sixteen B-25s took off from the *Hornet*'s dangerously short flight deck. Hours later Doolittle's bombers shocked the Japanese by hitting Tokyo, Nagoya, Osaka, and Kobe before retreating as planned toward airfields in Nationalist China.

Not one of the bombers made it to its assigned airfield. Enemy warships had been operating off the Japanese coast that morning, so that Doolittle had to launch his planes farther out to sea than planned. Now, one by one, the U.S. B-25s dropped out of the sky for lack of fuel. Their crews bailed out or crash-landed the planes in China, some landing in areas controlled by the Japanese. Chinese citizens helped Doolittle and most of his men to safety but nine did not make it back.

The first American strike against the Japanese, Doolittle's raid produced an immediate sensation in the United States. Little real damage had been done to the Japanese cities, but the attack humiliated Japanese Grand Admiral Yamamoto, the commander of the Pearl Harbor attack four months earlier. And it made Doolittle one of the war's first and most famous heroes.

Doolittle was born in Alameda, California, in 1896. Interested in aviation for a time as a youth, he also developed his tough, combative side and in 1912 won the Pacific coast amateur bantamweight boxing championship. A few years later he entered the University of California to study mining engineering. World War I intervened, however, and after Doolittle enlisted, the army air corps trained him as a pilot and flight instructor.

That began Doolittle's long career in the rapidly developing field of aviation. Remaining in the air corps until 1930, he made a record-setting transcontinental flight in 1922 (for which he received the Distinguished Flying Cross), set a world speed record for seaplanes in 1925, and made the first-ever takeoff and landing using instruments in 1929. In addition to racing and testing planes, he earned his doctorate in aeronautical engineering at the Massachusetts Institute of Technology in 1925.

He continued racing planes while working for Shell Oil Company on the development of high-octane aviation fuel during the 1930s. Recalled to active duty as an Air Force major in 1940, he eventually took on the Tokyo raid. For his bravery, Doolittle won the Congressional Medal of Honor and was promoted to brigadier general, but his military career was far from over.

Sent to Europe in 1942, he commanded the Twelfth Air Force, which supported the Allied invasions of North Africa, Sicily, and Italy. From 1943 to 1945 he commanded the Eighth Air Force, which was based in England and was responsible for massive bombing attacks on Germany.

Again a civilian in 1946, Doolittle became a vice president for Shell Oil Company and also continued his involvement with the aviation industry. Between 1948 and 1958 he was a member of the National Advisory Committee for Aeronautics (the NASA forerunner), serving as its chairman from 1956 to 1958. He also was a member of the President's Science Advisory Committee in 1957 and 1958.

Doolittle retired from Shell Oil in 1959 but remained active in the aerospace industry for many years afterward. He died in 1993, at the age of ninety-six.

George F. Kennan

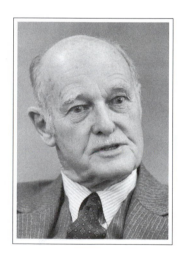

CAREER DIPLOMAT, HISTORIAN, EDUCATOR, GEORGE KENNAN HAS HELPED SHAPE AMERICAN FOREIGN POLICY SINCE 1933. HIS MANY YEARS IN GOVERNMENT SERVICE AND A LIFETIME OF SCHOLARLY WRITINGS REVEALED A DEEP INSIGHT INTO EAST-WEST RELATIONS, A RECOGNITION OF THE CHALLENGES OF TOTALITARIAN EXPANSION, AS WELL AS A MAN OF EXTRAORDINARY SENSITIVITY. FOR HIS SUCCESS IN ADVANCING OUR NATIONAL SECURITY AND FOR HIS MANY CONTRIBUTIONS TO THE STUDY OF INTERNATIONAL AFFAIRS, GEORGE KENNAN'S FELLOW AMERICANS PROUDLY HONOR HIM.

★ ★ ★

President George Bush awarded Kennan the Presidential Medal of Freedom with the above citation during a White House ceremony July 6, 1989.

A key figure in developing the early U.S. Cold War policy, George F. Kennan was born in Milwaukee, Wisconsin, in 1904. He had an uncle who was an expert and author on czarist Russia, and, while studying at Princeton University, Kennan chose history as his major. After graduating with his bachelor's degree in 1925, he entered the diplomatic corps and was given a series of assignments in Germany and the Baltic states during the late 1920s. At the time, the United States had no diplomatic relations with the Soviet Union, and diplomatic missions in the neighboring Baltic states were important as "listening posts."

Sent to Moscow when the United States established an embassy there in 1933, Kennan rose to second secretary before serving a two-year stint in Prague, Czechoslovakia (1938–1939). During World War II he held posts in Berlin, Germany, and Lisbon, Portugal.

Foreshadowing his later high-level policy work, Kennan served on the U.S. delegation to the European Advisory Commission in 1943 and 1944. The commission developed policy options on postwar Europe for leaders of the big three Allied powers, the United States, Britain, and the Soviet Union. Kennan returned to Moscow for a two-year assignment as minister-counselor in May 1944, a time when Soviet postwar relations with the West were already beginning to take shape.

Kennan's famous "long telegram" from Moscow in 1946 and a magazine article he published in 1947 after his return to the United States became key statements in formulating U.S. Cold War policy, particularly its determined opposition to Soviet expansionism. Citing both Soviet fears of Western ideas and the country's fanatical belief in spreading communism, Kennan said that diplomatic negotiations would prove fruitless. Soviet expansionism would have to be "contained" with deliberate tit-for-tat countermoves until the Soviet regime either proved willing to hold meaningful talks or broke down altogether.

Containment of communism became a key element of the Truman administration's foreign policy in the early Cold War years, a marked shift from previous efforts at appeasing the Soviets while the Allies needed their help with fighting the Nazis in World War II. Meanwhile, in 1947 Kennan took charge of the State Department's long-range foreign policy planning and in 1949 became a high-level adviser to Secretary of State Dean Acheson. By the end of the 1940s Kennan had come to believe that negotiations with the Soviets might be worthwhile, particularly on reunifying Germany.

That view proved unpopular with the Truman administration, and in 1950 Kennan left the State Department to lecture at the Institute for Advanced Study at Princeton. With his work at the institute as his base—he became permanent professor in 1956 and professor emeritus in 1974—Kennan launched his second career as an author, leading authority on the Soviet regime, and critic of U.S. foreign policy. His first two books, *American Diplomacy, 1900–1950* (1951) and *Realities of American Foreign Policy* (1954), were collections of lectures on U.S. foreign policy at the institute. *Russia Leaves the War* (1956), the first in his series on Soviet-American relations during World War I, won him both the National Book Award and the Pulitzer Prize.

While lecturing as a visiting professor at Oxford in 1957 and 1958, he did a controversial series of talks for the British Broadcasting Corporation in which he suggested that the United States and the

Soviet Union mutually withdraw their forces from European nations and allow reunification of Germany. Criticized as unrealistic at the time, Kennan's suggestions finally became an accomplished fact some three decades later, but not before the Soviet Union collapsed. A year later, in 1959, he advanced another controversial idea, that the United States stop relying on nuclear weapons for its defense and develop conventional forces instead. He further suggested negotiations with the Soviets to eventually abolish nuclear weapons.

Kennan briefly returned to foreign service between 1961 and 1963 as ambassador to Yugoslavia and in 1967 published *Memoirs, 1925–1950*, which won him a second Pulitzer Prize in 1968. He continued his writings in history and foreign policy, as well as writing additional books of memoirs, during the 1970s and 1980s. Among these books were *The Cloud of Danger: Current Realities of American Foreign Policy* (1977), *The Fateful Alliance: France, Russia and the Coming of the First World War* (1984), and *Sketches from a Life* (1989). He wrote *Around the Cragged Hill* in 1993.

Margaret Chase Smith

As the United States Representative for 8 years, as a 4-term Senator, Margaret Chase Smith served the people of Maine and the Nation with distinction. She influenced greatly the development of our postwar foreign and domestic policies, and her abilities and independent spirit made her one of the most admired women in America. A firm believer in a strong national defense, her efforts to improve the status of women in the Navy earned her the affectionate title Mother of the Waves. And for many years of outstanding public service, America proudly honors her.

★ ★ ★

President George Bush awarded Smith the Presidential Medal of Freedom with the above citation during a White House ceremony July 6, 1989.

The first woman elected to both chambers of Congress, Margaret Chase Smith was born Margaret Chase in Skowhegan, Maine, in 1897. Her father was the town barber, and as a youth she worked in his barbershop, as well as in the local five-and-dime store. After graduating from high school in 1916, she held a series of jobs, including newspaper circulation manager and office manager for a local woolen mill. In 1930 she married Clyde Harold Smith, a successful local businessman twenty-one years her senior.

When her husband became a Republican representative in the U.S. Congress, Smith served as his secretary in Washington. He died in 1940, though, and she won a special election to fill out the remainder of his term. Smith went on to serve four terms in the House (1941–1949), where, as an independent-minded Republican, she supported President Franklin D. Roosevelt's New Deal and foreign policies. She got herself appointed to the House Naval Affairs Committee in 1943 and became known as the "Mother of the Waves" for her efforts in behalf of women in the navy.

Smith ran successfully for the Senate in 1948 and went on to serve four terms (1949–1973). Soon after beginning her Senate term, she gained notoriety by joining six other senators in attacking Sen. Joseph McCarthy for his vicious anticommunist scare tactics. McCarthy sarcastically referred to her as "Snow White" and the others as the "six dwarfs." Smith outlasted McCarthy in the Senate by many years, though, and eventually became the ranking Republican on both the Armed Services and the Aeronautical and Space Sciences committees. She also was a member of the Appropriations Committee.

As during her House service, Smith was unafraid to buck the Senate Republican party line on issues in which she believed. She supported civil rights and federally funded health care for the aged, for example. A firm believer in a strong military, she also once openly criticized President John F. Kennedy for what she saw as his lack of will to use nuclear weapons. Reacting to reports of her remarks, Soviet leader Nikita Khrushchev called her "the devil in the disguise of a woman."

Toward the end of her fourth term Smith had grown increasingly frail with age—she was seventy-four at the time. Though she was still in good health and campaigned for reelection in 1972, her advancing age became an issue that contributed to her defeat that year. As if to prove the voters wrong, Smith lived another twenty-three years before succumbing to the effects of a stroke in 1995. She was ninety-seven.

Lech Walesa

LECH WALESA HAS SHOWN THROUGH HIS LIFE AND WORK THE POWER OF ONE INDIVIDUAL'S IDEAS WHEN COMBINED WITH THE IRRESISTIBLE FORCE OF FREEDOM. THROUGH MORAL AUTHORITY, FORCE OF PERSONALITY, AND DEMONSTRATED HEROISM, HE HAS INSPIRED A NATION AND THE WORLD IN THE CAUSE OF LIBERTY. THE UNITED STATES HONORS A TRUE MAN OF HIS TIMES AND OF

TIMELESS IDEALS: LECH WALESA, DISTINGUISHED SON OF
POLAND, CHAMPION OF UNIVERSAL HUMAN RIGHTS.

★ ★ ★

President George Bush awarded Walesa the Presidential Medal of
Freedom with the above citation during a White House ceremony
November 13, 1989.

A national hero and Poland's first freely elected president following
the collapse of its communist regime in 1990, Lech Walesa was born
in Popow, Poland, in 1943. His father was a carpenter, and Walesa
attended the state vocational school near Popow. After graduating,
Walesa got work in 1967 as an electrician at the Lenin Shipyard in
Gdansk. He married his wife, Miroslawa, in 1969.

The following year he witnessed the four-day bread riots outside
the shipyard, where fifty-five strikers protesting steep food price hikes
were massacred by police. The government hastily made concessions,
but like many other Polish workers, Walesa realized Poland needed
free trade unions outside the control of the Communist Party. He also
became more outspoken, and in 1976, after the government again
briefly imposed food price hikes, Walesa was fired for his boldness.

Now marked as a labor agitator, he went from job to job and was
periodically arrested for stirring up worker unrest. Undaunted,
Walesa signed a charter of workers' rights in 1979, calling for an
eight-hour day, independent trade unions, and other reforms. Then
serious food shortages (caused by high food exports) forced the
communist regime to double meat prices in mid–1980. Polish
workers, already seething with resentment at their repressive government, mounted angry protests around the country.

Walesa became head of the strike committee at Gdansk and soon
organized strikers in other parts of the country into the Solidarity
movement. Faced with these massive strikes, the government caved
in to worker demands, even allowing Solidarity to exist as a union
independent of government control. Walesa, now a national hero,
became chairman of Solidarity, which counted some 10 million of
the country's 17.3 million workers among its ranks.

A government crackdown in 1981 left Solidarity outlawed and
landed Walesa in jail for a year. The government resorted to martial
law to control labor agitation for the next few years, but the
Solidarity movement's past success provided a focus for widespread
unrest within Poland. The movement also had sparked intense
interest in the West. The irrepressible Walesa rankled Poland's communist regime when he won the Nobel Peace Prize in 1983 and again
in 1987 when he managed to smuggle his autobiography, *A Way of
Hope*, to a French publisher.

By the late 1980s Poland's Communist government was near
collapse because of the faltering national economy. Widespread

strikes forced communist leaders to bargain with Walesa and once again recognize Solidarity as a free union. In 1989 the communist regime fell, and the following year Walesa was elected president of Poland's new democratic republican government. Poland's communist Party, now in complete disarray, re-formed itself as the Social Democrat Party.

Many painful economic reforms had to be instituted as the country shifted to a free-market economy, and Walesa's first years in office were far from tranquil. He too had to deal with labor protests, this time resulting from high unemployment and inflation, and in 1993 angry voters gave former communists a majority in Poland's lower house. Walesa lost his bid for reelection in 1995.

Margaret Thatcher

THREE TIMES ELECTED PRIME MINISTER OF THE UNITED KINGDOM, MARGARET THATCHER LED HER COUNTRY WITH FEARLESSNESS, DETERMINATION, INTEGRITY, AND A TRUE VISION FOR BRITAIN. IN OVER A DECADE OF ACHIEVEMENT, SHE EXTENDED PROSPERITY AT HOME AND MADE SIGNAL CONTRIBUTIONS TO TRANSATLANTIC PARTNERSHIP, THE UNITY OF THE WEST, AND OVERCOMING THE POSTWAR DIVISION OF EUROPE. WITH A STRONG SENSE OF HER NATION'S HISTORY AND OF THE PRINCIPLES WHICH BROUGHT IT TO GREATNESS, SHE RESTORED CONFIDENCE TO THE BRITISH PEOPLE. THE UNITED STATES HONORS A STEADFAST AND TRUE ALLY AND A FIRM FRIEND OF POLITICAL AND ECONOMIC FREEDOM THROUGHOUT THE WORLD.

★ ★ ★

President George Bush awarded Thatcher the Presidential Medal of Freedom with the above citation during a White House ceremony March 7, 1991.

Britain's first woman prime minister and the longest-serving British prime minister since 1827, Margaret Thatcher was born Margaret Roberts in Grantham, England, in 1925. Her father ran a grocery store and held various posts in local government. She went on to graduate from Oxford as a chemistry major (1946) and while working as a research chemist also earned her master's degree there (1950).

Active in the Conservative Party from her student days, Thatcher, then just twenty-four, ran unsuccessfully for Parliament in 1950. The following year she married Dennis Thatcher, a wealthy businessman, and in 1953 gave birth to twins.

Her interest in a career and politics continued, though. She passed her bar examination in 1953 and practiced law until 1961. Elected to her first term in Parliament in 1959, she began her long career in government. When the Conservative Party regained a majority in Parliament, she served as the only woman member of Prime Minister Edward Heath's government (as secretary of education and science from 1970 to 1974). In 1975 she became the first woman Conservative Party leader, following the party's loss of its majority in Parliament and Heath's ouster from the party's top slot.

About this time Britain's economy had been nearly paralyzed by a wave of strikes, making Thatcher's brand of tough fiscal conservatism that much more attractive to voters. She promised to rein in unruly unions, restore the economy, cut Britain's excessive social welfare spending, and strengthen the military. Conservatives captured a majority in Parliament in 1979, and Thatcher became prime minister.

On the domestic front, Thatcher's eleven-year term as prime minister radically altered the British economy. Among her reforms were the privatization of state-owned enterprises and housing; the elimination of wage-price guidelines and subsidies to unviable industries; and new laws that curbed the power of unions. Between 1979 and 1987, inflation plummeted from 22 percent to 3.4 percent, the budget deficit dropped from 6 percent of gross domestic product to 3.4 percent, and the country enjoyed a 3 percent annual growth rate for all but two of those years. Those successes were accompanied by high unemployment early in her administration, though, along with a jump in bankruptcies and business losses.

Thatcher enjoyed considerable success in foreign policy. She oversaw the transition to an independent Zimbabwe in 1980. Two years later she ordered the recapture of the Falkland Islands from invading Argentine forces, a decisive military victory that restored a sense of pride among Britons and greatly increased her popularity. Thatcher maintained strong relations with the United States and reaffirmed Britain's commitment to the North Atlantic Treaty Organization, while also cultivating ties with the Soviet Union. Despite an attempt on her life by Irish terrorists in 1984, Thatcher also supported an agreement whereby Ireland was given some say in Northern Ireland's affairs.

Opposition to her proposed tax for funding local government, a faltering British economy, and concern about her proposed health-care reforms forced her resignation from office in 1990. Two years later Thatcher was awarded the title of baroness.

James Addison Baker III

As Secretary of State, James A. Baker III has guided American foreign policy through a period of extraordinary change. In the Gulf, Secretary Baker led, with great distinction, diplomatic efforts to resolve the crisis, pursuing every avenue and travelling tens of thousands of miles to seek Iraq's unconditional withdrawal from Kuwait. He helped forge an historic coalition of countries to stand against Iraq's aggression. His efforts were crowned by the passage of twelve United Nations Security Council resolutions, including a landmark resolution authorizing the use of force to expel Iraq from Kuwait. The United States honors a distinguished servant of our Nation, a clear voice for American principles, and a champion of peace and liberty around the world.

★ ★ ★

President George Bush awarded Baker the Presidential Medal of Freedom with the above citation during a White House ceremony July 3, 1991.

A Texas lawyer and longtime friend of George Bush, James Addison Baker III served as a high-ranking public official during the Reagan-Bush years. He also was a shrewd political manager, playing key roles in the campaigns of Bush, Gerald R. Ford, and Ronald Reagan.

The son of a prominent attorney in Houston, Baker was born in 1930. His father expected him to become an attorney as well, and after graduating from Princeton University in 1952, Baker earned his law degree from the University of Texas at Austin in 1957. He joined a prestigious Houston law firm and within ten years became a partner.

Following the death of his first wife, Mary McHenry, Baker entered politics as a district campaign manager for George Bush's 1970 Senate race in Texas. Bush lost to Democrat Lloyd Bentsen that year, but Baker remained active in the Republican Party. In 1973 he married Susan Garrett Winston. Two years later President Ford named him under secretary of commerce.

Ford's sagging presidential campaign in 1976 became Baker's next challenge, and he orchestrated a surprise comeback late in the race that brought Ford to just over 2 percent of the popular vote behind Jimmy Carter. Baker managed Bush's unsuccessful 1980 presidential primary bid before becoming a senior campaign adviser for the winning Reagan-Bush team.

Newly elected President Reagan surprised many observers by passing over longtime friend Edwin Meese and naming Baker his White House chief of staff. Baker held that post until 1985 and served as secretary of the Treasury from 1985 to 1988. He then directed Bush's successful 1988 presidential campaign, after which Bush named him secretary of state. In that post Baker helped forge a record of Bush administration foreign policy successes, including the agreement with the Soviet Union on the reunification of Germany in 1990 and the forming of the international coalition to repulse the Iraqi invasion of Kuwait in 1990.

Baker resigned as secretary in 1992 to become Bush's White House chief of staff. After managing Bush's unsuccessful reelection bid that year, he returned to his law practice in Houston and in 1995 published *The Politics of Diplomacy: Revolution, War and Peace, 1989–1992.*

Richard B. Cheney

As Secretary of Defense, Dick Cheney has been responsible for preserving America's defenses at a time of great change around the world. In the Persian Gulf, Secretary Cheney worked to bring together a formidable military coalition in response to Iraq's aggression against Kuwait and arranged one of the largest overseas deployments of troops in American history. At home, he worked with Congress to ensure the broadest possible support for our actions in the Gulf. When war came, his superb leadership of all our armed forces helped speed the way to victory. The United States honors a vigilant defender of our Nation's interests and a firm friend of freedom.

★ ★ ★

President George Bush awarded Cheney the Presidential Medal of Freedom with the above citation during a White House ceremony July 3, 1991.

A six-term Republican representative from Wyoming who also held important posts in the Nixon, Ford, and Bush administrations, Dick Cheney was born in 1941 and raised in Casper, Wyoming. After earning his bachelor's and master's degrees in political science from the University of Wyoming, in 1965 and 1966, he worked toward his doctorate at the University of Wisconsin until 1968, when an opening as a congressional staffer lured him to Washington, D.C. He has remained there in one capacity or another almost ever since.

In 1969 he moved from the legislative to the executive branch, becoming an assistant to Donald Rumsfeld, the director of the Office of Economic Opportunity in the Nixon administration. Cheney's association with Rumsfeld led to increasingly important staff jobs in the Nixon and Ford administrations over the next few years, and in 1975 he succeeded Rumsfeld as President Ford's White House chief of staff. After Ford lost his 1976 bid for a new term, Cheney returned to Casper, and in 1978 won his first term as Wyoming's sole member of the U.S. House of Representatives. A staunch supporter of President Ronald Reagan during the president's two terms, Cheney moved up steadily through Republican ranks in the House to become party whip in 1988, the then-minority party's second most powerful post in the House.

President George Bush named him defense secretary in 1989 amid the collapse of the Soviet bloc, giving Cheney the responsibility for reducing U.S. armed forces and redefining their role in the post-Cold War era. Cheney also oversaw the deployment and highly successful participation of U.S. troops in the 1991 Persian Gulf War.

Cheney's contribution to that remarkably successful military operation moved President Bush to award him the Presidential Medal of Freedom soon after the war's conclusion. Cheney remained defense secretary until the end of Bush's term and since 1993 has been a senior fellow at the American Enterprise Institute in Washington, D.C.

Colin Powell

IN A LONG AND DISTINGUISHED CAREER IN THE UNITED STATES ARMY, CULMINATING IN HIS SERVICE AS CHAIRMAN, JOINT CHIEFS OF STAFF, COLIN POWELL HAS PROVIDED UNSURPASSED LEADERSHIP AND JUDGMENT IN DIFFICULT TIMES. A DEFT MANAGER AND FORTHRIGHT COUNSELOR, HE PERSONIFIES THE IDEAL OF THE SOLDIER-STATESMAN, SERVING THE PRESIDENT AND THE NATION WITH PERSONAL INTEGRITY, POLITICAL JUDGMENT AND MILITARY SKILL. AS THE ARCHITECT AND MANAGER OF OPERATIONS DESERT SHIELD AND DESERT STORM, HE OVERSAW THE VINDICATION OF PRINCIPLE, THE DEFENSE OF SAUDI ARABIA, AND THE LIBERATION OF KUWAIT. THE UNITED STATES HONORS THIS PROFESSIONAL SERVANT OF PEACE AND FREEDOM.

★ ★ ★

President George Bush awarded Powell the Presidential Medal of Freedom with the above citation during a White House ceremony July 3, 1991. *[Powell was awarded a second Presidential Medal of Freedom on September 30, 1993. See p. 486.]*

One of only two people to have received the Presidential Medal of Freedom twice, Colin Powell was born in Harlem, New York, in 1937. *(See also the entry for Ellsworth Bunker, p. 49.)* His parents were Jamaican immigrants, and Powell was raised in the South Bronx. He graduated from City College of New York as a geology major in 1958 and, having been a member of the ROTC during college, went into the army as a second lieutenant that same year. He married Vivian Johnson in 1962.

Powell did two tours in South Vietnam. The first, as a military adviser from 1962 to 1963, ended in a rice paddy when Powell's foot was impaled by a Vietcong Punji-stick trap during a combat patrol. He returned to South Vietnam in 1968–1969 as a division operations officer, only to be injured again in 1969 during a helicopter crash landing. He was awarded a Soldiers Medal for rescuing fellow soldiers from the flaming wreckage.

Having earned his master's degree in business administration from George Washington University in 1971, Powell spent 1972 working for Frank Carlucci, President Richard Nixon's deputy director of the Office of Management and Budget (OMB). Both Carlucci and his boss, OMB director Caspar Weinberger, were impressed by Powell's quiet efficiency and competence. *(See also the entry for Weinberger, p. 402.)*

During the 1970s, Powell variously held purely military posts and had assignments in the Carter administration—senior military assistant to the deputy defense secretary (1979–1981) and assistant to the Energy Department secretary (1979). He later returned to Washington as Secretary of Defense Weinberger's senior military assistant (1983–1986). Weinberger's second in command, Powell played an important role in Reagan administration military operations, including the Grenada invasion and the 1986 raid against Libya.

When Carlucci became President Ronald Reagan's national security adviser in 1987, he named Powell his deputy. Powell reorganized the national security staff in the wake of the Iran-contra scandal to establish clear lines of authority. Later that same year, Powell was promoted to national security adviser, a post he held until Reagan left office.

Early in the Bush administration, Powell took over the Army Forces Command and was advanced to four-star general (1989). Later in 1989, President George Bush named him chairman of the Joint Chiefs of Staff, making him the first black to hold the nation's highest military post. Powell performed with characteristic efficiency and had a pivotal role in both the Panama invasion and the highly complex international military operations during the 1991 Persian Gulf War—Desert Shield and Desert Storm. President Bush awarded Powell his first Presidential Medal of Freedom shortly after the stunning allied victory in the Gulf War. President Bill Clinton gave him his second medal to mark his retirement from the army in 1993. Powell's book *My American Journey* was published in 1995.

H. Norman Schwarzkopf

CAPTAIN OF VICTORY IN THE GULF, GENERAL NORMAN
SCHWARZKOPF HAS SERVED HIS COUNTRY IN WAR AND PEACE WITH
SELFLESS DEVOTION AND DEDICATION THROUGHOUT A LONG AND
DISTINGUISHED CAREER IN THE UNITED STATES ARMY. AS
COMMANDER-IN-CHIEF, CENTRAL COMMAND, HE RESPONDED TO
THE UNPROVOKED AND UNLAWFUL AGGRESSION OF IRAQ AGAINST
KUWAIT WITH ENERGY AND IMAGINATION. HE LED THE LARGEST
COALITION SINCE WORLD WAR II, INTEGRATING THE ARMED
FORCES OF DISPARATE COUNTRIES, CULTURES, AND TRAINING INTO
A SINGLE MILITARY FORCE AND ACHIEVING SWIFT SUCCESS IN
OPERATION DESERT STORM. HE HAS SOUGHT TO BUILD BRIDGES OF
UNDERSTANDING BETWEEN THE UNITED STATES AND THE PEOPLES
OF THE MIDDLE EAST. THE UNITED STATES HONORS THIS SOLDIER,
WHO TAKES HIS PLACE IN HISTORY'S ROLL OF GREAT COMMANDERS.

★ ★ ★

*President George Bush awarded Schwarzkopf the Presidential Medal
of Freedom with the above citation during a White House ceremony
July 3, 1991.*

The son of a brigadier general, H. Norman Schwarzkopf was born in
Trenton, New Jersey, in 1934. After spending time abroad with his
father between 1946 and 1951, including a year in Iran, he went on to
graduate from the United States Military Academy at West Point in
1956. A strong student, he predicted to friends that someday he
would lead U.S. forces in a battle "decisive to the nation."

That day was still many years off, though, and after earning his
master's degree in guided-missile engineering at the University of
Southern California in 1963, he had his first taste of battle as a
military adviser in Vietnam (1965–1966). Not long after arriving in
Vietnam, he and fellow South Vietnamese soldiers withstood a ten-
day Vietcong siege of their base, and for the next year Schwarzkopf
fought alongside the South Vietnamese whenever they were called
into action. Three years later he returned to Vietnam as a battalion
commander in the Americal Division. It was during this tour
(1969–1970) that one of his companies was hit by misdirected
artillery fire, an incident that became the subject of the 1976 book
Friendly Fire, by C. D. B. Bryan.

After returning from Vietnam, he served in a succession of posts
and was promoted to general in 1983. That same year Schwarzkopf
commanded U.S. ground forces in the invasion of Grenada, the
Reagan administration's first major military operation. By 1988

Schwarzkopf had become a four-star general and the commander in chief of the U.S. Central Command, which was responsible for any U.S. military action in the Mideast. As part of his duties, he had drawn up contingency plans for the U.S. response to a war among Mideast nations. Then suddenly Iraq invaded oil-rich Kuwait in mid–1990.

Schwarzkopf's contingency plan became Operation Desert Shield, in which the United States deployed rapid-response forces to the Mideast to prevent Iraqi troops from moving into Saudi Arabia, a vital source of American oil imports. Continuing the buildup over the next months, Schwarzkopf eventually had under his command a coalition force of some 700,000 troops (540,000 American soldiers) in preparation for Desert Storm—his planned offensive to actually drive the Iraqis out of Kuwait. When Iraqi dictator Saddam Hussein refused diplomatic efforts to get him out of Kuwait, Schwarzkopf began the allied offensive with an intensive, six-week bombardment of Iraq and Kuwait in early 1991. Then in late February 1991 he launched the fierce ground attack that drove the 500,000-man Iraqi army to surrender in just one-hundred hours.

Having won the Persian Gulf War with lightning speed and remarkably few allied casualties, Schwarzkopf enjoyed a hero's welcome on returning to the United States later in 1991. The prediction from his student days fulfilled, he retired from the military that same year. In following years he became a sought-after public speaker and published his book (with Peter Petre) *It Doesn't Take a Hero* (1992).

Brent Scowcroft

THE IDEAL OF A STATESMAN, A QUIET YET PASSIONATE DEFENDER OF AMERICAN INTERESTS, BRENT SCOWCROFT'S SOUND COUNSEL HAS ENHANCED OUR NATIONAL SECURITY AND ADVANCED AMERICAN FOREIGN POLICY AND THE CAUSE OF FREEDOM AROUND THE WORLD. IN THE GULF, GENERAL SCOWCROFT NEVER WAVERED IN PURSUIT OF THIS NATION'S GOAL OF REVERSING IRAQ'S AGGRESSION AGAINST KUWAIT. HE SUPERBLY COORDINATED THE NATIONAL SECURITY AGENCIES AND THE DEVELOPMENT OF REC-OMMENDATIONS FOR THE PRESIDENT, ENABLING THE UNITED STATES TO CONDUCT AN EFFECTIVE AND UNITED FOREIGN POLICY AND A VICTORIOUS MILITARY CAMPAIGN. AMERICA HONORS AN OUTSTANDING GENERAL, TRUE PATRIOT, AND WISE STATESMAN.

★ ★ ★

President George Bush awarded Scowcroft the Presidential Medal of Freedom with the above citation during a White House ceremony July 3, 1991.

A top-level presidential adviser, Brent Scowcroft was born in Ogden, Utah, in 1925. After earning his bachelor's degree at the United States Military Academy at West Point in 1947, he was commissioned as an Air Force officer and spent the next sixteen years variously filling Air Force administrative posts, teaching Russian at West Point, serving as assistant air attaché in Yugoslavia (1959–1961), and heading the political science department at the United States Air Force Academy. Meanwhile, he married Marian Horner in 1951. Between 1964 and 1967 Scowcroft served at Air Force headquarters as a staffer in the long-range planning division and in 1967 he earned his doctorate in international relations from Columbia.

Scowcroft's career shifted to national security work in 1968. For the next three years he held various posts in the Defense Department, culminating in his assignment as a special assistant in the office of the Joint Chiefs of Staff. Then in 1971 he became President Richard Nixon's military aide. He accompanied President Nixon on the historic trip to China in 1971 and directed the advance preparations for Nixon's trip to the Soviet Union in 1972.

Scowcroft joined the Nixon administration's National Security Council as deputy assistant to the president for national security affairs in 1973. Promoted to lieutenant general, he became head of the National Security Council in 1975 when Henry Kissinger resigned to focus on his duties as secretary of state. Serving until the end of the Ford administration in 1977, Scowcroft played an important role in arranging the second Strategic Arms Limitation Talks (SALT II) interim agreement, planning the 1975 evacuation of Americans from Saigon, and the military response to Cambodia's capture of the *Mayaguez*, a U.S. cargo ship.

During the Carter administration, Scowcroft was a member of a presidential advisory committee for arms control (1977–1980). From 1982 to 1989 he was vice chairman of Kissinger Associates, an international consulting firm, but took time out in 1987 to serve on the three-member Tower Commission, which was charged with investigating the Iran-contra scandal.

During the Bush administration, Scowcroft returned to the White House as the assistant to the president for national security affairs. As a top Bush adviser, he played an important behind-the-scenes role in organizing the international effort to drive Iraqi forces out of Kuwait in the 1991 Persian Gulf War. President Bush awarded Scowcroft (and others involved) the Presidential Medal of Freedom soon after the allied military victory.

Scowcroft became president of the Forum for International Policy in Washington in 1992.

William F. Buckley, Jr.

WILLIAM F. BUCKLEY, JR. HAS LONG SERVED THIS NATION AS A PROLIFIC AUTHOR AND AS A THOUGHTFUL AND INSIGHTFUL COMMENTATOR ON PUBLIC AFFAIRS. HIS COLUMNS, BOOKS, NOVELS, AND TELEVISION PROGRAMS HAVE ENLIGHTENED AND ENTERTAINED MILLIONS WITH A STYLE MARKED BY GRACE, AN IRREPRESSIBLE WIT, AND VIBRANT ENERGY. THE MAGAZINE HE FOUNDED, NATIONAL REVIEW, IS ONE OF AMERICA'S LEADING JOURNALS OF OPINION AND HAS GREATLY CONTRIBUTED TO THE INTELLECTUAL FOUNDATION OF THE AMERICAN CONSERVATIVE MOVEMENT. THE UNITED STATES HONORS A MAN WHO HAS GIVEN MUCH TO THIS COUNTRY, A TIRELESS WORKER IN THE VINEYARDS OF LIBERTY.

★ ★ ★

President George Bush awarded Buckley the Presidential Medal of Freedom with the above citation during a White House ceremony November 18, 1991.

One of the conservative movement's most respected spokesmen, William F. Buckley, Jr., was born in New York City in 1925, the son of a Texas oil magnate. In his youth, Buckley attended Roman Catholic private schools in France and Germany, and soon displayed a bold, self-confident temperament that eventually became a Buckley trademark. For example, when the eight-year-old Buckley became incensed over Britain's failure to repay its war debts, he wrote to the King of England demanding action. Buckley later attended preparatory school in the United States and, after serving as an infantry officer during World War II, graduated from Yale University in 1950. He married Patricia Aldyn Austin Taylor that same year.

His Yale experiences and his already-determined conservative outlook provided the basis for his first book, *God and Man at Yale* (1951), a controversial work attacking the liberal bent of American colleges. After working briefly in Mexico for the Central Intelligence Agency and for *American Mercury* magazine as an editor, Buckley founded the *National Review* magazine in 1955 for the express purpose of revitalizing the conservative movement, which had been floundering since the advent of the liberal New Deal. With Buckley as editor in chief, the magazine reached a one-hundred-thousand-copy circulation by the early 1960s and was firmly established as a leading forum for conservative thought, a position it still holds today.

By 1962 he also was writing a syndicated newspaper column, *On the Right*, and in 1966, a year after his unsuccessful mayoral bid in

New York City, Buckley became a national celebrity as host of the television program "Firing Line." His *National Review* articles, newspaper columns, and other writings were republished in a series of books in the 1960s and 1970s, and he has written a series of best-selling spy novels that began with *Saving the Queen* (1976).

An articulate, thoughtful spokesman, he remains staunchly anti-communist, antiliberal and a traditionalist on social and moral issues. He greatly influenced the conservative movement from the 1950s onward and has supported the campaigns of conservative Republicans like Barry Goldwater, Richard Nixon, and Ronald Reagan. He served only briefly in public office, however, from 1969 to 1972 as a member of the U.S. Information Agency advisory board and in 1973 as a U.S. delegate to the UN General Assembly. Instead, he has focused on his writings and promoting his conservative viewpoint, which is to say he labored at being, as Arthur M. Schlesinger, Jr., once remarked, "the scourge of American liberalism."

Luis A. Ferré

LUIS A. FERRÉ HAS LED THE PEOPLE OF PUERTO RICO AS A DED-ICATED PUBLIC SERVANT, VISIONARY INDUSTRIALIST, AND PATRON OF THE ARTS. OVER THE COURSE OF HIS LIFE, LUIS FERRÉ HAS BEEN INVOLVED IN THE FAMILY BUSINESS, NEWSPAPER PUBLISHING, AND UNIVERSITY DEVELOPMENT. HE HAS ALSO BUILT AND DONATED PONCE'S MUSEUM OF ART AND FREE PUBLIC LIBRARY. LATER, THE PEOPLE OF PUERTO RICO ELECTED HIM, THE FOUNDER AND HEAD OF THE NEW PROGRESSIVE PARTY, THEIR GOVERNOR. LUIS FERRÉ EQUATES BUSINESS SUCCESS WITH SOCIAL RESPONSIBILITY AND DESCRIBES HIMSELF AS "REV-OLUTIONARY IN MY IDEAS, LIBERAL IN MY OBJECTIVES, AND CON-SERVATIVE IN MY METHODS." THE UNITED STATES HONORS ONE OF OUR PIONEERS OF FREEDOM.

★ ★ ★

President George Bush awarded Ferré the Presidential Medal of Freedom with the above citation during a White House ceremony November 18, 1991.

A millionaire industrialist and one-term governor of Puerto Rico, Luis A. Ferré was born in Ponce, Puerto Rico, in 1904. Some years later, in 1918, Ferré's father opened a foundry, beginning what was to become the multimillion-dollar family business, Ferré Industries. Eventually, Luis Ferré and his three brothers all moved into high-level positions in the expanding enterprise.

Ferré graduated from the Massachusetts Institute of Technology with a master's degree in electrical engineering in 1925 and then went to work for the family firm as its labor relations chief and head of the company's organization. The firm moved into cement manufacturing in the 1940s and in the following years grew into a diversified, multi-million-dollar operation that included cement, glass, clay, plastics, and steel manufacturing companies, as well as trucking and shipping firms. The Ferré's Puerto Rican Cement Company became the first Puerto Rican company listed on the New York Stock Exchange.

While continuing in the family business Ferré also became active in politics, serving as the elected representative at large in the Puerto Rican Assembly from 1953 to 1957. A member of the Republican Statehood party, he ran unsuccessfully for governor in 1956, 1960, and 1964, before leaving the party and forming his own New Progressive party in 1967. Ferré won the governorship in the 1968 election, breaking the twenty-year hold on the governorship by the Popular Democratic Party.

During his one term as governor, Ferré sought solutions to Puerto Rico's housing and narcotics problems, improved workers' wages and benefits, established programs to modernize agriculture, and initiated a massive development project to spur growth in Puerto Rico's lagging southwest region. Despite these efforts, however, Ferré was unable to prevent the Popular Democratic party from returning to power in 1973. Ferré's wife, the former Lorecita Ramirez de Arellano, whom he had married in 1933, died in 1970 while he was still in office.

In addition to his political and business enterprises, Ferré also is known for his philanthropy. Two of his largest gifts are in his hometown: the Ponce Museum of Art and the Ponce public library.

Betty Ford

BETTY FORD HAS CHAMPIONED MANY CAUSES, BOTH AS A FIRST LADY AND A LEADING CITIZEN OF THIS LAND. EVEN WHILE SHE SERVED AS A FULL PARTNER TO HER HUSBAND THROUGHOUT HIS YEARS IN CONGRESS AND THE WHITE HOUSE, SHE PROVIDED SELFLESS, STRONG, AND REFRESHING LEADERSHIP ON A NUMBER OF ISSUES, PARTICULARLY DRUG AND ALCOHOL DEPENDENCY. HER COURAGE AND CANDOR HAVE INSPIRED MILLIONS OF AMERICANS TO RESTORE THEIR HEALTH, PROTECT THEIR DIGNITY, AND SHAPE FULL LIVES FOR THEMSELVES. THE UNITED STATES HONORS A GENEROUS CITIZEN, A CREATIVE SPIRIT, A VALIANT WOMAN WHO HAS STRUGGLED FOR THE DIGNITY ESSENTIAL FOR TRUE FREEDOM.

★ ★ ★

President George Bush awarded Ford the Presidential Medal of Freedom with the above citation during a White House ceremony November 18, 1991.

The wife of President Gerald R. Ford and a candid and sometimes controversial first lady, Betty Bloomer Ford was born in Chicago in 1918. Raised in a fashionable neighborhood of Grand Rapids, Michigan, the young Betty Bloomer began taking dance lessons at age eight, and a career in dance remained a driving ambition throughout her youth. After graduating from high school she spent two summers, in 1937 and 1938, at the Bennington College School of Dance, where she studied under the noted choreographer and modern dancer Martha Graham.

Bloomer showed enough promise to win a place with the auxiliary concert group of Martha Graham's dance troupe and in 1939 moved to New York City. While continuing her dance training, she participated in public performances, including one at Carnegie Hall, and worked as a fashion model. In 1941, however, Bloomer decided to return home to Grand Rapids.

A five-year marriage to a Grand Rapids furniture dealer named William Warren ended in divorce in 1947, and later that year she met Gerald Ford, a former football star turned lawyer. They married in 1948 while he was campaigning as a Republican for his first term in the U.S. House of Representatives. After he won they moved to Washington, D.C., and remained there for the next three decades as he won an unbroken string of reelection victories. Betty Ford's three sons and one daughter were all born in Washington.

Betty, who had undergone psychotherapy for the pain she suffered from a pinched neck nerve, had already won a promise from her husband to leave politics after his House term ended in 1975. But no one expected President Richard Nixon to name him vice president after Spiro Agnew's resignation in 1973, much less that he would become president in mid–1974 after Nixon resigned over the Watergate scandal.

Extensively interviewed while serving as the vice president's wife, Ford already had a reputation for speaking frankly on controversial issues. She openly supported abortion in cases of rape, incest, or where the woman's health was threatened. And as the first lady she remained outspoken on women's issues and worked for adoption of the Equal Rights Amendment. An active supporter of the National Endowment for the Arts, she also worked on behalf of children and the mentally and physically handicapped. In addition, she focused national attention on the problem of breast cancer when she openly discussed her own radical mastectomy, performed just two months after she became first lady.

After her husband lost the presidency in 1976, she wrote two books, *The Times of My Life* (1978) and *Betty: A Glad Awakening* (1987), and became the chief executive of the Betty Ford Center.

Hanna Holborn Gray

As historian and humanist, teacher and university leader, Hanna Holborn Gray has assured that young generations learn the fundamentals of our civilization — truths that never bend to fashion. In the highest ranks of academic leadership, she has strengthened Yale University and the University of Chicago and ensured that they remain among the world's great teaching and research universities. The United States honors Hanna Gray for devoting her abundant talent and energy to the causes of excellence, truth, and freedom.

★ ★ ★

President George Bush awarded Gray the Presidential Medal of Freedom with the above citation during a White House ceremony November 18, 1991.

Born in Heidelberg, Germany, in 1930, Hanna Holborn was raised in a distinguished academic family. Her father was a highly regarded European historian and her mother held a doctorate in classical philology. With the rise of the Nazis, her parents were forced to leave

Germany and by the mid–1930s had settled in New Haven, Connecticut. Her father joined the Yale University faculty, and her family members all became U.S. citizens in 1940.

An exceptional student, she entered Bryn Mawr College at age fifteen and graduated summa cum laude in 1950. Continuing her education, she studied at Oxford University as a Fulbright scholar from 1950 to 1952 and completed her doctorate in Renaissance history at Harvard in 1957. She married Charles Montgomery Gray in 1954.

After teaching history at Harvard, she moved with her husband to Chicago in 1960 and soon after joined the University of Chicago history faculty. She rose to associate professor at Chicago before becoming Northwestern University's first woman dean of arts and sciences in 1972. Then in 1974 she returned to her hometown of New Haven as Yale's first woman provost. She proved to be a tough, frugal administrator and was widely expected to become Yale's next president, even though she had not graduated from the university. When the office fell vacant in 1977, she was in fact named acting president.

But before the search committee had completed its work, Gray accepted an offer from the University of Chicago in 1978, making her the first woman to head a major coeducational university in the United States. During her tenure she sought to maintain the university's high academic quality in an era of tightening budgets, strengthen the university's undergraduate liberal arts program, promote increased minority student enrollment, and increase faculty and administrative opportunities for women. She remained in office until 1993 and continues to teach at the university as a professor in the history department.

Gray holds honorary degrees from numerous academic institutions and with her husband edited the Journal of Modern History from 1965 to 1970. She is a member of the boards of directors of J. P. Morgan and Company, Morgan Guaranty Trust Company, Atlantic Richfield, and other corporations.

Friedrich August von Hayek

FRIEDRICH AUGUST VON HAYEK HAS DONE MORE THAN ANY THINKER OF OUR AGE TO EXPLORE THE PROMISE AND CONTOURS OF LIBERTY. HE GREW UP IN THE SHADOW OF HITLER'S TYRANNY AND DEVOTED HIMSELF AT AN EARLY AGE TO THE NURTURE OF INSTITUTIONS THAT PRESERVE AND EXPAND FREEDOM, THE LIFEBLOOD OF A FULL LIFE. THE ROAD TO SERFDOM STILL THRILLS READERS EVERYWHERE, AND HIS SUBSEQUENT WORKS INSPIRE PEOPLE THROUGHOUT THE WORLD BECAUSE THEY POSSESS THE

VIGOR AND FEEL OF REAL LIFE—NOT JUST THE HOLLOW RING OF ABSTRACT THEORY. PROFESSOR VON HAYEK HAS REVOLUTIONIZED THE WORLD'S INTELLECTUAL AND POLITICAL LIFE. FUTURE GEN-ERATIONS WILL READ HIS WORKS WITH THE SAME SENSE OF DIS-COVERY AND AWE THAT INSPIRE US TODAY.

★ ★ ★

President George Bush awarded Hayek the Presidential Medal of Freedom with the above citation during a White House ceremony November 18, 1991. Laurence Hayek received the award on his father's behalf.

A leading and for many years lonely critic of Keynesian economics, Friedrich August von Hayek was born in Vienna, Austria, in 1899. His father was a professor of botany at the University of Vienna, and Hayek earned his doctorate in economics there in 1923. Afterward, he worked for a time in the civil service, married Helen von Fritsch in 1926, and in 1929 became director of the Austrian Institute of Economic Research. Meanwhile, he also published his first book on theoretical economics, *Monetary Theory and the Trade Cycle* (1929).

Hayek moved to England in 1931, teaching first at the University of London and then at the London School of Economics. A conservative economist and free-market advocate, he opposed the Keynesian doc-trines of central economic planning, which were becoming a popular answer to the 1930s depression. In 1935 he edited *Collectivist Economic Planning*, a collection of articles by noted economists on the issue of central planning, and in his later writings warned that central planning was inherently inefficient and could help bring about a totalitarian government. Hayek's controversial book *The Road to Serfdom* (1944) further developed his idea that government inter-vention in a competitive market delays but does not cure a depression or other economic problems (such as inflation). Ultimately, he also said, Soviet-style collectivism would fail, a prediction that he not only lived to see fulfilled but also that vindicated his theories. A bestseller in the United States, his book helped establish Hayek as an important critic of Keynesian theories among free-market intellectuals.

Naturalized as a British citizen in 1938, he taught at the University of Chicago from 1950 to 1962. He was a professor at the University of Freiburg for the next six years and retired from teaching in 1968. He continued writing, though, including the books *Law, Legislation, and Liberty* (1978) and *Unemployment and Monetary Policy* (1979), and his theories influenced free-market proponents, including the noted American economist Milton Friedman, President Ronald Reagan, and British Prime Minister Margaret Thatcher.

Hayek shared the 1974 Nobel Prize in economics with Swedish economist Gunnar Myrdal and was awarded the Presidential Medal of Freedom in 1991. He died the following year, at age ninety-two.

Thomas P. "Tip" O'Neill, Jr.

IN HIS 50 YEARS OF PUBLIC SERVICE, THOMAS P. O'NEILL, JR., WAS NOT JUST A MAN OF THE HOUSE OF REPRESENTATIVES; HE WAS A MAN FOR THE AMERICAN PEOPLE. INHERITING THE PUBLIC SERVICE TRADITION FROM HIS FATHER, TIP O'NEILL HAD AN UNCANNY ABILITY TO UNDERSTAND PEOPLE AND POLITICS. HE WON 25 CONSECUTIVE ELECTIONS, RISING TO BECOME SPEAKER OF BOTH THE MASSACHUSETTS AND UNITED STATES HOUSE OF REPRESENTATIVES WHILE ALWAYS MAINTAINING HIS HUMOR, HUMILITY, AND TOUCH WITH THE PEOPLE HE SERVED. HE SAID, "ALL POLITICS IS LOCAL," BUT HE DEMONSTRATED THAT FAITHFUL SERVICE TO THE PEOPLE ALSO WELL SERVES THE NATION. THE UNITED STATES HONORS THIS DISTINGUISHED LEGISLATOR FOR HIS LEADERSHIP, AMITY, GOOD HUMOR, AND COMMITMENT TO SERVICE AND FREEDOM.

★ ★ ★

President George Bush awarded O'Neill the Presidential Medal of Freedom with the above citation during a White House ceremony November 18, 1991.

A master of old-style politics and an unabashed New Deal liberal, Thomas P. O'Neill, Jr., was born in a working-class neighborhood of Cambridge, Massachusetts, in 1912. His mother died when he was still young, and his father, an Irish Catholic active in local politics as a Democrat, eventually remarried. O'Neill's boyhood friends gave him the nickname "Tip," after a player on the former Saint Louis Browns who would hit foul tips until the pitcher finally gave up and walked him.

O'Neill entered politics as a campaign volunteer for the 1928 Democratic presidential candidate Al Smith. While in his last year at Boston College, he narrowly lost a race for the Cambridge City Council, the only election loss in his long career. He won a seat in the Massachusetts legislature just months after graduating from college in 1936 and remained in the state legislature for the next sixteen years, becoming speaker in 1948. O'Neill married Mildred Anne Miller in 1941.

Winning the House seat vacated by John F. Kennedy in 1952 (Kennedy became a senator), O'Neill moved to the U.S. House of Representatives in 1953. As a protégé of Massachusetts Rep. John McCormack, he soon joined the House Democrats' inner circle and by his second term in the House had won a seat on the powerful House Rules Committee.

During his long career in the House, O'Neill remained a loyal Democratic liberal, voting for the civil rights acts of 1956, 1957, and

1964; the Great Society social legislation—including Medicare, housing, aid to education, and anti-poverty programs—as well as consumer protection, environmental, and congressional reform measures. He could be fiercely protective of the interests of his Massachusetts constituents, but he went against them in 1967 by declaring his opposition to the Vietnam War.

Elected the House majority whip in 1971, O'Neill became majority leader the following year. During the Watergate scandal he was a leader in the fight to impeach President Richard Nixon and in 1976 was named Speaker of the House. O'Neill remained in the post through the Carter and Reagan administrations. As a loyal Democrat, he supported President Carter, but the two had significantly different political viewpoints. Nevertheless, O'Neill remained publicly neutral in the presidential primary battle between Carter and Sen. Edward M. Kennedy in 1980 and helped arrange the deal whereby Kennedy finally endorsed Carter.

During his term as House Speaker, he pushed for congressional reform and opposed a balanced budget because, as he said, it would mean cutting programs he had worked for over the years. Deeply opposed to President Reagan's ideas about a smaller federal government with less responsibility for social problems, O'Neill was often at odds with Reagan. During the partisan battling O'Neill publicly lambasted Reagan as "a cheerleader for selfishness" and dismissed him as "Herbert Hoover with a smile." O'Neill's closest friend, fellow Massachusetts Democratic Rep. Edward Boland, led the fight for passage of the short-lived Boland Amendment, which cut off U.S. aid to contra rebels in Nicaragua between 1984 and 1986. The Iran-contra scandal, a major embarrassment to President Reagan, stemmed from his administration's attempt to circumvent this amendment.

O'Neill retired in 1987, and his bestselling autobiography, *Man of the House* (with William Novak), was published the same year. He died seven years later, at age eighty-one.

Leon Howard Sullivan

THE REVEREND LEON SULLIVAN, A CIVIL RIGHTS LEADER AND PASTOR EMERITUS OF THE ZION BAPTIST CHURCH IN PHILADELPHIA, HAS DEVOTED HIS LIFE TO THE CAUSES OF LIBERTY AND JUSTICE. REVEREND SULLIVAN FOUNDED THE OPPORTUNITIES INDUSTRIALIZATION CENTERS OF AMERICA, ONE OF THE LARGEST AND MOST PRESTIGIOUS JOB TRAINING ORGANIZATIONS IN THE WORLD. HE LATER FOUNDED THE INTERNATIONAL

FOUNDATION FOR EDUCATION AND SELF-HELP. IN 1971, LEON SULLIVAN WAS ELECTED TO THE BOARD OF DIRECTORS OF GENERAL MOTORS, BECOMING THE FIRST BLACK AMERICAN TO PARTICIPATE IN THE DIRECTION OF A U.S. AUTO COMPANY. AMERICA HONORS THIS MAN OF PRINCIPLE, WHO IN WORD AND EXAMPLE HAS SHOWN SO MANY PEOPLE THE WAY TO FREEDOM.

★ ★ ★

President George Bush awarded Sullivan the Presidential Medal of Freedom with the above citation during a White House ceremony November 18, 1991.

Born to a broken home in a poor section of Charleston, West Virginia, in 1922, Leon Howard Sullivan was drawn to both religion and sports in his youth. He became an ordained Baptist minister at just seventeen years old and with an athletic scholarship played basketball and football at West Virginia State College. After losing his scholarship because of a serious knee injury, Sullivan worked nights in a steel mill to complete his education, graduating with a bachelor's degree in 1943. Continuing his studies, he spent the next two years at the Union Theological Seminary in New York City and got his master's degree in religion at Columbia University in 1947. He married Grace Banks in 1945.

In 1950 Sullivan began what became his lifelong ministry at the Zion Baptist Church in a poor black section of north Philadelphia. He proved a popular and inspiring speaker whose following eventually grew from six hundred to five thousand. But he also was determined to somehow help his fellow blacks pull themselves up to a better life. Concerned about job discrimination in the late 1950s, for example, he mounted a successful boycott campaign to force Philadelphia businesses to hire blacks. But unskilled black workers needed training before they could qualify for the jobs, and that prompted Sullivan to set up a job-training service.

With a donated building, equipment, technical help, and financial aid, he founded the Opportunities Industrialization Center in 1964 to teach black workers job skills in electronics, machine sewing, restaurant work, and other areas. Sullivan opened seven branch centers during the next five years, training six-thousand job seekers and finding work for all but a thousand of them. The success of the program also spawned federally funded centers modeled on Sullivan's plan in seventy-five cities nationwide.

While the job-training centers were probably his biggest success, Sullivan also founded the Zion Investment Associates in 1962 to help pioneer black capitalism. The group financed the country's first black-owned shopping center, a garment manufacturing company, an apartment complex, and an aerospace equipment subcontracting company. Later, in 1984, he set up the International Foundation for Education and Self-Help. Meanwhile, he also served on the boards of General Motors and other corporations.

Sullivan became pastor emeritus of the Zion Baptist Church in 1988, although he continues to head the organizations he founded.

Russell E. Train

As Chairman of the World Wildlife Fund, Russell E. Train has devoted himself to protecting our precious natural heritage. He has served the Nation as Administrator of the Environmental Protection Agency, as the first Chairman of the President's Council on Environmental Quality, and as Under Secretary of the Interior. Over the years, he has helped shape society's growing environmental awareness into sound policy. America honors an ardent conservationist, whose efforts help preserve Nature's treasures in this country and around the world.

★ ★ ★

President George Bush awarded Train the Presidential Medal of Freedom with the above citation during a White House ceremony November 18, 1991.

Born in Jamestown, Rhode Island, in 1920, Russell E. Train was the son of a U.S. Navy rear admiral and was largely raised in Washington, D.C. He went on to graduate cum laude from Princeton University in 1941 and spent World War II in the army as a field artillery officer. Deciding to study tax law, Train earned his law degree at Columbia University in 1948.

Admitted to the Washington, D.C., bar in 1949, he became a staffer for the congressional Joint Committee on Internal Revenue Taxation, a post he held from 1949 to 1953. Rising through a series of staff posts during the 1950s, Train served as chief counsel of the House Ways and Means Committee and as a staff assistant at the Treasury Department before becoming a U.S. Tax Court judge in 1957. Meanwhile, he married Aileen Bowdoin in 1954.

A hunting safari that Train went on in 1956 awakened his interest in conservation, and in 1961 he founded the African Wildlife Leadership Foundation. Four years later he resigned from the tax court to devote himself full time to conservation. That year he became president of the Conservation Foundation, a nonprofit group concerned about environmental problems in the United States.

President Richard Nixon named him undersecretary of the interior in 1969. Among Train's other duties at the Interior Department were setting up the government task force that studied ecological effects of the proposed Alaska oil pipeline and drawing up rules for the construction of the pipeline. Train next served as the first chairman of the newly established Council on Environmental Quality (1970–1973) and then became the Environmental Protection Agency administrator (1973–1977).

Returning to environmental advocacy, he headed the World Wildlife Fund in Washington, D.C., from 1978 to 1985 and thereafter has served as its board chairman. He also was board chairman for the Conservation Foundation (1985–1990). Train served on the National Commission on the Environment (1991–1993) and the President's Advisory Committee on Trade and Trade Negotiations (1991–1993).

Vernon A. Walters

As a soldier and statesman, General Vernon Walters has made service to his country his life's work. He served six Presidents with distinction during a half century of kaleidoscopic change, from World War II through the long Cold War to the fall of the Berlin Wall. He has served on the battlefields of Europe and in the councils of NATO, at the UN and CIA, as Ambassador and aide to Presidents. This extraordinary adventurer and intellectual has offered his diplomatic, linguistic, and tactical skills to the cause of world peace and individual liberty. America honors this steadfast defender of our interests and ideals, this true champion of freedom.

★ ★ ★

President George Bush awarded Walters the Presidential Medal of Freedom with the above citation during a White House ceremony November 18, 1991.

The son of a British-born insurance company executive, Vernon A. Walters was born in New York City in 1917. From age six he lived in Europe with his family, attending schools there and revealing his talent for learning languages. While still a teenager he became fluent in German, French, Spanish, and Italian. Walters's family returned to the United States in 1933, and after spending several unhappy years as an insurance adjuster, Walters joined the army in 1941.

As a young officer with exceptional language skills, Walters had a long series of prestigious assignments during his army career and was associated with many important people at home and abroad. He served both General Mark W. Clark and General George C. Marshall as an aide, attended several post–World War II summit conferences as President Harry S. Truman's interpreter, and went with Ambassador Averell Harriman on various diplomatic missions during the 1950s. From 1956 to 1960 he was President Dwight D. Eisenhower's staff assistant.

Walters was with Vice President Richard Nixon in Venezuela when an angry anti-U.S. mob attacked Nixon's limousine in 1958, and in 1964, while serving as a military attaché in Brazil, he was privy to advance knowledge of the military coup that removed President João Goulart from office that year. During the Vietnam War he was a senior military attaché to the American embassy in Paris and helped promote secret peace negotiations between the United States and North Vietnam by smuggling Henry A. Kissinger in and out of France more than a dozen times.

President Richard Nixon named him the Central Intelligence Agency (CIA) deputy director in 1972, though Walters soon had to fend off high-level White House staffers' attempts to use the CIA to block early phases of the Watergate investigation. Walters left the CIA in 1976 and that year also retired from the army as a lieutenant general. He spent the next four years doing consulting work and writing his autobiography, *Silent Missions* (1978).

Named ambassador at large by President Ronald Reagan in 1980, Walters traveled extensively, serving as a diplomatic trouble-shooter. Then in 1985 he became the permanent U.S. representative to the United Nations, where he spearheaded the administration's efforts to halt "the lynching of the United States" by UN resolutions passed to denounce American policies. He also attempted to negotiate the release of American hostages in Lebanon (1985) and to line up international support for diplomatically isolating Libya, which was promoting terrorism.

Walters, a lifelong bachelor, became U.S. ambassador to West Germany in 1989, the year the Berlin Wall was torn down. He remained in the post until 1991, when East Germany and West Germany were officially reunified as the Federal Republic of Germany.

Theodore "Ted" Williams

THEODORE SAMUEL WILLIAMS—TED WILLIAMS, THE "SPLENDID
SPLINTER"—IS PERHAPS THE GREATEST HITTER OF ALL TIME.
WILLIAMS MADE IT LOOK EASY. HE WON SIX BATTING TITLES,
BLASTED 521 HOME RUNS, AND HALF A CENTURY AGO AMAZED
AMERICA BY BECOMING THE LAST MAN TO BAT OVER .400. HE
ALSO GALLANTLY SERVED HIS COUNTRY IN TWO WARS AND
RETIRED FROM BASEBALL AS ONLY A HERO COULD—WITH A HOME
RUN IN HIS FINAL BAT. A CONSERVATIONIST, AVID FISHERMAN, AND
BASEBALL HALL OF FAMER, TED WILLIAMS IS A LIVING LEGEND.

★ ★ ★

*President George Bush awarded Williams the Presidential Medal of
Freedom with the above citation during a White House ceremony
November 18, 1991.*

An outfielder and home-run hitter for the Boston Red Sox, Ted Williams
was born in San Diego, California, in 1918. As a youth he dreamed of
playing professional baseball and practiced batting constantly. His ability
as a hitter was already apparent in high school, but during his first
season as a professional in 1936, with the San Diego Padres, his production at the plate was far from spectacular. In forty-two at-bats he did
not hit a single home run. If anything, though, Williams was
determined, and the next year his performance had improved enough to
get him a slot on the Red Sox minor league farm team in 1938.

A left-handed hitter, Williams then blasted his way into the Red
Sox lineup by leading the minor leagues that year with 43 home runs,
130 runs scored, 142 runs batted in, and a .366 batting average. In
1939, his first year with the Red Sox, he was named Outstanding
Rookie of the Year, and he scored an American-League-leading 134
runs in 1940. The following year his batting average reached .406,
making him the first player to top the .400 mark since 1930. Just
twenty-three years old, he also was the youngest to have done so.

World War II interrupted his playing career, and from 1942 to 1945
Williams served as a Marine Corps pilot and instructor. Meanwhile,
while still in the marines, he married Doris Soule.

Returning to the Red Sox, he was named the American League
Most Valuable Player in 1946 (and again in 1949). He stayed with the
team for the rest of his career as a professional baseball player, compiling an impressive 521 career home runs before retiring in 1960. He
was named to the Baseball Hall of Fame in 1966.

Williams became the manager of the Washington Senators in 1969
and was named American League Manager of the Year that year. He
stayed with the team until 1972, a year after it relocated to become the

Texas Rangers. In following years he has worked as a consultant and as a batting coach. Williams also published two books, *My Turn at Bat* (1969) and *The Science of Batting* (1971).

Javier Pérez de Cuéllar

FOR 10 YEARS OF EXCEPTIONALLY DISTINGUISHED SERVICE AS SECRETARY-GENERAL OF THE UNITED NATIONS, JAVIER PÉREZ DE CUÉLLAR PRESIDED OVER THE REBIRTH OF THAT INSTI- TUTION. WITH WISDOM, VISION, DIPLOMACY, AND SKILL, HE FORGED A U.N. WHERE COOPERATION IN REACHING COMMON GOALS IS REPLACING RHETORIC AND DIVISION.

* * *

President Geroge Bush awarded Pérez de Cuéllar the Presidential Medal of Freedom with the above citation during a White House ceremony December 12, 1991.

The United Nations secretary-general for nine years, Pérez de Cuéllar was born in Lima, Peru, in 1920. His father, a prosperous busi- nessman, died when he was just four. Educated in Catholic schools, Pérez de Cuéllar earned his law degree from Lima's Catholic University in 1943 and entered the foreign service the following year when he joined Peru's diplomatic staff in Paris.

He was a Peruvian delegate to the first-ever UN session (1946) and subsequently served in embassies in Britain, Bolivia, and Brazil. During the 1960s, between stints as a high-level official in Peru's Ministry of Foreign Affairs, he served as ambassador to Switzerland and the Soviet Union.

Pérez de Cuéllar returned to the United Nations in the 1970s. From 1971 to 1975 he was Peru's chief representative to the United Nations. Then, as the UN secretary-general's special representative (1976–1977) during the crisis in Cyprus, Pérez de Cuéllar succeeded in arranging talks between the rival Greek and Turkish factions. After serving as UN under- secretary-general for special political affairs (1979–1981), he retired briefly.

The retirement lasted less than three months and on January 1, 1982, he succeeded outgoing UN Secretary-General Kurt Waldheim. Soon after taking office, Pérez de Cuéllar weathered his first crisis in the Falkland Islands war between Britain and Argentina. Later he sought to use the UN Security Council in peacekeeping efforts and oversaw UN action on many other fronts during the 1980s and early 1990s, including in Afghanistan, the Mideast, and various African nations. He negotiated the 1988 cease-fire ending the fighting in the Iran-Iraq war and was deeply involved in the UN-sanctioned military action in the 1991 Persian Gulf War.

After a decade in office, Pérez de Cuéllar retired from the United Nations in December 1991. President Bush marked the occasion by awarding him the Presidential Medal of Freedom. Since his retirement, Pérez de Cuéllar has served as the director of the Republic National Bank of New York.

Sam Walton

THE PRESIDENTIAL MEDAL OF FREEDOM IS AWARDED TO SAM WALTON, AN AMERICAN ORIGINAL. SAM WALTON EMBODIES THE ENTREPRENEURIAL SPIRIT AND EPITOMIZES THE AMERICAN DREAM. CONCERN FOR HIS EMPLOYEES, A COMMITMENT TO HIS COMMUNITY AND A DESIRE TO MAKE A DIFFERENCE HAVE BEEN THE HALLMARK OF HIS CAREER. BY SPONSORING SCHOLARSHIPS FROM LATIN AMERICA HE HAS ALSO WORKED TO BRING PEOPLE CLOSER TOGETHER; AND TO SHARE WITH OTHERS THE AMERICAN IDEALS HE SO WELL REPRESENTS. A DEVOTED FAMILY MAN, BUSINESS LEADER AND STATESMAN FOR DEMOCRACY, SAM WALTON DEMONSTRATED THE VIRTUES OF FAITH, HOPE AND HARD WORK. AMERICA HONORS THIS CAPTAIN OF COMMERCE, AS SUCCESSFUL IN LIFE AS IN BUSINESS.

★ ★ ★

President George Bush awarded Walton the Presidential Medal of Freedom with the above citation during a ceremony at Wal-Mart Headquarters in Bentonville, Arkansas, on March 17, 1992.

A self-made billionaire and probably the most successful retail merchant of his day, Sam Walton was born in Kingfisher, Oklahoma, in 1918. The son of a mortgage broker, he was raised in Columbia, Missouri, and played quarterback on his high school football team, which he led to victory in the state championship. Walton graduated from the University of Missouri in 1940 with a bachelor's degree in economics and promptly went to work as a sales trainee for a J. C. Penney department store in Iowa. Helen Robson became his wife in 1943.

After serving in the Army Intelligence Corps during World War II, Walton decided to go into business for himself in 1945. With loans and his savings, he bought a Ben Franklin franchise store in Newport, Arkansas, parlaying his initial investment into fifteen Ben Franklin stores by 1960. Then in 1962 Ben Franklin franchise managers refused to back his idea to put large discount stores in small towns and rural areas. Walton was flying in the face of conventional retailing wisdom—stores were always sited in urban areas—but he believed large discount stores with smaller profit margins could thrive outside urban areas because they would have no competition.

Walton opened the first Wal-Mart Discount City in Rogers, Arkansas, in 1962, and just three decades later the Wal-Mart chain surpassed the venerable Sears and Roebuck as America's largest retailer. By 1991 Walton's chain—Wal-Mart, Sam's Club, and Wal-Mart Supercenters—included 1,735 stores in forty-two of the fifty states and was still growing at a rate of about 160 new stores a year. Sales topped $25 billion annually, and between 1985 and 1989 Walton was ranked as the nation's wealthiest individual.

Walton's stupendous success can be attributed to various factors, chief among them his basic strategy of rapid growth built on high sales volume and low prices. Another is the sophisticated marketing and logistical systems Walton used to meet his customers' demand for merchandise—regional warehouses took just two days to fill merchandise orders from Wal-Mart stores. He also knew how to get the most from his employees—Walton supplemented sales meeting pep talks about cutting costs and helping customers with profit-sharing and incentive bonus plans for the legions of low-paid Wal-Mart sales workers. Then, too, there was just plain hard work. Walton's day started at 4:30 a.m. and included regular stops at Wal-Mart stores around the country.

The formula created highly competitive stores, and this success can make the opening of a new Wal-Mart store a controversial event. Some small businesses simply cannot compete and have been forced out of business.

Having reached age seventy, Walton retired as president and chief executive in 1988. He remained Wal-Mart board chairman until his death in late 1992.

David Brinkley

THE NAME DAVID BRINKLEY IS SYNONYMOUS WITH TELEVISION NEWS. FROM HIS DAYS AS NBC'S WHITE HOUSE CORRESPONDENT TO HIS TIME AS CO-ANCHOR OF THE HUNTLEY-BRINKLEY REPORT TO HIS SUNDAY MORNING SHOW ON ABC, DAVID BRINKLEY HAS EXPLAINED THE COMPLEXITIES OF CURRENT EVENTS TO GENER-ATIONS OF AMERICANS. WITH THE WISDOM OF EXPERIENCE AND A

WRY WIT, HE HAS INFORMED THE NATION'S CITIZENS AND
HELPED HOLD ITS LEADERS ACCOUNTABLE. THE UNITED STATES
RECOGNIZES HIS CONTRIBUTIONS TO BROADCAST JOURNALISM.

★ ★ ★

President George Bush awarded Brinkley the Presidential Medal of
Freedom with the above citation during a White House ceremony
December 11, 1992.

A newsman who, as he once remarked, literally grew up with television broadcast journalism, David McClure Brinkley was born in Wilmington, North Carolina, in 1920, just six years before the invention of television. His father died when he was eight, and the young Brinkley became an avid reader, spending long hours at the local library after school. He also had a flair for writing that, during his high school years, led to an internship at the local paper.

When a full-time reporting job at the newspaper presented itself to him during his senior year, Brinkley dropped out of high school. Though he later attended classes at the University of North Carolina, Emory, and Vanderbilt, Brinkley's energies remained focused on his career as a journalist. After a stint in the army and as a radio copywriter for United Press, he began his long association with NBC in 1943. Working in Washington, D.C., he started out gathering news on Congress and the White House and writing copy for radio announcers.

Radio was still the mass medium in the mid–1940s, and opportunities to actually deliver radio news proved rare. Television, still in its infancy, was another matter, however. Because viewing audiences remained quite small, Brinkley found it easier to get started in television. By the early 1950s, when millions of Americans started watching television, Brinkley had already become an experienced hand in the emerging field of television broadcast journalism.

His first regular spot was delivering a Washington news roundup on John Cameron Swayze's "The Camel News Caravan" between 1951 and 1956. On the air Brinkley demonstrated a knack for succinct prose and had a dry, authoritative delivery that eventually would be widely imitated. In 1956 NBC teamed Brinkley (reporting from Washington) with Chet Huntley (based in New York) and on October 29, 1956, aired the first installment of "NBC News."

Later renamed the "Huntley-Brinkley Report" and expanded from fifteen minutes to a half hour, the show ranked first among news programs by 1958. By 1970, when Huntley retired, the show had garnered two Emmys in 1959 and 1960, and had led the ratings for most of its fourteen years on the air. Brinkley continued reporting for "NBC Nightly News" after 1970, appearing as a sometime co-anchor and as a commentator. He married Susan Melanie Benfer in 1972, having earlier divorced his first wife.

After "NBC Magazine with David Brinkley" failed, he moved over to ABC in 1981, where he did commentary for the nightly news program and began hosting his Sunday morning public affairs show "This Week with David Brinkley." From the first year onward, Brinkley's multifaceted program competed well against NBC's "Meet the Press" and CBS's "Face the Nation" in the Sunday morning slot. The program is now into its second decade with Brinkley at the helm.

Johnny Carson

ONE OF AMERICA'S GREATEST TELEVISION PERSONALITIES, JOHNNY CARSON LEFT THE NEBRASKA PLAINS TO PRESIDE OVER LATE NIGHT TV FOR ALMOST 30 YEARS. WITH A QUICK WIT AND A SURE GOLF SWING, JOHNNY'S GOOD-NATURED HUMOR KEPT THE PULSE OF THE NATION, AND ASSURED US THAT EVEN IN THE MOST DIFFICULT TIMES, IT WAS STILL OKAY TO LAUGH. THE UNITED STATES HONORS JOHNNY CARSON, WHO PERSONIFIES THE HEART AND HUMOR OF AMERICA.

★　★　★

President George Bush awarded Carson the Presidential Medal of Freedom with the above citation during a White House ceremony December 11, 1992.

Johnny Carson, one of television's most enduring personalities, was born in Corning, Iowa, in 1925. Two years after becoming interested in magic, the fourteen-year-old Carson staged his first magic show at his hometown Rotary Club in Norfolk, Nebraska, making three dollars in the process. His interest in performing lasted throughout high school, where Carson actively participated in student plays. He served in the navy during World War II and then graduated from the University of Nebraska in 1949.

Carson's first professional job was writing a Western comedy for a Lincoln, Nebraska, radio station in 1948, and after finishing college he joined radio station WOW in Omaha. Soon yearning for bigger opportunities, Carson moved to a Los Angeles television station in 1951, landing his own half-hour comedy show, "Carson's Cellar." The show lasted only thirty weeks, but Red Skelton, Groucho Marx, and Fred Allen all did guest spots with him, and Carson quickly moved to a comedy writing job on Skelton's CBS television show.

Next came what seemed like the big break in Carson's career. One day in 1954 Red Skelton suffered a last-minute injury that prevented him from appearing on his show. Carson filled in and made such a hit that

CBS gave him his own quiz show, "The Johnny Carson Show." That program lasted only thirty-nine weeks, however, and a discouraged Carson went to New York. But by 1957 he was back on television, hosting the ABC quiz show "Who Do You Trust?," and his talent for bantering with contestants soon made it ABC's most-watched daytime show.

While hosting "Who Do You Trust?," Carson did guest spots on various other shows, among them NBC's "Tonight Show," and at one point in 1958 he even substituted for host Jack Paar. When Paar finally quit in 1962, NBC handed Carson what would become his life's work. Carson revamped the show's format, introducing the opening monologue, and his affable, witty, and unflappable manner gave the show a cozy, late-night aura that drew viewers by the millions. Carson charmed his audiences with his just slightly off-color, bad-boy streak, and within five years the press was calling him an institution.

Carson took on all comers in the late-night slot, handily defeating rival talk shows in the ratings wars. And after being on the air for fifteen years—a feat in itself—he doubled his audience to an estimated 17.3 million viewers. By one estimate, the "Tonight Show" was earning fully 17 percent of NBC's pretax profits. With that kind of clout, Carson negotiated contracts during the 1970s and 1980s that consistently kept him among the highest paid television performers and gradually reduced the number of shows he did each week.

The venerable Johnny Carson finally retired in 1992 after thirty years on the "Tonight Show," though he still has ties to NBC. He married his fourth wife, Alexis Maas, five years before retiring.

Ella Fitzgerald

DISCOVERED AS A TEENAGER AT THE APOLLO THEATRE IN HARLEM, ELLA FITZGERALD AND HER SWING STYLE OF VOCAL JAZZ TRANSCEND THE TIMES. HER TRADEMARK SCAT CAPTIVATES AUDIENCES, AND AS A CULTURAL AMBASSADOR, HER IMPRESSIVE VOCAL RANGE STRETCHES ACROSS OCEANS AND POLITICAL BOUNDARIES. HONORED BY THE KENNEDY CENTER FOR HER LIFETIME ACHIEVEMENTS, INDUCTED INTO THE JAZZ HALL OF FAME, AND AWARDED THE NATIONAL MEDAL OF ARTS, IT IS FITTING THAT THE UNITED STATES HONORS THIS "FIRST LADY OF SONG".

★ ★ ★

President George Bush awarded Fitzgerald the Presidential Medal of Freedom with the above citation during a White House ceremony December 11, 1992. Fitzgerald was unable to attend due to illness.

Named *Down Beat* magazine's top female singer of the year twenty-one times during her nearly sixty-year singing career, Ella Fitzgerald was born in Newport News, Virginia, in 1917. Raised in Yonkers, New York, she soon acquired her mother's love of music and as a youth dreamed of becoming a performer—not a singer, but a dancer. Then one day in 1934 she and two friends drew straws to decide who would go on the amateur hour at Harlem's Apollo Theatre.

Fortunately for music lovers everywhere, Fitzgerald drew the short straw. But one problem remained: Ella planned a dance number, not a song. When she stepped out before the waiting audience, though, young Fitzgerald found herself paralyzed by stage fright. A desperate moment followed before she decided to sing instead, and she chose, prophetically, one of her favorites, "The Object of My Affection." The judges awarded her first prize and from that day forward singing became a lifetime object of her affection.

She had to win many more talent contests before getting her first big break in 1935, when she became the vocalist for Chick Webb's big band. Webb helped turn her into a polished performer, and she reached a wider audience through live radio broadcasts of the band's performances at the Savoy Ballroom. She also began recording in 1936, and two years later her swing rendition of the nursery rhyme "A-Tisket, A-Tasket" launched her as a nationally known star singer. Her solo singing career started in 1942, and at about that time she also began singing the *scats*, vocal imitations of instrumental sounds, for which she became famous.

Blessed with an acute musical sense and a wide vocal range that allowed her to "slither up or down a chromatic scale," Fitzgerald in 1946 began what became a lifelong association with jazz impresario Norman Granz, at first touring the world with his Jazz at the Philharmonic and then in 1955 moving to his newly founded Verve recording label. At Verve, Fitzgerald began recording a series of nine "songbook" albums that established her as a truly brilliant singer and made her a hit with the mainstream musical audience. Songbooks, containing two or more albums of songs written by a famous composer and sung by Fitzgerald, were recorded over a twelve-year span and included the music of Cole Porter, Irving Berlin, Duke Ellington, Rogers and Hart, and George and Ira Gershwin.

Meanwhile, she continued giving live performances and in 1949 married her second husband, Ray Brown, a double-bass player. She had a son before divorcing Brown in 1953 and raised her son, as well as nieces, on her own.

Maintaining a demanding schedule of singing engagements well into the 1980s, Fitzgerald was finally forced to cut back after major heart surgery. Singing remained the "object of her affection," however. She continued giving live performances and recording albums into the 1990s. Ella Fitzgerald died in 1996, at age 79.

Audrey Hepburn

AS A GIFTED ACTRESS, AUDREY HEPBURN CAPTURED THE
HEARTS OF MILLIONS. YET SHE HAS A MOST PROFOUND EFFECT
ON YOUNG PEOPLE WHO WILL NEVER KNOW HER AS A PRINCESS
IN ROMAN HOLIDAY, AS A MODEL IN FUNNY FACE, OR AS THE
WOMAN IN BLACK IN BREAKFAST AT TIFFANY'S. WITH A PASSION
THAT RIVALS HER BEAUTY, AUDREY HEPBURN IS A TIRELESS
WORKER AND A DEVOTED SPECIAL AMBASSADOR FOR THE
UNITED NATIONS INTERNATIONAL CHILDREN'S EMERGENCY
FUND. AMERICA IS PROUD TO HONOR AUDREY HEPBURN, A STAR
WHOSE LIGHT IS REFLECTED NOT ONLY ON MOVIE SCREENS BUT
IN THE BRIGHT SMILES OF CHILDREN AROUND THE WORLD.

★ ★ ★

*President George Bush awarded Hepburn the Presidential Medal of
Freedom with the above citation during a White House ceremony December
11, 1992. Hepburn was unable to attend due to failing health.*

The daughter of a Dutch mother and an English father, Audrey
Hepburn was born Edda van Heemstra Hepburn-Ruston in Brussels,
Belgium, in 1929. Educated in Britain, Hepburn happened to be in
Holland with her mother when the Nazis invaded. Trapped there for
the rest of World War II, they suffered many hardships. The Nazis
executed two of Hepburn's Dutch relatives and dragged a brother off to
a labor camp, and the rest of the family sometimes had to struggle to
feed themselves. At one point they even ate tulip bulbs just to survive.

Returning to London after the war, Hepburn spent her time as a
ballet student, model, dancer, and sometime actress in British films.
While on location in Monte Carlo, Hepburn caught the attention of
the French novelist Colette, who decided on the spot that Hepburn
was perfect for the starring role in the Broadway version of *Gigi*.
Hepburn proved an immediate smash hit when the play opened in
1951. She likewise took Hollywood by storm with her first movie,
Roman Holiday (1953), in which she played a princess hiding from
her duties. She enchanted audiences with her wistful beauty,
elegance, and childlike mischievousness and won an Academy Award
in 1954 for her role in *Roman Holiday*. She also won a Tony that same
year for her appearance in the Broadway play *Ondine*.

At the height of her acting career in the 1950s and 1960s, she played
opposite the most famous leading men of her day, including Humphrey
Bogart in *Sabrina* (1954), Fred Astaire in *Funny Face* (1957), Cary Grant
in *Charade* (1963), and Rex Harrison in *My Fair Lady* (1964). Among
her other most memorable films were *Breakfast at Tiffany's* (1961) and
Wait Until Dark (1967), in which she played a dramatic role.

Hepburn left Hollywood in 1967 to devote more time to her family, but her marriage to Mel Ferrer broke up the following year. Her second marriage, to psychiatrist Andrea Dotti, also ended in divorce. Meanwhile, she returned to the screen in the late 1970s and early 1980s but enjoyed only moderate success.

From 1988 onward, however, she threw herself into her work as a goodwill ambassador for the UN Children's Fund. Motivated by memories of her own childhood privations during World War II, she became a tireless traveler on behalf of UNICEF, frequently visiting Africa and Latin American countries where children were suffering hunger and starvation.

Hepburn died in early 1993 just over a month after receiving the Presidential Medal of Freedom from President Bush. She was sixty-three years old.

Ieoh Ming Pei

PERHAPS THE MOST FAMOUS ARCHITECT IN THE WORLD TODAY, I. M. PEI'S ARCHITECTURAL FEATS REPRESENT THE PINNACLE OF CLASSIC MODERNISM. HIS VERY NAME, IEOH MING, MEANS "TO INSCRIBE BRIGHTLY," AS HIS BUILDINGS HAVE ILLUMINATED SKYLINES WORLDWIDE. I. M. PEI HAS FOUND BEAUTY IN SIMPLICITY AND BOLDNESS IN GEOMETRY, SETTING THE STANDARD FOR MODERN ARCHITECTURE. FOR THE LEGACY OF ARTISTIC ELEGANCE HE HAS INSCRIBED IN OUR CITIES, AMERICA HONORS I. M. PEI.

★ ★ ★

President George Bush awarded Pei the Presidential Medal of Freedom with the above citation during a White House ceremony December 11, 1992.

A leading exponent of classic modernism, Ieoh Ming Pei was born in Canton, China, in 1917. His father was a banker, and Pei was raised in comfortable circumstances. Interested in architecture even as a youth, he went to the United States in 1935 to pursue his studies in the field. Though he had planned to return to China, the outbreak of World War II forced him to remain in the United States after his graduation from the Massachusetts Institute of Technology in 1940. He married Eileen Loo, a member of a prominent Chinese family, in 1942.

I. M. Pei worked as an architect in various American cities and joined the faculty of the Harvard University Graduate School of Design as an assistant professor in 1945. Continuing his graduate studies under the noted modernist architects Walter Gropius and Marcel Breuer at

Harvard, Pei earned his master's degree in architecture in 1946. Soon afterward, the Communist takeover in China eliminated any prospect of his returning home, and in 1954 he was granted U.S. citizenship.

Hired in 1948 as director of the architectural division of the New York City real estate development firm of Webb and Knapp, Pei began designing massive urban complexes connected with slum clearance projects. Among his projects were Denver's Mile High Center (completed in 1955), Chicago's Hyde Park Redevelopment (1959), and Philadelphia's Society Hill project (1964).

Pei formed his own architectural firm in 1955 and, with his former employer as a major client, went on to design a series of single-purpose buildings that helped him establish his reputation as a leading architect. He became famous for his high-prestige, large-scale buildings, as well as for his skill and boldness in grouping the geometric shapes making up the structures. From the 1960s onward he designed such prestigious buildings as New York City's John F. Kennedy International Airport (1970), the East Building Annex to the National Gallery of Art (1978), the John F. Kennedy Memorial Library at Harvard University (1979), the Fragrant Hill Hotel in Beijing, China, New York City's Jacob K. Javits Convention Center (1986), and one of his most controversial designs, a new glass-pyramid entrance as part of his renovation of the famed Louvre Museum in Paris (1988).

While continuing to work on smaller projects of personal interest, Pei after 1989 turned over the bulk of his firm's work to his longtime associates.

Richard Lee Petty

IN THE WORLD OF STOCK CAR RACING, THERE IS ONLY ONE KING. RICHARD PETTY IS MORE THAN RACING'S MONARCH, HE IS AN AMERICAN LEGEND. FROM HUMBLE BEGINNINGS IN LEVEL CROSS, NORTH CAROLINA, NUMBER 43 BECAME ONE OF RACING'S FINEST—AND FASTEST. WINNING A RECORD 200 RACES AND SEVEN DAYTONA 500 VICTORIES, RICHARD PETTY FOUND FREEDOM AT 175 MILES PER HOUR. THE UNITED STATES HONORS THIS AMERICAN HERO FOR EXEMPLIFYING THE DREAMS, DEDICATION, AND DRIVE THAT MAKE THIS NATION GREAT.

★ ★ ★

President George Bush awarded Petty the Presidential Medal of Freedom with the above citation during a White House ceremony December 11, 1992.

Born in Level Cross, North Carolina, in 1937, Richard Lee Petty literally grew up with the sport of stock-car racing. His father, Lee Petty, souped up old cars in his spare time and ran them in impromptu nighttime races on North Carolina's backcountry highways. By the 1940s, when Petty was still a young boy, racing modified street cars had become a popular pastime throughout much of the rural South, complete with established racetracks and a national organization. Petty's father, a three-time national title winner, was one of stock racing's first champions.

Young Petty grew up helping out at the track, and meanwhile watched stock car racing grow into a spectator sport of huge proportions, especially in his native South. After graduating from high school and taking a junior college business course, he started working fulltime for his father's auto-racing outfit, Petty Enterprises. Petty married Lynda Owens, a high school cheerleader, in 1958.

When Petty turned twenty-one, he decided to try driving stock cars competitively and in 1959, his second season of racing, was named Rookie of the Year. He won his first Grand National circuit victory in 1960. Two years later, when his father was seriously injured in a racing accident, the younger Petty became the sole driver for Petty Enterprises.

The year 1964 proved an important one in Petty's rising career as a race-car driver—he won his first super-speedway race, the Daytona 500, and claimed his first Grand National Championship as well. Two years later he became the first driver to ever win the Daytona 500 twice. Then in 1967 he established himself as stock-car racing's all-time best driver by winning twenty NASCAR races for the season, besting his father's career win total of fifty-four and winning his second Grand National Championship.

Petty was slowed by a serious accident in 1969 and a long losing streak (1977–1979) but went on racing, and winning, until he finally retired in 1992. By then he had driven in over one thousand Grand National races, had won some two hundred of them, and had been Grand National champion seven times (1964, 1967, 1971–1972, 1974–1975, 1979). He also won the Daytona 500 seven times.

A veritable legend among race-car fans, Petty published two autobiographies, *Grand National* (1971, with Bill Neely) and *King of the Road* (1977).

Harry W. Shlaudeman

Ambassador Harry Shlaudeman is one of America's most
decorated and masterful Foreign Service officers. In
almost four decades of service to eight Presidents,
through international crises and war, he has faced every
challenge with personal bravery and professional skill.
He has demonstrated his loyalty again in 1990, when at
the request of the President, he came out of retirement to
serve as Ambassador to Nicaragua and helped ensure that
nation's peaceful transition to democracy. For his decades
of meritorious service, courageous diplomacy, and protection of our interests abroad, the United States com-
memorates the service of Ambassador Harry Shlaudeman.

★ ★ ★

*President George Bush awarded Shlaudeman the Presidential Medal of
Freedom with the above citation during a White House ceremony
December 11, 1992.*

A diplomat whose career dealt almost exclusively with Central and
South America, Harry W. Shlaudeman was born in Los Angeles in 1926.
He served in the U.S. Marines during World War II, and in 1948 Carol
Jean Dickey became his wife. Graduating from Stanford University with
a bachelor's degree in 1952, he entered the foreign service two years later.

His first assignments abroad began the following year with
diplomatic staff posts in Colombia and, later, the Dominican
Republic. During the latter part of the 1960s Shlaudeman served as a
special assistant to the secretary of state (1967–1969) and then as
deputy assistant secretary of state for inter-American affairs
(1973–1975). In the interim he was deputy chief of the U.S. diplomatic
mission in Santiago, Chile (1969–1973).

President Gerald R. Ford appointed him to his first ambas-
sadorship, to Venezuela, in 1975, and the following year Shlaudeman
returned to the State Department for a brief stint as assistant secretary of state for inter-American affairs (1976–1977). In following
years he served as ambassador to Peru (1977–1980), Argentina
(1980–1983), and Brazil (1986–1989).

President Ronald Reagan named him ambassador at large and special
envoy to Central America in 1984, at a time when unrest in El Salvador
and Nicaragua were at a high point and when U.S. policy in Central
America had become a major domestic political issue. Shlaudeman
remained in the post until being named ambassador to Brazil in 1986.

Having retired in 1989, he nevertheless agreed to serve as

President George Bush's ambassador to Nicaragua in 1990, after the leftist Sandinista government was ousted in free elections. Shlaudeman served until 1992 and then again went into retirement.

Isaac Stern

Since his debut 56 years ago, Isaac Stern has become one of the world's preeminent violinists. His warm and vibrant interpretations have brought him international acclaim and our Nation's highest honor for artistic merit, the National Medal of Arts. But even beyond his triumphant career, Isaac Stern has enriched the human spirit by broadening the scope of music—supporting artists from all corners of the world; helping to found the National Endowment for the Arts; and rescuing Carnegie Hall from the wrecking ball. For his support of the arts and his lifetime achievement, the United States recognizes master violinist Isaac Stern.

★ ★ ★

President George Bush awarded Stern the Presidential Medal of Freedom with the above citation during a White House ceremony December 11, 1992.

Among the world's great violinists and the first American violin virtuoso, Isaac Stern was born in the Ukraine in 1920. The following year his parents emigrated to the United States to escape the Russian revolution and settled in San Francisco. There they encouraged him to start taking piano lessons at age six, and two years later he became interested in the violin. Stern studied violin at the San Francisco Conservatory from 1928 to 1931 and under the Russian violinist Naoum Blinder from 1932 to 1939.

Stern's recital debut came in 1934, and two years later, at age sixteen, he gave his orchestral debut with the San Francisco Symphony Orchestra. A lukewarm reception at his first New York appearance set the stage for several years of arduous practice, but when Stern returned to New York for his Carnegie Hall debut in 1943, he won high praise as a master violinist. Suddenly in demand, he steadily increased his concert schedule in the late 1940s and in 1948 made his first European tour. Meanwhile, in 1946, he appeared in the first of several movies that featured his playing *Humoresque*. In

1951 he married his second wife, Vera Lindenblit, his first marriage having ended in divorce three years earlier.

From the 1950s onward Stern was ranked among the world's leading violinists, as well as one of the most energetic—during the 1970s he was playing up to two-hundred concerts a year. He has made over one-hundred recordings and premiered works composed by Bernstein, Hindemith, Penderecki, and others. In addition, he has become known as an excellent judge of young musical talent and has nurtured the careers of numerous protégés.

Stern has done much to promote the arts. In 1956, before the era of cultural exchange programs, he gave the first concerts by an American musician in the postwar Soviet Union. When Carnegie Hall was threatened with demolition in 1960, he organized the successful fund-raising drive to save it. That year he also became president of Carnegie Hall Corporation, a post he continues to hold, and in 1964 he helped set up the National Endowment for the Arts.

Appearing more frequently on television from the 1970s ("Tonight at Carnegie Hall," "Live from Lincoln Center") he won an Emmy Award in 1987 for his performance in "Carnegie Hall: The Grand Reopening." Earlier, in 1981, he starred in the Academy-Award winning documentary *From Mao to Mozart: Isaac Stern in China*. More recently he was the subject of the television production "Isaac Stern—A Life" (1991).

John W. Vessey

GENERAL JOHN W. VESSEY WAS THE LAST FOUR-STAR COMBAT VETERAN OF WORLD WAR II TO RETIRE FROM ACTIVE DUTY. A SELF-DESCRIBED "MUD SOLDIER," THE FORMER CHAIRMAN OF THE JOINT CHIEFS OF STAFF NEVER FORGOT THE MEN IN THE FIELD, AND HE RETURNED FROM RETIREMENT TO SEARCH FOR SOLDIERS MISSING IN ACTION IN VIETNAM. HIS WISE COUNSEL TO TWO PRESIDENTS HAS HELPED TO BREAK AN IMPASSE WITH HANOI, CULMINATING IN VIETNAM'S RECENT OFFER TO PROVIDE ALL INFORMATION ABOUT AMERICANS MISSING IN ACTION. THE UNITED STATES HONORS GENERAL JOHN W. VESSEY, A SOLDIER/STATESMAN WHO COULD NOT LEAVE ANYONE BEHIND.

★ ★ ★

President George Bush awarded Vessey the Presidential Medal of Freedom with the above citation during a White House ceremony December 11, 1992.

The Joint Chiefs chairman for four years during the Reagan administration, John W. Vessey was born in 1922 and was raised in Crow Wing County, Minnesota. He was just under seventeen years old—and underage—when he enlisted in the Minnesota National Guard in 1939. His unit was activated, and by 1942 Vessey was fighting in Tunisia as part of the 34th Division artillery. A first sergeant in an artillery unit by the time he landed on the beachhead at Anzio, Italy, in 1944, Vessey was handed a field promotion to second lieutenant, along with the dangerous job of forward artillery observer.

Vessey finished the war as a lieutenant and married Avis C. Funk. In years following he held a series of army staff jobs and troop commands and, in addition to attending military schools, earned his bachelor's degree from the University of Maryland in 1963 at the age of forty-one. A lieutenant colonel by 1966, Vessey served in Vietnam in the 25th Division artillery. While commanding an artillery battalion there, he and his men held off an attack by five battalions of North Vietnamese regular soldiers, at one point firing their artillery at point blank range into the oncoming enemy. In 1971 he was promoted to brigadier general and given command of a unit working in Thailand to support anticommunist Laotians.

Other staff assignments and promotions followed, including a stint at the Pentagon as the number-three man on the army staff. Having been promoted to full general in 1976, he commanded U.S. military forces in Korea from 1976 to 1979. While serving in Korea, Vessey helped persuade President Jimmy Carter to reverse his controversial plan to withdraw American soldiers from South Korea. Then came his assignment as army vice chief of staff (1979–1982) and the crowning achievement to his long career, his four years as chairman of the Joint Chiefs of Staff (1982–1986).

Vessey worked closely with President Ronald Reagan, who appointed him, and Defense Secretary Caspar Weinberger to reassert the influence of the Joint Chiefs in the policy-making process and to gain operational control of military forces, once the president has set the strategy. (*See also the entry for Weinberger, p. 402.*) Thus in Grenada the White House let the military control the invasion once President Reagan decided in favor of the mission. Meanwhile, Vessey also used his time as chairman to push for more strategic mobility and for increased development of high-tech "smart weapons."

Vessey retired after his term as Joint Chiefs chairman, but in 1989 President George Bush called him out of retirement to serve as the U.S. envoy to Hanoi to oversee the search for any American soldiers, alive or dead, who were listed as missing in action during the Vietnam War. By the 1990s Vessey's work had effectively resolved that issue, and President Bill Clinton normalized relations with communist-ruled Vietnam in 1995.

Elie Wiesel

FEW PEOPLE HAVE SEEN A DARKER SIDE OF HUMANITY THAN ELIE WIESEL. DURING WORLD WAR II, HE SAW MOST OF HIS FAMILY KILLED WHILE IMPRISONED IN THE AUSCHWITZ AND BUCHENWALD CONCENTRATION CAMPS. AND YET THIS AUTHOR, PHILOSOPHER, AND WINNER OF THE 1986 NOBEL PEACE PRIZE STILL SEES THE PROMISE OF HUMAN TOLERANCE, LEARNING, AND FAITH. HE CHALLENGES PEOPLE OF ALL RELIGIONS TO REMEMBER THE HOLOCAUST, THAT IT MAY NEVER HAPPEN AGAIN. HIS DEEPLY SPIRITUAL LIFE AND LITERATURE REMIND US THAT TO PROTECT FREEDOM'S FLAME, WE MUST REMEMBER THAT WHICH THREATENS IT. THE UNITED STATES HONORS THIS KEEPER OF THAT FLAME, ELIE WIESEL.

★ ★ ★

President George Bush awarded Wiesel the Presidential Medal of Freedom with the above citation during a White House ceremony December 11, 1992.

The author of several books about the Holocaust and its survivors, Elie Wiesel was born to a Jewish family living in a small Romanian town in 1928. His father was a shopkeeper and encouraged Wiesel's early interest in religious studies. But Wiesel's rather quiet, almost hermitlike childhood was shattered in 1944 when the Nazis rounded up the town's fifteen-thousand Jews and sent them to Auschwitz, the Nazi concentration camp in Poland. Eventually his mother and one sister were murdered in the camp's gas chambers and his father died of starvation.

Somehow Wiesel, who was used as a slave laborer, and two older sisters survived until Allied troops liberated the concentration camps. Settling in France, Wiesel then studied literature and philosophy at the Sorbonne from 1948 to 1951, while also working as a journalist in France and Israel. He went to the United States in 1956, became a citizen seven years later, and married Marion Erster Rose in 1969.

Meanwhile, Wiesel completed his first book in 1958, a semiautobiographical work about the Holocaust. Originally published in France, it appeared two years later in the United States as *Night*. The book has been ranked among the most powerful literary treatments of the Holocaust, and in fact Wiesel is said to have been first to apply the term *Holocaust* to the Nazi's attempt to systematically exterminate Jews. In following years, Wiesel wrote a series of other semiautobiographical novels dealing with the emotional trials of those who survived the Holocaust. These books include *Dawn* (1961), *The Accident* (1962), *The Town Beyond the Wall* (1964), and *The Gates of the Forest* (1966).

Wiesel's novel about the Six-Day War, *A Beggar in Jerusalem* (1970), proved a bestseller in the United States and France. This was followed by *Souls on Fire* (1972), his highly praised collection of Hasidic tales; *The Testament* (1981), a novel dealing with the suffering of Soviet Jews; and collections of his writings.

A noted lecturer on the sufferings of the Holocaust, Wiesel has frequently spoken out against racism, oppression, and violence. For his many years of work to that end, he was awarded the 1986 Nobel Peace Prize.

From 1972 to 1976 Wiesel taught Judaic studies at City College of New York. He has been a professor at Boston University since 1976 and served as chairman of the President's Commission on the Holocaust (1979–1980) and of the United States Holocaust Memorial Council (1980–1986). He organized the Elie Wiesel Foundation for Humanity in 1987.

Strom Thurmond

FEW AMERICANS HAVE GIVEN AS MUCH TO THEIR COUNTRY AS HAS STROM THURMOND. AT NINETY YEARS YOUNG, HE HAS VIGOROUSLY SERVED SEVEN CONSECUTIVE TERMS AS SENATOR FROM SOUTH CAROLINA, AND HIS CAREER READS LIKE A ROLL CALL OF GOVERNMENT SERVICE: PRESIDENT PRO TEMPORE OF THE SENATE, GOVERNOR OF SOUTH CAROLINA, MAJOR GENERAL IN THE ARMY RESERVE, JUDGE AND TEACHER. THERE ARE FEW BETTER ADVOCATES IN CONGRESS THAN STROM THURMOND. HE HAS SPENT A LIFETIME SUPPORTING AMERICA'S FARMERS AND WORKERS, A STRONG NATIONAL DEFENSE, SPENDING RESTRAINT, AND LOWER TAXES. AMERICA PAYS TRIBUTE TO ITS MOST SENIOR SENATOR, STROM THURMOND, BY AWARDING HIM THE NATION'S HIGHEST CIVILIAN HONOR, THE PRESIDENTIAL MEDAL OF FREEDOM.

★ ★ ★

President George Bush awarded Thurmond the Presidential Medal of Freedom with the above citation during a White House ceremony January 12, 1993.

A senator for over four decades and a leading conservative voice in Congress, Strom Thurmond was born in Edgefield, South Carolina, in 1902. He was the son of a state legislator and went on to get his bachelor's degree from South Carolina's Clemson University in 1923. While teaching school during the 1920s, he studied law privately and in 1930 tied for the highest score on the state bar exam. His career in public service began during the 1930s, with such posts as state senator (1933–1938) and circuit court judge (1938–1941).

Thurmond was a highly decorated officer in the Eighty-second Airborne Division during World War II, and in 1946 he successfully ran for governor of South Carolina as a populist. He instituted a number of liberal reforms, including a ban on the poll tax and increased aid to education, but in 1948 led a revolt of southern delegates against a strong civil rights plank adopted by the Democratic National Convention. Leading the segregationists' hastily organized challenge to the regular Democrats, Thurmond ran as the States' Rights Democratic party candidate for president in 1948 and won thirty-nine electoral votes.

Though he faced determined opposition from the regular Democratic party, Thurmond nevertheless ran in a special Senate election in 1954 and became the only U.S. senator to ever win by write-in ballot. Reelected by wide margins ever since, he became a leading foe of civil rights legislation during the 1950s and 1960s and in 1957 his filibuster of civil rights legislation became the longest on record—twenty-four hours and eighteen minutes.

Then in 1964 he became the first southern Democrat to become a Republican. That year he threw his support behind Republican conservative presidential candidate Barry Goldwater, and in 1968 he backed Richard Nixon. That year he also married Nancy Moore, his first wife having died in 1960.

A staunch supporter of a strong military, Thurmond ranks as the senior member of the Senate Armed Services Committee. In that position he has backed virtually all the important weapons development legislation passed by Congress over the past two decades or so. In 1981, when the Republicans recaptured the majority in the Senate, Thurmond became Judiciary Committee chairman and also was elected president pro tempore of the Senate, a largely ceremonial post. (The president pro tempore presides over the Senate when the vice president of the United States is absent.) Thurmond held both these titles until 1987, when the Democrats again won a majority of Senate seats. Then in 1995, when the Republicans regained control of the Senate, he became Armed Services Committee chairman again.

Thurmond, who was ninety-three in mid-1995, will become the Senate's oldest-serving member if he finishes his current term, which ends in 1997.

Ronald Reagan

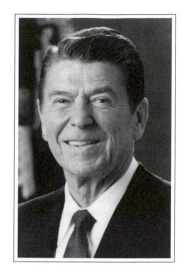

Ronald Reagan symbolizes all that is best in America. His is the story of a lifetime committed to individual freedom and liberty. As President he ennobled the American spirit of hope and optimism, faith and family. At home he championed free enterprise over big government and presided over the longest peacetime economic boom in our nation's history. Around the world he brandished America's lamp of liberty so those living in tyranny might secure freedom against darkness. His steadfast belief in peace through strength consigned imperial communism to the ash heap of history. Ronald Reagan's courage changed America and helped America change the world. America honors a man who has brought her great honor—the fortieth President of the United States.

★ ★ ★

President George Bush awarded Reagan the Presidential Medal of Freedom with the above citation during a White House ceremony January 13, 1993. The medal was accompanied with the added accolade "with distinction."

The fortieth president of the United States, Ronald Reagan was born in Tampico, Illinois, in 1911. His father was a shoe salesman, and the young Reagan was raised in the small Midwest town of Dixon, Illinois. He went on to graduate from Eureka College as an economics and sociology major in 1932 in the midst of the depression, and that same year found a job as a sports announcer at station WOC in Davenport, Iowa.

Five years later he landed a contract with Warner Brothers movie studio and began his film career with the starring role in *Love Is on the Air* (1937), a movie about a crusading radio announcer. Calling himself "the Errol Flynn of the B's," Reagan later made numerous other "B" movies for Warner Brothers, but his portrayal of the Gipper in *Knute Rockne—All American* (1940) established him as a serious actor. His performance in *Kings Row* (1941) was among his other notable roles, and in all he made fifty-two pictures.

During Reagan's early years, President Franklin D. Roosevelt had been his political hero. But while Reagan was serving as the Screen Actors Guild president (1947–1952), Reagan began shifting rightward in reaction to "rule or ruin" tactics communists were using in their bid to take over movie industry unions. Reagan's transition from a liberal Democrat to conservative Republican was completed during his years with General Electric (1952–1962), when he doubled as host of the "General Electric Theater" and traveling spokesman for the company. Meanwhile, he married his second wife, Nancy Davis, in 1952, having divorced his first wife, Jane Wyman, in 1948.

Reagan supported conservative Republican Barry Goldwater in the 1964 election, and his nationally televised speech backing Goldwater, "A Time for Choosing," helped establish him as a favorite among Republican conservatives. Two months later wealthy Reagan backers formed a committee to elect him governor of California. Reagan campaigned against big government and won the election handily in 1966. He was reelected governor in 1970 and succeeded in erasing a budget deficit inherited from the previous administration (through tax increases, a hiring freeze, and cutting expenditures for social programs).

A belated bid for the Republican presidential nomination failed in 1968, as did his full-fledged campaign in 1976 against incumbent Republican president Gerald R. Ford. But his 1976 primary run produced a strong turnout in the South and set up his successful 1980 campaign, in which he easily took the nomination and went on to soundly defeat President Jimmy Carter. At age sixty-nine, he became the oldest president ever sworn in to office.

Taking office in the midst of a serious inflationary recession (the prime interest rate had hit 21.5 percent) and with American prestige abroad at a low ebb, President Reagan promised "an era of national renewal" through his conservative policies. His plan was to cut government spending (except for defense), freeze hiring, and cut taxes to stimulate growth in the private sector. After recovering rapidly from a would-be assassin's bullet early in 1981, President Reagan won a massive tax cut, but the House, controlled by Democrats, adamantly refused to approve significant budget cuts, especially in social programs. Reagan, fighting for a balanced budget, countered by opposing tax increases in order to force Congress to cut spending. The battle continued throughout the Reagan years, with Reagan orchestrating a massive military buildup despite a rapidly rising national debt. Congress, for its part, ignored the billowing costs for Social Security and federal health-care programs that it had expanded, largely without regard to cost, over the years.

President Reagan, personally a very popular president and a much more astute politician than his opposition frequently wanted to admit, won reelection by a landslide in 1984. An economic boom, begun in 1983, continued through his second term, and the national political consensus edged inexorably rightward as Reagan and the much-maligned "Reagan revolution" set a new agenda of national priorities. Reagan's hard-line approach to negotiating with the Soviet Union softened in his second term after Soviet leader Mikhail Gorbachev took office, resulting in the historic Intermediate Nuclear Forces Treaty (1987) eliminating a whole class of nuclear weapons.

The most serious misstep in Reagan's two terms arose from his determined opposition to the spread of communism in Central America. For a time, Democrats in Congress cut off aid to the contras, anticommunist rebels in Marxist-controlled Nicaragua, but they did an about-face in 1986 by restoring funding. This victory, and the later ouster of the Nicaraguan Marxists in free elections, came too late for the Reagan administration, which found itself embroiled in the Iran-contra scandal over illicit funding of the contras during the congressional funding moratorium. Investigators never proved President Reagan had any direct link to the scandal, though some high-level White House subordinates were convicted of wrongdoing.

After his second term, Reagan retired to his ranch near Santa Barbara, California. He was later diagnosed as having Alzheimer's disease.

Bill Clinton

BILL CLINTON, A DEMOCRAT, WAS SWORN INTO OFFICE ON JANUARY 20, 1993.

MEDAL CEREMONIES

MAY 5, 1993 *ANA Hotel, Washington, D.C.*

JUNE 20, 1993 *Constitution Hall, Washington, D.C.*

SEPTEMBER 30, 1993 *Fort Meyers, Virginia*

NOVEMBER 2, 1993 *Announced at The White House*

NOVEMBER 30, 1993 *The White House East Room*

AUGUST 8, 1994 *The White House East Room*

SEPTEMBER 29, 1995 *The White House East Room*

James William Fulbright

FEW PUBLIC CAREERS MATCH THAT OF SENATOR J. WILLIAM
FULBRIGHT. A RHODES SCHOLAR, A TEACHER, LAWYER, UNI-
VERSITY PRESIDENT, CONGRESSMAN AND SENATOR, HIS
ENDURING LEGACY INCLUDES THE FLAGSHIP PROGRAM FOR
INTERNATIONAL EXCHANGE THAT CARRIES HIS NAME. HE LED
THE SENATE TO APPROVE SEVERAL ARMS REDUCTION TREATIES,
HE HELPED ESTABLISH THE UNITED NATIONS, AND HE PLAYED A
CRITICAL ROLE IN THE CREATION OF THE JOHN F. KENNEDY
CENTER FOR THE PERFORMING ARTS. ON THE SQUARE IN
SENATOR FULBRIGHT'S HOMETOWN IS A FLOWER GARDEN IN
WHICH STANDS A BUST INSCRIBED TO THE TOWN'S FAVORITE
SON. THE INSCRIPTION READS:

> *"In the beauty of these gardens, we honor the beauty of his dream...*
> *peace among nations and the free exchange of knowledge and ideas*
> *across earth."*

THE UNITED STATES HONORS THIS MAN OF PEACE AND PRINCIPLE
WHO HAS HELPED MAKE THIS WORLD A BETTER PLACE TO LIVE.

★ ★ ★

President Bill Clinton awarded Fulbright the Presidential Medal of
Freedom with the above citation during a ceremony at the ANA Hotel
in Washington, D.C., May 5, 1993.

Born in Sumner, Missouri, in 1905, James William Fulbright was
raised in Fayetteville, Arkansas. His father became a successful businessman there and eventually acquired interests in real estate, banks,
a lumber company, a newspaper, and other businesses. The young
Fulbright was a bright student, graduating from the University of
Arkansas at age nineteen. As a Rhodes scholar, he earned another
bachelor's degree (1928) and his master's degree (1931) from Oxford
University in England. Fulbright married Elizabeth Williams in 1932
and then earned his law degree at George Washington University,
graduating with distinction in 1934.

After a stint as a Justice Department attorney and an instructor at
George Washington University, Fulbright returned to Arkansas in 1936
to help run the family businesses and teach law at the University of
Arkansas. When the university president died after an auto accident in
1939, Fulbright was named his successor. Then only thirty-four years
old, he was the country's youngest university president.

Elected to the House of Representatives in 1942, the Arkansas
Democrat embarked on what became a thirty-two-year career in

Congress. During his one term as a representative, his most important legislation was the 1943 Fulbright Act, which urged U.S. participation in an international peacekeeping organization. The act helped pave the way for creation of the United Nations.

Two years later he was elected to the Senate. During his five terms, from 1945 to 1975, Fulbright helped pass numerous important bills and gained a national reputation as an independent-minded critic of U.S. foreign policy, particularly as chairman of the Senate Foreign Relations Committee. One of his most lasting contributions was to higher education, however. As a freshman senator he sponsored legislation creating the highly successful Fulbright scholarship program, an international exchange program for young scholars. By 1994 the program had provided fellowships to more than two hundred thousand students.

During the 1950s he was among the first senators to oppose Sen. Joseph McCarthy's fanatical anticommunist activities and increasingly questioned the prevailing belief that communism was a monolithic force always bent on aggressive expansion. Two years after becoming chairman of the Senate Foreign Relations Committee, he alone advised President John F. Kennedy against what became the humiliating failure of the Bay of Pigs invasion of Cuba in 1961. Meanwhile, however, Fulbright voted with other southern senators against school integration and civil rights legislation in the 1950s and 1960s.

In 1964, when he was still a loyal ally of President Lyndon B. Johnson, Senator Fulbright sponsored the 1964 Gulf of Tonkin Resolution, which allowed Johnson to dramatically expand U.S. involvement in Vietnam. He later regretted taking part in its passage and fell out with the president the following year, after Johnson ordered military intervention in the Dominican Republic. In 1966 Fulbright began openly criticizing U.S. involvement in Vietnam. His televised Foreign Relations Committee hearings on Vietnam and China that same year helped legitimize antiwar protest.

Continuing his attacks on President Johnson, Fulbright published the best-selling *The Arrogance of Power* (1966), criticizing the administration's efforts to turn the Vietnam War into a moral crusade. He again attacked the government's reliance on excessive force in foreign policy with *The Crippled Giant*, which was published in 1972.

Two years later, with the Vietnam War all but over, Arkansas voters rejected his bid for a sixth term. When Fulbright left the Senate in 1975, he had sixteen years as Foreign Relations Committee chairman behind him, the longest service ever for a head of that committee. Remaining in Washington, Fulbright practiced with a private law firm until retiring in 1993. Harriet Mayor became his second wife in 1990, his first having died some years earlier. Fulbright died in 1995 at the age of eighty-nine.

Arthur Ashe

Arthur Ashe's extraordinary accomplishments in tennis and philanthropy and human rights were matched only by the elegance and the intelligence with which he pursued them. A pioneering African American athlete and champion, he co-founded Artists and Athletes against Apartheid, and founded the Arthur Ashe Foundation for the Defeat of AIDS. An historian, writer and passionate advocate of education, his enduring legacy includes the award that bears his name for public service by an athlete. The United States honors this deeply moral man, who used his voice and his example to offer hope and inspiration to people everywhere.

★ ★ ★

President Bill Clinton awarded Ashe a posthumous Presidential Medal of Freedom during the National Sports Award ceremony at Constitution Hall in Washington, D.C., on June 20, 1993. Jeanne Ashe accepted the medal on her late husband's behalf.

Arthur Ashe was the first African-American ranked as the world's top tennis player and the first to win a major men's singles championship. He was born in Richmond, Virginia, in 1943. His mother died when he was just six, and a year later he started playing tennis at a segregated playground for blacks. Ashe showed early promise and soon found a patron in Dr. Walter Johnson, a black physician noted for developing talented young black tennis players.

Coached by Johnson in his courtside manner as well as his playing skills, young Ashe began competing with the 1958 U.S. junior national championship and won the indoor singles title in 1960 and 1961. He won a tennis scholarship to the University of California, Los Angeles, where tennis great Pancho Gonzalez, among others, tutored him. Ashe won various intercollegiate titles while at UCLA and began a long stint as a member of the U.S. Davis Cup team (1963–1970, 1975, and 1977–1978). Already Ashe's play demonstrated he belonged among the world's top-ranked tennis players.

By 1966, when he graduated with his bachelor's degree in business administration, Ashe had established his graceful playing style and was challenging opponents with his blistering serve and dismaying variety of backhand styles (sixteen in all). Then in 1968 he became the first black to win the U.S. men's singles championships and the U.S. Open at Forest Hills.

Two years later he captured the Australian Open and turned pro, but his outspoken criticism of South Africa's apartheid policies prompted that government to refuse him a visa to participate in the 1970 Davis Cup play there. Dropped from Davis Cup competition, South Africa finally relented in 1973, and Ashe promptly became the first black tennis player to reach the final of the South African Open.

Ashe's best year was 1975 when he won the Wimbledon singles and the World Championship singles. Ranked the world's leading tennis player that year, he was the first African-American to reach the top of the tennis profession. In 1979 his health began to decline.

After suffering his first heart attack, Ashe underwent two major heart operations in 1979 and 1983. Though barred from playing tennis because of his heart, he refused to give up. Ashe served as the U.S. Davis Cup team captain from 1981 to 1984 and in 1985 was inducted into the Tennis Hall of Fame. He also set up tennis programs for inner-city youths and wrote a history of black American athletes, *A Hard Road to Glory* (1988). In 1988 Ashe discovered he had been infected by the AIDS virus, probably through blood transfusions administered during his heart surgery.

Finally forced to publicly reveal his condition in 1992, he devoted his remaining time to educating the public about AIDS and raising funds for AIDS research. Ashe died of complications arising from AIDS in 1993. He was forty-nine years old.

Colin Powell

THIRTY-FIVE YEARS OF DEDICATED AND SELFLESS SERVICE TO AMERICA MARK THE CAREER OF COLIN POWELL. HE VIGILANTLY GUARDED OUR NATION'S INTERESTS IN A TIME OF AWESOME CHANGE, AS THE WALLS OF TOTALITARIANISM BEGAN TO CRUMBLE AND NEW NATIONS GRAPPLED WITH THE CHALLENGE OF DEMOCRACY. HIS FORESIGHT AND VISION HAVE HELPED TRANSFORM OUR ARMED FORCES INTO THE UNIFIED FIGHTING FORCE NECESSARY TO MEET THE CHALLENGES OF A NEW CENTURY. IN THE MIDST OF HIS HEAVY RESPONSIBILITIES, HE FOUND TIME TO ENCOURAGE AMERICA'S YOUNG PEOPLE TO DEVOTE THEIR LIVES TO PUBLIC SERVICE. THE UNITED STATES HONORS THIS SOLDIER-STATESMAN WHOSE ACCOMPLISHMENTS HAVE EARNED THE RESPECT AND ADMIRATION OF A GRATEFUL NATION.

★ ★ ★

President Bill Clinton awarded Powell the Presidential Medal of Freedom with the above citation during a White House ceremony September 30, 1993. The medal was presented with the additional accolade, "with distinction." (For the biography of Powell and his first Presidential Medal of Freedom citation, see p. 440.)

Martha Raye

A TALENTED PERFORMER WHOSE CAREER SPANS THE BETTER PART OF A CENTURY, MARTHA RAYE HAS DELIGHTED AUDIENCES AND UPLIFTED SPIRITS AROUND THE GLOBE. SHE BROUGHT HER TREMENDOUS COMEDIC AND MUSICAL SKILLS TO HER WORK IN FILM, STAGE, AND TELEVISION, HELPING TO SHAPE AMERICAN ENTERTAINMENT. THE GREAT COURAGE, KINDNESS, AND PATRIOTISM SHE SHOWED IN HER MANY TOURS DURING WORLD WAR II, THE KOREAN CONFLICT, AND THE VIETNAM CONFLICT EARNED HER THE NICKNAME "COLONEL MAGGIE." THE AMERICAN PEOPLE HONOR MARTHA RAYE, A WOMAN WHO HAS TIRELESSLY USED HER GIFTS TO BENEFIT THE LIVES OF HER FELLOW AMERICANS.

★ ★ ★

President Bill Clinton awarded Raye the Presidential Medal of Freedom with the above citation on November 2, 1993.

Martha Raye was born Margie Yvonne Reed in Butte, Montana, in 1916. Her parents were Irish immigrants whose song-and-dance routine took them to vaudeville houses, saloons, and carnivals around the country. Their home, Raye later remembered, was an old Pierce Arrow that her father drove from town to town looking for bookings. They lived out of the car and cooked on a sterno stove.

Raye began performing at age three and by her fifteenth birthday was singing, dancing, and doing comedy. She adopted the name Martha Raye at about this time, having found it in a phone book, and over the next years made a name for herself on the vaudeville circuit.

Her Hollywood debut in 1936 was one of those storybook tales of overnight success. A producer happened to see her performing an impromptu comedy routine one Sunday evening at a Hollywood nightclub and the following day put her to work in a film with Bing Crosby, *Rhythm on the Range*. Her comedy scene and one song established her as a star when the film was released later that year, and

Raye went on to do such films as *Hideaway Girl* (1937), *Give Me a Sailor* (1938), and *Four Jills in a Jeep* (1944).

Meanwhile, she costarred in a Broadway musical with Al Jolson, *Hold onto Your Hats* (1940), and was a guest on various radio comedy shows. During World War II she began her extensive travels with USO road shows to entertain American soldiers. Considering it her patriotic duty, Raye again devoted considerable time to the morale-boosting tours during both the Korean and Vietnam wars.

She achieved what was probably her greatest fame in the early 1950s through the new medium of television. Raye first appeared on Milton Berle's "Texaco Show," and after other appearances landed her own weekly program, the "Martha Raye Show." Reaching the height of her popularity in the 1953–1954 season, Raye was then ranked as the country's top comedienne.

In following years she toured on the cabaret circuit, starred in her own Miami nightclub, and made television appearances from time to time. In her last years she appeared in commercials.

Raye married more than a half-dozen times, the last time in 1991 to her manager, Mark Harris. She died in 1994, at age seventy-eight.

William Joseph Brennan

EVER DEVOTED TO PROTECTING THE RIGHTS OF THE INDIVIDUAL, WILLIAM J. BRENNAN HAS LEFT HIS INDELIBLE MARK ON THE JURISPRUDENCE OF THE NATION. DURING MORE THAN THREE DECADES ON THE SUPREME COURT, JUSTICE BRENNAN ARTICULATED AND DEFENDED THE SACRED CONSTITUTIONAL GUARANTEES OF FREE SPEECH, VOTING EQUALITY, AND PRIVACY, AND BOLDLY FOUGHT FOR THE RIGHTS OF THE UNDERPRIVILEGED AND EXCLUDED. JUSTICE BRENNAN'S FIERCELY HELD CONVICTIONS, HIS REVERENCE FOR CIVIL LIBERTIES, COMBINED WITH HIS ESSENTIAL KINDNESS, ARE NOW REFLECTED IN THE CONSTITUTION HE HELPED TO INTERPRET. A GRATEFUL NATION PROUDLY HONORS THE UNPARALLELED ACHIEVEMENTS OF JUSTICE WILLIAM J. BRENNAN, CHAMPION OF THE CONSTITUTION.

★ ★ ★

President Bill Clinton awarded Brennan the Presidential Medal of Freedom with the above citation during a White House ceremony November 30, 1993.

Considered by observers to be one of the Supreme Court's great justices, William Brennan was born in 1906 and raised in Newark, New Jersey. One of eight children of Irish immigrant parents, he was strongly influenced by his father, a labor leader and municipal reformer. After graduating cum laude from the University of Pennsylvania's Wharton School in 1928, he went to Harvard Law School on scholarship and finished in the top ten of his class. Brennan married Marjorie Leonard in 1928 and entered private practice in New Jersey after graduating from Harvard.

A labor trouble-shooter in the War Department during World War II, he returned to private practice until his appointment to the New Jersey Superior Court in 1949. Soon after, in 1952, Brennan moved up to the state's Supreme Court, and in 1956 Republican President Dwight D. Eisenhower named him to the Supreme Court, even though Brennan was a Democrat.

Brennan proved himself a skilled coalition builder. Aligning himself with the Court's liberal wing in the late 1950s and 1960s, he became a close colleague of Chief Justice Earl Warren, and a principal architect of many of the Warren Court's important decisions. Brennan continued to be an influential leader of the Court's liberal wing under Chief Justice Warren Earl Burger but he had less success under Chief Justice William H. Rehnquist as the Court became more conservative. Nevertheless, he remained a strong advocate on various issues before the Court, even though he voted with the minority with increasing frequency in his last years on the bench.

Among the most notable opinions he wrote were: *Baker v. Carr* in 1962, which began the massive legislative redistricting based on the principle of "one person, one vote"; and *New York Times v. Sullivan* in 1964, sharply restricting libel cases brought by public officials to encourage "robust" public debate. Other opinions included those seeking to restrain government regulation of pornography, restrict loyalty oaths, and curb school prayer.

Justice Brennan retired in 1990 at age eighty-four. Three years later President Clinton selected him as one of five notable American reformers to receive the Presidential Medal of Freedom.

Marjory Stoneman Douglas

An extraordinary woman who has devoted her long life to protecting the fragile ecosystem of the Everglades, and to the cause of equal rights for all Americans, Marjory Stoneman Douglas personifies passionate commitment. Her crusade to preserve and restore the

EVERGLADES HAS ENHANCED OUR NATION'S RESPECT FOR OUR PRECIOUS ENVIRONMENT, REMINDING ALL OF US OF NATURE'S DELICATE BALANCE. GRATEFUL AMERICANS HONOR THE "GRANDMOTHER OF THE GLADES" BY FOLLOWING HER SPLENDID EXAMPLE IN SAFEGUARDING AMERICA'S BEAUTY AND SPLENDOR FOR GENERATIONS TO COME.

★ ★ ★

President Bill Clinton awarded Douglas the Presidential Medal of Freedom with the above citation during a White House ceremony November 30, 1993.

Among America's best-known and oldest-living environmentalists, Marjory Stoneman Douglas was born in 1890 in Minneapolis, Minnesota. Her mother, who died while she was still a child, was a concert violinist, and her father practiced law until the family moved to Miami, Florida, where he founded the *Miami Herald*.

Douglas graduated from Wellesley College in 1912 with a degree in English and began reporting for her father's newspaper two years later. She was among the few women reporters in her day. Her marriage in 1914 lasted only three years, and during the closing years of World War I, she served overseas in Europe with the American Red Cross. Again in Miami by 1920, she worked another three years for the *Miami Herald* before quitting to take up writing short stories full time.

Advised by *Saturday Evening Post* editors to focus on Florida and life there, she followed their recommendation and for the next twenty years or so regularly published short stories in the *Post*, *Reader's Digest*, and other national magazines. She also taught at the University of Miami from 1925 to 1929.

With her reputation as a short-story writer secure, Douglas spent four years in the early 1940s researching a book about the Everglades. At the time this great alligator-infested, saw-grass swamp at Florida's southern tip was under heavy pressure from farmers and developers looking for cheap land and quick profits. Vast wetland tracts in the Everglades were being drained, destroying wildlife habitats and threatening the very existence of a unique natural resource.

Douglas's book, *The Everglades: River of Grass*, became a bestseller in 1947 and both increased public awareness of the plight of the Everglades and won her national recognition as a writer. Among the early crusaders for creation of the Everglades National Park, Douglas went on working to preserve the Everglades long after her book was published.

She also continued writing about Florida. Her first novel, *Road to the Sun*, was published in 1951. Other books followed, and when she celebrated her one-hundredth birthday in 1990, she was reportedly working on a biography of the naturalist W. H. Hudson.

Thurgood Marshall

THURGOOD MARSHALL TENACIOUSLY DEDICATED HIS EXCEP-
TIONAL LIFE TO OUR NATION'S MOST SACRED PRINCIPLES OF
LIBERTY, JUSTICE, AND EQUALITY. HIS UNPRECEDENTED VIC-
TORIES WITH THE N.A.A.C.P., INCLUDING THE LANDMARK
BROWN V. BOARD OF EDUCATION DECISION, DRAMATICALLY AND
FOREVER ALTERED THE COURSE OF AMERICAN LAW AND HISTORY.
HE BUILT ON THESE VICTORIES AS SOLICITOR GENERAL, AS AN
APPELLATE COURT JUDGE AND ULTIMATELY AS THE FIRST
AFRICAN AMERICAN TO SIT ON THE SUPREME COURT OF THE
UNITED STATES. INSISTING ON DIGNITY, RESPECT, AND CIVIL
RIGHTS FOR ALL, JUSTICE MARSHALL HAS BECOME LEGENDARY
AS A MAN WHOSE BRILLIANCE AND COURAGE ADVANCED AND
SECURED THE LIBERTIES WE CHERISH AS A NATION.

★ ★ ★

*President Bill Clinton awarded Marshall a posthumous Presidential
Medal of Freedom with the above citation during a White House
ceremony November 30, 1993. Thurgood Marshall, Jr., accepted the
award on his late father's behalf.*

Considered with Martin Luther King, Jr., a pillar of the civil rights
movement, Thurgood Marshall was born in Baltimore, Maryland, in
1908. His father was a yacht-club steward and his mother taught in
an elementary school. Excelling in school, Marshall went on to
graduate from the prelaw program at Pennsylvania's all-black
Lincoln University in 1930. He was turned down by the University of
Maryland Law School because of his race, but Marshall got his law
degree anyway, graduating first in his class from Howard University
in Washington, D.C., in 1933.

Entering private practice in Baltimore, Marshall also became a
counsel to the Baltimore branch of the National Association for the
Advancement of Colored People (NAACP). By 1935 he had used his
newly acquired legal knowledge to force the University of Maryland
Law School to accept its first black student. Moving up through the
ranks at the NAACP he became its national chapter counsel in 1938
and a year later helped found the NAACP Legal Defense and
Educational Fund (LDF), of which he became director.

Mounting a concerted effort by the LDF to desegregate the
country's school systems, Marshall traveled extensively in the South
seeking out lawyers willing to take on civil rights cases and coordinating court challenges against segregation. Marshall personally
argued civil rights cases that reached the Supreme Court and won

twenty-nine of the thirty-two cases he presented. By far his most important victory was the landmark Supreme Court ruling in *Brown v. Board of Education of Topeka* (1954), which overturned the "separate but equal" doctrine and ended the legal basis for public school segregation. He remained director of the LDF until the early 1960s, continuing his campaign in the courts against discrimination. Meanwhile, he married his second wife, Cecelia S. Suyat, in 1955, his first wife having died earlier that year.

President John F. Kennedy appointed him to the U.S. Court of Appeals, and despite opposition from segregationists in the Senate, Marshall joined the court in 1962. Three years later President Lyndon B. Johnson named him the first black to serve as U.S. solicitor general, one of the top Justice Department posts. Then in 1967 President Johnson appointed Marshall to the Supreme Court, making him the first black to sit on the nation's highest court.

During his first years as an associate justice, Marshall provided a crucial vote for the Court's liberal activist majority. But new appointments during the Nixon years swung the Court back to a conservative majority, and Marshall increasingly found himself in the minority. He remained a steadfast liberal throughout his twenty-four years on the bench, however, and became a tireless dissenter. Over the years Justice Marshall regularly dissented in cases involving such issues as limiting affirmative action programs, permitting restrictions on the right to abortion, upholding capital punishment, and limiting the rights of criminal defendants.

Marshall spoke out publicly against the Supreme Court's increasingly conservative makeup in the 1980s and was one of its last consistent liberals when he retired in 1991. He died two years later, at age eighty-four.

Joseph L. Rauh, Jr.

THROUGHOUT HIS LIFELONG CRUSADE FOR EQUAL JUSTICE, JOSEPH L. RAUH, JR., WAS AMONG THE FOREMOST DEFENDERS OF THE CONSTITUTION AND THE LIBERTIES ENSHRINED IN ITS WORDS. FROM HIS EARLY CAREER IN PUBLIC SERVICE DURING THE NEW DEAL TO HIS WORK IN THE LABOR AND CIVIL RIGHTS MOVEMENTS, HE CONSISTENTLY APPLIED THE POWER OF THE LAW TO RECTIFY INJUSTICE AND BUILD THE MORAL STRENGTH OF THIS NATION. ALWAYS MORE DEVOTED TO PUBLIC INTEREST THAN TO PRIVATE GAIN, HE DEDICATED HIS CONSIDERABLE TALENTS TO BATTLING

SEGREGATION AND RACIAL INJUSTICE, AND TO PROMOTING
DEMOCRACY IN THE LABOR MOVEMENT. A MAN OF ACTION WHO
EMBRACED THE NOBLE IDEALS ON WHICH THE UNITED STATES WAS
FOUNDED, JOSEPH RAUH'S BOLD ACHIEVEMENTS HAVE AN
HONORED PLACE IN THIS NATION'S HISTORY.

★ ★ ★

*President Bill Clinton awarded Rauh a posthumous Presidential
Medal of Freedom with the above citation during a White House
ceremony November 30, 1993.*

A champion of civil rights and liberal causes, Joseph L. Rauh, Jr., was
born in Cincinnati in 1911. Rauh went on to graduate from Harvard
University magna cum laude as an economics major in 1932 and
finished at the top of his class at Harvard Law School in 1935. After
marrying Olie Westheimer, he served as senior Supreme Court law
secretary, first to Justice Benjamin N. Cardozo and then to Justice
Felix Frankfurter. Rauh also provided legal counsel for federal
agencies, including the Federal Communications Commission and
the Lend-Lease Administration.

After World War II, in 1947, Rauh and a few other liberals founded
Americans for Democratic Action (ADA). *(See also the entry for
Reinhold Niebuhr, p. 120.)* Created as a liberal but staunchly anticommunist organization, the ADA named Rauh its executive committee
chairman (1947–1952). He became a vice-chairman in 1952 and
remained active in the ADA until his death.

Meanwhile, he was active in the Democratic party and at the 1948
Democratic National Convention was instrumental in writing the
party's strong civil rights plank of that year. Later he became an
effective civil rights lobbyist on Capitol Hill, figuring in the passage
of such notable legislation as the 1964 Civil Rights Act, the 1965
Voting Rights Act, and the 1968 Fair Housing Act. Rauh also served as
general counsel for the Leadership Conference on Civil Rights and
was a member of the NAACP executive board.

During the 1950s he was the country's top civil liberties lawyer,
often defending clients caught up in the anticommunist hysteria.
Among his high-profile clients were Lillian Hellman, a writer subpoenaed by the House Un-American Activities Committee; and
Arthur Miller, the noted playwright who was charged with contempt
of Congress for refusing to name associates with communist leanings.

Rauh's other legal work included acting as a counsel for labor
unions. He represented the United Automobile Workers on various
occasions and in the late 1950s successfully defended the union
against federal charges of corruption. He also counseled the
Brotherhood of Sleeping Car Porters, among other unions.

Rauh died in 1992, at age eighty-one.

John Minor Wisdom

COUPLING INTELLECT WITH COMPASSION, JUDGE JOHN MINOR WISDOM HAS, THROUGHOUT HIS DISTINGUISHED MILITARY CAREER AND NEARLY FOUR DECADES ON THE FEDERAL BENCH, USED HIS ELOQUENCE AND EXPERTISE TO ILLUMINATE THE ESSENCE OF AMERICAN JUSTICE. RENOWNED FOR THEIR CLARITY AND REASON, JUDGE WISDOM'S OPINIONS ADVANCED CIVIL RIGHTS AND ECONOMIC JUSTICE, AND HIS INSPIRED WORDS ECHO THROUGHOUT MANY OF THIS CENTURY'S MOST SIGNIFICANT SUPREME COURT DECISIONS. AS A GIFTED TEACHER AND RESPECTED MENTOR, HE HAS INFLUENCED AND ENLIGHTENED GENERATIONS OF YOUNGER LAWYERS, REFLECTING HIS EXTRAOR- DINARY SKILLS AS AN ATTORNEY AND HIS REPUTATION AS A MAN OF EXEMPLARY CHARACTER. THE UNITED STATES HONORS JUDGE WISDOM'S IMMEASURABLE CONTRIBUTIONS TO HUMANITY.

★ ★ ★

President Bill Clinton awarded Wisdom the Presidential Medal of Freedom with the above citation during a White House ceremony November 30, 1993.

The federal appeals court judge who in 1962 ordered the University of Mississippi opened to black students, John Minor Wisdom was born in New Orleans, Louisiana, in 1905. Raised in the ways of the Old South, he went on to graduate from Virginia's Washington and Lee University in 1925 and earned a law degree from his hometown Tulane University in 1929. That same year Wisdom went into private practice with a New Orleans law firm, and two years later he married Bonnie Stewart Mathews.

Wisdom was an adjunct professor of law at Tulane from 1938 to 1957. After serving in the army air force during World War II, he became the Republican national committeeman for Louisiana (1952–1957). A moderate Republican who supported President Dwight D. Eisenhower, Wisdom served as a member of the President's Commission on Government Contracts (1953–1957) while continuing his private practice. Then in 1957 President Eisenhower appointed Wisdom to the Fifth Circuit Court of Appeals.

Wisdom gained a reputation as an outstanding legal scholar while on the appeals court, but two key decisions of his in the early 1960s rank among his most famous. Both were important to advancing inte- gration in the Old South. The first was *Meredith v. Fair* in 1962, which forced the previously all-white University of Mississippi to accept black students. President John F. Kennedy sent federal troops to enforce desegregation at the university. A year later Judge Wisdom issued a landmark opinion in the voting rights case of *United States v. Louisiana.*

Judge Wisdom continues to serve on the Fifth Circuit court as a senior judge. He also sat as a member of the Special Court on Regional Railroad Reorganization from 1975 to 1986 and is currently the court's presiding judge. Wisdom has been a trustee of Washington and Lee University since 1953.

Herbert Block

COMBINING HUMOR, SATIRE, AND AN INCISIVE WIT, HERBERT BLOCK, BETTER KNOWN BY HIS PEN NAME HERBLOCK, HAS ENDOWED EDITORIAL PAGES WITH HIS SKILLED ARTISTRY FOR NEARLY HALF A CENTURY. HIS POLITICAL CARTOONS CONTINUE TO ENLIVEN THE MINDS AND TWEAK THE SENSIBILITIES OF MILLIONS OF AMERICANS. USUALLY SELECTING HIS TARGETS FROM AMONG THE POWERFUL OF WASHINGTON, EVERY PRESIDENT SINCE HERBERT HOOVER HAS KNOWN THE STING OF HERBLOCK'S PEN. HE INSTILLS IN OUR NATION'S LEADERS A DOSE OF HUMILITY, REMINDING ALL OF US THAT PUBLIC SERVICE IS A PRIVILEGE.

★ ★ ★

President Bill Clinton awarded Block the Presidential Medal of Freedom with the above citation during a White House ceremony August 8, 1994.

A three-time Pulitzer Prize winner for his political cartoons, Herbert Lawrence Block was born in Chicago in 1909. The son of a research chemist, he began drawing as a young boy and at age twelve won a scholarship for evening classes at the Art Institute of Chicago. While still a high school student, Block landed his first paid work as a cartoonist for the Illinois Republican party. He went on to Lake Forest College but dropped out after two years when the *Chicago Daily News* offered him a full-time job as a political cartoonist.

Having already taken the pen name Herblock at his father's suggestion, Block stayed with the *Daily News* until 1933. Then for the next ten years he worked for the Newspaper Enterprise Association (NEA) doing political cartoons out of its Cleveland, Ohio, office. While at NEA Block won his first Pulitzer Prize (1942), for a cartoon about the German occupation of France.

After spending three years drawing cartoons for the Army Information and Education Division during World War II, Block in

1946 landed a job doing political cartoons for the *Washington Post* and he has been working there ever since. The *Post* provided an ideal situation for Block, because it was close to Capitol Hill and so provided the steady flow of material he needed for his cartoons. His reputation as an incisive wit was already well established, though, and by the early 1950s his cartoons were syndicated in over 180 newspapers nationwide.

Collections of his cartoons began appearing in books as early as 1952, the first being *The Herblock Book*. Subsequent volumes, nine in all, appeared every few years until the late 1980s. His most recent book was his autobiography, *Herblock: A Cartoonist's Life*, which appeared in 1993.

Meanwhile, Block won his second Pulitzer Prize in 1954 for a political cartoon about Stalin's grisly reputation as a Communist dictator. In 1966 he designed a special stamp for the U.S. Post Office to commemorate the 175th anniversary of the bill of rights, and in 1979 won a third Pulitzer Prize for his cartoons. A lifelong bachelor, Block received numerous other honors and awards during his more than sixty years as a political cartoonist.

Cesar E. Chavez

WITH FEW MATERIAL POSSESSIONS, BUT GUIDED BY HIS PARENTS' STEADY EXAMPLE, HIS CATHOLIC FAITH, THE LESSONS OF GANDHI, AND AN UNSHAKABLE BELIEF IN JUSTICE, CESAR CHAVEZ BROUGHT ABOUT MUCH NEEDED CHANGE IN OUR COUNTRY. AN AGRICULTURAL WORKER HIMSELF SINCE CHILDHOOD, HE POSSESSED A DEEP PERSONAL UNDERSTANDING OF THE PLIGHT OF MIGRANT WORKERS, AND HE LABORED ALL HIS YEARS TO LIFT THEIR LIVES. AS THE LEADER OF UNITED FARM WORKERS OF AMERICA, HE FACED FORMIDABLE, OFTEN VIOLENT OPPOSITION WITH DIGNITY AND NONVIOLENCE. AND HE WAS VICTORIOUS. CESAR CHAVEZ LEFT OUR WORLD BETTER THAN HE FOUND IT, AND HIS LEGACY INSPIRES US STILL.

★ ★ ★

President Bill Clinton awarded Chavez a posthumous Presidential Medal of Freedom with the above citation during a White House ceremony August 8, 1994. Helen Chavez accepted the medal on her late husband's behalf.

The second of five children, Cesar E. Chavez was born near Yuma, Arizona, in 1927. During the depression his family lost their 160-acre

Arizona farm and moved to California seeking work. Chavez, then only ten years old, learned firsthand about the hardships migrant workers suffered, as he and his family traveled from place to place in California picking cotton, carrots, and other crops. Though he attended some sixty-five schools during his family's travels, Chavez never graduated from high school.

After spending two years in the navy during World War II, he went back to migrant farmwork and married Helen Fabela in the little southern California town of Delano. Chavez was picking apricots in a San Jose orchard when recruiters for the Community Service Organization approached him in 1952. His decision to join the group, dedicated to helping Mexican-Americans, was a pivotal moment in his life. Through it he met Saul Alinsky, the group's founder and self-styled professional radical, and also learned how to organize.

Leaving the Community Service Organization in 1958, he founded the National Farm Workers Association—later the United Farm Workers—in Delano. Unions had been trying for years to organize migrants working for California growers, and now Chavez took up the task of challenging both the powerful growers and the government officials who supported them. Using many tactics employed by the civil rights and antiwar movements, Chavez inspired an almost religious zeal in his followers.

Shy, humble, and small in stature, Chavez was something of a Mexican-American David taking on Goliath when he started out. But in 1965 he made a fateful commitment to back a nearly defunct AFL-CIO agricultural workers group in demanding higher wages for grape pickers in Delano. The strike expanded, and for five years he battled grape growers through work stoppages and other means. But it was his nationwide boycott of table grapes, begun in 1968, that finally forced growers to accept union contracts for migrant workers in 1970.

During the 1970s, Chavez led the United Farm Workers into the AFL-CIO and helped win passage of the Agricultural Labor Relations Act in California, which guaranteed farmworkers the right to collective bargaining. While he definitely improved conditions for migrant workers and expanded his union activities across the Southwest, he was never able to create the national farmworkers union he once envisioned. Competition from the Teamsters union during the 1970s and disputes between Chavez and his followers in later years caused union membership to decline.

Chavez died in 1993, at age sixty-six.

Arthur Flemming

THE HIGHEST ATTRIBUTES OF GOVERNMENT SERVICE ARE CLEARLY EVIDENT IN THE BRILLIANT CAREER OF ARTHUR FLEMMING. SERVING EVERY PRESIDENT FROM FRANKLIN ROOSEVELT TO RONALD REAGAN, HE IS A PROVEN RESOURCE OF ASTUTE INTELLIGENCE AND STEADFAST LOYALTY. ON THE FIRST TWO HOOVER COMMISSIONS, HE STROVE TO RENEW AND REINVIGORATE ESTABLISHED PRINCIPLES OF GOVERNMENTAL POWER AND RESPONSIBILITY. FROM HIS ROLE AS SECRETARY OF HEALTH, EDUCATION, AND WELFARE, TO HIS LANDMARK EFFORTS AS CHAIRMAN OF THE COMMISSION ON CIVIL RIGHTS, HE CONSISTENTLY CHALLENGED THE STATUS QUO. HE NOT ONLY SOUGHT HEALTH CARE REFORM, BUT HE ALSO SUMMONED OUR NATION TO UPHOLD ITS PROMISE OF EQUALITY. ARTHUR FLEMMING HAS SELFLESSLY LABORED FOR DECADES TO MAKE AMERICAN GOVERNMENT MORE EFFECTIVE AND EFFICIENT. A GRATEFUL NATION THANKS HIM.

★ ★ ★

President Bill Clinton awarded Flemming the Presidential Medal of Freedom with the above citation during a White House ceremony August 8, 1994.

A surrogate court judge's son, Arthur Flemming was born in Kingston, New York, in 1905. He went to Ohio Wesleyan University, became involved in politics as president of the school's Republican Club, and graduated with a bachelor's degree in 1927. Flemming moved to Washington, D.C., to continue his education, getting his master's degree in political science at American University the following year and his law degree at George Washington University in 1933. Meanwhile, from 1930 to 1934, he also worked as an editor on the staff of what became *U.S. News & World Report*. American University named Flemming director of its School of Public Affairs in 1934 and that same year he married Bernice Virginia Moler.

Flemming began his long career in government service when President Franklin D. Roosevelt made him the Republican member of the three-member Civil Service Commission in 1939. Remaining on the commission until 1948, he also held high-level posts in the Office of Production Management and War Manpower Commission during World War II and on the Hoover Commission under President Harry S. Truman.

Flemming left the government on being named president of Ohio

Wesleyan in 1948, but he was not away from Washington for long. President Truman named him to the Office of Defense Mobilization in 1951, and under President Dwight D. Eisenhower Flemming served as its head until 1957. Flemming again tried returning to the academic world, but in 1958 President Eisenhower appointed him secretary of health, education, and welfare, a post Flemming held until the Eisenhower administration left office in early 1961.

As secretary Flemming oversaw the first stages of school desegregation, announced groundbreaking studies on the health hazards of pollution from auto exhaust, and launched an attack on water pollution. He also single-handedly stirred up the 1959 cranberry scare by announcing just before Thanksgiving that cranberries in certain areas had been contaminated by carcinogens found in a weedkiller.

Over the next decades Flemming variously served as president of the University of Oregon, Ohio Wesleyan University, and Macalester College in Saint Paul, between stints on various commissions under every president from John F. Kennedy to Ronald Reagan. His most important post was as head of the Civil Rights Commission (under Richard Nixon, Gerald R. Ford, Jimmy Carter, and Reagan), but he also served on the national advisory commission of the Peace Corps and the White House Commission on Aging. His well-publicized criticisms of President Reagan's scaling back of the affirmative action program resulted in his being fired from the Civil Rights Commission in 1981.

Since then Flemming has worked as a public interest activist on Capitol Hill. Steadfastly refusing to retire despite his advancing years, he continues to testify before congressional committees and travel the lecture circuit, talking about such issues as aging and health care.

James Grant

RECOGNIZING THAT OUR CHILDREN ARE OUR MOST IMPORTANT RESOURCE AND MOST PROFOUND RESPONSIBILITY JAMES GRANT HAS DEVOTED HIS LIFE TO MAKING THE WORLD A BETTER PLACE FOR ITS YOUTH. HE HAS PROVEN TO BE A COMPASSIONATE AND VISIONARY EXECUTIVE AT UNICEF, TEACHING US THE DISASTROUS EFFECTS OF POVERTY, POPULATION GROWTH, AND ENVIRONMENTAL DEGRADATION UPON THE VULNERABLE AND DISPOSSESSED CHILDREN OF OUR WORLD. UNDER HIS LEADERSHIP, UNICEF HAS FOUGHT TO REDUCE DISEASE, MALNUTRITION, DISABILITY, AND ILLITERACY ON A GLOBAL SCALE. HIS WISE STEWARDSHIP HAS POINTED THE WAY TOWARD A FUTURE IN WHICH THESE ADVER-

SITIES MAY NO LONGER THREATEN OUR CHILDREN. JAMES GRANT CONTINUES TO CREATE HOPE AND OPPORTUNITY WHERE THERE WAS ONCE ONLY DESPAIR, EARNING OUR ETERNAL GRATITUDE AND ENSURING A BRIGHTER TOMORROW FOR OUR WORLD.

★ ★ ★

President Bill Clinton awarded Grant the Presidential Medal of Freedom with the above citation during a White House ceremony August 8, 1994.

The son of an American public health expert stationed in Asia, James Grant was born in Beijing, China, in 1922. He graduated from the University of California at Berkeley in 1943 and married Ethel Henck that same year. Grant began his career in the foreign service with a stint in China as a United Nations aid worker in the late 1940s. Returning to the United States, he earned his law degree at Harvard in 1951, and after three years with a Washington law firm, he held a series of posts connected with U.S. overseas aid programs.

President John F. Kennedy made him deputy assistant secretary of state for Near East and South Asian affairs in 1962. Two years later Grant went overseas as head of the U.S. aid mission in Turkey and in 1967 became an assistant administrator of the U.S. Agency for International Development. Grant helped found the Overseas Development Council in 1969 and for the next decade served as the organization's president.

His long term as executive director of the United Nations Children's Fund (UNICEF), which began in 1980, marked the high point of his career, however. Grant has been credited with making UNICEF an effective force for helping the world's needy children, and under his direction the organization had a hand in saving millions of them. His self-styled "child survival revolution" promoted simple, practical methods for curing childhood diseases and preventing their spread. He also organized the 1990 World Summit for Children as part of his continuing drive to focus public attention on the needs of children in poor and underdeveloped countries.

Following the death of his first wife, Grant married Ellan Young in 1989. He remained UNICEF executive director until shortly before his own death in 1995. He was seventy-two years old.

Dorothy Irene Height

DOROTHY HEIGHT HAS SPENT A LIFETIME PROVIDING LEAD-
ERSHIP IN THE STRUGGLE TO MAKE THE PROMISE OF EQUALITY
FOR PEOPLE AROUND THE WORLD. BEGINNING AS A CIVIL RIGHTS
ADVOCATE IN THE 1930S, SHE SOON GAINED PROMINENCE
THROUGH HER TIRELESS EFFORTS TO PROMOTE INTERRACIAL
SCHOOLING, TO REGISTER AND EDUCATE VOTERS, AND TO
INCREASE THE VISIBILITY AND STATUS OF WOMEN IN OUR
SOCIETY. SHE HAS LABORED TO PROVIDE HOPE FOR INNER-CITY
CHILDREN AND THEIR FAMILIES, AND SHE CAN CLAIM RESPONSI-
BILITY FOR MANY OF THE ADVANCES MADE BY WOMEN AND
AFRICAN AMERICANS OVER THE COURSE OF THIS CENTURY. FOR
HELPING OUR NATION TO MORE ACCURATELY REFLECT THE
NOBLE PRINCIPLES ON WHICH IT WAS FOUNDED, WE HONOR
DOROTHY HEIGHT.

★ ★ ★

*President Bill Clinton awarded Height the Presidential Medal of
Freedom with the above citation during a White House ceremony
August 8, 1994.*

Born in Richmond, Virginia, in 1912, Dorothy Irene Height was the
daughter of an African American building contractor and a nurse.
She was raised in a small town near Pittsburgh named Rankin and
proved a bright student, graduating from New York University in
three years and completing her master's degree there the following
year. She did additional postgraduate course work at the New York
School of Social Work.

Height's first job was as a caseworker for the New York City Welfare
Department (1934–1935), and during this time she also began her civil
rights work, focusing on such issues as desegregation of the armed
forces and free access to public accommodations for blacks. Her long
association with the Young Women's Christian Association (YWCA)
started when she joined the staff of the Harlem YWCA in 1938. She
rose quickly through the ranks to executive positions and served on
the YWCA national board from 1944 to 1977, when she retired. She
founded the YWCA Center for Racial Justice in 1965 and led it from
then until 1977 and oversaw integration of YWCA staff and facilities.

At about the same time she joined the YWCA staff, Height also
met her friend and mentor Mary Bethune, who had founded the
National Council of Negro Women (NCNW) in 1935. As a volunteer,
Height began a second career at the NCNW, an umbrella group concerned with equal employment and education for women. The

NCNW eventually represented some four million people in various groups and sponsored voter education and registration drives, monitored civil rights abuses, and set up civil rights workshops.

Height became president of the NCNW in 1957, a position she continues to hold today. During her time in office, she has developed various community-based and national programs aimed at such concerns as hunger, child care, housing, career training, and education. Though she herself has never married, Height has been concerned in recent years with strengthening black family life.

Named Woman of the Year in human rights by *Ladies' Home Journal* in 1974, Height has received numerous other awards and honors. President Ronald Reagan presented her with the Citizens Medal Award in 1989 for her humanitarian work, and five years later President Clinton gave her the Presidential Medal of Freedom.

Barbara Jordan

TEACHING BY DEED, AS WELL AS BY WORD, BARBARA JORDAN HAS DRAMATICALLY ARTICULATED AN ENDURING STANDARD OF MORALITY IN AMERICAN POLITICS. GUIDED BY AN UNSHAKABLE FAITH IN THE CONSTITUTION, SHE INSISTS THAT IT IS THE SACRED DUTY OF THOSE WHO HOLD POWER TO GOVERN ETHICALLY AND TO PRESERVE THE RULE OF LAW. AS THE FIRST AFRICAN AMERICAN WOMAN ELECTED TO THE TEXAS STATE SENATE, HER CONSPICUOUS ABILITIES LED HER TO THE UNITED STATES CONGRESS, WHERE HER BRILLIANT ORATORY AND METICULOUS JUDGEMENT EARNED OUR LASTING RESPECT. SHE CONTINUES HER LIFE'S WORK AS TEACHER, EXPLAINING AND ANALYZING COMPLEX ISSUES OF MORAL RESPONSIBILITY IN POLITICS AND IMBUING THE LEADERS OF TOMORROW WITH THE ABILITY TO FOLLOW HER FORMIDABLE LEAD.

★ ★ ★

President Bill Clinton awarded Jordan the Presidential Medal of Freedom with the above citation during a White House ceremony August 8, 1994.

The first African American woman elected to Congress from the South, Barbara Jordan was born in Houston, Texas, in 1936. She was the daughter of a Baptist minister, and her mother was often a featured speaker at the church. Jordan revealed her talent for public speaking in high school, and at Houston's all-black Texas Southern University she became a leader on the debating team. After graduating magna cum laude from Texas Southern in 1956 she earned her law degree from Boston University and was admitted to the bar in both Texas and Massachusetts in 1959.

Jordan returned to Houston, where she practiced law and also worked as a judge's administrative assistant. Her volunteer work in Houston for the Kennedy-Johnson ticket in 1960 led to two unsuccessful election bids for seats in the Texas legislature (1962, 1964). But after court-mandated redistricting in 1966, she became the first black state senator in Texas since Reconstruction. She served in the state senate until 1972 and then went on to three terms in the U.S. House of Representatives (1973–1979).

Jordan established herself as an effective legislator with a solid liberal voting record in Congress, supporting such measures as raising the minimum wage, using school busing to promote desegregation, and extending the school lunch program. But she did not win significant national exposure until the House Judiciary Committee hearings on President Richard Nixon's impeachment. As a committee member she delivered a moving speech, televised nationally, in which she reaffirmed her faith in the Constitution and then eloquently argued for articles of impeachment against Nixon.

A keynote speaker at the Democratic National Convention in 1976, Jordan unsuccessfully sought an appointment as attorney general under President Jimmy Carter. Then she unexpectedly retired from Congress in 1978 and began teaching at the University of Texas at Austin. About this time she contracted a neuromuscular disease that left her largely dependent on a wheelchair.

She continued to teach and to make occasional public appearances, however, including a keynote address at the 1992 Democratic National Convention. Selected by *Time* magazine as one of the ten women of the year in 1976, she was inducted into the National Women's Hall of Fame in Seneca Falls, New York, in 1990. Barbara Jordan died in 1995.

Joseph Lane Kirkland

LANE KIRKLAND IS A HERO OF THE MODERN LABOR MOVEMENT—A MAN WHO HAS SPENT HIS LIFE FORGING SOLIDARITY AMONG THE MEN AND WOMEN WHOSE SWEAT AND TOIL HAVE BUILT OUR WORLD. EVER RESOLUTE IN HIS QUEST TO ENHANCE OPPORTUNITIES FOR WORKING PEOPLE, HE HAS TIRELESSLY WORKED TO STRENGTHEN DEMOCRACY AND TO FURTHER THE CAUSE OF HUMAN RIGHTS. DURING THE COLD WAR, HIS VITAL ASSISTANCE TO THE SOLIDARITY MOVEMENT IN POLAND SPURRED THE FORCES OF FREEDOM TOWARD VICTORY IN EASTERN EUROPE, JUST AS HIS GUIDANCE HERE AT HOME HELPED TO RENEW AND FORTIFY THE AMERICAN ECONOMY. AS A PEOPLE, WE ARE INDEBTED TO LANE KIRKLAND FOR HIS TALENTED LEADERSHIP EFFORTS AS AN ADVOCATE FOR UNITY AND SOCIAL JUSTICE.

★ ★ ★

President Bill Clinton awarded Kirkland the Presidential Medal of Freedom with the above citation during a White House ceremony August 8, 1994.

The son of a cotton buyer, Joseph Lane Kirkland was born in Camden, South Carolina, in 1922 and was raised in the nearby cotton mill town of Newberry. Unlike a number of his schoolmates, he decided against working at the mill and instead went into the merchant marines. Kirkland graduated from the U.S. Merchant Marine Academy in 1942 and served aboard freighters carrying U.S. military supplies during World War II. Near war's end, he joined the International Organization of Masters, Mates and Pilots, gaining what would be his only experience as a rank-and-file union member.

After the war Kirkland got his bachelor's degree from the Georgetown University School of Foreign Service (1948) and became a staff researcher at the American Federation of Labor (AFL). He proved an exceptional speechwriter and so was loaned first to Harry S. Truman's vice-presidential running mate, Alben Barkley, in 1948 and then to Democratic presidential candidate Adlai Stevenson in 1952 and 1956. Meanwhile, Kirkland also was working his way up through the ranks of the AFL and, after the union's 1955 merger with the Congress of Industrial Organizations (CIO), the AFL-CIO.

AFL-CIO president George Meany named Kirkland his executive assistant in 1960, making him the chief watchdog for daily operations and the trouble-shooter for disputes between member unions. *(See also the entry for Meany, p. 69.)* Nine years later Kirkland became the number-two man at the AFL-CIO when he was elected secretary-treasurer. With a bigger role in policy-making, he criticized President Richard Nixon's wage and price controls during the early 1970s and backed hefty wage increases to keep workers' pay in step with inflation. Like Meany, Kirkland was a hard-line anticommunist and believed in a strong military. He also was a civil rights advocate and supported integration of AFL-CIO membership.

When Meany retired in 1979, Kirkland succeeded him as AFL-CIO president. While he largely continued past policies, which he had helped formulate, Kirkland presided over a union hurt by declining membership and a less than favorable political climate. During the 1980s he criticized President Ronald Reagan's cuts in social programs and made the AFL-CIO an active participant in the Democratic party, something Meany had avoided in the past.

Kirkland also sought greater unity within the union movement and in 1981 helped bring the United Automobile Workers back into the AFL-CIO. The Teamsters union returned in 1988. Meanwhile, Kirkland also engaged in international politics during the 1980s, strongly backing the workers' Solidarity movement in (then) communist-ruled Poland. Demands by the Polish union workers crippled and finally helped topple Poland's communist regime in 1989.

Kirkland resigned as AFL-CIO president in 1995.

Robert H. Michel

DEMONSTRATING LOYAL DEVOTION TO OUR COUNTRY, BOB MICHEL HAS WORKED CEASELESSLY TO MOVE OUR NATION FORWARD. AFTER VALIANT ARMY SERVICE DURING WORLD WAR II, HE CHOSE TO SERVE HIS COMMUNITY AND COUNTRY IN THE CONGRESS, EARNING THE TRUST OF HIS CONSTITUENTS, ELECTION AFTER ELECTION FOR NEARLY FOUR DECADES. RAISING HIS VOICE, SOMETIMES IN SONG, BUT ALWAYS IN THE SPIRIT OF CREATIVE COMPROMISE AND COOPERATION, HE HAS WON THE ENDURING RESPECT OF HIS COLLEAGUES ON CAPITOL HILL AND OF THE NINE PRESIDENTS WITH WHOM HE HAS SERVED. HE RETIRES AS HOUSE MINORITY LEADER, LEAVING A HISTORY OF LEGISLATIVE VICTORIES THAT OFTEN BROKE GRIDLOCK IN TIMES OF CRISIS. AMERICA THANKS HIM FOR DEMONSTRATING THE

HIGHEST STANDARDS OF PUBLIC SERVICE, PUTTING THE

INTERESTS OF THE NATION AHEAD OF HIS OWN.

★ ★ ★

President Bill Clinton awarded Michel the Presidential Medal of Freedom with the above citation during a White House ceremony August 8, 1994.

A House member for thirty-eight years and the Republicans' minority leader for fourteen of them, Robert H. Michel was born in Peoria, Illinois, in 1923. He was the son of a French immigrant and, after graduating from high school, served in the U.S. Army as an infantryman during World War II. Michel saw considerable combat in Europe and was decorated with two Bronze Stars, the Purple Heart, and four battle stars by the time of his discharge in 1946. Two years later he earned his bachelor's degree in business administration from Peoria's Bradley University and married Corinne Woodruff, his college sweetheart.

A conservative Republican, Michel entered politics in 1949, the heyday of the anticommunist witch-hunts, and landed squarely in the middle of the fray. His first job was as an administrative assistant to Illinois Rep. Harold Velde, then chairman of the House Un-American Activities Committee and a staunch anticommunist. After his boss decided to retire in 1956, Michel joined the race for Velde's seat and won his first term in the House by a substantial margin. Voters eventually reelected him to eighteen more consecutive terms, making him the second-longest-serving Republican of all time in the House.

A staunch conservative throughout his long career in the House, he consistently voted with the conservative coalition of Republicans and southern Democrats and actively campaigned for Barry Goldwater's presidential candidacy in 1964. While backing President Lyndon B. Johnson's growing involvement in Vietnam, Michel opposed the bulk of the president's Great Society programs. After 1969, when Michel became the ranking Republican on the House Appropriations Committee's subcommittee dealing with health, education, and welfare, he actively sought to curb the mushrooming costs of these social programs. Forced to deal with the long-standing House Democratic majority, however, Michel became a skilled negotiator, adept at arranging compromise measures.

Unscathed by the Watergate scandal, Michel moved up in the party ranks during the mid-1970s. Named minority whip in 1974, the second-most-powerful Republican post in the House, he kept up good relations with party moderates and with his Democratic adversaries. His preference for compromise and avoidance of partisan rhetoric were key factors in maintaining those working relationships.

Michel won election as the Republican minority leader in 1980 following Ronald Reagan's victory in the presidential race. With a newly won Republican majority in the Senate and the fiscally conservative Reagan in the White House, Michel used his skills as a quiet, hard-working negotiator to help promote President Reagan's legislative program in the House, including increased defense funding, tax cuts, and cuts in social spending.

During the Bush administration, Michel backed the controversial 1990 budget deal with Democrats that was to have traded spending cuts for increased taxes, among other initiatives. He retired from Congress in 1994, the year Republican election victories finally broke the Democrats' decades-long control of the House.

President Clinton awarded Michel the Presidential Medal of Freedom in 1994 to mark his retirement and many years of government service. Michel's departure also marked the start of a new era of Republican leadership in the House, however, one with a distinctly more combative and partisan style.

Robert Sargent Shriver

ROBERT SARGENT SHRIVER HAS NOT ONLY SHARED, BUT SHAPED, THE ACTION AND PASSION OF HIS TIMES. IT WAS SARGE SHRIVER'S ENERGY, PERSUASION, AND LEADERSHIP THAT MADE THE GOALS OF THE PEACE CORPS ATTAINABLE—THAT LIVING REMINDER THAT THE ESSENCE OF AMERICAN POWER IS NOT MIGHT OF ARMS, BUT CONSTANCY OF IDEALS AND PERSEVERANCE OF EFFORT. THAT SO MUCH ENDURES WITH HIS INDELIBLE STAMP BOTH STUNS AND INVIGORATES: HEAD START, VISTA, FOSTER GRANDPARENTS, LEGAL SERVICES, THE JOB CORPS, AND MORE. HE RELEASED A TORRENT OF CREATIVE ENERGY—FROM SPECIAL OLYMPIC ATHLETES TO HEAD START STUDENTS TO NATIONAL SERVICE PIONEERS. "SERVE, SERVE, SERVE," SARGENT SHRIVER TOLD AMERICANS, "BECAUSE IN THE END, IT WILL BE THE SERVANTS WHO SAVE US ALL." HIS SERVICE HAS BEEN OUR LEGACY OF HOPE.

★ ★ ★

President Bill Clinton awarded Shriver the Presidential Medal of Freedom with the above citation during a White House ceremony August 8, 1994.

The organizer and first director of the Peace Corps, Robert Sargent Shriver was born in Westminster, Maryland, in 1915. The son of a banker whose family came to Maryland in 1693, Shriver went on to graduate from Yale University cum laude in 1938. He earned his law degree from Yale Law School three years later.

After serving as a navy officer during World War II, Shriver became an assistant editor at *Newsweek*. It was while working as a journalist that he was approached by Joseph P. Kennedy to edit the letters of Kennedy's son, Joseph, Jr., who had been killed in the war. By 1947, Shriver had joined Kennedy's business organization and from 1948 to 1961 served as assistant general manager of Kennedy's Chicago Merchandise Mart, then the world's largest commercial building. Meanwhile, he married Kennedy's daughter Eunice in 1953 and served as president of Chicago's Board of Education from 1956 to 1960. *(See also the entry for Eunice Shriver, p. 351.)*

An adviser to John F. Kennedy's 1960 presidential campaign, he headed the search for the new administration's top appointees. Then in the early months of the Kennedy presidency Shriver organized the Peace Corps, a volunteer service program to provide people with needed skills for work in underdeveloped countries. Shriver became director of the program in the spring of 1961 and developed it into a highly publicized and very successful Kennedy-era program. The idea of working to improve public health, agriculture, and education in foreign countries proved especially appealing to idealistic young college students.

While continuing as Peace Corps director (until 1966), Shriver also headed the Office of Economic Opportunity, a post he held during the Johnson administration from 1964 to 1968. A special assistant to President Johnson from 1965 to 1968, he was U.S. ambassador to France from 1968 to 1970. Shriver later made an unsuccessful bid for the vice presidency (1972) and then for the Democratic nomination for president (1976). He has served as a member of the American Committee on East-West Accord from 1978.

After leaving government service, Shriver became a senior partner of a law firm with offices in the United States and Britain. The president of the International Special Olympics in 1984 and 1986, he has been the group's board chairman since 1990 and the chief executive officer since 1992.

Peggy Charren

MAKING IT HER LIFE'S WORK TO PUT OUR CHILDREN FIRST, PEGGY CHARREN HAS RAISED AMERICA'S CONSCIOUSNESS ABOUT OUR RESPONSIBILITIES TO YOUNG PEOPLE. AS THE MOTHER OF PRESCHOOLERS, SHE RECOGNIZED YEARS AGO THE POWERFUL INFLUENCE OF TELEVISION AND BEGAN HER CRUSADE TO IMPROVE THE NATURE OF CHILDREN'S PROGRAMMING. HER CREATIVE LEADERSHIP AT ACTION FOR CHILDREN'S TELEVISION LED TO THE PASSAGE OF THE CHILDREN'S TELEVISION ACT OF 1990 AND CHALLENGED THE TELEVISION INDUSTRY TO FULFILL ITS RESPONSIBILITY TO EDUCATE OUR CHILDREN AS WELL AS ENTERTAIN THEM. WHILE MANY HAVE DECRIED THE QUALITY OF TELEVISION, PEGGY CHARREN HAS DONE SOMETHING ABOUT IT, MAKING A REAL AND POSITIVE DIFFERENCE IN THE LIVES OF YOUNG AMERICANS.

★ ★ ★

President Bill Clinton awarded Charren the Presidential Medal of Freedom with the above citation during a White House ceremony, September 29, 1995.

An author and visiting scholar at the Harvard University Graduate School of Education, as well as a leading force for reform of children's television, Charren was born Peggy Walzer in New York City in 1928. She graduated from Connecticut College with her B.A. in 1949 and two years later married Stanley Charren, a manufacturing company executive.

Charren raised her two children while also finding time to start up and run two business ventures, Art Prints Inc. (1951–1953) and Quality Book Fairs (1960–1965). From 1966 to 1968 she served as director of the local Creative Arts Council in Newton, Massachusetts.

Then, amid the widespread grassroots social and political activism of the late 1960s, Charren founded Action for Children's Television in Cambridge, Massachusetts, in 1968. The group's president since then, she built it up into a national organization with considerable clout in the broadcasting industry. Much of Charren's success came through her personal efforts at lobbying broadcasters and members of Congress, and she has played an important role in reforming programming for children's television. She won a Peabody Award and a special Emmy for her work.

Charren has published three books, *Changing Channels: Living Sensibly with Television* (1983), *The TV-Smart Book for Kids* (1986), and *Television, Children, and the Constitutional Bicentennial* (1986). She has been a visiting scholar at Harvard University since 1987, and has served on such commissions as the Carnegie Commission on the Future of Public Broadcasting (1977–1979) and the President's Commission on Mental Health (1977–1980).

William T. Coleman, Jr.

HOLDING FAST TO HIS CONVICTION THAT EQUAL ACCESS TO THE AMERICAN DREAM IS THE RIGHT OF ALL OUR CITIZENS, WILLIAM COLEMAN HAS ENDEAVORED THROUGHOUT HIS LIFE TO CLOSE THE GAP BETWEEN THE IDEALS ENSHRINED ON OUR CONSTITUTION AND THE REALITY OF OUR DAILY LIVES. HE IMPLEMENTED SOME OF OUR NATION'S FIRST AFFIRMATIVE ACTION PROGRAMS AND HAS WORKED TIRELESSLY FOR THEIR SUCCESS. AS CLERK FOR SUPREME COURT JUSTICE FELIX FRANKFURTER, AS A TALENTED ATTORNEY, AS SECRETARY OF TRANSPORTATION, AND AS CHAIRMAN OF THE BOARD OF THE NAACP LEGAL DEFENSE AND EDUCATIONAL FUND, WILLIAM COLEMAN HAS INSPIRED AND ENLIGHTENED US ON OUR JOURNEY TOWARD EQUALITY FOR ALL AMERICANS.

★ ★ ★

President Bill Clinton awarded Coleman the Presidential Medal of Freedom with the above citation during a White House ceremony September 29, 1995.

A lawyer and for many years a government official, Coleman was born in Philadelphia in 1920. Raised in a black middle-class family, he decided on becoming a lawyer when he was about twelve years old. After graduating from the University of Pennsylvania summa cum laude in 1941 and serving in the Army during World War II, Coleman earned his law degree at Harvard University in 1946, graduating first in his class. Lovida Hardin became his wife in 1945.

While clerking for Supreme Court Justice Felix Frankfurter (1948–1949), he began a long friendship with Elliot Richardson, who later became attorney general. Coleman went into private practice later in 1949, working for prestigious firms first in New York and then Philadelphia. He became known as an expert in transportation law, and also immersed himself in legal battles involving civil rights.

He helped write the brief submitted to the Supreme Court for the historic *Brown v. Board of Education* case, and defended civil rights activists in court cases in years following. His civil rights work resulted in his being elected president of the NAACP Legal Defense and Education Fund in 1971, and he later served as the fund's board chairman.

Meanwhile, he entered government service for the first time in 1959, beginning a two-year stint on the President's Commission on Employment Policy during the Eisenhower administration. A consultant to the United States Arms Control and Disarmament Agency from 1963 to 1975, Coleman also served as assistant counsel to the Warren Commission investigation of President John F. Kennedy's assassination. Among his other government posts were delegate to the UN (1969) and on two presidential commissions (1971–1972) during the Nixon administration.

Coleman gave up his lucrative private practice to become President Gerald Ford's secretary of transportation in 1975. Just the second black to attain a cabinet rank (after Robert Weaver, President Lyndon Johnson's Housing and Urban Development Secretary), he took office at a time when serious financial problems afflicted the country's railroads and airlines. Coleman oversaw preparation of *A Statement of National Transportation Policy,* the first concerted effort at setting national transportation priorities, and submitted the report to Congress in 1975.

Leaving public office at the end of the Ford administration, Coleman returned to private practice. He remained a senior partner of a law firm into the mid-1990s.

Joan Ganz Cooney

RECOGNIZING THAT THE CARE AND SUPPORT OF CHILDREN IS OUR SACRED TASK, JOAN GANZ COONEY HAS WORKED TO PROVIDE YOUNG PEOPLE WITH THE KNOWLEDGE AND MORAL GUIDANCE THEY NEED TO MAKE THE MOST OF THEIR LIVES. IN FOUNDING THE CHILDREN'S TELEVISION WORKSHOP, SHE UNDERSTOOD THAT THE MEDIA COULD BE A POWERFUL TOOL FOR HELPING PARENTS IN THE VITAL WORK OF RAISING THEIR CHILDREN. THE WORKSHOP'S INNOVATIVE PROGRAMS, SUCH AS "SESAME STREET," HAVE INSPIRED A GENERATION OF CHILDREN WITH A COMMON LOVE OF LEARNING, TOLERANCE, AND COOPERATION.

★ ★ ★

President Bill Clinton awarded Cooney the Presidential Medal of Freedom with the above citation during a White House ceremony September 29, 1995.

A banker's daughter, Joan Ganz was born in 1929 in Phoenix, Arizona. She became interested in social and political issues during high school and graduated as an education major from the University of Arizona in 1951. After working as a newspaper reporter in Arizona, she went to New York in 1954 as a television publicity writer. The New York educational television station WNDT hired her as a public affairs documentary producer in 1962, and two years later she married Timothy J. Cooney, an official with the Equal Employment Council.

One evening in 1966 during a dinner party, Cooney got into a conversation with a Carnegie Corporation official about the possibilities of educational television and suddenly found herself with an offer to do a study on television and preschool education. Cooney completed her study later that year and by 1968 had organized the Children's Television Workshop with federal and private funding.

As the group's executive director, she oversaw the work of the childhood learning experts, television producers, and other experts who transformed a set of learning objectives for preschoolers into the award-winning children's show "Sesame Street." The show began its first regular season in November 1969 and has remained a highly regarded children's show ever since.

Cooney remained active as head of the Children's Television Workshop in following years, overseeing the production of "Sesame Street," "Electric Company," and other shows. Five years after her divorce in 1975, she married her second husband, Peter Peterson, and since 1990 has served as chairman of the workshop's executive committee. Over the years Cooney served on numerous commissions and panels, including the Council on Foreign Relations, of which she has been a member since 1974. She was inducted into the Academy of Television Arts and Sciences Hall of Fame in 1989.

John Hope Franklin

HIS EXTRAORDINARY WORK IN THE FIELD OF AMERICAN HISTORY AND HIS STUDIES OF THE SOUTH HAVE EARNED JOHN HOPE FRANKLIN THE RESPECT AND ADMIRATION OF PEOPLE THROUGHOUT THE WORLD. HE HAS DEMONSTRATED THAT THE DIVERSITY OUR COUNTRY ENJOYS IS A SOURCE OF ENORMOUS STRENGTH. FRANKLIN TREASURES AMERICAN HISTORY AS HE TREASURES THE BEAUTIFUL ORCHIDS HE RAISES, AND HIS GENUINE PASSION AND COMMITMENT ARE REFLECTED BOTH IN HIS WRITINGS AND IN HIS DEVOTION TO THE NATURAL WORLD. FOLLOWING HIS MAXIM TO "LOOK HISTORY STRAIGHT IN THE FACE AND CALL IT LIKE IT IS," HE HAS HELPED TO DEFINE WHO WE ARE AND WHERE WE HAVE BEEN, AND HE HAS ENCOURAGED EACH OF US TO LOOK FORWARD TO WHERE WE ARE GOING.

★ ★ ★

President Bill Clinton awarded Franklin the Presidential Medal of Freedom with the above citation during a White House ceremony September 29, 1995.

A history professor whose fifty-year teaching career included posts at Howard University, the University of Chicago, and Duke University, Franklin was born in Rentiesville, Oklahoma, in 1915. His father was one of the first black lawyers to practice in Oklahoma. The young Franklin studied history at Tennessee's Fisk University, graduating magna cum laude in 1935. Continuing his studies at Harvard University, he earned his master's (1936) and Ph.D. (1941) in history there. Meanwhile, Aurelia Elizabeth Whittington became his wife in 1940.

Franklin began teaching history at St. Augustine's College in Raleigh, North Carolina, in 1939 and while there published his first book, *The Free Negro in North Carolina* (1943). New teaching posts and a national reputation as a scholar of black American history followed over the next two decades. Franklin was professor of history at North Carolina College (1943–1947), Howard University (1947–1956), Brooklyn College (1956–1964), and was the history department chairman at Brooklyn. His *From Slavery to Freedom: A History of American Negroes* (1947) was used widely as a college text and as of 1987 was in its seventh edition. His next book, *The Militant South, 1800–1860*, was published in 1956 by Harvard University Press. During the early 1960s he wrote two other books, *Reconstruction after the Civil War* (1961), and *The Emancipation Proclamation* (1963), about the near- and long-term significance of that document.

His reputation as a scholar now firmly established, Franklin became professor of American history at the University of Chicago in 1964. He chaired the history department from 1967 to 1970. Joining the Duke University faculty in 1982, he was named professor of legal history at the Duke University Law School in 1985 and remained in that post until retiring in 1992.

Meanwhile, he continued writing books on black history, including *A Southern Odyssey* (1976), *Racial Equality in America* (1976), *George Washington Williams: A Biography* (1985), and *Race and History* (1990). He coauthored a number of other books and is currently serving as a member of the *American Scholar* editorial board.

A. Leon Higginbotham, Jr.

KNOWING FIRST HAND THE PAIN OF RACIAL BIGOTRY, A. LEON HIGGINBOTHAM, JR., ENTERED THE PROFESSION OF LAW TO PROTECT AND BRING JUSTICE TO OUR NATION'S DISEMPOWERED. HE MOVED STEADILY THROUGH THE RANKS OF THE JUDICIAL SYSTEM, ULTIMATELY BECOMING CHIEF JUDGE OF THE U.S. COURT OF APPEALS FOR THE THIRD CIRCUIT AND A LEADING INTELLECTUAL VOICE ON ISSUES INVOLVING RACE AND THE LAW. COMBINING THE MIND OF AN IMPARTIAL ADJUDICATOR AND THE HEART OF A PASSIONATE ACTIVIST, JUDGE HIGGINBOTHAM HAS PROVEN TO BE ONE OF OUR CONSTITUTION'S GREATEST DEFENDERS AND ONE OF EQUALITY'S STAUNCHEST ALLIES.

★ ★ ★

President Bill Clinton awarded Higginbotham the Presidential Medal of Freedom with the above citation during a White House ceremony September 29, 1995.

A federal judge for nearly three decades, Higginbotham was born in Trenton, New Jersey, in 1928. He went on to earn his bachelor's from Antioch College in 1949 and his L.L.B. from Yale Law School three years later. Soon after graduating, he became assistant district attorney in Philadelphia, a post he held until 1954 when he went into private practice with a Philadelphia law firm.

Higginbotham entered federal government service in 1962 when he was named a commissioner of the Federal Trade Commission during the Kennedy administration. He was the first African American to head a federal regulatory agency. President Lyndon Johnson next appointed him to the federal judiciary in 1964, naming him to the United States District Court for the Eastern District of Pennsylvania. Meanwhile, Higginbotham remained active in the NAACP and in 1968 served on the National Commission on the Causes and Prevention of Violence, which investigated riots by blacks in cities across the country during the late 1960s.

After Higginbotham had served over a decade as district court judge, President Jimmy Carter elevated him to the United States Court of Appeals, Third Circuit in 1977. The following year Higginbotham also published his highly regarded book, *In the Matter of Color: The Colonial Period.*

He spent another sixteen years as a senior appeals court judge before retiring in 1993. Higginbotham remained active in following years though, teaching at Harvard University's Kennedy School for Government and serving as a counsel to a New York law firm.

Frank M. Johnson, Jr.

MARTIN LUTHER KING, JR., RECOGNIZED FRANK JOHNSON'S UNFLINCHING COMMITMENT TO EQUALITY UNDER LAW, ONCE OBSERVED THAT JUDGE JOHNSON "GAVE TRUE MEANING TO THE WORD 'JUSTICE.'" AND INDEED HE HAS. APPOINTED AMERICA'S YOUNGEST SITTING U.S. DISTRICT JUDGE IN 1955, JOHNSON WENT ON TO SHAPE AMERICAN LAW DURING SOME OF OUR NATION'S MOST TURBULENT TIMES. JOINING THE MAJORITY IN BROWDER V. GAYLE, HE HELPED END THE JIM CROW TRADITION THAT RELEGATED BLACK AMERICANS TO THE BACK OF THE BUS, HASTENING THE DEMISE OF SEGREGATION ACROSS THE COUNTRY. IN THE YEARS SINCE, HE HAS CONSISTENTLY PROTECTED THE RIGHTS OF THE UNEMPOWERED, ALWAYS WORKING TO ENSURE ALL HAVE EQUAL ACCESS TO THE AMERICAN DREAM. JUDGE FRANK JOHNSON IS AMONG OUR NATION'S GREATEST CHAMPIONS OF FREEDOM, AND HE HAS EARNED OUR LASTING GRATITUDE.

★ ★ ★

President Bill Clinton awarded Johnson the Presidential Medal of Freedom with the above citation during a White House ceremony September 29, 1995.

Born in Haleyville, Alabama, in 1918, Johnson was the son of a farmer who served as a probate judge and, during the 1940s, the only

Republican in Alabama's state legislature. Young Johnson eventually entered the prelaw program at the University of Alabama and went on to graduate with his law degree in 1943, finishing first in his class. During World War II he served in the Army and was wounded in the 1944 Normandy invasion. Meanwhile, the former Ruth Jenkins became his wife in 1938.

Johnson went into private practice after the war, founding a law firm in Jasper, Alabama, with two other lawyers in 1946. He soon became known as a top-notch defense lawyer and in 1953 was named U.S. Attorney for Alabama's Northern District. Two years later he was appointed to a federal judgeship, as district judge for Alabama's Middle District. It was in this post, which he held for the next twenty-four years, that Johnson became a key figure in the dismantling of segregation in the Deep South.

Just three months after being appointed in 1955, Johnson joined another judge on a three-judge panel to rule in favor of expanding the Supreme Court's historic 1954 school integration decision, *Brown v. Board of Education,* to areas outside the schools.

In doing so, Johnson and the other judge upheld a civil suit by none other than Rosa Parks, who challenged Montgomery, Alabama's segregated seating for public buses in both a highly publicized incident on a bus and in a subsequent court case. The court ruling opened the way for desegregation of public facilities throughout the South.

During the 1950s and 1960s Johnson established a reputation as an innovative and often controversial champion of civil rights. He incurred the wrath of Alabama segregationists, most notably Alabama's segregationist governor, George Wallace, and Johnson's rulings prompted cross burnings in front of his home, death threats, and even the firebombing of his mother's house. One by one though, Johnson desegregated Montgomery's public facilities, from the bus depot to the parks and museums. He ruled against the poll tax and in 1962 issued the first-ever court-ordered reapportionment of legislative districts, overturning Alabama's biased apportionment system. A year later he ordered Alabama schools integrated, though he was careful to preserve neighborhood schools and to restrict busing.

During the 1970s, Judge Johnson struck out in new directions. In 1971 he found that Alabama's mental patients had a right to "adequate treatment" and ordered the state's mental hospitals reorganized and reformed. Five years later, he issued a similarly sweeping order to clean up the state's prisons. He surprised civil libertarians in 1978 though, by issuing the first-ever federal court order against a black institution for discriminating against whites. Here he ruled that traditionally black Alabama State University must open staff and faculty positions to whites.

Judge Johnson was appointed to the United States Court of Appeals in 1979 by President Jimmy Carter. As of the mid-1990s, he was a semi-retired senior judge for the eleventh circuit of the appeals court.

C. Everett Koop

C. EVERETT KOOP HAS ALWAYS RECOGNIZED THAT SCIENCE MUST NOT BE GOVERNED BY POLITICS, BUT RATHER BY SOBER REASONING BASED ON HARD FACTS AND RESEARCH. AS SURGEON GENERAL, HE STAYED TRUE TO HIS CONVICTIONS. CONSCIOUS OF HIS RESPONSIBILITIES AS THE NATION'S CHIEF HEALTH OFFICER, HE CANDIDLY ADDRESSED SUCH CONTROVERSIAL ISSUES AS AIDS EDUCATION, A BAN ON SMOKING, AND EFFORTS TO REDUCE TEEN PREGNANCY. WHILE HE EARNED THE IRE OF SOME, HE WON THE GRATITUDE OF MILLIONS BY HELPING TO MAKE THEIR LIVES SAFER AND HEALTHIER. A GIFTED SURGEON, A COMPASSIONATE SPOKESPERSON FOR THE YOUNG, AND AN EXTRAORDINARY PUBLIC SERVANT WHO INSISTS ON PLACING INTEGRITY ABOVE IDEOLOGY, C. EVERETT KOOP EXEMPLIFIES WHAT IS BEST ABOUT THE AMERICAN CHARACTER.

★ ★ ★

President Bill Clinton awarded Koop the Presidential Medal of Freedom with the above citation during a White House ceremony September 29, 1995.

A pioneering pediatric surgeon who became the country's leading spokesperson on public health matters, Koop was born in Brooklyn in 1916. A precocious student, he entered Dartmouth College at sixteen and graduated in 1937 with a B.A. Cornell Medical College awarded him an M.D. degree in 1941 and the University of Pennsylvania Graduate School of Medicine, his Sc.D. degree in 1947. Meanwhile, Koop married Elizabeth Flanagan in 1938.

While still an intern in the early 1940s, Koop had begun to focus on pediatric surgery, and in 1948 the Children's Hospital in Philadelphia named him surgeon-in-chief. Koop was one of the few specialists in this emerging field, and over the next decades he became a pioneer of new surgical and diagnostic techniques. He drastically improved the rate of successful surgery on newborns, helped make anesthesia safe for children, drew attention to the growing problem of cancer in children, and established the country's first neonatal intensive surgical care unit and first total-care unit for pediatric patients. He gained a nationwide reputation by successfully correcting birth defects once considered inoperable, including surgically sepa-rating Siamese twins on three occasions and saving a baby born with its heart outside its body (by surgically rebuilding the infant's chest).

An instructor at the University of Pennsylvania School of Medicine from 1942, he was appointed an assistant professor in 1949 and, while continuing at the Children's Hospital, became a full professor in 1959. He taught at the university until 1985, four years after giving up his post at the Children's Hospital.

Koop, who had become a Christian soon after beginning his medical practice, also became known for his opposition to abortion and antifamily trends in society. In 1979 he coauthored the antiabortion book *Whatever Happened to the Human Race?* with theologian Fleming H. Revell and for two years toured the country with a multimedia presentation. That work helped bring Koop to President Ronald Reagan's attention, and to an appointment in 1981 as deputy assistant secretary for health. The following year President Reagan named him surgeon general, and Koop served until the end of President Reagan's second term in 1989.

Koop quickly became a controversial figure in the administration by taking a tough stand against cigarette smoking early in 1982. At one point he even equated nicotine with heroin and cocaine addiction. Koop also spoke out on various other health issues, such as warning Americans about fat in their diets, but probably was at his most controversial in 1986 with statements supporting elementary school sex education courses and the use of condoms by adults to help stop the spread of AIDS.

Since 1993 he has been affiliated with the C. Everett Koop Institute at the Dartmouth-Hitchkock Medical Center in New Hampshire. He has written several books, including *The Right to Live, The Right to Die* (1976), *Sometimes Mountains Move* (1979, with Elizabeth Koop), *Koop: The Memoirs of America's Family Doctor* (1991), and *Let's Talk* (1992).

Gaylord Nelson

THROUGHOUT AN INSPIRING LIFETIME OF PUBLIC SERVICE, GAYLORD NELSON HAS DISTINGUISHED HIMSELF BY USING THE POWER OF GOVERNMENT TO FULFILL ONE OF HUMANITY'S SOLEMN RESPONSIBILITIES — THE PROTECTION OF EARTH'S FRAGILE ENVIRONMENT. HAVING PROUDLY SERVED HIS HOME STATE OF WISCONSIN AS A LEGISLATOR AND AS GOVERNOR, HE BROUGHT HIS TALENTS TO THE UNITED STATES SENATE IN 1963, WHERE HE AUTHORED AND CHAMPIONED A SERIES OF PROPOSALS TO PROTECT AMERICA'S NATURAL RESOURCES. HIS EFFORTS TO HELP CREATE EARTH DAY SET OUR NATION ON A PATH OF INCREASING CONCERN FOR THE ENVIRONMENT, ENCOURAGING ALL AMERICANS TO TAKE GREATER RESPONSI-

BILITY FOR THE WELL-BEING OF OUR PLANET. GAYLORD NELSON'S LIFELONG COMMITMENT HAS ENABLED MILLIONS TO RECOGNIZE AND TREASURE NATURE'S PRICELESS BEAUTY, PRESERVING IT FOR GENERATIONS OF AMERICANS TO COME.

★ ★ ★

President Bill Clinton awarded Nelson the Presidential Medal of Freedom with the above citation during a White House ceremony September 29, 1995.

An elected government official for most of his long career, Nelson was born at Clear Lake, Wisconsin, in 1916. Politics figured in Nelson's family heritage: his great-grandfather had a hand in organizing the Republican Party, and his father strongly supported the Progressive Party, an offshoot of the Republican Party in the early 1900s. Nelson went on to graduate with a degree in economics from San Jose State College in California in 1939 and received his law degree from Wisconsin Law School three years later.

After seeing combat with the Army in the Pacific campaign, he entered private practice in Madison, Wisconsin, and in 1947 married Carrie Lee Dotson. By this time he had also switched parties to become a Democrat and won his first term as a Wisconsin state senator in 1948. Reelected to two more terms, Nelson served from 1949 to 1958, when he became the first Democrat to win the Wisconsin governorship in some twenty-five years. Setting his sights on the United States Senate, he next won his first term to that office in the 1962 elections.

Nelson served in the Senate for eighteen years (1963-1981) and during his term of office was chairman of the Select Committee on Small Business and the Special Committee on Official Conduct. He became recognized as a leading proponent of environmental legislation and authored the Environmental Education Act of 1970 and the National Environmental Education Act of 1972. But Nelson achieved what is his best known success as the founder of Earth Day, which began as a teach-in on the environment at schools and colleges nationwide. Earth Day has been held annually since then and is now an international event.

Nelson lost his bid for reelection in 1980 and after leaving office became a counselor to the Wilderness Society in Washington, D.C. He remained in the post through the mid-1990s.

Walter Reuther

THROUGHOUT THE MOST PRODUCTIVE AND TUMULTUOUS YEARS IN THE HISTORY OF AMERICAN LABOR AND UNTIL HIS DEATH IN 1970, WALTER REUTHER STRIVED TIRELESSLY TO ADVANCE THE NEEDS OF WORKING MEN AND WOMEN. HE BROUGHT TOGETHER WORKERS IN THE AUTOMOBILE INDUSTRY AND SPENT MUCH OF HIS LIFE MOBILIZING, ENERGIZING, AND LEADING THE UNITED AUTOMOBILE WORKERS, BRINGING TO THE UNION A POWERFUL UNITY, A NEW EFFECTIVENESS, AND A STRONG SOCIAL CONSCIENCE. AS A FORCEFUL ADVOCATE FOR FAIRNESS AND DIGNITY IN THE WORKPLACE, REUTHER WAS A DEVOTED FRIEND OF WORKERS AROUND THE WORLD AND AN ARDENT FOE OF CORRUPTION AND RACISM. OUR COUNTRY IS STRONGER AND WISER BECAUSE OF HIS PASSIONATE AND HONEST LEADERSHIP.

★ ★ ★

President Bill Clinton awarded Reuther a posthumous Presidential Medal of Freedom with the above citation during a White House ceremony September 29, 1995.

The son of a local brewer's union leader, Reuther was born in Wheeling, West Virginia, in 1907. He left school at fifteen to work in a Wheeling steel mill, but was fired not long after for trying to organize a protest against working Sundays. Reuther then went to Detroit and wound up at the Ford Motor Company, where after five years he became foreman of the tool and die making section (1931). Meanwhile, he devoted his evenings to completing high school and three years of college courses at Wayne University as a sociology and economics major.

Ford laid him off in 1933 because of his union activities, and for the next two years Reuther and his brother toured Europe by bicycle, spending over a year working at a Ford plant in the Soviet Union. Reuther returned to Detroit in 1935 strongly opposed to communist theories, but convinced of the need for organized labor. Joining what was then the fledgling United Auto Workers (UAW) union, he began organizing auto workers and by 1936 had been elected to the union's executive board. That same year he married May Wolf, a former teacher.

Late in 1936 he led a sit-down strike at the Kelsey-Hayes Wheel Company, the first major strike in the Detroit auto industry, and from 1937 to 1941 took part in most of the UAW-backed sit-down strikes. Along the way he substantially increased UAW membership, took part in negotiating labor contracts, and rose through the union's executive ranks to become first vice president in 1942. Reuther, by then known as an ardent anticommunist, became president in 1946 following a hard-fought campaign marked by outbreaks of violence. In 1947 he forced out leftwing members and secured firm control over the union. The following year Reuther was seriously wounded when an unknown assailant fired a shotgun through the window of his home.

Though he lost the use of his right arm, Reuther recovered and in 1949 joined with the United Steelworkers union in negotiating groundbreaking employer-paid pension plans, as well as other fringe benefits. He also helped found the anticommunist International Confederation of Free Trade Unions in 1949. Three years later he became Congress of Industrial Organizations (CIO) president and in 1955 helped arrange the AFL-CIO merger. While remaining UAW president, he became an AFL-CIO vice president, second only to federation president George Meany.

Long recognized as a tough negotiator, Reuther won the auto industry's first profit-sharing plan for the UAW in 1961 and during the 1960s won big new contracts from automakers, giving auto workers higher wages, longer vacations, bigger pensions, and earlier retirement. But Reuther's relations with Meany soured and in 1968 Reuther led the 1.3 million member UAW out of the AFL-CIO. *(See also the entry for Meany, p. 69.)*

Merging the UAW with the International Brotherhood of Teamsters, Reuther created the 3.6-million member Alliance for Labor Action in 1969. But both Reuther and his wife were killed the following year when their plane crashed during an attempted landing in bad weather. Reuther was sixty-two years old.

James Rouse

GUIDED BY AN ABIDING BELIEF THAT CITIES SHOULD BE AMONG OUR PROUDEST ACHIEVEMENTS, JAMES ROUSE HAS USED HIS DESIGN AND DEVELOPMENT SKILLS TO BREATHE NEW LIFE INTO URBAN AREAS. TODAY, LIVELY AND INNOVATIVE PROJECTS LIKE BOSTON'S FANEUIL HALL MARKETPLACE AND BALTIMORE'S HARBORPLACE, AS WELL AS THE PLANNED COMMUNITY OF COLUMBIA, MARYLAND, STAND AS MONUMENTS TO ROUSE'S TALENT AND VISION. ADVISING SEVERAL PRESIDENTS ON HOUSING POLICIES, HE HAS WORKED IN BOTH THE PUBLIC AND PRIVATE SECTORS TO REVITALIZE OUR CITIES, STRENGTHEN

LOCAL ECONOMIES, AND FUNDAMENTALLY IMPROVE THE
QUALITY OF LIFE FOR CITIZENS ACROSS AMERICA.

★ ★ ★

*President Bill Clinton awarded Rouse the Presidential Medal of
Freedom with the above citation during a White House ceremony
September 29, 1995.*

Born in Easton, Maryland, in 1914, Rouse was the son of a canned
foods broker. His childhood was like that of many other youngsters,
though his family was probably somewhat more well-to-do than
most—Rouse grew up in a large Victorian mansion. But tragically,
when he was almost sixteen, Rouse's world collapsed. Both his
mother and father died within months of each other, and even the
house he had grown up in was taken from him when the bank fore-
closed to cover his father's business debts.

Rouse began his college studies in the early 1930s at the height of
the Depression. Over the next several years, he worked and attended
various colleges, eventually earning his law degree from the
University of Maryland (1937) by taking night classes and working
days as a legal clerk at the Baltimore office of the Federal Housing
Administration. By that time the ambitious Rouse had already
provided a start for himself in the mortgage business by convincing a
Baltimore bank to open a mortgage department in 1936. The bank
hired him to run the department that year.

Three years later Rouse borrowed $20,000 and with a real estate
appraiser set up the Moss-Rouse Company, a mortgage banking
firm. At first concentrating on FHA loans for single-family homes,
Rouse and his partner amassed some $6 million in mortgage loans
by the early 1940s. Rouse served as an air force officer during World
War II and returned to his business after the war. Then he began
underwriting shopping centers and apartment houses and in 1954
bought out his partner to form James W. Rouse and Company, Inc.

With his mortgage business mushrooming, Rouse became
involved in improving urban housing. He chaired a Baltimore committee on the city's urban decay, one of the first attempts at renewing
slum neighborhoods, and coauthored the book *No Slums in Ten
Years* (1955), which outlined a plan to redevelop Washington, D.C. In
the late 1950s he also founded with other businessmen the Ameri-
Council to Improve Our Neighborhood, which eventually became
the Urban Coalition.

Meanwhile, Rouse also turned to developing and constructing his
first regional shopping center in 1955. Three years later he completed
the country's second enclosed shopping mall—second by just a few
months—and by the end of the 1960s had built seventeen shopping
centers in all. But Rouse's crowning achievement was the building of an
entire city, Columbia, located between Baltimore and Washington, D.C.

Rouse wanted the city designed with people in mind, to make it "a garden for growing people," and the resulting plan was for a self-sufficient community of 110,000 residents to be completed in fifteen years. Work began in 1966, but the 1974–1975 recession forced Rouse to refinance the project and trim back the plans. Nevertheless, by the early 1990s, Columbia had grown to about 76,000 inhabitants.

During the 1970s, he turned to a new theme, successfully redeveloping inner city neighborhoods by creating what he called "festival marketplaces" like Boston's Faneuil Hall Marketplace and Baltimore's Harborplace. In 1974 he married his second wife, Patricia Traugott, having divorced his first wife two years earlier.

Rouse founded the Enterprise Foundation in 1981 to help fund the construction and rehabilitation of housing for the nation's poor. Over the next decade the group arranged funding for low-income housing in over one hundred cities and helped with the building or refurbishing of nearly 28,000 homes.

In his late seventies by the early 1990s, Rouse relinquished his post as Rouse Company's chief executive in 1991 and retired as chairman of the Enterprise Foundation in 1993. James Rouse died in 1996.

Willie Velasquez

WILLIE VELASQUEZ LABORED THROUGHOUT HIS CAREER TO INFUSE AMERICAN PUBLIC LIFE WITH THE VIBRANT HISPANIC HERITAGE. WITH VISION AND THE SKILLS HE DEVELOPED AS A MEMBER OF CESAR CHAVEZ' FARM WORKER MOVEMENT, VELASQUEZ FOUNDED THE SOUTHWEST VOTER REGISTRATION EDUCATION PROJECT IN 1974. HIS UNTIRING EFFORTS NEARLY DOUBLED HISPANIC VOTER REGISTRATION AND DRAMATICALLY INCREASED THE NUMBER OF LATINO ELECTED OFFICIALS IN THIS COUNTRY. THOUGH CANCER TOOK HIM FROM US TOO SOON, WILLIE VELASQUEZ' LEGACY LIVES ON IN ALL WHO SEEK TO MAKE OUR DEMOCRACY TRULY REPRESENTATIVE OF AMERICA'S DIVERSITY.

★ ★ ★

President Bill Clinton awarded Velasquez a posthumous Presidential Medal of Freedom with the above citation during a White House ceremony September 29, 1995.

A butcher's son, Velasquez was born in San Antonio, Texas, in 1944. He eventually became involved in fighting for the rights of Hispanic

Americans, and during the 1960s worked with Cesar Chavez, the leader of migrant farm workers. Chavez and Velasquez led a strike by farm workers in south Texas in 1968, but by the 1970s Velasquez had turned from labor organizing to the political arena.

Though active in the Hispanic American political party La Raza Unida during the 1970s, Velasquez built his reputation as a Latino activist through the Southwest Voter Registration Education Project. When he founded the group in 1974, there were just 1,566 Hispanics who were elected officials in the United States. Over the next fourteen years, Velasquez and his group launched some 1,000 voter registration drives aimed at increasing registered Hispanic American voters. The group eventually canvassed over 200 cities and Native American reservations in Texas, New Mexico, Colorado, and California and thereby earned recognition as the country's largest Hispanic American voter registration program.

In addition to increasing the Hispanic vote in these states, Velasquez and his organization also figured in several court battles aimed at election practices that diluted the Hispanic vote. Among these court decisions were bans on gerrymandering of political districts and the practice of at-large voting for city and county officials. Allowing candidates to field votes from a whole city or county (at large) had been used to prevent minority candidates from being elected.

Probably Velasquez's greatest achievement lay in significantly increasing the number of elected Hispanic officials. His Southwest Voter Registration Education Project had not only sought to increase Hispanic voting, but also to prod Hispanics into running for office. The group actively polled voters in support of campaigns by Hispanics, and by 1987 had helped boost the number of elected Hispanics to 3,038, an increase of 82 percent over the 1974 total of 1,566.

By 1981 Velasquez was a widely known political activist and in that year began teaching a course on politics in the Southwest at Harvard University. By the late 1980s though, he was stricken with cancer. He died in 1988 at age forty-four.

Lew Wasserman

A FIGURE OF LEGENDARY STRENGTH AND VISION IN HOLLYWOOD, LEW WASSERMAN HAS HELPED TO MAKE AMERICA THE WORLD'S LEADER IN THE ENTERTAINMENT INDUSTRY. WITH SKILL AND DETERMINATION, HE WAS INSTRUMENTAL IN TURNING A SMALL BOOKING AGENCY INTO A MULTIMEDIA EMPIRE, WINNING RESPECT FOR HIS TENACITY AND DEVOTION TO HARD

WORK. ON HIS STEADY RISE TO THE TOP, HE NEVER FORGOT THOSE IN OUR COUNTRY WHO STILL STRUGGLE. A GENEROUS FRIEND TO MANY HUMANITARIAN EFFORTS, WASSERMAN HAS TAKEN PARTICULAR INTEREST IN ASSISTING THOSE WHO ARE BLIND AND VISUALLY IMPAIRED, HELPING TO PRESERVE THE PRECIOUS GIFT OF SIGHT FOR COUNTLESS AMERICANS. HIS LIFE OF ACHIEVEMENT AND SERVICE REFLECTS THE BEST QUALITIES OF THE AMERICAN DREAM.

★ ★ ★

President Bill Clinton awarded Wasserman the Presidential Medal of Freedom with the above citation during a White House ceremony September 29, 1995.

Once described as one of the last larger-than-life movie barons, Wasserman was born in Cleveland, Ohio, in 1913. He got his start in show business early, as a movie usher working nights during high school. Soon after his high school graduation in 1930, a Cleveland nightclub hired him to handle promotion. There Wasserman met Jules Stein, a highly successful band musician's agent who owned the talent agency Music Corporation of America (MCA), and in 1936 Wasserman began what became virtually a lifelong association with MCA. Earlier that year he had married Edith Beckerman.

By 1938 Wasserman had become an MCA vice president and during the 1940s, the company emerged as Hollywood's leading talent agency for movie actors and actresses. Wasserman, named MCA president in 1946, eventually represented such stars as Clark Gable, Errol Flynn, Bette Davis, and Joan Crawford, and was responsible for important innovations like paying actors a percentage of the film's gross and the agent-packaged movie, in which an agency not only sold a studio the stars for a film, but the writer and director as well.

Meanwhile, Wasserman had come to believe in the vast possibilities of television, then an emerging new medium. In 1940 he had one of the only two privately owned television sets in California, at a time when there was little more to watch than test patterns. With the TV broadcasting boom during the early 1950s, though, he formed Revue Productions, MCA's television program production division, which by the mid-fifties was producing such highly profitable primetime programs as "Alfred Hitchcock Presents," "Bachelor Father," and "General Electric Theater." He made shrewd investments as well, by buying Paramount Studio's pre-1948 movies (which he then rented to TV stations) and Universal Pictures' 367-acre back lot (which eventually became the site of MCA's office tower, its Universal Studios amusement park, an amphitheater, and shopping mall).

Forced to divest MCA's talent agency by the federal government in 1961, he expanded MCA by buying Universal Studios and Decca Records. During the 1960s and 1970s, Wasserman pioneered the made-for-television movie (1966, *Fame Is the Name of the Game*) and the miniseries (1976, *Rich Man, Poor Man*). While the company took in millions from such hit movies as *The Sting, American Graffiti,* and *Day of the Jackal* during the 1970s, it was Wasserman who devised the summer blockbuster movie to raise the stakes even higher. For the first blockbuster, the 1975 smash hit *Jaws,* Wasserman revamped the whole system of movie distribution.

Jaws proved a stunning success and the blockbuster was born. MCA enjoyed further successes with blockbusters, including *E.T.* and *Back to the Future,* as well as such hit television programs as *Magnum P.I.* and *Miami Vice.* By the late 1980s though, the company had clearly passed its peak. MCA's movie box office share had dropped sharply and the market for its television programs was shrinking as well.

Late in 1990, Wasserman engineered the company's sale to Matsushita Corporation of Japan for $6.13 billion, the largest buyout by a Japanese firm up to that time. Wasserman got about $355 million in stock and was named to the MCA executive committee, but his relationship with Matsushita soon soured. When the Japanese finally sold most of MCA to the Canadian liquor giant Seagram Company in 1995, Wasserman retired, ending nearly six decades at MCA.

Bibliography

Extensive use was also made of periodicals, including *Current Biography*, the *New York Times*, the *Washington Post*, and other newspapers and magazines. Appropriate volumes of *Public Papers of Presidents* and relevant files in various presidential libraries also were consulted.

Axelrod, Alan. *The Environmentalists: A Biographical Dictionary from the 18th Century to Today*. New York: Facts on File, 1993.

Benet, William Rose. *Benet's Reader's Encyclopedia*. New York: Harper and Row, 1987.

Blaug, Mark. *Who's Who in Economics: A Biographical Dictionary*. Cambridge, Massachusetts: MIT Press, 1986.

Bowden, Henry. *Dictionary of American Religious Biography*. Westport, Connecticut: Greenwood Press, 1993.

Bowker. *American Men and Women of Science*. New York: R. R. Bowker, 1976.

Britannica. *Encyclopedia Britannica*. Chicago: Encyclopedia Britannica, 1995.

Brown, Les. *Les Brown's Encyclopedia of Television*, 3d ed. Detroit: Gale Research, 1992.

Brownstein, Ronald, and Nina Easton. *Reagan's Ruling Class: Portraits of the President's Top 100 Officials*. Washington, D.C.: Presidential Accountability Group, 1982.

Chernow, Barbara, and George Vallasi. *The Columbia Encyclopedia*, 5th ed. New York: Columbia University Press, 1993.

Clarke, Donald. *The Penguin Encyclopedia of Popular Music*. New York: Viking Penguin, 1982.

Congressional Quarterly. *Guide to Congress*, 4th ed. Washington, D.C.: Congressional Quarterly, 1991 .

Davis, Richard C. *Encyclopedia of American Forestry and Conservation History*. New York: MacMillan, 1983.

Delaney, John. *Dictionary of American Catholic Biography*. Garden City, New York: Doubleday, 1984.

Dupuy, Trevor, et. al. *The Harper Encyclopedia of Military Biography*. New York: HarperCollins, 1992.

Educational Communications. *Who's Who Among Black Americans*, 4th ed. Lake Forest, Illinois: Educational Communications, Inc., 1985.

Foner, Eric, et al. *The Reader's Companion to American Literature*. Boston: Houghton Mifflin, 1991.

Europa. *The International Who's Who of Women.* London: Europa Publications, 1992.

Fink, Gary M., ed. *Biographical Dictionary of American Labor.* Westport, Connecticut: Greenwood Press, 1984.

Flanders, Stephen A. *Dictionary of American Foreign Affairs.* New York: Maxwell Macmillan, 1993.

G. and C. Merriam. *Webster's American Military Biographies.* Springfield, Massachusetts: G. and C. Merriam Co., 1978.

Gale Research. *Dictionary of Literary Biography.* Detroit: Gale Research, 1978.

Gammond, Peter. *The Oxford Companion to Popular Music.* Oxford: Oxford University Press, 1991.

Golemba, Beverly E. *Lesser-known Women: A Biographical Dictionary.* Boulder, Colorado: Lyne Rienner Publishers, 1992.

Hall, Kermit L. *The Oxford Companion to the Supreme Court of the United States.* New York: Oxford University Press, 1992.

Hine, Darlene Clark, ed. *Black Women in America: An Historical Encyclopedia.* Brooklyn, New York: Carlson Publishing Inc., 1993.

H. W. Wilson. *Nobel Prize Winners.* Bronx, New York: H. W. Wilson, 1987.

Jeremy, David. *Dictionary of Business Biography.* London: Butterworths, 1984.

Judicial Conference of the United States. *Judges of the United States.* Washington, D.C.: U.S. Government Printing Office, 1983.

Kanellos, Nicolas. *Hispanic American Almanac.* Detroit: Gale Research, 1993.

Kerrigan, Evans E. *American War Medals and Decorations.* New York: Viking Press, 1964.

Low, W. Augustus, ed. *Encyclopedia of Black America.* New York: McGraw-Hill, 1981.

Melton, J. Gordon. *Religious Leaders of America.* Detroit: Gale Research, 1991.

Ohles, John F. *Biographical Dictionary of American Educators.* Westport, Connecticut: Greenwood Press, 1978.

Ragan, David. *Who's Who in Hollywood.* New York: Facts on File, 1992.

Rees, Philip. *Biographical Dictionary of the Extreme Right Since 1890.* New York: Simon and Schuster, 1990.

Sadie, Stanley. *The New Grove Dictionary of Music and Musicians.* New York: Grove Press, 1980.

Salem, C., ed. *African American Women: A Biographical Dictionary.* New York: Garland, 1993.

Scribner's. *Dictionary of American Biography.* New York: Scribner's, 1990.

Sobel, Robert, ed. *Biographical Directory of the United States Executive Branch, 1774–1989.* Westport, Connecticut: Greenwood Press, 1981.

Spiller, Roger, ed. *Dictionary of American Military Biography.* Westport, Connecticut: Greenwood Press, 1984.

Thomson, David. *A Biographical Dictionary of Film.* New York: Knopf, 1994.

Uglow, Jennifer S. *The Continuum Dictionary of Women's Biography.* New York: Continuum, 1982.

Utter, Glenn, and Charles Lockhart. *American Political Scientists: A Dictionary.* Westport, Connecticut: Greenwood Press, 1993.

Wetterau, Bruce. *World History, A Dictionary of Important People, Places, and Events, from Ancient Times to the Present.* New York: Henry Holt, 1994.

White, Edward G. *The American Judicial Tradition: Profiles of Leading American Judges.* Oxford: Oxford University Press, 1988.

Whitman, Alden. *American Reformers.* Bronx, New York: Wilson, 1985.

Wilson, Clyde N., ed. *Dictionary of Literary Biography: Twentieth-Century American Historians.* Detroit: Gale Research, 1983.

Illustration Credits

LYNDON B. JOHNSON LBJ Library Collection **47** Library of Congress **48** Library of Congress **51** Library of Congress **53** Library of Congress **55** Collection of the Supreme Court of the United States **58** John F. Kennedy Library **67** Moberg Studio **72** Illinois Institute of Technology **77** Bettmann **79** Library of Congress **81** Amil Romano, CBS **88** Bettmann Archive **91** Library of Congress **92** National Archives **101** Bettmann **103** Yoichi R. Okamoto, LBJ Library **104** University of Notre Dame **108** no credit **109** Bettmann **111** Harris & Ewing **118** Library of Congress **123** Library of Congress **124** Library of Congress **126** Yoichi R. Okamoto, LBJ Library Collection **127** Science Year, The World Book Science Annual **139** The White House **146** Library of Congress **149** Library of Congress **152** Library of Congress **155** Library of Congress **166** NAACP

RICHARD NIXON Courtesy of the White House **172** NASA **176** The University of Pennsylvania **182** NASA **193** Library of Congress **197** Reader's Digest **203** National Archives

GERALD R. FORD Gerald R. Ford Library **215** Library of Congress **217** Library of Congress **220** Library of Congress **223** National

Index